REA's Test Prep Books Are The Best!

(a sample of the <u>hundreds of letters</u> REA receives each year)

" REA's GED study guide helps people get that chance to receive that special gift [of a high school diploma]. "

GED Test-Taker, Rock Hill, SC

" I did well because of your wonderful prep books... I just wanted to thank you for helping me prepare for these tests. "

Student, San Diego, CA

" My students report your chapters of review as the most valuable single resource they used for review and preparation. "

Teacher, American Fork, UT

" Your book was such a better value and was so much more complete than anything your competition has produced — and I have them all! "

Teacher, Virginia Beach, VA

" Compared to the other books that my fellow students had, your book was the most useful in helping me get a great score. "

Student, North Hollywood, CA

" Your book was responsible for my success on the exam, which helped me get into the college of my choice... I will look for REA the next time I need help. "

Student, Chesterfield, MO

(more on next page)

(continued from front page)

" I just wanted to thank you for helping me get a great score
on the AP U.S. History exam... Thank you for making great test preps! "

Student, Los Angeles, CA

" Your *Fundamentals of Engineering Exam* book was the absolute best
preparation I could have had for the exam, and it is one of the major
reasons I did so well and passed the FE on my first try. "

Student, Sweetwater, TN

" I used your book to prepare for the test and found that the advice and the
sample tests were highly relevant... Without using any other material, I earned
very high scores and will be going to the graduate school of my choice. "

Student, New Orleans, LA

" What I found in your book was a wealth of information sufficient to shore up
my basic skills in math and verbal... The practice tests were challenging and
the answer explanations most helpful. It certainly is the
Best Test Prep for the GRE! "

Student, Pullman, WA

" I really appreciate the help from your excellent book.
Please keep up the great work. "

Student, Albuquerque, NM

" I am writing to thank you for your test preparation... your book helped me
immeasurably and I have nothing but praise for your *GRE* preparation. "

Student, Benton Harbor, MI

(more on back page)

The Best Test Preparation for the

GED

High School Equivalency Diploma

Scott Cameron, M.S.
Science Department Chairperson
San Marino High School, San Marino, California

Janet G. Emmons, Ed.M.
Instructor of English
McCullough High School, The Woodlands, Texas

Mel Friedman, M.S.
Professor of Mathematics
Delaware Valley College, Doylestown, Pennsylvania

Linda Gregory, Ph.D.
Scientific Consultant and Tutor
Cobble Hill, British Columbia

Linda Wiley Jackson, M.A.T.
English Department Chairperson
Raleigh-Egypt High School, Memphis, Tennessee

Mary Ann Kay, M.S.
Science Department Chairperson
Resurrection High School, Chicago, Illinois

Deloris K. Klug, M.A.
Science Department Chairperson
Westside High School, Anderson, South Carolina

Gary Land, Ph.D.
Professor of History
Andrews University, Berrien Springs, Michigan

Charles M. Mallek, M.A.
Social Studies Department Chairperson
Lakeview High School, St. Clair Shores, Michigan

Sandra A. Marona, Ed.M., M.A.
Reading Specialist
Agawam High School, Agawam, Massachusetts

June A. Niimi
Mathematics Department Chairperson
Pahoa High School, Pahoa, Hawaii

Joe D. Reed, Jr., M.S.
Science Department Chairperson
Big Spring High School, Big Spring, Texas

Thomasene W. Thomas, M.A.
Social Studies Department Chairperson
Lincoln High School, Port Arthur, Texas

Robert B. Truscott, M.A.
Former Assistant Director
Douglass/Cook College Writing Center
Rutgers University, New Brunswick, New Jersey

Brian Walsh, M.A.
English Department
Rutgers University, New Brunswick, New Jersey

Robert E. Winstead, Ed.M.
Instructor of Mathematics
Burges High School, El Paso, Texas

Research & Education Association
Visit our website at
www.rea.com

Research & Education Association
61 Ethel Road West
Piscataway, New Jersey 08854
E-mail: info@rea.com

The Best Test Preparation for the
GED High School Equivalency Diploma Tests

Published 2010

Copyright © 2004 by Research & Education Association, Inc.
Prior editions copyright © 2002, 2000, 1999, 1996, 1992 by
Research & Education Association, Inc. All rights reserved.
No part of this book may be reproduced in any form without
permission of the publisher.

Printed in the United States of America

Library of Congress Control Number 2004102770

ISBN-13: 978-0-87891-430-2
ISBN-10: 0-87891-430-7

REA® is a registered trademark of
Research & Education Association, Inc.

CONTENTS

About Research & Education Association

Founded in 1959, Research & Education Association (REA) is dedicated to publishing the finest and most effective educational materials—including software, study guides, and test preps—for students in middle school, high school, college, graduate school, and beyond.

REA's Test Preparation series includes books and software for all academic levels in almost all disciplines. Research & Education Association publishes test preps for students who have not yet entered high school, as well as high school students preparing to enter college. Students from countries around the world seeking to attend college in the United States will find the assistance they need in REA's publications. For college students seeking advanced degrees, REA publishes test preps for many major graduate school admission examinations in a wide variety of disciplines, including engineering, law, and medicine. Students at every level, in every field, with every ambition can find what they are looking for among REA's publications.

REA presents tests that accurately depict the official exams in both degree of difficulty and types of questions. REA's practice tests are always based upon the most recently administered exams, and include every type of question that can be expected on the actual exams.

REA's publications and educational materials are highly regarded and continually receive an unprecedented amount of praise from professionals, instructors, librarians, parents, and students. Our authors are as diverse as the fields represented in the books we publish. They are well known in their respective disciplines and serve on the faculties of prestigious high schools, colleges, and universities throughout the United States and Canada.

We invite you to visit us at *www.rea.com* to find out how REA is making the world smarter.

Acknowledgments

In addition to our authors, we would like to thank Larry B. Kling, Vice President, Editorial, for his overall direction; Pam Weston, Vice President, Publishing, for setting the quality standards for production integrity and managing the publication to completion; Anita Price Davis, David Gracer, and Jay Templin for developmental editing; Mike Reynolds, Senior Editor, for coordinating revisions; Christine Saul, Senior Graphic Designer, for cover design; and Caragraphics for pre-press electronic file mapping.

INTRODUCTION

Chapter 1

Introduction

ABOUT THIS BOOK

This book provides you with an accurate and complete representation of the GED. REA's three full-length practice tests are based on the latest editions of the GED tests, which were overhauled for 2002. Our topical reviews and drills are designed to prepare you for the very kind of material you will see when taking the actual test. You are allowed 7 hours and 5 minutes to complete each of our sample tests. That's the same amount of time you will be given during the actual exam. (Don't panic! The actual exam is usually administered during two or three sittings over a period of two days. Check with your state's department of education for information on GED test centers, test times, and test dates.) Our sample tests have been carefully calibrated to match the GED's level of difficulty, format, and content. Following each model test you will find an answer key along with detailed explanations designed to help you master the material and score high.

ABOUT THE TEST

Who takes the test and what is it used for?

The GED is taken by people who did not complete their high school education and would like to obtain a state-issued high school diploma. The diploma is awarded upon successful completion of the five GED tests. Candidates may choose to take the GED to fulfill requirements for admission to colleges or other schools, to further their careers, or even just for the sake of self-satisfaction. The GED is taken by nearly 800,000 people every year across the United States and Canada, as well as at more than 100 testing sites around the globe.

Who administers the test?

The GED is developed and administered by the GED Testing Service of the American Council on Education (ACE). Questions for the GED are created by writers and reviewers who are experienced in secondary or adult education. They follow standardized procedures, developed by the GED Testing Service, to ensure that the content and difficulty levels are appropriate. According to the American Council on Education, the writers and reviewers represent a wide variety of ethnic groups and are selected from many geographic areas. All questions are reviewed by a number of people, revised as necessary, and then are standardized based on a nationally selected sample of graduating high school seniors.

When and where is the test given?

The GED is administered on a regular basis in the United States and Canada. To accommodate all candidates, there are many versions of the exam, including administrations in English, French, Spanish, Braille, large print, and on audiotape.

To receive information on upcoming administrations of the GED, contact your local high school, adult school, GED Testing Center, or the GED Testing Service at:

1-800-62 MY GED (1-800-626-9433) or
(202) 939-9300

General Educational Development
GED Testing Service
American Council on Education
One Dupont Circle, N.W.
Washington, DC 20036

Website: *www.gedtest.org*
Email: comments@ace.nche.edu

HOW TO USE THIS BOOK

What do I study first?

Before you do anything else, take Practice Exam I to help you determine what areas may cause you the most difficulty. After you are done with the first practice exam, go through and check your answers against the answer keys found at the end of the practice test. It is also suggested that you read through the detailed explanations of answers found at the end of each practice test, as this will help you to understand what you are doing wrong. Once you have taken a practice test, you should first study the reviews which cover your problem areas. The reviews will cover the information you will need to know when taking the exam.

When you have done this, you should go back and study all of the remaining reviews and the test-taking tips which appear at the end of this introduction. Make sure you take the review drills that are interspersed within each review. Both the reviews and the drills will be very useful in helping you brush up on your skills. It will be also be beneficial to read through the Appendix, which includes the Periodic Table, a math reference table, the Constitution of the United States, and the Declaration of Independence.

After studying REA's review, take Practice Exam II and Practice Exam III. When you take our GED practice tests, be sure to do your best to simulate testing conditions: sit at a table in a room free of distractions and time yourself. Doing this will make you less nervous on the day of the actual test and, more importantly, you will develop a sense of pacing. After timing yourself for all of the practice tests, you will have a very good idea of how much time you can spend on each question during the actual GED.

When should I start studying?

It is never too early for you to start studying for the GED—the earlier the better. You should start studying as soon as possible so that you will be able to learn more. Starting early will allow you the time necessary to strengthen your problem areas. Do not procrastinate! Cramming is not an effective way to study since it does not allow you the time needed to learn the exam material.

The GED at a Glance			
TEST	**NO. OF QUESTIONS**	**MINUTES TO TAKE TEST**	**SUBJECT AREAS COVERED**
TEST 1 Language Arts: Writing			
Part I	50	75	Part I deals with sentence structure, usage, mechanics, and organization.
Part II	One essay	45	Part II is an essay of about 250 words.
TEST 2 Social Studies	50	70	History, geography, economics, and political science.
TEST 3 Science	50	80	Life science (biology), physical science (chemistry and physics), and Earth and space science.
TEST 4 Language Arts: Reading	40	65	Literary fiction and nonfiction prose.
TEST 5 Mathematics			Arithmetic (measurement, number relationships, and data analysis), algebra, and geometry.
Part 1	25	45	Part 1 allows the use of a calculator.
Part 2	25	45	Part 2 does not allow the use of a calculator.

Total Testing Time: 7 hours, 5 minutes

FORMAT FOR THE GED

All of the questions in the GED (except for the essay in the Writing test and several alternate format questions in the Mathematics test), will be in multiple-choice format. Each question will have five answers, numbered one through five, from which to choose. You should be aware of the amount of time you have to complete each section of the test, so that you do not waste too much time working on difficult questions, while neglecting to answer easy questions. Speed is very important. Using the practice tests will help you prepare for this task. Taking as many of the practice tests as possible, and making sure to time yourself, will help you become accustomed to the time constraints. Repeating this process will help you develop speed in answering the questions because you will become more familiar with the format.

Test 1: Language Arts: Writing (Two Parts)

Part I of the Writing Skills test consists of 50 multiple-choice items, which will require you to read passages and then answer a series of questions that follow. You will have 75 minutes in which to complete this section. This test is composed of 30% sentence structure questions, 30% usage questions, 25% mechanics (punctuation, capitalization, and spelling) questions, and 15% organization questions. The spelling portion of the test focuses squarely on homonyms, contractions, and possessives. Comma usage is tested only in the context of avoiding confusion in sentence construction. Approximately 50% of the questions on this test deal with sentence correction and 35% with sentence revision, while 15% of the sentence structure and usage questions will deal with construction shift.

Part II of the Writing Skills test is a 45-minute essay. Your essay must be written on the topic listed in your test booklet and is expected to be about 250 words in length. You will be expected to follow all of the rules for sentence structure, usage, and mechanics in writing your essay. You will be graded on several different aspects of your essay, such as how well you addressed and answered the question, the organization of your essay, how well you developed your essay and if you provided details and examples to back your main idea up, how well you followed the rules for standard written English, and how varied and appropriate your word choice is.

Test 2: Social Studies

The Social Studies test has 50 multiple-choice questions. You will have 70 minutes in which to answer questions based on an information document, graph, map, chart, or figure. The information tested within these questions can be found within the corresponding information document, graph, map, chart, or figure. The test consists of 40% history questions, 20% economics questions, 25% political science questions, and 15% geography questions. The types of items break down like this: 20% evaluation; 30% analysis; 30% application; and 20% with comprehension.

Test 3: Science

The Science test runs 80 minutes and consists of 50 multiple-choice items. The questions on the test are based on figures, charts, graphs, information documents, and other written information. This test deals with 45% life-science (biology) questions, 35% physical-science (physics and chemistry) questions, and 20% Earth- and space-science questions. Roughly half the test is composed of conceptual-understanding questions, while the other half presents problem-solving questions.

Test 4: Language Arts: Reading

The Language Arts: Reading test is a 65-minute test, containing 40 multiple-choice items. The questions on this test are based on excerpts from poetry, essays, biographies, plays, critical reviews (of television, film, literature, dance, art, music, sculpture, and theater), commentary, and business-related documents. This test consists of 75% literary-fiction questions and 25% nonfiction-prose questions. Nonfiction prose includes commentary, reviews, nonfiction essays, biographies, autobiographies, and business documents. In this test, 20% of the questions deal with comprehension, requiring you to restate the ideas or information presented or summarize what you read. Application questions make up 15% of the items; these require you to draw your own conclusions, understand the effects or importance of a situation, or identify the implications involved in the situation presented. Synthesis questions account for 30-35% of the test questions. The test also consists of 30–35% analysis questions, which will ask you to define stylistic and structural techniques in terms of concept.

Test 5: Mathematics

The Mathematics test is a 90-minute test. The 50 questions on this test are divided equally among the following content categories: number operations and number sense; measurement and geometry; data analysis, statistics, and probability; and algebra, functions, and patterns. The Mathematics test is divided into two parts. Part 1 (Item Nos. 1–25) *allows* calculator use. Part 2 (Item Nos. 26–50) does not allow the use of a calculator.

Part 1 only allows the use of a specific calculator, the Casio fx-260 Solar Calculator. Although you may find it helpful to use the Casio fx-260 while taking our Mathematics practice test, you needn't buy one. This calculator will be provided at the testing center. You will be given a brief overview of the calculator and time to practice on it before the Mathematics test begins. For more information about the Casio fx-260 Solar Calculator, contact the American Council on Education.

The Mathematics test has both multiple-choice questions and alternate-format questions. Unlike GED multiple-choice questions, which provide five possible answers for you to choose from, alternate-format questions require you to come up with your own answer. A total of 10 alternate-format questions are featured on the entire Mathematics test: You'll find seven in Part 1 and three in Part 2. One of these alternate-format questions will take the form of a coordinate plane. You'll have to grid in the correct answer on your answer sheet.

ABOUT THE REVIEW SECTIONS

Our reviews are written to help you understand the concepts behind the questions which will be asked on the actual GED. They will help you to prepare for the actual test by teaching you what you need to know. Each review is complete with drills which will help to reinforce the subject matter. The five review sections in this book correspond to the tests of the actual GED. By using the reviews in conjunction with the practice tests, you will be able to sharpen your skills and score well on the GED.

Language Arts: Writing Test Review

This section reviews correct sentence structure, usage, spelling, punctuation, and capitalization, and includes drills to help reinforce these rules. Studying these rules will help you do well on both parts of the Writing Skills test. Also discussed in this review are essay writing techniques to aid you in developing a strong, well-organized essay for Part II of the Writing Skills test.

Social Studies Test Review

This review provides a rundown of what you will need to know to pass the Social Studies test. Included are reviews of history, economics, political science, and geography. Drills are also provided to help you enhance your skills to pass this test. Our review will familiarize you with Social Studies and help you to become accustomed to reading Social Studies documents and answering questions concerning such documents. It is important to remember that the GED Social Studies test does not require you to memorize the large volume of information that is covered on the test. The test questions will be based on information documents, tables, graphs, or charts provided within the test.

Science Test Review

Discussed in this review is everything you need to know to pass the Science test. Our review goes over the basics of biology (including cell biology, anatomy, ecology, and genetics), physics, space science, Earth science, and chemistry. Included are drills on biology, earth science, space science, physics, and chemistry. Like the Social Studies test, the Science test does not require you to memorize all of science. The questions are based on information documents, tables, or graphs.

Language Arts: Reading Test Review

This review will help you become familiar with the type of material that you will encounter on the actual GED. The extensive reviews and drills cover writing forms including fiction and nonfiction prose, poetry, drama, essay, and commentary. Studying the Language Arts: Reading Review will help you do well on this test.

Mathematics Test Review

The Math test review covers the basics of what you need to know to pass this test from arithmetic all the way to geometry. Our reviews will take you through problems step-by-step and will show you how to use important mathematical equations in certain math problems. At the end of each section, there are valuable drills which will help you to thoroughly familiarize yourself with the math concepts that will appear on the Mathematics test.

SCORING THE EXAM

How is the GED scored?

When you receive your GED score report from ACE, it will contain six scores. Five individual scores will be reported, one for Parts I and II of the Language Arts: Writing test, one for the Social Studies test, one for the Science test, one for the Language Arts: Reading test, and one for the Mathematics test. The sixth score listed on the score report will be an average of the five individual test scores.

During the scoring process, an individual test is first given a raw score, which is your total number of correct answers. The raw score is then converted into a standard score, which ranges from a minimum of 200 to a high of 800. The standard score is what appears on your score report. Since each test has a different number of questions, raw scores must be converted into standard scores so that your performance on each of the individual tests may be accurately compared. Since various forms of the GED are administered during any one examination, the use of standard scores also corrects for changes in difficulty level between the different forms of the test. In other words, your score should be about the same no matter what form of the test you are given.

Most states require a minimum standard score of 410 on each individual test and a minimum average score of 450 for all 5 tests. To pass the five-test battery, the GED candidate must currently demonstrate a level of skill that meets or surpasses that of approximately 60 percent of graduating high school seniors.

How is my score obtained for the Writing test?

In order to obtain your score for the Writing Skills test, your raw score for both Parts are combined to form one raw score. Then, the raw score is converted into a standard score to give you a single, composite score for this test. Generally, the multiple-choice section of the Writing test is weighed more heavily than the essay. The composite score will consist of 60 to 65 percent of the multiple choice section and 35 to 40 percent of the essay.

Scoring your essay will require you to use the same technique used by the actual essay readers. A holistic method will be used to score your essay, in which two trained readers will read your paper and each assign it a score. The readers will judge your essay on its overall effectiveness and proper use of the rules of English, although they will not be keeping track of each and every mistake. Their overall impression of the essay will be the basis for your score.

Each essay will be graded using a four-point scale, with a score of four (4) being the highest and a score of one (1) being the lowest. The table below outlines what a GED essay reader will consider to be elements characterizing an essay at each score level.

GED ESSAY SCORES

Score of 4   An essay with a score of four will address the question with a strong main idea (thesis) and will continue to address the question throughout the essay. An essay with a score of a 4 will not drift in its focus. This essay will also be extremely well organized. It will be concise and easy to understand. The topic will be effectively supported with examples that illustrate the point of the essay. Very few errors in the use of Standard Written English will be noted. Word choice will be varied, clear, and appropriate.

Score of 3   An essay with a score of three will be thoughtfully organized and present adequate support for the main idea. Some errors in the use of standard written English will appear, however, they will not be consistent.

Score of 2   An essay with a score of two will be underdeveloped and not extensively organized, although the essay will show some signs of planning and organization. The ideas used to support the main idea will often be weak and repetitive. There will be many errors in the use of standard written English.

Score of 1   An essay with a score of one will have virtually no structure and the numerous errors in the use of standard written English will make the essay difficult to understand. The essay will not be developed and will have no apparent purpose.

Once each reader has assigned the essay a score, the two scores are added together, provided they do not differ by more than one point. A score between 2 and 8 will be obtained. This is your raw score.

In some cases, one reader will assign an essay a low score, while the other reader will assign the same essay a high score. When such discrepancies occur with the two scores differing by more than one point, a third reader is called in to score the essay. The three scores are averaged (to do this, add the three scores together and divide by 3), then the average is doubled and rounded off to the nearest whole number. In such a case, this number would be your raw score.

You may want to find two or three people who are willing to score your essay so you can obtain an objective raw score using the process described above. Should you decide to grade your own essay, assign the essay a score, using the chart, then double that number to determine the raw score. If you feel that your essay is between two scores (perhaps it is between a 3 and a 4 essay), add both numbers together to obtain your raw score (3 + 4 = 7) and divide by two. After determining your essay's score, record the score in the *Scoring Worksheet*.

If you score your own essay, be objective! Most of us like to think that our work is excellent, but we must learn to see where there is room for improvement. On the other hand, some people have a tendency to automatically decide that their work is poor, when it may not be at all. Try to see your writing for what it is whether it is excellent, below average, or average.

SCORING WORKSHEET

	Exam I	Exam II	Exam III
Test 1: Language Arts: Writing			
Multiple Choice	_____	_____	_____
Essay	_____	_____	_____
Test 2: Social Studies	_____	_____	_____
Test 3: Science	_____	_____	_____
Test 4: Language Arts:			
Reading	_____	_____	_____
Test 5: Mathematics	_____	_____	_____

Remember, you want to be able to answer at least 50% of the questions in each test correctly so that you can ensure yourself a passing score.

What is a passing score for the GED?

Every state has its own requirements for what constitutes a passing score for the GED. Generally, each state will require that you obtain a certain score for each of the individual subject tests, and then also obtain a certain average (total) score, which is a combination of all of your individual scores.

Listed on the following pages are the current GED requirements for each of the fifty states, U.S. territories, and Canada. Also included are age and residency requirements, testing fee amounts, and the title of the certificate which you will be awarded. For further information, you should contact your state's department of education.

STUDYING FOR THE GED

It is important for you to choose the time and place for studying that works best for you. Some students may set aside a certain number of hours every morning to study, while others may choose to study at night before going to sleep. Other students may study during the day, while waiting in a line, or they may even study while eating lunch. Only you will be able to determine when and where your studying is most effective. The most important factor to keep in mind is consistency. Use your time wisely. Work out a study routine—and stick to it!

When you take the practice tests, try to make your practice conditions similar to actual testing conditions. Make sure you turn the television and radio off. Sit down at a quiet table which is free from distraction and **time yourself**! Afterwards, you should check each answer and thoroughly review the reasoning behind each question that you missed. You should not review too much at one time. Concentrate on each of your problem areas individually, until you feel comfortable with your ability in each of those areas.

Do not write in the margins and spaces of this book when practicing, since you will not be allowed to write in the test booklet when taking the actual test. Also, make sure you do not write anything on your answer sheet, except to mark the answer you choose. Make sure the question numbers correctly correspond to the question numbers on the answer sheet.

Keep track of your scores! You will be able to gauge your progress and discover general weaknesses in particular sections. You should carefully study the reviews that cover the areas which are causing you difficulty. This will help you build your skills in those areas.

GED TEST-TAKING TIPS

You may be unfamiliar with standardized tests, such as the GED. There are many ways for you to familiarize yourself with this type of examination. Listed below are points to help you become familiar with the GED, some of which may be applied to other standardized tests, as well.

How to Beat the Clock

Become comfortable with the standardized format. When you are practicing to take the GED, pretend that you are under the same time constraints as you would be during the test. Stay calm, pace yourself, and pay attention to the clock. Practice these techniques thoroughly. After simulating the test only a few times, you will boost your chances of doing well and you will be able to sit down for the actual GED much more confidently.

Become familiar with the directions. Make sure you read and understand the directions before you take the exam, so that you do not waste valuable testing time.

Know the format for each section before you actually take the test. This will not only save you valuable time, but also ensure that you are familiar enough with the exam to avoid anxiety (and the mistakes that come from being anxious). Be sure to see details on the GED format elsewhere in this introduction.

Work on the easier questions first. Mark the very difficult questions (in the test booklet, not on the answer sheet) and continue. Remember, only correct answers will be counted in your score. You will not be penalized for guessing, so when you have either answered or marked all of the questions, go back and answer any of the difficult questions that you may have skipped. If you find yourself working too long on one question, mark it and go on. Be sure that you are marking your answer in the space that corresponds to the number of the question in the test booklet.

Know how much time is allowed for each section. Remember that you are racing against the clock. This is why you should not spend too much time on a single question. Budget your time. Every question has the same value, whether it is difficult or easy, so it is important to move on if a question becomes too time consuming. Pace yourself and make sure to check your time periodically to make sure that you are progressing at a swift, steady rate.

Should I guess?

If you don't know the answer to a question, guess! Eliminate answers that you know are wrong, and then pick the best answer from the ones that remain. Even if you can't eliminate any answers, guess anyway! Remember that there is no penalty for guessing, and only correct answers are counted. This means that you should never leave an answer choice blank. If you guess correctly, you will increase your number of correct answers, and if you guess wrong, you will not lose any points.

THE DAY OF THE TEST

On the day of the test, you should wake up early (hopefully after a decent night's rest) and have a good breakfast. Make sure you dress comfortably, so that you are not distracted by being too hot or too cold while taking the exam. You should plan on arriving at the test center early. By being early, you will spare yourself the anxiety of being late for the test. It will also allow you to collect your thoughts and to relax before taking the exam.

Before you leave for the test center, make sure that you have **two** forms of identification. You will not be admitted to the test center without identification. Acceptable forms of identification include a driver's license, Social Security card, birth certificate, passport, and green card.

Make sure you bring at least two sharpened No. 2 pencils, with erasers, to the exam. You may want to wear a watch to the test center; however, only ordinary watches will be permitted. Watches with alarms, calculator functions, flashing lights, beeping sounds, etc., will not be allowed. In addition, neither food nor calculators will be allowed into the examination room.

During the Test

When you arrive at the test center, try to sit in a seat where you feel you will be comfortable. The GED is usually administered during two or three sittings, depending on your test center. No breaks are given during the exam. If you need to use the rest room, or if you become ill, you may leave the examination room, but you will not be allowed to make up any lost time.

Once you enter the test center, follow all of the rules and instructions given by the test supervisor. If you do not, you risk being dismissed from the examination or having your GED scores voided (they will not be scored).

When all of the test materials have been passed out, the test instructor will give you directions for filling out your answer sheet. You must fill out this sheet carefully since this information will be printed on your score report. Fill out your name exactly as it appears on your identification documents and admission ticket, unless otherwise instructed.

Make sure you do not write in your test booklet or on your answer sheet, except to fill in the circle corresponding to the answer you choose. Scratch paper will be provided. You will be marking your answers on side two of your answer sheet. Each numbered row will contain five circles corresponding to each answer choice for that question. Fill in the circle which corresponds to your answer darkly, completely, and in a neat manner. You can change your answer, but remember to completely erase your old answer. Only one answer should be marked. This is very important, as your answer sheet will be machine scored, and stray lines or unnecessary marks may cause the machine to score your answers incorrectly.

Only work on the test section on which the test instructor has instructed you to work. You should begin only when instructed to do so, and stop, immediately, when instructed to stop. Do not turn to the next section of the test until you are told to do so. When all of the sections have been completed, you should remain seated until all of the test materials have been collected.

Good Luck on the GED!

GED STUDY
SCHEDULE

GED Study Course Schedule

This study course schedule allows for thorough preparation for the GED. Although it is designed for 12 weeks, it can be halved by collapsing each two-week period into a more ambitious one-week time line. If you are not enrolled in a structured course, be sure to set aside enough time each day to study. Depending on your schedule, you may find it easier to study throughout the weekend. Ultimately, however, the key to your success boils down to this: ***The more time you devote to studying for the GED, the more prepared and relaxed you will be on the day of the exam.***

Week	Activity
1	Read and study the introduction sections on studying for the GED on the following pages. Take Exam I to determine your strengths and weaknesses. You may wish to take one subject part of the test each day. For example, take the Language Arts: Writing on Monday, Social Studies on Tuesday, Science on Wednesday, etc. Score each section by using the score chart found in the introduction. (You may need the help of a counselor or teacher to read your essay in order to score your essay.) You can then determine the subjects in which you will need to strengthen your skills. Compare your score to the average score needed to pass in your state found in the score chart information. If you should score lower than the average (around 35–40) on any particular subject, you will want to concentrate on that area as you study each review section in this book.
2	Study the Language Arts: Writing Review: Part I. Be sure to complete every drill and study the list of commonly misspelled words.
3	Study the Language Arts: Writing Review: Part II. Take the essay writing drill. Rework the essay until you believe it would receive a top score according to the qualifications found in this introduction in the scoring section, and in the review. You may want to request the help of a teacher or counselor to score your essay since the actual essay will be read by just such a person.
4	Study the Social Studies Review. Be sure to complete all the drills.

Week	Activity
5	Study the Science Review in Biology and Chemistry. Take all the drills.
6	Study the Science Review in Earth Science and Physics. Take all the drills.
7	Study the Language Arts: Reading Review. Complete all the drills.
8	Study the Math Review in Arithmetic and Algebra. Complete all the drills.
9	Study the Math Review in Algebra and Geometry. Complete all the drills.
10	Take Exam II and after scoring your exam, review thoroughly all your incorrect answer explanations to determine your strengths and weaknesses.
11	Take Exam III and after scoring your exam, compare any improvement in comparison with the previously scored exam.
12	Determine your weaknesses based on Exam III and review thoroughly all your incorrect answer explanations. Then review the subjects in which you need to make gains by reading over the appropriate reviews.

Your Test-Day Checklist

☐ Get a good night's sleep. Tired test-takers consistently perform poorly.

☐ Wake up early.

☐ Dress comfortably. Keep your clothing temperature appropriate. You'll be sitting in your test clothes for hours. Clothes that are itchy, tight, too warm, or too cold take away from your comfort level.

☐ Eat a good breakfast.

☐ Take these with you to the test center:
- Several sharpened No. 2 pencils. Pencils are not provided at the test center.
- A ballpoint pen
- Admission ticket
- Two forms of ID. One must be a current, government-issued identification bearing your photograph and signature.

☐ Arrive at the test center early. Remember, many test centers do not allow you into a test session after the test has begun.

☐ Compose your thoughts and try to relax before the test.

Remember that eating, drinking, and smoking are prohibited. Calculators, dictionaries, textbooks, notebooks, briefcases, and packages are also prohibited.

LANGUAGE ARTS: WRITING REVIEW

Chapter 2

LANGUAGE ARTS: WRITING PART I REVIEW

I.   WRITING I STRATEGIES
II. STANDARD WRITTEN ENGLISH
III. CAPITALIZATION
IV. PUNCTUATION
V.   SPELLING AND WORD USAGE

Although we constantly come into contact with the English language, mastery is another story. The Writing I section of the GED will test how well you understand and recognize correct standard written English. You will want to review the information we have provided for you in this section to ensure that you will do well on this section of the exam. Our review concentrates on the common errors that you should avoid in your writing and presents practice exercises in recognizing and correcting errors when they occur in the written language.

Although the new GED Language Arts: Writing I no longer places special focus on the areas of spelling or comma usage, it is still important to study these areas to do well on the Essay section of the test.

With this knowledge will come the speed and accuracy you'll need to answer the questions successfully. Another way to save time is to memorize the directions; this will also cut your chances of making careless mistakes. Above all, however, be sure to complete the practice drills that are included in our topical review, as they will help you build your competence and confidence as you prepare for our practice tests and, ultimately, for the GED itself.

I. WRITING I STRATEGIES

If you can determine that there is an error somewhere in the sentence, this is your plan of attack:

> Sentence 1: **Many people say that their time spent in high school—despite the well-known ups and downs of being a teenager—were the best time of their lives.**

What correction should be made to this sentence?

   (1)   Change the spelling of high school to highschool.

   (2)   Change were to was.

   (3)   Insert a comma after say.

   (4)   Change lives to life.

   (5)   Change their time to their times.

➤ **Step 1** | Using your sense of "ear," scan the sentence for an error.

Here the phrase "were the best time of their lives" does not sound right, making it suspect.

➤ **Step 2** | Can you replace the questionable part with one of the choices?

In the example, the subject of the verb "were" is "time," which requires a singular verb. "Were" must be changed to "was" in order for the sentence to be correct due to the fact that "time" is a singular noun. Ignore the words that intervene between subject and verb ("despite the well-known ups and downs of being a teenager"); they do not affect the number of the verb.

➤ **Step 3** | Re-read the sentence with the answer choice you chose substituted for the part of the sentence in question. If it holds up according to your knowledge of correct standard written English, this is your answer.

The sentence would now read:

Many people say that their time spent in high school—despite the well-known ups and downs of being a teenager—was the best time of their lives.

If you cannot determine that there is an error somewhere in the sentence, this is your plan of attack:

Sentence 2: **Mr. Parker is <u>one of the professors who are teaching</u> students the importance of good grades and a good attitude.**

Which of the following is the best way to write the underlined portion of this sentence? If you think the original is the best way, choose option (1).

(1) one of the professors who are teaching
(2) one of the professors who is teaching
(3) one of the professor that has taught
(4) the professor that is to be teaching
(5) the professor that taught

➤ Step 1 | Look at the answer choices to see what has been changed from the original sentence. This helps you to focus on the type of problem being tested in the question.

The changes that occur are related to the form of the verb **are** or the use of the phrase **one of**.

➤ Step 2 | Go back into the example sentence and try to find the error.

➤ Step 3 | Eliminate any answer choices that repeat the error that you have found.

➤ Step 4 | Eliminate any answer choices that are obviously incorrect.

There are two subjects in this sentence. Mr. Parker is a singular noun, modified by the verb "is" in "Mr. Parker is one of the professors..." Professors, the second subject, is a plural noun modified by the second verb, which in this case should be "are," to allow for the subject and verb to agree. Therefore, answer choice (1) is correct. Answer choices (3), (4), and (5) are incorrect due to the improper use of the word "that."

➤ **ADDITIONAL HINTS**

- **Learn and understand the DIRECTIONS so you don't waste valuable time reading them on the day of the exam.**

- **Be sure to read the sentence exactly as it is written.**

- **Look for the most common errors in the sentence first. These are listed in the Review of Standard Written English.**

- **Do not pay attention simply to the underlined words. The words that are not underlined can determine whether or not the underlined words are correct.**

- **If you still do not know the correct answer, try the shortest choice in the sentence first. Good writing tends to be concise.**

- **Do not waste time looking for errors that are not there—a correction may not be necessary.**

- **If all else fails, make an educated guess.**

LANGUAGE ARTS: WRITING I TOPICS

The topics listed below should be reviewed in order to accurately answer the questions appearing on the Writing I section of the GED. See the Review of Standard Written English on the following pages.

SENTENCE STRUCTURE (30% of Test)

1. Sentence Fragments
2. Run-on Sentences
3. Comma Splices
4. Sentence Coordination
5. Use of the Subordinate Clause
6. Parallelism

USAGE (30% of Test)

1. Subject/Verb Agreement
2. Verb Tense
3. Pronouns

MECHANICS (25% of Test)

1. Capitalization
2. Punctuation (Commas are only tested if they are being used to eliminate confusion.)
3. Spelling (Only the spelling of homonyms, contractions, and possessions is tested.)

ORGANIZATION (15% of Test)

1. Topic sentences
2. Creating text divisions
3. Topic sentences
4. Unity/Coherence

II. REVIEW OF STANDARD WRITTEN ENGLISH

SUBJECT-VERB AGREEMENT

NO: The arrival of many friends promise good times.

Always remember to make the verb agree with the subject of the sentence. Be wary of the words that come between the subject and the verb. They may distract you.

YES: The **arrival** of many friends **promises** good times.

NO: Into the darkness stares her black cats.

Don't be fooled by sentences where the subject follows the verb. Be especially careful to determine the subject and make it agree with the verb.

YES: Into the darkness **stares** her black **cat**.

NO: Either the principal or the football coach usually attend the dance.

When singular subjects are joined by *either... or, neither... nor, or* or *nor*, the verb is also singular.

YES: Either the principal or the football **coach** usually **attends** the dance.

NO: Neither the cat nor the dogs is eating today.

If one of the subjects is plural and one is singular, make the verb agree with the subject nearest it.

YES: Neither the **cat** nor the **dogs are** eating today.

NO: Politics weigh heavily on him.

Don't assume that subjects ending with an *s* are necessarily plural.*

YES: Politics **weighs** heavily on him.

* **Beware of subjects that may appear to be plural but need to be construed as singular either 1) because of their meaning, 2) because they're used as words (e.g., *Women* is the plural of *woman*, or 3) because you're dealing with the title of a work (e.g., Joe Henderson's *Best Runs* is an outstanding motivational book).**

☞ Drill: Subject-Verb Agreement

DIRECTIONS: The following group of sentences may contain errors in subject-verb agreement. Make any necessary corrections.

1. Either her mother or her father usually drive her to school on rainy days.

2. There is, if I calculated right, two hundred dollars left in my bank account.

3. Mary and her friends was late for the test.

4. Economics are a major taught in many colleges.

5. The first years of high school is the most difficult.

6. Aristotle's *Poetics* have always been read widely.

7. The noise from all those fans were distracting.

8. Neither the chorus nor the actors knows their parts.

9. Each of us are going away for the weekend.

10. Neither the grass nor the flowers was growing well.

COMPARISON OF ADJECTIVES

NO: That was the most bravest thing he ever did.

Do not combine two superlatives.

YES: That was the **bravest** thing he ever did.

_____

NO: Mary was more friendlier than Susan.

Do not combine two comparatives.

YES: Mary was **friendlier** than Susan.

_____

NO: I can buy either the shirt or the scarf. The shirt is most expensive.

The comparative should be used when only two things are being compared.

YES: I can buy either the shirt or the scarf. The shirt is **more** expensive.

☞ Drill: Comparison of Adjectives

DIRECTIONS: In the following sentences, make the changes indicated in the parentheses. Also indicate if the comparative or superlative form is an adverb or an adjective.

1. He was sad to leave. (superlative)

2. She ran as fast as the others on the team. (comparative)

3. Throughout school, they were good in math. (superlative)

4. This class is as interesting as the European history class. (comparative)

5. He arrived as soon as I did. (comparative)

6. The test was as difficult as we expected. (comparative)

7. He responded to the interviewer as candidly as Tom. (comparative)

8. The beggar had less possessions than she. (superlative)

9. That answer is perfectly correct. (superlative)

10. She read the part best. (comparative)

POSSESSIVE NOUNS

A common error to avoid is to write *it's* (the contraction for *it is*) for *its* (the possessive form) or vice versa.

Form the possessive singular of nouns by adding *'s*.

> Mary's book
> the Jones's family car
> the sun's rays
> my mother-in-law's suitcase

☞ Drill: Possessive Nouns

DIRECTIONS: The following group of sentences may contain errors in possession. Make any necessary corrections.

1. His suit, like James, was grey.

2. The president's adviser's past was investigated.

3.　The pitcher's job is more difficult than the fielders.

4.　The woman's cat's kittens were given away.

5.　The majority leader of the House of Representatives' speech was well received.

6.　The final plans of the Boy Scouts of America's meeting were made.

7.　It was Susan, Ann, Joan, and my idea.

8.　The amateurs' life differs from the professionals.

9.　That is Dr. White and her new house.

10.　The plays' ending satisfied the audience.

PREPOSITIONS

NO:　She just couldn't start in to do her homework.

Do not overuse prepositions.

YES:　She just couldn't start to do her homework.

☞ Drill: Prepositions

DIRECTIONS: The following group of sentences may contain prepositional errors. Make any necessary corrections.

1.　Let's finish up the assignment.

2.　He was interested and fascinated with physics.

3.　She had learned of his life and his times through reading.

4.　They were both repelled and driven toward the space creature.

5.　Tell me on what he left it.

6.　Let's go over to James' house tomorrow.

7.　She always had an interest and an aptitude for science.

8.　It took a long time to get at the problem.

9.　She looked like her sister and her mother.

10.　Her belief and dedication to the cause were total.

CONJUNCTIONS

NO: She loved him dearly but not his dog.

When using a conjunction, be sure that the sentence parts you are joining are in agreement.

YES: She loved him dearly but **she did not love his dog**.

NO: They complimented them both for their bravery and they thanked them for their kindness.

When using conjunctions, a common mistake that is made is to forget that each member of the pair must be followed by the same kind of construction.

YES: They both **complimented them for their bravery** and **thanked them for their kindness**.

NO: While I'm usually interested in Fellini movies, I'd rather not go tonight.

While refers to time and should not be used as a substitute for *although, and,* or *but*.

YES: **Although** I'm usually interested in Fellini movies, I'd rather not go tonight.

NO: We read in the paper where they are making great strides in DNA research.

Where refers to a place or location. Be careful not to use it when it does not have this meaning.

YES: We read in the paper **that** they are making great strides in DNA research.

☞ Drill: Conjunctions

DIRECTIONS: The following group of sentences may contain errors in the use of conjunctions. Make any necessary corrections.

1. John's best assets are his personality and swimming ability.

2. I heard on the radio where the play is closing this week.

3. I was reading the paper and the phone rang.

4. Susan ate vegetables often but not fruits.

5. Please send me an answer to the question or opinions on the project.

6. While I'm tired from the trip, I'll attend the concert tonight.

7. Mary's goal is to study hard and pass the test.

8. He produced the play while she directed it.

9. A good essay is where the ideas are clearly articulated.

10. The class wanted neither to read the book nor do the assignment.

MISPLACED MODIFIERS

NO: Harold watched the painter gaping in astonishment.

The dangling participle is an error that results in an unclear sentence. The participle should appear immediately before or after the subject of the sentence.

YES: Gaping in astonishment, Harold watched the painter.

NO: On correcting the test, his errors became apparent.

Many modifiers cause confusion when they are out of place.

YES: His errors became apparent when the test was corrected.

NO: Jane almost polished the plate until it shined.

Words such as *almost, only, just, even, nearly, hardly, not,* and *merely* must appear immediately before the word they modify or they will cause confusion.

YES: Jane polished the plate until it almost shined.

☞ Drill: Misplaced Modifiers

DIRECTIONS: The following group of sentences may contain misplaced modifiers. Make any necessary corrections.

1. I saw a stray dog riding the bus this afternoon.

2. The clothing was given to the poor in large packages.

3. I found five dollars eating lunch in the park.

4. We saw two girls riding bicycles from our car.

5. Reading my book quietly, I jumped up when the car crashed.

6. He ran the mile with a sprained ankle.

7. The history majors only were affected by the new requirements.

8. Running quickly to catch the bus, Susan's packages fell out of her arms onto the ground.

9. He just asked the man directions to make sure.

10. He discovered a new route driving home.

PARALLEL STRUCTURE

NO: The janitor stopped, listened a moment, then he locked the door.

When ideas are similar, they should be expressed in similar forms. When elements of a sentence are similar, they too should appear in similar form.

YES: The janitor stopped, listened a moment, then locked the door.

☞ Drill: Parallel Structure

DIRECTIONS: The following group of sentences may contain errors in parallel structure. Make any necessary corrections.

1. In the summer I usually like swimming and to water-ski.

2. The professor explained the cause, effect, and the results.

3. Mary read the book, studied the examples, and takes the test.

4. Mark watched the way John started the car, and how he left the curb.

5. They bought the house because of location and its affordability.

6. The movie was interesting and had a lot of excitement.

7. Shakespeare both wrote beautiful sonnets and complex plays.

8. The painting is done either in watercolors or with oils.

9. The lecturer spoke with seriousness and in a concerned tone.

10. Either we forget those plans or accept their proposal.

RUN-ON SENTENCES

NO: It was a pleasant drive the sun was shining.

A run-on sentence is a sentence with too much in it. It usually contains two complete sentences separated by a comma, or two complete sentences merged together.

YES: It was a pleasant drive because the sun was shining.

_____

NO: Talk softly, someone is listening.

Sometimes a writer will try to correct a run-on sentence by inserting a comma between the clauses, but this creates another error, a *comma splice*. The following examples illustrate various ways to correct the comma splice.

YES: Talk softly; someone is listening.

or

Talk softly, because someone is listening.

SENTENCE FRAGMENTS

NO: A tree as old as your father.

This is just the opposite of a run-on sentence. A sentence fragment does not have enough in it to make it a complete thought. It is usually missing a subject or a verb.

YES: The tree is as old as your father.

☞ Drill: Run-On Sentences/Sentence Fragments

DIRECTIONS: The following sentences may be either run-on sentences or sentence fragments. Make any necessary corrections.

1.   After the rain stopped.

2.   Mow the lawn, it is much too long.

3.   The settlement you reached it seems fair.

4.   When I read, especially at night. My eyes get tired.

5.   It was impossible to get through on the phone, the lines were down because of the storm.

6.   Is this the only problem? The leaky pipe?

7. Everyone saw the crime, no one is willing to come forth.

8. The weather was bad, she played in the rain.

9. Ellen paced the floor. Worrying about her economics final.

10. Their season was over, the team had lost the playoffs.

TENSE OF VERBS

Tense means time. Verbs have the ability to tell us not only what action is occurring, but also when it is occurring. The form of the verb changes to indicate when an action takes place.

NO: I swum two miles last week.

Do not confuse the past participle for the past tense.

YES: I swam two miles last week.

☞ Drill: Tense of Verbs

DIRECTIONS: For the following sentences, fill in the indicated form of the verb in parentheses.

1. I _____ fifty pages by tomorrow. (*to read, future*)

2. We _____ in the concert. (*to sing, past*)

3. He _____ class on Mondays and Wednesdays. (*to teach, present*)

4. You _____ the dress without permission. (*to take, past*)

5. It _____ once spring arrives. (*to grow, future*)

6. The bee _____ her while she was on vacation. (*to sting, past*)

7. He _____ many plays. (*to cast, past perfect*)

8. He _____ the plane tomorrow if the skies are clear. (*to fly, future progressive*)

9. They _____ furniture all afternoon. (*to choose, present perfect progressive*)

10. You _____ your ticket before the train arrived. (*to buy, past perfect progressive*)

STANDARD WRITTEN ENGLISH

ANSWER KEY

Drill: Subject-Verb Agreement

1. Either her mother or her father usually drives her to school on rainy days.

2. There are, if I calculated right, two hundred dollars left in my bank account.

3. Mary and her friends were late for the test.

4. Economics is a major taught in many colleges.

5. The first years of high school are the most difficult.

6. Aristotle's *Poetics* has always been read widely.

7. The noise from all those fans was distracting.

8. Neither the chorus nor the actors know their parts.

9. Each of us is going away for the weekend.

10. Neither the grass nor the flowers were growing well.

Drill: Comparison of Adjectives

1. He was **saddest** to leave. (adjective)

2. She ran **faster** than the others on the team. (adverb)

3. Throughout school, they were **the best** in math. (adjective)

4. This class is **more interesting** than European history class. (adjective)

5. He arrived **sooner** than I did. (adverb)

6. The test was **more difficult** than we expected. (adjective)

7. He responded to the interviewer **more candidly** than Tom. (adverb)

8. This sentence (referring to "she") **cannot** be put in the superlative form.

9. The answer is **most perfectly** correct. (adverb)

10. She read the part **better**. (adjective)

Drill: Possessive Nouns

1. His suit, like James', was grey.
2. The past of the president's adviser was investigated.
3. The pitcher's job is more difficult than the fielders'.
4. The kittens of the woman's cat were given away.
5. The House of Representatives majority leader's speech was well received.
6. The final plans of the meeting of the Boy Scouts of America were made.
7. It was Susan's, Ann's, Joan's, and my idea.
8. The amateur's life differs from the life of the professional.
9. That is her and Dr. White's new house.
10. The play's ending satisfied the audience.

Drill: Prepositions

1. Let's finish the assignment.
2. He was interested and fascinated by physics.
3. She had learned of his life and of his times through reading.
4. They were both repelled by and driven toward the space creature.
5. Tell me what he left it on.
6. Let's go to James' house tomorrow.
7. She always had an interest in and an aptitude for science.
8. It took a long time to get through the problem.
9. She looked like her sister and like her mother.
10. Her belief in and dedication to the cause were total.

Drill: Conjunctions

1. John's best assets are his personality and his swimming ability.
2. I heard on the radio that the play is closing this week.
3. I was reading the paper when the phone rang.
4. Susan often ate vegetables but not fruits.
5. Please send me either an answer to the questions or opinions on the project.
6. Although I'm tired from the trip, I'll attend the concert tonight.

7.   Mary's goal is not only to study hard but also to pass the test.

8.   He produced the play and she directed it.

9.   A good essay is one in which the ideas are clearly articulated.

10. The class wanted neither to read the book nor to do the assignment.

Drill: Misplaced Modifiers

1.   I saw a stray dog while I was riding the bus this afternoon.

2.   The clothing was given in large packages to the poor.

3.   I found five dollars while I was eating lunch in the park.

4.   While we were in our car we saw two girls riding bicycles.

5.   When the car crashed, I jumped up from quietly reading my book.

6.   He ran the mile although his ankle was sprained.

7.   Only the history majors were affected by the new requirements.

8.   Susan's packages fell out of her arms onto the ground as she was running quickly to catch the bus.

9.   He asked the man for directions just to make sure.

10. While driving home, he discovered a new route.

Drill: Parallel Structure

1.   In the summer I usually like to swim and water-ski.

2.   The professor explained the cause, the effect, and the results.

3.   Mary read the book, studied the examples, and took the test.

4.   Mark watched how John started the car, and how he left the curb.

5.   They bought the house because of its location and its affordability.

6.   The movie was both interesting and exciting.

7.   Shakespeare wrote both (optional) beautiful sonnets and complex plays.

8.   The painting is done with either watercolor or oils.

9.   The lecturer spoke in a serious, concerned tone.

10. Either we forget those plans, or we accept their proposal.

Drill: Run-on Sentences/Sentence Fragments

1.   Fragment: We went out after the rain stopped.

2.   Run-on: Mow the lawn. It is much too long.

3. Run-on: The settlement you reached seems fair.

4. Fragment: My eyes get tired when I read, especially at night.

5. Run-on: It was impossible to get through on the phone, since the lines were down because of the storm.

6. Fragment: Is the leaky pipe the only problem?

7. Run-on: Everyone saw the crime, but no one is willing to come forth.

8. Run-on: The weather was bad. She played in the rain.

9. Fragment: Eileen paced the floor and worried about her economics final.

10. Run-on: The team had lost the playoffs; their season was over.

Drill: Tense of Verbs

1.	shall read	6.	stung
2.	sang	7.	had cast
3.	teaches	8.	will be flying
4.	took	9.	have been choosing
5.	will grow	10.	had been buying

III. CAPITALIZATION

When a letter is capitalized, it calls special attention to itself. This attention should be for a good reason. There are standard uses for capital letters as well as much difference of opinion as to what should and should not be capitalized. In general, capitalize 1) all proper nouns, 2) the first word of a sentence, and 3) a direct quotation.

NAMES OF SHIPS, AIRCRAFT, SPACECRAFT, AND TRAINS:

Apollo 13	*Mariner IV*
DC-10	*S. S. United States*
Sputnik 11	*Boeing 767*

NAMES OF DEITIES AND RELIGIOUS ENTITIES:

God	*Jupiter*
Allah	*Holy Ghost*
Buddha	*Diana*
Jehovah	*Shiva*

GEOLOGICAL PERIODS:

Neolithic Age	*Cenozoic era*
late Pleistocene times	*Age of Reptiles*
Ice Age	*Tertiary period*

NAMES OF ASTRONOMICAL BODIES:

Venus	*Big Dipper*
the Milky Way	*Halley's comet*
Ursa Major	*North Star*
Scorpio	*Deneb*
the Crab nebula	*Pleiades*

(Note that sun, moon, and earth are not capitalized unless they are used with other astronomical terms that are capitalized.)

PERSONIFICATIONS:

*Reliable **Nature** brought her promise of Spring.*

*Bring on **Melancholy** in his sad might.*

***Morning** in the bowl of night has flung the stone
that set the stars to flight.*

HISTORICAL PERIODS:

the Middle Ages	*World War I*
Reign of Terror	*Great Depression*
Christian Era	*Roaring Twenties*
Age of Louis XIV	*Renaissance*

ORGANIZATIONS, ASSOCIATIONS, AND INSTITU-TIONS:

Girl Scouts of America	*Loyal Order of Moose*
Young Men's Christian Association	*North Atlantic Treaty Organization*
New York Yankees	*League of Women Voters*
Smithsonian Institution	*Unitarian Church*
the Library of Congress	*Common Market*
the Illinois Central	*New York Philharmonic*
Franklin Glen High School	

GOVERNMENT AGENCIES AND INSTITUTIONS:

Little Rock City Council	*Committee on Foreign Affairs*
Senate	*House of Commons*
Arkansas Supreme Court	*Parliament*
Peace Corps	*House of Representatives*
Muncipal Court of Chicago	*Department of State*
Census Bureau	*Iowa Board of Education*
United States Court of Appeals	

A general term that accompanies a specific name is capitalized only if it follows the specific name. If it stands alone or comes before the specific name, it is put in lowercase.

Washington State	*the state of Washington*
Senator Dixon	*the senator from Illinois*
Central Park	*the park*
the Golden Gate Bridge	*the bridge*
President Andrew Jackson	*the president of the U.S.*
Pope John XXIII	*the pope*
Queen Elizabeth I	*the queen, Elizabeth I*
Tropic of Capricorn	*the tropics*
Glen Brook High School	*the high school in Glen Brook*
Monroe Doctrine	*the doctrine originated by Monroe*
the Milky Way Galaxy	*our galaxy, the Milky Way*
the Mississippi River	*the river*
Easter Day	*the day we celebrated Easter*
Treaty of Versailles	*the treaty signed at Versailles*
Webster's Dictionary	*a dictionary by Webster*

Use a capital to start a sentence or a sentence fragment.

Our car would not start.

When will you leave? I need to know right away.

Never!

Let me in! Right now!

When a sentence appears within a sentence, start it with a capital.

The main question is, Where do we start?

We had only one concern: When would we eat?

My sister said, "I'll find the Monopoly set."

He answered, "We can only stay a few minutes."

In poetry, it is usual practice to capitalize the first word of each line even if the word comes in the middle of a sentence.

> *When I consider everything that grows*
> *Holds in perfection but a little moment,*
> *That this huge stage produceth naught but shows,*
> *Whereon the stars in secret influence comment.*
>
> > —*William Shakespeare*

> *She dwells with Beauty—Beauty that must die;*
> *And Joy, whose hand is ever at his lips*
> *Bidding Adieu.*
>
> > —*John Keats*

The most important words of titles are capitalized. Those words not capitalized are conjunctions (e.g., *and, or, but*), articles (e.g., *a, the, and*), and short prepositions (e.g., *of, on, by, for*). The first and last word of a title must always be capitalized.

A Man for All Seasons	*Crime and Punishment*
Of Mice and Men	"Let Me In"
Rise of the West	"What to Look For"
"Sonata in G-Minor"	"The Ever-Expanding West"
Strange Life of Ivan Osokin	"Rubaiyat of Omar Khayyam"
"Law and Order"	*Symphony No. 41*
"Ode to Billy Joe"	"Piano Concerto No. 5"

☞ Drill: Capitalization

DIRECTIONS: The following sentences contain errors in capitalization. Correct these sentences by making words capital where necessary, and other words lowercase where necessary.

1. Where is the crab Nebula?

2. The girl scouts of America sell delicious cookies.

3. This year, senator Burns will visit our school.

4. Barbara said, "let me know when you are off the phone."

5. beth's new car is a black dodge neon, which she purchased at the dodge dealership in freeport.

6. mike and jackie are both graduates of edison high school.

7. glaciers from the ice age still exist.

8. Today in class, the Professor lectured on the Neolithic Age.

9. sergeant bruce whisman of the united states marine corps is stationed in hawaii.

10. We will be spending easter day with our aunt clara who lives near the mississippi river.

11. Helen asked, "when will betty and Rich be returning from yellowstone park?"

12. our english teacher will be reviewing the first twenty pages of the book *of mice and men* with the class.

13. The case went as high as the United States court of appeals.

14. at the baseball game last night, the Los Angeles dodgers beat the New York yankees by Ten runs.

15. Eric asked the teacher, "do you have a Webster's dictionary?"

CAPITALIZATION

ANSWER KEY

Drill: Capitalization

1. Where is the Crab nebula?

2. The Girl Scouts of America sell delicious cookies.

3. This year, Senator Burns will visit our school.

4. Barbara said, "Let me know when you are off the phone."

5. Beth's new car is a black Dodge Neon, which she purchased at the Dodge dealership in Freeport.

6. Mike and Jackie are both graduates of Edison High School.

7. Glaciers from the Ice Age still exist.

8. Today in class, the professor lectured on the Neolithic age.

9. Sergeant Bruce Whisman of the United States Marine Corps is stationed in Hawaii.

10. We will be spending Easter Day with our Aunt Clara who lives near the Mississippi River.

11. Helen asked, "When will Betty and Rich be returning from Yellowstone Park?"

12. Our English teacher will be reviewing the first twenty pages of the book *Of Mice and Men* with the class.

13. The case went as high as the United States Court of Appeals.

14. At the baseball game last night, the Los Angeles Dodgers beat the New York Yankees by ten runs.

15. Eric asked the teacher, "Do you have a Webster's Dictionary?"

IV. PUNCTUATION

Try to read this paragraph:

> *take some more tea the march hare said to alice very earnestly ive had nothing yet alice replied in an offended tone so i cant take more you mean you cant take less said the hatter its very easy to take more than nothing lewis carroll*

Now try again:

> *"Take some more tea," the March Hare said to Alice, very earnestly.*
>
> *"I've had nothing yet," Alice replied in an offended tone, "so I can't take more."*
>
> *"You mean you can't take <u>less</u>," said the Hatter, "it's very easy to take <u>more</u> than nothing."*

> *—Lewis Carroll*

This example illustrates how much punctuation helps the reader understand what the writer is trying to say. The most important role of punctuation is clarification.

In speech, words are accompanied by gesture, voice, tone, and rhythm that help convey a desired meaning. In writing, it is punctuation alone that must do the same job.

There are many rules about how to use the various punctuation marks. These are sometimes difficult to understand because they are described with so much grammatical terminology. Therefore, this discussion of punctuation will avoid as much terminology as possible. If you still find the rules confusing, and your method of punctuation is somewhat random, try to remember that most punctuation takes the place of pauses in speech.

Keeping this in mind, it is helpful to read your sentences aloud as you write; if you punctuate according to the pauses in your speech, you will do much better than if you put in your commas, periods, and dashes at random, or where they look good.

STOPS

There are three ways to end a sentence:
1. period
2. question mark
3. exclamation point

THE PERIOD

Periods end all sentences that are not questions or exclamations. In speech, the end of a sentence is indicated with a full pause. The period is the counterpart of this pause in writing.

Go get me my paper. I'm anxious to see the news.

Into each life some rain must fall. Last night some fell into mine.

The moon is round. The stars look small.

Mary and Janet welcomed the newcomer. She was noticeably happy.

When a question is intended as a suggestion and the listener is not expected to answer, or when a question is asked indirectly as part of a sentence, a period is also used.

Mimi wondered if the parade would ever end.

Will you please send the flowers you advertised.

We'll never know who the culprit was.

Periods also follow most abbreviations and contractions.

N.Y.	*Dr.*	*Jr.*	*Sr.*
etc.	*Jan.*	*Mrs.*	*Mr.*
Esq.	*cont.*	*A.M.*	*A.D.*

Periods (or parentheses) are also used after a letter or number in a series.

a.	*apples*	*1.*	*reading*
b.	*oranges*	*2.*	*writing*
c.	*pears*	*3.*	*arithmetic*

Errors to Avoid

Be sure to omit the period after a quotation mark preceded by a period. Only one stop is necessary to end a sentence.

She said, "Hold my hand." (no period after the final ")

"Don't go into the park until later."

"It's not my fault," he said. "She would have taken the car anyway."

After many abbreviations, particularly for organizations or agencies, no period is used (check your dictionary if in doubt).

AFL-CIO	NAACP	GM
FBI	NATO	IBM
TV	UN	HUD

THE QUESTION MARK

Use a question mark to end a direct question even if it is not in the form of a question. The question mark in writing is the same as the rising tone of voice used to indicate a question in speech. If you read the following two sentences aloud, you will see the difference in tone between a statement and a question composed of the same words.

Mary is here.

Mary is here?

Here are some more examples of correct use of question marks; pay special attention to the way they are used with other punctuation.

Where will we go next?

Would you like coffee or tea?

"Won't you," he asked "please lend me a hand?"

"Will they ever give us our freedom?" the prisoner asked.

"To be or not to be?" was the question asked by Hamlet.

Who asked "When?"

Question marks indicate a full stop and lend a different emphasis to a sentence than do commas. Compare these pairs of sentences:

Was the sonata by Beethoven? or Brahms? or Chopin?

Was the sonata by Beethoven, or Brahms, or Chopin?

Did they walk to the park? climb the small hill? take the bus to town? or go skating out back?

Did they walk to town, climb the small hill, take the bus to town, or go skating out back?

Sometimes question marks are placed in parentheses. This indicates doubt or uncertainty about the facts being reported.

The bombing started at 3:00 A.M. (?)

She said the dress cost 200,000 (?) dollars.

Harriet Stacher (18 (?)–1914) was well thought of in her time.

Hippocrates (460 (?)–377 (?) B.C.) is said to be the father of modern medicine.

THE EXCLAMATION POINT

An exclamation point ends an emphatic statement. It should be used only to express strong emotions such as surprise, disbelief, or admiration. If it is used too often for mild expressions of emotion, it loses its effectiveness.

Let go of me!

Help! Fire!

It was a wonderful day!

What a beautiful woman she is!

Who shouted "Fire!" (Notice no question mark is necessary.)

Fantastic!

"Unbelievable!" she gasped. (Notice no comma is necessary.)

"You'll never win!" he cried.

Where else can I go! (The use of the exclamation point shows that this is a strong statement even though it is worded like a question.)

Avoid Overuse

The following is an example of the overuse of exclamation points:

Dear Susan,

I was so glad to see you last week! You looked better than ever! Our talk meant so much to me! I can hardly wait until we get together again! Could you believe how long it has been! Let's never let that happen again! Please write as soon as you get the chance! I can hardly wait to hear from you!

Your friend,

Nora

☞ Drill: Periods, Question Marks, Exclamation Points

DIRECTIONS: In the following sentences correctly supply periods, question marks, and exclamation points.

1. "Good gracious" she said "Didn't you know that I was coming"

2. Mr. Morgan works for the CIA

3. Alexander wondered if it was time to go

4. Leave me alone Can't you see that I'm busy

5. "How many boxes did you buy" asked Dr. Jones

6. "Be careful" he shouted "Didn't you see the car coming"

7. Impossible I have never seen anything like that before

8. Lynn asked if anyone had the time

9. What else can I do I lost all my money

10. Who cried "Help"

INTERJECTIONS

An interjection is a word or group of words used as an exclamation to express emotion. It need not be followed by an exclamation point. Often an interjection is followed by a comma (see "THE COMMA") if it is not very intense. Technically, the interjection has no grammatical relation to other words in the sentence, yet it is still considered a part of speech.

Examples:

Oh dear, I forgot my keys again.

Ah! Now do you understand?

Ouch! I didn't realize that the stove was hot.

Oh, excuse me. I didn't realize that you were next on line.

PAUSES

There are five ways to indicate a pause shorter than a period:
1. dash
2. colon
3. semicolon
4. parentheses
5. comma

THE DASH

Use the dash to indicate a sudden or unexpected break in the normal flow of the sentence. It can also be used in the place of parentheses or of commas if the meaning is clarified. Usually the dash gives the material it sets off special emphasis. (On a typewriter and in some word-processing programs, two hyphens (--) indicate a dash.)

Could you—I hate to ask!—help me with these boxes?

When we left town—a day never to be forgotten—they had a record snowfall.

She said—we all heard it—"The safe is not locked."

These are the three ladies—Mrs. Jackson, Miss Harris, and Ms. Forrester—you hoped to meet last week.

The sight of the Andromeda Galaxy—especially when seen for the first time—is astounding.

That day was the longest in her life—or so it seemed to her.

A dash is often used to summarize a series of ideas that have already been expressed.

Freedom of speech, freedom to vote, and freedom of assembly—these are the cornerstones of democracy.

Carbohydrates, fats, and proteins—these are the basic kinds of food we need.

Jones, who first suggested we go; Marshall, who made all the arrangements; and Kline, who finally took us there— these were the three men I admired most for their courage.

James, Howard, Marianne, Angela, Catherine—all were displeased with the decision of the teacher.

The dash is also used to note the author of a quotation that is set off in the text.

Nothing is good or bad but thinking makes it so.

> *—William Shakespeare*

Under every grief and pine
Runs a joy with silken twine.

> *—William Blake*

☞ Drill: The Dash

DIRECTIONS: Read the following sentences. What effect does the dash have on the writing, especially the tone and mood?

1. Can you?—I would be ever so grateful—I'm having so much difficulty.

2. Could it be—no it can't be—not after all these years.

3. Time and patience—two simple words—yet why are they so hard for me to remember?

4. Most of the paintings in the gallery—in fact all but one— were done in the nineteenth century.

5. According to John Locke, these are man's inalienable rights—life, liberty, and property.

COLONS

The colon (:) is the sign of a pause about midway in length between the semicolon and the period. It can often be replaced by a comma and sometimes by a period. Although used less frequently now than it was 50 to 75 years ago, the colon is still convenient to use, for it signals to the reader that more information is to come on the subject of concern. The colon can also create a slight dramatic tension.

It is used to introduce a word, phrase, or complete statement (clause) that emphasizes, illustrates, or exemplifies what has already been stated.

He had only one desire in life: to play hockey.

The weather that day was the most unusual I'd ever seen: It snowed and rained while the sun was still shining.

In his speech, the president surprised us by his final point: The conventional grading system would be replaced next year.

Jean thought of only two things the last half hour of the hike home: a bath and a bed.

Notice that the word following the colon can start with either a capital or a small letter. Use a capital letter if the word following the colon begins another complete sentence. But when the words following the colon are part of the sentence preceding the colon, use a small letter.

May I offer you a suggestion: Don't drive without your seatbelts fastened.

The thought continued to perplex him: Where will I go next?

When introducing a series that illustrates or emphasizes what has already been stated, use the colon.

Only a few of the graduates were able to be there: Jamison, Mearns, Linkley, and Commoner.

For Omar Khayyam, a Persian poet, three things are necessary for a paradise on earth: a loaf of bread, a jug of wine, and his beloved.

In the basement, he kept some equipment for his experiments: the test tubes, some chemical agents, three sunlamps, and the drill.

Long quotes set off from the rest of the text by indentation rather than quotation marks are generally introduced with a colon.

The first line of Lincoln's Gettysburg address is familiar to most Americans:

Fourscore and seven years ago our fathers brought forth on this continent a new nation, conceived in liberty and dedicated to the proposition that all men are created equal.

I quote from Shakespeare's Sonnets:

When I do count the clock that tells the time,
And see the brave day sunk in hideous night;
When I behold the violet past prime,
And sable curls all silver'd o'er with white...

It is also customary to begin a business letter with a colon.

Dear Senator Jordan:

To Whom It May Concern:

Gentlemen:

Dear Sir or Madam:

But in informal letters, use a comma.

Dear Colin,

Dear Father,

The colon is also used to introduce a list.

Please send the following:
1. *50 index cards,*
2. *4 staplers, and*
3. *8 erasers.*

Prepare the recipe as follows:
1. *Slice the oranges thinly.*
2. *Arrange them in a circle around the strawberries.*
3. *Pour the liqueur over both fruits.*

At least three ladies will have to be there to help:
1. *Mrs. Goldman, who will greet the guests;*
2. *Harriet Sacher, who will serve the lunch; and*
3. *my sister, who will do whatever else needs to be done.*

Finally, the colon is used between numbers when writing the time, between the volume and number or volume and page number of a journal, and also between the chapter and verse in the Bible.

4:30 P.M.

The Nation, 34:8

Genesis 5:18

SEMICOLONS

Semicolons (;) are sometimes called mild periods. They indicate a pause midway in length between the comma and the colon. Writing that contains many semicolons is usually in a dignified, formal style. To use them correctly, it is necessary to be able to recognize main clauses—complete ideas. When two main clauses occur in a single sentence without a connecting word (*and, but, or, nor, for*), the appropriate mark of punctuation is the semicolon.

It is not a good idea for you to leave the country right now; you should actually try to stay as long as you possibly can.

Music lightens life; literature deepens it.

In the past, boy babies were often dressed in blue; girls in pink. ("were often dressed" is understood in the second part of the sentence.)

Can't you see it's no good to go on alone; we'll starve to death if we keep traveling this way much longer.

Burgundy and maroon are very similar colors; scarlet is altogether different.

Notice how the use of the comma, period, and semicolon each gives a sentence a slightly different meaning.

Music lightens life; literature deepens it.

Just as music lightens life, literature deepens it.

Music lightens life. Literature deepens it.

The semicolon lends a certain balance to writing that would otherwise be difficult to achieve. Nonetheless, you should be careful not to overuse it. A comma can just as well join parts of a sentence with two main ideas; the semicolon is particularly appropriate if there is a striking contrast in the two ideas expressed.

Ask not what your country can do for you; ask what you can do for your country.

It started out as an ordinary day; it ended being the most extraordinary of her life.

Our power to apprehend truth is limited; to seek it, limitless.

If any one of the following words or phrases are used to join together compound sentences, they are generally preceded by a semicolon:

then	*however*	*thus*	*furthermore*
hence	*indeed*	*so*	*consequently*
also	*that is*	*yet*	*nevertheless*
anyhow	*in addition*	*in fact*	*on the other hand*
likewise	*moreover*	*still*	*meanwhile*
instead	*besides*	*otherwise*	*in other words*
henceforth	*for example*	*therefore*	*at the same time*
even now			

For a long time, people thought that women were inferior to men; **even now** *it is not an easy attitude to overcome.*

Being clever and cynical, he succeeded in becoming president of the company; **meanwhile** *his wife left him.*

Cigarette smoking has never interested me; **furthermore**, *I couldn't care less if anyone else smokes or not.*

Some say Bach was the greatest composer of all time; **yet** *he still managed to have an ordinary life in other ways.*

> *We left wishing we could have stayed much longer; **in other words**, they showed us a good time.*

When a series of complicated items are listed or if there is internal punctuation in a series, the semicolon is sometimes used to make the meaning more clear.

> *You can use your new car for many things: to drive to town or to the country; to impress your friends and neighbors; to protect yourself from rain on a trip away from home; and to borrow against should you need money right away.*

> *The scores from yesterday's games came in late last night: Pirates-6, Zoomers-3; Caterpillars-12, Steelys-8; Crashers-9, Links-8; and Greens-15, Uptowns-4.*

> *In October a bag of potatoes cost 69¢; in December 99¢; in February $1.09; in April $1.39. I wonder if this inflation will ever stop.*

The semicolon is placed outside quotation marks or parentheses, unless it is a part of the material enclosed in those marks.

> *I used to call him "my lord and master"; it made him laugh every time.*

> *The weather was cold for that time of year (I was shivering wherever I went); nevertheless, we set out to hike to the top of that mountain.*

☞ Drill: Colons and Semicolons

DIRECTIONS: Correctly place the colon and the semicolon in the following sentences.

1. I have only one thing to say don't do it.

2. They seemed compatible yet they did not get along.

3. She had only one goal in life to be a famous pianist.

4. He thought the problem was solved instead his solution proved to be entirely wrong.

5. By the end of the day there were only two things on her mind rest and relaxation.

6. Only a few members were able to attend the convention Henry, Karen, David, Mark, and Susan.

7. They were willing to accept the proposal he was not.

8. The art students were expected to supply the following brushes, paints, pallets, and pads.

9. The time is now the time is right.

10. The highest scores on the final exam are as follows Linda Jones 96 John Smith 94 Susan Green 90. These grades are unusually high they must have studied well.

PARENTHESES

To set off material that is only loosely connected to the central meaning of the sentence, use parentheses ( ).

Most men (at least most that I know) like wine, women, and song, but have too much work and not enough time for such enjoyments.

On Tuesday evenings and Thursday afternoons (the times I don't have classes), the television programs are not too exciting.

Last year at Vale (we go there every year), the skiing was the best I've ever seen.

In New York (I've lived there all my life and ought to know), you have to have a license for a gun.

What must be done to think clearly and calmly (is it even possible?) and then make the decision?

Watch out for other punctuation when you use parentheses. Punctuation that refers to the material enclosed in the parentheses occurs inside the marks. Punctuation belonging to the rest of the sentence comes outside the parentheses.

I thought I knew the poem by heart (boy, was I wrong!).

For a long time (too long as far as I'm concerned), women were thought to be inferior to men.

We must always strive to tell the truth. (Are we even sure we know what truth is?)

☞ Drill: Parentheses

DIRECTIONS: Read the following sentences. What effect does the use of parentheses have on the writing? Also make any necessary corrections.

1. The choice (in my opinion,) was a good one.

2. Linda's comment ("Where did you get that dress")? wasn't intended to be sarcastic.

3. After today (and what a day it was!) I will begin to work harder.

4. Last summer in Cape Cod (this is the first year we went there,) we did a lot of sightseeing.

5. The first time I went driving (do you remember the day)?, I was so scared.

THE COMMA

Of all the marks of punctuation, the comma (,) has the most uses. Before you tackle the main principles that guide its usage, be sure that you have an elementary understanding of sentence structure. There are actually only a few rules and conventions to follow when using commas; the rest is common sense. The worst abuse of commas comes from those who overuse them, who place them illogically. If you are ever in doubt as to whether or not to use a comma, do not use it.

In A Series

When more than one adjective (an adjective series) describes a noun, use a comma to separate and emphasize each adjective.

the long, dark passageway

another confusing, sleepless night

the bright, red dog

an elaborate, complex plan

the beautiful, starry night

the haunting, melodic sound

the old, grey, crumpled hat

In these instances, the comma takes the place of "and." To test if the comma is needed, try inserting "and" between the adjectives in question. If it is logical, you should use a comma. The following are examples of adjectives that describe an adjective-noun combination that has come to be thought of almost as one word. In such cases the adjective in front of the adjective-noun combination needs no comma.

a stately **oak tree**   my worst **report card**

an exceptional **wine glass**   a borrowed **record player**

a successful **garage sale**   a porcelain **dinner plate**

If you insert "and" between the adjectives in the above examples, it will not make sense.

The comma is also used to separate words, phrases, and whole ideas (clauses); it still takes the place of "and" when used this way.

an apple, a pear, a fig, and a banana

a lovely lady, an indecent dress, and many admirers

She lowered the shade, closed the curtain, turned off the light, and went to bed.

John, Frank, and my Uncle Harry all thought it was a questionable theory.

The only question that exists about the use of commas in a series is whether or not one should be used before the final item. Usually "and" or "or" precedes the final item, and many writers do not include the comma before the final "and" or "or." When first learning, however, it is advisable to use the comma because often its omission can be confusing; in such cases as these, for instance:

NO: *Would you like to shop at Saks, Nordstrom and Best and Less?*

NO: *He got on his horse, tracked a rabbit and a deer and rode on to Canton.*

NO: *We planned the trip with Mary and Harold, Susan, Dick and Joan, Gregory and Jean and Charles. (Is it Gregory and Jean, or Jean and Charles, or Gregory and Jean and Charles?)*

With a Long Introductory Phrase

Usually if a phrase of more than five or six words precedes the subject at the beginning of a sentence, a comma is used to set it off.

After last night's fiasco at the disco, she couldn't bear the thought of looking at him again.

Whenever I try to talk about politics, my husband leaves the room.

When it comes to actual facts, every generation makes the same mistakes as the preceding one.

Provided you have said nothing, they will never guess who you are.

It is not necessary to use a comma with a short sentence.

In January she will go to Switzerland.

After I rest I'll feel better.

At Grandma's we had a big dinner.

During the day no one is home.

If an introductory phrase includes a verb form that is being used as another part of speech (a "verbal"), it must be followed by a comma. Try to make sense of the following sentences without commas.

NO: *When eating Mary never looked up from her plate.*
(When eating, Mary never looked up from her plate.)

NO: *Because of her desire to follow her faith in James wavered.*
(Because of her desire to follow, her faith in James wavered.)

NO: *Having decided to leave Mary James wrote her a letter.*
(Having decided to leave Mary, James wrote her a letter.)

Above all, common sense is the best guideline when trying to decide whether or not to use a comma after an introductory phrase. Does the comma make the meaning more clear? If it does, use it; if not, there is no reason to insert it.

To Separate Sentences with Two Main Ideas (Compound Sentences)

To understand this use of the comma, you need to have studied sentence structure and be able to recognize compound sentences.

When a sentence contains more than two subjects and verbs (clauses) and the two clauses are joined by a connecting word (*and, but, or, yet, for, nor*), use a comma before the connecting word to show that another clause is coming.

I thought I knew the poem by heart, but he showed me three lines I had forgotten.

Are we really interested in helping the children, or are we more concerned with protecting our good names?

He is supposed to leave tomorrow, but who knows if he will be ready to go.

Jim knows you are disappointed, and he has known it for a long time.

If the two parts of the sentence are short and closely related, it is not necessary to use a comma.

He threw the ball and the dog ran after it.

Dena played the piano and Jonathan danced.

Errors to Avoid

Be careful not to confuse a sentence that has a compound verb and a single subject with a compound sentence. If the subject is the same for both verbs, there is no need for a comma.

NO: *Charles sent some flowers, and wrote a long letter explaining why he had not been able to come.*

NO: *Last Thursday we went to the concert with Julia, and afterwards dined at an old Italian restaurant.*

NO: *For the third time, the teacher explained that the literacy level of high school students was much lower than it had been in previous years, and, this time, wrote the statistics on the board for everyone to see.*

To Set Off Interrupting Material

There are so many different kinds of interruptions that can occur in a sentence that a list of them all would be quite lengthy. In general, words and phrases that stop the flow of the sentence or are unnecessary for the main idea are set off by commas. Some examples are:

Abbreviations after names:

Did you invite John Paul, Jr., and his sister?

Martha Harris, Ph.D., will be the speaker tonight.

Interjections: An exclamation added without grammatical connection.

Oh, I'm so glad to see you.

I tried so hard, alas, to do it.

Hey, let me out of here.

No, I will not let you out.

Direct address:

Roy, won't you open the door for the dog?

I can't understand, mother, what you are trying to say.

May I ask, Mr. President, why you called us together?

Hey, lady, watch out for the car!

Tag questions: A question that repeats the helping verb in a negative phrase.

I'm really hungry, aren't you?

Jerry looks like his father, doesn't he?

You'll come early, won't you?

We are expected at nine, aren't we?

Mr. Jones can chair the meeting, can't he?

Geographical names and addresses:

The concert will be held in Chicago, Illinois, on August 12.

They visited Tours, France, last summer.

The letter was addressed to Ms. Marion Heartwell, 1881 Pine Lane, Palo Alto, California 95824.

(No comma is needed before the ZIP code because it is already clearly set off from the state name.)

Transitional words and phrases:

On the other hand, I hope he gets better.

In addition, the phone rang six times this afternoon.

I'm, nevertheless, going to the beach on Sunday.

You'll find, therefore, no one is more loyal to me than you.

To tell the truth, I don't know what to believe.

Parenthetical words and phrases:

You will become, I believe, a great statesman.

We know, of course, that this is the only thing to do.

In fact, I planted corn last summer.

The Mannes affair was, to put it mildly, a surprise.

Bathing suits, generally speaking, are getting smaller.

Unusual word order:

The dress, new and crisp, hung in the closet. (Normal word order: The new, crisp dress hung in the closet.)

Intently, she stared out the window. (Normal word order: She stared intently out the window.)

Nonrestrictive Elements (Not Essential to the Meaning)

Parts of a sentence that modify other parts are sometimes essential to the meaning of the sentence and sometimes not. When a modifying word or group of words is not vital to the meaning of the sentence, it is set off by commas. Since it does not restrict the meaning of the words it modifies, it is called "nonrestrictive." Modifiers that are essential to the meaning of the sentence are called "restrictive" and are not set off by commas. Compare the following pairs of sentences:

*The girl **who wrote the story** is my sister. (essential)*

*My sister, **the girl who wrote the story**, has always been drawn to adventure. (nonessential)*

*John Milton's famous poem **"Paradise Lost"** tells a remarkable story. (essential—Milton has written other poems)*

*Dante's great work, **"The Divine Comedy,"** marked the beginning of the Renaissance and the end of the Dark Ages. (nonessential—Dante wrote only one great work)*

*The cup **that is on the piano** is the one I want. (essential)*

*The cup, **which my brother gave me last year**, is on the piano. (nonessential)*

*My parakeet **Simian** has an extensive vocabulary. (essential—because there are no commas, the writer must have more than one parakeet)*

*My parakeet, **Simian**, has an extensive vocabulary. (nonessential—the writer must have only one parakeet whose name is Simian)*

*The people **who arrived late** were not seated. (essential)*

*George, **who arrived late**, was not seated. (nonessential)*

*She always listened to her sister **Jean**. (essential—she must have more than one sister)*

*She always listened to her husband, **Jack**. (nonessential—obviously, she has only one husband)*

To Set Off Direct Quotations

Most direct quotes or quoted materials are set off from the rest of the sentence by commas.

"Please read your part more loudly," the director insisted.

"I won't know what to do," said Michael, "if you leave me now."

The teacher said sternly, "I will not dismiss this class until I have silence."

Mark looked up from his work, smiled, and said, "We'll be with you in a moment."

Be careful not to set off indirect quotations or quotes that are used as subjects or complements.

"To be or not to be" is the famous beginning of a soliloquy in Shakespeare's Hamlet. (subject)

Back then my favorite song was "A Summer Place." (complement)

She said she would never come back. (indirect quote)

"Place two tablespoons of chocolate in this pan" were her first words to her apprentice in the kitchen. (subject)

To Set Off Contrasting Elements

*His intelligence, **not his beauty**, got him the job.*

*Your plan will take you further from, **rather than closer to**, your destination.*

*It was a reasonable, **though not appealing**, idea.*

*He wanted glory, **but found happiness instead**.*

*James wanted an active, **not a passive**, partner.*

In Dates

(Both forms of the date are acceptable.)

She will arrive on April 6, 1981.

He left on 5 December 1980.

In January, 1967, he handed in his resignation.

In January 1967 he handed in his resignation.

☞ Drill: The Comma

DIRECTIONS: In the following sentences insert commas wherever necessary. You may also want to note the reason for your choice.

1.   However I am willing to reconsider.

2.   She descended the long winding staircase.

3.   Whenever I practice the violin my family applauds.

4.   While driving Francis never took his eyes off the road.

5.   The car which I bought last year is in the garage.

6.   "Answer the door" said his mother loudly.

7.   Miss can I ask you for the time?

8.   He was after all an ex-convict.

9.   I'm so bored aren't you?

10. The old tall shady tree is wonderful during the summer.

11. George Gary and Bill were on line early this morning. They bought their tickets read the newspaper and spoke for a while.

12. The author James Grey was awarded the prize.

13. She attended school in London England last year.

14. They said they would do the job.

15. His weight not his height prevented him from competing in the race.

16. The family who won the lottery lives in New Jersey.

17. She got in the car turned on the ignition and left the curb.

18. Incidentally he called last night.

19. The kitten small and cute was adopted by the Brown family.

20. Mary did you see James Jr. at the party last night?

21. Lisa saw the mailman and gave him the letter.

22. Last night I finished my essay and started on my next assignment.

23. Really I can't believe that is the truth.

24.   We thought it was time to leave but we arrived early.

25.   Monday she will leave for Boston.

26.   After he got home he read a magazine ate dinner and left for the movies.

27.   If you pass the test you will graduate.

28.   When she decided to leave everyone was disappointed.

29.   Hey John it's time to go.

30.   He seemed wrong for the part yet he turned out to be the best actor in the production.

☞ Drill: Mechanics

DIRECTIONS: All of the needed punctuation and other aspects of mechanics have been omitted from the following passage. In making the necessary corrections there will often be more than one way of correcting the error. Therefore, try taking into account the mood and tone of the writing and the overall coherence of the piece when punctuating the passage.

my sister amy had finally finished packing for college at about 11 am what a day it was as usual she had overpacked but this was clearly an understatement standing in the hallway were the following 7 large blue suitcases 3 borrowed trunks 4 old bulging macys shopping bags and 2 duffel bags but im going halfway across the united states how many times do you think ill be coming home she asked once every 5 years at christmas time i guessed i do hope youll write seriously do you know the difference between the words pack and hoard i said amy laughed self-consciously civilization does exist in chicago illinois i added trust me it really does really remarked amy with her own personal brand of sarcasm after all its only the 1990s its well known that 3 4 s of chicago is still unsettled territory i turned away in disgust it was useless

i went to help amy with her baggage picking up the large over stuffed green duffel bag i screamed whats in here is this a 50 or 100 pound bag you have got to be kidding i added she had filled the entire bag with books i knew shed want to take a couple of her favorite books and magazines albert camus the stranger charles dickens great expectations shakespeares king lear copies of keats and ts eliots best poems some national geographics but i realized i was all wrong instead she had packed 30 copies of tolstoys war and peace or so it seemed on her book shelf remained 1 lone copy of websters new collegiate dictionary in fact it was an extra one she had received it for her birthday last year i believe the rest of the move was sadly repetitious i realized amy was nuts i wasnt about to reason with her i was tired it was futile there was no time meanwhile amy was totally calm and relaxed as she went through the radio stations finally settling on wnbc as she listened to the beatles hey jude i seemingly all powerful carried the last trunk out the door the plane a 747 was scheduled to leave at 12 oclock we were 10 minutes off schedule when we arrived at kennedy airport furthermore i had to pay a $5.00 surcharge for the extra baggage amy said she only had large bills as she was about to board the plane after 101 good byes i handed her a package as if she really needed anything else its a green pull over sweater just like mine i said tearfully oh you really shouldn't have please take it back amy replied theres no time for humility your plane is about to take off i said really you should keep it yours is already on the plane along with a few other things it took me a few moments to realize what she meant then i said one last final good bye to amy my ex sister

PUNCTUATION

ANSWER KEY

Drill: Periods, Question Marks, Exclamation Points

1. "Good gracious!" she said. "Didn't you know that I was coming?"

2. Mr. Morgan works for the CIA.

3. Alexander wondered if it was time to go.

4. Leave me alone! Can't you see that I'm busy?

5. "How many boxes did you buy?" asked Dr. Jones.

6. "Be careful!" he shouted. "Didn't you see that car coming?"

7. Impossible! I have never seen anything like that before.

8. Lynn asked if anyone had the time.

9. What else can I do? I lost all my money.

10. Who cried "Help!"

Drill: The Dash

1. The use of the dash makes the sentence more urgent.

2. The use of the dash helps to convey a feeling of disbelief.

3. The words set off by dashes emphasize and modify the key words, "Time and patience."

4. The dashes help to emphasize and clarify the subject.

5. The dash is used to set off specifics.

Drill: Colons and Semicolons

1. I have only one thing to say: don't do it.

2. They seemed compatible; yet they did not get along.

3. She had only one goal in life: to be a famous pianist.

4. He thought the problem was solved; instead, his solution proved to be entirely wrong.

5. By the end of the day there were only two things on her mind: rest and relaxation.

6. Only a few members were able to attend the convention: Henry, Karen, David, Mark, and Susan.

7. They were willing to accept the proposal; he was not.

8. The art students were expected to supply the following: brushes, paints, pallets, and pads.

9. The time is now: the time is right.

10. The highest scores on the final exam are as follows: Linda Jones, 96; John Smith, 94; Susan Green, 90. These grades are unusually high: they must have studied well.

Drill: Parentheses

1. The choice (in my opinion) was a good one. The comma in the example is unnecessary.

   The choice, in my opinion, was a good one. The parentheses are unnecessary in the example. "In my opinion" is not very necessary, since the statements made in writing are usually considered to be the author's, unless otherwise indicated.

2. Linda's comment ("Where did you get that dress?") wasn't intended to be sarcastic. The parentheses are a clear, effective method for containing a quote.

3. The parentheses properly set off material that is loosely connected to the central meaning of the sentence.

4. Last summer on Cape Cod (that was the first year we went there) we did a lot of sightseeing. The parentheses effectively contain the additional information.

5. The first time I went driving (do you remember the day?), I was so scared. The parentheses smoothly incorporate an important aside from the speaker.

Drill: The Comma

1. However, I am willing to reconsider.
   Reason: "However" is a transitional word and requires a comma after it.

2. She descended the long, winding staircase.
   Reason: A comma is used in a series to emphasize each adjective.

3. Whenever I practice my violin, my family applauds.
   Reason: Use a comma after a long introductory phrase.

4. While driving, Francis never took his eyes off the road.
   Reason: When the introductory phrase includes a "verbal," a comma is necessary.

5. The car, which I bought last year, is in the garage.
   Reason: The modifying group of words ("which I bought last year") is not vital to the meaning of the sentence and, therefore, is set off by commas.

6. "Answer the door," his mother said loudly.
   Reason: Use a comma to set off direct quotations.

7. Miss, can I ask you for the time?
   Reason: Use a comma to set off direct address.

8. He was, after all, an ex-convict.
   Reason: Use commas to set off parenthetical words and phrases.

9. I'm so bored, aren't you?
   Reason: Use a comma to set off tag questions.

10. The old, tall, shady tree is wonderful during the summer.
    Reason: When an adjective series describes a noun, use a comma to separate and emphasize each adjective.

11. George, Gary, and Bill were on line early this morning. They bought their tickets, read the newspaper, and spoke for a while.
    Reason: (For both sentences) use a comma to separate words, phrases, and whole ideas (clauses).

12. The author, James Grey, was awarded the prize.
    Reason: Use commas to set off nonrestrictive words.

13. She attended school in London, England, last year.
    Reason: Use commas to set off geographical names.

14. No correction necessary.

15. His weight, not his height, prevented him from competing in the race.
    Reason: Use commas to set off contrasting elements.

16. No correction necessary.

17. She got in the car, turned on the ignition, and left the curb.
    Reason: A comma is used to separate words, phrases, and whole ideas.

18. Incidentally, he called last night.
    Reason: Use a comma to set off parenthetical words and phrases.

19. The kitten, small and cute, was adopted by the Brown family.
    Reason: Use commas to set off nonrestrictive elements.

20. Mary, did you see James, Jr., at the party last night?
    Reason: 1. Use a comma to set off direct address. 2. Use a comma to set off abbreviations after names.

21. No change necessary.

22. No change necessary.

23. Really, I can't believe that is the truth.
    Reason: Use a comma to set off an interjection.

24. We thought it was time to leave, but we arrived early.
    Reason: Use a comma to set off sentences with two main ideas.

25. Monday, she will leave for Boston.
    Reason: Use a comma to set off parenthetical words and phrases.

26. After he got home he read a magazine, ate dinner, and left for the movies.
    Reason: The comma is used to separate words, phrases, and clauses.

27. No correction necessary.

28. When she decided to leave, everyone was disappointed.
    Reason: Use a comma to set off a long introductory phrase.

29. Hey, John, it's time to go.
    Reason: Use commas to set off direct address.

30. He seemed wrong for the part, yet he turned out to be the best actor in the production.
    Reason: Use a comma to separate sentences with two main ideas.

Drill: Mechanics

My sister, Amy, had finally finished packing for college at about 11:00 A.M. What a day it was! As usual, she had over-packed—but this is an understatement. Standing in the hallway were the following: seven large, blue suitcases; three borrowed trunks; four old, bulging Macy's shopping bags; and two duffel bags.

"But I'm going halfway across the United States! How many times do you think I'll be coming home?" she asked.

"Once every five years at Christmas time?" I guessed.

"I hope you'll write," she said.

"Seriously, do you know the difference between the words 'pack' and 'hoard'?" I asked. Amy laughed self-consciously.

"Civilization does exist in Chicago, Illinois," I added. "Trust me; it really does."

"Really?" remarked Amy, with her own personal brand of sarcasm. "After all, it's only the nineteen-nineties: It's well-known that three-fourths of Chicago is still unsettled territory."

I turned away in disgust. It was useless.

I went to help Amy with her baggage. Picking up the large, overstuffed, green duffel bag, I screamed, "What's in here! Is this a fifty- or a hundred pound bag? You have got to be kidding," I added.

She had filled the entire bag with books and magazines. I knew she would want to take a few of her favorites—*The Stranger*, by Albert Camus; *Great Expectations*, by Charles Dickens; *King Lear*, by William Shakespeare; copies of Keats' and T.S. Eliot's best poems; some copies of *National Geographic*—but I realized I was all wrong; instead, she had packed 30 copies of Tolstoy's *War and Peace*, or so it seemed. One lone copy of *Webster's New Collegiate Dictionary* remained on her bookshelf; in fact, it was an extra one she had received for her birthday last year. I believe the rest of the move was sadly repetitious. I realized Amy was nuts.

I wasn't about to reason with her: I was tired, it was futile, and there was no time. Meanwhile, Amy was totally calm and relaxed as she went through the radio stations. She finally settled on WNBC, and she listened to the Beatles' "Hey Jude." I, seemingly all-powerful, carried the last trunk out the door.

The plane, a 747, was scheduled to leave at noon. We were ten minutes off schedule when we arrived at Kennedy airport; furthermore, I had to pay a five-dollar surcharge for the extra baggage: Amy said she only had large bills. As she was about to board the plane (after one hundred and one good-byes), I handed her a package—as if she really needed anything else!

"It's a green pullover sweater—just like mine," I said tearfully.

"Oh, you really shouldn't have. Please take it back," Amy replied.

"There's no time for humility: your plane is about to take off," I said.

"Really, you should keep it! Yours is already on the plane—along with a few other things."

It took me a few moments to realize what she meant; then I said one last, final good-bye to Amy, my ex-sister.

V. SPELLING AND WORD USAGE

FREQUENTLY MISSPELLED GED WORDS

The following list contains frequently misspelled words that may appear on the GED test. Study the spelling of each word by having a friend or counselor drill you flashcard style. Then mark down the words which you misspelled and study those select ones again. Be sure to take all the drills which follow the list of words. This will increase your accuracy in spelling. (The words appear in their most popular U.S. spellings.)

a lot	address	already
ability	addressed	although
absence	adequate	altogether
absent	advantage	always
abundance	advantageous	amateur
accept	advertise	American
acceptable	advertisement	among
accident	advice	amount
accommodate	advisable	analysis
accompanied	advise	analyze
accomplish	advisor	angel
accumulation	aerial	angle
accuse	affect	annual
accustomed	affectionate	another
ache	again	answer
achieve	against	antiseptic
achievement	aggravate	anxious
acknowledge	aggressive	apologize
acquaintance	agree	apparatus
acquainted	aisle	apparent
acquire	all right	appear
across	almost	appearance

appetite	avenue	burial
application	awful	buried
apply	awkward	bury
appreciate	bachelor	bushes
appreciation	balance	business
approach	balloon	cafeteria
appropriate	bargain	calculator
approval	basic	calendar
approve	beautiful	campaign
approximate	because	capital
argue	become	capitol
arguing	before	captain
argument	beginning	career
arouse	being	careful
arrange	believe	careless
arrangement	benefit	carriage
article	benefited	carrying
artificial	between	category
ascend	bicycle	ceiling
assistance	board	cemetery
assistant	bored	cereal
associate	borrow	certain
association	bottle	changeable
attempt	bottom	characteristic
attendance	boundary	charity
attention	brake	chief
audience	breadth	choose
August	breath	chose
author	breathe	cigarette
automobile	brilliant	circumstance
autumn	building	citizen
auxiliary	bulletin	clothes
available	bureau	clothing

coarse	considerable	decision
coffee	consistency	decisive
collect	consistent	deed
college	continual	definite
column	continuous	delicious
comedy	controlled	dependent
comfortable	controversy	deposit
commitment	convenience	derelict
committed	convenient	descend
committee	conversation	descent
communicate	corporal	describe
company	corroborate	description
comparative	council	desert
compel	counsel	desirable
competent	counselor	despair
competition	courage	desperate
compliment	courageous	dessert
conceal	course	destruction
conceit	courteous	determine
conceivable	courtesy	develop
conceive	criticism	development
concentration	criticize	device
conception	crystal	dictator
condition	curiosity	died
conference	cylinder	difference
confident	daily	different
congratulate	daughter	dilemma
conquer	daybreak	dinner
conscience	death	direction
conscientious	deceive	disappear
conscious	December	disappoint
consequence	deception	disappointment
consequently	decide	disapproval

disapprove	emphasize	explanation
disastrous	enclosure	extreme
discipline	encouraging	facility
discover	endeavor	factory
discriminate	engineer	familiar
disease	English	fascinate
dissatisfied	enormous	fascinating
dissection	enough	fatigue
dissipate	entrance	February
distance	envelope	financial
distinction	environment	financier
division	equipment	flourish
doctor	equipped	forcibly
dollar	especially	forehead
doubt	essential	foreign
dozen	evening	formal
earnest	evident	former
easy	exaggerate	fortunate
ecstasy	exaggeration	fourteen
ecstatic	examine	fourth
education	exceed	frequent
effect	excellent	friend
efficiency	except	frightening
efficient	exceptional	fundamental
eight	exercise	further
either	exhausted	gallon
eligibility	exhaustion	garden
eligible	exhilaration	gardener
eliminate	existence	general
embarrass	exorbitant	genius
embarrassment	expense	government
emergency	experience	governor
emphasis	experiment	grammar

grateful	incidental	jealous
great	increase	journal
grievance	independence	judgment
grievous	independent	kindergarten
grocery	indispensable	kitchen
guarantee	inevitable	knew
guess	influence	knock
guidance	influential	know
half	initiate	knowledge
hammer	innocence	labor
handkerchief	inoculate	laboratory
happiness	inquiry	laid
healthy	insistent	language
heard	instead	later
heavy	instinct	latter
height	integrity	laugh
heroes	intellectual	leisure
heroine	intelligence	length
hideous	intercede	lesson
himself	interest	library
hoarse	interfere	license
holiday	interference	light
hopeless	interpreted	lightning
hospital	interrupt	likelihood
humorous	invitation	likely
hurried	irrelevant	literal
hurrying	irresistible	literature
ignorance	irritable	livelihood
imaginary	island	loaf
imbecile	its	loneliness
imitation	it's	loose
immediately	itself	lose
immigrant	January	losing

loyal	narrative	oscillate
loyalty	natural	ought
magazine	necessary	ounce
maintenance	needle	overcoat
maneuver	negligence	paid
marriage	neighbor	pamphlet
married	neither	panicky
marry	newspaper	parallel
match	newsstand	parallelism
material	niece	particular
mathematics	noticeable	partner
measure	o'clock	pastime
medicine	obedient	patience
million	obstacle	peace
miniature	occasion	peaceable
minimum	occasional	pear
miracle	occur	peculiar
miscellaneous	occurred	pencil
mischief	occurrence	people
mischievous	ocean	perceive
misspelled	offer	perception
mistake	often	perfect
momentous	omission	perform
monkey	omit	performance
monotonous	once	perhaps
moral	operate	period
morale	opinion	permanence
mortgage	opportune	permanent
mountain	opportunity	perpendicular
mournful	optimist	perseverance
muscle	optimistic	persevere
mysterious	origin	persistent
mystery	original	personal

personality	preferential	quart
personnel	preferred	quarter
persuade	prejudice	quiet
persuasion	preparation	quite
pertain	prepare	raise
picture	prescription	realistic
piece	presence	realize
plain	president	reason
playwright	prevalent	rebellion
pleasant	primitive	recede
please	principal	receipt
pleasure	principle	receive
pocket	privilege	recipe
poison	probably	recognize
policeman	procedure	recommend
political	proceed	recuperate
population	produce	referred
portrayal	professional	rehearsal
positive	professor	reign
possess	profitable	relevant
possession	prominent	relieve
possessive	promise	remedy
possible	pronounce	renovate
post office	pronunciation	repeat
potatoes	propeller	repetition
practical	prophet	representative
prairie	prospect	requirements
precede	psychology	resemblance
preceding	pursue	resistance
precise	pursuit	resource
predictable	quality	respectability
prefer	quantity	responsibility
preference	quarreling	restaurant

rhythm	significant	surprise
rhythmical	similar	suspense
ridiculous	similarity	sweat
right	sincerely	sweet
role	site	syllable
roll	soldier	symmetrical
roommate	solemn	sympathy
sandwich	sophomore	synonym
Saturday	soul	technical
scarcely	source	telegram
scene	souvenir	telephone
schedule	special	temperament
science	specified	temperature
scientific	specimen	tenant
scissors	speech	tendency
season	stationary	tenement
secretary	stationery	therefore
seize	statue	thorough
seminar	stockings	through
sense	stomach	title
separate	straight	together
service	strength	tomorrow
several	strenuous	tongue
severely	stretch	toward
shepherd	striking	tragedy
sheriff	studying	transferred
shining	substantial	treasury
shoulder	succeed	tremendous
shriek	successful	tries
siege	sudden	truly
sight	superintendent	twelfth
signal	suppress	twelve
significance	surely	tyranny

undoubtedly	vengeance	weather
United States	versatile	Wednesday
university	vicinity	week
unnecessary	vicious	weigh
unusual	view	weird
useful	village	whether
usual	villain	which
vacuum	visitor	while
valley	voice	whole
valuable	volume	wholly
variety	waist	whose
vegetable	weak	wretched
vein	wear	

☞ Drill: Spelling

DIRECTIONS: Indicate if the word is spelled correctly or incorrectly. If you believe the word is misspelled, then spell it correctly in the space provided.

1. alot _____
2. abcent _____
3. axident _____
4. adviseable _____
5. agressive _____
6. angel _____
7. appropriate _____
8. arangement _____
9. auful _____
10. awkward _____
11. bargen _____
12. beautiful _____

13. beggining _____
14. benifit _____
15. breathe _____
16. bisness _____
17. cafeteria _____
18. capten _____
19. category _____
20. cheif _____
21. congradulate _____
22. coffee _____
23. compitition _____
24. concientious _____

25. controled _____
26. courage _____
27. curteous _____
28. curiosity _____
29. day break _____
30. decition _____
31. delishious _____
32. desend _____
33. desperate _____
34. develope _____
35. diferent _____
36. disappoint _____
37. dizease _____
38. distence _____
39. estatic _____
40. eliminate _____
41. english _____
42. exagerate _____
43. exhaustion _____
44. exorbitant _____
45. experence _____
46. fasinating _____
47. forehead _____
48. foreteen _____
49. friend _____
50. goverment _____
51. guess _____

52. hapiness _____
53. heroes _____
54. humurus _____
55. imaginery _____
56. independent _____
57. innoculate _____
58. intelligence _____
59. itself _____
60. gellous _____
61. kindergartan _____
62. knowlege _____
63. leson _____
64. liklihood _____
65. loyal _____
66. mariage _____
67. miscellaneous _____
68. mispelled _____
69. muscle _____
70. news stand _____
71. ocassion _____
72. omition _____
73. oporttunity _____
74. opinion _____
75. osillate _____
76. paralelism _____
77. pencil _____
78. perserverence _____

79.	persuede	98.	seasin
80.	playright	99.	separate
81.	poison	100.	shepheard
82.	posses	101.	siege
83.	potatos	102.	similiar
84.	predictible	103.	sophmore
85.	priviledge	104.	stomack
86.	persue	105.	successful
87.	pronounciation	106.	sinonim
88.	psychology	107.	technical
89.	quarel	108.	temperiture
90.	quarter	109.	title
91.	rebelion	110.	undoubtedley
92.	recipe	111.	vacume
93.	reccomend	112.	vengeance
94.	repeat	113.	visiter
95.	respectibility	114.	Wensday
96.	rythm	115.	wretched
97.	scedual		

☞ Drill: Homophones

DIRECTIONS: A homophone is a word that sounds the same as another word, but which has a different meaning. The following sentences have a pair or pairs of homophones in parentheses. Circle the word you believe is used correctly in the sentence.

1. Mary was so (board, bored) with the lecture that she almost fell asleep.

2. Washington, D.C., is the (capitol, capital) of the United States.

3. The sand felt (coarse, course) against his (bear, bare) feet.

4. You should (council, counsel) Harry on his inappropriate behavior.

5. I had (two, too) ice cream (sundaes, sundays) for dessert after lunch and now I can't eat a thing for dinner.

6. Ruby will graduate (fourth, forth) in her class.

7. You (great, grate) the cheese and I'll slice the tomatoes.

8. I would like to learn how to ride a (horse, hoarse).

9. The cat fed (it's, its) kittens.

10. The bride wanted to (where, wear) something old and something (knew, new).

11. Was there ever a time when (there, their) was (piece, peace) in the world?

12. I saw a good (sale, sail) on a (pear, pair) of shoes.

13. Someday, I will become a pilot of a (plane, plain).

14. Please put some more mustard on that hotdog (roll, role).

15. The (site, sight) of the conference was in a great location near the beach.

16. The (soul, sole) of my sneaker is wearing away.

17. (Where, Wear) will you be tonight?

18. That interview was really a (waist, waste) of time.

19. That virus made me feel so (weak, week).

20. (Whether, Weather) or not he wants to pursue his career for a lifetime is up to him.

21. I would like to (weigh, way) myself on the scale but I am afraid I did not (lose, loose) any pounds.

22. (Here, Hear) today, gone tomorrow.

23. (Which, Witch) way did he go, George?

24. There's a (hole, whole) in the bucket.

25. (Who's, Whose) turn is it anyway?

☞ Drill: Usage and Sentence Correction

DIRECTIONS: In each of the following sentences, some part or all of the sentence is underlined. Below each sentence you will find five ways of phrasing the underlined part. Select the answer that produces the most effective sentence, one that is clear and exact, without awkwardness or ambiguity. In choosing answers, follow the requirements of standard written English. Choose the answer that best expresses the meaning of the original sentence.

Answer (1) is always the same as the underlined part. Choose answer (1) if you think the original sentence needs no revision.

·EXAMPLE:

The children swam in the lake all day <u>and that is because it was so hot.</u>
- (1) and that is because it was so hot.
- (2) when it was so hot.
- (3) since it was so hot.
- (4) which is why it was so hot.
- (5) at the time when it was so hot.

---

1. When a customer requested whole wheat instead of white bread, <u>it was a simple matter to substitute it for them.</u>

   - (1) it was a simple matter to substitute it for them.
   - (2) it was simple to substitute it.
   - (3) a simple matter it was to make the substitution.
   - (4) substitution was made a simple matter for him or her.
   - (5) it was easy to serve it to him or her.

2. That some serious cuts would have to be made in the city's budget <u>was evident to most everyone on the city council.</u>

   - (1) was evident to most everyone on the city council.
   - (2) was in evidence to most all on the city council.
   - (3) was evident to almost everyone on the city council.
   - (4) was evidenced by most everyone on the city council.
   - (5) was evidencing to almost everyone on the city council.

3. The train roared into town <u>with a whistle so ear-shattering so as to frighten</u> the waiting cattle.

   - (1) with a whistle so ear-shattering so as to frighten
   - (2) with as ear-shattering and frightening a whistle
   - (3) with a whistle so ear-shattering that it frightened

(4)   with an ear-shattering whistle and to frighten
(5)   with an ear-shattering and frightening whistle

4.   <u>This kind of a problem</u> requires a knowledge of the tensile strength of steel.

(1)   This kind of a problem   (4)   Those kinds of problems
(2)   These kinds of a problem   (5)   This kind of problem
(3)   These kind of problems

5.   <u>The child who was the winner's voice had an incredulous tone.</u>

(1)   The child who was the winner's voice had an incredulous tone.
(2)   The child winner's voice had an incredulous tone.
(3)   The winner's child's voice had an incredulous tone.
(4)   The voice of the winner's child had an incredulous tone.
(5)   Winning excited the child's voice to sound incredulous.

6.   <u>This morning's meeting having gone well</u> because Mrs. Chen was prepared with information to answer all our questions.

(1)   This morning's meeting having gone well
(2)   This morning's meeting having gone good
(3)   The meeting of this morning went good
(4)   This morning's meeting went well
(5)   This meeting in the morning going well

7.   <u>If you would have called me</u>, I could have told you about the book-signing party at Swift's Restaurant.

(1)   If you would have called me
(2)   If you had called me
(3)   When calling me
(4)   In order to call me
(5)   During our phone conversation

8.   <u>During the summer, Lydia developed her skill in both diving and swimming.</u>

(1)   During the summer, Lydia developed her skill in both diving and swimming.
(2)   During the summer, Lydia's skill was developed in both diving and swimming.

(3) Lydia, during the summer, developed both her skill in diving and swimming.

(4) Lydia both developing her skill in diving and in swimming during the summer.

(5) Both in diving and swimming Lydia developed her skill during the summer.

9. In order to keep track of his costs, a detailed diary was kept by the salesman for his automobile expenses.

(1) costs, a detailed diary was kept by the salesman for his automobile expenses.

(2) costs; a detailed diary was kept by the salesman for his automobile expenses.

(3) automobile expenses, the salesman kept a detailed diary.

(4) expenses for his automobile, a detailed costs diary was kept by the salesman.

(5) automobile expenses, the salesman kept a detailed diary of costs.

10. After the hurricane, we were told to leave the tree laying on the house until an insurance inspector could assess the damage.

(1) to leave the tree laying

(2) to leave the tree lay

(3) about leaving the tree to lay

(4) about leaving the tree lying

(5) to leave the tree lying

11. Practicing his manners for the economic conference, Lincoln Henderson arrived at the hospitality training session.

(1) Practicing his manners for the economic conference, Lincoln Henderson arrived

(2) In order of arriving at good manners for the economic conference, Lincoln Henderson practiced

(3) Because of arriving at good manners for the economic conference, Lincoln Henderson practiced

(4) To practice his manners for the economic conference, Lincoln Henderson arrived

(5) When practicing his manners for the economic conference, Lincoln Henderson arrived

12. It's the same charm and politeness he <u>plans to extend to</u> conference visitors who ride in his cab.

    (1) plans to extend to
    (2) plans on extending for
    (3) plans in extending in
    (4) is planning for extension to
    (5) will plan at extensions of

13. The judges at state competition all agreed that our one-act play performance <u>was crisp, witty, and the entire cast appeared to be very mature in their interpretation.</u>

    (1) was crisp, witty, and the entire cast appeared to be very mature in their interpretation.
    (2) was very crisp, very witty, and very mature was the cast's interpretation.
    (3) seemed crisp and witty and mature in the cast's interpretations.
    (4) appeared to be crisp and witty, and the cast was very mature.
    (5) was crisp, witty, and mature.

14. <u>Such of his songs as was sentimental and romantic were successful.</u>

    (1) Such of his songs as was sentimental and romantic were successful.
    (2) Such of his songs, sentimental and romantic, were successful.
    (3) His songs such as were sentimental, romantic, and successful.
    (4) His sentimental and romantic songs were successful.
    (5) His songs were successful and romantic.

15. Because the two top contestants are so evenly matched, <u>it is difficult for me deciding which one to receive the trophy.</u>

    (1) it is difficult for me deciding which one to receive the trophy.
    (2) it is difficult for me deciding which to give the trophy to.
    (3) it is difficult for me to decide to whom to give the trophy.
    (4) I am having difficulty deciding who should receive the trophy.
    (5) I am having difficulty deciding whom should receive the trophy.

SPELLING AND WORD USAGE

ANSWER KEY

Drill: Spelling

1. Incorrect. a lot
2. Incorrect. absent
3. Incorrect. accident
4. Incorrect. advisable
5. Incorrect. aggressive
6. Correct. angel
7. Correct. appropriate
8. Incorrect. arrangement
9. Incorrect. awful
10. Correct. awkward
11. Incorrect. bargain
12. Correct. beautiful
13. Incorrect. beginning
14. Incorrect. benefit
15. Correct. breathe
16. Incorrect. business
17. Correct. cafeteria
18. Incorrect. captain
19. Correct. category
20. Incorrect. chief
21. Incorrect. congratulate
22. Correct. coffee
23. Incorrect. competition
24. Incorrect. conscientious
25. Incorrect. controlled
26. Correct. courage
27. Incorrect. courteous
28. Correct. curiosity
29. Incorrect. daybreak
30. Incorrect. decision
31. Incorrect. delicious
32. Incorrect. descend
33. Correct. desperate
34. Incorrect. develop
35. Incorrect. different
36. Correct. disappoint
37. Incorrect. disease
38. Incorrect. distance
39. Incorrect. ecstatic
40. Correct. eliminate
41. Incorrect. English
42. Incorrect. exaggerate
43. Correct. exhaustion
44. Correct. exorbitant
45. Incorrect. experience
46. Incorrect. fascinating
47. Correct. forehead
48. Incorrect. fourteen
49. Correct. friend
50. Incorrect. government
51. Correct. guess
52. Incorrect. happiness
53. Correct. heroes
54. Incorrect. humorous

55. Incorrect. imaginary
56. Correct. independent
57. Incorrect. inoculate
58. Correct. intelligence
59. Correct. itself
60. Incorrect. jealous
61. Incorrect. kindergarten
62. Incorrect. knowledge
63. Incorrect. lesson
64. Incorrect. likelihood
65. Correct. loyal
66. Incorrect. marriage
67. Correct. miscellaneous
68. Incorrect. misspelled
69. Correct. muscle
70. Incorrect. newsstand
71. Incorrect. occasion
72. Incorrect. omission
73. Incorrect. opportunity
74. Correct. opinion
75. Incorrect. oscillate
76. Incorrect. parallelism
77. Correct. pencil
78. Incorrect. perseverance
79. Incorrect. persuade
80. Incorrect. playwright
81. Correct. poison
82. Incorrect. possess
83. Incorrect. potatoes
84. Incorrect. predictable
85. Incorrect. privilege
86. Incorrect. pursue
87. Incorrect. pronunciation
88. Correct. psychology
89. Incorrect. quarrel
90. Correct. quarter
91. Incorrect. rebellion
92. Correct. recipe
93. Incorrect. recommend
94. Correct. repeat
95. Incorrect. respectability
96. Incorrect. rhythm
97. Incorrect. schedule
98. Incorrect. season
99. Correct. separate
100. Incorrect. shepherd
101. Correct. siege
102. Incorrect. similar
103. Incorrect. sophomore
104. Incorrect. stomach
105. Correct. successful
106. Incorrect. synonym
107. Correct. technical
108. Incorrect. temperature
109. Correct. title
110. Incorrect. undoubtedly
111. Incorrect. vacuum
112. Correct. vengeance
113. Incorrect. visitor
114. Incorrect. Wednesday
115. Correct. wretched

Drill: Homophones

1. bored
2. capital
3. coarse; bare
4. counsel
5. two; sundaes
6. fourth
7. grate
8. horse
9. its
10. wear; new
11. there; peace
12. sale; pair
13. plane
14. roll
15. site
16. sole
17. Where
18. waste
19. weak
20. Whether
21. weigh; lose
22. Here
23. Which
24. hole
25. Whose

Drill: Usage and Sentence Correction

1. (1)
2. (3)
3. (3)
4. (5)
5. (2)
6. (4)
7. (2)
8. (1)
9. (3)
10. (5)
11. (4)
12. (1)
13. (5)
14. (4)
15. (4)

LANGUAGE ARTS: WRITING PART II REVIEW

I.   THE ESSAY TEST

II. WHY ESSAYS EXIST

III. ESSAY STRATEGIES

IV. PRE-WRITING/PLANNING TIME

V.   WRITING YOUR ROUGH DRAFT

VI. REVISING, EDITING, AND PROOFREADING

I. THE ESSAY TEST

This review is meant to help you become familiar with the skills you will need to pass the essay portion of the Language Arts: Writing Test. This section of the GED will ask you to *produce* ideas, rather than to analyze them. Our review will guide you through a step-by-step process of how to write your essay, from writing strategies to budgeting your time during the exam. Even if you feel that you are a good writer, you should still use this review, as it will help you become familiar with the type of essay you will be expected to write. By reading through this review and going through the included drills, you will increase your chances of doing well on this section of the test.

As you begin reading each section of this review, try not to become frustrated if you feel that you are not a good writer. The strategies included are provided to help you write an essay which is to the point, easily understood, properly structured, well supported, and correct according to the rules of grammar. You will not be expected to write a best-selling book in order to pass this test. Remember, the more you practice the strategies provided in this review, the easier it will be for you to write a passing essay.

LANGUAGE ARTS: WRITING PART II TOPICS

Part II of the Language Arts: Writing Test will require you to be familiar with various aspects of good writing, all of which are listed below. The topics covered in the Language Arts: Writing Part I Review are also necessary elements of good writing. For a comprehensive review on writing skills, you should study both the Language Arts: Writing Part I Review, which preceeds this review, and the Language Arts: Writing Part II Review, which follows.

EVIDENCE OF THOUGHTFUL WRITING

1. Planning
2. Drafting
3. Revising
4. Proofreading

CORRECT USE OF STANDARD WRITTEN ENGLISH

1. Spelling (only for homonyms, contractions, and possessives)
2. Punctuation
3. Grammar
4. Word Choice
5. Sentence Structure

You must realize that your essay will not be scored on each of these skills directly. The person reading your essay will be grading it based on his or her overall impression of how you applied all of these skills to your essay.

II. WHY ESSAYS EXIST

People write essays for many reasons—not just to complete tests. Some of our best thinkers have written essays which we continue to read from generation to generation. Essays offer the reader a logical, coherent, and imaginatively written composition showing the nature or consequences of a single controlling idea considered from the writer's unique point of view. Writers use essays to communicate their opinion or position on a topic to readers who are not present at that time. Writers also use essays to help their readers understand or learn about something that readers should or might want to know or do. Essays always express more or less directly the author's opinion, belief, position, or knowledge (backed by evidence) about the idea or object in question.

III. ESSAY STRATEGIES

All of an essay's organizational strategies may be used to aid an argument in writing. The author offers reasons and/or evidence so an audience will be inclined to believe the position the author presents about the idea under discussion. Writers use seven basic strategies to organize information and ideas in essays to help prove their point (thesis). All of these strategies may be useful to you in arguing an idea, in persuading a reader to see the issue your way. Essays may:

(1) show how a **process** or a procedure does or should work step-by-step in time;

(2) **compare or contrast** two or more things or ideas to show important differences or similarities;

(3) **identify a problem** and then explain how to solve it;

(4) **analyze** into its components, or **classify** by its types or categories, an idea or thing to show how it is put together, how it works, or how it is designed;

(5) **explain** why something happens to produce a particular result or set of results;

(6) **describe** the particular individual characteristics, beauty, or features of a place, person(s), time, or idea; or

(7) **define** what a thing is or what an idea means.

In a given essay, one pattern tends to dominate the discussion, depending on the object or idea in question. (For example, I might use **description** and **explanation** in order to **define** the varied meanings of "love.")

COMPOSING YOUR ESSAY:
USING THE WRITING PROCESS

Most people wrongly think that writers just sit down and churn out wonderful essays or poems in one sitting, in a flash of genius and inspiration. This is not true! Writers use the writing process from start to finish to help them develop a well-composed document. If you do not reflect on your composition in stages and make changes as you develop it, you will not see all the problems or errors in it. Don't try to write an essay all at one time and then leave the room. Stay and look through it. Reflect upon it using the writing process in the following way.

The writing process has five steps: (1) pre-writing or planning time, (2) rough drafting, (3) organizing and revising the ideas (not the words or sentences themselves), (4) polishing or editing (making sure sentences themselves are sentences, that the words you use are the right words, and that the spelling and punctuation are correct), and (5) proofreading to make sure no littel mistakes are left (like the misspelling of the word "little" here).

Using this process does not mean that you have to write five drafts. You should write one draft (stages 1 and 2), leaving space for corrections; e.g., writing on every other line, and then working on the existing draft through the rest of the stages (3 through 5). If time allows, you may want to do the whole process on scrap paper and then copy the finished product onto the allotted test paper. But if you do copy it, make sure you proofread your copy to see if, while transcribing it, you left anything out or said a word twice twice (or something silly like that mistake).

Since you have 45 minutes for this test, you might allocate your time for all these steps in a manner similar to the following:

(1)	Pre-writing, planning:	5 minutes
(2)	Rough draft:	15 minutes
(3)	Organizing, paragraphing:	10 minutes
(4)	Polishing, editing:	5–10 minutes
(5)	Proofreading:	2–5 minutes

If you have more time or less time, adjust this schedule proportionately. When you practice, be sure to have someone time you—someone who can keep you concentrating on this task until you're done.

IV. PRE-WRITING/ PLANNING TIME

Read the essay question and **decide on your purpose**: Do you want to persuade your reader? Or, do you want to explain something?

Sample: "Television is bad for people." Do you agree or disagree with this statement?

Decide. Take a stand. Don't be wishy-washy. Write the statement of your position.

Sample: I agree that television is bad for people.

Or: Television is an excellent learning tool and is good for most people.

One of these is your thesis, depending on your point of view.

CONSIDER YOUR AUDIENCE

The writer's responsibility is to write clearly, honestly, and cleanly for the reader's sake. Essays would be pointless without an audience. Why write an essay if no one wants or needs to read it? Why add evidence, organize your ideas, or correct bad grammar? The reason to do any of these things is because someone out there needs to understand what you mean or say. What would the audience need to know in order to believe you or to come over to your position? Imagine someone you know listening to you declare your position or opinion and then saying, "Oh, yeah? Prove it!" When you write your essay, make sure you answer the following questions so that you will not be daunted by a person who says, "Prove it!"

What evidence do you need to prove your idea to this skeptic?

What would s/he disagree with you about?

What does s/he share with you as common knowledge? What does s/he need to be told by you?

CONTROL YOUR POINT OF VIEW

People may write essays from one of three points of view, depending upon the essay's audience. The points of view below are discussed from Informal → Formal.

(1) Subjective/Personal Point of View:

"I think
"I believe $\Big\}$ cars are more trouble than they are worth."
"I feel

(2) Second Person (We... You; I... You): "If **you** own a car, **you** will soon find out that it is more trouble than it is worth."

(3) Third Person Point of View: (focuses on the idea, not what "I" think of it): "**Cars** are more trouble than **they** are worth."

Stick with one or another; don't switch your point of view midstream.

CONSIDER YOUR EVIDENCE

During the pre-writing stage, jot down a few phrases that show ideas and examples which support your point of view. Do this quickly on a separate piece of paper, spending no more than 5 minutes on the task. Don't try to outline; just **list things** you think may be important to discuss. After you have listed several ideas, pick at least three to five things you want or need to discuss and number them in the order of importance to prove your point.

V. WRITING YOUR ROUGH DRAFT

Spend about 20 minutes writing your rough draft. Looking over at your pre-writing list, write down the ideas you think will be most useful in proving your point in the order you think is the best to convince the reader. Be sure to **use real evidence** from life experiences or knowledge to support what you say. It is not necessary to draw evidence from books. Look into your own life—it will do fine.

For example, don't just write, "Cars are more trouble to fix than bicycles," and then not show evidence to support your claim. Give **examples** of what you mean: "**For example**, my dad's car needs 200 parts to make one brake work, but the brakes on my bicycle consist only of four pieces, and I can replace those myself." Write naturally and quickly. Don't worry too much at this point about paragraphing, spelling, punctuation— just write down what you think or want to say in the order of your list.

WRITING PARAGRAPHS

In the examples below, two paragraphs are offered as exhibits. One is an example of a paragraph without concrete evidence, and the other is an example of a paragraph with evidence for the idea. Study each. Note the topic sentence (T) and how that sentence is or is not supported by evidence.

Paragraphing with evidence:

(T) Television is bad for people. **Watching television takes time away from other things.** Programs on television are often stupid and depict crimes that people later copy. Television takes time away from loved ones, and it often becomes addictive. So, television is bad for people because it is no good.

In this example, the author has not given any concrete evidence for any of the good ideas presented. S/he just declares her/his ideas to be true. However, any one of the sentences above might make a good opening sentence for a whole paragraph. Take the second sentence, for example:

(T) Television is bad for people. **Watching television takes time away from other things (first piece of evidence).** For example, all those hours people spend sitting in front of the television, they could be building a chair or fixing the roof **(second piece of evidence).** Maybe the laundry needs to be done, but because people watch television, they may end up not having time to do it. Then Monday comes around again and they have no socks to wear to work **(third piece of evidence).** Someone could be writing a letter to a friend in Miami who hasn't been heard from or written to for months **(fourth piece of evidence).** Or maybe someone misses the opportunity to take in a beautiful day in the park because s/he had to see the hockey game. They'll repeat the hockey game on the news, but this beautiful day only comes around once. Watching television definitely keeps people from getting things done.

Always supply evidence. Three examples or illustrations of your idea per paragraph is a useful number. Four is okay, but stop there. Don't go on and on about a single point. You don't have time. A typical test essay, then, should have about five paragraphs. It should be broken down like this:

Introduction: A paragraph which shows your point of view (thesis) about an issue and introduces your position with three general ideas which support this thesis.

Development: Three middle paragraphs which prove your position from different angles, using evidence from real life and knowledge. Each one of these paragraphs should support each of the three ideas you started out with in Paragraph 1.

Conclusion: The last paragraph, which sums up your position and adds one final reminder of what the issue was and perhaps points to a solution: "So, television takes away from the quality of life and is therefore bad for human beings. We should be watching the sun, the sky, the birds, and each other, instead.'"

Write a paragraph below using this sentence for your focus: (Have someone read it and comment critically on it when you are done.)

"Television takes valuable time away from our loved ones."

TRANSITIONS

To help the reader follow the flow of your ideas, and to help unify the essay, use transitions to show the connections among your ideas. You may use transitions either at the beginnings of paragraphs, or you may use them to show the connections among ideas within a single paragraph.

Here are some typical transitional words and phrases.

Linking similar ideas

again	*for example*	*likewise*
also	*for instance*	*moreover*
and	*further*	*nor*
another	*furthermore*	*of course*
besides	*in addition*	*similarly*
equally important	*in like manner*	*too*

Linking dissimilar/contradictory ideas

although	*however*	*otherwise*
and yet	*in spite of*	*provided that*
as if	*instead*	*still*
but	*nevertheless*	*yet*

conversely	on the contrary	
even if	on the other hand	

Indicating cause, purpose, result

as	for	so
as a result	for this reason	then
because	hence	therefore
consequently	since	thus

Indicating time or position

above	before	meanwhile
across	beyond	next
afterwards	eventually	presently
around	finally	second
at once	first	thereafter
at the present time	here	thereupon

Indicating an example or summary

as a result	in any event	in short
as I have said	in brief	on the whole
for example	in conclusion	to sum up
for instance	in fact	
in any case	in other words	

☞ Drill: Writing

DIRECTIONS: Each of the following phrases or sentences is incorrect. Determine what is wrong with each item and correct it in the space provided.

1. About the television.

2. I like television and I think people should watch it television is good because it is so real I think many people would die without it.

3. In my opinion, I believe that in order to be able to understand this issue many hours and a lot of time must be devoted to comprehending what the message is that the writer is trying to communicate with ideas due to the fact that s/he is so involved with them.

4. While waiting for the check, the doorbell rang in the living room.

5. I like eating fish and to go to the lake.

6. I bought a computer and some word processing software which was frightening.

7. We cannot reimburse you for moving boats over 14 feet.

8. We could of been contenders in the contest, but the sweep of events make us losers in the end.

9. I like ducks, however, I prefer swans.

10. In the long run, the most important thing is not to be effected by the affects of television commercials.

VI. REVISING, EDITING, AND PROOFREADING

REVISE AND ORGANIZE THE PARAGRAPHS

The unit of work for revising is "the paragraph." After you have written what you want to say based on your pre-writing list, spend about ten minutes revising your draft, looking to see if you need to indent for paragraphs anywhere. If you do, make a little proofreader's mark (¶) to indicate that you think a paragraph should begin at that point. Check to see if you want to add anything that would make your point of view more convincing. Be sure to supply useful transitions to keep up the flow of your ideas. If you don't have room on the paper, or if your new paragraph shows up out of order, add that paragraph and indicate with a number or some other mark where you want it to go. Check to make sure that you provide examples and illustrate your statements.

POLISHING AND EDITING THE ESSAY SENTENCES

If the unit of work for revising is the paragraph, the unit of work for editing is the sentence. In the last five to ten minutes, check your paper for mistakes by editing.

Polishing checklist:

- Are all your sentences really sentences, or have you written any fragments or run-on sentences?
- Are you using your vocabulary correctly?
- Have you used some inappropriate words that you would never use with a teacher?
- Did you leave out punctuation anywhere? Did you capitalize correctly? Did you check for commas, periods, and quotation marks?

Be sure to **read every word** during this time and make corrections as you go. To help you recognize what you should look for in polishing and editing, refer to the Language Arts: Writing Part I Review in this book.

PROOFREADING

In the last two or three minutes, read your paper, word for word, forward and then backward from the end to the beginning. Read it out loud if possible, but read it! By doing so, you will notice a certain number of errors that you may have missed by having red forward only. For example, read the sentence before this one backward, starting with "only," and see if you spot any more errors than you read the first time.

☞ Drill: Essay Writing

DIRECTIONS: Give yourself 45 minutes to write an essay on the topic below, using the lined space provided and making sure to time yourself. Write only on the topic provided. Write legibly, use a ball-point pen, and budget your space so you do not run out of room to write. (Remember to use the strategies that you learned in this review.)

Television often causes the viewer to lose touch with reality and become completely passive and unaware. Like other addictions, television provides a pleasurable escape route from action to inaction.

Is this statement true or false? Do you feel that television's effects are good or bad? Respond to this statement in an essay of approximately 250 words, making sure to support your view with examples using your own past experiences or knowledge of other people's experiences.

Write your essay on these lined pages.

WRITING II

ANSWER KEY

Drill: Writing

Since more than one answer may be obtained for each item, we will only identify what errors are present in each phrase and sentence rather than provide a single correct sentence among various correct answers.

1. This sentence is a fragment. It has no subject or verb to complete it.

2. This is a run-on sentence. It has many subject and verb units not correctly separated by punctuation.

3. This is a wordy sentence. It should be rewritten as a single short sentence.

4. This is an example of a dangling modifier. Reading this sentence, one would think that the doorbell was waiting for the check.

5. This sentence does not link up the phrases that begin "eating…" and "to go…." They are not parallel.

6. This sentence suggests that either or both the computer or the software is frightening. Which is it? The reader cannot be sure because s/he cannot tell to which word the word "which" refers.

7. This sentence is confusing because the meaning of "14 feet" is ambiguous. Does the writer mean 14-foot long boats? Surely, moving boats over a distance of 14 feet is not such a costly proposition.

8. This sentence has two major flaws:

   (1) The phrase "could of" should be "could have." "Of" is never part of a verb.

   (2) In the second half, "make" should be "makes" to agree with the real subject, "sweep."

   The trouble is the writer probably thought "events" was the subject as s/he wrote the sentence.

9. This sentence is incorrectly punctuated with commas. It is actually two sentences on either side of the "however." Consequently, a semicolon [;] could be placed after "ducks." You can also use a

period [.] to separate the two sentences, or you can replace "however" with "but" and leave the commas as they appear.

10. Which "effect" word is correct? Neither. Make sure you use the right words in the right place. For example, don't write "red" for "read," or "there" for "their."

Drill: Essay Writing

SAMPLE ESSAY I

In the past thirty years, television has become a very popular pastime for almost everyone. From the time the mother places the baby in his jumpseat in front of the television so that she can relax and have a second cup of coffee until the time the senior citizen in the retirement home watches Vanna White turn the letters on "Wheel of Fortune," Americans spend endless hours in front of the "boob tube." I believe that television can become an addiction that provides an escape from the problems of the world and from facing responsibility for your own life.

When my mother was a little girl, what did children do to entertain themselves? They played. Their games usually involved social interaction with other children as well as imaginatively creating entertainment for themselves. They also developed hobbies like woodworking and sewing. Today, few children really know how to play with each other or entertain themselves. Instead, they sit in front of the television, glued to cartoons that are senseless and often violent. Even if they watch educational programs like "Sesame Street," they don't really have to do anything but watch and listen to what the answer to the question is.

Teenagers, also, use television as a way of avoiding doing things that will help them mature. How many kids do much homework anymore? Not many. Why not? Because they work part-time jobs and come home from work tired and relax in front of the television. Even if they watch a controversial program about some problem in the world like AIDS or the war in the Middle East, they don't usually do anything about it.

In addition, young mothers use television to escape their problems. The terrible woes of the people on the soap operas make their problems seem less important. This means that they don't need to solve their own problems.

Although it may seem as if television is really great for older people, I think even my grandma would have more fun if she had more interests rather than just watching quiz shows. I know she has blotted out the "real world" when she expects us to act like the Cosby kids when she comes to visit.

In conclusion, I believe that television really can become an addiction that allows people of all ages to avoid facing their own problems and lose themselves in the problems of other people.

Analysis of Sample Essay I

This essay scores a 4 (effective). The writer appears largely in control of the discussion and the mechanics of writing.

In the past thirty years, television has become a very popular pastime for almost everyone. From the time the mother places the baby in his jumpseat in front of the television so that she can relax and have a second cup of coffee until the time the senior citizen in the retirement home watches Vanna White turn the letters on "Wheel of Fortune," Americans spend endless hours in front of the "boob tube." [1—I believe that television can become an addiction that provides an escape from the problems of the world and from facing responsibility for your own life.]

> 1. The essay has a traditional structure; the first paragraph introduces the topic, even suggesting the organization of the essay. This last sentence states the writer's thesis clearly.

[2—When my mother was a little girl, what did children do to entertain themselves? They played.] Their games usually involved social interaction with other children as well as imaginatively creating entertainment for themselves. [3—They also developed hobbies like woodworking and sewing.] Today, few children really know how to play with each other or entertain themselves. Instead, they sit in front of the television, glued to cartoons that are senseless and often violent. Even if they watch educational programs like "Sesame Street," they don't really have to do anything but watch and listen to what the answer to the question is.

> 2. Each of the following paragraphs has a clear topic sentence. Here, it is in the form of a question which the writer immediately answers. The reader feels as though s/he is really taking part in the writer's thought process.
>
> 3. The writer's consistent use of specific, concrete evidence supports the general ideas effectively. Readers begin to feel convinced of the writer's opinion (thesis).

[4—Teenagers, also, use television as a way of avoiding doing things that will help them mature. How many kids do much homework anymore? Not many. Why not? Because they work part-time jobs and come home from work tired and relax in front of the television. Even if they watch a controversial program about some problem in the world like AIDS or the war in the Middle East, they don't usually do anything about it.]

> 4. This paragraph explores a new, interesting angle in support of the thesis.

[5—In addition,] young mothers use television to escape their problems. The terrible woes of the people on the soap operas make their problems seem less important. This means that they don't need to solve their own problems.

> 5. Effective transitions keep the flow of ideas going for the reader.

[6—Although it may seem as if television is really great for older people, I think even my grandma would have more fun if she had more interests rather than just watching quiz shows.] I know she has blotted out the "real world" when she expects us to act like the Cosby kids when she comes to visit.

> 6. Varied sentence structure helps create emphasis and changes the pace for the reader, helping to relieve monotony of tone and to keep the writing interesting.

[7—In conclusion, I believe that television really can become an addiction that allows people of all ages to avoid facing their own problems and lose themselves in the problems of other people.]

> 7. The concluding paragraph, although only one sentence long, restates the main idea. The writer may have run out of time and so could not write more, but at least s/he rounded out the thesis with a clear control of the main idea.

SAMPLE ESSAY II

I do not agree with the given statement. I think that instead of being bad for people, television not only does not blot out the real world but, instead, gives the person watching it a chance to experience the real world, even places he can't possibly go and may never get a chance to go.

For instance, I've learned a lot about the Vietnam War by watching TV. For a while, I heard things about it, about how some of the veterans didn't feel as if they were welcomed right when they came back from that war. I didn't understand what was the matter. Then they built a special memorial in Washington for the veterans that didn't come back. Since then, I have seen a lot of programs that showed what went on in Vietnam, and I've heard Vietnam vets talk about what happened to them. I think that that war has became very real to me because of TV.

Television educates us about the dangers of growing up in America today. I've seen good programs about the dangers of using drugs, about teenage pregnancy and what happens if you try to keep the baby, about eating too much cholesterol (That doesn't matter to me yet, but my dad needs to watch that!), and also anorexia. These are things we all need to know about, and TV has told about them so we know what to do.

I really am convinced that television brings the real world into your house. I think us kids today know a lot more about the real world than our grandparents did who grew up without television.

Analysis of Sample Essay II

This essay scores a 3 (adequate). The writer appears to have good control over the discussion and fairly good control over grammar and mechanics.

I do not agree with the given statement. [1—I think that instead of being bad for people, television not only does not blot out the real world but, instead, gives the person watching it a chance to experience the real world, even places he can't possibly go and may never get a chance to go.]

> 1. The writer takes one position and develops it. The first paragraph provides a clear introduction, and paragraphs two and three below develop this thesis.

[2—For instance, I've learned a lot about the Vietnam War by watching TV.] For a while, I heard things about it, about how some of the veterans didn't feel as if they were welcomed right when they came back from that war. I didn't understand what was the matter. Then they built a special memorial in Washington for the veterans that didn't come back. Since then, I have seen a lot of programs that showed what went on in Vietnam, and I've heard Vietnam vets talk about what happened to them. [3—I think that that war has became very real to me because of TV.]

> 2. This generalized example is not supported with specific evidence. The lack of specifics pulls this essay down.
>
> 3. Occasional weak sentence structure and a failure to proofread effectively take the essay down another step because the style and mechanics appear to be only fairly under control.

Television educates us about the dangers of growing up in America today. I've seen good programs about the dangers of using drugs, about teenage pregnancy and what happens if you try to keep the baby, about eating too much cholesterol (That doesn't matter to me yet, but my dad needs to watch that!), and also anorexia. These are things we all need to know about, and TV has told about them so we know what to do.

[5—I really am convinced that television brings the real world into your house. I think us [4—kids] today know a lot more about the real world than our grandparents did who grew up without television.]

> 4. The occasional use of slang such as this makes the writer's style inconsistent and less literate than it could be.
>
> 5. This last paragraph concludes, but weakly, and seems to wander off onto a possible new area of discussion not called for by the thesis.

SAMPLE ESSAY III

On the one hand, I think television is bad, But it also does some good things for all of us. For instants, my little sister thought she wanted to be a policeman until she saw NYPD Blue. Then she learned how dangerous it is and now she wants to be an astronaut. She is too young to remember the Challenger explosion.

But the bad thing about television programs are the ideas it puts in kids heads. Like violent things happen on television, and little kids see it and don't know that other people hurt when they are hit, battered up, beat. shot, etc. Then the kids go out and try to knock their friends around and think if they are strong and handsome that they can get their own way whatever happens. Even parents sometimes have trouble controling their own kids because of too much TV. Of course that's partly because the parents watch too much too when they should of been taking care of the kids they necklected them watching television.

So I think that television has both it's good and it's bad points. I'd hate to see us get rid of it all together, but I wonder if I'll let my kids watch it when I have them. It sometimes puts bad ideas in their heads.

Analysis of Sample Essay III

This essay scores between 2 and 1 (marginal—inadequate). The writer appears largely out of control of both the controlling idea, evidence to support the opinions expressed, and the grammar and mechanics of English itself.

[1—On the one hand, I think television is [2—bad, But] it also does some good things for all of us. For [3—instants], my little sister thought she wanted to be a policeman until she saw NYPD Blue. Then she learned how dangerous it is and now she wants to be an astronaut. She is too young to remember the Challenger explosion.]

> 1. The writer's failure to take one opinion (thesis) and clearly develop it weakens the whole essay. Some specific examples are

attempted, but the details in this paragraph would be better stated in later paragraphs.

2. Punctuation errors plague the essay and cause the writer to appear illiterate to the reader.

3. Poor spelling contributes to a sloppy, illiterate appearance.

[5—[4—But the bad thing about television programs are the ideas it puts in kids heads.] Like violent things happen on television, and little kids see it and don't know that other people hurt when they are hit, battered up, beat. shot, etc. Then the kids go out and try to knock their friends around and think if they are strong and handsome that they can get their own way whatever happens. Even parents sometimes have trouble controling their own kids because of too much TV. [6—Of course that's partly because the parents watch too much too when they should of been taking care of the kids they necklected them watching television.]]

4. Weak subject/verb agreement makes this sentence sound careless to the reader.

5. The lack of specificity forces the writer to blend what should be at least two paragraphs into one. The writer comes across as rambling and as not having thought through the ideas.

6. Persistent spelling and grammatical errors ("should of" instead of "should have") point to a writer who is out of control of his medium—language. This exasperates the reader and drives him or her away.

[8—So I think that television has both [7—it's] good and it's bad points. I'd hate to see us get rid of it all together, but I wonder if I'll let my kids watch it when I have them. It sometimes puts bad ideas in their heads.]

7. A typical apostrophe error that only the careless or rushed would let get by them.

8. In this weak "conclusion," the writer doesn't take a clear stand, plays it safe, probably hoping that a risk-free, wishy-washy ending will go well with the teachers reading this. That is a big mistake. Stick to your guns! The stronger your stand, the better your chances. But prove what you claim.

SOCIAL STUDIES REVIEW

Chapter 3

SOCIAL STUDIES REVIEW

I. SOCIAL STUDIES TOPICS

II. U.S. HISTORY

III. ECONOMICS

IV. POLITICAL SCIENCE

V. GEOGRAPHY

The following review has been created to help you become familiar with the types of questions you will encounter in the Social Studies section of the GED. Prior knowledge of the subjects tested is not necessary in order for you to do well on this exam. This test will require you to read a passage and/or interpret information from a graph, map, or chart, and then answer questions based on this information. Our review concentrates on presenting passages and questions similar to those appearing on the GED. By studying this review, you can familiarize yourself with the type of vocabulary which will appear on the test, as well as the content covered.

I. SOCIAL STUDIES TOPICS

The breakdown below shows the areas covered on the Social Studies test. You should review these topics in order to accurately answer the questions appearing in this section.

HISTORY (40% of Test)

1. North American Native People
2. The New World and the New Nation
3. Growth and Change
4. Industrialization
5. Crisis and Reform
6. The United States as a World Power
7. Challenges of the Modern World

ECONOMICS (20% of Test)

1. Scarcity
2. Economic Systems: Capitalism, Communism, Socialism
3. Free Enterprise
4. Production
5. The Consumer
6. Financial Institutions
7. Government and the Economy
8. The Economy
9. Labor and the Economy
10. Foreign Trade

POLITICAL SCIENCE (25% of Test)

1. Political Systems
2. The U.S. Political System

GEOGRAPHY (15% of Test)

1. Basic Principles
2. Regions of the U.S.
3. Themes and Issues in the U.S.
4. Cultural regions
5. Utilizing World Resources

The more familiar you are with the format of the Social Studies test, the better you will perform. Our review will present you with maps, charts, graphs, and various passages similar to those found on the actual test. You will be asked to answer questions based on the information given. Although you may feel that you are well prepared for this test, you should still read this review to brush up on your skills, and develop speed and accuracy in answering the questions. Various passages from important historical documents have been provided at the back of this book to help familiarize you with such documents. Also, make sure to memorize the directions to this section, so that valuable time is not wasted.

II. U.S. HISTORY

THE NEW WORLD

In 1606, three ships, the *Discovery*, *Godspeed*, and *Susan Constant*, left England with over 100 passengers aboard. The ships arrived in Jamestown, Virginia, in 1607 with people of various professions, such as doctors, bricklayers, carpenters, and farmers, among others.

The name Virginia was chosen because Queen Elizabeth I of England, who died in 1603, was known as the "Virgin Queen." Thick forests loomed everywhere in the new colony. Farms were begun only after a wilderness of trees and brush had been cleared. Times were indeed hard for the first colonists, but despite the hardships new settlers continued to make the long and arduous journey to the new land.

Many settlers of all nationalities settled in the colonies after 1607. A steady stream of French, Swedish, Portuguese, Dutch, English, and other nationalities settled up and down the eastern seaboard between 1607 and 1776. In 1619, the first 20 black immigrants arrived in Jamestown, and they accumulated land and did quite well despite the inevitable hardships of getting established in the new world. (Slavery came about 40 years later.)

The first law-making governmental structure in the new world was called the Virginia House of Burgesses. In 1619, two men from each of the eleven settlements made up the first representative Congress in Virginia. This bold step of setting up a representative government in 1619, in Virginia, served as a landmark achievement which other colonies emulated.

☞ Drill: The New World

DIRECTIONS: The following questions are based on the passage above. Read each question and choose the correct answer.

1. One of the conclusions that we can draw from the passage is that
   (1) thick forests of trees made it difficult to start farms in colonial Virginia.
   (2) thick forests of trees made it easy to get farms started.
   (3) new settlers stopped coming to the New World.
   (4) life was easy in colonial Virginia.
   (5) Queen Elizabeth I of England was alive when the first settlers founded Jamestown, Virginia.

2. One conclusion that can be drawn is that
    (1) each ship had over 100 passengers aboard.
    (2) most people went to the New World for adventure.
    (3) a variety of skilled people went to the new world in order to build houses, plant farms, and to take care of the sick.
    (4) the *Discovery, Godspeed,* and *Susan Constant* were forts in Virginia.
    (5) the *Discovery, Godspeed,* and *Susan Constant* were lakes in Virginia.

3. The three ships that landed in Jamestown, Virginia, were
    (1) *Susan Constant, Discovery,* and *Virgin Queen.*
    (2) *Susan Constant, Pinta,* and *Godspeed.*
    (3) *Pinta, Godspeed,* and *Susan Constant.*
    (4) *Nina, Pinta,* and *Santa Maria.*
    (5) *Discovery, Godspeed,* and *Susan Constant.*

4. The main idea of the passage is that
    (1) black immigrants settled in the country in 1619.
    (2) many nationalities settled in America after 1607.
    (3) the English were the first settlers in the New World.
    (4) slavery came about 40 years after 1619.
    (5) other colonies also settled on the Eastern seaboard.

5. The first colony was established in
    (1) 1607.   (4) 1492.
    (2) 1620.   (5) 1916.
    (3) 1619.

6. Which of the following statements is an opinion?
    (1) Twenty-two members made up the first representative Congress.
    (2) In 1619, the Virginia House of Burgesses was established.
    (3) Only men were elected to the representative assembly.
    (4) Eleven settlements were represented.
    (5) The setting up of the Virginia House of Burgesses was a landmark achievement.

7. In which colony did the House of Burgesses begin?
    (1) Maryland   (4) South Carolina
    (2) Virginia   (5) Rhode Island
    (3) Massachusetts

RAILROADS,
1783–1860

8. According to the map, which of the following statements is most correct?
   (1) The South had the most extensively developed railroad system.
   (2) The transportation system ran primarily east-west.
   (3) The West had a poorly developed transportation system.
   (4) The South depended upon canals for transportation.
   (5) The United States had developed few railroad lines prior to 1860.

THE INDUSTRIAL REVOLUTION

The industrial revolution began with inventions such as the flying shuttle of 1733, the spinning jenny of 1764, the water frame of 1769, the power loom of 1785, and the cotton gin of 1793. In 1784, wrought iron was made from pig iron, and in 1785, the cotton mill was first operated by steam power. These inventions, among others, made it much easier for products to be produced at a much faster pace.

The industrial revolution, which introduced machine labor, began in England around 1760 and changed the face of America and Europe. A shift in population from the rural areas to the cities began as new technology provided more and more jobs. Some of the inventions that fueled the industrial revolution were the cotton gin, the spinning jenny, the power loom, the steamboat, Morse's telegraph, and others.

The industrial revolution continues to play a major role today in many parts of the world. Computers have revolutionized the way that goods are produced. An example of this would be in the making of garments. There are sewing machines on the market today that can be programmed to actually make a garment to exact proportions and specifications.

Bales of Cotton
1790-1830

1790 1800 1810 1820 1830	750000 500000 250000 0

☞ Drill: The Industrial Revolution

DIRECTIONS: The following questions are based on the information above.
Read each question and choose the correct answer.

9. Based on the passage, which of the following is the best example of a
   new invention being used to change the way things were made in the
   1700s?
   (1) The assembly line being introduced
   (2) Oxen being used to plow fields
   (3) Shoes being made by hand by a cobbler
   (4) Fabric being made with a machine in a mill instead of by hand
   (5) Furniture being carved by hand

10. The new industrial revolution is continuing because of the advent of
    (1) computers.   (4) knitting needles.
    (2) the spinning jenny.   (5) the stock market.
    (3) the loom.

11. Which of the following statements expresses an opinion rather than a
    fact?
    (1) Computers can improve productivity.
    (2) Computers are difficult to operate.
    (3) Computers are used only in America.
    (4) Computers are not a part of the industrial revolution.
    (5) Computers can be programmed for specific tasks.

12. One profession that was least likely to flourish during the industrial revolution was the
    (1) factory worker.
    (2) steamboat captain.
    (3) city housing worker.
    (4) telegraph operator.
    (5) farmer.

13. The industrial revolution began in
    (1) America.
    (2) England.
    (3) France.
    (4) Germany.
    (5) Japan.

14. An invention that was not a part of the industrial revolution was the
    (1) cotton gin.
    (2) radio.
    (3) telegraph.
    (4) steamboat.
    (5) power loom.

15. According to the graph, how many bales of cotton were produced in 1830?
    (1) 200,000
    (2) 500,000
    (3) 750,000
    (4) 50,000
    (5) 75,000

16. In what year was more cotton produced than in 1830?
    (1) 1790
    (2) 1800
    (3) 1830
    (4) All of the above.
    (5) None of the above.

THE CIVIL WAR

The Civil War, which started in 1861 and ended in 1865, was the bloodiest war in all of U.S. history. It tore the country apart and, in some instances, pitted brother against brother. The war was fought over political and social differences between the Union and Confederacy. The war essentially brought down the tragic institution of slavery. To this day, the scars of the Civil War are evident in American society.

At the beginning of the hostilities between the North and South, the states of South Carolina, Georgia, Florida, Alabama, Mississippi, Texas, Louisiana, North Carolina, Arkansas, Tennessee, and eventually Virginia, decided to secede from the Union.

After the Civil War ended and the Union forces were victorious, there remained monumental tasks that had to be tackled in reuniting the country. Some states were not admitted to the Union until the Fourteenth and Fifteenth Amendments, granting citizenship rights and the right to vote to blacks, were approved. As a result of the new freedoms, black men became office holders in the deep South between 1868 and 1877.

☞ Drill: The Civil War

DIRECTIONS: The following questions are based on the passage above. Read each question and choose the correct answer.

17. The Civil War began in
    (1) 1865.
    (2) 1860.
    (3) 1866.
    (4) 1861.
    (5) 1862.

18. A civil war means a war that is fought
    (1) between citizens of the same country.
    (2) between two or more countries.
    (3) between the army ground forces and naval forces.
    (4) between adjacent countries.
    (5) between allied countries.

19. Secede may be defined as
    (1) to leave or get out of.
    (2) to become an ally of another country.
    (3) to make peace.
    (4) to become successful.
    (5) to stay behind or remain.

20. One result of the ratification of the Fourteenth and Fifteenth Amendments was the
    (1) ratification of the Congressional Plan of Reconstruction.
    (2) end of Reconstruction.
    (3) election of blacks to political office.
    (4) Civil War.
    (5) the assassination of Abraham Lincoln.

THE ELECTION OF 1912

The election of 1912 was one of the most dramatic in American history. President Taft's inability to maintain party harmony led Theodore Roosevelt to return to national politics. When denied the Republican nomination, Roosevelt and his supporters formed the Progressive Party (Bull Moose) and nominated Roosevelt for president and Hiram Johnson (California) for vice president on a political platform nicknamed "The New Nationalism." It called for stricter regulation of large corporations; creation of a tariff commission; woman's suffrage; minimum wages and benefits; direct election of senators; initiative, referendum and recall; presidential primaries; and prohibition of child labor. Roosevelt also called for a Federal Trade Commission to regulate the broader economy, a stronger executive, and more government planning. Theodore Roosevelt did not see big business as evil, but as a permanent development that was necessary in a modern economy.

☞ Drill: The Election of 1912

DIRECTIONS: The following questions are based on the passage above. Read each question and choose the correct answer.

21. The Progressive movement started in
    (1) 1914.
    (2) 1912.
    (3) 1915.
    (4) 1965.
    (5) 1913.

22. Which was **not** a part of Theodore Roosevelt's political platform in 1912?
    (1) The formation of the "Bull Moose" party
    (2) A stronger chief executive
    (3) Annexation of Cuba
    (4) Minimum wages
    (5) Women's suffrage

THE GREAT DEPRESSION

The Great Depression began in 1929 with the crash of the stock market. This brought on a period of approximately twenty-five percent unemployment and very bleak times for millions of people. Banks closed and many people lost all of their savings.

Long soup lines in cities became a common sight. It became extremely difficult for families to get by without some government assistance.

Franklin Roosevelt was elected to the presidency in 1932 during the Great Depression. He had many "new deal" ideas about how to turn the economy around. Many work programs were instituted, such as the Works Progress Administration (WPA) and the Civilian Conservation Corps (CCC). Such programs put large numbers of people to work on public projects. The government became their employer. Congress also passed a social security law in 1935 at the urging of President Roosevelt.

☞ Drill: The Great Depression

DIRECTIONS: The following questions are based on the passage above. Read each question and choose the correct answer.

23. One of the conclusions that can be drawn from the above passage is that
    (1) many businesses failed for lack of customers during the Great Depression.
    (2) many people did not want to work.
    (3) employment was high.
    (4) few people lived in the city.
    (5) many people left the country.

24. The Great Depression started because of
    (1) the stock market crash of 1929.
    (2) runaway inflation.
    (3) a migration of people from the farm to the city.
    (4) adverse economic conditions in foreign countries.
    (5) Roosevelt's "new deal" ideas.

25. Which of the following statements is an example of a "new deal" program?
    (1) Changing the laws governing the states
    (2) Recruits being drafted into the armed forces
    (3) Volunteers working in soup kitchens
    (4) Politicians making speeches
    (5) Masses of people being hired by the government to build and repair bridges and highways

26. In the above passage, one of the conclusions that can be drawn is that
     (1) the government had little to do with ending the depression.
     (2) President Roosevelt helped to bring the country out of the depression.
     (3) the depression ended before President Roosevelt took office.
     (4) the depression did not cause many hardships.
     (5) Roosevelt was a very popular president.

THE POPULATION

Comparison of Population in Selected Cities in the United States – 1988

City	Population
New York	7,352,700
Los Angeles	3,352,710
Chicago	2,977,520
Houston	1,698,090
Philadelphia	1,647,000
San Diego	1,070,310

Demographic Statistics of Selected States in the United States—1989

State	Population	Approx. Pop. Density	Land Area Sq. Mi.	Per Capita Income
Virginia	6,098,000	149	39,704	$16,399
Rhode Island	998,000	823	1,055	$18,061
Massachusetts	5,913,000	713	7,824	$22,196
Georgia	6,436,000	109	58,056	$16,188
New York	17,950,000	366	47,377	$20,540

☞ Drill: The Population

DIRECTIONS: The following questions are based on the graph above. Read each question and choose the correct answer.

27. How many cities listed above have populations less than 3 million?
     (1) 3   (4) 1
     (2) 5   (5) 2
     (3) 4

28. Which state has the second smallest population of the states listed?
    (1) Georgia   (4) Virginia
    (2) New York   (5) Massachusetts
    (3) Rhode Island

29. Of the states listed, which state has the highest population density (number of people per square mile)?
    (1) Rhode Island   (4) New York
    (2) Virginia   (5) Georgia
    (3) Massachusetts

30. The state with the third highest per capita income is
    (1) Virginia.   (4) Georgia.
    (2) Rhode Island.   (5) New York.
    (3) Massachusetts.

NATION AND STATE: A BALANCE OF POWER

Powers Reserved for the Federal Government

✔ Regulate foreign commerce
✔ Regulate interstate commerce
✔ Mint money
✔ Create and establish post offices
✔ Grant copyrights and patents
✔ Declare and wage war; declare peace
✔ Admit new states
✔ Fix standards for weights and measures
✔ Raise and maintain an army and navy
✔ Govern the federal city (Washington, D.C.)
✔ Conduct relations with foreign powers
✔ Universalize bankruptcy laws

Shared Powers

✔ Taxation, borrowing and spending
✔ Control of the militia
✔ Acting directly on individuals

Powers Reserved for the States

✔ Conduct and monitor elections
✔ Set voter qualifications
✔ Provide for local governments
✔ Ratify proposed amendments to the U.S. Constitution
✔ Regulate intrastate commerce
✔ Maintain police power over public health, safety, morals
✔ Provide education for their citizens
✔ Levy direct taxes (a power the federal government also has under the 16th Amendment)
✔ Maintain integrity of state borders
✔ Regulate contracts and wills

U.S. HISTORY

ANSWER KEY

Drill: The New World

1.	(1)	3.	(5)	5.	(1)	7.	(2)
2.	(3)	4.	(2)	6.	(5)	8.	(2)

Drill: The Industrial Revolution

9.	(4)	11.	(2)	13.	(2)	15.	(3)
10.	(1)	12.	(5)	14.	(2)	16.	(5)

Drill: The Civil War

17.	(4)	18.	(1)	19.	(1)	20.	(3)

Drill: The Election of 1912

21.	(2)	22.	(3)

Drill: The Great Depression

23.	(1)	24.	(1)	25.	(5)	26.	(2)

Drill: The Population

27.	(3)	28.	(5)	29.	(1)	30.	(2)

III. ECONOMICS

THE IMPORTANCE OF ECONOMICS

A study of economics is crucial to the fiscal well-being of a nation and can be defined as the effectiveness with which people use limited resources to meet unlimited wants. Macroeconomics is a study of looking at the economy as a whole. Microeconomics is a method of looking at the economy in small units or parts. Economics, as a formalized discipline, is a little over two hundred years old. Adam Smith, the father of economics, paved the way in 1776 with the writing of his seminal book *The Wealth of Nations*.

The Wealth of Nations served as the impetus for synthesizing the various elements of the industrial society into the discipline of economics. He believed that the free market system inherently works to produce the best products in the most efficient manner possible. He felt that the competitors who were less efficient would be driven out of business. Adam Smith also espoused *laissez-faire* economics, which means that the free market system should be unrestricted by government controls.

The reality of making choices in economics is very meaningful. One makes many choices on a daily basis. Earning and spending money and deciding how to spend your time are all involved in daily decision making. Suppose, for example, you had decided to go to college and had applied and been accepted to several schools. The choice you make will depend on several factors, such as tuition, courses offered, and distance from home.

Scarcity is the reason that choices have to be made. Since there is a limited supply of goods and services, it is very important to make the right choices.

Every decision you make has an opportunity cost. An opportunity cost of a good refers to the good or service you had to forego in order to choose another. When you choose one item or service over another, it costs you the one you did not choose.

☞ Drill: The Importance of Economics

DIRECTIONS: The following questions are based on the passage above. Read each question, then choose the correct answer.

1.   Economics as a scholarly discipline can be traced back to about
     (1)   the American Revolutionary War.
     (2)   the Roaring Twenties.
     (3)   the Sixties.
     (4)   the Classical Age.
     (5)   the Civil War.

2.   The study of how people use limited natural resources to meet unlimited wants is
     (1)   political science.   (4)   microeconomics.
     (2)   economics.   (5)   sociology.
     (3)   macroeconomics.

3.   A method of looking at individual parts of the economy is
     (1)   macroeconomics.   (4)   technology.
     (2)   scarcity.   (5)   fiscal well-being.
     (3)   microeconomics.

4.   *Laissez-faire* stated that there should be
     (1)   government controls in business.
     (2)   no government controls in the free market system.
     (3)   competition in all businesses.
     (4)   pacts between labor and the government.
     (5)   state-owned factories.

5.   According to the passage above, which is an example of *laissez-faire*?
     (1)   State-run trash collection
     (2)   Government-subsidized hospital care
     (3)   The government's dismantling of Bell Telephone
     (4)   Privately run stock market
     (5)   Public transportation systems

6.   The cost of tuition will be one of the factors considered in
     (1)   choosing a college.
     (2)   deciding on a major field of study.
     (3)   buying a car.
     (4)   moving.
     (5)   making a decision.

7.   Economic decisions
     (1)   do not affect most people.

(2) are made only in the government.
(3) are easy decisions to make.
(4) must be made by everyone.
(5) are only made by college graduates.

8. Scarcity is
   (1) a limited supply of goods and services.
   (2) an economic unreality.
   (3) pluralism.
   (4) opportunity cost.
   (5) the supply of goods and services.

9. When you forego one good or service in favor of another, this is known as
   (1) relative scarcity.   (4) decision making.
   (2) economizing.   (5) favoritism.
   (3) opportunity cost.

BUSINESS

The factors of production are essential to producing and distributing goods and services. The three primary factors of production are land, labor, and capital. The two secondary factors of production are entrepreneurship and technology. Land includes the soil and all natural resources. Labor is defined as the physical and mental effort used to produce goods and services. Capital, as a factor of production, refers to the tools and equipment used in making goods and services. Entrepreneurship is defined as directing and managing a business. Technology means the application of knowledge and skills to production.

A market system is the method of producing and distributing goods and services as a result of individuals making decisions in the market place.

A command economy is defined as one wherein all decisions of an economic nature are in the hands of the government. A mixed economy is one in which some industries are government regulated and co-exist along with free markets.

The three major kinds of business organizations are sole proprietorship, partnership, and corporation. A sole proprietorship is owned by one person. Some advantages of a sole proprietorship are: all decisions are made by one person, all profits go to the owner, and the owner is the sole boss. Some disadvantages of a sole proprietorship are: the owner is liable for all debts, business expertise is limited to one person, and limited capital. A partnership is composed of two or more persons. The advantages of a partnership are: more than one person can offer ideas, more capital, and any liability is spread among partners. Some disadvantages are: if one person leaves the partnership, the company dissolves, partners are responsible for all debts of the business, and profits must be divided. In a corporation, the organization is set up as an artificial individual which pays income taxes. The advantages are: increased capital, increased managerial ability, and limited liability. The disadvantages of the corporation are: increased taxes, unwieldy size, and government restrictions.

☞ Drill: Business

DIRECTIONS: The following questions are based on the passage above. Read each question, then choose the correct answer.

10. The three primary factors of production are
    (1) land, labor, and technology.
    (2) labor, capital, and entrepreneurship.
    (3) land, labor, and capital.
    (4) technology, capital, and land.
    (5) labor, capital, and technology.

11. Entrepreneurship is defined as
    (1) directing and managing a business.
    (2) a circular flow of activity.
    (3) a production unit.
    (4) an economic model.
    (5) a supply-based system.

12. A market economy is one in which
    (1) decisions about production and distribution are made by individuals.
    (2) supply and demand are equal.
    (3) supply is larger than demand.
    (4) supply is always up.
    (5) all decisions are made by the government.

13. The three major kinds of businesses are
    (1) cooperative, corporation, and partnership.

    (2)   partnership, coalition, and sole proprietorship.
    (3)   corporation, sole proprietorship, and partnership.
    (4)   sole proprietorship, coalition, and corporation.
    (5)   coalition, corporation, and cooperative.

14.   One advantage of a corporation is
    (1)   increased capital.   (4)   government restrictions.
    (2)   unlimited liability.   (5)   increased profits.
    (3)   double taxation.

15.   One disadvantage of a sole proprietorship is
    (1)   limited liability.
    (2)   increased managerial ability.
    (3)   limited capital.
    (4)   lack of restrictions.
    (5)   decreased profits.

16.   A partnership is composed of
    (1)   one owner.   (4)   no more than two owners.
    (2)   two or more owners.   (5)   three owners only.
    (3)   not less than ten owners.

INSURANCE

The Federal Reserve System, established in 1913, regulates the banking industry. It is mandatory that all national banks be members of the Federal Reserve System.

There are a dozen Federal Reserve districts located in San Francisco, Kansas City, Dallas, Chicago, Minneapolis, St. Louis, Atlanta, Richmond, Philadelphia, New York, Cleveland, and Boston. The Federal Reserve Bank in each district is owned by the member banks in that district.

Authorized by Congress in 1933, the Federal Deposit Insurance Corporation (FDIC) insures depositors' money. All national banks must also belong to the FDIC as well as to the Federal Reserve System. At this time, deposits are guaranteed by the FDIC for up to $100,000.

Insurance is a means of sharing risk. There are many types of insurance policies, including term insurance and whole insurance. Term insurance is paid for a certain period of time and then renewed. Whole, or straight life, insurance is paid for a lifetime. The premiums for whole insurance are usually small. Limited payment life insurance means the policyholder pays the insurance for a limited number of years and then the policy is paid up for life.

Endowment policies are used basically as a savings plan as well as insurance protection. The endowment policies provide funds for college and also additional income when a policyholder retires.

☞ Drill: Insurance

DIRECTIONS: The following questions are based on the passage above. Read each question, then choose the correct answer.

17. The Federal Reserve System is made up of
    (1) twenty Federal Reserve districts.
    (2) five Federal Reserve districts.
    (3) fourteen Federal Reserve districts.
    (4) twelve Federal Reserve districts.
    (5) nine Federal Reserve districts.

18. A conclusion that can be drawn from the above passage is
    (1) that a depositor's money up to $100,000 is safe in a bank if it is a member of the FDIC.
    (2) that every bank is a member of the FDIC.
    (3) that deposits of $200,000 are guaranteed by the FDIC.
    (4) that all state banks are members of the FDIC.
    (5) that anyone can withdraw $100,000 from the FDIC.

19. The Federal Reserve Banks are
    (1) located only on the East Coast.
    (2) spread throughout the United States.
    (3) located only on the West Coast.
    (4) found in all fifty states.
    (5) found only in coastal cities.

20. Congress established the Federal Deposit Insurance Corporation in
    (1) 1935.   (4) 1933.
    (2) 1920.   (5) 1913.
    (3) 1965.

21. A straight life policy is
    (1) paid over a lifetime.
    (2) paid for a limited period of time.
    (3) a savings policy.
    (4) very expensive.
    (5) usually reserved for married couples.

22. A term insurance policy is
    (1) paid for a lifetime.
    (2) paid for a certain number of years.
    (3) a hospitalization policy.
    (4) a savings.
    (5) for college tuition.

TAXES

Some of the different kinds of taxes that are paid to the federal government are excise taxes on the sale of goods like cigarettes, liquor, and gasoline. Other types of taxes include income taxes, corporate income taxes, and payroll taxes which are social security taxes.

An excise tax is also called a regressive tax because the tax is the same for everyone, while the income tax is called a progressive tax because it is prorated according to income.

☞ Drill: Taxes

DIRECTIONS: The following questions are based on the passage above. Read each question, then choose the correct answer.

23. The tax one has to pay on gasoline is
    (1) an excise tax.   (4) a payroll tax.
    (2) an income tax.   (5) an expensive tax.
    (3) a corporate tax.

24. One conclusion that can be drawn from the above passage is that
    (1) the federal government's expenses are so large that it needs taxes from many sources.
    (2) the deferral government has a balanced budget.
    (3) everyone pays the same taxes.
    (4) taxes are not necessary.
    (5) the federal government taxes everything.

25. A progressive tax is
    (1) aimed solely at the middle class.
    (2) the same as an excise tax.
    (3) put on products.
    (4) the same for everyone.
    (5) based on earnings.

INFLATION

Inflation is a rise in the general level of prices.

Deflation is a decline in the general level of prices.

FIGURE A—INFLATION

Year	Total Bank Failures	Year	Total Bank Failures
1980	10	1985	120
1981	10	1986	138
1982	42	1987	184
1983	48	1988	200
1984	79	1989	208

FIGURE B—BANK FAILURES 1980–89

Banks have been deregulated since 1980 when the Depository Institutions Deregulation and Monetary Control Act was passed. Ceilings on interest rates were removed.

Formula for Calculating the Time it Will Take for Prices to Double

$$\frac{70}{\text{Annual rate of inflation}} = \text{Years it will take for prices to double}$$

FIGURE C

☞ **Drill: Inflation**

DIRECTIONS: The following questions are based on the information above. Read each question then choose the correct answer.

Questions 26 through 28 are based on Figure A.

26. What three years had the same inflation rate?
    (1) 1988, 1989, 1980   (4) 1986, 1981, 1980
    (2) 1981, 1985, 1987   (5) 1980, 1985, 1988
    (3) 1982, 1983, 1985

27. What year experienced the lowest inflation rate?
    (1) 1989   (4) 1986
    (2) 1981   (5) 1985
    (3) 1984

28. What year had the second highest inflation rate?
    (1) 1984   (4) 1980
    (2) 1989   (5) 1981
    (3) 1986

Questions 29 through 31 are based on Figure B.

29. Based on the above statistics, the conclusion can be drawn that
    (1) banks made riskier investments after 1980.
    (2) all banks were on sound financial footing.
    (3) there was a growth of banks.
    (4) all banks are covered by the Federal Deposit Insurance Corporation.
    (5) deregulation was a success.

30. The biggest jump in bank failures took place from
    (1) 1983–84.
    (4) 1988–89.
    (2) 1984–85.
    (5) 1986–87.
    (3) 1982–83.

31. Which year had the fourth highest number of bank failures?
    (1) 1988
    (4) 1983
    (2) 1982
    (5) 1987
    (3) 1986

Questions 32 and 33 are based on Figure C.

32. If the inflation rate is 10%, how many years will it take for prices to double?
    (1) 10 years
    (4) 7 years
    (2) 20 years
    (5) 8 years
    (3) 5 years

33. If the inflation rate is 7%, how many years will it take for prices to double?
    (1) 5 years
    (4) 15 years
    (2) 12 years
    (5) 10 years
    (3) 7 years

ECONOMICS

ANSWER KEY

Drill: The Importance of Economics

1.	(1)	4.	(2)	7.	(4)
2.	(2)	5.	(4)	8.	(1)
3.	(3)	6.	(1)	9.	(3)

Drill: Business

10.	(3)	12.	(1)	14.	(1)	16.	(2)
11.	(1)	13.	(3)	15.	(3)		

Drill: Insurance

17.	(4)	19.	(2)	21.	(1)
18.	(1)	20.	(4)	22.	(2)

Drill: Taxes

23.	(1)	24.	(1)	25.	(5)

Drill: Inflation

26.	(3)	28.	(5)	30.	(5)	32.	(4)
27.	(4)	29.	(1)	31.	(3)	33.	(5)

IV. POLITICAL SCIENCE

THE CONSTITUTION

The Constitution of the United States was written in 1787, and by June 1788 at least nine states had approved it. The great document has stood the test of time and is as contemporary now as it was when it was written, over 200 years ago. It is the chief law of the land.

The Constitution requires three main branches of government: the executive, legislative, and judicial branches. It has a checks and balances system which keeps any one branch from becoming too powerful.

The Constitution may be amended when changes or additions are needed. So far, there are twenty-six amendments to the Constitution. The first ten amendments are called the Bill of Rights and were added in 1791.

The first four amendments are listed:

Amendment I—protects the basic freedoms of religion, speech, press, the right to assemble, and the right to petition.

Amendment II—gives people the right to bear arms.

Amendment III—forbids any soldier from being lodged in a citizen's home during peace time.

Amendment IV—disallows search or seizure of a person's property without "probable cause" and a warrant.

☞ Drill: The Constitution

DIRECTIONS: The following questions are based on the passage above. Read each question, then choose the correct answer.

1. The Constitution of the United States is
    - (1) the chief law of the land.
    - (2) written in 1687.
    - (3) not very flexible.
    - (4) no longer being used.
    - (5) becoming too powerful.

2. The government outlined by the Constitution has
   (1) two branches.
   (4) no real branches.
   (2) three branches.
   (5) one branch.
   (3) four branches

3. An example of freedom of speech is
   (1) speaking before a city council meeting.
   (2) making a speech to an audience.
   (3) disagreeing with proposed legislation.
   (4) All of the above.
   (5) None of the above.

4. The four basic freedoms are contained in
   (1) the Second Amendment.
   (4) the Fourth Amendment.
   (2) the Third Amendment.
   (5) the Eighth Amendment.
   (3) the First Amendment.

5. The first ten amendments are called
   (1) the basic freedoms.
   (4) the Civil Liberties Amendments.
   (2) the basic amendments.
   (5) the Constitution.
   (3) the Bill of Rights.

THE PRESIDENCY

The President is the head of the executive branch. He has to carry out the laws of the land. The President is elected every four years and can be elected for two four-year terms.

Although he has many powers, the President must consult with Congress before declaring war on another country. The President has the power to recommend legislation to Congress. The President has certain bills passed in order to carry out the agenda he has set forth. He sometimes calls key members of the House of Representatives and Senate to the White House to try to persuade them to pass legislation that he favors.

Any person running for President has to be at least thirty-five years old and be a natural-born citizen of the United States. He or she also must have resided in the country for 14 years prior to being elected.

☞ Drill: The Presidency

DIRECTIONS: The following questions are based on the passage above. Read each question, then choose the correct answer.

6. The office of the President falls under which branch of government?
    (1) Executive Branch   (4) Political Branch
    (2) Legislative Branch   (5) Republican Branch
    (3) Judicial Branch

7. Which of the following statements is a fact?
    (1) The President is the head of the executive branch.
    (2) The President is the most powerful man in the world.
    (3) The President is elected every two years.
    (4) The President is able to be elected for four years.
    (5) The President can declare war on his own.

8. Which of the following is incorrect?
    (1) The President has an agenda.
    (2) The President can recommend legislation to Congress.
    (3) The President never tries to sway House members' votes.
    (4) The President favors certain bills.
    (5) The President often persuades Congress to vote a certain way.

9. A candidate for the presidency must be at least
    (1) 35 years old.   (4) 30 years old.
    (2) 25 years old.   (5) 21 years old.
    (3) 40 years old.

GOVERNMENT

The United States Congress is composed of two houses: the House of Representatives and the Senate. The House is composed of 435 members. The Senate is composed of 100 members. This august body is a part of the legislative branch. The members of the Senate must be at least 30 years old and a citizen of the United States at least nine years prior to being elected. The members of the House must be at least 25 years old and a citizen of the United States for at least seven years.

Bills introduced in the Senate and the House of Representatives are recommended by citizens, the President, or the members of Congress themselves. If the bill is passed by both houses of Congress, it is sent to the President for his signature. He may sign the bill or veto the bill or use the pocket veto (the bill remains on the President's desk for ten days). If he vetoes the bill, it goes back to the house from which it originated. If both Houses have a two-thirds majority voting for the bill, the President's veto is overridden.

The Senate has the following specific powers: to approve appointments made by the President; to ratify treaties; to try cases of impeachment. The House has the following specific powers: create bills to raise money for the government; elect the President from the top three candidates if neither gets a majority of the electoral college votes; bring charges of impeachment.

Congress has the power to promote the progress of science and useful arts by securing the authors and inventors exclusive right to their respective writings and discoveries for limited times. Congress has the power to regulate commerce with foreign nations and among the several states. It also has the power to borrow on the credit of the United States.

The judicial branch of the government is composed of federal courts and judges. The Supreme Court is composed of nine justices and is the supreme law of the land. There are eleven United States Courts of Appeals and almost 100 United States District Courts.

The Supreme Court has original jurisdiction in two kinds of cases: cases in which a state is one of the parties involved and cases where ambassadors or other foreign officials are involved.

A unicameral legislature's body consists of one house. (The only example is the Nebraska state legislature.) A bicameral legislature's body consists of two houses.

All states have patterned their legislatures after the United States Congress. Each state has three branches of government and has a system of checks and balances.

All states have a governor who is the head of the state executive branch.

Most states have divisions of local governments called counties. Louisiana calls its divisions parishes. Some of the county officials are: a treasurer, a county auditor, a district attorney, a sheriff, and others.

Three kinds of city governments are in existence in this country. They are the commission, council-manager, and mayor-council systems.

In a weak mayor-council system, the council makes most of the major decisions. In a strong mayor-council system, the mayor has many important powers, including the power to veto acts passed by the council. Most large cities have the strong mayor-council system whose mayor works full time.

☞ Drill: Government

DIRECTIONS: The following questions are based on the passage above. Read each question, then choose the correct answer.

10. The legislative branch is composed of
     (1)   the House of Representatives and the Senate.
     (2)   the President.
     (3)   the judges.
     (4)   the President and judges.
     (5)   Congress and the President.

11. The Senate is composed of
     (1)   100 members.   (4)   101 members.
     (2)   435 members.   (5)   50 members.
     (3)   200 members.

12. A candidate for the Senate must be at least
     (1)   30 years old.   (4)   18 years old.
     (2)   25 years old.   (5)   21 years old.
     (3)   40 years old.

13. A candidate for the House of Representatives must be a citizen of the United States for at least
     (1)   five years prior to election.
     (2)   seven years prior to election.
     (3)   nine years prior to election.
     (4)   five months prior to election.
     (5)   nine weeks prior to election.

14. A bill can be recommended for consideration by
     (1)   the President.   (4)   All of the above.
     (2)   a citizen.   (5)   None of the above.
     (3)   a congressman.

15. If the President vetoes a bill, it will still become law if
    (1) two-thirds of the members of the Senate and the House vote to override this veto.
    (2) three-fourths of the members of the Senate and the House vote to override his veto.
    (3) one house votes to override his veto.
    (4) neither house votes to override his veto.
    (5) both houses unanimously vote to override his veto.

16. The word veto means to
    (1) accept.
    (2) reject.
    (3) compromise.
    (4) override.
    (5) change.

17. An example of an event that would fall under the powers of the Senate is
    (1) introducing a bill to raise money.
    (2) bringing charges of impeachment.
    (3) electing a President if neither of the candidates receives a majority of electoral votes.
    (4) approving an appointee to a cabinet position.
    (5) appointing a new President in the event of the death of the President.

18. An example of an event that would fall under the powers of the House of Representatives is
    (1) ratifying treaties.
    (2) confirming an appointment to the Supreme Court.
    (3) bringing charges of impeachment.
    (4) electing the Vice President if there is a tie in the voting in the electoral college for the top candidate.
    (5) declaring official holidays.

19. Which of the following is an example of the power of Congress to promote science and art by giving authors and inventors the exclusive use of their product for a specified period of time?
    (1) A speech made to a public audience
    (2) An essay written for a class project
    (3) The invention of a new way to do something
    (4) The singing of a solo on a musical program
    (5) Controlling a Broadway musical

20. Which of the following is an example of the power of Congress to regulate commerce with foreign nations?
    (1) Senate proposal to limit the number of foreign-made goods coming into the U.S.
    (2) The limitation of the number of farms in existence
    (3) The growth of the gross national product
    (4) Subsidies for farmers
    (5) Declare war on another country

21. The Supreme Court is comprised of
    (1) eight justices.   (4) five justices.
    (2) nine justices.   (5) one justice.
    (3) seven justices.

22. The judicial branch is made up of
    (1) federal courts and judges.
    (2) the lower courts only.
    (3) the House of Representatives and the Senate.
    (4) the President.
    (5) the Supreme Court only.

23. In which one of the following cases would original jurisdiction be in the Supreme Court?
    (1) An ambassador from another country has violated a civil law
    (2) A citizen has a dispute with a neighbor
    (3) A newspaper slanders one of the politicians in the community
    (4) A mayor is involved
    (5) None of the above.

24. All of the following states have a bicameral legislature except
    (1) Texas.   (4) Nebraska.
    (2) Louisiana.   (5) New York.
    (3) Massachusetts.

25. Each state has
    (1) three branches of government.
    (2) one branch of government.
    (3) two branches of government.
    (4) different numbers of branches of government.
    (5) three executive branches of government.

26. In most states, divisions of local governments are called
    (1) counties.
    (2) states.
    (3) boards.
    (4) auditors.
    (5) sheriffs.

27. In Louisiana, the local division is called a
    (1) county.
    (2) parish.
    (3) board.
    (4) township.
    (5) territory.

28. A strong mayor-council system gives many powers to the
    (1) council.
    (2) cities.
    (3) state.
    (4) country.
    (5) mayor.

POLITICAL SCIENCE

ANSWER KEY

Drill: The Constitution

1.	(1)	3.	(4)	5.	(3)
2.	(2)	4.	(3)		

Drill: The Presidency

6.	(1)	7.	(1)	8.	(3)	9.	(1)

Drill: Government

10.	(1)	15.	(1)	20.	(1)	25.	(1)
11.	(1)	16.	(2)	21.	(2)	26.	(1)
12.	(1)	17.	(4)	22.	(1)	27.	(2)
13.	(2)	18.	(3)	23.	(1)	28.	(5)
14.	(4)	19.	(3)	24.	(4)		

V. GEOGRAPHY

UNITED STATES

STATE	Student Dropout Rate
Connecticut	17.8%
Iowa	13.1%
Massachusetts	30.1%
Michigan	27.1%
Missouri	24.5%
New York	33.7%
Tennessee	31.4%
Texas	35.1%
Wisconsin	16.7%

FIGURE A—Student Dropout Rate—1988 (Selected States)

San Diego, California	1,070,310
Omaha, Nebraska	353,170
Baltimore, Maryland	751,400
Houston, Texas	1,698,090
Boston, Massachusetts	577,830
New York City, New York	7,352,700

FIGURE B—U.S. City Populations—1988 (Selected Cities)

Year	Population	Year	Population
1860	31,443,321	1930	123,202,624
1870	38,558,371	1940	132,164,569
1880	50,189,209	1950	151,325,798
1890	62,979,766	1960	179,323,175
1900	76,212,168	1970	203,302,031
1910	92,228,496	1980	226,547,082
1920	106,021,537		

FIGURE C—Population of the United States

The United States is a relatively young country made up of immigrants from all over the world. It's composed of 50 states. Each state has its own capital. The nation's capital is the District of Columbia (Washington D.C.). This country serves as a leader of the free world and has many allies around the world.

The United States is located in the Western Hemisphere on the continent of North America. The United States touches both the Pacific Ocean and the Atlantic Ocean. It shares its borders with two countries, with Mexico to the south and Canada to the north. Its land area totals 3,679,192 square miles. As of the 2000 decennial census, its population stood at 281.42 million. The geography of the United States is quite diverse. The middle of the continental Unites States is mostly a vast central plain. The Rocky Mountains can be found in the western states, while the Appalachian Mountains can be found throughout the eastern states, extending northward through Maine (and into the Canadian province of Newfoundland) and as far south as central Alabama.

The Middle Atlantic states, which include New York, West Virginia, Delaware, Maryland, New Jersey, and Pennsylvania, are a hub of activity. This area is highly industrialized and includes a skilled work force. The financial center of the nation is found in and immediately around New York City, and cultural activities of all kinds are found in this area.

Known as the Plains states are North Dakota, South Dakota, Nebraska, Kansas, Minnesota, Iowa, Missouri, Wisconsin, Illinois, Michigan, Indiana, and Ohio. This area is also referred to as the Midwest Region of the United States. It is known as a great agricultural region. Some of the crops grown are wheat, corn, and oats.

The Plains states are highly industrialized. Easy access to major waterways and the close proximity to coal and iron deposits have made it attractive to industry. Skilled laborers are available and are necessary to work in manufacturing plants.

The South includes the following states: Texas, Oklahoma, Louisiana, Arkansas, Mississippi, Alabama, Florida, Georgia, South Carolina, North Carolina, Tennessee, Kentucky, and Virginia. This area is known for its relatively mild weather and good, rich soil. Agriculture and oil are two of the most important industries in the South. Some of the crops grown are cotton, corn, tobacco, peanuts, and rice. Cattle raising is also very important in some of these states. Five of these states border on the Gulf of Mexico.

The Pacific states include Washington, Oregon, and California. California has the largest population of any state in the United States. It is known for its agriculture and leads all other states in this regard. Oregon and Washington also are known for farming. All three states also have very developed industries.

Some of the major cities located in the Pacific states are Seattle, Spokane, Portland, Olympia, San Francisco, Los Angeles, Salem, and San Diego. There are many interesting places to visit in this area and thus tourism is a major industry.

The Mountain states are Montana, Idaho, Wyoming, Nevada, Utah, Colorado, Arizona, and New Mexico. These states are sparsely populated, even though the combined square mileage is over 800,000. The Rocky Mountains stretch through this area and most people feel they are a beautiful sight to behold.

The New England states include Maine, Massachusetts, New Hampshire, Vermont, Rhode Island, and Connecticut. Territorially, this is a very small region. The total size is about 67,000 square miles. The main industries in this area are fishing, shipping, manufacturing, and dairy farming.

Alaska and Hawaii, the 49th and 50th states, joined the United States in 1959. Neither of these states is part of the continental United States; that is, they are not connected to any other state. Alaska is the largest state. It is 586,412 square miles, or about two and a half times the size of Texas (the second largest state). Alaska is located in the far northwest of North America and is separated from the 48 continental states by Canada. Alaska's main industries are oil, tourism, fishing, timber, and mining. Alaska experiences very cold temperatures throughout most of the year. Glaciers cover five percent of the state. Hawaii is composed of 137 islands in the South Pacific Ocean. Its main industries are tourism, sugar, pineapples, and defense. Hawaii experiences a warm climate throughout the year.

☞ Drill: United States

DIRECTIONS: The following questions are based on the information above. Read each question, then choose the correct answer.

Questions 1 and 2 are based on Figure A.

1. Of the states listed in the first chart, which state has the lowest dropout rate?
   (1) Wisconsin
   (2) New York
   (3) Connecticut
   (4) Michigan
   (5) Iowa

2.   Of the states listed, which two states have the highest dropout rates?
     (1)   Tennessee and Massachusetts
     (2)   New York and Massachusetts
     (3)   Michigan and Texas
     (4)   New York and Texas
     (5)   Iowa and Missouri

Questions 3 and 4 are based on Figure B.

3.   Which city has the third largest population?
     (1)   Houston   (4)   San Diego
     (2)   Boston   (5)   Baltimore
     (3)   Omaha

4.   Arrange the following five cities in order of their population, placing the
     city with the largest population first, etc.

     Baltimore, New York, Houston, San Diego, Boston

     (1)   New York, Boston, Baltimore, San Diego, Houston
     (2)   Baltimore, New York, Houston, San Diego, Boston
     (3)   Houston, Baltimore, Boston, New York, San Diego
     (4)   San Diego, Boston, Baltimore, New York, Houston
     (5)   New York, Houston, San Diego, Baltimore, Boston

Questions 5 through 7 are based on Figure C.

5.   What was the United States population in 1910?
     (1)   151,325,798   (4)   92,228,496
     (2)   203,302,031   (5)   151,325,798
     (3)   50,189,209

6.   How much did the population increase between 1970 and 1980?
     (1)   By approximately 20,000
     (2)   By approximately 200,000
     (3)   By approximately 2,000,000
     (4)   By approximately 20,000,000
     (5)   By approximately 200,000,000

7.   The population of the United States has
     (1)   steadily declined.
     (2)   remained about the same.
     (3)   dropped markedly.
     (4)   fluctuated widely.
     (5)   steadily increased.

Questions 8 through 21 are based on the passage.

8. Which of the following statements is based on fact?
    (1) Texas is the second largest state.
    (2) Texas weather is ideal most of the time.
    (3) Texas is an extremely beautiful state.
    (4) Dallas is the nicest city in Texas.
    (5) Texas is too diverse.

9. The United States shares its land boarders with
    (1) Canada.
    (2) Mexico.
    (3) Brazil.
    (4) Both Canada and Mexico.
    (5) None of the above.

10. What main industry do Alaska and Hawaii have in common?
    (1) Tourism
    (2) Defense
    (3) Farming
    (4) Mining
    (5) None of the above.

11. The United States
    (1) is one of the oldest countries in the world.
    (2) is a young country by comparison.
    (3) is located in South America.
    (4) is the only country in North America.
    (5) is located entirely on the North American continent.

12. One conclusion that can be drawn from the passage is that
    (1) an unskilled work force is necessary for an area to become industrialized.
    (2) cultural activities are necessary for a city or state to thrive.
    (3) highly industrialized areas are found only on the East Coast.
    (4) cultural activities are only found in New York.
    (5) the financial center of the United States can be found in the region of Middle Atlantic states.

13. One reason for the growth of industry in the Plains states is
    (1) its location near waterways and coal and iron deposits.
    (2) the rolling plains.

(3)   the mild climate.

(4)   the unskilled workforce.

(5)   its proximity to the nation's financial center.

14.   The area of the South includes
 (1)   13 states.   (4)   10 states.
 (2)   5 states.   (5)   9 states.
 (3)   12 states.

15.   Most of the states in the South border on
 (1)   the Atlantic Ocean. (4)   the Indian Ocean.
 (2)   the Gulf of Mexico. (5)   Lake Michigan.
 (3)   the Pacific Ocean.

16.   Two of the main industries of the South are
 (1)   oil and agriculture. (4)   oil and cattle raising.
 (2)   oil and mining.   (5)   cotton and corn.
 (3)   agriculture and fishing.

17.   The Pacific states have one thing in common. They are
 (1)   farming centers.
 (2)   extremely cold in the winter.
 (3)   located in the Southwest.
 (4)   not highly populated.
 (5)   prone to natural disasters.

18.   One of the major industries in the Pacific states is
 (1)   auto manufacturing. (4)   travel.
 (2)   tourism.   (5)   airline.
 (3)   oil refining.

19.   The mountain range that stretches throughout the Mountain states are the
 (1)   Appalachian Mountains. (4)   None of the above.
 (2)   Rocky Mountains. (5)   All of the above.
 (3)   Himalayan Mountains.

20.   The Mountain states do not include
 (1)   Arizona.   (4)   Idaho.
 (2)   New Mexico.   (5)   Nevada.
 (3)   Louisiana.

21. Which of the two industries listed are very important in New England?
    (1) Dairy farming and shipping
    (2) Oil refining and shipping
    (3) Shipping and farming
    (4) Oil refining and farming
    (5) Fishing and oil refining

MEXICO

Mexico borders the United States on the south and has about 88,000,000 people. The land area is about 762,000 square miles. The capital is Mexico City. Some of the chief crops are coffee, cotton, corn, sugar cane, and rice.

Mexico has an abundance of natural resources, such as oil, gold, silver, and natural gas. Textiles, steel production, tourism, and petroleum are the major industries in Mexico.

☞ Drill: Mexico

DIRECTIONS: The following questions are based on the previous passage. Read each question, then choose the correct answer.

22. Mexico borders the United States on the
    (1) north.   (4) south.
    (2) east.   (5) southeast.
    (3) west.

23. The population of Mexico is about
    (1) 8 billion people.   (4) 18 million people.
    (2) 80 million people.   (5) 80 hundred thousand people.
    (3) 88 million people.

24. Mexico has an abundance of
    (1) oil and gold.   (4) diamonds and natural gas.
    (2) natural gas and nickel. (5) oil and diamonds.
    (3) nickel and diamonds.

CANADA

Canada is the United States' neighbor to the north. It includes the second largest territory in the world. The current population is about 27 million people. The capital of Canada is Ottawa.

The United States and Canada are two sprawling countries that make up North America. Each country is an industrial giant and provides a very high standard of living for its population. The population of the United States is about nine or ten times larger than that of Canada.

The United States and Canada have large supplies of natural resources. In the United States, the minerals include coal, copper, gold, nickel, silver, zinc, and others. In Canada, the minerals found are nickel, gold, lead, silver, zinc, and others.

☞ Drill: Canada

DIRECTIONS: The following questions are based on the passage above. Read each question, then choose the correct answer.

25. Canada
     (1) is the largest country in the world.
     (2) is located to the south of the United States.
     (3) includes the second largest territory in the world.
     (4) is a part of the United States.
     (5) is the capital of Ohio.

26. The population of Canada is near
     (1) 25,000,000.   (4) 127,000,000.
     (2) 7,000,000.   (5) 2,700,000.
     (3) 27,000,000.

27. Based on the above passage, the conclusion that can be drawn is that
     (1) the United States produces and consumes far more than Canada.
     (2) Canada's population is larger than that of the United States.
     (3) the standard of living in Canada is higher than that in the United States.
     (4) the climate in the United States is better than the climate in Canada.
     (5) All of the above.

28. The main idea of the third paragraph is
    (1) Canada has a large supply of natural resources.
    (2) the United States has a large supply of natural resources.
    (3) the United States and Canada have large quantities of natural resources.
    (4) the United States is the largest producer of coal.
    (5) Canada is the largest producer of lead.

MAPS

FIGURE A

FIGURE B

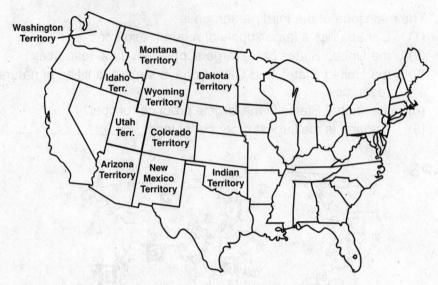

FIGURE C — Election of 1868

☞ Drill: Maps

<u>DIRECTIONS</u>: The following questions are based on the maps above. Read each question, then choose the correct answer.

Questions 29 through 31 are based on Figure A.

29. Using Figure A choose which letter represents the continent of North America.
    (1) A   (4) D
    (2) B   (5) E
    (3) C

30. The area marked as letter "F" on Figure A represents the continent of
    (1) North America.   (4) Africa.
    (2) South America.   (5) Antarctica.
    (3) Europe.

31. Which continent is not shown on Figure A?
    (1) North America.   (4) South America.
    (2) Antarctica.   (5) Asia.
    (3) Europe.

Questions 32 and 33 are based on Figure B.

32. Using Figure B, which country can be found at the intersection of the coordinates 20 degrees North, 100 degrees West?
    - (1) Paraguay
    - (2) United States
    - (3) Mexico
    - (4) Panama
    - (5) Nicaragua

33. Which of the following countries, on Figure B, is not bordered by an ocean?
    - (1) Bolivia
    - (2) Peru
    - (3) Chile
    - (4) Costa Rica
    - (5) Canada

Questions 34 and 35 are based on Figure C.

34. According to Figure C, which of the following had achieved statehood by 1868?
    - (1) Montana
    - (2) Oregon
    - (3) Washington
    - (4) Arizona
    - (5) New Mexico

35. According to Figure C, which state was bordered by three territories in 1868?
    - (1) Texas
    - (2) Oregon
    - (3) California
    - (4) New York
    - (5) Nevada

SOUTH AND CENTRAL AMERICA

Selected South American Countries

Country	Population	Square Miles
Argentina	32,291,000	1,065,189
Brazil	153,771,000	3,286,470
Chile	13,000,000	292,257
Venezuela	29,753,000	352,143
Ecuador	10,506,000	109,483

Central America is the connecting point between North and South America. The countries in Central America have an extremely long coastline. The main industry of this area is agriculture, and most people who live in this area are extremely poor. Bananas, coffee, and corn are some of their chief crops.

The seven nations that make up Central America are Belize, Guatemala, Honduras, El Salvador, Panama, Costa Rica, and Nicaragua.

☞ Drill: South and Central America

DIRECTIONS: The following questions are based on the passage above. Read each question, then choose the correct answer.

36.   Which two countries have the closest population?
    (1)   Chile and Ecuador   (4)   Brazil and Chile
    (2)   Brazil and Chile   (5)   Venezuela and Argentina
    (3)   Argentina and Ecuador

37.   Which country is the largest in both population and square miles?
    (1)   Ecuador   (4)   Argentina
    (2)   Brazil   (5)   Chile
    (3)   Venezuela

38.   One of the chief crops in Central America is
    (1)   wheat.   (4)   rice.
    (2)   bananas.   (5)   beans.
    (3)   barley.

39.   The number of countries in Central America is
    (1)   six.   (4)   five.
    (2)   two.   (5)   eight.
    (3)   seven.

CLIMATE AND WEATHER

Weather and climate conditions affect the way of life for people everywhere and in a variety of ways. A definition of weather refers to day-to-day conditions, such as how hot or cold it is or how dry or humid. Climate refers to the overall condition of the atmosphere over a period of time.

☞ Drill: Climate and Weather

DIRECTIONS: The following questions are based on the passage above. Read each question, then choose the correct answer.

40. Which of the following is an example of weather?
    (1) A forecast of rain
    (2) Tropical rain forest conditions
    (3) Tropical rain forest
    (4) Ice in the Arctic
    (5) Seasons in New England

41. Which of the following is an example of climate?
    (1) Changes in the temperature from time to time
    (2) Long, extended periods of little or no rainfall in certain areas
    (3) A forecast of sunshine
    (4) An electrical storm
    (5) A temporary drought

GEOGRAPHY

ANSWER KEY

Drill: United States

1.	(5)	7.	(5)	13.	(1)	19.	(2)
2.	(4)	8.	(1)	14.	(1)	20.	(3)
3.	(4)	9.	(4)	15.	(2)	21.	(1)
4.	(5)	10.	(1)	16.	(1)		
5.	(4)	11.	(2)	17.	(1)		
6.	(4)	12.	(5)	18.	(2)		

Drill: Mexico

22.	(4)	23.	(3)	24.	(1)

Drill: Canada

25.	(3)	26.	(3)	27.	(1)	28.	(3)

Drill: Maps

29.	(5)	31.	(2)	33.	(1)	35.	(5)
30.	(4)	32.	(3)	34.	(2)		

Drill: South and Central America

36.	(1)	37.	(2)	38.	(2)	39.	(3)

Drill: Climate and Weather

40.	(2)	41.	(2)

▼
SCIENCE REVIEW

Chapter 4

SCIENCE REVIEW

I. STRATEGIES FOR SCIENCE SECTIONS

II. BIOLOGY

III. CHEMISTRY

IV. EARTH SCIENCE

V. PHYSICS

Your first step in preparing for the GED science sections is to study our science review. Included are hints to help you quickly and accurately answer the questions which will appear in this test. Remember that the more you know about science, the more accurately you will be able to answer the questions. By studying the science review and our hints, you will greatly increase your chances of achieving a passing score on the GED Science Test.

GED science problems test your basic knowledge of life sciences and physical sciences. In order to accurately answer the science sections of the GED, the following topics should be reviewed.

LIFE SCIENCES (45% of Test)

1. Biology

PHYSICAL SCIENCES (35% of Test)

1. Physics
2. Chemistry

EARTH SCIENCE (20% of Test)

1. Earth Science
2. Space Science

The more familiar you are with the topics that will appear on this section of the test, the more likely you are to do well. Our review covers only the topics which will appear on the test. Since the GED presents concepts with which you should already be familiar, a review of the topics presented may be all that is needed in preparation for this test.

Make sure to memorize the directions for this section of the test, as speed and accuracy are just as important as knowledge of the subject matter. Even if you are sure you know all of the information provided in our review, still complete the included drills. These drills will help you become accustomed to the types of questions presented on this test, as well as sharpen your overall thinking skills.

I. STRATEGIES FOR SCIENCE SECTIONS

➤ Step 1 Carefully read the passage, graph, chart, figure, and/or other information on which the questions are based. Then read the first question.

➤ Step 2 Make sure you clearly understand what the question is asking. Misinterpreting a question will cost you time and points. Scan the passage, graph, chart, or figure again to make sure the answer is accurately based upon this given information.

If you know the answer to the question, this is your plan of attack:

> ➤ Step 3 | Quickly find your answer among the answer choices, making sure to fill in the circle correctly corresponding to your answer.

If you do not know the answer to the question, this is your plan of attack:

> ➤ Step 3 | Use the process of elimination, based on the following hints, to narrow down the answer choices. Then, make an educated guess.

> ➤ ADDITIONAL HINTS

- **If a word is unfamiliar to you, try to figure out its meaning from the context in which it is used.**

- **When a question asks you to apply an unfamiliar idea or principle, try to apply it to a familiar situation first. Next, apply the principle, in the same manner, to the given question. This often aids in the understanding of the problem.**

- **Often, when an answer choice repeats information from a passage, it is a trick. Be sure to read all of the choices before making a hasty decision.**

- **Although the answer you choose may seem logical and correct, make sure it is supported by the given information.**

II. BIOLOGY

A. THEMES AND GENERAL VOCABULARY

Biology is an independent set of explanatory concepts. Thus, we describe biology as the study of living organisms/things.

A hypothesis is very tentative and is something to be proven; it is only tentatively held and must be checked out fully and possibly proven. A hypothesis is an educated guess.

There are many fields of study in the biological sciences. Zoology, for example, is the study of animal life. Botany is the study of plant life; ecology is the study of the relationship of living things to their environment; embryology is the study of embryos; anatomy is the study of structures of the body; physiology is the study of the functions of the body; genetics is the study of heredity; cytology is the study of the cell; histology is the study of tissues; and bacteriology is the study of bacteria and/or one-celled plant life.

☞ Drill: Themes and General Vocabulary

<u>DIRECTIONS</u>: Carefully read and answer each of the following questions which are based on the information which you have just read.

1. Biology is the study of
    (1) life.   (4) All of the above.
    (2) living things.   (5) None of the above.
    (3) explanatory concepts.

2. A hypothesis explains and relates
    (1) conclusions.   (4) guesses.
    (2) facts.   (5) myths.
    (3) theories.

3. A hypothesis that has survived a number of independent tests becomes a
    (1) law.   (4) principle.
    (2) fact.   (5) strong guess.
    (3) theory.

B. THE CELL

The cell is the basic structure of all living things. This is the foundation of the cell theory. Some cells are total living organisms while other cells are the basic units of structure of other living things. All cells reproduce from identical cells by reproduction. Sex cells reproduce by meiosis while somatic cells (autosomes or body cells) reproduce by mitosis.

Cells are of two types: prokaryotic or eukaryotic. Prokaryotes are cells that do not have a nuclear membrane or a membrane surrounding its organelles. Bacteria and blue-green bacteria are examples of prokaryotes. Eukaryote refers to most cells making up all other living organisms.

A generalized cell will contain:
1. a cell membrane which is a double layer of lipids that surrounds the cell, thus acting as a "gatekeeper," controlling what moves into and out of the cell.
2. a nucleus which is separated from the cytoplasm by a thickened membrane that is more selective than the cell membrane.
3. cytoplasm, the gel-like material that surrounds and protects by cushioning the organelles. It also contains all the chemicals for that particular cell to carry out its living activities.

Depending upon the kind of cell and the function of the cell, any cell can contain any number of the following organelles:
1. Mitochondria: the powerhouse of the cell. It is the site where energy is obtained from food consumed and made available for the cell's use.
2. Chloroplast: the site of photosynthesis.
3. Plastids: store chlorophyll for use by the chloroplasts.
4. Lysosomes: carry out digestive functions and store digestive enzymes as needed by the cell.
5. Smooth endoplasmic reticulum: does not have ribosomes attached and is the transportation system of the cell.
6. Rough endoplasmic reticulum: has ribosomes attached and also carries out cell transportation but mainly of necessary protein materials needed by the cell.
7. Golgi apparatus: manufactures, synthesizes, stores, and distributes hormone and enzyme materials needed by the cell.
8. Peroxisomes: manufacture, store and secrete oxidation enzymes needed by the cell.
9. Vacuoles: spaces that act as a vacuum cleaner to rid the cell of

wastes and water. Also, when not cleaning the cell, the vacuole will act as a storehouse for chemicals and compounds needed by the cell.

10. Basal bodies: structures that clean the cell.

11. Cell wall: a tough outer membrane that supports and protects the plant cell.

12. Centrioles: rod-shaped structures responsible for animal cell reproduction.

13. Nucleolus: the center of the nucleus that resembles a golf ball and houses the genes, chromosomes, and their needed materials.

14. Chromosomes: hereditary structures that contain the genes which determine the hereditary information contained in the cell.

Generalized Plant Cell

Generalized Animal Cell

Cells maintain a balance or working equilibrium that is optimum for their needs. This balance, obtained by this internal control, is called homeostasis. This accounts for all movement into and out of the cell. Though the cell can adjust to a wide range of environmental needs and amounts, there is a limit to how much and how often it can adjust.

To understand homeostasis, one must understand how molecules move by osmosis and diffusion. When molecular movement has met needed concentrations of materials on either side of the cell membrane, the state of equilibrium exists. It is in this state that the cell operates most efficiently.

Materials move into and out of the cell either by active transport, passive transport, endocytosis, phagocytosis, or exocytosis. The exact method used depends on the type, function, and environment of the cell. A cell exists in a constantly changing environment and has constantly changing needs which must be met in order to stay alive and function. All transport occurs over a semipermeable membrane. Turgor pressure is necessary for the cell to adjust to its needs and environment. This pressure determines the amount of water maintained inside the cell to counterbalance the environment outside the cell. It is by the maintaining of this pressure that all transportation needed in the cell is determined.

Proteins are used by the cell or organism to provide energy, general maintenance, growth, and reproduction functions. All living material needs carbon, nitrogen, hydrogen, and oxygen to survive. Also, these elements are essential for the construction of organic molecules that constitute what it means to be "living." Only protein will supply the necessary nitrogen for life within a cell or organism. Protein degradation is the process by which proteins are broken down into the smallest units, called amino acids. Then, the amino acids are reconstructed into peptide chains (by the process of protein synthesis) that can be used by cell organelles or other materials as needed by the cell. This process of combining amino acids to produce peptide chains to reconstruct proteins is called protein synthesis.

Reproduction is a process that is necessary for life to continue. Reproduction is the process the organism or cell utilizes to create an offspring like itself. Reproduction can be asexual or sexual. Asexual reproduction occurs when one split produces a carbon-copy of the cell itself. Asexual processes are called fission, budding, fragmentation, regeneration, conjugation, or sporulation. The asexual methods of reproduction are used by one-cell organisms or lower life organisms.

Mitosis is the division of a body cell. The division or reproduction is for the purpose of maintaining life as a productive and efficient organism. Meiosis is the division of sex cells, namely, production of the egg or the sperm. Meiosis is a double process like mitosis.

CELL DIVISION

MITOSIS

Mitosis is a form of cell division whereby each of two daughter nuclei receives the same chromosome complement as the parent nucleus. All kinds of asexual reproduction are carried out by mitosis; it is also responsible for growth, regeneration, and cell replacement in multicellular organisms.

Interphase—Interphase is no longer called the resting phase because a great deal of activity occurs during this phase. In the cytoplasm, oxidation and synthesis reactions take place. In the nucleus, DNA replicates itself and forms messenger RNA, transfer RNA and ribosomal RNA.

Interphase

Prophase—Chromatids shorten and thicken during this stage of mitosis. The nucleoli disappear and the nuclear membrane breaks down and disappears as well. Spindle fibers begin to form. In an animal cell, there is also division of the centrosome and centrioles.

Late prophase in plant cell mitosis

Prophase in animal cell mitosis

Metaphase—During this phase, each chromosome moves to the equator, or middle of the spindle. The paired chromosomes attach to the spindle at the centromere.

Metaphase in plant cell mitosis

Metaphase in animal cell mitosis

Anaphase—Anaphase is characterized by the separation of sister chromatids into a single-stranded chromosome. The chromosomes migrate to opposite poles of the cell.

Anaphase in plant cell mitosis

Anaphase in animal cell mitosis

Telophase—During telophase, the chromosomes begin to uncoil and the nucleoli as well as the nuclear membrane reappear. In plant cells, a cell plate appears at the equator which divides the parent cell into two daughter cells. In animal cells, an invagination of the plasma membrane divides the parent cell.

Late telophase in plant cell mitosis

Late telophase in animal cell mitosis

MEIOSIS

Meiosis consists of two successive cell divisions with only one duplication of chromosomes. This results in daughter cells with a haploid number of chromosomes or one-half of the chromosome number in the original cell. This process occurs during the formation of gametes and in spore formation in plants.

Spermatogenesis—This process results in sperm cell formation with four immature sperm cells with a haploid number of chromosomes.

Oogenesis—This process results in egg cell formation with only one immature egg cell with a haploid number of chromosomes, which becomes mature and larger as yolk forms within the cell.

FIRST MEIOTIC DIVISION

Interphase I—Chromosome duplication begins to occur during this phase.

Prophase I—During this phase, the chromosomes shorten and thicken and synapsis occurs with pairing of homologous chromosomes. Crossing-over between non-sister chromatids will also occur. The centrioles will migrate to opposite poles and the nucleolus and nuclear membrane begin to dissolve.

Metaphase I—The tetrads, composed of two doubled homologous chromosomes, migrate to the equatorial plane during Metaphase I.

Anaphase I—During this stage, the paired homologous chromosomes separate and move to opposite poles of the cell. Thus, the number of chromosomes types in each resultant cell is reduced to the haploid number.

Telophase I—Cytopolasmic division occurs during telophase I. The formation of two new nuclei with half the chromosomes of the original cell occurs.

Prophase II—The centrioles that had migrated to each pole of the parental cell, now incorporated in each haploid daughter cell, divide, and a new spindle forms in each cell. The chromosomes move to the equator.

Metaphase II—The chromosomes are lined up at the equator of the new spindle, which is at right angles to the old spindle.

Anaphase II—The centromeres divide and the daughter chromatids, now chromosomes, separate and move to opposite poles.

Telophase II—Cytoplasmic division occurs. The chromosomes gradually return to the dispersed form and a nuclear membrane forms.

A living organism could be called a chemical factory. More chemical activity is carried on inside the cell or inside the living organism than any other place. Chemical bonds are broken, constructed and reconstructed in a continuous operation. Chemical reactions occur simultaneously throughout the organism so that life will be an ongoing process. Carbohydrates, starches, lipids, proteins, water, and nucleic acids are the chemicals (organic molecules) and compounds that are basic to all life.

DNA was discovered in 1869. It was not until the development of the electron microscope in the mid-1940s that scientists gained a true realization of the functioning of DNA.

DNA (deoxyribonucleic acid) is the basic chemical of life. It is a giant molecule made of four different nitrogenous bases (adenine, guanine, cytosine, thymine), phosphate groups, and 5- carbon sugars that collectively are called a nucleotide. It is a self-duplicating molecule that is in a double helix (spiral staircase appearance). It is found inside the nucleus of the cell. It contains the directions, or "blueprints," for the making of all the proteins that a cell needs. Proteins play a major role in cell metabolism and are the basic building blocks of a cell. DNA is the controller of heredity and all life activities of the cell. Its function is linked to the functioning of a companion chemical called RNA (ribonucleic acid).

The Chemical Composition of DNA

* = site of attachment to deoxyribose

Structural formulas of purines (adenine and guanine), pyrimidines (thymine and cytosine), and a nucleotide.

Ribonucleic acid differs from DNA in that uracil replaces thymine as a nitrogenous base, and the sugar bond used by RNA has one less oxygen present. Also, RNA is a straight chain. The genetic information in DNA is carried out of the nucleus by what is called messenger RNA (mRNA). Protein synthesis is carried out in the cytoplasm of the cell by transfer RNA (tRNA) using ribosomes composed of ribosomal RNA and proteins.

The DNA acts as an interpreter or decoder for the many chemical messages that are carried through the cell as a part of the life activities. The DNA cannot leave the nucleus and, therefore, must have a messenger and translator working directly with it. In addition, the tRNA picks up and delivers necessary amino acids to complete the needed activity. This process enables the cell to carry out digestion, oxidation, assimilation, synthesis, and other necessary cell activities.

The basic functions of life comprising total cell metabolism are:
1. Ingestion: taking in of food.
2. Digestion: breaking down of food by enzymes to simpler, soluble forms.
3. Secretion: formation of useful substances.
4. Absorption: diffusion of dissolved material through cell membranes.
5. Respiration: release of energy by oxidation of food.
6. Excretion: getting rid of wastes of the cells.
7. Transportation: circulation of materials throughout the organism.
8. Assimilation: formation of more protoplasm, resulting in growth and repair.
9. Regulation: maintaining stability of organism's chemical makeup under constantly changing internal and external environment (homeostasis).
10. Synthesis: building up of complex molecules from simple compounds.
11. Reproduction: production of more living individuals.
12. Irritability: response to stimuli.
13. Movement: the ability to change position. In some rare cases, as in plants, movement is coupled with irritability.
14. Bioluminescence: production of internal light within some organisms.

Photosynthesis is a process that occurs within all plant cells which supply all of the carbohydrates used by both plants and animals. Not only are essential organic compounds formed, but needed water and oxygen are given off as by-products in this autotrophic nutrition process.

Chloroplasts absorb light energy from the sun. Carbon dioxide and water are present as raw materials at the chloroplast manufacturing site.

An overall chemical description of photosynthesis is the equation

$$6\ CO_2 + 6\ H_2O \xrightarrow[\text{chlorophyll}]{\text{light}} C_6H_{12}O_6 + 6\ O_2$$

Photosynthesis is a two-step process involving light reactions and dark reactions. In the light reaction process, light must be present along with chlorophyll to start the chemical reaction. Carbon dioxide and water are broken down into free atoms. Then the dark reaction can happen. Light is not necessary for this chemical reaction to occur. Carbon, acting as a centerpiece, joins with oxygen and hydrogen to form carbohydrates. Water and unused oxygen are given off as waste products.

photolysis
(light reaction)

light   energy   chlorophyll
$\longrightarrow$ $\downarrow$
$2H_2O$ energy $2H_2 + O_2$
$\longrightarrow$

CO_2 fixation
(dark reaction)

$CO_2 + 2H_2 \longrightarrow [CH_2O]$
$+ H_2O$
carbohydrates

Photolysis and CO_2 fixation

Cellular respiration is the process by which the cell or organism gets energy for all of its activities. It is through this respiration process that chemical energy is released. This process occurs in the mitochondria through a series of steps.

The steps are summarized as follows:
Step 1 – Activation of glucose
Step 2 – Formation of sugar diphosphate
Step 3 – Formation and oxidation of PGAL, phosphoglyceraldehyde
Step 4 – Formation of pyruvic acid ($C_3H_4O_3$)
       Net gain of two ATP molecules

Cellular respiration can be either aerobic or anaerobic. In aerobic respiration, release of energy from organic compounds occurs in the presence of oxygen. The oxidation, or process of breaking down and releasing energy, is stimulated by enzymes and acids present in and around the mitochondria. In anaerobic respiration, there is no oxygen present and it must occur by a fermentation process. Lactic acid is produced as a by-product of this process. Lactic acid in muscles results in muscle fatigue and soreness.

Everyone is aware of how offspring will resemble their parents. Yet, the offspring may have traits that are not present in either parent. In 1857, Gregor Mendel developed his Laws of Genetics after seven years of studying the garden green pea. Mendel's Laws of Genetics are:

1. Law of Dominance: Every organism receives a trait from the mother and a trait from the father. One trait may have dominance over the other and mask the recessive trait to keep it from showing in the offspring. Dominant traits are normally the darker, heavier, or larger of the two traits.

2. Law of Segregation: Genes separate into single units at the time the egg and sperm unite. Each character links with a like character to form a gene. It is segregation that ensures each parent contributes equally to the offspring.

3. Law of Independent Assortment: Each unit or character for a trait is independently distributed to link with a like gene to form another pair. There is no pattern to their separation and rejoining to form the genes for the potential offspring. Genes on separate chromosomes are inherited independently.

In 1900, Walter Sutton began further studies based on Mendel's studies. Sutton compared the behavior of the chromosomes to the principles of inheritance. He confirmed all that Gregor Mendel had formulated. Sutton learned that the "factors" Mendel referred to were units located in the chromosomes. Sutton named these factors "genes." The chromosomal theory of inheritance, established by Sutton, states that genes are located on chromosomes and forms the basis for the study of genetics.

The Sutton Law was followed by the Hardy-Weinberg Law, which was based on population studies. The law states that in a population at equilibrium, both genes and genotypic frequencies remain constant from generation to generation. Each trait, whether dominant or recessive, has an equal chance to exert its influence.

Basic Language of Genetics:

1. A gene is the part of a chromosome that codes for a certain hereditary trait.
2. A chromosome is a rod-shaped body formed from the genes found in the cell nucleus.
3. A genotype is the genetic makeup of an organism or the set of genes that it possesses. This is always expressed in capital letters to express dominant traits or small letters to express recessive traits.
4. The phenotype is the outward visible appearance or expression of gene action. It is the hereditary makeup of an organism that we see or measure.
5. Homologous chromosomes are chromosomes bearing genes for the same characters.
6. A homozygous trait is an identical pair of alleles on homologous chromosomes for any given trait.
7. A heterozygous trait is a mixed pair of alleles on homologous chromosomes for any given trait.
8. Hybrid refers to an organism carrying unlike genes for certain traits. This is a preferred trait when breeding for the "best of both" traits.
9. Mutation is a sudden appearance of a new trait or variation which is inherited.
10. Lethal means deadly. This trait will cause death of the organism.

Each gene has a particular location on a chromosome (allele). Genes carried on the X chromosome are called sex-linked genes. Males carrying a recessive allele on their single X chromosome express a recessive phenotype.

Females must carry recessive alleles on both X chromosomes to express a recessive phenotype.

Mutations can affect either chromosomes or individual genes. Chromosomal aberrations like mutations occur in reproductive cells and may be passed on to the offspring. Nondisjunction of the chromosomes results in gametes that have too few or too many chromosomes. In polyploidy, organisms have an extra set of chromosomes. In the disease called trisomy 21, or Down's Syndrome, a person has an extra twenty-first chromosome. Gene mutations occur due to a change in the DNA sequence for that particular gene at that particular time. A mutated gene does not give correct directions for protein synthesis and normally harms the organism. There are a few mutations that have proven to be beneficial, however.

The Punnett Square is a method used to predict the probable outcome of a particular genetic cross. This testcross will help determine information about an organism or potential organism. Study the basis crosses worked out below.

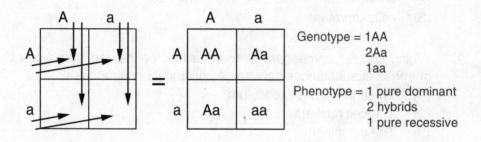

☞ Drill: The Cell

DIRECTIONS: Carefully read and answer each of the following questions which are based on the information which you have just read.

4.   How do body cells, such as muscle or bone cells, reproduce?
    (1)   Osmosis   (4)   Meiosis
    (2)   Mitosis   (5)   Spore formation
    (3)   Diffusion

5.   Which of the following is part of the cell theory?
    (1)   All cells are eukaryotes.   (4)   All cells come from other cells.
    (2)   All cells are prokaryotes.   (5)   All cells undergo meiosis.
    (3)   All cells have nuclei.

6. According to the cell theory,
   (1) all living things are composed of cells.
   (2) the number of cells in an organism is set before birth.
   (3) cell activity is controlled by the nucleus.
   (4) cells can be neither created or destroyed.
   (5) eukaryotic cells have a cell wall for protection.

7. Prokaryotic cells have no
   (1) need for energy.
   (2) metabolism.
   (3) DNA.
   (4) cell membrane.
   (5) membrane to separate nuclear components from the rest of the cell.

8. Most living cells are
   (1) prokaryotes.
   (2) eukaryotes.
   (3) cellokaryotes.
   (4) pentokaryotes.
   (5) sex cells.

9. Which cellular component is responsible for the regulation of exchanges of substances between a cell and its environment?
   (1) The endoplasmic reticulum
   (2) The cell nucleus
   (3) The cytoplasm
   (4) The cell membrane
   (5) The nuclear membrane

10. Which of the cellular components contains all of the cell except the nucleus and possesses substances for functioning organelles?
    (1) Cytoplasm
    (2) Cell membrane
    (3) Nucleus
    (4) Vacuole
    (5) Mitochondria

11. Which of the following is a cytoplasmic structure attached to the endoplasmic reticulum?
    (1) Plastid
    (2) Mitochondria
    (3) Lysosome
    (4) Ribosome
    (5) Chromosome

12. Which of the following is a cytoplasmic organelle associated with cellular digestion?
    (1) Plastid
    (2) Mitochondria
    (3) Lysosome
    (4) Golgi bodies
    (5) Stomach

13. Golgi apparatus are most common in
    (1) glandular tissue.
    (2) nervous tissue.
    (3) muscle tissue.
    (4) blood tissue.
    (5) striated tissue.

14. An organelle associated with protein synthesis is
    (1) plastids.
    (2) Golgi apparatus.
    (3) mitochondria.
    (4) ribosome.
    (5) nucleolus.

15. Diffusion of particles across a semipermeable membrane
    (1) is called osmosis.
    (2) always involves carriers.
    (3) results in dynamic equilibrium.
    (4) occurs from lesser to greater concentrations.
    (5) is not strictly controlled.

16. Maintaining a balanced internal control is called
    (1) homeostasis.
    (2) osmosis.
    (3) diffusion.
    (4) movement.
    (5) pump balance.

17. Osmosis and diffusion are processes that are used in homeostasis. They serve the purpose of
    (1) meeting a need of nutrition for the cell.
    (2) protein synthesis.
    (3) establishing a state of equilibrium.
    (4) using energy.
    (5) moving the cell through a solution.

18. The pressure that plant cells exert against cell walls is called
    (1) osmotic pressure.
    (2) isotonic pressure.
    (3) turgor pressure.
    (4) wall pressure.
    (5) exocytosis.

19. Even though glucose concentration is higher in our liver cells than in our bloodstream, glucose will still move into our liver by
    (1) facilitated diffusion.
    (4) endocytosis.
    (2) active transport.
    (5) osmosis.
    (3) osmotic pressure.

20. Which type of transport requires energy from the breakdown of ATP?
    (1) Active transport
    (4) Osmosis
    (2) Bulk flow
    (5) Exocytosis
    (3) Facilitated diffusion

21. An organic molecule is any molecule
    (1) containing carbon.
    (4) containing zinc.
    (2) containing phosphorus.
    (5) that is naturally grown.
    (3) found in dead organisms.

22. One kind of organic molecule is a
    (1) protein.
    (4) All of the above.
    (2) carbohydrate.
    (5) None of the above is organic.
    (3) lipid.

23. The type of organic molecule that is the basic structure of protein is
    (1) glucose.
    (4) glycerol.
    (2) amino acid.
    (5) carbohydrate.
    (3) starch.

24. Asexual reproduction produces offspring
    (1) with the same features.
    (2) with most of the same features.
    (3) with one of the parent features.
    (4) with adapted features.
    (5) that vary in genotype and size.

25. Sexual reproduction involves
    (1) mitosis.
    (4) All of the above.
    (2) fission.
    (5) None of the above.
    (3) chromosomes from each parent.

26. Formation of chains of yeast cells is an example of
    (1) conjugation.
    (4) budding.
    (2) fragmentation.
    (5) polymerization.
    (3) fission.

27. Mitosis results in
    (1) offspring cells exactly like the parent cell.
    (2) offspring cells different from the parent cell.
    (3) new combinations of father cells.
    (4) new combinations of mother cells.
    (5) a smaller number of cells.

28. Meiosis produces
    (1) zygotes.   (4) sex cells.
    (2) gametes.   (5) 2 and 4
    (3) body cells.

29. Meiosis produces
    (1) two genes for each trait joined together.
    (2) two genes for each trait separated.
    (3) only female traits.
    (4) only male traits.
    (5) a zygote with two genes for each trait.

30. The breaking of chemical bonds
    (1) ends life.
    (2) is an ongoing process.
    (3) does not occur simultaneously.
    (4) has no effect on life.
    (5) may be painful to an organism.

31. The greatest amount of chemical activity is found
    (1) inside the cell.   (4) at birth.
    (2) outside the cell.   (5) during cell fusion.
    (3) at death.

32. A DNA nucleotide is named on the basis of its
    (1) base.   (4) shape.
    (2) phosphate.   (5) rate of mutation.
    (3) sugar.

33. DNA is found in the
    (1) cytoplasm.   (4) ribosome.
    (2) nucleus.   (5) 2 and 3
    (3) mitochondria.

34. The sequence of the DNA sets up a(n)
    (1) electrochemical reaction.
    (2) blueprint for supplying cells with protein.
    (3) way to convert DNA to carbohydrates.
    (4) mutation.
    (5) method for analyzing the number of hydroxyl groups on the 2' carbon.

35. RNA contains
    (1) uracil.
    (2) deoxyribose phosphate.
    (3) thymine.
    (4) proteins.
    (5) a dideoxyribose sugar.

36. A particular tRNA molecule attaches to a particular
    (1) amino acid.   (4) nucleotide.
    (2) gene.   (5) rRNA.
    (3) protein.

37. Genetic information that needs to move out of the nucleus can not leave by way of the DNA. Therefore, it is carried out by the
    (1) tRNA.   (4) mRNA.
    (2) mDNA.   (5) mPNA.
    (3) tDNA.

38. The RNA molecule that transcribes (receives information) from DNA and carries the information to code for a particular protein chain is called
    (1) hRNA.   (4) sRNA.
    (2) mRNA.   (5) DNA.
    (3) tRNA.

39. The interpretations of DNA enable the cell to
    (1) carry out living processes.   (4) direct its own death.
    (2) grow to an infinite size.   (5) develop a brain.
    (3) leave the nucleus.

40. During cellular respiration, energy is transferred from
    (1) ATP to glucose.   (4) glucose to CO_2.
    (2) enzymes to CO_2.   (5) CO_2 to O_2.
    (3) glucose to ATP.

41. The working and functioning of a cell is called
    (1) cell metabolism.　　　　　(4) cell oxidation.
    (2) cell catabolism.　　　　　(5) cell anabolism.
    (3) cell reduction.

42. Movement within a cell is its ability to
    (1) stir its cytoplasm.
    (2) move from place to place.
    (3) respond to irritability.
    (4) respond to sound.
    (5) oxygenate its blood.

43. Photosynthesis supplies the major portion of
    (1) proteins.　　　　　　　　(4) amino acids.
    (2) lipids.　　　　　　　　　(5) light.
    (3) carbohydrates.

44. During photosynthesis, light energy is trapped by
    (1) sugar.　　　　　　　　　(4) carbon dioxide.
    (2) water.　　　　　　　　　(5) leaf stomata.
    (3) chlorophyll.

45. The structural unit of photosynthesis is the
    (1) chloroplast.　　　　　　(4) matrix.
    (2) stroma.　　　　　　　　(5) mitochondriam.
    (3) cristae.

46. When water is split to provide raw ingredients for the chemical process of photosynthesis,
    (1) oxygen is freed.　　　　(4) carbon is freed.
    (2) hydrogen is freed.　　　(5) carbon dioxide is freed.
    (3) nitrogen is freed.

47. Cells release energy by a process called
    (1) breathing.　　　　　　　(4) photosynthesis.
    (2) metabolism.　　　　　　(5) exocytosis.
    (3) respiration.

48. Cell respiration is responsible for supplying the cell with needed
    (1) energy.　　　　　　　　(4) protein.
    (2) nutrition.　　　　　　　(5) reproductive structures.
    (3) water.

49. Anaerobic respiration in humans is commonly carried out in the _____ tissue.
    (1) heart   (4) muscle
    (2) liver   (5) kidney
    (3) brain

50. The passing of traits from parents to offspring is called
    (1) genetic.   (4) maturation.
    (2) heredity.   (5) DNA transcription.
    (3) development.

51. The principle of independent assortment requires the observation of
    (1) one contrasting trait.
    (2) at least two contrasting traits.
    (3) one contrasting trait in two different plants.
    (4) the same trait tested twice in one plant.
    (5) one trait tested for four generations.

52. The process that enables the principle of segregation to occur is known as
    (1) meiosis.   (4) growth.
    (2) mitosis.   (5) fusion.
    (3) development.

53. Which pair of terms are most identical in meaning?
    (1) Chromosomes and genes
    (2) DNA and mitosis
    (3) Protein and ribosomal RNA
    (4) Mendel's "factors" and chromosomes
    (5) Genes and Mendel's "factors"

54. What happens to traits as a population grows?
    (1) Most recessive traits quickly become extinct.
    (2) Dominant traits combine to form a trait exhibiting hyperdominance.
    (3) Fluctuations in genotypic frequencies do not occur.
    (4) Dominant traits will permanently mask recessive traits in all future generations.
    (5) The Hardy-Weinberg Law no longer is applicable.

55. A change in the genetic coding is called
    (1) an anticodon.   (2) a procodon.
    (3) lethal.   (4) a mutation.
    (5) an evolving gene.

56. The phenotype of an organism
    (1) represents its genetic composition.
    (2) is all the traits that are actually expressed.
    (3) occurs only in dominant pure organisms.
    (4) cannot be observed.
    (5) is equivalent to the genotype.

57. A hybrid organism would have a genotype of
    (1) Aa.   (4) AaA.
    (2) AA.   (5) AAbb.
    (3) aa.

58. Each gene has a particular location on a chromosome. This seat, or
    location, is called a(n)
    (1) autosome.   (4) chromosome.
    (2) gene locus.   (5) allele.
    (3) gene.

59. A trait that is carried on the X chromosome and has no allele on the Y
    chromosome is considered
    (1) normal autosomal.   (4) sex-influenced.
    (2) mutation.   (5) female.
    (3) sex-linked.

60. The failure of a chromosome pair to separate during meiosis or mitosis
    is called
    (1) sex-linked.   (4) polysomy.
    (2) mutation.   (5) Down's Syndrome.
    (3) nondisjunction.

61. Trisomy 21, a genetic defect whereby an organism has an extra twenty-
    first chromosome, is a
    (1) defect caused by a mutation of one base pair.
    (2) correctable defect.
    (3) case where the extra chromosome takes the place of chromo-
        some 22.
    (4) sex-linked trait seen only in males.
    (5) nondisjunctive genetic trait.

62. A testcross results in all the offspring being one color. We can predict that parent was
    (1) inbred.   (4) homozygous.
    (2) hybrid.   (5) heterozygous.
    (3) impure.

63. Lobed ears are dominant over attached ears as a human trait. What would the predicted results be if two hybrid lobed ear parents mated?
    (1) 4 lobed   (4) 1 lobed, 1 attached, 2 split
    (2) 3 lobed, 1 attached   (5) 4 attached
    (3) 2 lobed, 2 attached

C. BREAKING THE CODE OF LIFE

More is being learned about the code of life that is locked into the DNA of every cell. Every living organism has its own unique pattern of DNA that accounts for the individualism in each organism. Prior to mitosis or meiois occurring within the cell, that is the reason for organisms to grow, develop, and reproduce, so replication of the DNA must occur. In this process, DNA unspirals, unzips, and separates, and new strands of DNA are constructed from nucleotides present in the nucleus. Then the process of cell division may occur. This occurrence is what holds the code of life. Never is the code altered in any replication that totally alters the organism. Although this may be the key to answering questions about cancer and other life-threatening diseases that affect certain organisms, much research still needs to be done.

☞ Drill: Breaking the Code of Life

DIRECTIONS: Carefully read and answer each of the following questions which are based on the information which you have just read.

64. A nucleotide consists of
    (1) a sugar, a protein, and uracil.
    (2) a sugar, a phosphate group, and a nitrogenous base.
    (3) a starch, a nitrogenous base, and a sugar.
    (4) a protein, a starch, and a sugar.
    (5) a nucleus and a sugar.

65. The process by which DNA copies itself is called
    (1) transcription.   (2) replication.
    (3) nucleotide.   (4) codon.
    (5) translation.

66. It has been determined that chromosomes are made of genes, and genes are composed of

    (1) DNA. (4) DNA and lipoproteins.
    (2) DNA and carbohydrates. (5) amino acids.
    (3) DNA and starches.

D. EVOLUTION OF ORGANISMS

Several theories have been formulated on how life evolves. One such theory was proposed by Jean Lamarck in 1809 when he proposed that an organism evolves in response to its environment by acquiring a trait which would adapt them to live in its changing environment. For instance, if a giraffe's neck was too short, by the constant stretching during the parent's life, offspring would be born with longer necks.

In 1859, Darwin formulated his theory in his book called *On the Origin of Species*. The book supported the theory of evolution but gave a completely different twist to the evolution idea. After studying many plants and animals, Darwin concluded that no two organisms are exactly alike, but instead differ in size, shape, color, etc., and that these traits are inherited from the parents to the offspring and not acquired. Individuals who inherit adaptive traits have a greater chance for survival. Thus, Darwin called his theory natural selection.

Evidence that supports evolutionary theories includes adaptations to the environment, homologous organs, vestigial organs, similarity of embryonic development, similarity of nucleic acids, and similar protein structure. With the groundwork laid by Lamarck and Darwin, modern evolutionists include speciation, adaptive radiation, convergent evolution, divergent evolution, and population genetics as phenomena that support evolutionary theory.

Over time, there have been marked changes in atmospheric content, climate, and environment. If a species did not have the necessary adaptive traits to change with the external changes, the species became extinct.

Fossils are evidence of living things that existed long ago. The most common fossils are found in sedimentary rock that can be dated by using radioactive isotopes to measure the amount of carbon in the remains. This amount determines a close approximation to the exact age of the fossil remains.

It is proposed by evolutionary theory that each era is briefly marked by rapid adaptive radiation normally followed by mass extinction that ended each era. Stanley Miller provided evidence that life-supporting molecules arose under abiotic conditions. He produced the exact atmosphere that was thought to have first existed and showed how heterotrophs used the available organic substances for food.

Geological evolution is as follows:

Precambrian Era	unicellular organisms originated
Paleozoic Era	multicellular animals and fern-like plants originated
Mesozoic Era	birds, mammals, reptiles, and flowering plants originated
Cenozoic Era	radiation of birds, mammals, reptiles, and flowering plants occurred

☞ Drill: Evolution of Organisms

<u>DIRECTIONS</u>: Carefully read and answer each of the following questions which are based on the information which you have just read.

67. According to Lamarck,
    (1) evolution was slow.
    (2) organisms passed acquired traits to offspring.
    (3) evolution was a mutation.
    (4) each organism adapted quickly to survive.
    (5) giraffes with short necks can stretch and never produce long-necked offspring.

68. After long study, Darwin proposed that
    (1) acquired traits are passed.
    (2) all organisms are alike.
    (3) no two organisms are exactly alike.
    (4) all organisms will reproduce.
    (5) an organism with a long lifetime will evolve mostly during its youth.

69. Natural selection is a process by which
    (1) organisms compete for food.
    (2) organisms with traits well-suited to the environment will survive and reproduce.
    (3) acquired traits will be passed on from parent to offspring.
    (4) the phenomenon of mutation kills all organisms it afflicts.
    (5) animals choose to eat only those foods which are non-toxic.

70. The general effect of migration upon the Hardy-Weinberg principle is
    (1) to increase the differences in populations.
    (2) to cause mutations.
    (3) to reduce differences in populations by mixing genes.
    (4) to discourage the movement of organisms into or out of a population.
    (5) to eliminate recessive alleles from a population.

71. A group of the same species living in the same place at the same time that is genetically studied is an example of
    (1) community study.   (4) a genealogical study.
    (2) ecosystem genetics.   (5) niche work.
    (3) population genetics.

72. The type of evolution that explains the polar bear and the brown bear is called
    (1) divergent evolution.   (4) disruptive evolution.
    (2) convergent evolution.   (5) convolution.
    (3) directional evolution.

73. Extinction refers to an organism's
    (1) parents dying before it is born.
    (2) species dying out.
    (3) death.
    (4) parents deciding again to have offspring.
    (5) escape from an environment by migrating.

74. Fossils are
    (1) remains found in sedimentary rock.
    (2) dried organisms.
    (3) old animals still around.
    (4) something that is old.
    (5) perfectly preserved animals that died during a narrow time period of the earth's history.

75. What simple components were combined in Miller's experiment to find biologically important molecules?
    (1) DNA, RNA, and protein
    (2) Ammonia, methane, water, and hydrogen
    (3) Purines and pyrimidines
    (4) Oxygen, hydrogen, and chlorophyll extract
    (5) Urea and lactic acid

76. An era is
    (1) a period of evolutionary time.
    (2) an evolution theory.
    (3) a short period of time filled with rapid changes.
    (4) a period of time something lived.
    (5) usually about 20 years in length.

77. Man probably first evolved during the
    (1) Mesozoic Era.   (4) Cenozoic Era.
    (2) Precambrian Era.   (5) era following the Cenozoic Era.
    (3) Paleozoic Era.

78. Geological evolution began with the
    (1) Precambrian Era.
    (2) unicellular organisms living on land.
    (3) multicellular organisms living in water.
    (4) Paleozoic Era.
    (5) Cenozoic Era.

E. CLASSIFICATION

Classification is a method of organizing information based on similarities. Aristotle was the first scientist to attempt to classify living things by grouping them into two major groups—plants or animals. Then they were divided into three major sub-groups as to their habitat—land, water, or air. Since Aristotle's first attempt at classification, man has used various systems of classifying living things in an effort to identify them. With so many languages and word meanings, a standard language had to be developed so that the use of common names in each language could be avoided. Thus, scientists began to use the genus and species names as this would be a consistent language in any nation. This classification system is called binomial nomenclature.

The levels of classification from largest to smallest are kingdom, phylum class, order, family, genus, and species. All living organisms are classified into one of five kingdoms to start the identifying procedure. Then the organism will be studied, compared to specific requirements, and placed in an appropriate level until a species is finally established. The biological name would be the genus and species.

A classification key can be used as an aid to identify organisms. It uses an organism's general characteristics and special features to find its appropriate placement. (Study the following mini-key.)

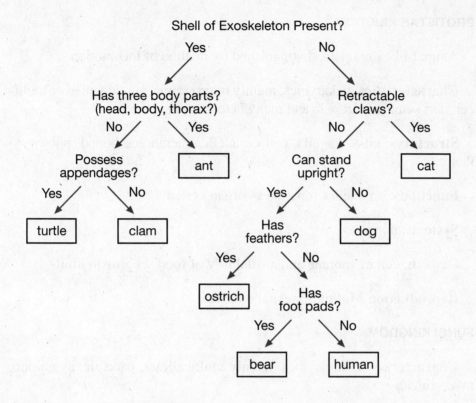

Shell of Exoskeleton Present?

Often, as seen throughout time, organisms change in order to survive. Natural selection causes all species to adapt to changing environmental conditions. This change is called adaptation. The organisms change to adapt to their new environments and through time they evolve into entirely different organisms. This is called speciation.

MONERAN KINGDOM

Bacteria and blue-green bacteria

Characteristics: prokaryotes, microscopic, live as a single cell or in colonies in water, autotrophic, few heterotrophic

Structures: flagella, capsules

Functions:: food getting, respiration, reproduction

Systems: none

Growth: cell membrane and availability of food set growth limit

Reproduction Method: binary fission

PROTISTAE KINGDOM

Animal-like organism, distinguished by method of locomotion

Characteristics: eukaryotes, mainly microscopic, single-celled or multi-cellular; some autotrophic and many heterotrophic

Structures: cilia, flagella, cell organelles membrane bound, photosynthetic

Functions: organelles function as organ systems

Systems: none

Growth: cell membrane and availability of food set growth limit

Reproduction Method: asexual or sexual

FUNGI KINGDOM

Characteristics: eukaryotes, mainly multicellular, parasitic, symbiotic, mycorrhizae

Structures: root-like, caps, filaments, reproductive

Functions: digestive-like, respiration, reproductive

Systems: beginning to develop

Growth: based on food source and availability

Reproduction Method: asexual, sexual

PLANTAE KINGDOM

Characteristics: eukaryotes, multicellular, nonmotile, autotrophic

Structures: cellulose cell walls

Functions: based on cell and tissue chemistry

Systems: all present and functioning

Growth: based on hormone action

Reproduction Method: asexual, sexual by spores, seeds, flowers, and cones

ANIMALAE KINGDOM

Characteristics: eukaryotes, multicellular, heterotrophic, most are motile at some point in lifetime

Structures: all present and unique to organism

Functions: based on nutrition, cell and tissue chemistry, and individual demands

Systems: all present and functioning

Growth: based on hormone action and nutrition

Reproduction Method: asexual, sexual

☞ Drill: Classification

<u>DIRECTIONS</u>: Carefully read and answer each of the following questions which are based on the information which you have just read.

79. Aristotle would have classified which two organisms in the same grouping?
    (1) Ferns and feathered birds
    (2) Algae and whales
    (3) Roses and mushrooms
    (4) Cats and carnations
    (5) Dogs and dandelions

80. The practice of giving organisms two names is known as
    (1) binomial nomenclature.   (4) binomial species.
    (2) common name.   (5) Arabic numerals.
    (3) family name.

81. Which of the following do modern taxonomists study to determine relationships among organisms?
    (1) Chromosome structure   (4) All of the above.
    (2) Embryology   (5) None of the above.
    (3) Biochemical similarities

82. A human being is known as *Homo sapiens*. Its species name is
    (1) man.   (4) sapiens.
    (2) human.   (5) Mammalia.
    (3) Homo.

83. To use a classification key, one must
    (1) study structures and features of organisms.
    (2) be able to see well.
    (3) know a lot about plants.
    (4) study many books.
    (5) memorize the names used in binomial nomenclature.

84. Organisms change to adapt to their new environments and through
    time they evolve into entirely different organisms. This process is called
    (1) specialization.   (4) convergent evolution.
    (2) speciation.   (5) divergent evolution.
    (3) special evolution.

85. Monerans do not have a true nucleus or membrane-bound organelles;
    therefore they are called
    (1) eukaryotes.   (4) nokaryotes.
    (2) cokaryotes.   (5) anucleotic.
    (3) prokaryotes.

86. Autotrophic bacteria
    (1) depend on other organisms for food.
    (2) depend on other organisms for nitrogen.
    (3) always need oxygen.
    (4) produce their own food.
    (5) are parasitic.

87. Protozoa are mostly heterotrophic. This means they
    (1) produce their own food.
    (2) obtain energy by feeding on other organisms.
    (3) are harmful to prokaryotes.
    (4) require sunlight constantly.
    (5) eat various sources of food (originating from plants and animals).

88. Protozoans are classified by their method of
    (1) reproduction.   (4) food-getting.
    (2) growth.   (5) protein synthesis.
    (3) locomotion.

89. An example of a fungus is
    (1) mushroom.
    (2) bread mold.
    (3) penicillum.
    (4) All of the above.
    (5) None of the above.

90. Most fungi spread through the world by
    (1) air.
    (2) water.
    (3) spores.
    (4) organisms.
    (5) moving by the use of cilia.

91. One cellular characteristic that results in plant and animal differences is
    (1) plants have cellulose-filled cell walls.
    (2) plants are autotrophic.
    (3) plants have roots.
    (4) plants are green.
    (5) plants bend towards light.

92. Plants are unique in that their growth is based on
    (1) water.
    (2) food.
    (3) hormone action.
    (4) enzyme action.
    (5) exercise.

93. To be classified an animal, an organism must
    (1) have a cell membrane.
    (2) have hormone functions.
    (3) be motile at some point in life.
    (4) reproduce at some point in life.
    (5) eat meat.

94. Most organisms classified as animals reproduce
    (1) asexually.
    (2) sexually.
    (3) by a combination of asexual and sexual.
    (4) once a year.
    (5) by the fission of sperm with an ovary.

F. HUMAN SYSTEMS BIOLOGY

DIGESTIVE SYSTEM

The digestive system is responsible for both mechanical and chemical digestion that break down food into molecules so they can move into the cell and be used for the living process. The mouth, teeth, and tongue begin the chemical digestion by mechanically breaking down the food through the chewing process and the addition of saliva. The enzyme amylase breaks down carbohydrates and starts the breakdown of starches. Food moves from the mouth to the stomach by way of the esophagus. In the stomach, other digestive enzymes and hydrochloric acid begin the breakdown of proteins. The stomach churns and mixes the food. Food, now in a liquid-like state, moves from the stomach into the small intestine, where it is absorbed through the villa into the bloodstream where it is delivered and assimilated by the cells of the body. Waste materials and unused food are carried back to the large intestine where they mix with roughage and water. The undigested materials are excreted from the body.

CIRCULATORY SYSTEM

The circulatory system is composed of the heart, arteries, veins, red blood cells, white blood cells, antibodies, thrombin, water, and plasma. A four-chambered heart, controlled by the pacemaker, rhythmically controls the pumping action by alternating contractions of the atria and ventricles. Blood circulates through the body in two loops—arteries carrying oxygenated blood away from the heart to all parts of the body, and veins returning deoxygenated blood to the heart and lungs to be reoxygenated. An auxiliary portion is the lymphatic system, which drains excess tissue fluids back into the circulatory system along with white blood cells that destroy harmful microorganisms.

SKELETAL SYSTEM

The skeleton is the basic framework of the human body and is made of connective tissue—bones and cartilage. Bone is living tissue with vitamins, collagen, and minerals to give it strength and hardness. The process by which the bones harden is called ossification. Bones are joined by cartilage at joints. Joints are classified as to the amount of movement they allow: stationary (skull), hinge (elbow), or ball and socket (hip).

MUSCULAR SYSTEM

Three human muscle types are skeletal, cardiac, and smooth. All muscle tissue exerts force when it contracts; therefore, muscles are responsible for all movement of the body, voluntary or involuntary. Energy for all movement is derived from an ample supply of mitochondria in the muscle cell. ATP, a high level energy carrier, is produced by the mitochondria for use by other cells and tissue parts during movement or exercise. Muscles are paired to accomplish full movement. Each contracting muscle will be paired with an antagonistic muscle, and tendons attach paired muscle groups to bones to complete the movement action. The skeletal muscles make up this grouping of muscles and are mainly voluntary.

Cardiac muscle is found only in the heart. The heart is the strongest muscle of the body. It is responsible for keeping the blood flowing through the circulatory system at a given pressure. The cardiac muscle is an involuntary muscle.

Smooth muscles are found in the linings of the body such as the digestive system and internal organs. They are generally involuntary muscles.

NERVOUS SYSTEM

The basic unit of the nervous system is the neuron (nerve cell). Its structure allows electrochemical signals to travel across synapses to activate muscles, glands, or organ tissue. The nervous system is divided into two parts. One part, the central nervous system, includes the brain, spinal cord, and the peripheral nervous system, which is a vast network of nerves that totally connect all parts of the body. Receptors located in sense organs and in the skin send information along the sensory neurons to the spinal cord and then to the brain where the information is chemically interpreted, causing a motor response.

RESPIRATORY SYSTEM

Respiration involves actions started by nerves stimulating muscles and bones to mechanically enlarge the respiratory cavity of the body. The breathing rate is controlled by nerves originating in the brain based on carbon dioxide content. The human nasal passages are adapted to clean, moisten, and warm the air before it enters the lungs by way of the trachea and bronchi. The lungs are made up of many tiny air sacs called alveoli that are found at the end of the bronchiole in clusters. The exchange of gases between the lungs and circulatory system occurs in the alveoli.

REPRODUCTIVE SYSTEM

The male and female reproductive systems produce sex cells. In addition, the female system provides the internal environment for fertilization and for the development of the embryo and fetus. The male reproductive system consists of a pair of testes, ducts, glands, and the penis. The female reproductive system consists of a pair of ovaries, the Fallopian tubes, the uterus, and the vagina.

EXCRETORY SYSTEM

The excretory system is made up of the kidney, bladder, connecting tubes, and capillaries joined to the kidney. Urine is collected by structures in the kidney called nephrons. From the nephrons, the liquid wastes are collected and stored in the bladder. Urine leaves the body through the urethra.

ENDOCRINE SYSTEM

The endocrine system produces hormones which travel by way of the bloodstream to specific target cells. The manner in which the hormone acts on the target cells depends on whether it is a protein or steroid. Each will cause a feedback, which is one way to regulate hormones secreted into the body. Homeostasis depends on the actions of the nervous and endocrine systems. Organs, like the kidney, function based on endocrine stimulation.

INTEGUMENTARY SYSTEM

The integumentary covering of the body is called the skin. Skin consists of two layers, the epidermis and the dermis. Skin protects the body, rids the body of mineral salts and wastes, regulates body temperature, and picks up environmental signals. The skin is the bonding or holding agent that keeps the body intact and functioning. Also part of the integumentary system are the hair and nails.

IMMUNITY AND DISEASES

IMPORTANT LYMPHATIC ORGANS —
A defense against pathogens

Adenoids and Tonsils—Organs that filter out antigens (substances, such as viruses, which stimulate antibody synthesis) that enter the body via the upper-respiratory and gastro-intenstinal tracts.

Thymus—Produces cells that eventually become what are called peripheral T cells, which possess surface receptors for antigens.

Bone Marrow—Produces blood-forming stem cells.

Spleen—Has three functions:

(1) Can mount an immune response to antigens in the blood stream.

(2)   Scavenges old red blood cells.

(3)   Functions as a reserve site for making blood forming stem cells.

DISORDERS OF THE IMMUNE SYSTEM

Lupus—People develop immune reactions to their own nucleic acids.

Allergies—People become hypersensitive to environmental substances, called allergens.

AIDS (Acquired Immune Deficiency Syndrome)—

(1)   People have reduced numbers of helper T cells.

(2)   People may not be able to form antibodies against diseases like pneumonia.

☞ Drill: Human Systems Biology

DIRECTIONS: Carefully read and answer each of the following questions which are based on the information which you have just read.

95.   Food is broken down into essential nutrients in the
    (1)   digestive system.   (4)   nervous system.
    (2)   circulatory system.   (5)   oral cavity.
    (3)   skeletal system.

96.   Although humans can not digest cellulose, the fiber helps us by
    (1)   providing antibiotic activity in the intestines.
    (2)   stimulating muscle action in the digestive system.
    (3)   providing a padding medium.
    (4)   providing energy for the digestive system.
    (5)   expanding so that the stomach feels extremely full.

97.   Mechanical digestion involves
    (1)   converting food particles into molecules.
    (2)   building usable food molecules.
    (3)   obtaining food.
    (4)   tearing and grinding food into small bits.
    (5)   using tools, such as blenders, to break down food.

98. The circulatory system is responsible for all of the following except
    (1) the distribution of oxygen.
    (2) carrying nutrients.
    (3) providing for natural defenses of the body.
    (4) removing urea from the body.
    (5) stopping the flow of blood after an injury.

99. Vessels that carry deoxygenated blood to the heart are called the
    (1) arteries.   (4) vesicles.
    (2) veins.   (5) aorta and vena cava.
    (3) capillaries.

100. Minerals normally found in bone tissue are
    (1) iron and mercury.   (4) strontium and phosphorus.
    (2) calcium and iron.   (5) calcium and strontium.
    (3) iron only.

101. During the process of ossification,
    (1) calcium is lost from bone tissue.
    (2) phosphorus is lost from bones.
    (3) bones are changed to cartilage.
    (4) cartilage is changed to bone.
    (5) bones may fracture easily.

102. The type of muscle tissue found in the walls of many internal organs is identified as
    (1) striated.   (4) skeletal.
    (2) voluntary.   (5) cardiac.
    (3) smooth.

103. The point where two bones meet is called
    (1) point of connection.   (4) growth plane.
    (2) joint.   (5) cartilage.
    (3) point of insertion.

104. The central nervous system consists of
    (1) the brain and spinal cord.
    (2) spinal nerves only.
    (3) the medulla and cerebrum.
    (4) the cerebrum and spinal column.
    (5) the brain and skin.

105. The junction where an impulse travels from one neuron to another is called the
    (1) synapse.
    (2) stimuli.
    (3) nerve message.
    (4) affector node.
    (5) nervous system.

106. The actual exchange of gases occurs at the
    (1) trachea.
    (2) nostrils.
    (3) alveoli.
    (4) bronchioles.
    (5) bronchi.

107. The breathing center of the brain is sensitive to
    (1) the concentrations of oxygen.
    (2) contractions of carbon dioxide in body cells.
    (3) the amount of oxygen in the blood.
    (4) the concentration of carbon dioxide in the blood.
    (5) pollutants in the carbon dioxide we breathe.

108. Maintenance of the body's fluid and chemical balance is dependent upon the proper functioning of the
    (1) digestive system.
    (2) excretory system.
    (3) nervous system.
    (4) circulatory system.
    (5) skeletal system.

109. Metabolic wastes include all of the following except
    (1) water.
    (2) urea.
    (3) carbon dioxide.
    (4) feces.
    (5) None of the above.

110. Chemical messengers called hormones are found in the .
    (1) endocrine system.
    (2) digestive system.
    (3) nervous system.
    (4) integumentary system
    (5) skeletal system.

111. Homeostasis depends primarily on the actions of the
    (1) nervous and endocrine systems.
    (2) nervous and muscular systems.
    (3) digestive and nervous systems.
    (4) circulatory and nervous systems.
    (5) endocrine and digestive systems.

112. Skin, hair, and nails are part of the
    (1) skeletal system.   (4) endocrine system.
    (2) circulatory system.   (5) nervous system.
    (3) integumentary system.

113. Skin protects the body and
    (1) rids the body of mineral salts and wastes.
    (2) regulates body temperature.
    (3) picks up environmental signals.
    (4) All of the above.
    (5) None of the above.

114. Infectious diseases are caused by
    (1) bacteria, fungi, and protozoans.
    (2) bacteria only.
    (3) fungi only.
    (4) protozoans only.
    (5) antibodies.

115. The only group of diseases or disorders for which there are no known cures is the group that includes
    (1) infectious diseases.   (4) STDs.
    (2) degenerative diseases.   (5) psychological disorders.
    (3) genetic disorders.

G. ECOLOGY

Ecology can be defined as the study of interactions between groups of organisms and their environment. Groups are referred to as populations. Ecology is the basis of all life and all support systems of life. It is made up of chains—the food chain, carbon/oxygen chain, energy chain, and water chain. It is through the linking of the chains that life continues. Each organism has a specific habitat in an ecosystem carrying out a specific role (niche).

Ecology and behavior are closely linked. It is because of learned and innate behaviors that that organisms are equipped to meet the ever-changing environmental demands and the interactions with other living organisms.

Life on earth exists in a thin layer known as the biosphere. The land, air, and water that make up the biosphere each have their own areas where life exists. The land, or terrestrial, biomes are determined mainly by climate. Water, or aquatic, biomes are classified as freshwater or marine, depending upon the amount of salt (salinity) in the water. Marine life occurs in various zones depending on depth, temperature, and light intensity. Freshwater abiotic factors are depth, turbidity, temperature, and light intensity. Estuaries are mixtures of salt and fresh water. They are more protected than the ocean, but more nutrient-rich than rivers and support a wide variety of species.

The size of a population at a given time is determined by its growth rate. Growth rate is determined by the factors of birth rate, immigration, death rate, and emigration. Other factors like natural disasters, availability of food, and disease also independently affect population. Environmental resistance to increased population often depends on population density. Crowding of organisms can reduce nutrients, spread disease, and interfere with reproduction. Competition for an environment's limited resources occurs between members of a population (intraspecific competition) and between different species in an area (interspecific competition). Competition also limits population size.

Humans are unique in their ability to modify the carrying capacity of their environment to be favorable for population growth. Most scientists agree that it is only a matter of time before humans will be unable to increase the earth's carrying capacity any further. At that time, the birth rate must decrease and the death rate must increase to balance population growth.

Natural resources are necessary for human survival and the making of necessary products. The natural resources are water, soil, air, wildlife, and forests. Problems that are now being faced are related to erosion, soil depletion, species extinction, deforestation, desertification, and water shortages. Efforts to reverse these problems and their environmental damages are found in the planned programs of reforestation, captive breeding, biological harvesting, or planned farming through efficient plowing and planting procedures.

Pollution is damaging both the ecosystems and living organisms. Air, water, soil, and food resources are being affected by pollution. Pollutants include automobile exhaust, fertilizers, pesticides, industrial wastes, radioactive wastes, and most of all, household wastes. The growing population and modern conveniences greatly contribute to this insurmountable problem. Government regulations, community efforts, and changes in the habits of industries and individuals are necessary to solve pollution problems.

☞ Drill: Ecology

DIRECTIONS: Carefully read and answer each of the following questions which are based on the information which you have just read.

116. The areas of earth where life exists collectively is called
    (1)   the ecosystem.   (4)   an ecosystem.
    (2)   a biome.   (5)   a niche.
    (3)   a biosphere.

117. An organism's niche is composed of
    (1)   what he eats.   (4)   All of the above.
    (2)   how he sleeps.   (5)   None of the above.
    (3)   how he reproduces.

118. Learned and innate behaviors function to
    (1)   allow flexibility to meet environmental changes.
    (2)   allow interactions with other living organisms.
    (3)   choose lifestyles.
    (4)   Both 1 and 2.
    (5)   Both 1 and 3.

119. The abiotic parts of an ecosystem include
    (1)   bacteria.   (4)   temperature.
    (2)   plants.   (5)   algae.
    (3)   animals.

120. The biotic potential of a population is
    (1)   the rate at which a population would reproduce if every individual lived.
    (2)   the rate at which a population would die.
    (3)   the rate at which a population would over-populate.
    (4)   None of the above.
    (5)   All of the above.

121. All of the following are limiting factors except
    (1)   habitat.   (4)   population density.
    (2)   food.   (5)   shelter.
    (3)   water.

122. The carrying capacity means the ability
    (1) to carry a load.   (4) to supply occupations.
    (2) to support life.   (5) to hold a very heavy weight.
    (3) to support offspring.

123. Cities near the ocean may meet their demands for water by using a procedure called
    (1) water recovery.   (4) water recycling.
    (2) desalination.   (5) beach cleaning.
    (3) irrigation.

124. A substance that is nonbiodegradable is
    (1) paper waste.   (4) food waste.
    (2) plastic.   (5) an aluminum can.
    (3) wood.

125. The ecosystem and living organisms are being damaged by
    (1) changing environmental conditions.
    (2) pollution.
    (3) pesticides.
    (4) acid rain.
    (5) All of the above.

BIOLOGY

ANSWER KEY

Drill: Themes and General Vocabulary

1. (4)	2. (2)	3. (3)

Drill: The Cell

4. (2)	19. (2)	34. (2)	49. (4)
5. (4)	20. (1)	35. (1)	50. (2)
6. (1)	21. (1)	36. (1)	51. (2)
7. (5)	22. (4)	37. (4)	52. (1)
8. (2)	23. (2)	38. (2)	53. (5)
9. (4)	24. (1)	39. (1)	54. (3)
10. (1)	25. (3)	40. (3)	55. (4)
11. (4)	26. (4)	41. (1)	56. (2)
12. (3)	27. (1)	42. (3)	57. (1)
13. (1)	28. (5)	43. (3)	58. (2)
14. (4)	29. (2)	44. (3)	59. (3)
15. (3)	30. (2)	45. (1)	60. (3)
16. (1)	31. (1)	46. (1)	61. (5)
17. (3)	32. (1)	47. (3)	62. (4)
18. (3)	33. (5)	48. (1)	63. (2)

Drill: Breaking the Code of Life

64. (2)	65. (2)	66. (1)

Drill: Evolution of Organisms

67. (2)	70. (3)	73. (2)	76. (1)
68. (3)	71. (3)	74. (1)	77. (4)
69. (2)	72. (1)	75. (2)	78. (1)

Drill: Classification

79. (3)	83. (1)	87. (2)	91. (1)
80. (1)	84. (2)	88. (3)	92. (3)
81. (4)	85. (3)	89. (4)	93. (3)
82. (4)	86. (4)	90. (3)	94. (2)

Drill: Human Systems Biology

95. (1)	101. (4)	107. (4)	113. (4)
96. (2)	102. (3)	108. (2)	114. (1)
97. (4)	103. (2)	109. (4)	115. (3)
98. (4)	104. (1)	110. (1)	
99. (2)	105. (1)	111. (1)	
100. (2)	106. (3)	112. (3)	

Drill: Ecology

116. (3)	119. (4)	122. (2)	125. (5)
117. (4)	120. (1)	123. (2)	
118. (4)	121. (4)	124. (2)	

III. CHEMISTRY

A. INTRODUCTION TO CHEMISTRY

Chemistry is one of the oldest branches of science. The study of chemistry can be traced back as far as the Babylonian Period. The field of chemistry seeks to transform one molecule into another to tailor or refine such chemicals as plastics, drugs, food technology, fuels, and dyes. Out of these raw materials, countless products required to meet our needs of daily living can be manufactured. Chemistry is defined as the study of the composition and behavior of elements in combination with each other.

Chemistry began to grow as knowledge spread about the atomic theory proposed by Thomas Dalton about 1807. He advocated that all matter is composed of small indivisible particles which he named "atoms" and described as little round balls. He believed these particles could combine with one another in many forms to produce all possible substances. It was remarkable how close his theory was to being correct considering the lack of experimental techniques available at that time. He was correct in stating that atoms join together to form complex substances. Dalton was incorrect in his assumption that all atoms are alike.

A great growth was experienced in the field of chemistry after the discovery of the group-forming pattern by D. L. Mendeleev in 1896. With the newly acquired information, a listing of all of the known chemical elements was placed on a chart in the order of their increasing atomic weights and number of energy levels. This charted information was the first periodic table.

As information in the field of chemistry grew, studies branched into the areas of organic chemistry and inorganic chemistry. Organic chemistry deals with the carbon compounds while inorganic chemistry deals with all the other elements and compounds.

The field of chemistry has vastly expanded based on the study of the atomic structure of elements and their behavior. Atomic structure is related to the properties and arrangement of elements in the periodic chart. The elements are classified into groups, periods, and families. It is from these groupings that matter is classified and its behavior is studied based on the ability of an element to combine or react with other elements. The study of the behavior of matter is based on properties of the elements and their ability to combine through the transfer and sharing of electrons to form compounds and other matter. This is commonly referred to as the process of bonding.

Every element has its own letter symbol. With these letter symbols and atomic numbers used together correctly, one can construct a formula. The formulas can be combined to show the composition of compounds, reactions between elements, chemical equilibrium, and oxidation and reaction rates. This is accomplished by the process of balancing equations.

It is necessary that everyone understands the basics of chemistry since our lives are centered around this subject. Also, how far we can progress is based on our ability to understand chemical concepts and apply them to our everyday life.

☞ Drill: Introduction to Chemistry

DIRECTIONS: Carefully read and answer each of the following questions which are based on the information which you have just read.

1. Which one of the following is NOT the job of a chemist?
   (1) Changing one material into another
   (2) Turning raw materials into products
   (3) Selling new chemicals
   (4) Refining materials
   (5) Studying the behavior of elements

2. In making bread, a mixture of flour, water, and yeast are baked in an oven. The raw materials of bread baking are
   (1) an oven.   (4) yeast and flour.
   (2) water, flour, and yeast.   (5) yeast and an oven.
   (3) water, flour, and an oven.

3. Which one of the following is a synthetic food?
   (1) An apple
   (2) Water
   (3) A cherry pie made of flour, fruit, sugar, and fat
   (4) A diet supplement made of wheat protein, BHT, artificial colors, and other ingredients
   (5) Tofu, made of soybeans, sea salt, and water

4. The atomic theory states that all matter is composed of
    (1) carbon.
    (2) atoms.
    (3) molecules.
    (4) compounds.
    (5) complex substances.

5. According to Dalton's theory, which of the following is NOT assumed?
    (1) Atoms can be broken into subatomic particles
    (2) All matter is made of atoms
    (3) Atoms are round
    (4) Atoms can join together
    (5) Atoms of the same substance are identical

6. Dalton was incorrect in some assumptions concerning the atom. This error can be based on his experimentation technique. One incorrect assumption was
    (1) all atoms are alike.
    (2) all atoms are not alike.
    (3) some atoms are more alike than others.
    (4) atoms are not found everywhere.
    (5) atoms can combine with each other.

7. In the periodic table, elements increase in
    (1) both mass and number of energy levels.
    (2) mass only.
    (3) number of energy levels.
    (4) atomic structure.
    (5) mass number at energy levels.

8. Mendeleev discovered there was a pattern when one started to arrange elements based on their
    (1) name.
    (2) atomic weights.
    (3) particulate composition.
    (4) period.
    (5) melting point.

9. An element near the bottom of the periodic table would have
    (1) electrons in low energy levels only and low atomic weight.
    (2) electrons in high energy levels and low atomic weight.
    (3) electrons in high energy levels and high atomic weight.
    (4) one energy level and high atomic weight.
    (5) no energy levels and low atomic weight.

10. Organic differs from inorganic in that the organic
    (1)   contains only one distinguishable phase.
    (2)   contains no specific elements.
    (3)   is uniform.
    (4)   . deals with carbon compounds.
    (5)   deals with naturally occurring compounds.

11. In the following formulas, the symbol "C" indicates carbon. Which formulas represent organic compounds?
    a. H_2O b. C_2H_2 c. H_2O_2 d. $C_6H_{12}O_6$
    (1)   a only   (4)   b and d
    (2)   b only   (5)   d only
    (3)   a and c

12. Which is the most likely reason why organic and inorganic chemistry have become separate studies?
    (1)   Fights among chemists
    (2)   Lack of lab space
    (3)   Chemical knowledge is too great for one person to master it all
    (4)   Salaries are better for chemists who specialize
    (5)   Schools prefer organic chemists

13. The study of matter is based on
    (1)   evaluating properties of one element.
    (2)   evaluating types and abilities of properties of one element.
    (3)   the ability to transfer through the sharing of electrons.
    (4)   the ability to transfer through the sharing of neutrons.
    (5)   elements that cannot bond.

14. The sharing of electrons or transfer of electrons is called
    (1)   bonding.   (4)   effect of gravity.
    (2)   transference.   (5)   kinetic flow.
    (3)   boiling.

15. Matter is group-based on its ability to
    (1)   react with itself in the presence of other elements.
    (2)   be studied.
    (3)   react and combine with other elements.
    (4)   change.
    (5)   bond irreversibly with other elements.

16. Bonding is the process by which atoms
    (1) behave in the presence of heat.
    (2) only transfer electrons.
    (3) only share electrons.
    (4) either share or transfer electrons.
    (5) share and transfer properties.

17. When one balances a chemical equation, they are showing
    (1) combination of compounds.
    (2) equilibrium.
    (3) oxidation and reaction rates.
    (4) reactions between different elements.
    (5) All of the above.

18. Equilibrium can be expressed as the point at which
    (1) all the chemicals present stop reacting.
    (2) the chemicals start to react.
    (3) the chemical reactants are used up.
    (4) the products react together at the same rate as the reactants.
    (5) the reactants are chemically reacting at maximum velocity.

19. For a chemical equilibrium involving gaseous reactants and products,
    an increase in pressure
    (1) always displaces the equilibrium in the direction in which the
        number of molecules decrease.
    (2) displaces the equilibrium to form more of the reactants.
    (3) displaces the equilibrium to form more of the products.
    (4) has no effect on the equilibrium.
    (5) leads to extremely rapid formation of reactant molecules.

20. Formulas can be combined to show the composition of
    (1) compounds.   (4) reactions.
    (2) atomic numbers.   (5) oxidation and reduction rates.
    (3) symbols.

21. A chemical formula is constructed by correctly combining
    (1) compounds.   (4) equilibrium.
    (2) elements.   (5) symbols and atomic numbers.
    (3) symbols.

22. Every element has its own
    (1) symbol.
    (2) color.
    (3) emblem.
    (4) insignia.
    (5) six-digit serial number.

23. Chemistry is a study that
    (1) only deals with mixing chemicals.
    (2) only shows reactions.
    (3) only relates to electrons and protons.
    (4) deals with everyday life.
    (5) does not affect biology.

B. STRUCTURE OF MATTER

Matter is anything that occupies space and has mass. Matter resists changes in motion. It takes force to accelerate matter. There are four states of matter—solid, liquid, gas, and a fourth state called the plasma state. This state only exists at extremely high temperatures, such as those found on the sun. Plasma consists of high-energy, electrically charged particles. Plasma is created when a fluorescent lamp is turned on. Most of the matter in the universe is in the plasma state.

The structure of matter depends on the number and types of atoms that combine or react to form the matter. Matter is measured by the force with which gravity pulls on the mass toward the center of the earth. Matter can also be measured by its capacity for doing work, or the energy that it contains. This energy can be either activation, potential, or kinetic energy. Activation energy is that energy necessary to start a reaction. Potential energy is stored energy, while kinetic energy is the energy that matter possesses due to motion.

It can be shown experimentally that potential energy can be transformed into kinetic energy without any energy loss. This is an illustration of the Law of Conservation of Matter or Energy, which states that under ordinary conditions, matter or energy can neither be created nor destroyed but can be converted from one form to another.

One method of classifying matter is to find out if it is a substance or a mixture of substances. If a substance is composed of only one kind of atom, it is an element. If the substance is composed of two or more kinds of atoms, the matter can be a mixture or a compound, depending on how the atoms are joined and react to each other under normal conditions.

Mixtures do not follow the law of definite proportions, which means that the two substances can be mixed in almost any proportion. Thus, the properties of a mixture vary with composition. If the substances in a mixture are spread out evenly, it is considered to be a homogeneous mixture. If the substances in a mixture are not spread out evenly, it is considered to be a heterogeneous mixture. Vinegar is a homogeneous mixture as the substances are spread out evenly throughout. A homogeneous mixture can be called a solution. Other solutions include seawater, soft drinks, tea, or milk.

A suspension is a heterogeneous mixture in which the particles are large enough to be seen by a microscope or the eye. These particles are affected by gravity and may settle out of the mixture. The particles can be temporarily suspended again by shaking. The mixing of water and pepper is an example of a suspension. Stirring up the bottom of a river will produce a suspension. With time, the action of gravity on the sand and soil will cause the particles to settle back to the bottom of the river.

If particles of a mixture are larger than those found in a solution, yet smaller than particles found in a suspension, the mixture is referred to as a colloid. Colloidal particles appear to be evenly distributed and they will not settle out. The small size of the particles causes gravity to have less of an effect. Thus, there is less possibility of settling out caused by gravity.

All matter can be identified as having either physical or chemical properties. A physical property is a characteristic of matter that can be observed without changing the makeup of the substance. Boiling points and freezing points are examples of physical properties. Other physical properties are color, odor, hardness, density, and the ability to conduct heat or electricity. Physical properties can be used to separate mixtures. A mixture of iron and sand can be separated by a magnet. Iron is magnetic. Sand is not, and thus they can be separated with ease.

A physical change occurs when matter changes in size, shape, color, or state. A physical change does not change the chemical composition of a substance. When a glass breaks, the size and shape of the glass change, but the chemical makeup remains the same no matter in how many pieces the glass might exist.

A chemical property is a characteristic that determines how a substance reacts to form other substances. Chemical properties are determined by chemical changes. When a chemical change occurs, the substance seldom will, if ever, return to its original state. For example, iron will rust in the presence of water and oxygen. Rusting is an example of the chemical property known as corrosion. Corrosion occurs when metals are destroyed as they combine chemically with other substances.

In a chemical change, a substance is changed to a new substance which has different properties. Chemical changes may release thermal energy, light, or electricity. Some chemical changes need energy. All changes, chemical and physical, involve an energy change of some kind. Many compounds are formed from elements by chemical changes. In the same respect, many compounds are broken down by a chemical change.

When wood burns, heat is given off and a small amount of ashes is left. The substance of the wood has changed. Wood is made of carbon, hydrogen, and oxygen. When wood burns, the elements unite with atmospheric oxygen resulting in the formation of carbon dioxide and water. Also, carbon is the element of the ash substance that remains. This is a chemical change as energy is used to bring about the change and heat (an energy form) is given off; other compounds have been formed and the elements can never return to the state of wood (unless they again become integrated into the growth of a tree).

☞ Drill: Structure of Matter

DIRECTIONS: Carefully read and answer each of the following questions which are based on the information which you have just read.

24. Anything that takes up space, has mass, and resists change is called
    (1) a solid.   (4) matter.
    (2) a liquid.   (5) energy.
    (3) plasma.

25. The particles of a compound are most strongly held together when it is in the state of a
    (1) solid.   (4) plasma.
    (2) liquid.   (5) gel.
    (3) gas.

26. A scientist discovers a substance that possesses a high temperature under normal conditions. The substance is most likely
    (1) liquid.   (4) gas.
    (2) plasma.   (5) not matter.
    (3) solid.

27. Matter can be measured
    (1) by its capacity to do work.
    (2) by the energy that it could contain.
    (3) by the energy that it did contain.
    (4) by its constant movement.
    (5) by counting the number of atoms which make up the matter.

28. Activation energy is
    (1) the energy necessary to move an object.
    (2) the energy necessary to cause motion.
    (3) the energy that measures an activity.
    (4) the energy necessary.to start a reaction.
    (5) the energy needed to keep a reaction under control.

29. Potential energy is possessed by
    (1) a book on a high shelf.   (4) an electric generator.
    (2) a bullet in motion.   (5) X-rays.
    (3) a hot wire.

30. A substance which cannot be further decomposed by ordinary chemical means is
    (1) water.   (4) copper.
    (2) air.   (5) wood.
    (3) sugar.

31. When 30 grams of mercury are heated with oxygen, the mercury unites with 3 grams of oxygen to form 33 grams of mercuric oxide. This reaction illustrates
    (1) the fact that the elements always combine.
    (2) a nuclear transformation.
    (3) the Law of Conservation of Matter.
    (4) the formation of mixtures.
    (5) the reduction of mercury to mercuric oxide.

32. The Law of Conservation of Energy states that
    (1) either energy or mass may be destroyed.
    (2) energy may neither be created nor destroyed.
    (3) energy can be converted to only one form.
    (4) energy may either be created or destroyed.
    (5) energy must be maintained in one form.

33. A substance composed of two or more elements that are chemically united is called
    (1) an isotope.
    (2) a compound.
    (3) an element.
    (4) a mixture.
    (5) a solution.

34. A can of baking powder carries the ingredient statement, "cornstarch, sodium bicarbonate, calcium acid phosphate, and sodium aluminum sulfate." This baking powder is
    (1) a compound.
    (2) a mixture.
    (3) a mixture or a compound.
    (4) a mixture or an atom.
    (5) a complex element.

35. Which one of the following is not an element?
    (1) Aluminum
    (2) Water
    (3) Tin
    (4) Oxygen
    (5) Gold

36. All solutions
    (1) contain water.
    (2) are liquids.
    (3) contain dissolved molecules.
    (4) are heterogeneous.
    (5) contain electrolytes.

37. If a sample of a material contains oxygenated water and dissolved salt, the sample is what type of mixture?
    (1) A compound
    (2) A substance
    (3) An element
    (4) A proportional mixture
    (5) Homogeneous

38. A heterogeneous mixture is
    I.   a type of matter
    II. a pure substance
    III. a type of mixture
    IV. a solution

    (1) I, II, III, IV
    (2) I, III, IV
    (3) I only
    (4) III, IV
    (5) I, III

39. A certain material contains three kinds of matter and has properties that vary from one point in the material to another. The material should be classified as
    (1) an element.
    (2) a mixture.
    (3) a liquid.
    (4) a solid.
    (5) a compound.

40. Suspensions can be reproduced by
    (1) shaking.
    (2) mixing.
    (3) stirring.
    (4) All of the above.
    (5) None of the above.

41. A suspension will have solid particles to settle out after a period of time due to
    (1) chemical action.
    (2) heat.
    (3) gravity.
    (4) continuous agitation during settling.
    (5) a change in the solubility of the particles.

42. If particles can be suspended for a short period of time by stirring, the mixture is called a
    (1) suspension.
    (2) colloid.
    (3) compound.
    (4) chemical solution.
    (5) whirlpool.

43. A dessert that is a colloid is
    (1) pie.
    (2) gelatin.
    (3) pudding.
    (4) ice cream.
    (5) chocolate cake.

44. A mixture is noted to have suspended particles evenly dispersed throughout and there is no evidence of sedimentation. This mixture is referred to as a
    (1) suspension.
    (2) homogeneous compound.
    (3) mixture.
    (4) colloid.
    (5) solution.

45. The properties that can be used to separate mixtures are
    (1) chemical.
    (2) acid.
    (3) alkaline.
    (4) physical.
    (5) unstable.

46. The ability to conduct electricity is
    (1) a chemical property.
    (2) a physical change.
    (3) a chemical change.
    (4) a physical property.
    (5) a biological property only.

47. A physical property is
    (1) an observable fact.
    (2) a characteristic of matter that can be observed without changing the makeup of the substance.
    (3) a characteristic of matter that cannot be observed without changing the makeup of the substance.
    (4) not useful for separating two substances.
    (5) based on the physical shape of the substance being analyzed.

48. Which of the following involves a physical change?
    (1) The melting of wax
    (2) The corroding of iron
    (3) The breaking of glass
    (4) The burning of wood
    (5) The breaking of bonds between sodium and chloride in table salt

49. A student observes that when a solid is heated in contact with air and remains hot, a liquid is formed. He may reasonably conclude that
    (1) a chemical change took place.
    (2) a physical change took place.
    (3) both physical and chemical changes took place.
    (4) no decision can be made concerning the change that occurred from this single observation.
    (5) the air is causing the liquid to remain hot.

50. Jon watches a match burn. Which of the following is true?
    (1) This is a chemical change because chemical properties of the match are unchanged.
    (2) This is a chemical change because burning is a chemical reaction.
    (3) This is a physical change because chemical properties of the match are unchanged.
    (4) This is neither a chemical nor a physical change.
    (5) This is both a chemical and physical change.

51. Chemical action may involve all of the following except
    (1) combining of atoms of the elements to form a molecule.
    (2) separation of the molecules in a mixture.
    (3) breaking down compounds into elements.
    (4) reacting a compound and an element to form an element and a new compound.
    (5) None of the above.

52. All chemical changes involve
    (1) a decreased stability in a solution.
    (2) an increased stability in a solution.
    (3) breaking of bonds and forming new ones.
    (4) formation of ion reactants.
    (5) a change of state.

53. When a chemical change takes place, a new _____ is always formed.
    (1) substance   (4) solution
    (2) element   (5) colloid
    (3) mixture

54. When an ice cube melts to form water, this change is an example of
    (1) a chemical change, because water is not the same material as ice.
    (2) a chemical change, because heat is needed to make it happen.
    (3) a physical change.
    (4) forming a solution.
    (5) creating a gas.

55. Which of the following involves a chemical change?
    (1) The rusting of iron
    (2) The breaking of glass
    (3) The evaporation of water
    (4) The melting of ice
    (5) An ice cube floating in a glass of water

56. A chemical change may involve all of the following except
    (1) combining of atoms of elements to form compounds.
    (2) the separation of the molecules in a mixture.
    (3) breaking down of compounds into elements.
    (4) reacting a compound and an element to form a new compound and a new element.
    (5) burning a piece of paper.

57. An example of a chemical change is
    (1) breaking of a glass bottle.
    (2) sawing of a piece of wood.
    (3) burning of wood.
    (4) melting of an ice cube.
    (5) crushing a boulder into pebbles.

58. In a chemical reaction like burning wood,
    (1) heat is given off.
    (2) no heat is given off.
    (3) heat is absorbed.
    (4) heat is a useless by-product.
    (5) oxygen is liberated.

C. SIMPLE EQUATIONS SHOWING STRUCTURE OF MATTER

Matter can be identified not only by name, but by the way the element fits together with other elements to form matter. It is important for one to know if the proposed combination actually exists. For example, no chemist has ever been able to prepare hydrogen nitrate. Additionally, in making combinations, one must have a positive and a negative component. Generally speaking, metals are positive components, while nonmetals are negative components (with the exception of ammonia and radicals). When elements combine in varying proportions, prefixes are used for the naming of the compound and for formula writing. Mono- means one, bi- or di- means two, tri- means three, tetra- means four, pent- means five, and so on. Common suffixes and meanings are -ide (for naming monatomic anions), -ous (for the ion with the lower charge), and -ic (for the ion with the higher charge).

☞ Drill: Simple Equations Showing Structure of Matter

DIRECTIONS: Carefully read and answer each of the following questions which are based on the information which you have just read.

59. A scientist combines hydrogen, oxygen, and sodium to make a compound. Which of these four substances is the name of the compound?
    (1) Hydrogen
    (2) Lye
    (3) Oxygen
    (4) Sodium
    (5) Table salt

60. The formula for ferrous chloride or iron (II) chloride is
    (1) $FeCl_2$
    (2) $2FeCl_2$
    (3) Fe_2Cl
    (4) $2FeCl$
    (5) $FeCl$

61. When hydrogen is burned with oxygen, water is produced. This can be written

(1) $H_2 + O_2 \rightarrow HO$ (4) $H_2 + O \rightarrow H_3O$

(2) $H_2 + O \rightarrow H_2O$ (5) $2H_2 + O_2 \rightarrow 2H_2O$

(3) $2H + O_2 \rightarrow HO$

62. Which of the following is classified as a monatomic element?

(1) Water   (4) Helium

(2) Milk   (5) Bicarbonate

(3) Benzene

D. PERIODICITY OF ELEMENTS

The latter half of the 19th century brought about the updating of the Periodic Law: the properties of the elements are periodic functions of their atomic numbers. Atomic numbers represent the number of protons and also the number of electrons in a neutral atom. The electron structures of the atoms provide information showing the properties of the elements. Vertical columns represent the chemical families while horizontal columns represent the period or row. Proceeding across a row, the ability to hold electrons decreases. For example, lithium is the most metallic while fluorine is the least metallic. Study the Periodic Table which appears in the appendix of this book.

Some atoms tend to join with other atoms, while others will show no tendency to join with like atoms or like elements. The results of this tendency or attraction of the atoms involved in joining is called a chemical bond. When atoms combine to form new molecules, there is a shifting or transfer of valence electrons found in the outer shell of each atom. This usually results in the completing of outer shells by each atom. A more stable compound or form is achieved by the gaining, losing, or sharing of pairs of electrons. In forming chemical bonds, there is a release of energy or an absorption of energy. The bonds can be ionic, covalent, or metallic.

The kinetic model explains the forces between molecules and the energy they possess in three basic assumptions:

1. All matter is composed of extremely small particles.

2. The particles making up all matter are in constant motion.

3. When these particles collide with each other or with the walls of the container, there is no loss of energy.

☞ Drill: Periodicity of Elements

<u>DIRECTIONS</u>: Carefully read and answer each of the following questions which are based on the information which you have just read.

63. Metallic ions are _____ their corresponding atoms.
    (1) smaller than
    (2) the same size as
    (3) larger than
    (4) heavier than
    (5) darker in color than

64. In a horizontal (series) row, the ionization energy tends to _____ with increasing atomic number.
    (1) increase
    (2) decrease
    (3) remain constant
    (4) increase in frequency
    (5) become kinetic

65. Molecular mass and formula mass are similar because both represent the mass of the smallest
    (1) atom that makes up the element.
    (2) element that combines to form a molecule.
    (3) unit that makes up a compound.
    (4) ion that makes up an atom.
    (5) formula that makes up an equation.

66. The tendency or attraction of the atoms involved in joining is called a(n)
    (1) covalent bond.
    (2) metallic bond.
    (3) chemical bond.
    (4) stable bond.
    (5) ionic bond.

67. A more stable compound is achieved when atoms
    (1) gain electrons to fill their outer shell.
    (2) share pairs of electrons.
    (3) absorb energy.
    (4) Both 1 and 2.
    (5) 1, 2, and 3.

68. When an ionic bond occurs between two atoms,
    (1) the forces of repulsion are greater than the forces of attraction.
    (2) a pair of electrons join or are simultaneously attracted.
    (3) an increase in energy results.

(4) the atoms become unstable.

(5) two cations are attracted and bond together.

69. The kinetic model implies that oxygen molecules would have _____ average kinetic energy than/as hydrogen molecules at the same temperature.
    (1) higher
    (2) the same
    (3) lower
    (4) not the same
    (5) sixteen times the

70. According to the kinetic model, matter is not made of
    (1) atoms.
    (2) extremely small particles.
    (3) atoms in constant motion.
    (4) particles moving without collisions.
    (5) atoms that do not lose energy during rebounding.

71. Under ideal gas circumstances, when atoms collide together
    (1) there is no energy loss.
    (2) there is an energy gain.
    (3) there is energy exchanged.
    (4) there is no source of comparison.
    (5) they will stick together.

E. BEHAVIOR OF MATTER

The behavior and classification of matter is dependent upon the electron attraction and interaction of electrons forming the matter. When atoms react with one another, it is the electrons that are involved in bonding, whether it be ion or covalent.

All reactions need to receive a certain amount of energy before they can start. The amount of energy needed or received to start the chemical reaction is called activation energy. Some reactions require so little energy that it can be absorbed from the surroundings. This is called a spontaneous reaction which takes place with so little energy that it seems as if no energy was needed. A reaction that gives off energy is called an exothermic reaction. A reaction that absorbs energy is called an endothermic reaction. Combustion is a decomposition reaction. A catalyst can be added to a chemical reaction to control the reaction rate.

ACIDS

Acid properties are:

1. Water solutions of acids conduct electricity.
2. Acids will react actively with metals.
3. Acids will change blue litmus to pink.
4. Acids will react with bases resulting in both a loss of water and leaving a salt (neutralization).
5. Weak acid solutions taste sour.
6. Acids react with carbonates to release carbon dioxide.

BASES

Bases properties are:

1. Bases are conductors of electricity in strong solutions.
2. Bases change red litmus paper blue.
3. Bases react with acids to neutralize each other and to form a salt and water.
4. Bases react with fats to form a class of compounds called soaps.
5. Bases feel slippery and strong solutions are caustic to the skin.

SALTS

A salt is an ionic compound containing positive ions other than hydrogen and a negative ion other than hydroxide ions. It is usually formed by neutralization when certain acids and bases are combined and form water and salt as the products.

A formula is a sort of road map, or a detailed description, of how something is organized or produced. A formula will not reveal the hidden structures of substances. In some reactions, no product is formed at completion, or reactants and products may react both ways. The reaction is said to have reached equilibrium when the rate of the forward reaction is equal to the rate of the reverse reaction. Factors that affect chemical equilibrium are changing concentration, temperature, and pressure.

Reactions that do not occur spontaneously can be forced by an external supply of energy. This is called an electrolytic reaction. Many chemicals and useful products are produced in this manner. Electroplating, electrolysis of water or salts, and the cathode functioning of a battery all are examples of electro-chemistry.

Simple electrochemical cells, in which electrons produced by the oxidation of zinc atoms are transferred through an external circuit into a copper solution, are called galvanic cells or voltaic cells. All electrochemical cells have the same general components: an oxidation half-cell, a reduction half-cell, and a means of separation so that the electrons produced by the oxidation reaction can be supplied through an external circuit into the reduction reaction. The voltage of the cell is the net voltage or potential voltage of two half-cell reactions. Lead storage cells contain a series of lead grids separated by an insulating material. The grids are alternately filled with spongy lead and lead dioxide that compose what are called dry cells. As long as the grids remain intact, the cell will deliver about two volts of electric current.

☞ Drill: Behavior of Matter

DIRECTIONS: Carefully read and answer each of the following questions which are based on the information which you have just read.

72. The behavior of matter is dependent upon
    (1)   the proton attraction.   (4)   the ion attraction.
    (2)   the neutron attraction.   (5)   covalent interactions.
    (3)   the electron attraction.

73. The addition of a catalyst to a reaction
    (1)   changes the chemicals.
    (2)   changes the temperature.
    (3)   changes the rate of reaction.
    (4)   changes the ingredients of the reaction.
    (5)   can make previously impossible reactions work.

74. In a(n) _____ reaction, the products are lower in energy than the reactants.
    (1)   exothermic   (4)   chemothermic
    (2)   endothermic   (5)   mesothermic
    (3)   isothermica

75. Which of the following reactions is considered to be spontaneous?
    (1)   The conversion of copper to gold
    (2)   The conversion of water to steam
    (3)   The conversion of carbon dioxide to methane
    (4)   The conversion of hydrogen and oxygen to form water
    (5)   The conversion of iron to its oxide

76. Combustion is a(n)
    (1) reaction where things are broken down to products with less potential energy.
    (2) reaction where things are combined together to form a more complex product.
    (3) endothermic reaction.
    (4) exothermic reaction.
    (5) reaction characterized by lack of energy transfer.

77. A lemon has a sour taste because
    (1) all fruits are sour.   (4) it does not contain sugar.
    (2) it contains a base.   (5) carbon dioxide is being released.
    (3) it contains an acid. .

78. Soap contains what kind of a substance?
    (1) Acid   (4) Neutralized ion
    (2) Base   (5) Caustic
    (3) Salt

79. A student determines that an unknown substance conducts electricity, tastes sour, and reacts with another substance to produce a salt. Most likely, the substance is a
    (1) base.   (4) solution.
    (2) acid.   (5) salt.
    (3) catalyst.

80. A salt derived from a strong base and a weak acid will undergo hydrolysis and give a solution that will be
    (1) basic.   (4) volatile.
    (2) acidic.   (5) caustic.
    (3) neutral.

81. A formula will
    (1) describe the organization and composition of a substance.
    (2) tell the rate of the chemical reaction.
    (3) construct hidden structures.
    (4) show when equilibrium is reached.
    (5) describe the physical properties of each element involved.

82. Equilibrium can be expressed as the point at which
    (1) all the chemicals present stop reacting.
    (2) the chemicals start reacting.

(3)   the chemical reactants are used up.

(4)   the products react together at the same rate as the reactants.

(5)   the number of reactant molecules equals the number of product molecules.

83.   In a chemical reaction at equilibrium, which of the following changes would always increase the concentration of the product?

(1)   Add a catalyst

(2)   Increase pressure

(3)   Increase temperature

(4)   Increase concentration of reactant

(5)   Decrease pressure

84.   Which of the following objects are made by the process of electroplating?

        I. silver-plated spoon

        II. chromium-plated automobile bumper

        III. radioactive carbon

(1)   I, II, III   (4)   II only

(2)   II, III   (5)   I, II

(3)   I only

85.   Which one of the following metals does not undergo corrosion and thus does not need to be electroplated?

(1)   iron   (4)   nickel

(2)   aluminum   (5)   gold

(3)   copper

86.   A galvanic cell has a porous barrier between the half-cell on the left and the half-cell on the right in order to

(1)   halt the movement of ions.

(2)   allow the two solutions to mix completely.

(3)   preserve the strong acid nature of the solutions.

(4)   allow movement of ions for preserving neutrality.

(5)   measure the quantity of current.

87.   A galvanic cell

(1)   produces an electrical current that can be used to perform work.

(2)   is very different from a flashlight battery.

(3)   converts chemical energy to electrical energy.

(4)   1, 2, and 3

(5)   1 and 3

F. SOLUTIONS

Forces of attraction between particles produce a solution. One must mix a solute and a solvent to produce a solution. The particles making up each have certain forces of attraction that produce bonds. The bonds produced by these forces of attraction will determine the solubility of the solute. Temperature also affects the solubility of a solution. If the solution is made of gases, the solubility will be affected by pressure. Pressure does not affect the solubility of solids and liquids. If no more solute can be dissolved in the solvent, the solution is said to be saturated. In an unsaturated solution, more solute can be added to the solvent, while in a supersaturated solution, the solution is holding more dissolved solute than normal at that given temperature.

Matter exists as a substance or a mixture. If a substance is made of only one kind of atom, it is an element. If it is made of two or more kinds of atoms in a definite grouping, it is a compound. A compound always occurs in a definite composition based on the Law of Definite Composition, which states, "A compound is composed of two or more elements chemically combined in a definite ratio by weight." Compounds always have a fixed composition and will be classified as ionic or covalent depending on the type of bonding that occurs when the atoms are combined. The ability to combine is dependent upon the valence of the atom or element. An ionic compound contains ionic bonds—a force of attraction between oppositely charged ions. A covalent compound is a compound that is composed of covalent bonds—a bond in which the electrons are shared between atoms. When a compound is formed, the elements or atoms making up the compound lose their properties and take on the properties of the compound formed.

It is important to remember that the gain of electrons is reduction, and the loss of electrons is oxidation. The oxidation number of a bonded atom is the number of electrons gained, lost, or shared in a chemical reaction. The metal elements that lose electrons easily and become positive ions are placed high in the electromotive series.

The metal elements that lose electrons with greater difficulty are placed lower on the periodic chart. The energy required to remove electrons from metallic atoms can be assigned numeral values called electrode potentials. Binary compounds are named by changing the name of the element that has the negative oxidation number to end in -ide.

The rate of the reaction is defined as the quantity of product formed in some stated interval or the rate at which the reaction will take place. The rate of the chemical reaction can be defined in terms of the change in concentration of any species in the reaction with respect to time. The rate of the reaction can be determined by measuring how fast the product is formed after the reactants are mixed, or how many moles are formed per second. Also, increase in temperature will increase frequency of molecular collision and increase rate of reaction. Activation energy is necessary to produce enough energy to break or weaken bonds before new bonds can be formed. Some reactions produce energy in the formation of new compounds or the products have more energy than the reactants (exothermic reactions) while other reactants need a greater amount of energy than the activation energy (endothermic reactions). The study of reaction rate factors is called chemical kinetics.

☞ Drill: Solutions

DIRECTIONS: Carefully read and answer each of the following questions which are based on the information which you have just read.

88. Solution rate of a solid solute dissolving in a liquid solvent may be increased by
    (1) changing the temperature.   (4) All of the above.
    (2) stirring the solution.   (5) None of the above.
    (3) shaking the solution.

89. A solution can be both
    (1) diluted and concentrated simultaneously.
    (2) saturated yet diluted simultaneously.
    (3) saturated and unsaturated simultaneously.
    (4) supersaturated and saturated simultaneously.
    (5) acidic and neutral simultaneously.

90. The solubility of a solute must indicate
    (1) the temperature of the solution.
    (2) the quantity of solute.
    (3) the quantity of solvent.
    (4) All of the above.
    (5) None of the above.

91. The most common solvent is
    (1) alcohol.   (4) an acid.
    (2) benzene.   (5) acetone.
    (3) water.

92. The ability to combine is dependent upon the _____ of the atom or element.
     (1) valence
     (2) molecular count
     (3) atomic number
     (4) atomic mass
     (5) proton number

93. The Law of Definite Composition is based on definite composition by
     (1) weight.
     (2) volume.
     (3) density.
     (4) specific weight.
     (5) temperature.

94. Which of the following substances are joined by ionic bonds?
     (1) O_2
     (2) NaCl
     (3) formaldehyde
     (4) Cl_2
     (5) Na_2

95. The number of bonds formed by an atom is most closely associated with
     (1) its atomic weight.
     (2) the number of electrons in the atom.
     (3) the number of electron shells.
     (4) the number of electrons in the outer shell.
     (5) the number of electrons in the innermost shell.

96. A binary compound can be identified by the _____ ending.
     (1) -ous
     (2) -ide
     (3) -ic
     (4) -ion
     (5) -ate

97. A reduction reaction always involves the
     (1) loss of electrons.
     (2) gain of electrons.
     (3) addition of oxygen.
     (4) removal of oxygen.
     (5) gain of electrons and protons.

98. Which of the following formulas shows a naturally occurring reduction?
     (1) $Fe^{+2} \rightarrow Fe^{+3} + e-$
     (2) $Mg \rightarrow Mg^{+2} + 2e-$
     (3) $Fe^{+2} + e- \rightarrow Fe^{+1}$
     (4) $Fe^{+3} + e- \rightarrow Fe^{+2}$
     (5) $Mg + e- \rightarrow Mg^{-1}$

99. An ion with an oxidation number of 3+ can combine with three identical ions, each having an oxidation number of
    (1) 1+   (4) 3-
    (2) 1-   (5) 2+
    (3) 3+

100. In a(n) _____ reaction, the products are lower in energy than the reactants.
    (1) endothermic   (4) exothermic
    (2) moles   (5) kinetic
    (3) chemical

101. When the energy released by the products of a reaction is greater than the energy of activation,
    (1) the reaction stops.
    (2) the reaction is exothermic.
    (3) the reaction always forms products.
    (4) the product is unstable.
    (5) the reaction needs excessive heat to begin.

102. The effect of an increase in temperature on a chemical reaction is to increase the
    (1) energy of activation.
    (2) concentration of reactants.
    (3) frequency of collision.
    (4) potential energy barrier.
    (5) heat of formation.

103. Chemical action may involve all of the following except
    (1) combining of atoms of elements to form a molecule.
    (2) separation of the molecules in a mixture.
    (3) breaking down compounds into elements.
    (4) reacting a compound and an element to form a new compound and a new element.
    (5) combusting a compound to form a new substance.

CHEMISTRY

ANSWER KEY

Drill: Introduction to Chemistry

1.	(3)	7.	(1)	13.	(3)	19.	(1)
2.	(2)	8.	(2)	14.	(1)	20.	(1)
3.	(4)	9.	(3)	15.	(3)	21.	(5)
4.	(2)	10.	(4)	16.	(4)	22.	(1)
5.	(1)	11.	(4)	17.	(5)	23.	(4)
6.	(1)	12.	(3)	18.	(4)		

Drill: Structure of Matter

24.	(4)	33.	(2)	42.	(1)	51.	(2)
25.	(1)	34.	(2)	43.	(2)	52.	(3)
26.	(2)	35.	(2)	44.	(4)	53.	(1)
27.	(1)	36.	(3)	45.	(4)	54.	(3)
28.	(4)	37.	(5)	46.	(4)	55.	(1)
29.	(1)	38.	(5)	47.	(2)	56.	(2)
30.	(4)	39.	(2)	48.	(3)	57.	(3)
31.	(3)	40.	(4)	49.	(2)	58.	(1)
32.	(2)	41.	(3)	50.	(2)		

Drill: Simple Equations Showing Structure of Matter

59.	(2)	60.	(1)	61.	(5)	62.	(4)

Drill: Periodicity of Elements

63.	(1)	66.	(3)	69.	(2)	71.	(1)
64.	(2)	67.	(4)	70.	(4)		
65.	(3)	68.	(2)				

Drill: Behavior of Matter

72.	(3)	76.	(1)	80.	(1)	84.	(5)
73.	(3)	77.	(3)	81.	(1)	85.	(5)
74.	(1)	78.	(2)	82.	(4)	86.	(4)
75.	(5)	79.	(2)	83.	(4)	87.	(5)

Drill: Solutions

88. (4)	92. (1)	96. (2)	100. (4)
89. (2)	93. (4)	97. (2)	101. (2)
90. (4)	94. (2)	98. (4)	102. (3)
91. (3)	95. (4)	99. (2)	103. (2)

IV. EARTH SCIENCE

A. ASPECTS OF EARTH SCIENCE

An understanding of the beginnings of the solar system and the Earth's development is essential to environmental survival. This understanding is filled with curiosity, and may be the price of environmental survival. A lack of curiosity and understanding may signal the environment's demise.

1. THEORIES

Hipparchus, in 150 B.C., determined the distance of the moon based on his calculations on the Earth's diameter. The Greeks added to the study of astronomy by determining that an eclipse was caused by the Earth passing between the sun and the moon, and, the sun was at the center of the solar system. These and other basic studies concerning the sun, moon, planets, galaxies, and solar system have led to questions like, "Does the universe go on forever? Where does it all end? Is space infinite?" It is because of such challenging questions that astronomy has developed into an exact science.

The theory developed by Sir Isaac Newton is in direct opposition to the theory developed by Albert Einstein. Newton stated that a planet moves around the sun because of the gravitational force exerted by the sun. This theory holds true if one is studying the velocities of small objects compared to light. Einstein's theory of relativity states that the planet chooses the shortest possible path throughout the four-dimensional world which is defined by the presence of the sun. According to this theory, if you were to leave home and walk in a straight line, you would eventually end up back where you started. Both these theories were inventions by human minds and have been used to create many of our scientific explanations (theories). New theories will show weaknesses and limitations to each theory.

Most scientists tend to believe the theory stating the solar system probably developed as a nebula (cloud of gas and dust) that once swirled around the sun and slowly flattened out. Sections of the cloud began to spin like eddies in a stream, collecting gases and dust and causing the sections to grow and form planets. They slowly developed into spinning planets that now travel around the sun.

The most widely held theory on how the universe came into existence is called the Big Bang Theory. This theory states that it was from a colossal explosion 10 to 14 billion years ago that a highly concentrated mass of gaseous matter formed and then radiated outward, creating the universe. It is widely believed that the life on Earth is a natural consequence of the events set in motion by the Big Bang. It is also generally thought that the universe continues to expand today. The Big Bang, however, is not universally accepted. Among the things that cause it to be called into question are observations (a) that some globular clusters appear to be older than the universe itself and (b) that galaxies exist in superclumps, with enormous voids between them.

In the early 1700s, Abraham Werner presented his theory that an ocean once covered the Earth. The chemicals in the water slowly settled to the bottom of the water where they formed granite and other forms of rock layers. The Earth was completely formed with the settling of the water and no other changes occurred. All life, according to Werner, began with the settling of the water and the formation of the Earth.

The Hutton Theory of 1785 claimed that the Earth was gradually changing and would continue to change in the same ways. According to Hutton, these changes could be used to explain the past. He died before he could get other scientists to accept his ideas, yet after his death and publication of his ideas, they became a leading guide for the geological thinkers.

The Creation Theory with which we are most familiar is that given in the first chapters of Genesis. Various attempts have been made to work out the date of the creation on the basis of the data given in the Bible and the date of creation has been set at 3760 B.C. The creation, as explained in Genesis, is accepted by some people as the formation of the Earth and the origin of life.

Battle lines have been drawn. One theorist will research and develop a possible strategy for solving the age-old question, only for another theorist to come along and find a flaw in that research and then develop a new theory. Thus new theories are constantly developed. Each theory developed is viewed in a manner to gain an understanding of the information presented pertaining to the Earth's formation for the purpose of survival and prosperity of the universe.

2. SOLAR SYSTEM

The solar system includes the sun, nine planets with their moons, asteroids, meteoroids, comets, interplanetary dust, and interplanetary plasma that is circular in shape. The sun is the center of the solar system with a mass 750 times greater than that of all of the planets combined. The planets rotate around the sun with Mercury being the closest to and Pluto being the farthest from the sun. The terrestrial (earth-like) planets—Mercury, Venus, Mars, and the Earth—are composed chiefly of iron and rock. These planets are smallest in comparison to the four largest planets, Jupiter, Saturn, Uranus, and Neptune, which are called the Major planets. They are composed chiefly of hydrogen, helium, ammonia, and methane. Pluto is believed to be less than one-fifth the size of Earth, which makes it smaller than our moon.

Asteroids or planetoids are small, irregularly-shaped objects orbiting between Jupiter and Mars. Meteoroids are chunks of iron resulting from collisions between asteroids. Comets are round heads consisting of dust particles mixed with frozen water, frozen methane, and frozen ammonia, and a tail made of dust and gases escaping from the head.

3. METEORS AND METEORITES

A meteor is a metallic or stony mass belonging to the solar system that is hurtled into the Earth's atmosphere. The meteor cannot be seen until it enters the atmosphere, at which time the friction with the air makes it glow and shine for only a few seconds as it falls to the Earth. Thus, it is called a falling, or shooting, star.

Meteorites seldom do damage, yet they have devastating potentiality. Meteorites are pieces of extraterrestrial matter that are studied to determine the origins of the universe and the solar system. Meteorites make up only a tiny fraction of the matter falling into the Earth's atmosphere from space. They sometimes explode into fragments with a noise that can be heard for many miles when they strike the surface of the Earth.

4. STARS

When you look at the sky, you see only a tiny part of the universe consisting mainly of stars, clouds of dust, and the solar system. Astronomers study the brightness and color of the stars. Brightness indicates the mass of the stars, while the color indicates the temperature of the star's surface. The distance is difficult to determine as most stars are so far away. Stars have been studied as early as 3000 B.C.; yet, they still remain a mystery.

Stars and star groupings (constellations) are used as compasses at night, as a navigational aid, as a basis for astrology, for study, and for viewing at the planetarium. What appears as movement of the stars and the nearly 80 constellations is actually the spinning and placement of the Earth. Seasonally and yearly, the constellations that can be seen will differ, causing the sky to appear to move west during the year.

5. GALAXIES

Galaxies are groups or systems of stars located millions to billions of light-years from Earth. Sometimes called stellar universes, galaxies include billions of stars, and are classified as to their appearance. Irregular systems have no special form or symmetry. The spiral system resembles a large pinwheel with arms extending from the dense central core. Elliptical systems appear round without the spiral arms.

Our solar system is in the Milky Way Galaxy. The Milky Way is a spiral galaxy and is held together by gravity. It slowly rotates, with its spiral arms turning once in about 200 million years. The Milky Way contains clouds of gas, dust, and millions or billions of star clusters which form their own distinct patterns. Bands of stars making-up the spiral arms of our galaxy can be seen in the night sky. The Andromeda Nebula Galaxy, first studied in 1612, resembles the Milky Way. It is the nearest galaxy that northern hemisphere observers can see.

In the past few decades, radio astronomy has played a great role in studying celestial objects. In 1959, the first quasar was discovered. It was noticed that some sources of celestial radio waves appeared to be point-like—"quasi-stellar"—instead of looking like radio waves emitted by galaxies. These "quasi-stellar radio sources," or quasars as they are known, give off radio waves and light at a rate over 100,000 billion times as fast as the sun. Quasars appear to be far smaller than ordinary galaxies, and are believed by some astronomers to be the core of violently exploding galaxies. Quasars appear to be among the most distant objects in the universe. Today, astronomers have identified over 1,000 quasars.

☞ Drill: Aspects of Earth Science

DIRECTIONS: Carefully read and answer each of the following questions which are based on the information which you have just read.

1. When the Earth passes between the sun and the moon, this causes the occurrence of a(n)
   - (1) phase.
   - (2) ellipse.
   - (3) darkness.
   - (4) eclipse.
   - (5) None of the above.

2. The first to study astronomy was/were
   (1) Hipparchus.
   (2) Greeks.
   (3) Aristotle.
   (4) Plato.
   (5) All of the above.

3. The survival of planet Earth could possibly be based on the study of the
   (1) eclipse occurrences.
   (2) sun and moon relationships.
   (3) solar system.
   (4) galaxies.
   (5) the moon.

4. A theory can be defined as
   (1) an educated guess.
   (2) an invention of the human mind.
   (3) a possible idea that would lead to scientific explanation.
   (4) a scientific explanation.
   (5) a fact.

5. "Planets move around the sun because of the gravitational force exerted by the sun" is part of which scientist's theory?
   (1) Aristotle
   (2) Newton
   (3) Einstein
   (4) Hipparchus
   (5) Copernicus

6. A planet chooses its shortest path through a four-dimensional world which is defined by the presence of the sun would be the theory of which scientist?
   (1) Aristotle
   (2) Newton
   (3) Einstein
   (4) Hipparchus
   (5) Copernicus

7. Possibly, a planet could have begun as
   (1) a nebula.
   (2) eddies.
   (3) a collection of gases.
   (4) a spinning dust collection.
   (5) a galaxy.

8. The difference between a nebula and an eddy would be their
   (1) shape.
   (2) movement.
   (3) shape and movement.
   (4) type of gas forming mass.
   (5) None of the above.

9. The solar system probably first developed as
   (1) a nebula.   (4) lost terrestrial material.
   (2) a galaxy.   (5) the sun.
   (3) another planet.

10. A factor that dispels the Big Bang Theory is
    (1) the escape of dust and gases.
    (2) the speed at which the planets are traveling.
    (3) the expanding of the universe.
    (4) that galaxies exist in superclumps with large voids between them.
    (5) All of the above.

11. According to the Big Bang Theory, the universe was created
    (1) 10 to 14 billion years ago.
    (2) 200 million years ago.
    (3) in 3760 B.C.
    (4) in 3000 B.C.
    (5) None of the above.

12. The type of rock formed on the ocean's floor is
    (1) granite.   (4) marble.
    (2) limestone.   (5) conglomerate.
    (3) phosphate.

13. _____ developed the theory stating that the ocean covered the entire Earth.
    (1) Benjamin Warner   (4) Alexander Bell
    (2) Joseph Copernicus   (5) None of the above.
    (3) Abraham Werner

14. The theory that all life began with the settling of the water was formulated in the
    (1) 1940s.   (4) 1800s.
    (2) 1850s.   (5) 1700s.
    (3) 1650s.

15. According to Hutton, changes would be explained by the
    (1) past.
    (2) present.
    (3) future.
    (4) social attitudes.
    (5) None of the above.

16. Hutton's theory stated
    (1) how to explain the past.
    (2) how the sun and moon were the same.
    (3) how the Earth was gradually changing and would cease the gradual changing.
    (4) how the Earth was gradually changing and would continue to change in the same ways.
    (5) that the Earth is not changing.

17. Hutton _____ before he was able to get his fellow scientists to accept his ideas.
    (1) left the scientific field
    (2) was institutionalized
    (3) died
    (4) disappeared
    (5) quit

18. The Creation Theory is based on the
    (1) findings on the bottom of the ocean.
    (2) first chapter of Genesis.
    (3) first chapter of Matthew.
    (4) first happenings on Earth.
    (5) Adam and Eve.

19. According to the Creation Theory, the beginning of the Earth was
    (1) 1796 B.C.
    (2) 3706 B.C.
    (3) 3760 B.C.
    (4) 2796 B.C.
    (5) 1 B.C.

20. Various attempts have been made to establish the correct order of beginnings based on
    (1) data in the Bible.
    (2) data in the Koran.
    (3) dates in the Bible.
    (4) dates in the Koran.
    (5) data and dates in the Koran.

21. Theories are developed for the purpose of
    (1) further discussion and experimentation.
    (2) gaining an understanding of information for survival.

(3)   momentary gains.
(4)   solving world peace.
(5)   settling disputes.

22.   The major battle is
(1)   which strategy is most correct.
(2)   which research is best developed.
(3)   which theory is best presented.
(4)   which strategy solves the problem.
(5)   None of the above.

23.   When considering evolution and change, survival and prosperity of the universe is the basis for
(1)   all theories.   (4)   all debates.
(2)   all experimentations.   (5)   All of the above.
(3)   all research.

24.   Galaxies are groups or systems of
(1)   moons.   (4)   rockets.
(2)   stars.   (5)   asteroids.
(3)   planets.

25.   The Earth is a planet in the galaxy called the
(1)   Quasar.   (4)   Solar System.
(2)   Orion.   (5)   Milky Way.
(3)   Nebula.

26.   Galaxies are located _____ of light-years from the Earth.
(1)   hundreds   (4)   trillions
(2)   thousands   (5)   tens
(3)   billions

27.   Elliptical systems appear to lack spiral arms but possess
(1)   round bodies.   (4)   rectangular bodies.
(2)   square bodies.   (5)   oval bodies.
(3)   triangular bodies.

28.   The Earth is a
(1)   galaxy.   (4)   moon.
(2)   planet.   (5)   satellite.
(3)   star.

29. The band of starlight coming from our own galaxy forms the
    (1) sun.
    (2) moon.
    (3) spiral arms.
    (4) Milky Way.
    (5) planets.

30. Located in the center of the solar system is the
    (1) earth.
    (2) moon.
    (3) sun.
    (4) comet.
    (5) Orion Nebula.

31. The Milky Way is a(n)
    (1) elliptical galaxy.
    (2) flattened galaxy.
    (3) spiral galaxy.
    (4) pinwheel galaxy.
    (5) round galaxy.

32. The Milky Way contains
    (1) clusters of stars forming their own distinct pattern.
    (2) clusters of dust forming their own distinct pattern.
    (3) clusters of planetoids forming their own distinct pattern.
    (4) clusters of comets forming their own distinct pattern.
    (5) clusters of meteors forming their own distince pattern.

33. The galaxy that is closest in resemblance to the Milky Way is
    (1) Quasar.
    (2) Nebula.
    (3) Earth.
    (4) Andromeda.
    (5) Orion.

34. The discovery of quasars has been aided by
    (1) radio astronomy.
    (2) telescopes.
    (3) light waves.
    (4) clouds of gas.
    (5) Star clusters.

35. The first quasar was located in 1959. Since that date, scientists have located more than _____ quasars.
    (1) 20,000
    (2) 1,000
    (3) 1,959
    (4) 100,000
    (5) 100

36. A star's mass is indicated by its
    (1) color.
    (2) surface.
    (3) distance.
    (4) brightness.
    (5) density.

37. The temperature of a star is indicated by its
    (1) surface.   (4) brightness.
    (2) mass.   (5) density.
    (3) color.

38. A person who studies the stars is called a(n)
    (1) astrologer.   (4) star searcher.
    (2) astronomer.   (5) astrologist.
    (3) astrophysicist.

39. A group of stars is called a(n)
    (1) compass.
    (2) navigational instrument aid.
    (3) consolation.
    (4) constellation.
    (5) installation.

40. What appears as star movement is actually
    (1) spinning and placement of the Earth.
    (2) spinning and placement of the sun.
    (3) spinning and placement of the moon.
    (4) spinning and placement of the star grouping.
    (5) None of the above.

41. The place where stars are viewed and studied is called the
    (1) atmosphere.   (4) planetoid.
    (2) laboratory.   (5) telescope.
    (3) planetarium.

42. Upon entering the atmosphere, metallic masses glow due to friction
    with the atmosphere and cause the mass to glow; hence, we are able
    to see a(n)
    (1) sun.   (4) star.
    (2) meteor.   (5) eclipse.
    (3) moon.

43. A meteor is
    (1) a comet.   (4) glowing air.
    (2) a star falling.   (5) a metallic mass.
    (3) a falling comet.

44. A meteor is sometimes called a
    (1) falling comet.   (4) failing sun.
    (2) falling sun.   (5) exploding star.
    (3) shooting star.

45. A meteor will glow for
    (1) a few days.   (4) a month.
    (2) a few hours.   (5) years.
    (3) a few seconds.

46. Damage to the Earth by meteorites occurs
    (1) at the changing of the moon.
    (2) at times of devastation.
    (3) seldomly, but could be devastating.
    (4) at changing of the seasons.
    (5) during hail storms.

47. To determine the origins of the universe and the solar system, one could study
    (1) mentors.   (4) mentalities.
    (2) meteorites.   (5) oceans.
    (3) cometrites.

48. Meteorites are
    (1) extrametal matter.
    (2) fractions of moon beams.
    (3) extraterrestrial matter.
    (4) fractions of sun beams.
    (5) satellites.

49. The Earth-like planets are made up of
    (1) lava and stone.   (4) hydrogen and methane.
    (2) tin and copper.   (5) oxygen and carbon dioxide.
    (3) iron and rock.

50. The sun has a mass of 750 times greater than
    (1) all terrestrial planets.
    (2) the four largest planets.
    (3) the Earth, moon, and sun combined.
    (4) all planets combined.
    (5) Mercury.

51. Which planet is the farthest from the sun?
     (1)   Earth   (4)   Jupiter
     (2)   Mars   (5)   Pluto
     (3)   Saturn

52. Which planet is the closest to the sun?
     (1)   Earth   (4)   Pluto
     (2)   Mars   (5)   None of the above.
     (3)   Mercury

53. Which of the following planets is the largest?
     (1)   Earth   (4)   Pluto
     (2)   Mars   (5)   Moon
     (3)   Saturn

54. Asteroids are irregularly-shaped objects orbiting between Jupiter and
     Mars that are _____ in size.
     (1)   tiny   (4)   medium
     (2)   large   (5)   planet-like
     (3)   small

55. Meteoroids are chunks of iron resulting from collisions between
     (1)   asteroids.   (4)   stars.
     (2)   comets.   (5)   meteorites.
     (3)   planetoids.

56. Asteroids orbit between
     (1)   Neptune and Venus.   (4)   Neptune and Jupiter.
     (2)   Jupiter and Mars.   (5)   Earth and the moon.
     (3)   Mars and Venus.

B. PHYSICS AND CHEMISTRY OF THE EARTH

1. PHYSICAL PROPERTIES

   The Earth has three motions: it spins like a top, moves in the spinning motion around the sun, while moving through the Milky Way with the rest of the solar system. The Earth spins around on its axis, an imaginary line that connects the North and South poles at either end of the planet Earth. The spinning motion has a path it follows around the sun (orbit), making the sun seem to move from east to west and causing the occurrences of day and night.

The Earth has only one moon. The sun's gravity acts on both the Earth and the moon, causing the moon to travel in an oval-like orbit around the Earth. Because of this movement, we have the seasons of spring, summer, fall, and winter. The seasons are a result of the tilting of the Earth on its axis, movement, and position of the moon in relation to the sun.

2. CHEMICAL COMPOSITION

The Earth's surface is about 70% water, with most of the water being oceans with depths extending to 12,450 feet. The land surface makes up the remaining 30% and extends an average of 2,757 feet above the division of land and water. The highest peak is Mount Everest in Asia at 29,028 feet above sea level. Oceans, lakes, rivers, and all other bodies of water and ice make up a part of the Earth called the hydrosphere. Land bodies surrounded by water make up the continents. Together, land and water surfaces that support life are called the biosphere.

The chemical composition of the Earth is 46.6% oxygen, 27.72% silicon, 8.13% aluminum, 5.0% iron, 3.60% calcium, 2.83% sodium, 2.59% potassium, 2.09% magnesium, 0.44% titanium, and all other elements total 1.0%. A geologist is a person who studies the Earth and its contents. It is through the work of geologists that the chemical composition of the Earth has been established.

3. ROCKS

The hard, solid part of the Earth's surface is called rock. Rock may be exposed from its soil cover when highways are cut through hillsides or mountain regions. River channels or shorelines frequently cut through rock beds. Some mountain chains expose rock beds when weathering exposes the rock base. Rocks are useful in many ways as granite (igneous), marble (metamorphic), or limestone (sedimentary) can be used in buildings, dams, highways, or the making of cement. Metals like aluminum, iron, lead, and tin are removed from rock that is called ore.

4. MINERALS

Minerals are the most common form of solid material found in the Earth's crust. Even soil contains bits of minerals that have broken away from its rock source. Minerals are dug from the Earth and are used to make a variety of products. To be considered a mineral, the element must be found in nature and never have been a part of any living organism. Atoms making up the element or substance must be arranged in regular patterns to form crystals and must have the same chemical makeup as the area where it is found.

5. ORES

Ores are mineral deposits high enough in an element content that it would be economically feasible to be mined and sold for a profit. Ore deposits are located from geological knowledge about crustal movements and ore formations along with sophisticated instruments and a lot of luck. Once the ore has been located, the mining process is based on the most economical method to remove the highest amount of the mineral from the rock with the least amount of environmental damage. Processes include leaching or separating the mineral from the rock by heat, brine solutions, evaporation of seawater, or chemically removing the metal from the ore.

6. EARTH'S MAGNETISM

Imaginary lines curve from the North pole to the South pole, making up the Earth's magnetic field. The Earth acts as though its center is a large magnet. These imaginary lines aid the compass needle to determine directions based on the Earth's natural magnetic field. Scientists have identified enormous electric currents that are deep within the Earth as being responsible for the Earth's magnetic fields.

☞ Drill: Physics and Chemistry of the Earth

DIRECTIONS: Carefully read and answer each of the following questions which are based on the information which you have just read.

57. The Earth spins around on its
    (1) equator.
    (2) poles.
    (3) axis.
    (4) orbit.
    (5) rotation.

58. An axis is
    (1) a definite line.
    (2) a connecting line at the equator.
    (3) a connecting line between the poles.
    (4) a connecting line between orbits.
    (5) a pole.

59. The Earth has
    (1) no moon.
    (2) two moons.
    (3) three moons.
    (4) four moons.
    (5) one moon.

60. An orbit is the
    (1) spinning motion of the Earth.
    (2) axis of the Earth.
    (3) movement and position of the Earth around the sun.
    (4) gravity action of the Earth.
    (5) time of year.

61. The percentage of the Earth's surface that is water is
    (1) 30%.   (4) 90%.
    (2) 50%.   (5) 25%.
    (3) 70%.

62. The highest point in the world is located in
    (1) North America.   (4) Africa.
    (2) Europe.   (5) Antarctica.
    (3) Asia.

63. The highest altitude on Earth is Mount Everest, which is
    (1) 28,028 ft. above sea level.
    (2) 29,028 ft. above sea level.
    (3) 29,208 ft. above sea level.
    (4) 28,208 ft. above sea level.
    (5) 20,928 ft. above sea level.

64. The hydrosphere is
    (1) land surrounded by bodies of water.
    (2) areas of atmosphere with water present.
    (3) oceans, land, and lakes.
    (4) oceans, lakes, and rivers, and all other bodies of water and ice.
    (5) where glaciers are present.

65. The biosphere is
    (1) land and water surfaces that support life.
    (2) land that supports life.
    (3) living parts of the atmosphere.
    (4) water surfaces that support life.
    (5) the highest level of the atmosphere.

66. How much greater is the Earth's oxygen content compared to silicon content?
     (1)   18.8%   (4)   8.9%
     (2)   19.8%   (5)   18.88%
     (3)   21.1%

67. A geologist is a person who studies
     (1)   geography.   (4)   chemical composition.
     (2)   rocks only.   (5)   soil.
     (3)   gaseous composition.

68. The element that makes up the greater percentage of the Earth's atmosphere is
     (1)   oxygen.   (4)   magnesium.
     (2)   silicon.   (5)   carbon dioxide.
     (3)   calcium.

69. The solid part of the Earth is called
     (1)   ore.   (4)   metals.
     (2)   rock.   (5)   air.
     (3)   highways.

70. Igneous rock forms are commonly called
     (1)   marble.   (4)   cement.
     (2)   limestone.   (5)   stalagmites.
     (3)   granite.

71. Metamorphic rock forms are commonly called
     (1)   cement.   (4)   limestone
     (2)   iron.   (5)   sandstone.
     (3)   marble.

72. The sedimentary rock forms are commonly called
     (1)   limestone.   (4)   cement.
     (2)   granite.   (5)   conglomerate.
     (3)   marble.

73. Minerals are found
     (1)   in the atmosphere.   (4)   only in your body.
     (2)   in the Earth's crust. (5)   None of the above.
     (3)   at the ocean bottom.

74. To be considered a mineral, the substance must never have been a part of a living organism and must be found in
    (1) water.
    (2) rock.
    (3) ore.
    (4) nature.
    (5) sand.

75. Elements are made up of
    (1) atoms.
    (2) particles.
    (3) minerals.
    (4) soil.
    (5) elementary.

76. Minerals are the most common form of _____ found in the Earth's crust.
    (1) aquatic material
    (2) solid material
    (3) living organisms
    (4) soil material
    (5) All of the above.

77. Ores are
    (1) minerals beneath Earth's surface.
    (2) mineral deposits high enough in element content to be profitable to dig.
    (3) materials that are removed from minerals.
    (4) mineral deposits low in element content.
    (5) used in water.

78. One process used to separate mineral from rock is
    (1) heating the rock.
    (2) chemical evaporation.
    (3) environmental leaching.
    (4) boiling seawater.
    (5) freezing the rock.

79. Mineral deposits are located by studying
    (1) mining areas.
    (2) crustal movements.
    (3) geographical rises.
    (4) ocean beds.
    (5) volcanic eruptions.

80. The Earth acts as though its center is a large
    (1) rock.
    (2) black hole.
    (3) magnet.
    (4) curve.
    (5) empty space.

81.   Imaginary lines curve from
       (1)   east to west.
       (2)   north to east.
       (3)   north to west.
       (4)   south to east.
       (5)   north to south.

82.   The cause of the Earth's magnetic field is
       (1)   enormous currents.
       (2)   space satellites.
       (3)   a lost secret.
       (4)   in the Earth's crust.
       (5)   unknown.

C. EVOLUTION AND CRUSTAL PROCESS

1. CHANGING OF THE EARTH

The moon's gravitational pull produces tides both in the ocean and in the Earth's solid crust. Throughout time, slow evolutionary changes have taken place and continue to take place. As shorelines are inched away in one location, mud and silt build up in other areas, adding to the land surface. With all these changes occurring slowly over long periods of time, little difference can be recorded as to variations in land or water surfaces of the Earth.

2. CONTINENTAL DRIFTS

The continental shelves are zones of relatively shallow portions of the continent extending out under the oceans. The continental shelves or edges are a part of the continent they adjoin and the edge of the shelf is the true boundary of the continent. The continental shelf is not a small area. In some areas, they may contain the same area as the size of the former Soviet Union under the waters of the ocean. The shelves were formed eighteen to twenty thousand years ago due to the melting of the glaciers, along with time, wave-cutting terraces, erosion and sedimentation—all are part of the formation explanation. At the edge of the shelf, the continental slope leads downward to the deep ocean. At the bottom of the slope, an area of deposition called the continental rise may form a gentler slope. Other features included in the continental margin are trenches, ridges, and submarine canyons. A reef is a rocky or coral elevation dangerous to the surface navigation which may or may not be uncovered by water. A rocky reef is always detached from shore; a coral reef may or may not be connected to the shoreline.

3. NATURE'S RECYCLING

Nature's method of recycling is evident through many processes. Some processes are the water cycle, carbon cycle, oxygen cycle, and energy cycle as demonstrated by prey and predators. These concepts are explained through the following drawings.

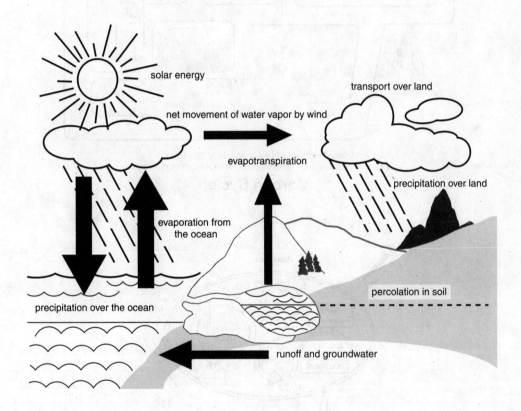

solar energy

net movement of water vapor by wind

transport over land

evapotranspiration

precipitation over land

evaporation from
the ocean

percolation in soil

precipitation over the ocean

runoff and groundwater

The Hydrologic (Water) Cycle

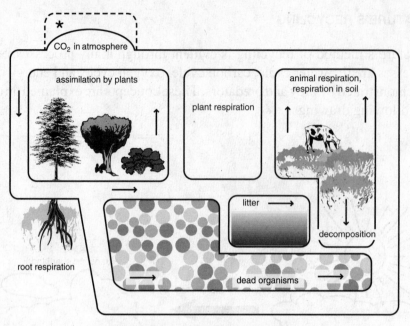

* A seasonal change in the atmospheric CO_2 levels
is caused by variations in the distribution of vegetation on the earth.

Carbon Cycle

Oxygen Cycle

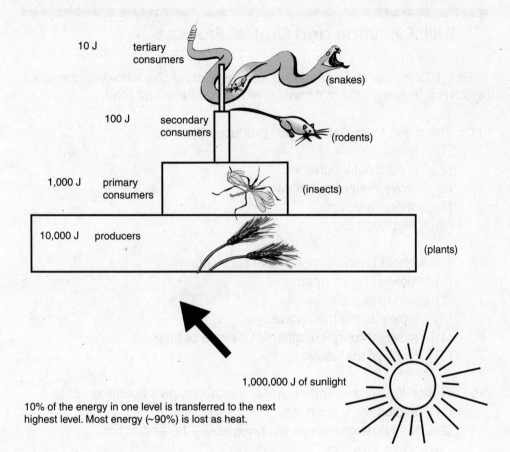

10 J — tertiary consumers (snakes)

100 J — secondary consumers (rodents)

1,000 J — primary consumers (insects)

10,000 J — producers (plants)

1,000,000 J of sunlight

10% of the energy in one level is transferred to the next highest level. Most energy (~90%) is lost as heat.

Energy Cycle

☞ Drill: Evolution and Crustal Process

DIRECTIONS: Carefully read and answer each of the following questions which are based on the information which you have just read.

83. The moon's gravitational pull produces the
    (1) tides.
    (2) solid crustal surfaces.
    (3) movement of surface water.
    (4) shore build-up.
    (5) weather.

84. Throughout time, changes have taken place
    (1) slowly and stopped.
    (2) slowly and continually.
    (3) slowly along the shores.
    (4) slowly throughout different periods of time.
    (5) None of the above.

85. The shifting of the Earth's surface locations gives some proof to
    (1) evolutionary changes.
    (2) land changes which will bring about the end of time.
    (3) shore build-up.
    (4) shore erosion.
    (5) the Big Bang Theory.

86. Shorelines are made of
    (1) mud and silt.   (4) silt and soil.
    (2) sand and mud.   (5) sand and snow.
    (3) rock and silt.

87. Terracing, erosion, and sedimentation are responsible for forming the
    (1) continental rise.   (4) continental margin.
    (2) continental slope.   (5) None of the above.
    (3) continental shelf.

88. An area that is always detached from a shore would be a
    (1) peninsula.   (4) marginal reef.
    (2) coral reef.   (5) rocky reef.
    (3) barrier reef.

89. A shelf that leads downward is called a
    (1) continental drop.
    (2) continental reef.
    (3) continental slope.
    (4) continental margin.
    (5) All of the above.

90. When compared, the water cycle, carbon cycle, oxygen cycle, and energy cycle have
    (1) only a few minor differences.
    (2) only one major difference.
    (3) nothing that can be compared among the four cycles.
    (4) evidence of recycling.
    (5) many major problems.

91. All, except the _____ cycle, use various forms of life.
    (1) energy
    (2) oxygen
    (3) carbon
    (4) rinse
    (5) water

92. The two cycles that involve gaseous exchanges are
    (1) carbon and energy.
    (2) energy and oxygen.
    (3) carbon and water.
    (4) oxygen and carbon.
    (5) oxygen and water.

D. SURFACE PROCESSES

1. ATMOSPHERE

Air, an odorless and colorless gas, surrounds the Earth and extends approximately 1,000 miles above the surface of the Earth. This is called the atmosphere. It is made up of 78% nitrogen and 21% oxygen; the remaining 1% consists mainly of argon, water vapor, dust particles, and other gases. Cloud formations float in the lowest portion of the atmosphere, called the troposphere. Weather occurrences are formed in the troposphere. It is also the more dense portion of the atmosphere, followed by the stratosphere, mesosphere and exosphere.

The ionosphere is a belt of radiation surrounding the Earth. Outside the atmosphere, in what used to be considered "empty" space, man's satellites in 1958 disclosed the existence of magnetism. The aurora borealis or "northern dawn/lights" is a beautiful display of moving, colored streamers or folds of light. Its counterpart in the Antarctic is the aurora australis, or "southern dawn/lights," both connected to the Earth's magnetic field or lines of force. During magnetic storms, aurora borealis can be seen as far south as Boston and New York.

2. WATER

The most important source of sediment is Earth and rock material carried to the sea by rivers and streams; the same materials may also have been transported by glaciers and winds. Other sources are volcanic ash and lava, shells and skeletons of organisms, chemical precipitates formed in seawater, and particles from outer space.

Water is a most unusual substance because it exists on the surface of the Earth in its three physical states: ice, water, and water vapor. There are other substances that might exist in a solid and liquid or gaseous state at temperatures normally found at the Earth's surface, but there are fewer substances which occur in all three states.

Water is odorless, tasteless, and colorless. It is the only substance known to exist in a natural state as a solid, liquid, or gas on the surface of the Earth. It is a universal solvent. Water does not corrode, rust, burn, or separate into its components easily. It is chemically indestructible. It can corrode almost any metal and erode the most solid rock. A unique property of water is that it expands and floats on water when frozen or in the solid state. Water has a freezing point of 0°C (or 32°F) and a boiling point of 100°C (or 212°F). Water has the capacity for absorbing great quantities of heat with relatively little increase in temperature. When distilled, water is a poor conductor of electricity but when salt is added, it is a good conductor of electricity.

Sunlight is the source of energy for temperature change, evaporation, and currents for water movement through the atmosphere. Sunlight controls the rate of photosynthesis for all marine plants, which are directly or indirectly the source of food for all marine animals. Migration, breeding, and other behaviors of marine animals are affected by light.

Water, as the ocean or sea, is blue because of the molecular scattering of the sunlight. Blue light, being of short wavelength, is scattered more effectively than light of longer wave lengths. Variations in color may be caused by particles suspended in the water, water depth, cloud cover, temperature, and other variable factors. Heavy concentrations of dissolved materials cause a yellowish hue, while algae will cause the water to look green. Heavy populations of plant and animal materials will cause the water to look brown.

3. WEATHERING

Weathering is the natural wearing away of rock or soil due to chemical or physical actions on these Earth surfaces. This occurs very slowly over a long period of time. Through chemical weathering, rocks break down as oxygen, carbon dioxide, and water vapor react with rock until it is finally changed into soil. Physical weathering occurs in dry regions by the wind action constantly wearing away the surface of the rock.

4. EROSION

The first concept of erosion was that natural weathering that we call erosion led to the formation of mountains and mountain chains. The main causes of erosion are air and/or water movement across rock or soil, changes in the temperature, or any combination of these factors. Chemical erosion can occur as carbon dioxide and water vapor are removed from dead organic matter. These are all natural forms of erosion. Man can cause erosion with poor crop-planting procedures, lack of crop rotation, and the cutting of trees without planning or replacement.

5. TEMPERATURE

Temperature is controlled by the position of the Earth on its axis and its distance from the sun at rotation. At the equator, the air would be warmest and always pushing upward while cold air would be flowing in to be warmed. The constant changing of air will cause changes in the temperature.

6. PRESSURE

Air pressure also plays an important role in the movement of air and the changing of air temperatures and weather changes. Next to the equator, a low pressure cell is formed because the air is warmer, lighter, and moving upward. The low pressure is a result of the molecules of air being further apart. The colder air has closer air molecules; thus, a high pressure cell is formed. Extreme weather conditions, such as flooding, may result when both low cells and high cells occupy the same air space.

7. CLIMATE

Climate is the usual weather that occurs in a general area over a period of time. The study of climate is called climatology. When referring to climate, one takes into consideration air temperature, wind speed, sunshine, humidity, amount of precipitation, air pressure, and general geographic conditions.

Climate has a direct effect upon living organisms and the type(s) of life that can exist in the region being considered. Climate also affects our method of transportation, outdoor activities, choices for employment, type of clothing, type of housing, and food naturally available or that can be grown.

8. ALTERNATE ENERGY FORMS

About 90% of today's energy is supplied from fossil fuels as crude oil, natural gas, and coal. These materials are a result of nature providing such supplies for man's use. Thus, these are considered our nonrenewable resources as they cannot be replaced after they have been used. With conservation and suitable alternate energy sources, our natural resources will last longer and these fossil fuels can be usable for many more years. Alternate energy sources include methanol, ethanol, wood and wood wastes, garbage and plant material, corn, other grains, solar energy, photovoltaic cells, hydroelectricity, nuclear power, wind energy (windmills), tidal energy, geothermal energy (geysers), and fusion using nuclear waste materials.

☞ Drill: Surface Processes

DIRECTIONS: Carefully read and answer each of the following questions which are based on the information which you have just read.

93.   The atmosphere is partially made up of
    (1)   78% oxygen.   (4)   1% nitrogen.
    (2)   78% carbon dioxide.   (5)   78% nitrogen.
    (3)   21% argon.

94.   Cloud formations float in the lowest portion of the atmosphere, called the
    (1)   stratosphere.   (4)   exosphere.
    (2)   mesophere.   (5)   ozone layer.
    (3)   troposphere.

95.   An odorless, colorless gas that surrounds the Earth is commonly called
    (1)   nitrogen.   (4)   air.
    (2)   oxygen.   (5)   carbon dioxide.
    (3)   argon.

96. A belt of radiation surrounding the Earth is called the
    (1) stratosphere.   (4) mesophere.
    (2) ionosphere.   (5) ozone layer.
    (3) trophosphere.

97. Aurora borealis, the beautiful display of colored streamers, is commonly called
    (1) southern lights.   (4) eastern lights.
    (2) western lights.   (5) None of the above.
    (3) northern lights.

98. The aurora australis is seen in the
    (1) Arctic region.   (4) northern region.
    (2) Antarctic region.   (5) eastern region.
    (3) southern region.

99. Sediment is transported by
    (1) oceans and trees.   (4) earth and rock.
    (2) rivers and streams.   (5) wind.
    (3) lava and streams.

100. Sediment can be formed from
    (1) water and snow.
    (2) snails.
    (3) shells and skeletons of organisms.
    (4) volcanic ash and rock from Mars.
    (5) dirt.

101. One of the few substances that can exist in all three states is
    (1) nitrogen.   (4) oxygen.
    (2) sediment.   (5) water.
    (3) soil.

102. The three physical states matter can exist in are
    (1) solid, liquid, and gas.   (4) soil, liquid, and gas.
    (2) solid, gas, and water.   (5) solid, liquid, and air.
    (3) solid, liquid, and oxygen.

103. Water can corrode and erode
    (1) any solid.   (4) when distilled.
    (2) the most solid rock.   (5) All of the above.
    (3) only metals.

104. Water can
    (1)   corrode, rust, burn, and separate.
    (2)   freeze at 100°C.
    (3)   be destroyed by chemical means.
    (4)   expand and float.
    (5)   boil at 32°F.

105. When salt water is distilled, it
    (1)   is a poor conductor of electricity.
    (2)   is doubled in power to conduct electricity.
    (3)   is a very good conductor of electricity.
    (4)   is not able to conduct electricity.
    (5)   converts electricity into stored energy.

106. Temperature change, rate of photosynthesis, and migration are all
    (1)   affected by sunlight.
    (2)   least affected by sunlight.
    (3)   most affected by sunlight.
    (4)   not controlled by sunlight.
    (5)   not affected by sunlight.

107. The source of evaporation is the
    (1)   movement of air.   (4)   currents.
    (2)   atmosphere.   (5)   ozone.
    (3)   sunlight.

108. An indirect source of food for all marine plants is
    (1)   temperature changes.
    (2)   sunlight.
    (3)   breeding.
    (4)   migration behaviors of aquatic life.
    (5)   water.

109. Marine animal behavior is greatly affected by
    (1)   water movement.   (4)   migration.
    (2)   sunlight.   (5)   warm weather.
    (3)   photosynthesis.

110. According to the passage, water, as in the ocean or sea, is
    (1)   blue-green.   (4)   blue.
    (2)   red-brown.   (5)   green.
    (3)   yellowish.

111. Water displays a blue color because of
    (1)   scattered sunlight.
    (2)   heavy plant growth.
    (3)   organic material in water.
    (4)   lack of organic material in water and presence of inorganics.
    (5)   dyes.

112. A control of water color is the
    (1)   population present.   (4)   lack of water movement.
    (2)   amount of oxygen.   (5)   level of pollution.
    (3)   types of minerals present.

113. The natural wearing away of rock or soil due to chemical or physical actions is called
    (1)   weather.   (4)   corrosion.
    (2)   weathering.   (5)   fading.
    (3)   erosion.

114. Rocks break down as oxygen, carbon dioxide, and water vapor due to
    (1)   physical weathering.   (4)   chemical weathering.
    (2)   chemical weather.   (5)   None of the above.
    (3)   physical weather.

115. Physical weathering occurs in
    (1)   wet, windy regions.   (4)   dry, hot regions.
    (2)   dry, windy regions.   (5)   dry, stagnant regions.
    (3)   dry, cold regions.

116. Man can control erosion by
    (1)   adding chemicals to the soil.
    (2)   cutting trees and clearing land.
    (3)   rotating crops.
    (4)   removing dead organic matter.
    (5)   never rotating crops.

117. Erosion actually
    (1)   destroys the Earth.
    (2)   does not affect the Earth.
    (3)   leads to forest growth.
    (4)   only occurs with water movement.
    (5)   creates soil.

118. Erosion is a form of natural weathering that
    (1) led to the forming of mountain chains.
    (2) formed only a few mountains out west.
    (3) was proven false.
    (4) is caused by chemical, physical, and psychological means.
    (5) has no important impact on the environment.

119. Temperature is controlled by
    (1) weather.   (4) pressure.
    (2) position of the axis.   (5) the sun.
    (3) time.

120. One of the factors that causes a change in temperature is
    (1) time.   (4) rainy weather.
    (2) changing air currents.   (5) the moon.
    (3) wind blowing hard.

121. Air is the warmest at the
    (1) North pole.   (4) axis.
    (2) South pole.   (5) equator.
    (3) poles.

122. Air temperature, movement of air, and weather changes are all affected by
    (1) air pressure.   (4) high pressure cells.
    (2) low pressure only.   (5) clouds.
    (3) high pressure only.

123. Colder air has close air molecules that form a
    (1) low pressure cell.   (4) dry condition.
    (2) high pressure cell.   (5) None of the above.
    (3) flooding condition.

124. Warmer air has molecules of air that are far apart. Therefore, it produces
    (1) a low pressure cell.   (4) dry conditions.
    (2) a high pressure cell.   (5) not conditions.
    (3) rainy weather.

125. A low pressure cell is the result of the molecules
    (1) blowing upward.   (2) being close together.
    (3) being far apart.   (4) bouncing up and down.
    (5) blowing downward.

126. Usual weather that occurs in a general area is called
    (1) rain.   (4) conditions.
    (2) snow.   (5) stability.
    (3) climate.

127. The study of climate is called
    (1) air temperature.   (4) astrology.
    (2) geography.   (5) meterology.
    (3) climatology.

128. Climate affects all of the following except:
    (1) number of human chromosomes.
    (2) transportation.
    (3) organisms.
    (4) outdoor activities.
    (5) living conditions.

129. An alternate energy source is
    (1) crude oil.   (4) coal.
    (2) ethanol.   (5) petroleum.
    (3) natural gas.

130. Fossil fuels are considered to be nonrenewable because
    (1) they are easily and quickly replaced.
    (2) they can be replaced within a normal lifetime.
    (3) they can never be replaced.
    (4) they can be replaced with an alternate energy source.
    (5) they do not need to be renewed because they are abundant.

131. A geyser is considered
    (1) wind energy.   (4) nuclear energy.
    (2) solar energy.   (5) hydrolic energy.
    (3) geothermal energy.

132. Crude oil, natural gas, and coal are called
    (1) nuclear energy sources.
    (2) alternate energy sources.

    (3)   natural sources.

    (4)   renewable energy sources.

    (5)   fossil fuel sources.

133. Conservation of nonrenewable energy sources means
    (1)   not using fossil fuels.
    (2)   using less fossil fuels.
    (3)   using all fossil fuels as they are found.
    (4)   recycling fossil fuels.
    (5)   None of the above.

E. EARTH'S HAZARDS AND RESOURCES

1. EARTHQUAKES

Earthquakes are vibrations due to the movements within and beneath the Earth's crust. They occur as a result of faulting or other structural processes happening as a result of a strain on the rocks at the edge of the crust. A long series of quakes with none being greater than the others is called an Earth swarm and occurs near volcanic regions. Imperial Valley, California, is known for having Earth swarms. Earth tremors are vibrations of low intensity and can be felt only by those located directly over the affected area.

Earthquake intensity is measured on a scale from 0 to 9, where each number represents an energy release ten times that of the number. This energy release is measured by the "Richter Scale" as it was introduced by Charles F. Richter in 1935. Richter was an American seismologist. About 80% of Earthquake energy is released in the areas bordering the vast Pacific Ocean, with 15% released in an east-west band across the Mediterranean. The remaining 5% occur sporadically throughout the remaining parts of the world bordering large bodies of water.

2. VOLCANOES

Volcanoes are a natural phenomenon with their effects confined to a small area. About 500 volcanoes are known to have been active, with two-thirds of them in the Pacific Ocean area. Modern research into volcanoes and their role in forming much of the Earth's crust began with the French geologist Jean Etienne Guettard in the mid-eighteenth century.

Volcanoes discharge a large amount of carbon dioxide into the air; the weathering of rocks utilizes carbon dioxide. This presents a pair of mechanisms for possible long-term climatic changes. A period of greater than normal volcanic action might initiate a warming of the Earth. The mountains built by the volcanic ash might expose large areas of new and unweathered rock to the air, which will lower the carbon dioxide levels, thus reducing the atmospheric temperature.

3. OCEANS

It is estimated the world's oceans extend over 328 million cubic miles with the greatest depth being 36,198 feet off the coast of Guam. The deepest of all oceans is the Pacific Ocean, averaging 14,048 feet. The Baltic Sea is only 180.4 feet deep. Sedimentary rock at the bottom of the oceans has been dated at 3 billion years old with the water dated at 4 billion years old.

The oceans supply man with a means of transportation, habitat for aquatic life that is used for food, a source of minerals, and a means of weather control. Also, the ocean offers various sources of energy for consumption and use in the future. Presently, oil and gas are being derived from the ocean as sources of energy. Much research is presently being conducted as to the feasibility of waves or water of the ocean being used to produce power. Also, the ocean is being used to simulate islands of lush plant growth to increase the photosynthesis process as a possible way to reduce the depletion of the ozone layer.

4. HOT SPRINGS

Hot springs are naturally occurring bodies of water that are warmer than their surrounding air. Hot springs (thermal springs) occur in regions of faulted or folded rock due to volcanic action. The water that comes from underground where the rocks are hot will produce hot water that rises to the Earth's surface in the form of a spring. Not all hot springs are a direct result of volcanoes, but are produced by geysers.

5. MIGRATION

Migration is the movement of people or animals from one area to another area. Migration occurs because of seasonal changes, wars, famines, floods, volcanic eruptions, weather, and other natural disasters for the purpose of survival. Migration practices began with prehistoric man. Little is known about the pattern of movement or why migrations took place. It is believed the first migrations were to escape the spread of the great glaciers and ice sheets. The most common application of migration is that of birds and other animals moving to survive winters or for the purpose of reproduction as illustrated by the salmon moving into the colder waters.

6. FLOODING

Flooding is the natural occurrence of an extremely large amount of water flowing into a given area faster than it can leave the area. As a result, the stream, lake, or river will overflow its natural level. Estuary zones and sand dunes are natural flood control devices. Man-made devices include dams and sandbagging to control flood waters. The control of flood waters is important to the survival of coastal habitats for wading marsh birds, birds of prey, migratory birds, water fowl, and other aquatic life, as well as man.

7. WATER-BASED FORMATIONS

The commonly seen waves on the surface of water are caused principally by wind. When a breeze blows over calm water, it forms small ripples or capillary waves. As the wind speed increases, larger, more visible gravity waves are formed. When the wind reaches high speeds, whitecaps are formed. However, submarine Earthquakes, volcanic eruptions, and tides also cause waves. Waves will always break parallel to the shoreline.

The tide is the continuous cycle of alternating rise and fall of the sea level observed along the coastlines and bodies of water connected to the sea. On most coastlines, the cycle occurs about every 12 hours. Along the Gulf coastline, a tidal cycle can occur about every 24–25 hours. The rise and fall of sea level observed along coastlines is produced by waves of extreme length; high water is the crest of the wave; low water is the trough. Tides can be predicted once observations have been mathematically related to the positions of Earth, moon, and sun. Tides are caused by the gravitational interaction between the sun, moon, and Earth. The moon exercises the greatest influence on our tide; although its mass is much less than the sun's, it is closer to the Earth and its tide-producing effect is more than twice as great.

The maximum height reached by a rising tide is called high water. This is due solely to the periodic tidal force, but at times, the meteorological effects of severe storms or strong winds may be superimposed on the normal tide to produce high water.

Low water is the minimum height reached by a falling tide. Usually this is due solely to the influence of a periodic tidal force, but sometimes the influence of severe storms or strong winds may be superimposed on the normal tide to produce low water.

Tides are classified as semidiurnal, diurnal, and mixed. Areas having semidiurnal tides have two high waters and two low waters each day; this is the most common type. Diurnal tides consist of one high water and one low water each day. Tides are classified as mixed when they are diurnal on some days and semidiurnal on others.

Hurricanes occur when the atmospheric conditions, tail movements, winds, and pressure change severely. Hurricanes begin with winds moving in a circular motion over bodies of water, picking up both speed and rainy weather conditions. When a hurricane approaches a coastline, the sea level will go 20 feet above normal tide level. The months of June through November are considered hurricane season. August, September, and October normally have more hurricanes documented than any other months with September having the greatest number of hurricanes. May and December, on rare occasions, have logged hurricanes. Hurricanes can cause both property damage and personal damage when they move from the water to land surfaces with a tornado resulting from its wind force as it moves further inland.

A typhoon is a severe storm over the oceans that is made of rain, wind, and water and will affect tidal movements of shorelines of islands near their occurrences.

Currents are water movements in horizontal or vertical flow occurring at differing depths of the water. Currents stabilize the climate of adjacent land areas, preventing extremes of temperatures. Currents are also influenced/affected by the moon and its position relative to the equator.

Density differences may produce both horizontal and vertical movement of water, causing modifications to the wind-driven surface currents. Water tends to flow from an area of low density to an area of high density. Water may tend to become of greater density as the temperature decreases.

Fog is a hydrometeor which consists of a visible collection of minute water droplets suspended in the atmosphere near the Earth's surface. It will interfere with the ability to see at a distance over the area that it covers. It is caused by atmospheric humidity and a warm temperature layer being transported over a cold body of water or land surface.

8. ECONOMICS OF EARTH'S RESOURCES

Conservation is the protection and wise management of Earth's resources or natural resources, for the benefit of not only man, but all living things. Without wise practices of conservation and concern for the quality of the environment, all natural resources necessary for life, such as air, animals, energy, minerals, plants, soil, water, and other elemental forms would be damaged, wasted, or destroyed. With greater conservation enforcement, the cost of living will be lower for everyone and more ideal surroundings will be present. The Earth not only has limited resources, but the demands are greater as populations increase, which means there must be a wiser use of Earth's resources if they are to last as long as man or if man is to survive. The cost of man's poor resource management can be life itself.

☞ Drill: Earth's Hazards and Resources

DIRECTIONS: Carefully read and answer each of the following questions which are based on the information which you have just read.

134. Vibrations due to movements within and beneath the Earth's crust are called
    (1) shifting plates.   (4) fault lines.
    (2) volcanic eruptions.   (5) seismic encounters.
    (3) earthquakes.

135. Earth swarms are
    (1) a long series of quakes with none being greater than the others.
    (2) a group of quakes which occur at the same time.
    (3) large tidal waves that occur because of an Earthquake.
    (4) bees which form colonies along the fault line.
    (5) aftershocks.

136. Imperial Valley, California, is known for having
    (1) Earth swarms.   (4) Earthquakes.
    (2) Earth trimmers.   (5) None of the above.
    (3) volcanic regions.

137. If vibrations are felt directly over the area affected, then one has experienced a(n)
    (1) volcano.   (4) Earth trimmer.
    (2) Earthquake.   (5) Earth tremor.
    (3) Earth swarm.

138. Earthquake intensity is measured on a scale called the
    (1) Friction Scale.   (4) Pitcher Scale.
    (2) Vibration Scale.   (5) Pitch Scale.
    (3) Richter Scale.

139. _____ % of the energy of earthquakes is released in areas bordering the vast Pacific Ocean.
    (1) 8   (4) .8
    (2) 18   (5) 81
    (3) 80

140. Earthquakes are measured on a scale of
    (1) 0-9.   (4) 0-1,000.
    (2) 1-10.   (5) 1-5
    (3) 10-100.

141. The Richter Scale was introduced in
    (1) 1934.   (4) 1955.
    (2) 1844.   (5) 1975.
    (3) 1935.

142. Two-thirds of all known active volcanos have occurred in the
    (1) Atlantic Ocean.   (4) Red Sea.
    (2) Pacific Ocean.   (5) Baltic Sea.
    (3) Gulf of Mexico.

143. The number of known active volcanoes is about
    (1) 700.   (4) 600.
    (2) 900.   (5) 400.
    (3) 500.

144. Modern research of volcanoes was begun by Jean Etienne Guettard in the mid-eighteenth century as he analyzed volcanoes' role in
    (1) forming much of the Earth's crust.
    (2) forming the plates the Earth now rests on.
    (3) formation of Earth from atmospheric wastes.
    (4) rock formations.
    (5) changes in the atmosphere.

145. Volcanoes discharge a large amount of
    (1) random types of gas.   (4) carbon dioxide.
    (2) acids.   (5) mud.
    (3) oxygen.

146. A period of greater than normal volcanic action might
    (1) lower carbon dioxide levels, thus reducing temperature.

(2) lower carbon dioxide levels, thus raising temperature.

(3) warm the Earth immediately and for an extended period.

(4) initiate a warming of the Earth.

(5) cool the Earth.

147. Mountains built by volcanic ash might expose large areas of new and unweathered rock to the air, causing

(1) a warming of the Earth for an extended period.

(2) an increase in the carbon dioxide levels, thus raising the temperature.

(3) a decrease in the carbon dioxide levels, thus lowering temperature.

(4) a rise in carbon dioxide levels, thus lowering temperature.

(5) All of the above.

148. It is estimated that the world's oceans extend over

(1) 323 cubic million miles.　(4) 328 million cubic miles.

(2) 328 million miles.　(5) 328 cubic miles.

(3) 323 million miles.

149. The trench with the greatest depth is located off the coast of

(1) Cuba.　(4) Guatemala.

(2) Asia.　(5) Iraq.

(3) Guam.

150. The deepest of the oceans is the

(1) Indian Ocean.　(4) Baltic Ocean.

(2) Pacific Ocean.　(5) North Sea.

(3) Atlantic Ocean.

151. Water in the ocean dates about

(1) 4 million years old.　(4) 4 thousand years old.

(2) 4 billion years old.　(5) 4 hundred thousand years old.

(3) 4 trillion years old.

152. The _____ is very shallow, measuring only 180.4 feet deep.

(1) Baltic Sea.　(4) Arctic Ocean.

(2) Baltic Ocean.　(5) Pacific Ocean.

(3) Atlantic Ocean.

153. Presently oil and _____ are being derived from the ocean as sources of energy.
    (1) minerals
    (2) hydroelectric power
    (3) gas
    (4) food
    (5) fish

154. The oceans supply man with a variety of things, including
    (1) a place for water sports.
    (2) a natural site for photosynthesis.
    (3) a means of transportation.
    (4) All of the above.
    (5) None of the above.

155. The ocean can be of assistance to the maintaining of the ozone layer by
    (1) being a breeding area for more fish.
    (2) being a site of increased photosynthesis.
    (3) acting as a weather controller.
    (4) decreasing evaporation processes.
    (5) creating ozone.

156. Hot springs are
    (1) located in Mississippi.
    (2) man-made bodies of water.
    (3) located only in mountainous areas.
    (4) naturally occurring bodies of water.
    (5) found in arid areas.

157. Hot springs occur mainly
    (1) in colder regions of the nation.
    (2) in warmer regions of the nation.
    (3) in faulted or folded rock and tornado regions.
    (4) in faulted or folded rock and volcanic regions.
    (5) All of the above.

158. Some hot springs are produced by
    (1) wheezers.
    (2) underground seepages.
    (3) geysers.
    (4) naturally occurring water rocks.
    (5) whirlpools.

159. Migration occurs because of
     (1)   famines.
     (2)   the need for cold weather.
     (3)   the need to escape cavemen.
     (4)   the need to develop a pattern of movement to be studied.
     (5)   the need to escape floods.

160. The most common animal that practices migration is the
     (1)   buffalo.   (4)   bird.
     (2)   crane.   (5)   elephant.
     (3)   cow.

161. Migration is the
     (1)   movement of a family from house to house.
     (2)   movement of people or animals from one area to another.
     (3)   movement of birds to reproduce.
     (4)   movement of people to room together.
     (5)   None of the above.

162. One natural flood control device is the
     (1)   man-made dam.   (4)   sand dune.
     (2)   sandbagged river.   (5)   beaver.
     (3)   flood gate.

163. The control of flood waters is important for the
     (1)   a survival of coastal habitats.
     (2)   survival of wading birds.
     (3)   providing of recreational areas.
     (4)   All of the above.
     (5)   None of the above.

164. An extremely large amount of water flowing into a given area faster than
     it can leave the area describes a
     (1)   tornado.   (4)   flood.
     (2)   hurricane.   (5)   tidal wave.
     (3)   volcano.

165. Capillary waves occur in
     (1)   the ocean.   (4)   all types of water.
     (2)   the sea.   (5)   sequences of five.
     (3)   a pond.

166. Whitecaps usually begin to occur when the wind speed is
    (1)   high speed.
    (2)   medium speed.
    (3)   slow speed.
    (4)   varying.
    (5)   diminishing.

167. Waves are normally caused by
    (1)   the moon.
    (2)   the sun.
    (3)   the Earth's rotation.
    (4)   the current.
    (5)   the wind.

168. Tides are caused by
    (1)   the moon.
    (2)   the Earth.
    (3)   the sun.
    (4)   All of the above.
    (5)   None of the above.

169. The continuous cycle of alternating rise and fall of the sea level observed along the coastlines and bodies of water connected to the sea is called
    (1)   the tide.
    (2)   moon exercises.
    (3)   sun exercises.
    (4)   a waterfall.
    (5)   a tidal wave.

170. A tidal cycle along the Gulf coastline will occur about every
    (1)   12 hours.
    (2)   24 hours.
    (3)   28 hours.
    (4)   36 hours.
    (5)   6 hours.

171. Tides are caused by the gravitational interaction between the sun, moon, and
    (1)   Mars.
    (2)   the oceans.
    (3)   the mountains.
    (4)   Earth.
    (5)   Jupiter.

172. Low water is the
    (1)   trough.
    (2)   crest of the wave.
    (3)   lowest tidal cycle.
    (4)   bottom of the water.
    (5)   crest.

173. The maximum height reached by a rising tide is called
    (1)   low water.
    (2)   high water.
    (3)   flood.
    (4)   hurricane.
    (5)   peak.

174. The minimum height water can reach during the falling tide is called the
    (1) high water.   (4) forced water.
    (2) cold water.   (5) trough.
    (3) low water.

175. Tides are classified as
    (1) one high and low water.
    (2) two high and one low water.
    (3) semidiurnal.
    (4) antidiurnal.
    (5) diurnal.

176. Mixed tides are
    (1) those that change from day to day.
    (2) either diurnal or semidiurnal.
    (3) semidiurnals only in certain areas.
    (4) seasonal changes of tides.
    (5) None of the above.

177. Tides are classified as diurnal if they are composed of
    (1) two high waters and two low waters.
    (2) one high water and one low water.
    (3) one high water and two low waters.
    (4) two high waters and one low water.
    (5) All of the above.

178. Hurricanes occur when
    (1) atmospheric conditions change slowly.
    (2) severe climate changes occur at the poles.
    (3) the sky changes color.
    (4) atmosphere and pressure change is severe.
    (5) the weather turns cold.

179. Hurricanes occur over
    (1) land.   (4) water and land.
    (2) water.   (5) the polar caps only.
    (3) land during the day.

180. August, September, and October normally have more hurricanes documented than any other months with
    (1) September having the greatest number of hurricanes.
    (2) August having the greatest number of hurricanes.
    (3) October having the greatest number of hurricanes.
    (4) August and October having the greatest number of hurricanes.
    (5) all three months having the same approximate number of hurricanes.

181. A typhoon is a severe storm that occurs over
    (1) bodies of water making up rivers.
    (2) bodies of land and water.
    (3) bodies of land.
    (4) bodies of water making up oceans.
    (5) the polar ice caps.

182. According to the passage, rain, wind, and water make up
    (1) tornadoes.   (4) severe storms.
    (2) volcanoes.   (5) blizzards.
    (3) typhoons.

183. Currents prevent extremes of temperature by
    (1) eroding the land.
    (2) stabilizing the climate over water areas.
    (3) stabilizing the climate over land areas.
    (4) wind movement.
    (5) None of the above.

184. Currents are influenced by the
    (1) moon and planets.   (4) sun and gravity.
    (2) sun and wind.   (5) moon and equator.
    (3) sun.

185. Currents are
    (1) movements in horizontal or vertical flow occurring at all depths.
    (2) movements in a horizontal flow occurring at all depths.
    (3) movements in a vertical flow occurring at all depths.
    (4) movements in horizontal or vertical flow occurring at one certain depth.
    (5) movements in a vertical flow occurring at shallow depths.

186. Differences in density may be produced
    (1) by horizontal movements of water.
    (2) by vertical movements of water.
    (3) both by vertical and horizontal movements of water.
    (4) both by horizontal and vertical movements of air.
    (5) the magnetic field.

187. A decrease in temperature will cause the density of water to
    (1) be cut in half.   (4) weaken.
    (2) decrease.   (5) increase.
    (3) remain the same.

188. Water tends to flow from an area of
    (1) low density to high density.   (4) hotness to coldness.
    (2) high density to low density.   (5) None of the above.
    (3) coldness to hotness.

189. Fog will interfere with one's ability to
    (1) see over a small area.   (4) see large moving objects.
    (2) see at a distance.   (5) see anything.
    (3) see colors.

190. Fog is
    (1) the same as smog.
    (2) caused when cold air moves over warm air.
    (3) a collection of minute water droplets.
    (4) extremely rare on Earth.
    (5) associated with a tornado.

191. Fog is also called a
    (1) geyser.   (4) hydrometeor.
    (2) hydrotherapy.   (5) black cloud.
    (3) fallen cloud.

192. Conservation is
    (1) protection and wise use of animals.
    (2) protection and wise use of all Earth's resources.
    (3) protection and wise use of some of the Earth's resources.
    (4) management of natural resources only.
    (5) the using up of all resources.

193. Conservation is concerned with the following:
    (1) air, food, water, and heat.
    (2) air, minerals, gas, and oil.
    (3) food, water, oil, and gas.
    (4) None of the above.
    (5) All of the above.

194. The cost of living will be lower for everyone and more ideal surround-
    ings will be present
    (1) with legislation to get better conservation laws.
    (2) with or without conservation enforcement.
    (3) after forgetting the conservation laws.
    (4) with conservation enforcement.
    (5) None of the above.

195. Whom does conservation benefit?
    (1) All living things including man
    (2) All living things but not necessarily man
    (3) All animal life only
    (4) All plants only
    (5) No one

EARTH SCIENCE

ANSWER KEY

Drill: Aspects of Earth Science

1. (4)	15. (1)	29. (3)	43. (5)
2. (1)	16. (4)	30. (3)	44. (3)
3. (3)	17. (3)	31. (3)	45. (3)
4. (4)	18. (2)	32. (1)	46. (3)
5. (2)	19. (3)	33. (4)	47. (2)
6. (3)	20. (1)	34. (1)	48. (3)
7. (1)	21. (2)	35. (2)	49. (3)
8. (3)	22. (4)	36. (4)	50. (4)
9. (5)	23. (1)	37. (3)	51. (5)
10. (4)	24. (2)	38. (2)	52. (3)
11. (1)	25. (5)	39. (4)	53. (3)
12. (1)	26. (3)	40. (1)	54. (3)
13. (3)	27. (1)	41. (3)	55. (1)
14. (5)	28. (2)	42 (2)	56. (2)

Drill: Physics and Chemistry of the Earth

57. (3)	64. (4)	71. (3)	78. (1)
58. (3)	65. (1)	72. (1)	79. (2)
59. (5)	66. (5)	73. (2)	80. (3)
60. (3)	67. (4)	74. (4)	81. (5)
61. (3)	68. (1)	75. (1)	82. (1)
62. (3)	69. (2)	76. (2)	
63. (2)	70. (3)	77. (2)	

Drill: Evolution and Crustal Process

83. (1)	86. (1)	89. (3)	92. (4)
84. (2)	87. (3)	90. (4)	
85. (1)	88. (5)	91. (5)	

Drill: Surface Processes

93. (5)	104. (4)	115. (2)	126. (3)
94. (3)	105. (1)	116. (3)	127. (3)
95. (4)	106. (1)	117. (1)	128. (1)
96. (2)	107. (3)	118. (1)	129. (2)
97. (3)	108. (2)	119. (2)	130 (3)
98. (2)	109. (2)	120. (2)	131. (3)
99. (2)	110. (4)	121. (5)	132. (5)
100. (3)	111. (1)	122. (1)	133. (2)
101. (5)	112. (1)	123. (2)	
102. (1)	113. (2)	124. (1)	
103. (2)	114. (4)	125. (3)	

Drill: Earth's Hazards and Resources

134. (3)	150. (2)	166. (1)	182. (3)
135. (1)	151. (2)	167. (5)	183. (3)
136. (1)	152. (1)	168. (4)	184. (5)
137. (5)	153. (3)	169. (1)	185. (1)
138. (3)	154. (4)	170. (2)	186. (3)
139. (3)	155. (2)	171. (4)	187. (5)
140. (1)	156. (4)	172. (3)	188. (1)
141. (3)	157. (4)	173. (2)	189. (2)
142. (2)	158. (3)	174. (3)	190. (3)
143. (3)	159. (1)	175. (3)	191. (4)
144. (1)	160. (4)	176. (2)	192. (2)
145. (4)	161. (2)	177. (2)	193. (4)
146. (4)	162. (4)	178. (4)	194. (1)
147. (3)	163. (4)	179. (4)	195. (1)
148. (4)	164. (4)	180. (1)	
149. (3)	165. (4)	181. (4)	

V. PHYSICS

A. BASIC CONCEPTS OF PHYSICS

Physics is the study of matter, energy, and the relationships between the two phenomenal areas of study. Relationships between matter and energy have existed as long as the universe has existed, though man has not totally understood all relationships. Every time you lift a baby, push a wheelbarrow, or physically work out, you are demonstrating or applying the principles of physics. Basic principles or concepts of physics may be divided into eight general areas: mechanics (motion and force), energy, magnetism, sound, light, heat, waves, and electricity.

A scientific law is usually constructed after a limited number of experiments or observations have been tried. It summarizes the order that is believed to exist within certain prescribed conditions and can only occasionally be modified or extended to fit new situations. A scientific law is a statement that (1) fits new facts, (2) uses inductive and deductive reasoning, and (3) successfully predicts what is found in nature.

LAW OF ACCELERATION

The amount of acceleration is directly proportional to the acting force and inversely proportional to mass:

$$F = ma.$$

Drop a rock and it falls to the ground. The rock starts its fall from a resting position and gains speed as it falls. This gain in speed indicates the acceleration of the rock as it falls. Gravity (acting force) causes the rock to fall downward once it moves from its resting position. Remember, acceleration is equal to the change in speed divided by the time interval.

ARCHIMEDES' LAW OF BUOYANCY OR ARCHIMEDES' PRINCIPLE

The relationship between buoyancy and displaced liquid was discovered in ancient times by the Greek philosopher Archimedes in the third century B.C. It states that "an immersed object is pushed up by a force equal to the weight of the fluid it displaces." When an object is suspended in water, the pressures on opposite sides cancel each other. The pressure increases with depth, and the upward force on the bottom of the object will be greater than the downward forces on the top. Thus, an object is lighter in water than in air. This relationship, called Archimedes' Principle, is found to be true of both liquids and gases.

BERNOULLI'S LAW

"A moving stream of gas or liquid appears to exert less sideways pressure than if it were at rest." Bernoulli studied the relationship of fluid speed and pressure, and wondered how the fluid got the energy for extra speed. He discovered that the pressure in a fluid decreases as the speed of the fluid increases. This principle is a consequence of the conservation of energy and supports the concept of steady flow. If the flow speed is too great, then it becomes turbulent and follows changing, curling paths known as eddies. Also, this same principle application accounts for the flight of birds and aircraft abilities.

BOYLE'S LAW

If the temperature of a gas remains constant,

$$\frac{V_1}{V_2} = \frac{P_2}{P_1}$$

where P and V are the pressure and volume, respectively. When the density of the gas increases in a given space, the pressure is increased. The density of the gas also can be doubled by simply compressing the air to half its volume. This law is applied when one inflates a tire, balloon, or any other such object.

CHARLES' LAW

"The volume of gas increases as its temperature increases if the pressure stays the same." Charles' measurements suggested that the volume of a gas would become zero at a temperature of -273° C. Thus, this temperature is called absolute zero. This law applies only to gases. Scientists have found all gases become liquids or solids before they are cooled to the temperature of -273°C. Charles' Law is used to explain the kinetic theory as four factors are needed to describe a gas—the mass, the volume, the pressure, and the temperature. Charles' Law explains the increase in volume within tires after traveling long distances or traveling on hot days.

HOOKE'S LAW

The amount of stretch or compression, x, is directly proportional to the applied force F:

$$(x = F).$$

This law is used to explain the property of elasticity. Elasticity is the ability of a body to change shapes when a force is applied and then return to its original shape when that force is removed. Steel is an example of an elastic material. It can be stretched and it can be compressed. Because of its strength and elastic properties, it is used to make springs for construction girders. Also, spring construction and functioning is based on Hooke's Law.

NEWTON'S LAWS

Sir Isaac Newton's laws describe how forces change the motion of an object and are stated in the Three Laws of Motion.

The First Law (Law of Inertia) states that every body remains in a state of rest or uniform motion unless acted upon by forces from the outside.

The Second Law (Law of Constant Acceleration) states that the acceleration of an object increases as the amount of net force applied from outside the object increases. The formula of this law is

Force = mass × acceleration

Force = mass × meter divided by seconds squared (m/s^2) $= \dfrac{kg \cdot m}{s^2}$.

Therefore, applying the formula to determine one newton is the force needed to give a mass of one kilogram an acceleration of one meter per second squared, or:

Force (1 newton) = mass 1(kg) × acceleration ($1m/s^2$) $1\ N = 1kg \times 1\ m/s^2$

Newton's Third Law (Law of Conservation of Momentum) states that forces always come in pairs: to every action there is an equal and opposite reaction. When one object exerts a force on a second object, the second object exerts a force that would be equal to and opposite the force of the first object. Mass is a measure of the amount of inertia of a body. The product of mass and velocity is the amount of momentum an object possesses. A quantity that is not changed is said to be conserved. In a collision the total momentum of the colliding bodies is not changed. This is the Law of Conservation of Momentum or Newton's Third Law. Momentum is conserved provided there are no outside forces acting on a set of objects.

LAW OF CONSERVATION OF ENERGY

Energy cannot be created or destroyed; it changes forms but does not cease to exist. This law explains how energy can change from one form to another. As energy can never be created or destroyed, the total energy of the universe remains the same.

LAW OF CONSERVATION OF MECHANICAL ENERGY

In the absence of friction, energy stored in a machine remains constant and work done by the machine is equal to the work done on it. The energy of an object enables it to do work. Mechanical energy is due to the position of something (potential energy) or the movement of something (kinetic energy). Mechanical energy is produced by a machine that is a device for multiplying forces or changing the directions of forces.

LAW OF GRAVITATION

Any two bodies in the universe attract each other with a force (F) that is directly proportional to their masses (m) and inversely proportional to the square of their distance (d) apart:

$$F = \frac{Gm_1m_2}{d^2}$$

Forces are always applied at several different places under normal circumstances, not just at one point. This force on objects found on the Earth is what we call gravity.

LENZ'S LAW

The direction of an induced current is always such that its magnetic field opposes the operation that causes it. This law is the basis for the design of a generator and its ability to function by converting mechanical energy into electrical energy. A changing magnetic field induces an electric field. A generator uses the electromagnetic induction to convert mechanical energy into electrical energy.

OHM'S LAW

The current in a wire is proportional to the potential difference between the ends of the wire:

V (voltage) = I (current) × R (resistance)

Ohm's Law determines the strength of the current that flows into the circuit and the basis for the concept of electrical current. Any path along which electrons can flow is a circuit. A complete circuit is needed to maintain a continuous electron flow.

LAW OF REFLECTION

The angle of the incidence equals the angle of reflection. This law explains how a wave changes its direction or how it is reflected back. When light is reflected from a flat surface or plane such as a mirror, the incoming light ray (incident ray) and the reflected ray of light (reflected ray) are measured with respect to a line perpendicular to the flat surface. When a light ray strikes a flat surface, the angle of incidence always equals the angle of reflection. Sunlight is an example showing this law.

LAW OF REFRACTION

Light rays passing through a transparent substance are bent, or refracted; the thicker the substance is, the farther apart its actual and apparent locations will be. The law also states that the incident ray and the refracted ray both lie on one plane.

A theory applies to a broad range of phenomena and is applied to a small aspect of nature. A theory attempts to explain the "how's" and "why's" of science. It is in the establishing and testing of theories that discoveries are made. The primary purpose of a theory is to enable us to see a natural phenomenon as a part of a simple, unified whole as it

1. correlates many facts in a single concept or reasonable assumption;

2. suggests or accommodates new ideas;

3. stimulates research;

4. is useful in solving long-range problems; and

5. makes predictions.

Albert Einstein developed the Theory of Relativity, which is often referred to as Einstein's Theory. The relativity theory is based on mathematical formulas and calculations dealing with gravitation, mass, motion, space, and time. Basic principles of this theory are:

1. Motion in a straight line will have constant velocity. All other motion is judged from this frame of reference.

2. The speed of light in empty space will always have the same value regardless of the motion of the source or the motion of the observer.

Before a hypothesis can be scientific, it must conform to the scientific rule of being testable. Then, one must test by following the scientific method:

1. recognize the problem;

2. formulate your hypothesis;

3. complete related research;

4. perform test-to-test prediction;

5. collect data while performing the test;

6. summarize research and test results in an orderly manner; and

7. draw conclusions.

☞ Drill: Basic Concepts of Physics

DIRECTIONS: Carefully read and answer each of the following questions which are based on the information which you have just read.

1. Physics is the most basic science because
    (1) you can better understand science if you understand physics principles.
    (2) the physics ideas extend into more complex science ideas.
    (3) underneath biology and chemistry concepts lie the physics concepts.
    (4) All of the above.
    (5) None of the above.

2. Which of the following statements is not true?
    (1) Science is a method of answering theoretical questions.
    (2) Technology is a method of solving practical problems.
    (3) Science excludes the human factor.
    (4) A good scientist is influenced by his likes and dislikes as well as friends' opinions.
    (5) A good scientist is not influenced by his likes and dislikes as well as friends' opinions.

3. A scientific law is
   (1) an educated guess that has yet to be proven by experiment.
   (2) a synthesis of a limited number of experiments or observations that summarizes a belief.
   (3) close agreements among observations made by competent observers about different ideas.
   (4) a guess that has been tested and proven without any limitations.
   (5) usually incorrect.

4. To test a scientific law,
   (1) set up one experiment and analyze the results.
   (2) set up many experiments and analyze the results.
   (3) use inductive and deductive reasoning in analyzing new facts.
   (4) find the best result and report only that result.
   (5) make assumptions based on your opinions.

5. If the force acting on a cart is doubled, what happens to the cart's acceleration?
   (1) It is quadrupled.   (4) It is quartered.
   (2) It is tripled.   (5) It is doubled.
   (3) It is halved.

6. Acceleration is defined as the
   (1) change in position divided by the time needed to make that change.
   (2) change in velocity divided by the time needed to make that change.
   (3) time it takes to move from one speed to another speed.
   (4) time it takes to move from one place to another place.
   (5) change in time.

7. The acceleration due to gravity _____ over the Earth's surface.
   (1) is constant
   (2) is faster than the base rate
   (3) is slower than the base rate
   (4) varies
   (5) creates rain

8. Archimedes' Principle says that an object is buoyed up by a force that is equal to
   (1) the weight of the fluid displaced.

    (2)   the volume of the fluid displaced.
    (3)   the mass of the fluid displaced.
    (4)   the mass of the object.
    (5)   the speed at which the object is moving.

9.   Pressure in a liquid depends on the
    (1)   density of the liquid.   (4)   Both 1 and 3.
    (2)   volume of the liquid.   (5)   Both 1 and 2.
    (3)   depth of the measuring point.

10.   The main difference between gases and liquids is that in gases,
    (1)   molecules are moving faster.
    (2)   forces between molecules are greater.
    (3)   distances between molecules are greater.
    (4)   molecules collide more frequently.
    (5)   molecules are moving slower.

11.   When a river narrows, the water in the river flows
    (1)   faster.   (4)   at the same rate.
    (2)   more slowly.   (5)   in the reverse direction.
    (3)   at varying rates.

12.   Bernoulli's Principle states that
    (1)   internal fluid pressure decreases as fluid speed increases.
    (2)   as the volume of a gas increases at constant temperature, the pressure decreases.
    (3)   an object in air is buoyed up by a force equal to the weight of the air displaced.
    (4)   internal fluid pressure increases as fluid speed increases.
    (5)   force is equal to mass.

13.   The total energy of a liquid depends in part on the liquid's
    (1)   specific heat.   (4)   heat of vaporization.
    (2)   volume.   (5)   color.
    (3)   heat of fusion.

14.   Boyle's Law relates
    (1)   pressure and temperature.   (4)   temperature and volume.
    (2)   pressure and volume.   (5)   volume and mass.
    (3)   pressure and mass.

15. The reason a shower curtain will pull to the inside of a bathtub during a shower is that
    (1) there is more air inside the shower curtain.
    (2) there is less air inside the curtain.
    (3) the pressure is higher inside the curtain.
    (4) the pressure is lower inside the curtain.
    (5) there is a draft in the bathtub.

16. The change in volume of a gas with a change in temperature
    (1) is directly proportional to its volume.
    (2) depends on the nature of the gas.
    (3) is directly proportional to the coefficient of volume expansion.
    (4) All of the above.
    (5) None of the above.

17. As a substance is heated steadily, its temperature increases for a while, then the temperature stops increasing. The temperature stops increasing because
    (1) the molecules are losing kinetic energy.
    (2) the substance is changing from a liquid to a gas.
    (3) the substance is changing from a gas to a liquid.
    (4) the molecules are moving closer together.
    (5) None of the above.

18. Charles' Law can be used to explain
    (1) why car tires are slightly larger after a long trip on a hot day.
    (2) how a liquid-filled thermometer works.
    (3) why a bottle of water cracks when it freezes.
    (4) how large amounts of gas are stored in small containers.
    (5) the Theory of Relativity.

19. The law that explains the principle of elasticity is
    (1) Charles' Law.   (4) Marshall's Law.
    (2) Newton's Law.   (5) Einstein's Law.
    (3) Hooke's Law.

20. The ability of a body to change shapes when a force is applied and then return to its original shape when that force is removed is
    (1) elasticity.   (4) girders.
    (2) compression.   (5) chameleon.
    (3) springforce.

21. Which of the following is made of an elastic material?
    (1) A piece of cookie dough (4) A telephone pole
    (2) Biscuit dough   (5) A bridge girder
    (3) Skis

22. The resistance of an object to changes in its state of motion is called
    (1) momentum.   (4) acceleration.
    (2) inertia.   (5) deceleration.
    (3) torque.

23. The Law of Inertia states that an object
    (1) at rest will remain at rest unless acted on by an outside force.
    (2) will move at the same velocity from an inside force.
    (3) will continue to move in a straight line.
    (4) has more mass when moving.
    (5) All of the above.

24. The Law of Inertia applies to
    (1) only moving objects.
    (2) only objects that are not moving.
    (3) both moving and nonmoving objects.
    (4) all objects at rest only.
    (5) all objects.

25. The acceleration produced by a net force on an object is
    (1) directly proportional to the magnitude of the net force.
    (2) in the same direction as the net force.
    (3) inversely proportional to the mass of the object.
    (4) All of the above.
    (5) None of the above.

26. When an automobile is accelerated forward,
    (1) the tires exert a forward action force on the road.
    (2) the road exerts a forward reaction force on the tires.
    (3) the road exerts a rearward reaction on the tires.
    (4) the tires exert a rearward reaction on the road.
    (5) the tires deflate.

27. The acceleration of a body is
    (1) directly proportional to the force exerted.
    (2) inversely proportional to the mass of the body.
    (3) in the same direction as the applied force.

(4)   All of the above.

(5)   None of the above.

28.   The force required to accelerate an object of known weight is
       (1)   related to velocity and gravity.
       (2)   not related to acceleration due to gravity.
       (3)   directly proportional to the acceleration due to gravity.
       (4)   directly proportional to the weight of the object.
       (5)   the force of gravity itself.

29.   Newton's Third Law of Motion deals with
       (1)   one object and two forces.
       (2)   two objects and one force.
       (3)   two objects and two forces.
       (4)   three objects and two forces.
       (5)   three objects and three forces.

30.   According to Newton's Third Law, if you push on something, providing
       there are no outside forces acting on you or the object, it will push
       (1)   back on you with equal force.
       (2)   gently on something else.
       (3)   away from you.
       (4)   on you if you are not moving.
       (5)   back with a doubled force.

31.   Energy is
       (1)   the capacity for doing work.
       (2)   acquired by an object raised to an elevated position.
       (3)   acquired by an object which is set in motion.
       (4)   All of the above.
       (5)   None of the above.

32.   Energy can
       (1)   not be created.   (4)   All of the above.
       (2)   not be destroyed.   (5)   None of the above.
       (3)   be changed in form.

33.   Mechanical energy is produced by a machine that is a device for
       (1)   multiplying forces or changing the directions of forces.
       (2)   dividing forces or changing the direction of forces.
       (3)   adding forces.

(4)   subtracting the direction of the force.

(5)   changing speed.

34.   Which of the following is NOT an example of a simple machine?
       (1)   Pulley   (4)   Lever
       (2)   Fulcrum   (5)   Computer
       (3)   Inclined plane

35.   Friction acts parallel to the surfaces which are sliding over one another and in the
       (1)   same direction as the motion.
       (2)   opposite direction of the motion.
       (3)   contact line and circular motion.
       (4)   direction of the sliding force.
       (5)   None of the above.

36.   It can be reasoned that the gravitational attraction between the Earth and the moon must be
       (1)   directly proportional to the square of the distance between them.
       (2)   inversely proportional to the square of the distance between them.
       (3)   the same at all distances.
       (4)   independent of distance.
       (5)   related to their speeds.

37.   The gravitational force between two masses
       (1)   is always an attraction.
       (2)   depends on how large the masses are.
       (3)   depends inversely on the square of the distances between the masses.
       (4)   All of the above.
       (5)   None of the above.

38.   Gravitational forces are the weakest forces found in nature. Because of this,
       (1)   the gravitational effect between a pencil and the Earth cannot be seen.
       (2)   there is no gravitational force between two 1-kg masses.
       (3)   there is no movement between two 1-kg masses located near each other in space.
       (4)   gravitational effects can only be observed when a large mass is involved.
       (5)   gravity's effect on humans cannot be seen.

39. A generator uses electromagnetic induction to convert
    (1) mechanical energy into electric energy.
    (2) electric energy into mechanical energy.
    (3) magnetic energy into electromagnetic energy.
    (4) electromagnetic energy into electric energy.
    (5) magnetic energy into electromagnetic energy.

40. The induction of voltage by a change in the magnetic field around a conductor is called
    (1) generated voltage.
    (2) Faraday's induction.
    (3) transformer induction.
    (4) electromagnetic induction.
    (5) transformer voltage.

41. According to Ohm's Law,
    (1) $V = I/R$.
    (2) $V = IR$.
    (3) $R = VI$.
    (4) $I = R/V$.
    (5) $R = I/V$

42. When two light bulbs are connected in series,
    (1) the same amount of current flows through each light bulb.
    (2) the current through each light is proportional to the resistance of the bulb.
    (3) the light bulbs will not work unless there is a fuse in the circuit.
    (4) there are at least two branches in the circuit.
    (5) All of the above.

43. Ohm's Law determines the strength of the current that flows
    (1) through the circuit.
    (2) out of the circuit.
    (3) around the circuit.
    (4) into and through the circuit.
    (5) into the circuit.

44. The Law of Reflection states that
    (1) all waves incident on a mirror are reflected.
    (2) waves incident on a mirror are partially reflected.
    (3) the angle at which a ray is reflected from a mirror is unpredictable.
    (4) the angle of reflection from a mirror equals the angle of incidence.
    (5) what you see is what you get.

45. Reflection occurs
    (1)   when the image is located in front of the mirror.
    (2)   when one part of the wave travels more slowly than another part.
    (3)   when the wave incidence is deflected.
    (4)   None of the above.
    (5)   All of the above.

46. The reason we can read print from any direction is that
    (1)   letters emit black light in all directions.
    (2)   letters absorb black light from all directions.
    (3)   the white part of a page reflects light in all directions.
    (4)   the image is decolored.
    (5)   our brain can process information quickly.

47. When refraction occurs, part of a wave
    (1)   is bent more than another part.
    (2)   slows down before another part.
    (3)   is pushed to one side.
    (4)   is closer together than it appears.
    (5)   is crushed.

48. A rainbow occurs because sunlight
    (1)   is refracted by water in the raindrops.
    (2)   is refracted by the atmosphere.
    (3)   is bent by layers of hot air in the atmosphere.
    (4)   falls on different size raindrops.
    (5)   has conquered the storm.

49. When light is refracted,
    (1)   the rays all lie on different planes.
    (2)   the rays lie on one plane.
    (3)   the rays lie on one thickness.
    (4)   the rays lie behind the plane.
    (5)   the rays disappear.

50. Testing
    (1)   and establishing theories lead to discoveries.
    (2)   explains how discoveries are made.
    (3)   correlates all discoveries.
    (4)   and establishing myths lead to great discoveries.
    (5)   is expensive and dangerous.

51. A major purpose of the theory is to
    (1) bring fame to the scientist.
    (2) prove another scientist wrong.
    (3) stimulate research.
    (4) supply reading material.
    (5) give scientists something to study.

52. Einstein reasoned
    (1) all motion is relative.
    (2) a spaceship can measure its speed only relative to other objects.
    (3) there is no unique spot relative to which all motion can be measured.
    (4) All of the above.
    (5) None of the above.

53. According to the Theory of Relativity, all laws of nature are the same in reference frames that
    (1) accelerate.   (4) oscillate.
    (2) vibrate.   (5) decelerate.
    (3) move at constant speeds.

54. To insure that a hypothesis is scientific, it must conform to the
    (1) ideas of the scientist.
    (2) rule of having been tested before.
    (3) scientific rule of being testable.
    (4) scientific rule of categorizing.
    (5) scientist's opinion.

55. A testing of a hypothesis is accomplished by following the scientific method which includes:
    (1) recognizing the problem.
    (2) formulating a hypothesis.
    (3) completing related research.
    (4) All of the above.
    (5) None of the above.

B. MATTER, MASS, AND DENSITY

Matter is found in everything. Everything is made of atoms. All matter, living or nonliving, is a combination of elements (atoms). Matter is anything that has mass and occupies space. Matter can exist in four states dependent upon its Brownian Motion:(1) solid, (2) liquid, (3) gas, or (4) plasma, which makes up the greatest quantity of matter.

Mass is the quantity of matter in a body that exhibits a response to any effort (energy or movement) made to start it, stop it, or change in any way its state of motion. Mass is measured by the amount of inertia an object has. The greater the mass, the greater the force necessary to change its state of motion. Mass is often confused with weight. Weight is a specific numerical measurement or unit, while mass is anything that takes up space and has weight.

Density is the measure of compactness of a material. It being as light as a feather or heavy as a rock is dependent upon its density. Density is not mass nor is it volume. Density cannot be equated to size in all cases; rather, it is the compactness of the mass per unit of volume. Both the mass of the atoms making up the substance or material and the spacing between the atoms determine the density of materials or state of materials.

☞ Drill: Matter, Mass, and Density

<u>DIRECTIONS</u>: Carefully read and answer each of the following questions which are based on the information which you have just read.

56. Most of the matter of the universe is in which state?
    (1) Liquid   (4) Plasma
    (2) Solid   (5) Air
    (3) Gas

57. Atoms combine to form
    (1) nucleon.   (4) isotopes.
    (2) elements.   (5) molecules.
    (3) more atoms.

58. Mass is measured by the amount of
    (1) inertia an object has.
    (2) motion an object has.
    (3) weight an object has.

(4)   specific numbers of an object.

(5)   force an object exerts.

59. The greater the mass of an object, the greater the force necessary

    (1)   to change its position.

    (2)   to change its force.

    (3)   to change its weight.

    (4)   to change its state of motion.

    (5)   to change its shape.

60. If an object has the density of water and is placed into water, it will

    (1)   float.

    (2)   sink.

    (3)   bounce up and down.

    (4)   neither float nor sink, but stay anywhere it is put.

    (5)   fill up with water.

61. The reason an iron ship does not sink is that

    (1)   iron is less dense than water.

    (2)   iron in the shape of a ship's hull displaces more water than if the same amount of iron were in a solid block.

    (3)   the ship is so big.

    (4)   the buoyant force equals the volume of the boat.

    (5)   iron is waterproof.

C. MOTION

Motion is all around us. Our bodies, no matter how still we think we are, are in a constant state of motion. Motion is easy to see but almost impossible to describe or define. Therefore, when speaking of motion, one must address it as relative to an object rate.

1. VELOCITY

Velocity is the speed in a given direction. Speed and velocity can be used interchangeably if the description is asking for how fast a movement occurs in a certain direction. Velocity can be described as constant or changing. A constant velocity requires that both the speed stay the same and direction not be changed or altered. Motion at constant velocity is motion in a straight line at a constant speed. A body may be moving at a constant speed along a curved path or the speed may vary along a constant path. The latter is referred to as changing velocity.

2. ACCELERATION

Acceleration is a rate that applies to a decreasing speed (deceleration) as well as an increasing speed (acceleration). Acceleration applies to a change in direction as well as the change in speed. Pressing the gas pedal of a car will accelerate the speed of the car; pressing the brakes will retard the speed, or decelerate the car. Like velocity, acceleration is directional.

3. MOMENTUM

Momentum is the mass of an object multiplied by its velocity

$$momentum = mass \times velocity = m \times v.$$

If the momentum of an object changes, either the mass or the velocity or both change. Thus, acceleration occurs.

Gravity causes a rock to fall downward once it has been dropped. This action on movement is referred to as gravitational motion. If there were no gravitational action, the motion would be called free fall. The time that it takes an object to fall from the beginning of the fall to the point of rest is called elapsed time. The concept of gravity effects was first credited to Isaac Newton after he was hit on the head with an apple that fell from a tree he was sitting beneath.

4. SPEED

Speed is a measure of how fast something is moving or the rate at which a distance is being covered. Speed is calculated as the distance covered divided by the unit of time. Speed is the rate of change of the position of an object. The average speed describes the motion of objects even if they are not moving at a constant speed. This average speed can be calculated by the total distance traveled divided by the total time taken for travel.

5. INERTIA

Inertia is the resistance an object has to a change in its state of motion. Inertia can be measured by its mass depending upon the amount and type of matter in it. The idea of inertia while in motion is called momentum in reference to moving objects.

☞ Drill: Motion

DIRECTIONS: Carefully read and answer each of the following questions which are based on the information which you have just read.

62. Motion is
    (1) a constant state.
    (2) relative to an object.
    (3) all around us.
    (4) All of the above.
    (5) None of the above.

63. Uniform motion in a straight line is the only motion possible for
    (1) a space ship.
    (2) an automobile accelerating.
    (3) an isolated object.
    (4) a relative force.
    (5) a boat.

64. If a moving van changes direction, which of the following also changes?
    (1) mass.
    (2) speed.
    (3) weight.
    (4) inertia.
    (5) velocity.

65. Velocity can be described as
    (1) constant.
    (2) changing.
    (3) the force exerted.
    (4) speed.
    (5) Both 1 and 2.

66. The value of the acceleration due to gravity
    (1) depends on the mass of an object.
    (2) depends on the shape of the earth.
    (3) depends on smaller surfaces.
    (4) depends on the deceleration factor.
    (5) depends on the weight of an object.

67. Deceleration applies to
    (1) an increasing speed with a change in velocity.
    (2) a decreasing speed with a change in velocity.
    (3) a rate showing decreasing speed.
    (4) a rate showing increasing speed.
    (5) inertia.

68. Momentum is conserved in all collisions in which no external forces are acting except
    (1) those in which heat is regenerated.
    (2) those that are nonelastic.
    (3) when all changes are equal.
    (4) when no change occurs.
    (5) None of the above.

69. An object falling under the influence of gravity with no air resistance is said to be in
    (1) free fall.   (4) free motion.
    (2) elapsed time.   (5) fall motion.
    (3) gravitational motion.

70. The time that it takes an object to fall from the beginning of the fall to the point of rest is called
    (1) free fall time.   (4) velocity.
    (2) concept gravity time.   (5) deceleration.
    (3) elapsed time.

71. The motion of objects, even if they are not moving at a constant speed, is called the
    (1) potential speed.   (4) average speed.
    (2) calculated speed.   (5) kinetic speed.
    (3) rate of change.

72. Speed is calculated by the following formula:
    (1) speed divided by distance.
    (2) distance multiplied by the time.
    (3) adding time, distance, and weight.
    (4) distance divided by time.
    (5) force multiplied by mass.

73. The resistance an object has against change in its state of motion is called
    (1) force.   (4) friction.
    (2) velocity.   (5) acceleration.
    (3) inertia.

74. Mass can be defined as
    (1) the amount of matter in an object.
    (2) the type of matter in an object.

(3)   the amount and type of matter in an object.
(4)   the amount and density of matter in an object.
(5)   None of the above.

75.   The idea of inertia while in motion is called
      (1)   momentum in reference to moving objects.
      (2)   inertia frame of reference.
      (3)   measurement of momentum.
      (4)   momentum in reference to nonmoving objects.
      (5)   All of the above.

D. FORCE

Force is the push or pull one body exerts on another body. "For every action, there is an equal and opposite reaction" is another way of describing force. Force is the product of acceleration. The combination of all the forces that act on an object is called the net force. When a body is at rest, a force is at work. The fact that the body is at rest rather than accelerating shows another force at work. Force is necessary to maintain balance and reach net force zero. For a book to be at rest on a table, the sum of the forces acting upon the book must equal zero.

The process of determining the components of a vector is called resolution. A person pushes a lawn mower. This in turn applies force against the ground causing the lawn mower to roll forward. In this example, the vector is a combination of two components. Any vector can be represented by a pair of components that are at right angles to each other.

Friction is the name given to the force that acts between materials that are moving past each other. Friction is a result that arises from irregularities in the surfaces of sliding objects. If no friction was present, a moving object would need no force whatever for its motion to continue. Even for a surface that appears to be smooth, there are microscopic irregularities causing friction to occur.

PARALLEL

When the forces on two opposite sides are equal, this is said to be a parallel force. Thus, this produces, considering all forces are equal, an action-reaction situation.

☞ Drill: Force

<u>DIRECTIONS</u>: Carefully read and answer each of the following questions which are based on the information which you have just read.

76. A net force
    (1) changes the state of motion of an object.
    (2) must be a contact force.
    (3) may act over long distances.
    (4) produces a constant velocity.
    (5) grosses change.

77. For a book resting on the horizontal surface of a desk,
    (1) the weight of the book on the desk is a force.
    (2) the force of gravity is only on the book.
    (3) the desk pushes up on the book.
    (4) Both 1 and 3.
    (5) Both 1 and 2.

78. When pushing a lawn mower, with force at an angle of 30° to the ground,
    (1) the desired motion is in the direction of the vertical component.
    (2) the effective force in the direction of the motion is less than the applied force.
    (3) the applied force varies if the handle is raised, but the vertical component becomes less.
    (4) None of the above.
    (5) All of the above.

79. A vector is a quantity that has
    (1) magnitude and time.
    (2) magnitude and direction.
    (3) time and direction.
    (4) magnitude, direction, and time.
    (5) only direction.

80. The weight of a person can be represented by a vector that acts
    (1) perpendicular to the ground underneath the person.
    (2) parallel to the ground.
    (3) straight down, even if the person is standing on a hill.

(4) in a direction that depends on where the person is standing.

(5) All of the above.

81. Friction

(1) acts in a direction opposite to the direction of motion of an object.

(2) comes from microscopic bumps that act as obstructions to an object's motion.

(3) is the name given to the force acting between surfaces sliding past one another.

(4) All of the above.

(5) None of the above.

82. Which of the following two forces oppose each other when a block of wood slides down a ramp?

(1) Gravitational force and electrical force

(2) Electrical force and magnetic force

(3) Magnetic force and frictional force

(4) Frictional force and gravitational force

(5) Electrical force and frictional force

83. The idea of parallel force can be applied to circuits. A parallel circuit would

(1) have equal currents.

(2) have action-reaction forces producing static electricity.

(3) have a constant supply of electricity.

(4) would have an on-off supply of electricity depending on all forces being constant.

(5) have unequal currents.

84. When forces on two opposing sides are equal, you have

(1) an AC circuit.   (4) Both 1 and 3.

(2) a DC circuit.   (5) an AC/DC circuit.

(3) a parallel force.

E. ENERGY

Energy is the ability of an object to cause change; energy is the ability to do work. Energy is produced when forces are at work. Objects in motion cause change. The greater the speed, the greater the change that occurs. If you experience an energy surge, then you can work more or move faster. Objects as well as people can have energy. Energy can exist in various forms and can change from one form to another form. This energy and its changes can be measured. The unit of measurement of energy is called a joule.

Energy exists in three states: potential, kinetic, and activation energies. An object possessing energy because of its motion has kinetic energy. The energy that an object has as the result of its position or condition is called potential energy. The energy necessary to transfer or convert potential energy into kinetic energy is called activation energy.

Study the diagram to see that a rock at rest is considered to be potential energy. If a force is used to set that rock in motion, that force would be the activation energy. The rock rolling down the hill until it reaches a point of rest (potential energy) is considered kinetic energy.

Other forms of energy are a result of conditions or combinations of the states of energy. When kinetic and potential energy of lifting, bending, and stretching are grouped together, they are called mechanical energy. If one considers the total energy of the particles that make up an object or body, this is thermal energy. A raised weight possesses potential energy called gravitational potential energy. When it is released, it will return to its former level. This is the principle applied to the functioning of a spring or stretching an object.

Work is the transfer of energy as the result of motion. Most people think of work as an amount of effort exerted. However, if you attempted to move a boulder without any success, you expended energy but no work was accomplished. Work is a derived unit; it may be expressed as any force unit times any distance unit. The only thing that matters in calculating work is the distance moved in the direction of the force.

A machine is any device by which energy can be transferred from one place to another or one form to another. Think back to the diagram of the rock rolling down the hill. This is an example of a machine. Often, when we think of a machine or using a machine, some outside agent—a motor, a battery, your muscles—does the work on the machine. The machine then delivers work to something on which it acts.

The principle of conservation of mechanical energy deals with the functioning of a machine. This principle dictates how two kinds of work are related. "In the absence of other forces that dissipate energy, the total mechanical energy of a system remains constant." So long as any energy that is stored within a machine remains constant, and in the absence of friction, the work done by the machine is exactly equal to the work done on it.

Power is the rate of doing work per unit of time. This is calculated by:

P (power) = W (work) divided by t (time).

Suppose two workers are pushing identical boxes up an inclined plane. One pushes his box up the plane in 20 seconds while the other pushes his box up the plane in 40 seconds. Both do the same amount of work. The difference is the rate of time in which the work is done. The unit for power is watt. One watt is one joule of work per second.

☞ Drill: Energy

DIRECTIONS: Carefully read and answer each of the following questions which are based on the information which you have just read.

85. Objects in motion cause change. The faster the motion,
     (1)   the lesser the change that occurs.
     (2)   the greater the change that occurs.
     (3)   the less the speed increases.
     (4)   the more the ability to work has decreased.
     (5)   All of the above.

86. Energy is
    (1) the ability to do work.
    (2) objects in motion.
    (3) produced when forces are at work.
    (4) Both 1 and 3.
    (5) Both 2 and 3.

87. As a pendulum swings back and forth,
    (1) potential energy is transformed into kinetic energy.
    (2) its energy is all kinetic at the lowest part of its swing.
    (3) its energy is all potential at the end points of its swing.
    (4) All of the above.
    (5) None of the above.

88. Kinetic energy is
    (1) energy due to the possible position of the mass.
    (2) energy due to the motion of the mass.
    (3) energy due to the orientation of the particles in a mass.
    (4) proportional to the weight of the object.
    (5) energy due to the mass of the motion.

89. Kinetic energy is the energy an object has because of its
    (1) mass.   (4) density.
    (2) location.   (5) speed.
    (3) size.

90. Potential energy
    (1) is due to the potential of the mass.
    (2) is energy due to the motion of a mass.
    (3) is energy due to the orientation of the particles in a mass.
    (4) of position is proportional to the weight of the object concerned.
    (5) is energy due to the mass of the motion.

91. Energy can be transferred
    (1) by the movement of materials in one direction.
    (2) by the movement of cooled gas.
    (3) through matter by mechanical machines.
    (4) through space by electromagnetic waves.
    (5) through gas.

92. A pulse moving along a spiral spring
    (1) carries particles of matter along with it.
    (2) is a method of energy transfer.
    (3) can be a crest or trough of a wave.
    (4) can be compression or a rarefaction in transverse wave motion.
    (5) will die.

93. In physics, work is done
    (1) in lifting an object from the floor to the table.
    (2) in supporting an object on our shoulder.
    (3) in preparing school lessons.
    (4) in earning wages.
    (5) in the laboratory.

94. The two factors which determine the amount of work done are
    (1) magnitude of the force exerted and the weight of the object moved.
    (2) the distance of the object moved in the time required.
    (3) the displacement of the object and the magnitude of the force in the direction of the displacement.
    (4) the magnitude of the force in the direction of the displacement and the time required.
    (5) All of the above.

95. A teacher pushes a stack of papers across the desk. The teacher is showing
    (1) the body used as a machine.
    (2) resistance of papers.
    (3) lever and wheel action.
    (4) the desk's resistance to holding papers.
    (5) None of the above.

96. Machines may be used
    (1) to divide the force.
    (2) to multiply speed.
    (3) to divide force and speed simultaneously.
    (4) to keep the direction of the force constant.
    (5) to change mass.

97. The principle of conservation of mechanical energy dictates how two kinds of work are related. They are
    (1) friction and mechanical energy.
    (2) absence of friction and work by a machine.
    (3) speed and type of machine.
    (4) time and speed of machine.
    (5) mass and speed of machine.

98. The law of conservation of mechanical energy
    (1) is illustrated in suspending a pendulum.
    (2) states that the sum of the potential and kinetic energies of an ideal energy system remains constant.
    (3) involves frictional forces.
    (4) involves systems where the work done is dependent on the path length.
    (5) Both 1 and 4.

99. In science, power is
    (1) the capacity for doing work.
    (2) the time rate of doing work.
    (3) the product of a displacement and the force in the direction of the displacement.
    (4) the force acquired as an object is being moved.
    (5) money.

100. Power is the rate of doing work per unit of time. This can be calculated by applying the formula
    (1) power equals work divided by time.
    (2) work equals power.
    (3) power equals work added to time.
    (4) power equals time divided by number participating in the work.
    (5) force equals mass multiplied by time.

F. HEAT

Heat is a necessity of life. It is also a very valuable tool that cooks our food, frees metals from ores, and creates usable products (to mention a few of its uses). Heat is a form of energy and that energy is created by the motion of the molecules making up an object. Heat is the transfer of energy from an object of high temperature to one of lower temperature.

Heat has several properties: it is a conductor, it can be measured, heat can be transferred or radiated, and heat can travel by convection. Nearly all materials will either expand or contract when heat is added or taken away. When the amount of heat within an object or around an object varies, that object will vary. There is an exact point at which the variation will occur. We call this the specific heat. The specific heat of any substance is defined as the quantity of heat required to raise the temperature of a unit of mass of that substance by one degree. For instance, a gram of water requires one calorie of energy to raise the temperature 1°C.

Heat is commonly measured in calories or kilocalories, although scientifically the SI or joule is preferred. SI is the abbreviation of Le Système International d'Unites (French), which is the international system of measurement. The term applied here would be the degree. The degree is a measure of temperature. Temperature is a measure of the average kinetic energy of the particles in a body. The degree might be stated in terms of Fahrenheit (F), Kelvin (K), or Celsius (C).

Celsius is based on the freezing temperature of a body or substance being 0 degrees. To totally remove all possible internal heat within a body or substance, one must reduce the temperature to –273 degrees. This point is considered to be 0 on the Kelvin scale and is called absolute zero. The Fahrenheit scale measures the freezing point at 32°F. To convert from the Fahrenheit scale to the Celsius scale use the formula:

$$(°F – 32)\,^5\!/_9 = °C$$

unless the temperature is below zero on either scale. In that case, you must place a minus sign in front of its number in the equation.

Heat and work are similar when discussing the transfer of energy. Heat is transferred by convection, conduction, or radiation. As work is accomplished, heat is transferred. One way that heat passes from one object to another is by conduction. Not all objects will conduct heat at the same rate; therefore, they are considered poor heat conductors. A very poor conductor of heat is called an insulator.

Most gases and liquids are poor conductors. They can transfer heat by convection, the mass movement of the heated gas or liquid. This is accomplished by spurring, or sporadic movement of molecules in the mass that pass heat when they bump together. Another method of heat transfer is called radiation. Unlike conduction and convection, radiation does not require direct contact between bodies or masses. Almost all of the energy that comes to Earth is by radiation from the sun. The amount of heat that a body can radiate depends not only on its temperature but on the nature of its surface. Dark, rough surfaces tend to send out more heat than smooth, light-colored surfaces.

☞ Drill: Heat

DIRECTIONS: Carefully read and answer each of the following questions which are based on the information which you have just read.

101. Heat transfer occurs
    (1) from an object of a lower temperature to one of higher temperature.
    (2) from an object of a higher temperature to one of lower temperature.
    (3) when expansion takes place.
    (4) when electrons bump into each other.
    (5) the temperature rises.

102. Heat travels from the sun to the Earth by a process called
    (1) conduction.   (4) insulation.
    (2) convection.   (5) radiation.
    (3) connection.

103. Specific heat is related to the amount of heat
    (1) a specific object has.
    (2) one molecule contains.
    (3) transferred by one molecule.
    (4) needed to change the temperature of one gram of a substance by one degree Celsius.
    (5) two molecules contain.

104. Heat transfer by convection occurs when
    (1) electrons bump into other electrons.
    (2) large numbers of atoms move from place to place.
    (3) atoms give off heat in the form of electromagnetic waves.
    (4) electromagnetic waves travel from one place to another through a vacuum.
    (5) an electron bumps into a neutron.

105. Compared to any other substances, water has
    (1) a high specific heat.
    (2) a low specific heat.
    (3) an average specific heat.
    (4) a high average specific heat.
    (5) no temperature.

106. Heat can be measured in
    (1) joule.
    (2) calories.
    (3) kilocalories.
    (4) All of the above.
    (5) None of the above.

107. Temperature is a measure of
    (1) the total energy in a substance.
    (2) the total kinetic energy in a substance.
    (3) the average kinetic energy in a substance.
    (4) the average molecular kinetic energy in a substance.
    (5) air.

108. Internal energy is the
    (1) total amount of energy contained in an object.
    (2) average amount of energy contained in an object.
    (3) amount of energy that is transferred from one object to another object.
    (4) amount of kinetic energy each molecule has.
    (5) amount of potential energy minus the amount of kinetic energy a moledule possesses.

109. Which temperature scale designates the freezing point of water as 0 degrees?
    (1) Celsius.
    (2) Fahrenheit.
    (3) Kelvin.
    (4) joule.
    (5) All of the above.

110. Which temperature scale reads a measurement of 0 at absolute zero?
    (1) Celsius.
    (2) joule.
    (3) Kelvin.
    (4) Fahrenheit.
    (5) None of the above.

111. If the weather reporter stated that it was −10 degrees Fahrenheit outside, what would the temperature be on the Celsius scale?
    (1) 10 degrees
    (2) −5 degrees
    (3) 9 degrees
    (4) None of the above.
    (5) All of the above.

112. Heat transfer by conduction occurs when
    (1) electrons bump into atoms and other electrons.
    (2) large numbers of atoms move from place to place.

    (3)   atoms give off heat in the form of electromagnetic waves.

    (4)   the atoms are placed in a vacuum.

    (5)   atoms are sucked into a vacuum.

113. Styrofoam is a good heat

    (1)   emitter.   (4)   insulator.

    (2)   absorber.   (5)   None of the above.

    (3)   conductor.

114. A piece of metal will feel colder to the touch than a piece of wood at the same temperature. Why is this so?

    (1)   Metal is colder than wood.

    (2)   Metal, in general, has a higher heat capacity than wood.

    (3)   Metal, in general, is a better heat conductor than wood.

    (4)   Wood, in general, is a poor insulator.

    (5)   Metal cools quicker than wood.

115. Heat transfer that does not require direct contact between two objects is called

    (1)   conduction.   (4)   All of the above.

    (2)   radiation.   (5)   None of the above.

    (3)   convection.

116. Two pots are filled with boiling water. The pots are exactly the same size, but one pot is white and the other pot is black. Which pot will cool faster?

    (1)   The white pot

    (2)   The black pot

    (3)   They will cool at the same rate

    (4)   A comparison cannot be made as shape is not stated

    (5)   None of the above.

G. WAVES

A British physicist, Edward Victor Appleton, received a Nobel Prize in 1947 for his work dealing with waves. His discoveries led to defining an important region of the atmosphere called the "ionosphere." It was established that there were definite layers that would reflect and absorb various radio waves, and thus, the Appleton layers were established. These layers reflect and absorb only the long radio waves used in ordinary radio broadcasts. The shorter waves, used for television broadcasting, pass through, and that is why televisions have a limited range and must use satellite relay stations. The ionosphere is the strongest at the end of the day, after the day long effect of the sun's radiation, and weakens by dawn because many ions and electrons have recombined. Storms on the sun, intensifying the streams of particles and high-energy radiation sent to the Earth, cause the ionized layers to strengthen and thicken. The regions above the ionosphere also flare up into aurora displays.

A wave is a wiggle in space and time that can extend from one place to another. Light and sound are both forms of energy that move through space as waves. If this wiggle only occurs in time, it is called a vibration. A wave is measured in wavelengths. The high points are called the crests, the low points the troughs, and the distance from the midpoint to the crest is the amplitude. How frequently a vibration occurs is described by its frequency. The time necessary for the wave to complete one cycle is called a period.

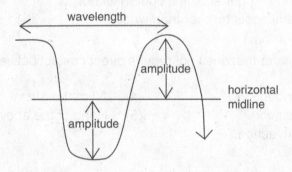

MICROWAVES

Microwaves, having wavelengths shorter than radio waves, are used in communications and to cook food.

☞ Drill: Waves

DIRECTIONS: Carefully read and answer each of the following questions which are based on the information which you have just read.

117. The wave theory assumes that
　　(1)　light is a train of waves having wave fronts in the same direction as the paths of light rays.
　　(2)　each point of a wave on a wave front may be regarded as a new source of disturbance.
　　(3)　the speed of sound in audio-dense media is less than that in air.

    (4)   a wave of sound is the line of direction of waves sent out from the base source.

    (5)   All of the above.

118. A wave
    (1)   is a disturbance that moves only through solids, liquids, and gases.
    (2)   produces a transfer of energy and matter.
    (3)   involves a quantity which changes location.
    (4)   involves a disturbance which changes in magnitude from place to place at a given time.
    (5)   is made of water.

119. A wave
    (1)   carries energy from one place to another.
    (2)   has a period.
    (3)   has a wavelength.
    (4)   All of the above.
    (5)   None of the above.

120. The time needed for a wave to make one complete cycle is called the wave's
    (1)   frequency.   (4)   velocity.
    (2)   rotation.   (5)   period.
    (3)   wavelength.

121. The distance between successive identical parts of a wave is called the wave's
    (1)   frequency.   (4)   amplitude.
    (2)   period.   (5)   trough.
    (3)   wavelength.

122. The wiggle formed by a wave in time is called the
    (1)   amplitude.   (4)   period.
    (2)   frequency.   (5)   interference.
    (3)   vibration.

123. Microwaves are waves that
    (1)   are shorter.
    (2)   are closer together.
    (3)   are longer.
    (4)   occur less frequently than usual.
    (5)   are flat.

H. LIGHT

The only thing that we can really see is light. Most objects are made visible by the light they reflect from such light sources. Scientists agree that light has a dual nature—part particle and the other part wave. The particles may be measured as photons. The waves are measured by the distance the light travels in one year. This is called a light-year. Light is defined as the only visible portion of the electromagnetic spectrum. Light is produced by vibrating electrically charged atoms that have the ability to absorb energy and emit it as light. The transfer of energy by electromagnetic waves is called radiation.

PROPERTIES

The properties of light are reflection, refraction, diffraction, and interference. The amount of the property being demonstrated depends on the amount of light, angle of the light ray, object composition and density. Material that allows all the light to pass through is called transparent. Material that blocks the light is called opaque.

Quantum is an elemental unit that describes the smallest amount of anything. One quantum of light energy is called a photon. In the micro-world, one quantum of anything is an atom. The Quantum Theory is the study of the behavior of the basic elemental form of anything. This can be adapted to all branches of science to explain behavior of matter.

Reflection occurs when a wave bounces off an object. Waves that strike the object are called incident waves, while waves that bounce off are called reflected waves. The angle between the reflected wave and the normal is called the angle of reflection. When the waves are reflected from a surface, the angle of incidence always equals the angle of reflection.

Refraction is the bending of waves toward the direction of slower wave velocity. When wavelengths become shorter, the frequency does not change. Thus, the material will determine the amount of light that is refracted.

DIFFRACTION

The bending of light around the edge of the object blocking its path is called diffraction . The effects of diffraction occur when waves pass either through an opening or around an object that blocks their path.

Light travels in waves that are transverse. This is called polarization. Other waves are longitudinal as they travel. Polarized light waves are waves that travel on one plane. Light vibrating parallel to a molecule is absorbed. The light vibrating at right angles to the rows pass through. This concept is used in the sunglass industry—sunglass lenses are designed to reduce glare.

Illumination is the process of making an object bright by increasing the amount of light per unit of area of a surface.

X-rays are electromagnetic waves with the shortest wavelength and the highest amount of energy. Electrically charged particles are filled with kinetic energy that is changed to radiation when these rays crash into other matter.

Lasers are a source of light that produces a bright and narrow beam of light of one color length and is coherent. Coherent light has the troughs and crests of the light lined up together. Lasers convert one form of energy into light energy. The laser is very bright but extremely inefficient as a light source. They are used extensively by surveyors, welders, surgeons, and by code interpreters for barcoding, as a method of ringing up sales at the supermarket.

☞ Drill: Light

DIRECTIONS: Carefully read and answer each of the following questions which are based on the information which you have just read.

124. Light is measured as
    (1)   a light-year.
    (2)   amps.
    (3)   photons.
    (4)   a light spectrum.
    (5)   amperes.

125. When you approach a light source, the wavelength of emitted light appears
    (1)   longer.
    (2)   shorter.
    (3)   the same.
    (4)   to be short and long.
    (5)   bright.

126. The energy of a photon is directly proportional to its
    (1)   period.
    (2)   photos.
    (3)   wavelength.
    (4)   amplitude.
    (5)   frequency.

127. The composition and density of an object will
    (1)   directly affect the amount of light passed.
    (2)   indirectly affect the amount of light passed.
    (3)   not affect light passing.
    (4)   cause the object to become opaque.
    (5)   enhance light.

128. Glass is transparent to light because
    (1)   light beams do not interact with glass molecules.
    (2)   glass molecules are relatively far apart.
    (3)   glass molecules have a natural frequency in the visible region.
    (4)   glass molecules reradiate absorbed light in a relatively short time.
    (5)   None of the above.

129. Electron energy states are quantized because
    (1)   electrons behave as particles.
    (2)   electrons behave as waves.
    (3)   the nucleus is quantized.
    (4)   only so many electrons will fit in one region of space.
    (5)   they are in large quantities.

130. The Quantum Theory assumes that a transfer of energy between light and matter occurs only in discrete quantities proportionate to
    (1)   the intensity of the light.
    (2)   the frequency of the radiation.
    (3)   the quantity of matter.
    (4)   the temperature of matter.
    (5)   the mass of matter.

131. The energy states available to an electron are
    (1)   continuous.   (4)   nonquantized.
    (2)   noncontinuous.   (5)   unlimited.
    (3)   quantized.

132. When an image is created by reflection from a plane mirror,
    (1)   reflected rays diverge.
    (2)   the image is located behind the mirror.
    (3)   the image is upright.
    (4)   All of the above.
    (5)   None of the above.

133. The angle between the reflected wave and the normal is called the
    (1) angle of reflection.
    (2) angle of refraction.
    (3) angle of diffraction.
    (4) angle of inference.
    (5) angle of deflection.

134. The bending of waves toward the direction of slower wave velocity is called
    (1) reflection.
    (2) diffraction.
    (3) optifraction.
    (4) refraction.
    (5) deflection.

135. A ray of light passing from one medium into another along the normal is not
    (1) deflected.
    (2) reflected.
    (3) refracted.
    (4) rerefracted.
    (5) inflicted.

136. Diffraction occurs only for
    (1) radio waves.
    (2) light.
    (3) X-rays.
    (4) Can occur for any wave.
    (5) Will not occur for any wave.

137. The effects of diffraction occur either when waves pass through an opening or around an object that
    (1) blocks their path.
    (2) opens their path.
    (3) clears their path.
    (4) leads to their path.
    (5) signals their path.

138. Light traveling in waves that are transverse and travel on one plane is called
    (1) diffracted light.
    (2) refracted light.
    (3) polarized light.
    (4) distracting light.
    (5) reflected light.

139. Light reflected from a lake surface is polarized
    (1) vertically.
    (2) horizontally.
    (3) randomly.
    (4) by refraction.
    (5) equally.

140. Illumination is the process of making an object bright by
    (1) decreasing the area of surface.
    (2) increasing the area of surface.

(3) decreasing the amount of light per unit of area of a surface.

(4) increasing the amount of light per unit of area of a surface.

(5) None of the above.

141. X-rays are electromagnetic waves with the shortest wavelength and

(1) the lowest amount of energy.

(2) the highest amount of energy.

(3) no energy.

(4) All of the above.

(5) None of the above.

142. Electrically charged particles are filled with kinetic energy that is changed to radiation when these rays

(1) crash into other matter.

(2) avoid other matter.

(3) change angles of travel.

(4) change to potential energy.

(5) Both 2 and 4.

143. Coherent light consists of light rays that all have the same

(1) frequency.   (2) phase.

(3) wavelength.   (4) All of the above.

(5) None of the above.

144. Light emitted by a laser is

(1) more coherent.   (4) coherent.

(2) less coherent.   (5) not coherent.

(3) incoherent.

I. SOUND

Sound travels about 4-1/2 times faster in seawater than in air. Its speed is affected by temperature, salinity, and pressure; an increase in any of these results in an increase in the speed of sound.

Sound energy does not travel in straight lines in the ocean because of density differences in water. It is refracted, or bent, by variations in sound speed of the water, scattered by suspended material or marine organisms, reflected and scattered by the surface and bottom, and attenuated by the water through which it travels.

Ambient noise refers to any noise or sound produced by the environment or living creatures or organisms.

There are many varieties of sounds that are produced to be captured by the ear and interpreted by the brain. The brain easily distinguishes one sound from another, yet sound is only a longitudinal wave, a rhythmic disturbance of the air that carries energy. Sound waves are compression waves produced by vibrating matter. Ultrasound is used extensively in medical treatment. One way is through picturing a fetus in the womb without any danger to the fetus or the mother.

When any frequency of forced vibrations on an object matches the natural frequency of the object, the measure of the sound increases. The use of tuning forks adjusted to the same frequency and spaced a meter apart is the most common way to demonstrate resonance.

☞ **Drill: Sound**

DIRECTIONS: Carefully read and answer each of the following questions which are based on the information which you have just read.

145. Sounds are produced by
    (1) matter at rest.
    (2) liquids in motion.
    (3) solids only.
    (4) solids, liquids, or gases.
    (5) your eardrum.

146. An increase in temperature results in
    (1) an increase in the speed of sound.
    (2) a decrease in the speed of sound.
    (3) an increase in the pressure of sound waves.
    (4) a decrease in the pressure of sound waves.
    (5) None of the above.

147. Compared to the speed of light, the speed of sound is
    (1) faster.
    (2) slower.
    (3) the same.
    (4) Cannot be compared.
    (5) Has not been determined.

148. Ambient noise refers to
    (1) wavelengths of sound vibration.
    (2) any sound produced one does not want to hear.
    (3) any noise or sound produced by the environment or living creatures or organisms.

(4)   noise that cannot be heard.
(5)   loud sounds.

149. The most common transmitting medium for sound vibrations is
     (1)   metal wires.   (4)   clay.
     (2)   earth.   (5)   air.
     (3)   water.

150. Ultrasound is a(n)
     (1)   type of radio wave.
     (2)   sound wave.
     (3)   X-ray wave.
     (4)   combination of sound and light waves.
     (5)   vibration.

151. Resonance occurs when you
     (1)   push an object.
     (2)   hit an object with a hammer.
     (3)   vibrate an object.
     (4)   force an object to vibrate at its natural frequency.
     (5)   hit your vocal cords.

152. The use of the tuning forks demonstrates
     (1)   sound.   (4)   resonance.
     (2)   amplitude.   (5)   pitch.
     (3)   frequency.

J. ELECTRICITY

An electrical charge resting on an object is called static electricity. If this static electricity is placed in motion, it becomes an electrical current. It is the electrical current that we use in most electrical appliances. This same static electricity can be produced by rubbing a hard rubber rod or sealing wax with a piece of fur or flannel. Also, the same result can be accomplished by rubbing a glass rod with a piece of silk.

Electricity can be carried by matter that is a conductor. Sometimes this is accomplished by a spark, which is a static discharge, or a transfer of static electricity. Materials that are poor conductors, such as wood, plastic, rubber, or glass, are used as insulators or grounds which allow an object to lose its charge in a given direction.

A flow of electrons or charged particles through a conductor is called an electric current. This is demonstrated by use of an electroscope.

Electrical circuits function very efficiently within homes. Most circuits are either alternating current (AC) or direct current (DC). Electricity can be supplied to a water heater to heat water, or through wiring and a bulb to produce artificial light. The energy is carried by means of electrical current from a power plant. One common electrical circuit is the series circuit. A path is formed by electric conductors in the form of wire to carry the current. The series circuit has only one path for the current so the current will be the same through every part.

Another circuit is the parallel circuit, in which there are two or more separate branches for the current to flow. This is the type of circuit used in string lights for a Christmas tree such that when one light goes out, the rest of the lights will stay on. Also, this type of wiring pattern is used for the outlets in our homes. It is not necessary for all the outlets to be in use at all times for electricity to be available at the flip of a switch.

One electronic device that is commonly used is the battery. A battery acts like a pump forcing electrons through a conductor. There are two types of batteries: wet cell battery and dry cell battery. A wet cell battery contains two different metals in a solution containing an electrode. The car battery is an example of the wet cell battery. The dry cell battery contains a carbon rod set in the middle of a zinc holder. A moist paste sets up a chemical reaction that causes electrons to be released.

☞ Drill: Electricity

DIRECTIONS: Carefully read and answer each of the following questions which are based on the information which you have just read.

153. Static electricity compressed will become
    (1)   a kilowatt.   (4)   sound current.
    (2)   static energy.   (5)   a shock.
    (3)   an electrical current.

154. Electric energy is measured in
    (1)   a kilowatt hour.   (4)   number of wavelengths.
    (2)   Celsius.   (5)   volts.
    (3)   currents.

155. A property of electricity is that it can
    (1) be carried by a conductor.
    (2) not be carried by a conductor.
    (3) act like static.
    (4) be carried by an insulator.
    (5) change form.

156. An electric current is produced when electrons or charged particles flow through
    (1) an insulator.   (4) an oscilloscope.
    (2) a conductor.   (5) a microscope.
    (3) an electroscope.

157. Alternating current is made by
    (1) alternating the voltage at the energy source.
    (2) alternating current and voltage.
    (3) using huge batteries.
    (4) emptying chemical batteries.
    (5) turning the light switch on and off.

158. One type of current may be carried in only one path. This is called a(n)
    (1) direct current.   (4) parallel circuit.
    (2) alternating current.   (5) one-way charge.
    (3) series circuit.

159. Electrical elements in our homes are connected in
    (1) series circuits.   (4) switches.
    (2) parallel circuits.   (5) wires.
    (3) outlets.

160. Where there are two or more separate branches for the current to flow, this is called
    (1) current circuits.   (4) parallel circuits.
    (2) outlet circuits.   (5) forked circuits.
    (3) series circuits.

161. A battery acts like a pump forcing electrons through
    (1) a series circuit.   (4) series insulator.
    (2) a parallel circuit.   (5) a conductor.
    (3) an insulator.

162. There are two types of batteries:
    (1) wet cell battery and dry cell battery.
    (2) alternating current battery and direct current battery.
    (3) well cell battery and alternating current battery.
    (4) direct and dry cell batteries.
    (5) size AA and D batteries.

K. MAGNETISM

Magnetism is the ability to attract iron and certain other metals that have a molecular structure similar to iron. Magnetism is related to electricity in that it travels in currents. Magnets exert a force on another magnet just like an electrical charge. They can attract or repel each other without touching because of their electrical charges. The strength of their interaction depends on the distance of separation of the two magnets.

Magnetism was explained by Albert Einstein in 1905 in his theory of special relativity when he showed that a magnetic field is a by-product of the electric field. Charges in motion have associated with them both an electric and a magnetic field. A magnetic field is produced by the motion of the electric charge.

A voltmeter is a calibrated device used to measure the electric potential. This electrical current produces a magnetic field. The same principal construction is used in the making of an electric motor. The principal difference is that the current is made to change direction every time the coil makes a half revolution.

Speakers used in car radios, home stereos, and loudspeaker systems belong in the grouping of electromagnets. A speaker consists of a coil of thin wire that goes between the poles of a magnet. The coil is attached to a cone-shaped piece of stiff paper that converts the electrical current into sound.

☞ Drill: Magnetism

<u>DIRECTIONS</u>: Carefully read and answer each of the following questions which are based on the information which you have just read.

163. Magnetic fields are produced by
    (1) charges at rest.   (4) magnets.
    (2) moving particles.   (5) moving charged particles.
    (3) moving particles of Earth.

164. Magnetic domains are
    (1)   clusters of atoms randomly aligned.
    (2)   blocks of material.
    (3)   regions that may or may not be magnetized.
    (4)   regions of atoms magnetically aligned.
    (5)   clusters of magnets.

165. According to Einstein,
    (1)   all motion is relative.
    (2)   a planet moves around the sun because of the gravitational force exerted by the sun.
    (3)   there is a unique spot relative to which all motion can be measured.
    (4)   All of the above.
    (5)   None of the above.

166. The electromagnetic theory
    (1)   was developed by James Clark.
    (2)   describes the manner in which radiated energy spreads in dense space.
    (3)   predicts that heat radiation travels in space with the speed of light.
    (4)   states that the energy of electromagnetic radiations will not split.
    (5)   was developed by accident.

167. A speaker converts an electrical current into sound by
    (1)   a coil of thin wire that goes between the poles of a magnet.
    (2)   a coil of thin wire going around the poles of an electromagnet.
    (3)   changing energy forms.
    (4)   All of the above.
    (5)   None of the above.

PHYSICS

ANSWER KEY

Drill: Basic Concepts of Physics

1.	(4)	15.	(4)	29.	(3)	43.	(5)
2.	(4)	16.	(4)	30.	(1)	44.	(4)
3.	(2)	17.	(2)	31.	(4)	45.	(1)
4.	(3)	18.	(1)	32.	(4)	46.	(3)
5.	(5)	19.	(3)	33.	(1)	47.	(2)
6.	(2)	20.	(1)	34.	(2)	48.	(1)
7.	(4)	21.	(5)	35.	(2)	49.	(2)
8.	(1)	22.	(2)	36.	(2)	50.	(1)
9.	(4)	23.	(1)	37.	(4)	51.	(3)
10.	(3)	24.	(3)	38.	(4)	52.	(4)
11.	(1)	25.	(4)	39.	(1)	53.	(3)
12.	(1)	26.	(2)	40.	(4)	54.	(3)
13.	(2)	27.	(4)	41.	(2)	55.	(4)
14.	(2)	28.	(4)	42.	(1)		

Drill: Matter, Mass, and Density

56.	(4)	58.	(1)	60.	(4)	61.	(2)
57.	(5)	59.	(4)				

Drill: Motion

62.	(4)	66.	(1)	70.	(3)	74.	(3)
63.	(3)	67.	(3)	71.	(4)	75.	(1)
64.	(5)	68.	(3)	72.	(4)		
65.	(5)	69.	(1)	73.	(3)		

Drill: Force

76.	(1)	79.	(2)	82.	(4)	84.	(4)
77.	(4)	80.	(3)	83.	(3)		
78.	(2)	81.	(4)				

Drill: Energy

85. (2)	89. (5)	93. (1)	97. (2)
86. (4)	90. (3)	94. (3)	98. (2)
87. (4)	91. (4)	95. (1)	99. (2)
88. (2)	92. (2)	96. (2)	100. (1)

Drill: Heat

101. (2)	105. (1)	109. (1)	113. (4)
102. (5)	106. (4)	110. (3)	114. (3)
103. (4)	107. (4)	111. (4)	115. (2)
104. (2)	108. (1)	112. (1)	116. (1)

Drill: Waves

117. (2)	119. (4)	121. (3)	123. (1)
118. (4)	120. (5)	122. (3)	

Drill: Light

124. (3)	130. (2)	136. (4)	142. (1)
125. (2)	131. (3)	137. (1)	143. (4)
126. (5)	132. (4)	138. (3)	144. (4)
127. (1)	133. (1)	139. (2)	
128. (4)	134. (4)	140. (4)	
129. (1)	135. (3)	141. (2)	

Drill: Sound

145. (4)	147. (2)	149. (5)	151. (4)
146. (1)	148. (3)	150. (2)	152. (4)

Drill: Electricity

153. (3)	156. (2)	159. (2)	161. (5)
154. (1)	157. (1)	160. (4)	162. (1)
155. (1)	158. (3)		

Drill: Magnetism

163. (5)	165. (1)	167. (1)
164. (4)	166. (3)	

LANGUAGE ARTS: READING REVIEW

Chapter 5

LANGUAGE ARTS: READING REVIEW

I. LANGUAGE ARTS: READING TOPICS

II. READING PROSE

III. READING POETRY

IV. READING DRAMA

V. READING COMMENTARY

This review is meant to help you become familiar with the types of reading passages you will find on the Language Arts: Reading section of the GED. Each of these types of writing communicate ideas in a very distinct way. This review will help you understand how each type differs from the others. It will also help you learn how to handle types of writing that may be unfamiliar to you.

When you begin reading each section, do not become frustrated if some of the vocabulary is new to you. Before too long you will understand the new words. You do not have to try to memorize any of the literary terms that may come up, just so long as you understand them while you are reading the review. Relax and consider all of the points that the review sections make about the individual types of writing. This will train you to handle these same types of writing when you take the actual GED. Here is a breakdown of the questions on the GED Language Arts: Reading section.

I. LANGUAGE ARTS: READING TOPICS

The topics listed below should be reviewed in order to accurately answer the questions appearing on the Literature and the Arts test of the GED. See the review on the pages which follow.

LITERARY FICTION (75% of Test)

1. Fictional Prose
2. Poetry
3. Drama

NONFICTION PROSE (25% of Test)

1. Comments
2. Criticism
3. Reviews

The literature on the GED will range from primarily American authors to a representation of English and Canadian authors, as well as some translations from world literature. These works will include contemporary literature, works from the popular press, fiction, non-fiction, poetry, prose, and criticism, reviews, comments on literature, the fine arts, television, film, and dance.

A casual survey of recent years' exams reveals that the following authors' works are frequently offered for discussion: Edith Wharton, Robert Frost, D.H. Lawrence, Twain, Steinbeck, Emerson, Thoreau, Hemingway, Thomas Wolfe, Tennessee Williams, Stephen Crane, Carl Sandburg, Fitzgerald, Faulkner, Eugene O'Neill, Katherine Ann Porter, G.K. Chesterton, Ralph Ellison, William Golding, Joyce Carol Oates, Mary Gordon, Studs Terkel, James Baldwin, Ken Kesey, Betty Friedan, Gail Godwin, Robert Stone, John Irving, John LeCarré, Toni Morrison, Mary McCarthy, and Maya Angelou. What these authors' works have in common is their significance and relevance to the human condition, as well as their merit as literary works. They have something to say, and they say it well.

As you read this review, think about how each of the writing types differs from the rest. Keep in mind the objectives of each of the types (literary fiction and nonfiction prose). Finally, be sure you understand one section before you go on to the next. This understanding will do wonders for you when you take the actual GED.

II. READING PROSE

What is prose? Basically, prose is **not** poetry. Prose is what we write and speak most of the time in our everyday lives: unmetered, unrhymed language. Which is not to say that prose does not have its own rhythms—language, whether written or spoken, has cadence and balance. And certainly prose can have instances of rhyme and alliteration. After all, language is **phonic**, or meant to be heard.

Furthermore, **prose** may be either **fiction** or **nonfiction**. A novel (like a short story) is fiction; an autobiography is nonfiction. While a novel (or short story) may have autobiographical elements, an autobiography is presumed to be entirely factual. Essays are usually described in other terms: expository, argumentative; persuasive, critical, narrative. Essays may be either fiction or nonfiction. Prose may also include everyday material such as employee handbooks, business contracts, or memos.

READING NOVELS

What is a novel? A good description might be that a novel is a rather long story, filled with many characters and subplots, interlaced with motifs, symbols, and themes, with time and space to develop interrelationships and to present descriptive passages. Much "popular" literature today is formulaic—the endless series of romance novels by various publishers, the sequel upon sequel of sword-and-sorcery novels, and Western novels by genuine cowboys. But popularity alone is not the measure for significance nor for merit. Telling a story whose plot is probable yet refreshingly unpredictable is an art. Characters who seem real and familiar, yet unique and individual, are the creations of skilled writers.

Analyzing novels is a bit like asking the journalist's questions "the five W's and an H": who?, what?, when?, where?, why?, and how? The "**what**" is the story, the narrative, the plot, and subplots. Some students may be familiar with Freytag's Pyramid, originally designed to describe the structure of a five-act drama but now widely used to analyze fiction as well. The stages generally specified are **introduction** or **exposition, complication, rising action, climax, falling action,** and **denouement** or **conclusion**. As the novel's events are charted, the "change which structures the story" should emerge. There are many events in a long narrative, but generally only one set of events comprises the "real" or "significant" story; this is the plot.

Also important, subplots often parallel or serve as counterpoints to the main plot line, serving to enhance the central story. Minor characters sometimes have essentially the same conflicts and goals as the major characters, but the consequences of the outcome seem less important.

Sometimes an author divides the novel into chapters—named or unnamed, perhaps just numbered. Or he might divide the novel into "books" or "parts," with chapters as subsections. Readers should take their cue from these divisions; the author must have had some reason for them. Take note of what happens in each larger section, as well as within the smaller chapters. Whose progress is being followed? What event or occurrence is being foreshadowed or prepared for? What causal or other relationships are there between sections and events? Some writers, such as Steinbeck in *The Grapes of Wrath*, use *intercalary* chapters, alternating between the "real" story (the Joads) and peripheral or parallel stories (the Okies and migrants in general). Look for the pattern of such organization; try to see the interrelationships of these alternating chapters.

Of course, plots cannot happen in isolation from characters, the "who." Not only are there major and minor characters to consider; we need to note whether the various characters are **static** or **dynamic**. Static characters do not change in significant ways—that is, in ways which relate to the story which is structuring the novel. A character may die and still be static, unless his death is central to the narrative. For instance, in Golding's *Lord of the Flies*, the boy with the mulberry birthmark apparently dies in a fire early in the novel. Momentous as any person's death is, this boy's death is not what the novel is about. He is a static character. However, when Simon is killed, and later Piggy, the narrative is directly impacted because the reason for their deaths is central to the novel's theme regarding man's innate evil. Piggy and Simon are dynamic characters. A dynamic character may change only slightly in his attitudes, but those changes may be the very ones upon which the narrative rests.

We describe major characters or "actors" in novels as **protagonists** or **antagonists**. The *pro*tagonist struggles **toward** or for someone or something; the *an*tagonist struggles **against** someone or something. The possible conflicts are usually cited as man against himself, man against man, man against society, man against nature. Sometimes more than one of these conflicts appears in a story, but usually one is dominant and is the structuring device.

A character can be referred to as **stock**, meaning that he exists because the plot demands it. For instance, a Western with a gunman who robs the bank will require a number of **stock** characters: the banker's lovely daughter, the tough but kindhearted barmaid, the cowardly white-shirted citizen who sells out the hero to save his own skin, and the young freckle-faced lad who shoots the bad guy from a second-story hotel window.

Or a character can be a **stereotype**, without unique characteristics. For instance, a sheriff in a small Southern town; a football player who is all brawn; a librarian clucking over her prized books; the cruel commandant of a POW camp.

Characters often serve as **foils** for other characters, enabling us to see one or both of them better. A classic example is Tom Sawyer, the Romantic foil for Huck Finn's Realism. Or, in Harper Lee's *To Kill a Mockingbird*, Scout is the naive observer of events which her brother Jem, four years older, comes to understand from the perspective of the adult world.

Sometimes characters are **allegorical**, or **symbolic**, standing for qualities or concepts rather than for actual people. For instance, Jim Casey (initials "J. C.") in *The Grapes of Wrath* is often regarded as a Christ figure, pure and self-sacrificing in his aims for the migrant workers.

Other characters are fully three-dimensional, "rounded," examples of humans in all their virtue, vice, hope, despair, strength, and weakness. This rich variety aids the author in creating characters who are credible and plausible, without being dully predictable and mundane.

The interplay of plot and characters determines in large part the **theme** of a work, the **"why."** First of all, we must distinguish between a mere topic and a genuine theme or thesis; and then between a theme and contributing *motifs*. A **topic** is a phrase, such as "man's inhumanity toward man"; or "the fickle nature of fate." A **theme**, however, turns a phrase into a statement: "Man's inhumanity toward man is barely concealed by 'civilization'." Or "Man is a helpless pawn, at the mercy of fickle fate." Many writers may deal with the same **topic,** such as the complex nature of true love; but their **themes** may vary widely, from "True love will always win out in the end" to "Not even true love can survive the cruel ironies of fate."

To illustrate the relationship between plot, character, and theme, let's examine two familiar fairy tales. In "The Ugly Duckling," the structuring story line is "Once upon a time there was an ugly duckling, who in turn became a beautiful swan." In this case, the duckling did nothing to deserve his ugliness or his eventual transformation; but he did not curse fate. He only wept and waited, lonely and outcast. And when he became beautiful, he did not gloat; he eagerly joined the other members of his flock, who greatly admired him. Theme: "Good things come to him who waits," or "Life is unfair—you don't get what you deserve, nor deserve what you get"? What happens to the theme if the ugly duckling remains an ugly duckling: "Some guys just never get a break"?

Especially rewarding to examine for the connection between plot and theme is "Cinderella": "Once upon a time, a lovely, sweet-natured young girl was forced to labor and serve her ugly and ungrateful stepmother and two stepsisters. But thanks to her Fairy Godmother, Cinderella and the Prince marry, and live happily ever after."

We could change events (plot elements) at any point, but let's take the penultimate scene where the Prince's men come to the door with the single glass slipper. Cinderella has been shut away so that she is not present when the other women in the house try on the slipper. Suppose that the stepmother or either of the two stepsisters tries on the slipper—and it fits! Cinderella is in the back room doing the laundry, and her family waltzes out the door to the palace and she doesn't even get an invitation to the wedding. And imagine the Prince's dismay when the ugly, one-slippered lady lifts her wedding veil for the consummating kiss! Theme: "There is no justice in the world, for those of low or high station"; or "Virtue is not its own reward"?

Or let's say that during the slipper-test scene, the stepsisters, stepmother, and finally Cinderella all try on the shoe, but to no avail. And then in sashays the Fairy Godmother, who gives them all a knowing smirk, puts out her slipper-sized foot and cackles hysterically, like the Joker from "Batman." Theme: "You can't trust anybody these days"; or, a favorite statement of theme, "Appearances can be deceiving." The link between plot and theme is very strong, indeed.

Skilled writers often employ **motifs** to help unify their works. A motif is a detail or element of the story which is repeated throughout, and which may even become symbolic. Television shows are ready examples of the use of motifs. A medical show, with many scenes alternately set in the hospital waiting room and operating room, uses elements such as the pacing, anxious parent or loved one, the gradually filling ashtray, the large wall clock whose hands melt from one hour to another. And in the operating room, the half-masked surgeon whose brow is frequently mopped by the nurse; the gloved hand open-palmed to receive scalpel, sponge, and so on; the various oscilloscopes giving readouts of the patient's very fragile condition; the expanding and collapsing bladder manifesting that the patient is indeed breathing; and, again, the wall clock, assuring us that this procedure is taking forever. These are all **motifs**, details which in concert help convince the reader that this story occurs in a hospital, and that the mood is pretty tense, that the medical team is doing all it can, and that Mom and Dad will be there when the patient wakes up.

But motifs can become symbolic. The oscilloscope line quits blipping, levels out, and gives off the ominous hum. And the doctor's gloved hand sets down the scalpel and shuts off the oscilloscope. In the waiting room, Dad crushes the empty cigarette pack; Mom quits pacing and sinks into the sofa. The door to the waiting room swings shut silently behind the retreating doctor. All these elements signal "It's over, finished."

This example is very crude and mechanical, but motifs in the hands of a skillful writer are valuable devices. And in isolation, and often magnified, a single motif can become a controlling image with great significance. For instance, Emma Bovary's shoes signify her obsession with material things; and when her delicate slippers become soiled as she crosses the dewy grass to meet her lover, we sense the impurity of her act as well as its hopelessness. Or when wise Piggy, in *Lord of the Flies*, is reduced to one lens in his glasses, and finally to no glasses at all, we see the loss of insight and wisdom on the island, and chaos follows.

Setting is the "where" of the story: interior—what structure; exterior—in what locality; and even the world or realm—this world or another. But setting is also the "when": time of day, time of year, time period or year; it is the dramatic moment, the precise intersection of time and space when this story is being told. Setting is also the atmosphere: positive or negative, calm, chaotic, Gothic, Romantic. The question for the reader to answer is whether the setting is ultimately essential to the plot/theme, or whether it is incidental; i.e., could this story/theme have been told successfully in another time and/or place? For instance, could the theme in *Lord of the Flies* be made manifest if the boys were not on an island? Could they have been isolated in some other place? Does it matter whether the "war" which they are fleeing is WWII or WWIII or some other conflict, in terms of the theme?

Hopefully, the student will see that the four elements of plot, character, theme, and setting are intertwined and largely interdependent. A work must really be read as a whole, rather than dissected and analyzed in discrete segments.

The final question, "how," relates to an author's style. Style involves language (word choice), syntax (word order, sentence type and length), the balance between narration and dialogue, the choice of narrative voice (first person participant, third person with limited omniscience), use of descriptive passages, and other aspects of the actual words on the page which are basically irrelevant to the first four elements (plot, character, theme, and setting). Stylistic differences are fairly easy to spot among such diverse writers as Jane Austen, whose style is—to today's reader—very formal and mannered; Mark Twain, whose style is very casual and colloquial; William Faulkner, whose prose often spins on without punctuation or paragraphs far longer than the reader can hold either the thought or his breath; and Hemingway, whose dense but spare, pared-down style has earned the epithet, "Less is more."

READING SHORT STORIES

The modern short story differs from earlier short fiction, such as the parable, fable, and tale, in its emphasis on character development through scenes rather than summary: through *showing* rather than *telling*. Gaining popularity in the 19th century, the short story generally was realistic, presenting detailed accounts of the lives of middle-class people. This tendency toward realism dictates that the plot be grounded in *probability*. There was a good chance that these events could really happen. Furthermore, the characters are human with recognizable human motivations, both social and psychological. Setting—time and place—is realistic rather than fantastic. And, as Poe stipulated, the elements of plot, character, setting, style, point of view, and theme all work toward a single *unified* effect.

However, some modern writers have stretched these boundaries and have mixed in elements of nonrealism—such as the supernatural and the fantastic—sometimes switching back and forth between realism and nonrealism, confusing the reader who is expecting conventional fiction. Barth's "Lost in the Funhouse" and Allen's "The Kugelmass Episode" are two stories which are not, strictly speaking, *realistic*. However, if the reader will approach and accept this type of story on its own terms, he will be better able to understand and appreciate them fully.

Unlike the novel, which has time and space to develop characters and relationships, the short story must rely on flashes of insight and revelation to develop plot and characters. The "slice of life" in a short story is much narrower than that in a novel; the time span is much shorter, the focus much tighter. To attempt anything like the grandness available to the novelist would be to view fireworks through a soda straw: occasionally pretty, but ultimately not very satisfying or enlightening.

The elements of the short story are those of the novel, discussed earlier. However, because of the compression of time and concentration of effect, probably the short story writer's most important decision is **point of view**. A narrator may be *objective*, presenting information without bias or comment. Hemingway frequently uses the objective *third-person* narrator, presenting scenes almost dramatically, i.e., with a great deal of dialogue and very little narrative, none of which directly reveals the thoughts or feelings of the characters. We say that such a narrator is fully or partially *omniscient*, depending on how complete his knowledge is of the characters' psychological and emotional makeup. The least objective narrator is the *first-person* narrator, who presents information from the perspective of a single character who is a participant in the action. Such a narrative choice allows the author to present the discrepancies between the writer's/reader's perceptions and those of the narrator.

One reason the choice of narrator, the point of view from which to tell the story, is immensely important in a short story is that the narrator reveals character and event in ways which affect our understanding of theme. For instance, in Faulkner's "A Rose for Emily," the unnamed narrator who seems to be a townsperson tells the story out of order. The narrator withholds information which would explain the events being presented, letting the reader puzzle over Emily Grierson's motivations, a device common in detective fiction. In fact, the narrator presents contradictory information, making the reader alternately pity and resent the spinster. When we examine the imagery and conclude that Miss Emily and her house represent the decay and decadence of the Old South which resisted the invasion of "progress" from the North, we see the importance of setting and symbol in relation to theme.

Similarly, in Mansfield's "Bliss," the abundant description of setting creates the controlling image of the lovely pear tree. But this symbol of fertile life becomes ironic when Bertha Young belatedly feels sincere and overwhelming desire for her husband. The third-person narrator's omniscience is limited to Bertha's thoughts and feelings; otherwise, we would have seen her husband's infidelity with Miss Fulton.

In O'Connor's "Good Country People," the narrator is broadly omniscient, but the reader is still taken by surprise at the cruelty of the Bible salesman who seduces Joy-Hulga. That he steals her artificial leg is perhaps poetic justice, since she (with her numerous degrees) had fully intended to seduce him ("just good country people"). The story's title, the characters' names—Hopewell, Freeman, Joy; the salesman's professed Christianity, the Bibles hollowed out to hold whiskey and condoms, add to the irony of Mrs. Freeman's final comment on the young man: "Some can't be that simple... I know I never could."

The importance of tense is demonstrated in a short story by John Updike. The youthful narrator in "A & P" also uses present tense, but not consistently, which gives his narrative a very casual, even unschooled flavor. Sammy identifies himself in the opening paragraph: "In walks these three girls in nothing but bathing suits. I'm in the third checkout slot, with my back to the door, so I don't see them until they're over by the bread." And later, "Stokesie's married, with two babies chalked up on his fuselage already, but as far as I can tell that's the only difference. He's twenty-two, and I was nineteen this April." The girls incur the wrath of the store manager, who scolds them for their inappropriate dress. And Sammy, in his adolescent idealism, quits on the spot; although he realizes that he does not want to "do this" to his parents, he tells us "… it seems to me that once you begin a gesture it's fatal not to go through with it." But, his gesture is ill-spent: "I look around for my girls, but they're gone, of course… I could see Lengel in my place in the slot, checking the sheep through. His face was dark gray and his back stiff, as if he'd just had an injection of iron, and my stomach kind of fell as I felt how hard the world was going to be to me hereafter."

Answering GED exam questions on short stories is much the same as addressing questions on novels. The student must answer multiple choice questions which require close reading for such elements as tone, style, atmosphere, and inference. Knowing the story beforehand may help the student, but the ability to analyze is the major component of this type of exam.

READING ESSAYS

Essays fall into four rough categories: **speculative, argumentative, narrative**, and **expository**. Depending on the writer's purpose, his essay will fit more or less into one or these groupings.

The **speculative** essay is so named because, as its Latin root suggests, it *looks* at ideas; explores them rather than explains them. While the speculative essay may be said to be *meditative*, it often makes one or more points. But the thesis may not be as obvious or clear-cut as that in an expository or argumentative essay. The writer deals with ideas in an associative manner, playing with ideas in a looser structure than he would in an expository or argumentative essay. This "flow" may even produce *intercalary* paragraphs, which present alternately a narrative of sorts and thoughtful responses to the events being recounted, as in E.B. White's "The Ring of Time."

The purposes of the **argumentative** essay, on the other hand, are always clear: to present a point and provide evidence, which may be factual or anecdotal, and to support it. The structure is usually very formal, as in a debate, with counterpositions and counterarguments. Whatever the organizational pattern, the writer's intent in an argumentative essay is to persuade his reader of the validity of some claim, as Francis Bacon does in "Of Love."

Narrative and **expository** essays have elements of both the speculative and argumentative modes. The narrative essay may recount an incident or a series of incidents and is almost always autobiographical, in order to make a point, as in George Orwell's "Shooting an Elephant." The informality of the story-telling makes the narrative essay less insistent than the argumentative essay, but more directed than the speculative essay.

Students are probably most familiar with the **expository** essay, the primary purpose of which is to explain and clarify ideas. While the expository essay may have narrative elements, that aspect is minor and subservient to that of explanation. Furthermore, while nearly all essays have some element of persuasion, argumentation is incidental in the expository essay. In any event, the four categories—speculative, argumentative, narrative, and expository— are neither exhaustive nor mutually exclusive.

As nonfiction, essays have a different set of elements from novels and short stories: **voice, style, structure,** and **thought**.

Voice in nonfiction is similar to the narrator's tone in fiction; but the major difference is in who is "speaking." In fiction, the author is not the speaker— the **narrator** is the speaker. Students sometimes have difficulty with this distinction, but it is necessary if we are to preserve the integrity of the fictive "story." In an essay, however, the author speaks directly to the reader, even if he is presenting ideas which he may not actually espouse personally. This directness creates the writer's **tone**, his attitude toward his subject.

Style in nonfiction derives from the same elements as style in fiction word choice, syntax, balance between dialogue and narration, voice, use of description—those things specifically related to words on the page. Generally speaking, an argumentative essay will be written in a more formal style than will a narrative essay, and a meditative essay will be less formal than an expository essay. But such generalizations are only descriptive, not prescriptive (rules for writing the essay).

Structure and **thought**, the final elements of essays, are so intertwined as to be inseparable. Just as in our discussion of the interdependence of plot and theme, we must be aware that to change the structure of an essay will alter its meaning. For instance, in White's "The Ring of Time," to abandon the *intercalary* paragraph organization, separating the paragraphs which narrate the scenes with the young circus rider from those which reflect on the nature of time, would alter our understanding of the essay's thesis. Writers signal structural shifts with alterations in focus, as well as with visual clues (spacing), verbal clues (*but, therefore, however*), or shifts in the kind of information being presented (personal, scientific, etc.).

Thought is perhaps the single element which most distinguishes nonfiction from fiction. The essayist chooses his form not to tell a story but to present an idea. Whether he chooses the speculative, narrative, argumentative, or expository format, the essayist has something on his mind that he wants to convey to his readers. And it is this idea which we are after when we analyze his essay.

Often studied is Orwell's "Shooting an Elephant," a narrative essay recounting (presumably) the writer's experience in Burma as an officer of the British law that ruled the poverty-ridden people of a small town. Orwell begins with two paragraphs which explain that, as a white European authority figure, he was subjected to taunts and abuse by the natives. Ironically, he sympathized with the Burmese and harbored fairly strong anti-British feelings, regarding the imperialists as oppressors rather than saviors. He tells us that he felt caught, trapped between his position of authority, which he himself resented, and the hatred of those he was required to oversee.

The body of the essay—some eleven paragraphs—relates the incident with an otherwise tame elephant gone mad which had brought chaos and destruction to the village. Only occasionally does Orwell interrupt the narrative to reveal his reactions directly, but his descriptions of the Burmese are sympathetically drawn. The language is heavily connotative, revealing the helplessness of the villagers against both the elephant and the miserable circumstances of their lives.

Orwell recounts how, having sent for an elephant gun, he found that he was compelled to shoot the animal, even though its destruction was by now unwarranted and even ill-advised, given the value of the elephant to the village. But the people expected it, demanded it; the white man realized that he did not have dominion over these people of color after all. They were in charge, not he.

To make matters worse, Orwell bungles the "murder" of the beast, which takes half an hour to die in great agony. And in the aftermath of discussions of the rightness or wrongness of his action, Orwell wonders if anyone realizes he killed the elephant only to save face. It is the final sentence of the final paragraph which directly reveals the author's feelings, although he has made numerous indirect references to them throughout the essay. Coupled with the opening paragraphs, this conclusion presents British imperialism of the period in a very negative light: "the unable doing the unnecessary to the ungrateful."

Having discovered Orwell's main idea, we must look at the other elements (voice, style, structure) to see *how* he communicates it to the reader. The voice of the first-person narrative is fairly formal, yet remarkably candid, using connotation to color our perception of the events. Orwell's narrative has many complex sentences, with vivid descriptive phrases in series, drawing our eye along the landscape and through the crowds as he ponders his next move. Structurally, the essay first presents a premise about British imperialism. Next the essay moves to a gripping account of the officer's reluctant shooting of the elephant, and finally ends with an admission of his own guilt as an agent of the institution he detests. Orwell frequently signals shifts between his role as officer and his responses as a humane person by using the word *but* or by using dashes to set off his responses to the events he is recounting.

The GED essay exam could conceivably take any work and ask the student to discuss how the writer's attitude toward *time* is revealed; to compare/contrast the attitudes toward time in any pair of essays; to look at the writer's use of language in any essay and discuss the resulting *voice*. The most important thing, as always, is to read and reread the question carefully; the next most important thing is to read and reread the work(s) to be discussed. Try to find the *thought* which the writer means to communicate; then analyze for *voice*, *style*, and *structure*.

☞ Drill: Reading Prose

DIRECTIONS: Read the following passage and answer the questions which follow.

1   And it was at this moment, as I stood there with the rifle in my hands, that I first grasped the hollowness, the futility of the white man's dominion in the East. Here was I, the white man with his gun, standing in front of the unarmed native crowd—seemingly the

5   leading actor of the piece; but in reality I was only an absurd puppet pushed to and fro by the will of those yellow faces behind. I perceived in this moment that when the white man turns tyrant it is his own freedom that he destroys.

George Orwell, "Shooting an Elephant"

1. How is the narrator feeling at this moment?
   (1) Uncomfortable   (4) Arrogant
   (2) Joyous   (5) Resentful
   (3) Contented

2. What is the setting of the passage?
   (1) England   (4) Australia
   (2) Alaska   (5) Texas
   (3) Asia

3. "Absurd puppet" in line 5 refers to
   (1) the elephant.   (4) the government.
   (2) the native king.   (5) the gun.
   (3) the white man.

III. READING POETRY

Opening a book to study for an examination is perhaps the worst time to read poetry, or read about poetry, because above all, poetry should be enjoyed; it is definitely "reading for pleasure." This last phrase seems to have developed recently to describe the reading we do other than for information or for study. Perhaps you personally would not choose poetry as pleasure reading because of the bad name poetry has received over the years. Some students regard the "old" poetry, such as Donne's or Shelley's, as difficult or dull, or modern poetry as too weird. It is hard to imagine that poetry was the "current language" for students growing up in the Elizabethan or Romantic eras. Whereas in our world information can be retrieved in a nanosecond, in those worlds time was plentiful to sit down, clear the mind, and let poetry take over. Very often the meaning of a poem does not come across immediately and for the modern student this proves very frustrating. Sometimes it takes years for a poem to take on meaning—the reader simply knows that the poem sounds good and it provokes an emotional response that cannot be explained. With time, more emotional experience, more reading of similar experiences, more life, the reader comes to a meaning of that poem that satisfies. In a few more years that poem may take on a whole new meaning. Think of the way lyrics to certain songs affect you—poetry is no different.

This is all very well for reading for pleasure but you are now called upon, in your present experience, to learn poetry for an important examination. Perhaps the first step in the learning process is to answer the question, "Why do people write poetry?" An easy answer is that they wish to convey an experience, an emotion, an insight, or an observation in a startling or satisfying way, one that remains in the memory for years. But why not use a straightforward sentence or paragraph? Why wrap up that valuable insight in fancy words, rhyme, paradox, meter, allusion, symbolism, and all the other seeming mumbo-jumbo that poets use? Why not just come right out and say it like "normal people" do? An easy answer to these questions is that poetry is not a vehicle for conveying meaning alone. Gerard Manley Hopkins, one of the great innovators of rhythm in poetry, claimed that poetry should be "heard for its own sake and interest even over and above its interest or meaning." Poetry provides intellectual stimulus. Of course, one of the best ways of studying a poem is to consider it a jigsaw puzzle presented to you whole. It can then be taken apart piece by piece (word by word), analyzed scientifically, labelled, and put back together again into a whole. Then, the meaning is complete. But people write poetry to convey more than meaning.

T.S. Eliot maintained that the meaning of the poem existed purely to distract us "while the poem did its work." One interpretation of a poem's "work" is that it changes us in some way. We see the world in a new way because of the way the poet has seen it and told us about it. Maybe one of the reasons people write poetry is to encourage us to see things in the first place. Simple things like daffodils take on a whole new aspect when we read the way Wordsworth saw them in his poem "Daffodils." Why did Wordsworth write that poem? His sister had written an excellent account of the scene in her journal. Wordsworth not only evokes nature as we have never seen it before, alive, joyous, exuberant, he shows nature's healing powers, its restorative quality as the scene flashes "upon that inward eye/Which is the bliss of solitude." Bent over your books studying, how many times has a similar quality of nature's power in the memory come to you? Maybe for you a summer beach scene rather than daffodils by the lake is more meaningful, but the poet captures a moment that we have all experienced. The poet's magic is to make that moment new again.

If poets enhance our power of sight, they also awaken the other senses as powerfully. We can hear Emily Dickinson's snake in the repeated "s" sound of the lines:

His notice sudden is—
The Grass divides as with a Comb—
A spotted shaft is seen—

and because of the very present sense of sound, we experience the indrawn gasp of breath of fear when the snake appears. We can touch the little chimney sweep's hair "that curled like a lamb's back" in William Blake's poetry and because of that sense we are even more shocked to read that the child's hair is all shaved off so that the soot will not spoil its color. We can smell the poison gas as Wilfred Owen's soldiers fumble with their gas masks; we can taste the blood gurgling in the poisoned lungs. For that moment, you join those soldiers of WWI.

Poets write to awaken the senses. They have crucial ideas, but the words they use are often more important than the meaning. More important still than ideas and sense awakening is the poet's appeal to the emotions. And it is precisely this area that disturbs a number of students. Our modern society tends to block out emotions—we need reviews to tell us if we enjoyed a film, a critic's praise to see if a play or novel is worth our time. We hesitate to laugh at something in case it is not the "in" thing to do. We certainly do not cry— at least in front of others. Poets write to overcome that blocking (very often it is their own blocking of emotion they seek to alleviate), but that is not to say that poetry immediately sets us laughing, crying, loving, hating. The important fact about the emotional release in poetry is that poets help us explore our own emotions, sometimes by shocking us, sometimes by drawing attention to balance and pattern, sometimes by cautioning us to move carefully in this inner world.

Poets tell us nothing really new. They tell us old truths about human emotions that we begin to restructure anew, to reread our experiences in light of theirs, to reevaluate our world view. Whereas a car manual helps us understand the workings of a particular vehicle, a poem helps us understand the inner workings of human beings. Poets frequently write to help their emotional life—the writing then becomes cathartic, purging or cleansing the inner life, feeding that part of us that makes us human. Many poets might paraphrase Byron who claimed that he had to write or go mad. Writer and reader of poetry enter into a partnership, each helping the other to find significance in the human world, to find safety in a seemingly alien world.

This last point brings any reader of poetry to ask the next question: Why read poetry? One might contend that a good drama, novel, or short story might provide the same emotional experience. But a poem is much more accessible. Apart from the fact that poems are shorter than other genres, there is a unique directness to them which hinges purely on language. Poets can say in one or two lines what may take novelists and playwrights entire works to express. For example, Keats' lines—

Beauty is truth, truth beauty—that is all

Ye know on earth, and all ye need to know—

In your reading of poems remember that poetry is perhaps the oldest art and yet surrounds us without our even realizing it. Listeners thrilled to Homer's poetry; tribes chanted invocations to their gods; today we listen to song lyrics and find ourselves, sometimes despite ourselves, repeating certain rhythmic lines. Advertisements we say we hate have a way of repeating themselves as we use the catchy phrase or repetition. Both lyricists and advertisers cleverly use language, playing on the reader's/listener's/watcher's ability to pick up on a repeated sound or engaging rhythm or inner rhyme. Think of a time as a child when you thoroughly enjoyed poetry: nursery rhymes, ballgame rhythms, jump-rope patterns. Probably you had no idea of the meaning of the words ("Little Miss Muffet sat on a tuffet..." a tuffet?!), but you responded to the sound, the pattern. As adults we read poetry for that sense of sound and pattern. With more experience at reading poetry there is an added sense of pleasure as techniques are recognized: alliteration, onomatopoeia; forms of poetry become obvious—the sonnet, the rondelle. Even greater enjoyment comes from watching a poet's development, tracing themes and ideas, analyzing maturity in growth of imagery, use of rhythm.

To the novice reader of poetry, a poem can speak to the reader at a particular time and become an experience in itself. A freshman's experience after her mother's death exemplifies this. Shortly after the death, the student found Elizabeth Jenning's poem "Happy Families." Using the familiar names of the cards, Mrs. Beef and Master Bun, the poet describes how strangers try to help the family carry on their lives normally although one of the "happy family" is "missing." The card game continues although no one wants it to. At the end the players go back to their individual rooms and give way to their individual grief. The student described the relief at knowing that someone else had obviously experienced her situation where everyone in the family was putting up a front, strangers were being very kind, and a general emptiness prevailed because of that one missing family member. The poem satisfied. The student saw death through another's eyes; the experience was almost the same, yet helped the reader to reevaluate, to view a universal human response to grief as well as encourage her to deal with her own.

On reading a poem the brain works on several different levels: it responds to the sounds; it responds to the words themselves and their connotations; it responds to the emotions; it responds to the insights or learning of the world being revealed. For such a process, poetry is a very good training ground— a boot camp—for learning how to read literature in general. All the other genres have elements of poetry within them. Learn to read poetry well and you will be a more accomplished reader, even of car manuals! Perhaps the best response to reading poetry comes from a poet herself, Emily Dickinson, who claimed that reading a book of poetry made her feel "as if the top of [her] head were taken off!"

Before such a process happens to you, here are some tips for reading poetry before and during the examination.

BEFORE THE EXAM

1. Make a list of poets and poems you remember; analyze poems you liked, disliked, loved, hated, and were indifferent to. Find the poems. Reread them and for each one analyze your *feelings*, first of all, about the poetry itself. Have your feelings changed? Now what do you like or hate? Then paraphrase the meaning of each poem. Notice how the "magic" goes from the poem, i.e., "Daffodils": the poet sees many daffodils by the side of a lake and then thinks how the sight of them later comforts him.

2. Choose a poem at random from an anthology or one mentioned in this introduction. Read it a couple of times, preferably aloud, because the speaking voice will automatically grasp the rhythm and that will help

the meaning. Do not become bogged down in individual word connotation or the meaning of the poem—let the poetry do its "work" on you; absorb the poem as a whole jigsaw puzzle.

3. Now take the puzzle apart. Look carefully at the title. Sometimes a straightforward title helps you focus. Sometimes a playful title helps you get an angle on the meaning. "Happy Families," of course, is an ironic title because the family playing the card game of that name is not happy.

4. Look carefully at the punctuation. Does the sense of a line carry from one to another? Does a particular mark of punctuation strike you as odd? Ask why that mark was used.

5. Look carefully at the words. Try to find the meaning of words with which you are not familiar within the context. Familiar words may be used differently: ask why that particular use. If you have tapped into your memory bank of vocabulary and find you are still at a loss, go to a dictionary. Once you have the *denotation* of the word, start wondering about the *connotation*. Put yourself in the poet's position and think why that word was used.

6. Look carefully at all the techniques being used. You will gain these as you progress through the test preparation. As soon as you come across a new idea learn the word, see how it applies to poetry, where it is used. Be on the lookout for it in other poetry. Ask yourself questions such as why the poet used alliteration here; why the rhythm changes there; why the poet uses a sonnet form and which sonnet form is in use. Forcing yourself to ask the WHY questions, and answering them, will train the brain to read more perceptively. Poetry is not accidental; poets are deliberate people; they do things for specific reasons. Your task under a learning situation is to discover WHY.

7. Look carefully at the speaker. Is the poet using another persona? Who is that persona? What is revealed about the speaker? Why use that particular voice?

8. Start putting all the pieces of the puzzle together. The rhythm helps the meaning. The word choice helps the imagery. The imagery adds to the meaning. Paraphrase the meaning. Ask yourself simple questions: What is the poet saying? How can I relate to what is being said? What does this poet mean to me? What does this poem contribute to human experience?

9. Write a poem of your own. Choose a particular style; use the sonnet form; parody a famous poem; express yourself in free verse on a crucial,

personal aspect of your life. Then analyze your own poetry with the above ideas.

DURING THE EXAM

You will have established a routine for reading poetry, but now you are under pressure, you must work quickly, and will have no access to a dictionary. You cannot read aloud but you can:

1. Internalize the reading—hear the reading in your head. Read through the poem two or three times following the absorbing procedure.

2. If the title and poet are supplied, analyze the title as before and determine the era of the poetry. Often this pushes you toward the meaning.

3. Look carefully at the questions which should enable you to be able to "tap into" your learning process. Answer the ones that are immediately clear to you: form, technique, language perhaps.

4. Go back for another reading for those questions that challenge you—theme or meaning perhaps—analyze the speaker or the voice at work—paraphrase the meaning—ask the simple question, "What is the poet saying?"

5. If a question asks you about a specific line, metaphor, opening or closing lines, highlight or underline them to force your awareness of each crucial word. Internalize another reading emphasizing the highlighted area—analyze again the options you have for your answers.

6. Do not waste time on a super-tough question. Move onto another section and let the poetry do its "work." Very often the brain will continue working on the problem on another level of consciousness. When you go back to the difficult question, it may well become clear.

7. If you still are not sure of the answer, choose the option that you feel is the closest to correct.

☞ Drill: Reading Poetry

<u>DIRECTIONS</u>: Read the following poem, then answer the questions which follow.

Why could she not stop for death?

1   Because I could not stop for Death–
              He kindly stopped for me–
              The Carriage held but just Ourselves–
              And Immortality.

5   We slowly drove–He knew not haste
              And I had put away
              My labor and my leisure too,
              For His Civility–

              We passed the School, where Children strove
10   At Recess–in the Ring–
              We passed the Fields of Gazing Grain–
              We passed the Setting Sun–

              Or rather–He passed Us–
              The Dews drew quivering and chill–
15   For only Gossamer, my Gown–
              My Tippet–only Tulle–

              We paused before a House that seemed
              A Swelling of the Ground–
              The Roof was scarcely visible–
20   The Cornice-in the Ground–

              Since then–'tis Centuries–and yet
              Feels shorter than the Day
              I first surmised the Horses' Heads
              Were toward Eternity–

Emily Dickinson, 1863.

1.   What is the author's attitude toward dying in the poem?
    (1)   She is terrified   (4)   She is contented
    (2)   She is overjoyed   (5)   She is frustrated
    (3)   She is angry

2. Death is personified as
    (1) a horse.   (4) the devil.
    (2) a king.   (5) a carriage driver.
    (3) a child.

3. Lines 21–24 signify that
    (1) death is timeless.
    (2) the narrator died yesterday.
    (3) the narrator's horses have died.
    (4) Eternity is a nearby city.
    (5) the horses are lost.

IV. READING DRAMA

The Glass Menagerie by Tennessee Williams begins when one of its four characters, Tom, steps into the downstage light and addresses the audience directly as though he were the chorus from a much earlier play. "I have tricks in my pocket, I have things up my sleeve," says Tom. "But I am the opposite of a stage magician. He gives you illusion that has the appearance of truth. I give you truth in the pleasant disguise of illusion."

To sit among the audience and watch a skillful production of *The Glass Menagerie* is to visit Tom's paradoxical world of theater, a magic place in which known imposters and stagecraft trickery create a spectacle which we know is illusion but somehow recognize as truth. Theater, as a performed event, combines the talents and skills of numerous artists and craftspersons, but before the spectacle must come the playwright's work, the pages of words designating what the audience sees and hears. These words, the written script separate from the theatrical performance of them, is what we call *drama*, and the words give the spectacle its significance because without them the illusion has neither frame nor content. Truth requires boundaries and substance.

Although drama is literature written to be performed, it closely resembles the other genres. In fact, both poetry and prose also can be performed; but as captivating as these public readings sometimes are, only performed drama best creates the immediate living "illusion as truth" Tom promises. Like fiction and narrative poetry, drama tells a tale—that is, it has plot, characters, and setting—but the author's voice is distant, heard only through the stage directions and perhaps some supplementary notes. With rare exceptions, dialogue dominates the script. Some drama is poetry, such as the works of Shakespeare and Molière, and all plays resemble poems as abstractions because both forms are highly condensed, figurative expressions.

A scene set inside a house, for instance, requires a room with only three walls. No audience complains, just as no movie audience feels betrayed by film characters' appearing ridiculously large. Without a thought, audiences employ what Samuel Taylor Coleridge called "a willing suspension of disbelief"; in other words, they know that the images before them are not real but rather representations, reflections in the mirror of which Hamlet speaks, not the real world ("Nature").

A play contains conflict which can be **enacted** immediately on the stage without any alterations in the written word. **Enacted** means performed by an actor or actors free to use the entire stage and such theatrical devices as sets, costumes, makeup, special lighting, and props for support. This differs from the oral interpretation of prose or poetry. No matter how animated, the public reader is not acting. This is the primary distinction between drama and other literary forms. Their most obvious similarity is that any form of literature is a linguistic expression. There is, however, one other feature shared by all kinds of narratives: the pulsating energy which pushes the action along is generated by human imperfection. We speak of tragic characters as having "flaws," but the same is true about comic characters as well. Indeed, nothing is more boring either on a stage or in a written text than a consistently flawless personality, because such characters can never be the real people of our everyday experiences. The most fundamental human truth is human frailty.

Although it can be argued that a play, like a musical composition, must be performed to be understood, the script's linguistic foundation always gives the work potential as a literary experience. Moreover, there is never a "definitive" interpretation. The script, in a sense, remains unfinished because it never stops inviting new variations, and among those invited to participate are individual readers whose imaginations should not be discounted. For example, when *Death of a Salesman* was originally produced, Lee J. Cobb played Willy Loman. Aside from the character's age, Dustin Hoffman's Willy in the revival forty years later bore hardly any physical resemblance to Cobb's. Yet both portrayals "worked." The same could be said about the Willys created by the minds of the play's countless readers. Quite capable of composing its own visions and sounds, the human imagination is the original mirror, the place where all human truths evolve.

PLOT STRUCTURE

As with other narrative types, a play's **plot** is its sequence of events, its organized collection of incidents. At one time it was thought that all the actions within a play should be contained within a single twenty-four hour period. Few lengthy plays have plots which cover only the period of time enacted on the stage. Most plays condense and edit time much as novels do. Decades can be reduced to two hours. Included in the plot is the **exposition**, the revealing of whatever information we need in order to understand the conflict of the play. This exposed material should provide us with a sense of place and time (**setting**), the central participants, important prior incidents, and the play's overall mood. In some plays, such as Shakespeare's, the exposition comes quickly. Notice, for instance, the opening scenes in *Macbeth, Hamlet,* and *Romeo and Juliet*: not one presents us with a central character, yet each—with its witches or king's ghost or street brawl—clearly establishes an essential tension foreshadowing the main conflict to come.

These initial expositions attack the audience immediately and are followed by events in chronological order. The exposition must establish what has come previously, even for an audience familiar with the story, before the plot can advance. Arthur Miller, in his *Death of a Salesman*, continuously interrupts the central action with dislocated expositions from earlier times as though the past were always in the present. He carefully establishes character, place, mood, and conflict throughout the earliest scenes; however, whatever present he places on stage is always caught in a tension between the audience's anticipation of the future and its suspicions of the past. The plots in plays like *Death of a Salesman* tend not to attack us head-on but rather to surround us and gradually close in, the circle made tighter by each deliberately released clue to a mysterious past.

Fairly soon in a play we must experience some incident that incites the fundamental conflict when placed against some previously presented incident or situation. In most plays the conflict's abrasive conditions continuously chafe and even lacerate each other. The play's tempo might provide some interruptions or variations in the pace; nevertheless, conflicts generate the actions which make the characters' worlds worse before they can get better. Any plot featuring only repetitious altercations, however, would soon become tiresome. Potentially, anything can happen in a conflict. The **complication** is whatever presents an element capable of altering the action's direction. Perhaps some new information is discovered or a previously conceived scheme fails, creating a reversal of what had been expected. The plot is not a series of similar events but rather a compilation of related events leading to a culmination, a **crisis**.

In retrospect, we should be able to accept a drama's progression of actions leading to the crisis as inevitable. After the crisis comes the **resolution** (or **denouement**),which gives the play its concluding boundary. This does not mean that the play should offer us solutions for whatever human issues it raises. Rather, the playwright's obligation is to make the experience he presents to us seem filled within its own boundaries. George Bernard Shaw felt he had met this obligation when he ended *Pygmalion* with his two principal characters, Higgins and Eliza, utterly incapable of voicing any romantic affection for each other; and the resolution in Ibsen's *A Doll's House* outraged audiences a hundred years ago and still disturbs some people today, even though it concludes the play with believable consequences.

Terms such as **exposition, complication, crisis,** and **resolution,** though helpful in identifying the conflict's currents and directions, at best only artificially define how a plot is molded. If the play provides unity in its revelations, these seams are barely noticeable. Moreover, any successful play clearly shows that the artist accomplished much more than merely plugging components together to create a finished work. There are no rules which all playwrights must follow, except the central precept that the play's unified assortment of actions be complete and contained within itself.

CHARACTER

Essential to the plot's success are the characters who participate in it. Midpoint in *Hamlet* when Elsinore Castle is visited by the traveling theater company, the prince joyously welcomes the players, but his mood quickly returns to bitter depression shortly after he asks one actor to recite a dramatic passage in which the speaker recalls the fall of Troy and particularly Queen Hecuba's response to her husband's brutal murder. The player, caught by the speech's emotional power, becomes distraught and cannot finish. Left alone on stage, Hamlet compares the theatrical world created by the player with Hamlet's "real" world and asks: "What's Hecuba to him, or he to Hecuba,/ That he should weep for her!" Under ordinary circumstances Hamlet's anxiety would not overshadow his Renaissance sensibilities, because he knows well that fictional characters always possess the potential to move us. As though by instinct, we know the same. We read narratives and go to the theater precisely because we want to be shocked, delighted, thrilled, saddened, titillated, or invigorated by "a dream of passion." Even though some characters are more complex and interesting than others, they come in countless types as the playwright's delegates to our imaginations and as the imitations of reality seeking our response.

TYPES OF PLAYS

When Polonius presents the traveling players to Hamlet, he reads from the theater company's license, which identifies them as

> The best actors in the world, either for tragedy, comedy, history, pastoral, pastoral-comical, historical-pastoral, tragical-historical, tragi-cal-comical-historical-pastoral, scene individable or poem unlimited...

The joke is on those who think all plays somehow can be categorized according to preconceived definitions, as though playwrights follow literary recipes. The notion is not entirely ridiculous, to be sure, since audiences and readers can easily tell a serious play from a humorous one, and a play labeled "tragedy" or "comedy" will generate certain valid expectations from us all, regardless of whether we have read a word by Aristotle or any other literary critic. Still, if beginning playwrights had to choose between writing according to some rigid structures designating the likes of a "tragical-comical-historical-pastoral" or writing a play unrestricted by such rules (a "poem unlimited"), they would probably choose the latter.

We tend to categorize dramatic thought into three clusters: the serious, the comic, and the seriocomic. Thus, in our attempts to interpret life's complexities, it is tempting to place the art forms representing it in precise, fixed designations. After a few centuries, though, it would become clear that there is a better way of explaining what a play's form should be—not so much fixed as organic. In other words, we should think of a play as similar to a plant's growing and taking shape according to its own design. This analogy works well because the plant is not a mechanical device constructed from a predetermined plan, yet every plant is a species and as such contains qualities which identify it with others. So just as Shakespeare could ridicule overly precise definitions for dramatic art, he could still write dramas which he clearly identified as tragedies, comedies, or histories, even though he would freely mix two or more of these together in the same play.

COMEDY

The primary aim of comedy is to amuse us with a happy ending, although comedies can vary according to the attitudes they project, which can be broadly identified as either **high** or **low**, terms having nothing to do with an evaluation of the play's merit. Generally, the amusement found in comedy comes from an eventual victory over threats or ill fortune. Much of the dialogue and plot development might be laughable, yet a play need not be funny to be comic. **Farce** is low comedy intended to make us laugh by means of a series of exaggerated, unlikely situations that depend less on plot and character than on gross absurdities, sight gags, and coarse dialogue. The "higher" a comedy goes, the more natural the characters seem and the less boisterous their behavior. The plots become more sustained, and the dialogue shows more weighty thought. As with all dramas, comedies are about things that go wrong. Accordingly, comedies create deviations from accepted normalcy, presenting problems which we might or might not see as harmless. If these problems make us judgmental about the involved characters and events, the play takes on the features of **satire**, a rather high comic form implying that humanity and human institutions are in need of reform. If the action triggers our sympathy for the characters, we feel even less protected from the incongruities as the play tilts more in the direction of **tragi-comedy**. In other words, the action determines a figurative distance between the audience and the play. Such factors as characters' personalities and the plot's predictability influence this distance. The farther away we sit, the more protected we feel and usually the funnier the play becomes. Closer proximity to believability in the script draws us nearer to the conflict, making us feel more involved in the action and less safe in its presence.

A more consistent play is Oscar Wilde's *The Importance of Being Earnest*, which opened in 1895. In the following scene, Lady Bracknell questions Jack Worthing, who has just announced that Lady Bracknell's daughter, Gwendolyn, has agreed to marry him. Being satisfied with Jack's answers concerning his income and finding his upper-class idleness and careless ignorance about world affairs an asset, she queries him about his family background. In grave tones, the embarrassed Jack reveals his mysterious lineage. His late guardian, Thomas Cardew—"an old gentleman of a very charitable and kindly disposition"—had found the baby Jack in an abandoned handbag.

LADY BRACKNELL: A hand-bag?

JACK: (very seriously): Yes, Lady Bracknell. I was in a hand-bag—a somewhat large, black leather hand-bag, with handles to it—an ordinary hand-bag in fact.

LADY BRACKNELL: In what locality did this Mr. James, or Thomas, Cardew come across this ordinary hand-bag?

JACK: In the cloak-room at Victoria Station. It was given him in mistake for his own.

LADY BRACKNELL: The cloak-room at Victoria Station?

JACK: Yes. The Brighton line.

LADY BRACKNELL: The line is immaterial, Mr. Worthing. I confess I feel somewhat bewildered by what you have just told me. To be born, or at any rate bred, in a hand-bag, whether it had handles or not, seems to me to display a contempt for the ordinary decencies of family life that reminds one of the worst excesses of the French Revolution. And I presume you know what that unfortunate movement led to? As for the particular locality in which the hand-bag was found, a cloak-room at a railway station might serve to conceal a social indiscretion— has probably, indeed, been used for that purpose before now—but it could hardly be regarded as an assured basis for recognized position in good society.

JACK: May I ask you then what would you advise me to do? I need hardly say I would do anything in the world to ensure Gwendolyn's happiness.

LADY BRACKNELL: I would strongly advise you, Mr. Worthing, to try and acquire some relations as soon as possible, and to make a definite effort to produce at any rate one parent, of either sex, before the season is over.

JACK: Well, I don't see how I could possibly manage to do that. I can produce the hand-bag at any moment. It is in my dressing-room at home. I really think that should satisfy you, Lady Bracknell.

LADY BRACKNELL: Me, sir! What has it to do with me? You can hardly imagine that I and Lord Bracknell would dream of allowing our only daughter—a girl brought up with the utmost care—to marry into a cloak-room, and form an alliance with a parcel. Good morning, Mr. Worthing!

(LADY BRACKNELL sweeps out in majestic indignation.)

This dialogue between Lady Bracknell and Jack is typical of what runs throughout the entire play. It is full of exaggerations, in both the situation being discussed and the manner in which the characters, particularly Lady Bracknell, express their reactions to the situation. Under other circumstances an abandoned baby would not be the focus of a comedy, but we are relieved from any concern for the child since the adult Jack is obviously secure, healthy, and, with one exception, carefree. Moreover, we laugh when Lady Bracknell exaggerates Jack's heritage by comparing it with the excesses of the French Revolution. On the other hand, at the core of their discussion is the deeply ingrained and oppressive notion of English class consciousness, a mentality so flawed it almost begs to be satirized. Could there be more there than light, witty entertainment?

TRAGEDY

The term "tragedy" when used to define a play has historically meant something very precise, not simply a drama which ends with unfortunate consequences. This definition originated with Aristotle, who insisted that the play be an imitation of complex actions which should arouse an emotional response combining fear and pity. Aristotle believed that only a certain kind of plot could generate such a powerful reaction. Comedy, as we have seen, shows us a progression from adversity to prosperity. Tragedy must show the reverse; moreover, this progression must be experienced by a certain kind of character, says Aristotle, someone whom we can designate as the **tragic hero**. This central figure must be basically good and noble: "good" because we will not be aroused to fear and pity over the misfortunes of a villain, and "noble" both by social position and moral stature because the fall to misfortune would not otherwise be great enough for tragic impact. These virtues do not make the tragic hero perfect, however, for he must also possess **hamartia**—a tragic flaw—the weakness which leads him to make an error in judgment which initiates the reversal in his fortunes, causing his death or the death of others or both. These dire consequences become the hero's catastrophe. The most common tragic flaw is **hubris**, an excessive pride that adversely influences the protagonist's judgment.

Often the catastrophic consequences involve an entire nation because the tragic hero's social rank carries great responsibilities. Witnessing these events produces the emotional reaction Aristotle believed the audience should experience, the **catharsis**. Although tragedy must arouse our pity for the tragic hero as he endures his catastrophe and must frighten us as we witness the consequences of a flawed behavior which anyone could exhibit, there must also be a purgation, "a cleansing," of these emotions which should leave the audience feeling not depressed but relieved and almost elated. The assumption is that while the tragic hero endures a crushing reversal, somehow he is not thoroughly defeated as he gains new stature through suffering and the knowledge that comes with suffering. Classical tragedy insists that the universe is ordered. If truth or universal law is ignored, the results are devastating, causing the audience to react emotionally; simultaneously, the tragic results prove the existence of truth, thereby reassuring our faith that existence is sensible.

Sophocles' plays give us some of the clearest examples of Aristotle's definition of tragedy. Shakespeare's tragedies are more varied and more modern in their complexities. *Othello* is one of Shakespeare's most innovative and troublesome extensions of tragedy's boundaries. The title character commands the Venetian army and soon becomes acting governor of Cypress. He is also a Moor, a dark-skinned African whose secret marriage to the beautiful Desdemona has infuriated her father, a wealthy and influential Venetian, whose anger reveals a racist element in Venice which Othello tries to ignore. Iago hates Othello for granting a promotion to Cassio which Iago believes should rightfully be his. With unrelenting determination and malicious deception, Iago attempts to persuade Othello that Desdemona has committed adultery with Cassio. The following excerpt catches Iago in the early stages of his successful manipulation:

IAGO: In Venice they [wives] do let heaven see pranks
They dare not show their husbands; their best conscience
Is not to leave 't undone, but keep 't unknown.

OTHELLO: Dost thou say so?

IAGO: She did deceive her father, marrying you;

And when she seem'd to shake and fear your looks,
She lov'd them most.

OTHELLO: And so she did.

IAGO: Why, go to, then;
She that so young could give out such a seeming,
To see her father's eyes up close as oak,
He thought 'twas witchcraft; but I am much to blame;
I humbly do beseech you of your pardon
For too much loving you.

OTHELLO: I am bound to thee for ever.

IAGO: I see, this hath a little dash'd your spirits.

OTHELLO: Not a jot, not a jot.

IAGO: I' faith, I fear it has.
I hope you will consider what is spoke
Comes from my love. But I do see you're mov'd;
I am to pray you not to strain my speech
To grosser issues nor to larger reach
Than to suspicion.

OTHELLO: I will not.

IAGO: Should you do so, my lord,
My speech should fall into such vile success
As my thoughts aim not at. Cassio's my worthy friend—
My lord, I see you're mov'd.

OTHELLO: No, not much mov'd:
I do not think but Desdemona's honest.

IAGO: Long live she so! and long live you to think so!

OTHELLO: And yet, how nature erring from itself,—

IAGO: Ay, there's the point: as, to be bold with you,
Not to affect many proposed matches
Of her own clime, complexion, and degree,
Whereto, we see, in all things nature tends;
Foh! one may smell in such, a will most rank,

Foul disproportion, thoughts unnatural.
But pardon me; I do not in position
Distinctly speak of her, though I may fear
Her will, recoiling to her better judgment,
May fall to match you with her country forms
And happily repent.

OTHELLO: Farewell, farewell:
If more thou dost perceive, let me know more;
Set on thy wife to observe. Leave me, Iago.

IAGO: My lord, I take my leave. (Going)

OTHELLO: Why did I marry? This honest creature, doubtless,
Sees and knows more, much more, than he unfolds.

Notice that Iago speaks much more than Othello. This is typical of their conversations, as though Iago were the superior of the two. Dramatically, for Iago's scheme to compel our interests we must perceive in Othello tragic proportions, both in his strengths and weaknesses; otherwise, *Othello* would slip into a mean tale about a rogue and his dupe. Much of the tension in this scene stems from Othello's reluctance either to accept Iago's innuendos immediately or to dismiss them. This confusion places him on the rack of doubt, a torture made more severe because he questions his own desirability as a husband. Consequently, since Iago is not the "honest creature" he appears to be and Othello is unwilling to confront openly his own self-doubts, Iago becomes the dominant personality—a situation which a flawless Othello would never tolerate.

HISTORY

The playwright's raw material can spring from any source. A passion play, for instance, is a dramatic adaptation of the Crucifixion as told in the gospels. A history play is a dramatic perspective of some event or series of events identified with recognized historical figures. Television docudramas are the most recent examples.

Ever since the 16th century, history plays have seldom risen above the level of patriotic whitewash and political propaganda. Of course there are notable exceptions to this trend: Robert Bolt's *A Man for All Seasons* is one. The title character, Sir Thomas More, is beheaded at the play's conclusion, following his refusal to condone Henry VIII's break from the Roman Catholic Church and the king's establishment of the Church of England with the monarch as its head. Henry wants More to condone these actions because the Pope will not grant Henry a divorce from Queen Catherine so that he can marry Anne Boleyn, who the king believes will bear him the male heir he desperately wants. The central issue for us is not whether More's beliefs are valid but whether any person of conscience can act freely in a world dominated by others far less principled. In Henry's only scene he arrives at Sir Thomas' house hoping his Lord Chancellor will not disappoint him:

[music in background]

HENRY: Son after son she's borne me, Thomas, all dead at birth, or dead within a month; I never saw the hand of God so clear in anything…. I have a daughter, she's a good child, a well-set child—But I have no son. (He flares up.) It is my bounden duty to put away the Queen, and all the Popes back to St. Peter shall not come between me and my duty! How is it that you cannot see? Everybody else does.

MORE: (Eagerly) Then why does Your Grace need my poor support?

HENRY: Because you are honest. What's more to the purpose, you're known to be honest…. There are those like Norfolk who follow me because I wear the crown, and there are those like Master Cromwell who follow me because they are jackals with sharp teeth and I am their lion, and there is a mass that follow me because it follows anything that moves—and there is you.

MORE: I am sick to think how much I must displease Your Grace.

HENRY: No, Thomas, I respect your sincerity. Respect? Oh, man, it's water in the desert…. How did you like our music? That air they played, it had a certain—well, tell me what you thought of it.

MORE: (Relieved at this turn; smiling) Could it have been Your Grace's own?

HENRY: (Smiles back) Discovered! Now I'll never know your true opinion. And that's irksome, Thomas, for we artists, though we love praise, yet we love truth better.

MORE: (Mildly) Then I will tell Your Grace truly what I thought of it.

HENRY: (A little disconcerted) Speak then.

MORE: To me it seemed—delightful.

HENRY: Thomas—I chose the right man for Chancellor.

MORE: I must in fairness add that my taste in music is reputably deplorable.

(From *A Man for All Seasons* by Robert Bolt. Copyright ©1960, 1962 by Robert Bolt. Reprinted by permission of Random House Inc.)

To what extent Henry and More discussed the king's divorce and its subsequent events nobody knows, let alone what was actually said, although we can be certain they spoke an English distinctively different from the language in the play. Bolt's imagination, funnelled through the dramatist's obligation to tell an interesting story, presides over the historical data and dictates the play's projections of More, Henry, and the other participants. Thus, we do not have "history"; instead, we have a dramatic perception of history shaped, altered, and adorned by Robert Bolt, writing about 16th century figures from a 1960 vantage point. But as the scene above shows, the characters' personalities are not simple reductions of what historical giants should be. Henry struts a royal self-assurance noticeably colored by vanity and frustration; yet although he lacks More's wit and intelligence, the king clearly is no fool. Likewise, as troubled as More is by the controversy before him, he projects a formidable power of his own. *A Man for All Seasons* succeeds dramatically because Bolt provides only enough history to present a context for the characters' development while he allows the resultant implications to touch all times, all seasons. When we read any history play, we should search for similar implications; otherwise, the work can never become more than a theatrical précis with a narrow focus.

MODERN DRAMA

From the 1870's to the present, the theater has participated in the artistic movements reflecting accumulated theories of science, social science, and philosophy which attempt to define reality and the means we use to discern it. First caught in a pendulum of opposing views, modern drama eventually synthesized these perspectives into new forms, familiar in some ways and boldly original in others. Henrik Ibsen's plays began the modern era with their emphasis on **realism**, a seeking of truth through direct observation using the five senses. As objectively depicted, contemporary life received a closer scrutiny than ever before, showing everyday people in everyday situations. Before Ibsen, theatrical sets were limited, with rare exceptions, to castles and country estates. After Ibsen, the farmhouse and city tenement were suitable for the stage. Ibsen's work influenced many others, and from realism came two main variations. The first, **naturalism**, strove to push realism toward a direct transformation of life on stage, a "slice of life" showing how the scientific principles of heredity and environment have shaped society, especially in depicting the plights of the lower classes. The second variation, **expressionism**, moved in a different direction and actually denied realism's premise that the real world could be objectively perceived; instead—influenced by Sigmund Freud's theories about human behavior's hidden, subconscious motivations and by other modernist trends in the arts, such as James Joyce's fiction and Picasso's paintings—expressionism imitated a disconnected dream-like world filled with psychological images at odds with the tangible world surrounding it. While naturalism attempts to imitate life directly, expressionism is abstract and often relies on symbols.

A modern play can employ any number of elements found in the spectrum between these extremes as well as suggest divergent philosophical views about whether humanity has the power to change its condition or whether any of its ideas about the universe are verifiable. Moreover, no work of art is necessarily confined within a particular school of thought. It is quite possible that seemingly unrelated forms can appear in the same play and work well. *The Glass Menagerie, A Man for All Seasons*, and *Death of a Salesman* feature characters and dialogue indicative of realistic drama, but the sets described in the stage directions are expressionistic, offering either framed outlines of places or distorted representations. Conventions from classical drama are also available to the playwright. As previously noted, Tom acts as a Greek chorus as well as an important character in his play; the same is true of the Common Man, whose identity changes from scene to scene. In short, anything is possible in modern drama, a quality which is wholly compatible with the diversity and unpredictability of 20th century human experiences.

In a sense all good drama is modern. No label about a play's origin or form can adequately describe its content. Establishing the people, places, and thought within the play is crucial to our understanding. For the characters to interest us we must perceive the issues that affect their lives, and eventually we will discover why the characters' personalities and backgrounds, together with their social situations, inevitably converge with these issues and create conflicts. *Death of a Salesman* challenges the classical definitions of tragedy by giving us a modern American, Willy Loman, who is indeed a "low man," a person of little social importance and limited moral fiber. His delusionary values have brought him at age sixty-four to failure and despair, yet more than ever he clings to his dreams and painted memories for solace and hope. Late one night, after Willy has returned from an aborted sales trip, his rambling conversation with his wife Linda returns to the topic which haunts him the most, his son Biff.

WILLY: Biff is a lazy bum!

LINDA: They're sleeping. Get something to eat. Go on down.

WILLY: Why did he come home? I would like to know what brought him home.

LINDA: I don't know. I think he's still lost, Willy. I think he's very lost.

WILLY: Biff Loman is lost. In the greatest country in the world a young man with such—personal attractiveness, gets lost. And such a hard worker. There's one thing about Biff—he's not lazy.

LINDA: Never.

WILLY (with pity and resolve): I'll see him in the morning; I'll have a nice talk with him. I'll get him a job selling. He could be big in no time. My God! Remember how they used to follow him around in high school? When he smiled at one of them their faces lit up. When he walked down the street.... (He loses himself in reminiscences.)

LINDA (trying to bring him out of it): Willy, dear, I got a new kind of American-type cheese today. It's whipped.

WILLY: Why do you get American cheese when you know I like Swiss?

LINDA: I just thought you'd like a change—

WILLY: I don't want change! I want Swiss cheese. Why am I always being contradicted?

LINDA (with a covering laugh): I just thought it would be a surprise.

WILLY: Why don't you open a window in here, for God's sake?

LINDA (with infinite patience): They're all open dear.

WILLY: The way they boxed us in here. Bricks and windows, windows and bricks.

LINDA: We should have bought the land next door.

WILLY: The street is lined with cars. There's not a breath of fresh air in the neighborhood. The grass don't grow any more, you can't raise a carrot in the backyard. They should've had a law against apartment houses. Remember those two beautiful elms out there? When I and Biff hung the swing between them?

LINDA: Yeah, like a million miles from the city.

WILLY: They should've arrested the builder for cutting those down. They massacred the neighborhood. (Lost) More and more I think of those days, Linda. This time of year it was lilac and wisteria. And then the peonies would come out, and the daffodils. What fragrance in this room!

LINDA: Well, after all, people had to move somewhere.

WILLY: No, there's more people now.

LINDA: I don't think there's more people. I think—

WILLY: There's more people! That's what's ruining this country! Population is getting out of control. The competition is maddening! Smell the stink from that apartment house! And another on the other side…. How can they whip cheese?

In Arthur Miller's stage directions for *Death of a Salesman*, the Loman house is outlined by simple framing with various floors represented by short elevated platforms. Outside the house the towering shapes of the city angle inward presenting the crowded oppressiveness Willy complains about. First performed in 1949, the play continues to make a powerful commentary on modern American life. We see Willy as more desperate than angry about his condition, which he defines in ways as contradictory as his assessments of Biff. In his suffocating world, Willy gropes for peace while hiding from truth; and although his woes are uniquely American in some ways, they touch broader, more universal human problems as well.

☞ Drill: Reading Drama

DIRECTIONS: The following three questions are based on the previous passage. After reading the passage, answer the following questions.

1. Where does the dialogue in the passage take place?
    (1) At a country cottage   (4) At a seaside resort
    (2) At a city residence   (5) At a western ranch
    (3) At a European villa

2. Why is Willy upset that Linda bought American cheese?
   (1) Because Biff likes American cheese
   (2) Because Willy does not like cheese
   (3) Because the whole city stinks like cheese
   (4) Because Willy fears change
   (5) Because American cheese makes Linda sick

3. What would be a good description of Linda?
   (1) She is cruel   (4) She is selfish
   (2) She is dishonest   (5) She is patient
   (3) She is lazy

V. READING COMMENTARY

When you go to see a movie, and it turns out to be a movie that strikes you in many ways, you just cannot wait to talk about it. Right? That discussion after the movie is a commentary. It is a way of expressing your thoughts and impressions about the film you have just seen. If you were to write down your thoughts and impressions, rather than discuss them, you essentially would have an example of the type of commentary that turns up on the GED.

Commentary is not just about movies. It also takes as its subject dance, art, sculpture, theater, literature, and music. Commentary is a means of conveying feelings about the arts to an audience. The audience may be a teacher for whom you write a report. It may be a friend who receives a letter in which you talk about a play you have just seen. Most likely, the audience is the reader of a newspaper or magazine since this is where the majority of commentary makes its way to the general public. This type of commentary is the kind you will find in the entertainment section of your newspaper. It is also the kind you will encounter on the GED.

What are we looking for when we are presented with a review of something? There are a couple of standard items that we should use as guides when we attempt to understand a review. Here are some important questions to keep in mind as you read such a review:

- What is the author's attitude toward the work? Is the basic opinion favorable to the work or is it disapproving?

- Does the author back up his/her opinion with concrete examples? Are the examples descriptive enough that you understand the critic's point?

You should become able to see how a review works in terms of these points. A critic will *always* have an opinion, and they will *always* cite examples to demonstrate why they feel the way they do. Once you learn to recognize this system, you will be able to follow a reviewer's line of reasoning and understand his interpretations and opinions about a play, poem, or painting. The GED will not expect you to know the background of any of the artists, literature, or works of art discussed. Instead, it will present to you passages which are descriptive enough to answer all questions without any prior knowledge of the work being discussed.

Here is an example of a typical passage that might appear on the GED, with questions that would follow:

Superman, starring Christopher Reeve and Margot Kidder, has the look and feel of a comic book placed on screen. Throughout the movie we are presented with the clear, sharp colors of the original Superman as he was, and is, drawn in DC Comics. Not only are the colors clear-cut and bold, but so are the personalities of the characters. There is a simplicity to every character in the movie that lets us clearly know the good guys from the bad guys. In a comic book there just is not the room, nor the inclination, to develop a character in great depth, and so we get characters who are more like cardboard cut-outs than real people. This is what makes comic books so fun. Comic books allow us to escape from the world of real people and give us satisfying conclusions to superheroes' dilemmas. *Superman*, the movie, manages to do the same thing. This is what makes it great entertainment!

In *Superman*, nothing is beyond the hero's control. There is nothing terrible that can happen that Superman cannot fix. His character can bring back a loved one from the dead by turning back time. He is also able to avert nuclear destruction by being faster and more powerful that a ballistic missile. When we, the audience, see the character faced with these situations, we feel as if we are involved in them also. When we see Superman get through these situations and conquer these problems, we feel as if we are also a part of the solution. This gives us the kind power over problems that we do not have in real life. It is that feeling of power that we get by identifying with Superman that allows us a fantasy for just a while. *Superman*, like the comic book that came before it, is guaranteed to entertain with humor, drama, and most importantly, the kind of action that puts you in the sky right alongside the hero himself.

Drill: Reading Commentary

DIRECTIONS: The following questions are based on the passage above. Read each question and choose the correct answer.

1. Which of the following terms would the reviewer most likely use to describe the movie *Superman*?
    (1) Ridiculous   (4) Old-fashioned
    (2) Confusing   (5) Boring
    (3) Satisfying

2. According to the reviewer, the movie *Superman* is most like

    (1) a circus.   (4) a poem.
    (2) an auto race.   (5) a comic book.
    (3) a war.

3. The author believes that *Superman*

    (1) is an accurate portrayal of real life.
    (2) is an entertaining fantasy.
    (3) is a depressing drama.
    (4) is too wordy.
    (5) lacks humor.

You will notice that the commentator expresses a clear opinion about the movie and uses examples to explain why he felt the way he did. Every commentary will work in this way. Remember that the objective of any commentary is to express an opinion or explain an interpretation; learn to recognize this first in any commentary you pick up. After that, learn to pick out the concrete examples that the reviewer uses to back up his opinions. Knowing how to pick up these things will help you greatly on the GED. Buy a newspaper and read a review of a local play or current movie. Try to pick it apart. This will be good practice so that by the time you take the actual exam you will understand commentary on all of the arts.

LANGUAGE ARTS: READING

ANSWER KEY

Drill: Reading Prose

1. (1) 2. (3) 3. (3)

Drill: Reading Poetry

1. (4) 2. (5) 3. (1)

Drill: Reading Drama

1. (2) 2. (4) 3. (5)

Drill: Reading Commentary

1. (3) 2. (5) 3. (2)

MATH
REVIEW

Chapter 6

MATH REVIEW

I. STRATEGIES FOR MATH SECTIONS

II. ARITHMETIC

III. ALGEBRA

IV. GEOMETRY

In order to be successful on the mathematics section of the GED, you must first prepare yourself by studying the fundamental concepts in our math review. Our math hints can help increase your chances of answering the problems correctly. The methods that we provide consist of specific steps that illustrate for you the best way to approach particular math problems. These hints will pick up where your math knowledge leaves off. The more familiar you are with our math hints, the better your chances of achieving a top score on the GED Mathematics Exam.

GED math problems test your basic knowledge of arithmetic, algebra, and geometry. Our math review represents the various mathematical topics that will appear on the GED. You will not find any calculus, trigonometry, or imaginary numbers in our math review. The mathematical concepts presented on the GED are ones with which you are already familiar and simply need to review in order to score well.

Along with a knowledge to these topics, your speed and accuracy in answering the math questions will have an effect upon your success. Therefore, memorize the directions in order to save time and decrease your chances of making careless mistakes. Then, complete the practice drills that are provided for you in our review. Even if you are sure you know your fundamental math concepts, the drills will help to warm you up so that you can go into the math GED with quick, sharp math skills. Also, make sure to review the Reference Table of mathematical symbols and formulas which appears in the appendix of this book.

I. STRATEGIES FOR MATH SECTIONS

If you know how to solve the problem, this is your plan of attack:

> Solve for x:
>
> $3x + 4(x + 1) = 11$
>
> (A) -1 (B) 0 (C) $3/4$
>
> (D) 1 (E) $11/7$

➤ Step 1   Calculate the answer as quickly as possible.

$$3x + 4x + 4 = 11$$
$$7x + 4 + (-4) = 11 + (-4)$$
$$7x = 7$$
$$x = 1$$

➤ Step 2   Find your answer among the answer choices.

The answer is (D).

If you do not know how to solve the problem, this is your plan of attack:

> A computer generates three consecutive even integers each time it is turned on. If the sum of the three numbers is 54, what is the value of the largest number?
>
> (A) 10   (B) 14   (C) 20
>
> (D) 24   (E) 28

> **Step 1** Determine what the question is asking.

This question is asking you to find the largest of three even, consecutive integers.

> **Step 2** Try to formulate an equation that solves for the unknown value using all the necessary information given in the question. Look at the answer choices and eliminate any that are obviously wrong.

Let x = the first even integer
Let $x + 2$ = the second even integer
Let $x + 4$ = the third even integer (the largest)
Therefore,
$$x + (x + 2) + (x + 4) = 54$$

By immediately looking at the answer choices, we see that (A) is obviously wrong since if 10 were correct, the other two numbers would be 6 and 8 which, when added together equal only 24. In the same way, (E) is obviously wrong since if 28 was correct, the other two numbers would be 24 and 26 which, when added together, would be much greater than 54.

> **Step 3** Plug in the remaining answer choices to find the correct answer.

Plugging in the other choices, we find:

If $x + 4 = 14$, then $x = 10$. Therefore, 10 + 12 + 14 would have to equal 54. However, it only equals 36.

If $x + 4 = 20$, then $x = 16$. Therefore, 16 + 18 + 20 would have to equal 54. It does and therefore, (C) is the correct answer.

> **Step 4** If you cannot formulate an equation, try to make an educated guess among the remaining answer choices.

> **ADDITIONAL HINTS**

- **Know all important formulas and concepts in the Mathematics Review.**

- **Draw sketches. This allows you to visualize exactly what the question is asking and what information you need to find.**

- Always look at the answer choices before trying to work out the problem. If all the choices are in a specific format, you would want to do your work in the same format. For example, if the measurements in a problem are given in feet, but the answer choices are given in inches, you must change the feet to inches when working out the problem.

- Remember to work in only one unit and convert if more than one is presented in the problem. For example, if a problem gives numbers in decimals and fractions, convert one in terms of the other and then work out the problem.

- Avoid lengthy computations. If a problem is taking a long time to figure out, go on to another question and come back to it if time remains.

- Do not panic if something looks unusual; it may be easy.

- Use the scratch paper which will be provided.

- When given specific information for a problem, immediately plug these values into your equation.

- Be suspicious of choices that seem too obvious unless it is an easy level question. Many times choices will appear that are simply repetitions of numbers used in the problem. If the question is medium or hard, the chances are that these answers are incorrect.

- After working out an equation, make sure your result is actually answering the question. Otherwise, you may have to perform some extra steps. For example, although you may solve an equation for a specific variable, this may not be the final answer. You may have to use this answer to find another quantity.

Find the greatest of three consecutive integers whose sum is 36.

(A) 11   (B) 13   (C) 15

(D) 17   (E) 19

Let x = the first integer

Let $x + 1$ = the second integer

Let $x + 2$ = the third integer

$x + (x + 1) + (x + 2) = 36$

$3x + 3 = 36$

$3x = 33$

$x = 11$

Although $x = 11$ and answer choice (A) is 11, this is not the correct answer. The questions asks for the *greatest* of three consecutive integers. 11 is the smallest. Therefore, 11 must be plugged into $(x + 2)$ in order to find the greatest integer which is 13.

MATH TOPICS

The topics listed below should be reviewed in order to accurately answer the mathematical GED sections. See the math review on the following pages.

ARITHMETIC (50% of Test)

1. Integers and Real Numbers
2. Fractions
3. Decimals
4. Percentages
5. Radicals
6. Exponents
7. Averages

ALGEBRA (30% of Test)

1. Operations With Polynominals
2. Simplifying Algebraic Expressions
3. Equations
4. Two Linear Equations
5. Absolute Value Equations
6. Inequalities
7. Ratios and Proportions

GEOMETRY (20% of Test)

1. Points, Lines, and Angles
2. Regular Polygons
3. Triangles
4. Quadrilaterals

5. Circles
6. Solids
7. Coordinate Geometry

II. ARITHMETIC

1. INTEGERS AND REAL NUMBERS

Most of the numbers used in algebra belong to a set called the **real numbers** or **reals**. This set can be represented graphically by the real number line.

Given the number line below, we arbitrarily fix a point and label it with the number 0. In a similar manner, we can label any point on the line with one of the real numbers, depending on its position relative to 0. Numbers to the right of zero are positive, while those to the left are negative. Value increases from left to right, so that if *a* is to the right of *b*, it is said to be greater than *b*.

Negative   Positive
Numbers   Numbers   0

If we now divide the number line into equal segments, we can label the points on this line with real numbers. For example, the point 2 lengths to the left of zero is –2, while the point 3 lengths to the right of zero is + 3 (the + sign is usually assumed, so + 3 is written simply as 3). The number line now looks like this:

These boundary points represent the subset of the reals known as the **integers**. The set of integers is made up of both the positive and negative whole numbers: $\{... -4, -3, -2, -1, 0, 1, 2, 3, 4, ...\}$. Some subsets of integers are:

Natural Numbers or Positive Numbers—the set of integers starting with 1 and increasing: $\mathcal{N} = \{1, 2, 3, 4, ...\}$.

Whole Numbers—the set of integers starting with 0 and increasing: $\mathcal{W} = \{0, 1, 2, 3, ...\}$.

Negative Numbers—the set of integers starting with –1 and decreasing: $\mathcal{Z} = \{-1, -2, -3 ...\}$.

Prime Numbers—the set of positive integers greater than 1 that are divisible only by 1 and themselves: $\{2, 3, 5, 7, 11, ...\}$.

Even Integers—the set of integers divisible by 2: $\{..., -4, -2, 0, 2, 4, 6, ...\}$.

Odd Integers—the set of integers not divisible by 2: $\{..., -3, -1, 1, 3, 5, 7, ...\}$.

PROBLEM

Classify each of the following numbers into as many different sets as possible. Example: real, integer ...

(1) 0	(2) 9	(3) $\sqrt{6}$
(4) $\frac{1}{2}$	(5) $\frac{2}{3}$	(6) 1.5

SOLUTION

(1) Zero is a real number, and an integer, and a whole number.

(2) 9 is a real number, an odd number, and a natural number.

(3) $\sqrt{6}$ is a real number.

(4) $\frac{1}{2}$ is a real number.

(5) $\frac{2}{3}$ is a real number.

(6) 1.5 is a real number, and a decimal.

ABSOLUTE VALUE

The **absolute value** of a number is represented by two vertical lines around the number, and is equal to the given number, regardless of sign.

The absolute value of a real number A is defined as follows:

$$|A| = \begin{cases} A & \text{if } A \geq 0 \\ -A & \text{if } A < 0 \end{cases}$$

EXAMPLE

$$|5| = 5, |-8| = -(-8) = 8.$$

Absolute values follow the given rules:

(A) $|-A| = |A|$

(B) $|A| \geq 0$, equality holding only if $A = 0$

(C) $\left|\dfrac{A}{B}\right| = \dfrac{|A|}{|B|}, B \neq 0$

(D) $|AB| = |A| \times |B|$

(E) $|A|^2 = A^2$

Absolute value can also be expressed on the real number line as the distance of the point represented by the real number from the point labeled 0.

3 unit lengths

So $|-3| = 3$ because -3 is 3 units to the left of 0.

PROBLEM

Classify each of the following statements as true or false. If it is false, explain why.

(1) $|-120| > 1$

(4) $|12 - 3| = 12 - 3$

(2) $|4 - 12| = |4| - |12|$

(5) $|-12a| = 12|a|$

(3) $|4 - 9| = 9 - 4$

SOLUTION

(1) True

(2) False, $|4 - 12| = |4| - |12|$

$$|-8| = 4 - 12$$

$$8 \neq -8$$

In general, $|a + b| \neq |a| + |b|$

(3) True

(4) True

(5) True

PROBLEM

Calculate the value of each of the following expressions:

(1) $||2 - 5| + 6 - 14|$

(2) $|-5| \times |4| + \dfrac{|-12|}{4}$

SOLUTION

Before solving this problem, one must remember the order of operations: parenthesis, multiplication and division, addition and subtraction.

(1) $||-3| + 6 - 14| = |3 + 6 - 14| = |9 - 14| = |-5| = 5$

(2) $(5 \times 4) + {}^{12}/_4 = 20 + 3 = 23$

PROBLEM

Find the absolute value for each of the following:

(1) zero

(3) $-\pi$

(2) 4

(4) a, where a is a real number

SOLUTION

(1) $|0| = 0$

(2) $|4| = 4$

(3) $|-\pi| = \pi$

(4) for $a > 0, |a| = a$

for $a = 0, |a| = 0$

for $a < 0, |a| = -a$

$$\text{i.e., } |a| = \begin{cases} a \text{ if } a > 0 \\ 0 \text{ if } a = 0 \\ a \text{ if } a < 0 \end{cases}$$

POSITIVE AND NEGATIVE NUMBERS

A) **To add two numbers with like signs,** add their absolute values and write the sum with the common sign, So,

$$6 + 2 = 8, (-6) + (-2) = -8$$

B) **To add two numbers with unlike signs,** find the difference between their absolute values, and write the result with the sign of the number with the greater absolute value. So,

$$(-4) + 6 = 2, 15 + (-19) = -4$$

C) **To subtract a number b from another number a,** change the sign of b and add to a. Examples:

$$10 - (3) = 10 + (-3) = 7 \tag{1}$$
$$2 - (-6) = 2 + 6 = 8 \tag{2}$$
$$(-5) - (-2) = -5 + (+2) = -3 \tag{3}$$

D) **To multiply (or divide) two numbers having like signs**, multiply (or divide) their absolute values and write the result with a positive sign. Examples:

$$(5)(3) = 15 \tag{1}$$
$$(-6)/(-3) = 2 \tag{2}$$

E) **To multiply (or divide) two numbers having unlike signs,** multiply (or divide) their absolute values and write the result with a negative sign. Examples:

$$(-2)(8) = -16 \tag{1}$$
$$9/(-3) = -3 \tag{2}$$

According to the law of signs for real numbers, the square of a positive or negative number is always positive. This means that it is impossible to take the square root of a negative number in the real number system.

☞ Drill: Integers and Real Numbers

Addition

1. Simplify $4 + (-7) + 2 + (-5)$.

(A) –6   (B) –4   (C) 0   (D) 6   (E) 18

2. Simplify $144 + (-317) + 213$.

(A) -357 (B) -40 (C) 40 (D) 357 (E) 674

3. Simplify $|4 + (-3)| + |-2|$.

(A) -2 (B) -1 (C) 1 (D) 3 (E) 9

4. What integer makes the equation $-13 + 12 + 7 + ? = 10$ a true statement?

(A) -22 (B) -10 (C) 4 (D) 6 (E) 10

5. Simplify $4 + 17 + (-29) + 13 + (-22) + (-3)$.

(A) -44 (B) -20 (C) 23 (D) 34 (E) 78

Subtraction

6. Simplify $319 - 428$.

(A) -111 (B) -109 (C) -99 (D) 109 (E) 747

7. Simplify $91,203 - 37,904 + 1,073$.

(A) $54,372$ (B) $64,701$ (C) $128,034$ (D) $129,107$ (E) $130,180$

8. Simplify $|43 - 62| - |-17 - 3|$.

(A) -39 (B) -19 (C) -1 (D) 1 (E) 39

9. Simplify $-(-4 - 7) + (-2)$.

(A) -22 (B) -13 (C) -9 (D) 7 (E) 9

10. In Great Smoky Mountains National Park, Mt. LeConte rises from 1,292 feet above sea level to 6,593 feet above sea level. How tall is Mt. LeConte?

(A) 4,009 ft (B) 5,301 ft (C) 5,699 ft (D) 6,464 ft (E) 7,885 ft

Multiplication

11. Simplify $-3 * - 18 * - 1$.

(A) -108 (B) -54 (C) -48 (D) 48 (E) 54

12. Simplify $|-42| * |7|$.

(A) -294 (B) -49 (C) -35 (D) 284 (E) 294

13. Simplify –6 * 5 * – 10 * – 4 * 0 * 2.

(A) –2,400　(B) –240　(C) 0　(D) 280　(E) 2,700

14. Simplify –| –6 * 8 |.

(A) –48　(B) –42　(C) 2　(D) 42　(E) 48

15. A city in Georgia had a record low temperature of –3°F one winter. During the same year, a city in Michigan experienced a record low that was nine times the record low set in Georgia. What was the record low in Michigan that year?

(A) –31°F　(B) –27°F　(C) –21°F　(D) –12°F　(E) –6°F

Division

16. Simplify –24 ÷ 8.

(A) –4　(B) –3　(C) –2　(D) 3　(E) 4

17. Simplify (–180) ÷ (–12).

(A) –30　(B) –15　(C) 1.5　(D) 15　(E) 216

18. Simplify | –76 | ÷ | –4 |.

(A) –21　(B) –19　(C) 13　(D) 19　(E) 21.5

19. Simplify | 216 ÷ (–6) |.

(A) –36　(B) –12　(C) 36　(D) 38　(E) 43

20. At the end of the year, a small firm has $2,996 in its account for bonuses. If the entire amount is equally divided among the 14 employees, how much does each one receive?

(A) $107　(B) $114　(C) $170　(D) $210　(E) $214

Order of Operations

21. Simplify $\dfrac{4 + 8 * 2}{5 - 1}$

(A) 4　(B) 5　(C) 6　(D) 8　(E) 12

22. 96 ÷ 3 ÷ 4 ÷ 2 =

(A) 65　(B) 64　(C) 16　(D) 8　(E) 4

23. $3 + 4 * 2 - 6 \div 3 =$

(A) –1   (B) 5/3   (C) 8/3   (D) 9   (E) 12

24. $[(4 + 8) * 3] \div 9 =$

(A) 4   (B) 8   (C) 12   (D) 24   (E) 36

25. $18 + 3 * 4 \div 3 =$

(A) 3   (B) 5   (C) 10   (D) 22   (E) 28

26. $(29 - 17 + 4) \div 4 + | -2 | =$

(A) $2^2/_3$ (B) 4   (C) $4^2/_3$ (D) 6   (E) 15

27. $(-3) * 5 - 20 \div 4 =$

(A) –75   (B) –20   (C) –10   (D) $-8^3/_4$ (E) 20

28. $\dfrac{11 * 2 + 2}{16 - 2 * 2} =$

(A) 11/16   (B) 1   (C) 2   (D) 3 2/3   (E) 4

29. $| -8 - 4 | \div 3 * 6 + (-4) =$

(A) 20   (B) 26   (C) 32   (D) 62   (E) 212

30. $32 \div 2 + 4 - 15 \div 3 =$

(A) 0   (B) 7   (C) 15   (D) 23   (E) 63

---

2. FRACTIONS

The fraction, a/b, where the **numerator** is a and the **denominator** is b, implies that a is being divided by b. The denominator of a fraction can never be zero since a number divided by zero is not defined. If the numerator is greater than the denominator, the fraction is called an **improper fraction**. A **mixed number** is the sum of a whole number and a fraction, i.e., $4^3/_8 = 4 + {}^3/_8$.

OPERATIONS WITH FRACTIONS

A) **To change a mixed number to an improper fraction,** simply multiply the whole number by the denominator of the fraction and add the numerator. This product becomes the numerator of the result and the denominator remains the same. e.g.,

$$5\,\frac{2}{3} = \frac{(5 \cdot 3) + 2}{3} = \frac{15 + 2}{3} = \frac{17}{3}$$

To change an improper fraction to a mixed number, simply divide the numerator by the denominator. The remainder becomes the numerator of the fractional part of the mixed number, and the denominator remains the same, e.g.,

$$\frac{35}{4} = 35 \div 4 = 8\,\frac{3}{4}$$

To check your work, change your result back to an improper fraction to see if it matches the original fraction.

B) **To find the sum of two fractions having a common denominator**, simply add together the numerators of the given fractions and put this sum over the common denominator.

$$\frac{11}{3} + \frac{5}{3} = \frac{11+5}{3} = \frac{16}{3}$$

Similarly for subtraction,

$$\frac{11}{3} - \frac{5}{3} = \frac{11-5}{3} = \frac{6}{3} = 2$$

C) **To find the sum of the two fractions having different denominators**, it is necessary to find the **lowest common denominator (LCD)** of the different denominators using a process called **factoring**.

To **factor** a number means to find two numbers that when multiplied together have a product equal to the original number. These two numbers are then said to be **factors** of the original number; e.g., the factors of 6 are

   (1) 1 and 6 since $1 \times 6 = 6$.

   (2) 2 and 3 since $2 \times 3 = 6$.

Every number is the product of itself and 1. A **prime factor** is a number that does not have any factors besides itself and 1. This is important when finding the LCD of two fractions having different denominators.

To find the LCD of $^{11}/_6$ and $^5/_{16}$, we must first find the prime factors of each of the two denominators.

   $6 = 2 \times 3$

   $16 = 2 \times 2 \times 2 \times 2$

   $LCD = 2 \times 2 \times 2 \times 2 \times 3 = 48$

Note that we do not need to repeat the 2 that appears in both the factors of 6 and 16.

Once we have determined the LCD of the denominators, each of the fractions must be converted into equivalent fractions having the LCD as a denominator.

Rewrite 11/6 and 5/16 to have 48 as their denominators.

   $6 \times ? = 48$ $16 \times ? = 48$

   $6 \times 8 = 48$ $16 \times 3 = 48$

If the numerator and denominator of each fraction is multiplied (or divided) by the same number, the value of the fraction will not change. This is because a fraction b/b, b being any number, is equal to the multiplicative identity, 1.

Therefore,

$$\frac{11}{6} \cdot \frac{8}{8} = \frac{88}{48} \qquad\qquad \frac{5}{16} \cdot \frac{3}{3} = \frac{15}{48}$$

We may now find

$$\frac{11}{6} + \frac{5}{16} = \frac{88}{48} + \frac{15}{48} = \frac{103}{48}$$

Similarly for subtraction,

$$\frac{11}{6} - \frac{5}{16} = \frac{88}{48} - \frac{15}{48} = \frac{73}{48}$$

D) **To find the product of two or more fractions,** simply multiply the numerators of the given fractions to find the numerator of the product and multiply the denominators of the given fractions to find the denominator of the product. e.g.,

$$\frac{2}{3} \cdot \frac{1}{5} \cdot \frac{4}{7} = \frac{2 \times 1 \times 4}{3 \times 5 \times 7} = \frac{8}{105}$$

E) To find the quotient of two fractions, simply invert the divisor and multiply; e.g.,

$$\frac{8}{9} \div \frac{1}{3} = \frac{8}{9} \times \frac{3}{1} = \frac{24}{9} = \frac{8}{3}$$

F) **To simplify a fraction** is to convert it into a form in which the numerator and denominator have no common factor other than 1; e.g.,

$$\frac{12}{18} = \frac{12 \div 6}{18 \div 6} = \frac{2}{3}$$

G) A **complex fraction** is a fraction whose numerator and/or denominator is made up of fractions. To simplify the fraction, find the LCD of all the fractions. Multiply both the numerator and denominator by this number and simplify.

PROBLEM

If $a = 4$ and $b = 7$, find the value of $\dfrac{a + \frac{a}{b}}{a - \frac{a}{b}}$

SOLUTION

By substitution,

$$\frac{a + \frac{a}{b}}{a - \frac{a}{b}} = \frac{4 + \frac{4}{7}}{4 - \frac{4}{7}}$$

In order to combine the terms, we must find the LCD of 1 and 7. Since both are prime factors, the LCD $= 1 \times 7 = 7$.

Multiplying both numerator and denominator by 7, we get:

$$\frac{7(4 + \frac{4}{7})}{7(4 - \frac{4}{7})} = \frac{28 + 4}{28 - 4} = \frac{32}{24}$$

By dividing both numerator and denominator by 8, 32/24 can be reduced to 4/3.

☞ Drill: Fractions

Fractions

DIRECTIONS: Add and write the answer in simplest form.

1.   5/12 + 3/12 =

(A)   5/24   (B)   1/3   (C)   8/12   (D)   2/3   (E)   1 1/3

2.   5/8 + 7/8 + 3/8 =

(A)   15/24   (B)   3/4   (C)   5/6   (D)   7/8   (E)   1 7/8

3.   131 2/15 + 28 3/15 =

(A)   159 1/6   (B)   159 1/5   (C)   159 1/3   (D)   159 1/2   (E)   159 3/5

4.   3 5/18 + 2 1/18 + 8 7/18 =

(A)   13 13/18 (B)   13 3/4   (C)   13 7/9   (D)   14 1/6   (E)   14 2/9

5.   17 9/20 + 4 3/20 + 8 11/20 =

(A)   29 23/60   (B)   29 23/20   (C)   30 3/20

(D)   30 1/5   (E)   30 3/5

Subtract Fractions with the Same Denominator

DIRECTIONS: Subtract and write the answer in simplest form.

6.   4 7/8 – 3 1/8 =

(A)   1 1/4   (B)   1 3/4   (C)   1 12/16   (D)   1 7/8   (E)   2

7.   132 5/12 – 37 3/12 =

(A)   94 1/6   (B)   95 1/12   (C)   95 1/6   (D)   105 1/6   (E)   169 2/3

8.   19 1/3 – 2 2/3 =

(A)   16 2/3   (B)   16 5/6   (C)   17 1/3   (D)   17 2/3   (E)   17 5/6

9. 8/21 – 5/21 =

(A) 1/21   (B) 1/7   (C) 3/21   (D) 2/7   (E) 3/7

10. 82 7/10 – 38 9/10 =

(A) 43 4/5   (B) 44 1/5   (C) 44 2/5   (D) 45 1/5   (E) 45 2/10

Finding the LCD

<u>DIRECTIONS</u>: Find the lowest common denominator of each group of fractions.

11. 2/3, 5/9, and 1/6.

(A) 9   (B) 18   (C) 27   (D) 54   (E) 162

12. 1/2, 5/6, and 3/4.

(A) 2   (B) 4   (C) 6   (D) 12   (E) 48

13. 7/16, 5/6, and 2/3.

(A) 3   (B) 6   (C) 12   (D) 24   (E) 48

14. 8/15, 2/5, and 12/25.

(A) 5   (B) 15   (C) 25   (D) 75   (E) 375

15. 2/3, 1/5, and 5/6.

(A) 15   (B) 30   (C) 48   (D) 90   (E) 120

16. 1/3, 9/42, and 4/21.

(A) 21   (B) 42   (C) 126   (D) 378   (E) 4,000

17. 4/9, 2/5, and 1/3.

(A) 15   (B) 17   (C) 27   (D) 45   (E) 135

18. 7/12, 11/36, and 1/9.

(A) 12   (B) 36   (C) 108   (D) 324   (E) 432

19. 3/7, 5/21, and 2/3.

(A) 21   (B) 42   (C) 31   (D) 63   (E) 441

20. 13/16, 5/8, and 1/4.

(A) 4   (B) 8   (C) 16   (D) 32   (E) 64

Adding Fractions with Different Denominators

DIRECTIONS: Add and write the answer in simplest form.

21.   1/3 + 5/12 =

(A)   2/5   (B)   1/2   (C)   9/12   (D)   3/4   (E)   1 1/3

22.   3 5/9 + 2 1/3 =

(A)   5 1/2   (B)   5 2/3   (C)   5 8/9   (D)   6 1/9   (E)   6 2/3

23.   12 9/16 + 17 3/4 + 8 1/8 =

(A)   37 7/16   (B)   38 7/16   (C)   38 1/2   (D)   38 2/3   (E)   39 3/16

24.   28 4/5 + 11 16/25 =

(A)   39 2/3   (B)   39 4/5   (C)   40 9/25   (D)   40 2/5   (E)   40 11/25

25.   2 1/8 + 1 3/16 + 5/12 =

(A)   3 35/48   (B)   3 3/4   (C)   3 19/24   (D)   3 13/16   (E)   4 1/12

Subtraction with Different Denominators

DIRECTIONS: Subtract and write the answer in simplest form.

26.   8 9/12 – 2 2/3 =

(A)   6 1/12   (B)   6 1/6   (C)   6 1/3   (D)   6 7/12   (E)   6 2/3

27.   185 11/15 – 107 2/5 =

(A)   77 2/15   (B)   78 1/5   (C)   78 3/10   (D)   78 1/3   (E)   78 9/15

28.   34 2/3 – 16 5/6 =

(A)   16   (B)   16 1/3   (C)   17 1/2   (D)   17   (E)   17 5/6

29.   3 11/48 – 2 3/16 =

(A)   47/48   (B)   1 1/48   (C)   1 1/24   (D)   1 8/48   (E)   1 7/24

30.   81 4/21 – 31 1/3 =

(A)   47 3/7   (B)   49 6/7   (C)   49 1/6   (D)   49 5/7   (E)   49 13/21

Multiplication of Fractions

DIRECTIONS: Multiply and reduce the answer.

31. 2/3 * 4/5 =

(A) 6/8   (B) 3/4   (C) 8/15   (D) 10/12   (E) 6/5

32. 7/10 * 4/21 =

(A) 2/15   (B) 11/31   (C) 28/210   (D) 1/6   (E) 4/15

33. 5 1/3 * 3/8 =

(A) 4/11   (B) 2   (C) 8/5   (D) 5 1/8   (E) 5 17/24

34. 6 1/2 * 3 =

(A) 9 1/2   (B) 18 1/2   (C) 19 1/2   (D) 20   (E) 12 1/2

35. 3 1/4 * 2 1/3 =

(A) 5 7/12   (B) 6 2/7   (C) 6 5/7   (D) 7 7/12   (E) 7 11/12

Division of Fractions

DIRECTIONS: Divide and reduce the answer.

36. 3/16 ÷ 3/4 =

(A) 9/64   (B) 1/4   (C) 6/16   (D) 9/16   (E) 3/4

37. 4/9 ÷ 2/3 =

(A) 1/3   (B) 1/2   (C) 2/3   (D) 7/11   (E) 8/9

38. 5 1/4 ÷ 7/10 =

(A) 2 4/7   (B) 3 27/40   (C) 5 19/20   (D) 7 1/2   (E) 8 1/4

39. 4 2/3 ÷ 7/9 =

(A) 2 24/27   (B) 3 2/9   (C) 4 14/27   (D) 5 12/27   (E) 6

40. 3 2/5 ÷ 1 7/10 =

(A) 2   (B) 3 4/7   (C) 4 7/25   (D) 5 1/10   (E) 5 2/7

Changing an Improper Fraction to a Mixed Number

<u>DIRECTIONS</u>: Write each improper fraction as a mixed number in simplest form.

41. 50/4
(A) 10 1/4   (B) 11 1/2   (C) 12 1/4   (D) 12 1/2   (E) 25

42. 17/5
(A) 3 2/5   (B) 3 3/5   (C) 3 4/5   (D) 4 1/5   (E) 4 2/5

43. 42/3
(A) 10 2/3   (B) 12   (C) 13 1/3   (D) 14   (E) 21 1/3

44. 85/6
(A) 9 1/6   (B) 10 5/6   (C) 11 1/2   (D) 12   (E) 14 1/6

45. 151/7
(A) 19 6/7   (B) 20 1/7   (C) 21 4/7   (D) 31 2/7   (E) 31 4/7

Changing a Mixed Number to an Improper Fraction

<u>DIRECTIONS</u>: Change each mixed number to an improper fraction in simplest form.

46. 2 3/5
(A) 4/5   (B) 6/5   (C) 11/5   (D) 13/5   (E) 17/5

47. 4 3/4
(A) 7/4   (B) 13/4   (C) 16/3   (D) 19/4   (E) 21/4

48. 6 7/6
(A) 13/6   (B) 43/6   (C) 19/36   (D) 42/36   (E) 48/6

49. 12 3/7
(A) 87/7   (B) 164/14   (C) 34/3   (D) 187/21   (E) 252/7

50. 21 1/2
(A) 11/2   (B) 22/2   (C) 24/2   (D) 42/2   (E) 43/2

3. DECIMALS

When we divide the denominator of a fraction into its numerator, the result is a **decimal**. The decimal is based upon a fraction with a denominator of 10, 100, 1000, ... and is written with a **decimal point**. Whole numbers are placed to the left of the decimal point where the first place to the left is the units place; the second to the left is the tens; the third to the left is the hundreds, etc. The fractions are placed on the right where the first place to the right is the tenths; the second to the right is the hundredths, etc.

EXAMPLE

$$12\frac{3}{10} = 12.3 \qquad 4\frac{17}{100} = 4.17 \qquad \frac{3}{100} = .03$$

Since a **rational number** is of the form a/b, $b \neq 0$, then all rational numbers can be expressed as decimals by dividing b into a. The result is either a **terminating decimal**, meaning that b divides a with a remainder of 0 after a certain point; or **repeating decimal**, meaning that b continues to divide a so that the decimal has a repeating pattern of integers.

EXAMPLE

(A) $\quad \frac{1}{2} = .5$

(B) $\quad \frac{1}{3} = .333...$

(C) $\quad \frac{11}{16} = .6875$

(D) $\quad \frac{2}{7} = .285714285714...$

(A) and (C) are terminating decimals; (B) and (D) are repeating decimals. This explanation allows us to define **irrational numbers** as numbers whose decimal form is non-terminating and non-repeating, e.g.,

$$\sqrt{2} = 1.414...$$
$$\sqrt{3} = 1.732...$$

PROBLEM

Express $-\frac{10}{20}$ as a decimal.

SOLUTION

$$-\frac{10}{20} = -\frac{50}{100} = -.5$$

PROBLEM

Write $\frac{2}{7}$ as a repeating decimal.

SOLUTION

To write a fraction as a repeating decimal divide the numerator by the denominator until a pattern of repeated digits appears.

$$2 \div 7 = .285714285714...$$

Identify the entire portion of the decimal which is repeated. The repeating decimal can then be written in the shortened form:

$2/7 = .\overline{285714}$

OPERATIONS WITH DECIMALS

A) **To add numbers containing decimals,** write the numbers in a column making sure the decimal points are lined up, one beneath the other. Add the numbers as usual, placing the decimal point in the sum so that it is still in line with the others. It is important not to mix the digits in the tenths place with the digits in the hundredths place, and so on.

EXAMPLES

$2.558 + 6.391$ $57.51 + 6.2$

$$
\begin{array}{r}
2.558 \\
+\ 6.391 \\
\hline
8.949
\end{array}
\qquad
\begin{array}{r}
57.51 \\
+\ \ 6.20 \\
\hline
63.71
\end{array}
$$

Similarly with subtraction,

$78.54 - 21.33$ $7.11 - 4.2$

$$
\begin{array}{r}
78.54 \\
-\ 21.33 \\
\hline
57.21
\end{array}
\qquad
\begin{array}{r}
7.11 \\
-\ 4.20 \\
\hline
2.91
\end{array}
$$

Note that if two numbers differ according to the number of digits to the right of the decimal point, zeros must be added.

$.63 - .214$ $15.224 - 3.6891$

$$
\begin{array}{r}
.630 \\
-\ .214 \\
\hline
.416
\end{array}
\qquad
\begin{array}{r}
15.2240 \\
-\ 3.6891 \\
\hline
11.5349
\end{array}
$$

B) **To multiply numbers with decimals**, simply multiply as usual. Then, to figure out the number of decimal places that belong in the product, find the total number of decimal places in the numbers being multiplied.

EXAMPLES

$$
\begin{array}{rl}
6.555 & \text{(3 decimal places)} \\
\times\ \ \ \ 4.5 & \text{(1 decimal place)} \\
\hline
32775 & \\
26220\ \ & \\
\hline
294975 & \\
29.4975 & \text{(4 decimal places)}
\end{array}
\qquad
\begin{array}{rl}
5.32 & \text{(2 decimal places)} \\
\times\ \ \ .04 & \text{(2 decimal places)} \\
\hline
2128 & \\
000\ \ & \\
\hline
2128 & \\
.2128 & \text{(4 decimal places)}
\end{array}
$$

C) **To divide numbers with decimals,** you must first make the divisor a whole number by moving the decimal point the appropriate number of places to the right. The decimal point of the dividend should also be moved the same number of places. Place a decimal point in the quotient, directly in line with the decimal point in the dividend.

EXAMPLES

$$12.92 \div 3.4$$

$$
\begin{array}{r}
3.8 \\
3{,}4\overline{){)}12{,}9{,}2} \\
-102 \\
\hline
272 \\
-272 \\
\hline
0
\end{array}
$$

$$40.376 \div 7.21$$

$$
\begin{array}{r}
5.6 \\
7{,}21\overline{){)}40{,}37{,}6} \\
-3605 \\
\hline
4326 \\
-4326 \\
\hline
0
\end{array}
$$

If the question asks to find the correct answer to two decimal places, simply divide until you have three decimal places and then round off. If the third decimal place is a 5 or larger, the number in the second decimal place is increased by 1. If the third decimal place is less than 5, that number is simply dropped.

PROBLEM

Find the answer to the following to 2 decimal places:

(1) $44.3 \div 3$

(2) $56.99 \div 6$

SOLUTION

(1)
$$
\begin{array}{r}
14.766 \\
3\overline{)44.300} \\
-3 \\
\hline
14 \\
-12 \\
\hline
23 \\
-21 \\
\hline
20 \\
-18 \\
\hline
20 \\
-18 \\
\hline
2
\end{array}
$$

(2)
$$
\begin{array}{r}
9.498 \\
6\overline{)56.990} \\
-54 \\
\hline
29 \\
-24 \\
\hline
59 \\
-54 \\
\hline
50 \\
-48 \\
\hline
2
\end{array}
$$

14.766 can be rounded off to 14.77

9.498 can be rounded off to 9.50

D)   When comparing two numbers with decimals to see which is the larger, first look at the tenths place. The larger digit in this place represents the larger number. If the two digits are the same, however, take a look at the digits in the hundredths place, and so on.

EXAMPLES

.518 and .216

5 is larger than 2, therefore

.518 is larger than .216

.723 and .726

6 is larger than 3, therefore

.726 is larger than .723

☞ Drill: Decimals

Addition

1. $1.032 + 0.987 + 3.07 =$

(A) 4.089   (B) 5.089   (C) 5.189   (D) 6.189   (D) 13.972

2. $132.03 + 97.1483 =$

(A) 98.4686   (B) 110.3513   (C) 209.1783

(D) 229.1486   (E) 229.1783

3. $7.1 + 0.62 + 4.03827 + 5.183 =$

(A) 0.2315127   (B) 16.45433   (C) 16.94127

(D) 18.561   (E) 40.4543

4. $8 + 17.43 + 9.2 =$

(A) 34.63   (B) 34.86   (C) 35.63   (D) 176.63   (E) 189.43

5. $1,036.173 + 289.04 =$

(A) 382.6573   (B) 392.6573   (C) 1,065.077

(D) 1,325.213   (E) 3,926.573

Subtraction

6. $3.972 - 2.04 =$

(A) 1.932   (B) 1.942   (C) 1.976   (D) 2.013   (E) 2.113

7. $16.047 - 13.06 =$

(A) 2.887   (B) 2.987   (C) 3.041   (D) 3.141   (E) 4.741

8. $87.4 - 56.27 =$

(A) 30.27   (B) 30.67   (C) 31.1   (D) 31.13   (E) 31.27

9.   1,046.8 – 639.14 =

(A) 303.84   (B) 313.74   (C) 407.66   (D) 489.74   (E) 535.54

10.   10,000 – 842.91 =

(A) 157.09   (B) 942.91   (C) 5,236.09 (D) 9,057.91 (E) 9,157.09

Multiplication

11.   1.03 * 2.6 =

(A) 2.18   (B) 2.678   (C) 2.78   (D) 3.38   (E) 3.63

12.   93 * 4.2 =

(A) 39.06   (B) 97.2   (C) 223.2   (D) 390.6   (E) 3906

13.   0.04 * 0.23 =

(A) 0.0092   (B) 0.092   (C) 0.27   (D) 0.87   (E) 0.920

14.   0.0186 * 0.03 =

(A) 0.000348 (B) 0.000558 (C) 0.0548   (D) 0.0848   (E) 0.558

15.   51.2 * 0.17 =

(A) 5.29   (B) 8.534   (C) 8.704   (D) 36.352   (E) 36.991

Division

16.   123.39 ÷ 3 =

(A) 31.12   (B) 41.13   (C) 401.13   (D) 411.3   (E) 4,113

17.   1,428.6 ÷ 6 =

(A) 0.2381   (B) 2.381   (C) 23.81   (D) 238.1   (E) 2,381

18.   25.2 ÷ 0.3 =

(A) 0.84   (B) 8.04   (C) 8.4   (D) 84   (E) 840

19.   14.95 ÷ 6.5 =

(A) 2.3   (B) 20.3   (C) 23   (D) 230   (E) 2,300

20.   46.33 ÷ 1.13 =

(A) 0.41   (B) 4.1   (C) 41   (D) 410   (E) 4,100

Comparing

21. Which is the **largest** number in this set—{0.8, 0.823, 0.089, 0.807, 0.852}?

(A) 0.8   (B) 0.823   (C) 0.089   (D) 0.807   (E) 0.852

22. Which is the **smallest** number in this set—{32.98, 32.099, 32.047, 32.5, 32.304}?

(A) 32.98   (B) 32.099   (C) 32.047   (D) 32.5   (E) 32.304

23. In which set below are the numbers arranged correctly from smallest to largest?

(A) {0.98, 0.9, 0.993}   (D) {0.006, 0.061, 0.06}

(B) {0.113, 0.3, 0.31}   (E) {12.84, 12.801, 12.6}

(C) {7.04, 7.26, 7.2}

24. In which set below are the numbers arranged correctly from largest to smallest?

(A) {1.018, 1.63, 1.368}   (D) {16.34, 16.304, 16.3}

(B) {4.219, 4.29, 4.9}   (E) {12.98, 12.601, 12.86}

(C) {0.62, 0.6043, 0.643}

25. Which is the **largest** number in this set—{0.87, 0.89, 0.889, 0.8, 0.987}?

(A) 0.87   (B) 0.89   (C) 0.889   (D) 0.8   (E) 0.987

Changing a Fraction to a Decimal

26. What is 1/4 written as a decimal?

(A) 1.4   (B) 0.14   (C) 0.2   (D) 0.25   (E) 0.3

27. What is 3/5 written as a decimal?

(A) 0.3   (B) 0.35   (C) 0.6   (D) 0.65   (E) 0.8

28. What is 7/20 written as a decimal?

(A) 0.35   (B) 0.4   (C) 0.72   (D) 0.75   (E) 0.9

29. What is 2/3 written as a decimal?

(A) 0.23   (B) 0.33   (C) 0.5   (D) 0.6   (E) $0.\overline{6}$

30. What is 11/25 written as a decimal?

(A) 0.1125   (B) 0.25   (C) 0.4   (D) 0.44   (E) 0.5

4. PERCENTAGES

A **percent** is a way of expressing the relationship between part and whole, where whole is defined as 100%. A percent can be defined by a fraction with a denominator of 100. Decimals can also represent a percent. For instance,

$$56\% = 0.56 = 56/100$$

PROBLEM

Compute the value of

(1) 90% of 400

(3) 50% of 500

(2) 180% of 400

(4) 200% of 4

SOLUTION

The symbol % means per hundred, therefore $5\% = 5/100$

(1) 90% of $400 = 90/100 \times 400 = 90 \times 4 = 360$

(2) 180% of $400 = 180/100 \times 400 = 180 \times 4 = 720$

(3) 50% of $500 = 50/100 \times 500 = 50 \times 5 = 250$

(4) 200% of $4 = 200/100 \times 4 = 2 \times 4 = 8$

PROBLEM

What percent of

(1) 100 is 99.5

(2) 200 is 4

SOLUTION

(1) $99.5 = x \times 100$

$99.5 = 100x$

$.995 = x;$ but this is the value of x per hundred. Therefore,

$x = 99.5\%$

(2) $4 = x \times 200$

$4 = 200x$

$.02 = x.$ Again this must be changed to percent, so

$x = 2\%$

EQUIVALENT FORMS OF A NUMBER

Some problems may call for converting numbers into an equivalent or simplified form in order to make the solution more convenient.

1. Converting a fraction to a decimal:

$$^1/_2 = 0.50$$

Divide the numerator by the denominator:

$$\begin{array}{r} .50 \\ 2\overline{)1.00} \\ \underline{-10} \\ 00 \end{array}$$

2.   Converting a number to a percent:

   $0.50 = 50\%$

   Multiply by 100:

   $0.50 = (0.50 \times 100)\% = 50\%$

3.   Converting a percent to a decimal:

   $30\% = 0.30$

   Divide by 100:

   $30\% = 30/100 = 0.30$

4.   Converting a decimal to a fraction:

   $0.500 = \frac{1}{2}$

   Convert .500 to 500/1000 and then simplify the fraction by dividing the numerator and denominator by common factors:

$$\frac{2 \times 2 \times 5 \times 5 \times 5}{2 \times 2 \times 2 \times 5 \times 5 \times 5}$$

   and then cancel out the common numbers to get $\frac{1}{2}$.

PROBLEM

Express

(1)   1.65 as a percent

(2)   .07 as a fraction

(3) $-\,^{10}/_{20}$ as a decimal

(4) $^{4}/_{2}$ as an integer

SOLUTION

(1) $1.65 \times 100 = 165\%$

(2) $0.7 = {}^{7}/_{10}$

(3) $-{}^{10}/_{20} = -0.5$

(4) $^{4}/_{2} = 2$

☞ Drill: Percentages

Finding Percents

1.   Find 3% of 80.

(A)   0.24   (B)   2.4   (C)   24   (D)   240   (E)   2,400

2.   Find 50% of 182.

(A)   9   (B)   90   (C)   91   (D)   910   (E)   9,100

3.   Find 83% of 166.

(A)   0.137   (B)   1.377   (C)   13.778   (D)   137   (E)   137.78

4.   Find 125% of 400.

(A)   425   (B)   500   (C)   525   (D)   600   (E)   825

5.   Find 300% of 4.

(A)   12   (B)   120   (C)   1200   (D)   12,000   (E)   120,000

6.   Forty-eight percent of the 1,200 students at Central High are males. How many male students are there at Central High?

(A)   57   (B)   576   (C)   580   (D)   600   (E)   648

7.   For 35% of the last 40 days, there has been measurable rainfall. How many days out of the last 40 days have had measurable rainfall?

(A)   14   (B)   20   (C)   25   (D)   35   (E)   40

8.   Of every 1,000 people who take a certain medicine, 0.2% develop severe side effects. How many people out of every 1,000 who take the medicine develop the side effects?

(A)   0.2   (B)   2   (C)   20   (D)   22   (E)   200

9.   Of 220 applicants for a job, 75% were offered an initial interview. How many people were offered an initial interview?

(A)   75   (B)   110   (C)   120   (D)   155   (E)   165

10.   Find 0.05% of 4,000.

(A)   0.05   (B)   0.5   (C)   2   (D)   20   (E)   400

Changing Percents to Fractions

11. What is 25% written as a fraction?

(A) 1/25   (B) 1/5   (C) 1/4   (D) 1/3   (E) 1/2

12. What is 33 1/3% written as a fraction?

(A) 1/4   (B) 1/3   (C) 1/2   (D) 2/3   (E) 5/9

13. What is 200% written as a fraction?

(A) 1/2   (B) 2/1   (C) 20/1   (D) 200/1   (E) 2000/1

14. What is 84% written as a fraction?

(A) 1/84   (B) 4/8   (C) 17/25   (D) 21/25   (E) 44/50

15. What is 2% written as a fraction?

(A) 1/50   (B) 1/25   (C) 1/10   (D) 1/4   (E) 1/2

Changing Fractions to Percents

16. What is 2/3 written as a percent?

(A) 23%   (B) 32%   (C) 33 1/3% (D) 57 1/3% (E) 66 2/3%

17. What is 3/5 written as a percent?

(A) 30%   (B) 35%   (C) 53%   (D) 60%   (E) 65%

18. What is 17/20 written as a percent?

(A) 17%   (B) 70%   (C) 75%   (D) 80%   (E) 85%

19. What is 45/50 written as a percent?

(A) 45%   (B) 50%   (C) 90%   (D) 95%   (E) 97%

20. What is 1 1/4 written as a percent?

(A) 114%   (B) 120%   (C) 125%   (D) 127%   (E) 133%

Changing Percents to Decimals

21. What is 42% written as a decimal?

(A) 0.42   (B) 4.2   (C) 42   (D) 420   (E) 422

22. What is 0.3% written as a decimal?

(A) 0.0003   (B) 0.003   (C) 0.03   (D) 0.3   (E) 3

23. What is 8% written as a decimal?

(A) 0.0008   (B) 0.008   (C) 0.08   (D) 0.80   (E) 8

24. What is 175% written as a decimal?

(A) 0.175   (B) 1.75   (C) 17.5   (D) 175   (E) 17,500

25. What is 34% written as a decimal?

(A) 0.00034   (B) 0.0034   (C) 0.034   (D) 0.34   (E) 3.4

Changing Decimals to Percents

26. What is 0.43 written as a percent?

(A) 0.0043%   (B) 0.043%   (C) 4.3%   (D) 43%   (E) 430%

27. What is 1 written as a percent?

(A) 1%   (B) 10%   (C) 100%   (D) 111%   (E) 150%

28. What is 0.08 written as a percent?

(A) 0.08%   (B) 8%   (C) 8.8%   (D) 80%   (E) 800%

29. What is 3.4 written as a percent?

(A) 0.0034%   (B) 3.4%   (C) 34%   (D) 304%   (E) 340%

30. What is 0.645 written as a percent?

(A) 64.5%   (B) 65%   (C) 69%   (D) 70%   (E) 645%

5. RADICALS

The **square root** of a number is a number that when multiplied by itself results in the original number. Thus, the square root of 81 is 9 since $9 \times 9 = 81$. However, –9 is also a root of 81 since $(-9)(-9) = 81$. Every positive number will have two roots. The principal root is the positive one. Zero has only one square root, while negative numbers do not have real numbers as their roots.

A **radical sign** indicates that the root of a number or expression will be taken. The **radicand** is the number of which the root will be taken. The **index** tells how many times the root needs to be multiplied by itself to equal the radicand, e.g.,

index

radical sign → radicand

(1) $\sqrt[3]{64}$;

3 is the index and 64 is the radicand. Since $4 \cdot 4 \cdot 4 = 64$, $\sqrt[3]{64} = 4$

(2) $\sqrt[5]{32}$;

5 is the index and 32 is the radicand. Since $2 \cdot 2 \cdot 2 \cdot 2 \cdot 2 = 32$, $\sqrt[5]{32} = 2$

OPERATIONS WITH RADICALS

A) **To multiply two or more radicals**, we utilize the law that states,

$$\sqrt{a} \cdot \sqrt{b} = \sqrt{ab}.$$

Simply multiply the whole numbers as usual. Then, multiply the radicands and put the product under the radical sign and simplify, e.g.,

(1) $\sqrt{12} \cdot \sqrt{5} = \sqrt{60} = 2\sqrt{15}$

(2) $3\sqrt{2} \cdot 4\sqrt{8} = 12\sqrt{16} = 48$

(3) $2\sqrt{10} \cdot 6\sqrt{5} = 12\sqrt{50} = 60\sqrt{2}$

B) **To divide radicals**, simplify both the numerator and the denominator. By multiplying the radical in the denominator by itself, you can make the denominator a rational number. The numerator, however, must also be multiplied by this radical so that the value of the expression does not change. You must choose as many factors as necessary to rationalize the denominator, e.g.,

(1) $\dfrac{\sqrt{128}}{\sqrt{2}} = \dfrac{\sqrt{64} \cdot \sqrt{2}}{\sqrt{2}} = \dfrac{8\sqrt{2}}{\sqrt{2}} = 8$

(2) $\dfrac{\sqrt{10}}{\sqrt{3}} = \dfrac{\sqrt{10} \cdot \sqrt{3}}{\sqrt{3} \cdot \sqrt{3}} = \dfrac{\sqrt{30}}{3}$

(3) $\dfrac{\sqrt{8}}{2\sqrt{3}} = \dfrac{\sqrt{8} \cdot \sqrt{3}}{2\sqrt{3} \cdot \sqrt{3}} = \dfrac{\sqrt{24}}{2 \cdot 3} = \dfrac{2\sqrt{6}}{6} = \dfrac{\sqrt{6}}{3}$

C) **To add two or more radicals,** the radicals must have the same index and the same radicand. Only where the radicals are simplified can these similarities be determined.

EXAMPLE

(1) $6\sqrt{2} + 2\sqrt{2} = (6+2)\sqrt{2} = 8\sqrt{2}$

(2) $\sqrt{27} + 5\sqrt{3} = \sqrt{9}\sqrt{3} + 5\sqrt{3} = 3\sqrt{3} + 5\sqrt{3} = 8\sqrt{3}$

(3) $7\sqrt{3} + 8\sqrt{2} + 5\sqrt{3} = 12\sqrt{3} + 8\sqrt{2}$

Similarly, to subtract,

(1) $12\sqrt{3} - 7\sqrt{3} = (12-7)\sqrt{3} = 5\sqrt{3}$

(2) $\sqrt{90} - \sqrt{20} = \sqrt{16}\sqrt{5} - \sqrt{4}\sqrt{5} = 4\sqrt{5} - 2\sqrt{5} = 2\sqrt{5}$

(3) $\sqrt{50} - \sqrt{3} = 5\sqrt{2} - \sqrt{3}$

PROBLEM

Simplify $5\sqrt{2} + 3\sqrt{8}$

SOLUTION

To add two radicals we need a common radicand. Here the two radicands are 2 and 8. But 8 factors as $2 * 4$, so $5\sqrt{2} + 3\sqrt{8} = 5\sqrt{2} + 3\sqrt{4*2}$, and this can be rewritten as $5\sqrt{2} + 3\sqrt{4} * \sqrt{2}$. Finally we note that $\sqrt{4}$ is 2, so we obtain $5\sqrt{2} + 3*2*\sqrt{2}$, or $5\sqrt{2} + 6\sqrt{2} = 11\sqrt{2}$.

PROBLEM

Simplify the expression $\left(2\sqrt{8}\right) * \left(3\sqrt{2}\right) + \left(\sqrt{12}\right) * \left(7\sqrt{3}\right)$

SOLUTION

The order of operations indicates that we should multiply the radicals first, and then add. Toward that end, $\left(2\sqrt{8}\right) * \left(3\sqrt{2}\right) + \left(\sqrt{12}\right) * \left(7\sqrt{3}\right)$ is the same as $(2)*(3)*\left(\sqrt{8}\right)*\left(\sqrt{2}\right) + (7)*\left(\sqrt{12}\right)*\left(\sqrt{3}\right)$.

This equals $6 * \sqrt{8*2} + 7 * \sqrt{12*3}$ or $6 * \sqrt{16} + 7 * \sqrt{36}$. Finally, this can be simplified to $6 * 4 + 7 * 6 = 24 + 42 = 66$.

☞ DRILL: Radicals

Multiplication

<u>DIRECTIONS</u>: Multiply and simplify each answer.

1. $\sqrt{6} * \sqrt{5} =$

(A) $\sqrt{11}$ (B) $\sqrt{30}$ (C) $2\sqrt{5}$ (D) $3\sqrt{10}$ (E) $2\sqrt{3}$

2. $\sqrt{3} * \sqrt{12} =$

(A) 3   (B) $\sqrt{15}$ (C) $\sqrt{36}$ (D) 6   (E) 8

3. $\sqrt{7} * \sqrt{7} =$

(A) 7   (B) 49   (C) $\sqrt{14}$ (D) $2\sqrt{7}$ (E) $2\sqrt{14}$

4. $3\sqrt{5} * 2\sqrt{5} =$

(A) $5\sqrt{5}$ (B) 25   (C) 30   (D) $5\sqrt{25}$ (E) $6\sqrt{5}$

5. $4\sqrt{6} * \sqrt{2} =$

A) $4\sqrt{8}$ (B) $8\sqrt{2}$ (C) $5\sqrt{8}$ (D) $4\sqrt{12}$ (E) $8\sqrt{3}$

Division

<u>DIRECTIONS</u>: Divide and simplify the answer.

6. $\sqrt{10} \div \sqrt{2} =$

(A) $\sqrt{8}$ (B) $2\sqrt{2}$ (C) $\sqrt{5}$ (D) $2\sqrt{5}$ (E) $2\sqrt{3}$

7. $\sqrt{30} \div \sqrt{15} =$

(A) $\sqrt{2}$ (B) $\sqrt{45}$ (C) $3\sqrt{5}$ (D) $\sqrt{15}$ (E) $5\sqrt{3}$

8. $\sqrt{100} \div \sqrt{25} =$

(A) $\sqrt{4}$ (B) $5\sqrt{5}$ (C) $5\sqrt{3}$ (D) 2   (E) 4

9. $\sqrt{48} \div \sqrt{8} =$

(A) $4\sqrt{3}$ (B) $3\sqrt{2}$ (C) $\sqrt{6}$ (D) 6   (E) 12

10. $3\sqrt{12} \div \sqrt{3} =$

(A) $3\sqrt{15}$ (B) 6   (C) 9   (D) 12   (E) $3\sqrt{36}$

Addition

<u>DIRECTIONS</u>: Simplify each radical and add.

11. $\sqrt{7} + 3\sqrt{7} =$

(A) $3\sqrt{7}$ (B) $4\sqrt{7}$ (C) $3\sqrt{14}$ (D) $4\sqrt{14}$ (E) $3\sqrt{21}$

12. $\sqrt{5} + 6\sqrt{5} + 3\sqrt{5} =$

(A) $9\sqrt{5}$ (B) $9\sqrt{15}$ (C) $5\sqrt{10}$ (D) $10\sqrt{5}$ (E) $18\sqrt{15}$

13. $3\sqrt{32} + 2\sqrt{2} =$

(A) $5\sqrt{2}$ (B) $\sqrt{34}$ (C) $14\sqrt{2}$ (D) $5\sqrt{34}$ (E) $6\sqrt{64}$

14. $6\sqrt{15} + 8\sqrt{15} + 16\sqrt{15} =$

(A) $15\sqrt{30}$ (B) $30\sqrt{45}$ (C) $30\sqrt{30}$ (D) $15\sqrt{45}$ (E) $30\sqrt{15}$

15. $6\sqrt{5} + 2\sqrt{45} =$

(A) $12\sqrt{5}$ (B) $8\sqrt{50}$ (C) $40\sqrt{2}$ (D) $12\sqrt{50}$ (E) $8\sqrt{5}$

Subtraction

<u>DIRECTIONS</u>: Simplify each radical and subtract.

16. $8\sqrt{5} - 6\sqrt{5} =$

(A) $2\sqrt{5}$ (B) $3\sqrt{5}$ (C) $4\sqrt{5}$ (D) $14\sqrt{5}$ (E) $48\sqrt{5}$

17. $16\sqrt{33} - 5\sqrt{33} =$

(A) $3\sqrt{33}$ (B) $33\sqrt{11}$ (C) $11\sqrt{33}$ (D) $11\sqrt{0}$ (E) $\sqrt{33}$

18. $14\sqrt{2} - 19\sqrt{2} =$

(A) $5\sqrt{2}$ (B) $-5\sqrt{2}$ (C) $-33\sqrt{2}$ (D) $33\sqrt{2}$ (E) $-4\sqrt{2}$

19. $10\sqrt{2} - 3\sqrt{8} =$

(A) $6\sqrt{6}$ (B) $-2\sqrt{2}$ (C) $7\sqrt{6}$ (D) $4\sqrt{2}$ (E) $-6\sqrt{6}$

20. $4\sqrt{3} - 2\sqrt{12} =$

(A) $-2\sqrt{9}$ (B) $-6\sqrt{15}$ (C) 0 (D) $6\sqrt{15}$ (E) $2\sqrt{12}$

6. EXPONENTS

When a number is multiplied by itself a specific number of times, it is said to be **raised to a power**. The way this is written is $a^n = b$ where a is the number or **base**, n is the **exponent** or **power** that indicates the number of times the base is to be multiplied by itself, and b is the product of this multiplication.

In the expression 3^2, 3 is the base and 2 is the exponent. This means that 3 is multiplied by itself 2 times and the product is 9.

An exponent can be either positive or negative. A negative exponent implies a fraction such that if n is a negative integer

$$a^{-n} = \frac{1}{a^n}, \ a \neq 0. \ \text{So, } 2^{-4} = \frac{1}{2^4} = \frac{1}{16}.$$

An exponent that is zero gives a result of 1, assuming that the base is not equal to zero.

$$a^0 = 1, \ a \neq 0.$$

An exponent can also be a fraction. If m and n are positive integers,

$$a^{\frac{m}{n}} = \sqrt[n]{a^m}.$$

The numerator remains the exponent of a, but the denominator tells what root to take. For example,

(1) $4^{\frac{3}{2}} = \sqrt[2]{4^3} = \sqrt{64} = 8$

(2) $3^{\frac{4}{2}} = \sqrt[2]{3^4} = \sqrt{81} = 9$

If a fractional exponent were negative, the same operation would take place, but the result would be a fraction. For example,

(1) $27^{-\frac{2}{3}} = \dfrac{1}{27^{2/3}} = \dfrac{1}{\sqrt[3]{27^2}} = \dfrac{1}{\sqrt[3]{729}} = \dfrac{1}{9}$

PROBLEM

Simplify the following expressions:

(1) $\quad -3^{-2}$

(3) $\dfrac{-3}{4^{-1}}$

(2) $\quad (-3)^{-2}$

SOLUTION

(1) Here the exponent applies only to 3. Since

$$x^{-y} = \frac{1}{x^y}, \; -3^{-2} = -(3)^{-2} = -\frac{1}{3^2} = -\frac{1}{9}$$

(2) In this case the exponent applies to the negative base. Thus,

$$(-3)^{-2} = \frac{1}{(-3)^2} = \frac{1}{(-3)(-3)} = \frac{1}{9}$$

(3) $\dfrac{-3}{4^{-1}} = \dfrac{-3}{(\frac{1}{4})^1} = \dfrac{-3}{\frac{1}{4^1}} = \dfrac{-3}{\frac{1}{4}}$

Division by a fraction is equivalent to multiplication by that fraction's reciprocal, thus

$$\frac{-3}{\frac{1}{4}} = -3 \cdot \frac{4}{1} = -12 \text{ and } \frac{-3}{4^{-1}} = -12$$

General Laws of Exponents

A) $\quad a^p a^q = a^{p+q}$

$\quad 4^2 4^3 = 4^{2+3} = 1024$

B) $\quad (a^p)^q = a^{pq}$

$\quad (2^3)^2 = 2^6 = 64$

C) $\dfrac{a^p}{a^q} = a^{p-q}$

$\dfrac{3^6}{3^2} = 3^4 = 81$

D) $(ab)^p = a^p b^p$

$(3 \cdot 2)^2 = 3^2 \cdot 2^2 = (9)(4) = 36$

E) $\left(\dfrac{a}{b}\right)^p = \dfrac{a^p}{b^p}$, $b \neq 0$

$\left(\dfrac{4}{5}\right)^2 = \dfrac{4^2}{5^2} = \dfrac{16}{25}$

☞ Drill: Exponents

Multiplication

Simplify

1. $4^6 * 4^2 =$
(A) 4^4 (B) 4^8 (C) 4^{12} (D) 16^8 (E) 16^{12}

2. $2^2 * 2^5 * 2^3 =$
(A) 2^{10} (B) 4^{10} (C) 8^{10} (D) 2^{30} (E) 8^{30}

3. $6^6 * 6^2 * 6^4 =$
(A) 18^8 (B) 18^{12} (C) 6^{12} (D) 6^{48} (E) 18^{48}

4. $a^4 b^2 * a^3 b =$
(A) ab (B) $2a^7 b^2$ (C) $2a^{12}b$ (D) $a^7 b^3$ (E) $a^7 b^2$

5. $m^8 n^3 * m^2 n * m^4 n^2 =$
(A) $3m^{16}n^6$ (B) $m^{14}n^6$ (D) $3m^{14}n^5$ (D) $3m^{14}n^5$ (E) m^2

Division

Simplify

6. $6^5 \div 6^3 =$
(A) 0 (B) 1 (C) 6 (D) 12 (E) 36

7. $11^8 \div 11^5 =$

(A) 1^3 (B) 11^3 (C) 11^{13} (D) 11^{40} (E) 88^5

8. $x^{10}y^8 \div x^7y^3 =$

(A) x^2y^5 (B) x^3y^4 (C) x^3y^5 (D) x^2y^4 (E) x^5y^3

9. $a^{14} \div a^9 =$

(A) 1^5 (B) a^5 (C) $2a^5$ (D) a^{23} (E) $2a^{23}$

10. $c^{17}d^{12}e^4 \div c^{12}d^8e =$

(A) $c^4d^5e^3$ (B) $c^4d^4e^3$ (C) $c^5d^8e^4$ (D) $c^5d^4e^3$ (E) $c^5d^4e^4$

Power to a Power

Simplify

11. $(3^6)^2 =$

(A) 3^4 (B) 3^8 (C) 3^{12} (D) 9^6 (E) 9^8

12. $(4^3)^5 =$

(A) 4^2 (B) 2^{15} (C) 4^8 (D) 20^3 (E) 4^{15}

13. $(a^4b^3)^2 =$

(A) $(ab)^9$ (B) a^8b^6 (C) $(ab)^{24}$ (D) a^6b^5 (E) $2a^4b^3$

14. $(r^3p^6)^3 =$

(A) r^9p^{18} (B) $(rp)^{12}$ (C) r^6p^9 (D) $3r^3p^6$ (E) $3r^9p^{18}$

15. $(m^6n^5q^3)^2 =$

(A) $2m^6n^5q^3$ (B) m^4n^3q (C) $m^8n^7q^5$

(D) $m^{12}n^{10}q^6$ (E) $2m^{12}n^{10}q^6$

---

7. MEAN, MEDIAN

MEAN

The mean is the arithmetic average. It is the sum of the variables divided by the total number of variables. For example:

$$\frac{4+3+8}{3} = \frac{15}{3} = 5$$

PROBLEM

Find the mean salary for four company employees who make $5/hr., $8/hr., $12/hr., and $15/hr.

SOLUTION

The mean salary is the average.

$$\frac{\$5 + \$8 + \$12 + \$15}{4} = \frac{\$40}{4} = \$10/hr$$

PROBLEM

Find the mean length of five fish with lengths of 7.5 in., 7.75 in., 8.5 in., 8.5 in., 8.25 in.

SOLUTION

The mean length is the average length.

$$\frac{7.5 + 7.75 + 8.5 + 8.5 + 8.25}{5} = \frac{40.5}{5} = 8.1 \text{ in}$$

MEDIAN

The median is the middle value in a set when there is an odd number of values. There is an equal number of values larger and smaller than the median. When the set is an even number of values, the average of the two middle values is the median. For example:

The median of (2, 3, 5, 8, 9) is 5.

The median of (2, 3, 5, 9, 10, 11) is $\frac{5+9}{2} = 7$.

PROBLEM

For this series of observations find the mean and median.

500, 600, 800, 800, 900, 900, 900, 900, 900, 1000, 1100

SOLUTION

The mean is the value obtained by adding all the measurements and dividing by the numbers of measurements.

$$\frac{500 + 600 + 800 + 800 + 900 + 900 + 900 + 900 + 900 + 1000 + 1100}{11}$$

$$= \frac{9300}{11} = 845.45.$$

The median is the observation in the middle. We have 11 observations, so here the sixth, 900, is the median.

Both of these numbers are measures of central tendency. They describe the "middle" or "center" of the data.

PROBLEM

Nine rats run through a maze. The time each rat took to traverse the maze is recorded and these times (in minutes) are listed below.

1, 2.5, 3, 1.5, 2, 1.25, 1, .9, 30

Find the mean and the median.

SOLUTION

The mean is the sum of observations divided by the number of observations. In this case

$$\frac{1 + 2.5 + 3 + 1.5 + 2 + 1.25 + 1 + .9 + 30}{9} = \frac{43.15}{9} = 4.79.$$

The median is the "middle number" in an ordered array of the observations from the lowest to the highest.

0.9, 1.0, 1.0, 1.25, 1.5, 2.0, 2.5, 3.0, 30.0

The median is the fifth observation in this ordered array or 1.5. There are four observations larger than 1.5 and four observations smaller than 1.5.

☞ Drill: Averages

Mean

DIRECTIONS: Find the mean of each set of numbers:

1. 18, 25, and 32.

(A) 3   (B) 25   (C) 50   (D) 75   (E) 150

2. 4/9, 2/3, and 5/6.

(A) 11/18   (B) 35/54   (B) 41/54   (D) 35/18   (E) 54/18

3. 97, 102, 116, and 137.

(A) 40   (B) 102   (C) 109   (D) 113   (E) 116

4. 12, 15, 18, 24, and 31.

(A) 18   (B) 19.3   (C) 20   (D) 25   (E) 100

5. 7, 4, 6, 3, 11, and 14.

(A) 5   (B) 6.5   (C) 7   (D) 7.5   (E) 8

Median

DIRECTIONS: Find the median value of each set of numbers.

6.   3, 8, and 6.

(A) 3   (B) 6   (C) 8   (D) 17   (E) 20

7.   19, 15, 21, 27, and 12.

(A) 19   (B) 15   (C) 21   (D) 27   (E) 94

8.   1 2/3, 1 7/8, 1 3/4, and 1 5/6.

(A) 1 30/48   (B) 1 2/3   (C) 1 3/4   (D) 1 19/24   (E) 1 21/24

9.   29, 18, 21, and 35.

(A) 29   (B) 18   (C) 21   (D) 35   (E) 25

10. 8, 15, 7, 12, 31, 3, and 28.

(A) 7   (B) 11.6   (C) 12   (C) 14.9   (E) 104

ARITHMETIC DRILLS

ANSWER KEY

Drill: Integers and Real Numbers

1.	(A)	9.	(E)	17.	(D)	25.	(D)
2.	(C)	10.	(B)	18.	(D)	26.	(D)
3.	(D)	11.	(B)	19.	(C)	27.	(B)
4.	(C)	12.	(E)	20.	(E)	28.	(C)
5.	(B)	13.	(C)	21.	(B)	29.	(A)
6.	(B)	14.	(A)	22.	(E)	30.	(C)
7.	(A)	15.	(B)	23.	(D)		
8.	(C)	16.	(B)	24.	(A)		

Drill: Fractions

1.	(D)	14.	(D)	27.	(D)	40.	(A)
2.	(E)	15.	(B)	28.	(E)	41.	(D)
3.	(C)	16.	(B)	29.	(C)	42.	(A)
4.	(A)	17.	(D)	30.	(B)	43.	(D)
5.	(C)	18.	(B)	31.	(C)	44.	(E)
6.	(B)	19.	(A)	32.	(A)	45.	(C)
7.	(C)	20.	(C)	33.	(B)	46.	(D)
8.	(A)	21.	(D)	34.	(C)	47.	(D)
9.	(B)	22.	(C)	35.	(D)	48.	(B)
10.	(A)	23.	(B)	36.	(B)	49.	(A)
11.	(B)	24.	(E)	37.	(C)	50.	(E)
12.	(D)	25.	(A)	38.	(D)		
13.	(E)	26.	(A)	39.	(E)		

Drill: Decimals

1.	(B)	9.	(C)	17.	(D)	25.	(E)
2.	(E)	10.	(E)	18.	(D)	26.	(D)
3.	(C)	11.	(B)	19.	(A)	27.	(C)
4.	(A)	12.	(D)	20.	(C)	28.	(A)
5.	(D)	13.	(A)	21.	(E)	29.	(E)
6.	(A)	14.	(B)	22.	(C)	30.	(D)
7.	(B)	15.	(C)	23.	(B)		
8.	(D)	16.	(B)	24.	(D)		

Drill: Percentages

1.	(B)	9.	(E)	17.	(D)	25.	(D)
2.	(C)	10.	(C)	18.	(E)	26.	(D)
3.	(E)	11.	(C)	19.	(C)	27.	(C)
4.	(B)	12.	(B)	20.	(C)	28.	(B)
5.	(A)	13.	(B)	21.	(A)	29.	(E)
6.	(B)	14.	(D)	22.	(B)	30.	(A)
7.	(A)	15.	(A)	23.	(C)		
8.	(B)	16.	(E)	24.	(B)		

Drill: Radicals

1.	(B)	6.	(C)	11.	(B)	16.	(A)
2.	(D)	7.	(A)	12.	(D)	17.	(C)
3.	(A)	8.	(D)	13.	(C)	18.	(B)
4.	(C)	9.	(C)	14.	(E)	19.	(D)
5.	(E)	10.	(B)	15.	(A)	20.	(C)

Drill: Exponents

1.	(B)	9.	(B)
2.	(A)	10.	(D)
3.	(C)	11.	(C)
4.	(D)	12.	(E)
5.	(B)	13.	(B)
6.	(E)	14.	(A)
7.	(B)	15.	(D)
8.	(C)		

Drill: Averages

1.	(B)	6.	(B)
2.	(B)	7.	(A)
3.	(D)	8.	(D)
4.	(C)	9.	(E)
5.	(D)	10.	(C)

III. ALGEBRA

In algebra, letters or variables are used to represent numbers. A **variable** is defined as a placeholder, which can take on any of several values at a given time. A **constant**, on the other hand, is a symbol which takes on only one value at a given time. A **term** is a constant, a variable, or a combination of constants and variables. For example: 7.76, $3x$, xyz, $5z/x$, $(0.99)x^2$ are terms. If a term is a combination of constants and variables, the constant part of the term is referred to as the **coefficient** of the variable. If a variable is written without a coefficient, the coefficient is assumed to be 1.

EXAMPLE

$3x^2$
coefficient : 3
variable: x

y^3
coefficient: 1
variable: y

An **expression** is a collection of one or more terms. If the number of terms is greater than 1, the expression is said to be the sum of the terms.

EXAMPLE

9, $9xy$, $6x + x/3$, $8yz - 2x$

An algebraic expression consisting of only one term is called a **monomial**; of two terms is called a **binomial**; of three terms is called a **trinomial**. In general, an algebraic expression consisting of two or more terms is called a **polynomial**.

1. OPERATIONS WITH POLYNOMIALS

A) **Addition of polynomials** is achieved by combining like terms, terms which differ only in their numerical coefficients, e.g.,

$$P(x) = (x^2 - 3x + 5) + (4x^2 + 6x - 3)$$

Note that the parentheses are used to distinguish the polynomials.

By using the commutative and associative laws, we can rewrite $P(x)$ as:

$$P(x) = (x^2 + 4x^2) + (6x - 3x) + (5 - 3)$$

Using the distributive law, $ab + ac = a(b + c)$, yields:

$$(1 + 4)x^2 + (6 - 3)x + (5 - 3)$$

$$= 5x^2 + 3x + 2$$

B) **Subtraction of two polynomials** is achieved by first changing the sign of all terms in the expression which is being subtracted and then adding this result to the other expression, e.g.,

$$(5x^2 + 4y^2 + 3z^2) - (4xy + 7y^2 - 3z^2 + 1)$$

$$= 5x^2 + 4y^2 + 3z^2 - 4xy - 7y^2 + 3z^2 - 1$$

$$= (5x^2) + (4y^2 - 7y^2) + (3z^2 + 3z^2) - 4xy - 1$$

$$= (5x^2) + (-3y^2) + (6z^2) - 4xy - 1$$

C) **Multiplication of two or more polynomials** is achieved by using the laws of exponents, the rules of signs, and the commutative and associative laws of multiplication. Begin by multiplying the coefficients and then multiply the variables according to the laws of exponents, e.g.,

$$(y^2)\,(5)\,(6y^2)\,(yz)\,(2z^2)$$

$$= (1)\,(5)\,(6)\,(1)\,(2)\,(y^2)\,(y^2)\,(yz)\,(z^2)$$

$$= 60[(y^2)\,(y^2)\,(y)]\,[(z)\,(z^2)]$$

$$= 60(y^5)\,(z^3)$$

$$= 60\,y^5z^3$$

D) **Multiplication of a polynomial by a monomial** is achieved by multiplying each term of the polynomial by the monomial and combining the results, e.g.,

$$(4x^2 + 3y)\,(6xz^2)$$

$$= (4x^2)\,(6xz^2) + (3y)\,(6xz^2)$$

$$= 24x^3z^2 + 18xyz^2$$

E) **Multiplication of a polynomial by a polynomial** is achieved by multiplying each of the terms of one polynomial by each of the terms of the other polynomial and combining the result, e.g.,

$$(5y + z + 1)\,(y^2 + 2y)$$

$$[(5y)\,(y^2) + (5y)\,(2y)] + [(z)\,(y^2) + (z)\,(2y)] + [(1)\,(y^2) + (1)\,(2y)]$$

$$= (5y^3 + 10y^2) + (y^2z + 2yz) + (y^2 + 2y)$$

$$= (5y^3) + (10y^2 + y^2) + (y^2z) + (2yz) + (2y)$$

$$= 5y^3 + 11y^2 + y^2z + 2yz + 2y$$

F) **Division of a monomial by a monomial** is achieved by first dividing the constant coefficients and the variable factors separately, and then multiplying these quotients, e.g.,

$$6xyz^2 \div 2y^2z$$

$$= (6/2)\,(x/1)\,(y/y^2)\,(z^2/z)$$

$$= 3xy^{-1}z$$

$$= 3xz/y$$

G) **Division of a polynomial by a polynomial** is achieved by following the given procedure, called long division.

Step 1: The terms of both the polynomials are arranged in order of ascending or descending powers of one variable.

Step 2: The first term of the dividend is divided by the first term of the divisor which gives the first term of the quotient.

Step 3: This first term of the quotient is multiplied by the entire divisor and the result is subtracted from the dividend.

Step 4: Using the remainder obtained from Step 3 as the new dividend, Steps 2 and 3 are repeated until the remainder is zero or the degree of the remainder is less than the degree of the divisor.

Step 5: The result is written as follows:

$$\frac{\text{dividend}}{\text{divisor}} = \text{quotient} + \frac{\text{remainder}}{\text{divisor}}$$

divisor $\neq 0$

e.g. $(2x^2 + x + 6) \div (x + 1)$

$$
\begin{array}{r}
2x - 1 \\
(x+1)\overline{\smash{\big)}\,2x^2 + x + 6} \\
\underline{-(2x^2 + 2x)} \\
-x + 6 \\
\underline{-(-x - 1)} \\
7
\end{array}
$$

The result is $(2x^2 + x + 6) \div (x + 1) = 2x - 1 + \dfrac{7}{x + 1}$

PROBLEM

Simplify $p^2 + 2pq + q^2$ if $p + q = 1$.

SOLUTION

Since $p + q = 1, q = 1-p$. Thus $p^2 + 2pq + q^2 = p^2 + 2p(1 - p) + (1 - p)^2$. Opening parentheses we obtain $p^2 + (2p - p^2) + 1 + p^2 - 2p)$. Finally we combine like terms and obtain $(p^2 + p^2 - 2p^2) + (2P - 2p) + 1$, and this reduces to 1.

PROBLEM

Simplify $p^2 + 2pq + q^2$.

SOLUTION

Here we are not told that $p + q = 1$. So we rewrite $p^2 + 2pq + q^2$ as $p^2 + pq + pq + q^2 = p(p + q) + q(p + q)$, and this equals $(p + q)(p + q)$ or $(p + q)^2$.

☞ Drill: Operations With Polynomials

Addition

1. $9a^2b + 3c + 2a^2b + 5c =$

(A) $19a^2bc$ (B) $11a^2b + 8c$ (C) $11a^4b^2 + 8c^2$

(D) $19a^4b^2c^2$ (E) $12a^2b + 8c^2$

2. $14m^2n^3 + 6m^2n^3 + 3m^2m^3 =$

(A) $20m^2n^3$ (B) $23m^6n^9$ (C) $23m^2n^3$

(D) $32m^6n^9$ (E) $23m^8n^{27}$

3. $3x + 2y + 16x + 3z + 6y =$

(A) $19x + 8y$ (B) $19x + 11yz$ (C) $19x + 8y + 3z$

(D) $11xy + 19xz$ (E) $30xyz$

4. $(4d^2 + 7e^3 + 12f) + (3d^2 + 6e^3 + 2f) =$

(A) $23d^2e^3f$ (B) $33d^2e^2f$ (C) $33d^4e^6f^2$

(D) $7d^2 + 13e^3 + 14f$ (E) $23d^2 + 11e^3f$

5. $3ac^2 + 2b^2c + 7ac^2 + 2ac^2 + b^2c =$

(A) $12ac^2 + 3b^2c$ (B) $14ab^2c^2$ (C) $11ac^2 + 4ab^2c$

(D) $15ab^2c^2$ (E) $15a^2b^4c^4$

Subtraction

6. $14m^2n - 6m^2n =$

(A) $20m^2n$ (B) $8m^2n$ (C) $8m$ (D) 8 (E) $8m^4n^2$

7. $3x^3y^2 - 4xz - 6x^3y^2 =$

(A) $-7x^2y^2z$ (B) $3x^3y^2 - 10x^4y^2z$ (C) $-3x^3y^2 - 4xz$

(D) $-x^2y^2z - 6x^3y^2$ (E) $-7xyz$

8. $9g^2 + 6h - 2g^2 - 5h =$

(A) $15g^2h - 7g^2h$ (B) $7g^4h^2$ (C) $11g^2 + 7h$

(D) $11g^2 - 7h^2$ (E) $7g^2 + h$

9. $7b^3 - 4c^2 - 6b^3 + 3c^2 =$

(A) $b^3 - c^2$ (B) $-11b^2 - 3c^2$ (C) $13b^3 - c$

(D) $7b - c$ (E) 0

10. $11q^2r - 4q^2r - 8q^2r =$

(A) $22q^2r$ (B) q^2r (C) $-2\,q^2r$

(D) $-q^2r$ (E) $2\,q^2r$

Multiplication

11. $5p^2t * 3p^2t =$

(A) $15p^2t$ (B) $15p^4t$ (C) $15p^4t^2$ (D) $8p^2t$ (E) $8p^4t^2$

12. $(2r + s)\,14r =$

(A) $28rs$ (B) $28r^2 + 14sr$ (C) $16r^2 + 14rs$

(D) $28r + 14sr$ (E) $17r^2s$

13. $(4m + p)(3m - 2p) =$

(A) $12m^2 + 5mp + 2p^2$ (B) $12m^2 - 2mp + 2p^2$ (C) $7m - p$

(D) $12m - 2p$ (E) $12m^2 - 5mp - 2p^2$

14. $(2a + b)(3a^2 + ab + b^2) =$

(A) $6a^3 + 5a^2b + 3ab^2 + b^3$ (B) $5a^3 + 3ab + b^3$

(C) $6a^3 + 2a^2b + 2ab^2$ (D) $3a^2 + 2a + ab + b + b^2$

(E) $6a^3 + 3a^2b + 5ab^2 + b^3$

15. $(6t^2 + 2t + 1)\,3t =$

(A) $9t^2 + 5t + 3$ (B) $18t^2 + 6t + 3$ (C) $9t^3 + 6t^2 + 3t$

(D) $18t^3 + 6t^2 + 3t$ (E) $12t^3 + 6t^2 + 3t$

Division

16. $(x^2 + x - 6) \div (x - 2) =$

(A) $x - 3$ (B) $x + 2$ (C) $x + 3$ (D) $x - 2$ (E) $2x + 2$

17. $24b^4c^3 \div 6b^2c =$

(A) $3b^2c^2$ (B) $4b^4c^3$ (C) $4b^3c^2$ (D) $4b^2c^2$ (E) $3b^4c^3$

18. $(3p^2 + pq - 2q^2) \div (p + q) =$

(A) $3p + 2q$ (B) $2q - 3p$ (C) $3p - q$

(D) $2q + 3p$ (E) $3p - 2q$

19. $(y^3 - 2y^2 - y + 2) \div (y - 2) =$

(A) $(y - 1)^2$ (B) $y^2 - 1$ (C) $(y + 2)(y - 1)$

(D) $(y + 1)^2$ (E) $(y + 1)(y - 2)$

20. $(m^2 + m - 14) \div (m + 4) =$

(A) $m - 2$ (B) $m - 3 + \dfrac{-2}{m + 4}$ (C) $m - 3 + \dfrac{4}{m + 4}$

(D) $m - 3$ (E) $m - 2 + \dfrac{-3}{m + 4}$

2.   SIMPLIFYING ALGEBRAIC EXPRESSIONS

To factor a polynomial completely is to find the prime factors of the polynomial with respect to a specified set of numbers.

The following concepts are important while factoring or simplifying expressions.

1.   The factors of an algebraic expression consist of two or more algebraic expressions which, when multiplied together, produce the given algebraic expression.

2.   A **prime factor** is a polynomial with no factors other than itself and 1. The **least common multiple (LCM)** for a set of numbers is the smallest quantity divisible by every number of the set. For algebraic expressions the least common numerical coefficients for each of the given expressions will be a factor.

3.   The **greatest common factor (GCF)** for a set of numbers is the largest factor that is common to all members of the set.

4.   For algebraic expressions, the greatest common factor is the polynomial of highest degree and the largest numerical coefficient which is a factor of all the given expressions.

Some important formulas, useful for the factoring of polynomials are listed below.

$$a(c + d) = ac + ad$$
$$(a + b)(a - b) = a^2 - b^2$$
$$(a + b)(a + b) = (a + b)^2 = a^2 + 2ab + b^2$$
$$(a - b)(a - b) = (a - b)^2 = a^2 - 2ab + b^2$$

$$(x + a)(x + b) = x^2 + (a + b)x + ab$$

$$(ax + b)(cx + d) = acx^2 + (ad + bc)x + bd$$

$$(a + b)(c + d) = ac + bc + ad + bd$$

$$(a + b)(a + b)(a + b) = (a + b)^3 = a^3 + 3a^2b + 3ab^2 + b^3$$

$$(a - b)(a - b)(a - b) = (a - b)^3 = a^3 - 3a^2b + 3ab^2 - b^3$$

$$(a - b)(a^2 + ab + b^2) = a^3 - b^3$$

$$(a + b)(a^2 - ab + b^2) = a^3 + b^3$$

$$(a + b + c)^2 = a^2 + b^2 + c^2 + 2ab + 2ac + 2bc$$

$$(a - b)(a^3 + a^2b + ab^2 + b^3) = a^4 - b^4$$

$$(a - b)(a^4 + a^3b + a^2b^2 + ab^3 + b^4) = a^5 - b^5$$

$$(a - b)(a^5 + a^4b + a^3b^2 + a^2b^3 + ab^4 + b^5) = a^6 - b^6$$

$$(a - b)(a^{n-1} + a^{n-2}b + a^{n-3}b^2 + \ldots + ab^{n-2} + b^{n-1}) = a^n - b^n$$

where n is any positive integer (1, 2, 3, 4, ...).

$$(a + b)(a^{n-1} - a^{n-2}b + a^{n-3}b^2 - \ldots - ab^{n-2} + b^{n-1}) = a^n + b^n$$

where n is any positive odd integer (1, 3, 5, 7, ...).

The procedure for factoring an algebraic expression completely is as follows:

Step 1: First find the greatest common factor if there is any. Then examine each factor remaining for greatest common factors.

Step 2: Continue factoring the factors obtained in Step 1 until all factors other than monomial factors are prime.

EXAMPLE

Factoring $4 - 16x^2$,

$$4 - 16x^2 = 4(1 - 4x^2) = 4(1 + 2x)(1 - 2x)$$

PROBLEM

Express each of the following as a single term.

(A) $3x^2 + 2x^2 - 4x^2$

(B) $5axy^2 - 7axy^2 - 3xy^2$

SOLUTION

(A) Factor x^2 in the expression.

$$3x^2 + 2x^2 - 4x^2 = (3 + 2 - 4)x^2 = 1x^2 = x^2.$$

(B) Factor xy^2 in the expression and then factor a.

$$5axy^2 - 7axy^2 - 3xy^2 = (5a - 7a - 3)xy^2$$
$$= [(5 - 7)a - 3]xy^2$$
$$= (-2a - 3)xy^2.$$

PROBLEM

Simplify $\dfrac{\frac{1}{x-1} - \frac{1}{x-2}}{\frac{1}{x-2} - \frac{1}{x-3}}$.

SOLUTION

Simplify the expression in the numerator by using the addition rule:

$$\frac{a}{b} + \frac{c}{d} = \frac{ad + bc}{bd}$$

Notice bd is the Least Common Denominator, LCD. We obtain

$$\frac{x - 2 - (x - 1)}{(x - 1)(x - 2)} = \frac{-1}{(x - 1)(x - 2)}$$

in the numerator.

Repeat this procedure for the expression in the denominator:

$$\frac{x - 3 - (x - 2)}{(x - 2)(x - 3)} = \frac{-1}{(x - 2)(x - 3)}$$

We now have

$$\frac{\frac{-1}{(x-1)(x-2)}}{\frac{-1}{(x-2)(x-3)}},$$

which is simplified by inverting the fraction in the denominator and multiplying it by the numerator and cancelling like terms

$$\frac{-1}{(x - 1)(x - 2)} \cdot \frac{(x - 2)(x - 3)}{-1} = \frac{x - 3}{x - 1}.$$

☞ Drill: Simplifying Algebraic Expressions

1. $16b^2 - 25z^2 =$

(A) $(4b - 5z)^2$ (B) $(4b + 5z)^2$ (C) $(4b - 5z)(4b + 5z)$

(D) $(16b - 25z)^2$ (E) $(5z - 4b)(5z + 4b)$

2. $x^2 - 2x - 8 =$

(A) $(x - 4)^2$ (B) $(x - 6)(x - 2)$ (C) $(x + 4)(x - 2)$

(D) $(x - 4)(x + 2)$ (E) $(x - 4)(x - 2)$

3. $2c^2 + 5cd - 3d^2 =$

(A) $(c - 3d)(c + 2d)$ (B) $(2c - d)(c + 3d)$ (C) $(c - d)(2c + 3d)$

(D) $(2c + d)(c + 3d)$ (E) Not possible

4. $4t^3 - 20t =$

(A) $4t(t^2 - 5)$ (B) $4t^2(t - 20)$ (C) $4t(t + 4)(t - 5)$

(D) $2t(2t^2 - 10)$ (E) Not possible

5. $x^2 + xy - 2y^2 =$

(A) $(x - 2y)(x + y)$ (B) $(x - 2y)(x - y)$ (C) $(x + 2y)(x + y)$

(D) $(x + 2y)(x - y)$ (E) Not possible

6. $5b^2 + 17bd + 6d^2 =$

(A) $(5b + d)(b + 6d)$ (B) $(5b + 2d)(b + 3d)$ (C) $(5b - 2d)(b - 3d)$

(D) $(5b - 2d)(b + 3d)$ (E) Not possible

7. $x^2 + x + 1 =$

(A) $(x + 1)^2$ (B) $(x + 2)(x - 1)$ (C) $(x - 2)(x + 1)$

(D) $(x + 1)(x - 1)$ (E) Not possible

8. $3z^3 + 6z^2 =$

(A) $3(z^3 + 2z^2)$ (B) $3z^2(z + 2)$ (C) $3z(z^2 + 2z)$

(D) $z^2(3z + 6)$ (E) $3z^2(1 + 2z)$

9. $m^2p^2 + mpg - 6q^2 =$

(A) $(mp - 2q)(mp + 3q)$ (B) $mp(mp - 2q)(mp + 3q)$

(C) $mpq(1 - 6q)$ (D) $(mp + 2q)(mp + 3q)$

(E) Not possible

10. $2h^3 + 2h^2t - 4ht^2 =$

(A) $2(h^3 - t)(h + t)$ (B) $2h(h - 2t)^2$ (C) $4h(ht - t^2)$

(D) $2h(h + t) - 4ht^2$ (E) $2h(h + 2t)(h - t)$

3.   EQUATIONS

An **equation** is defined as a statement that two separate expressions are equal.

A **solution** to an equation containing a single variable is a number that makes the equation true when it is substituted for the variable. For example, in the equation $3x = 18$, 6 is the solution since $3(6) = 18$. Depending on the equation, there can be more than one solution. Equations with the same solutions are said to be **equivalent equations**. An equation without a solution is said to have a solution set that is the **empty** or **null** set and is represented by ϕ.

Replacing an expression within an equation by an equivalent expression will result in a new equation with solutions equivalent to the original equation. Suppose we are given the equation

$$3x + y + x + 2y = 15.$$

By combining like terms we get

$$3x + y + x + 2y = 4x + 3y.$$

Since these two expressions are equivalent, we can substitute the simpler form into the equation to get

$$4x + 3y = 15$$

Performing the same operation to both sides of an equation by the same expression will result in a new equation that is equivalent to the original equation.

A)   **Addition or subtraction**

$$y + 6 = 10$$

we can add (-6) to both sides

$$y + 6 + (-6) = 10 + (-6)$$

to get $y + 0 = 10 - 6 \rightarrow y = 4$

B)   **Multiplication or division**

$$3x = 6$$
$$3x/3 = 6/3$$
$$x = 2$$

$3x = 6$ is equivalent to $x = 2$.

C)   **Raising to a power**

$$a = x^2y$$
$$a^2 = (x^2y)^2$$
$$a^2 = x^4y^2$$

This can be applied to negative and fractional powers as well, e.g.,

$$x^2 = 3y^4$$

If we raise both members to the -2 power, we get

$$(x^2)^{-2} = (3y^4)^{-2}$$

$$\frac{1}{(x^2)^2} = \frac{1}{(3y^4)^2}$$

$$\frac{1}{x^4} = \frac{1}{9y^8}$$

If we raise both members to the $\frac{1}{2}$ power, which is the same as taking the square root, we get:

$$(x^2)^{1/2} = (3y^4)^{1/2}$$

$$x = \sqrt{3}\, y^2$$

D) The **reciprocal** of both members of an equation are equivalent to the original equation. Note: The reciprocal of zero is undefined.

$$\frac{2x + y}{z} = \frac{5}{2} \qquad\qquad \frac{z}{2x + y} = \frac{2}{5}$$

PROBLEM

Solve for x, justifying each step. $3x - 8 = 7x + 8$.

SOLUTION

$$3x - 8 = 7x + 8$$

Adding 8 to both members,	$3x - 8 + 8 = 7x + 8 + 8$
Additive inverse property,	$3x + 0 = 7x + 16$
Additive identity property,	$3x = 7x + 16$
Adding $(-7x)$ to both members,	$3x - 7x = 7x + 16 - 7x$
Commuting,	$-4x = 7x - 7x + 16$
Additive inverse property,	$-4x = 0 + 16$
Additive identity property,	$-4x = 16$
Dividing both sides by -4,	$x = {}^{16}/_{-4}$
	$x = -4$

Check: Replacing x with -4 in the original equation:

$$3x - 8 = 7x + 8$$

$$3(-4) - 8 = 7(-4) + 8$$

$$-12 - 8 = -28 + 8$$

$$-20 = -20$$

LINEAR EQUATIONS

A linear equation with one unknown is one that can be put into the form $ax + b = 0$, where a and b are constants, $a \neq 0$.

To solve a linear equation means to transform it in the form $x = {}^{-b}/_a$.

A)   If the equation has unknowns on both sides of the equality, it is convenient to put similar terms on the same sides, e.g.,

$$
\begin{aligned}
4x + 3 &= 2x + 9 \\
4x + 3 - 2x &= 2x + 9 - 2x \\
(4x - 2x) + 3 &= (2x - 2x) + 9 \\
2x + 3 &= 0 + 9 \\
2x + 3 - 3 &= 0 + 9 - 3 \\
2x &= 6 \\
{}^{2x}/_2 &= {}^6/_2 \\
x &= 3.
\end{aligned}
$$

B)   If the equation appears in fractional form, it is necessary to transform it, using cross-multiplication, and then repeating the same procedure as in A), we obtain:

$$\frac{3x + 4}{3} \quad\times\quad \frac{7x + 2}{5}$$

By using cross-multiplication we would obtain:

$3(7x + 2) = 5(3x + 4)$.

This is equivalent to:

$21x + 6 = 15x + 20$,

which can be solved as in A):

$$
\begin{aligned}
21x + 6 &= 15x + 20 \\
21x - 15x + 6 &= 15x - 15x + 20 \\
6x + 6 - 6 &= 20 - 6 \\
6x &= 14 \\
x &= {}^{14}/_6 \\
x &= {}^7/_3
\end{aligned}
$$

C)   If there are radicals in the equation, it is necessary to square both sides and then apply A)

$$
\begin{aligned}
\sqrt{3x + 1} &= 5 \\
(\sqrt{3x + 1})^2 &= 5^2
\end{aligned}
$$

$$3x + 1 = 25$$
$$3x + 1 - 1 = 25 - 1$$
$$3x = 24$$
$$x = {}^{24}/_3$$
$$x = 8$$

PROBLEM

Solve the equation $2(x + 3) = (3x + 5) - (x - 5)$.

SOLUTION

We transform the given equation to an equivalent equation in which we can easily recognize the solution set.

$$2(x + 3) = 3x + 5 - (x - 5)$$

Distribute, $\qquad\qquad 2x + 6 = 3x + 5 - x + 5$

Combine terms, $\qquad\qquad 2x + 6 = 2x + 10$

Subtract $2x$ from both sides, $\qquad 6 = 10$

Since $6 = 10$ is not a true statement, there is no real number x which will make the original equation true. The equation is inconsistent and the solution set is ϕ, the empty set.

PROBLEM

Solve the equation $2({}^2/_3\, y + 5) + 2(y + 5) = 130$.

SOLUTION

The procedure for solving this equation is as follows:

${}^4/_3 y + 10 + 2y + 10 = 130,$	Distributive property
${}^4/_3 y + 2y + 20 = 130,$	Combining like terms
${}^4/_3 y + 2y = 110,$	Subtracting 20 from both sides
${}^4/_3 y + {}^6/_3 y = 110,$	Converting $2y$ into a fraction with denominator 3
${}^{10}/_3 y = 110,$	Combining like terms
$y = 110 \cdot {}^3/_{10} = 33,$	Dividing by ${}^{10}/_3$

Check: Replace y with 33 in the original equation,

$$2({}^2/_3(33) + 5) + 2(33 + 5) = 130$$
$$2(22 + 5) + 2(38) = 130$$
$$2(27) + 76 = 130$$

$$54 + 76 = 130$$
$$130 = 130$$

Therefore the solution to the given equation is $y = 33$.

☞ Drill: Linear Equations

Solve for x:

1. $4x - 2 = 10$

(A) -1 (B) 2   (C) 3   (D) 4   (E) 6

2. $7z + 1 - z = 2z - 7$

(A) -2 (B) 0   (C) 1   (D) 2   (E) 3

3. $^1/_3 b + 3 = ^1/_2 b$

(A) 1/2   (B) 2   (C) 3 3/5   (D) 6   (E) 18

4. $0.4p + 1 = 0.7p - 2$

(A) 0.1   (B) 2   (C) 5   (D) 10   (E) 12

5. $4(3x + 2) - 11 = 3(3x - 2)$

(A) -3 (B) -1 (C) 2   (D) 3   (E) 7

4.   INEQUALITIES

An inequality is a statement where the value of one quantity or expression is greater than (>), less than (<), greater than or equal to (≥), less than or equal to (≤), or not equal to (≠) that of another.

EXAMPLE

$5 > 4$.

The expression above means that the value of 5 is greater than the value of 4.

A **conditional inequality** is an inequality whose validity depends on the values of the variables in the sentence. That is, certain values of the variables will make the sentence true, and others will make it false. $3 - y > 3 + y$ is a conditional inequality for the set of real numbers, since it is true for any replacement less than zero and false for all others.

$x + 5 > x + 2$ is an **absolute inequality** for the set of real numbers, meaning that for any real value x, the expression on the left is greater than the expression on the right.

$5y < 2y + y$ is inconsistent for the set of non-negative real numbers. For any y greater than or equal to 0, the sentence is always false. A sentence is inconsistent if it is always false when its variables assume allowable values.

The solution of a given inequality in one variable x consists of all values of x for which the inequality is true.

The graph of an inequality in one variable is represented by either a ray or a line segment on the real number line.

The endpoint is not a solution if the variable is strictly less than or greater than a particular value.

EXAMPLE

$x > 2$

2 is not a solution and should be represented as shown.

The endpoint is a solution if the variable is either (1) less than or equal to, or (2) greater than or equal to, a particular value.

EXAMPLE

$5 > x \geq 2$

In this case 2 is the solution and should be represented as shown.

PROPERTIES OF INEQUALITIES

If x and y are real numbers then one and only one of the following statements is true.

$$x > y, x = y, \text{ or } x < y.$$

This is the order property of real numbers.

If a, b, and c are real numbers:

A) If $a < b$ and $b < c$, then $a < c$.

B) If $a > b$ and $b > c$, then $a > c$.

This is the transitive property of inequalities.

If a, b, and c are real numbers and $a > b$, then $a + c > b + c$ and $a - c > b - c$. This is the **addition property of inequality**.

Two inequalities are said to have the same **sense** if their signs of inequality point in the same direction.

The sense of an inequality remains the same if both sides are multiplied or divided by the same positive real number.

EXAMPLE

$4 > 3$

If we multiply both sides by 5 we will obtain:

$4 \times 5 > 3 \times 5$

$20 > 15$

The sense of the inequality does not change.

The sense of an inequality becomes opposite if each side is multiplied or divided by the same negative real number.

EXAMPLE

$4 > 3$

If we multiply both sides by -5 we would obtain:

$4 \times -5 < 3 \times -5$

$-20 < -15$

The sense of the inequality becomes opposite.

If $a > b$ and a, b, and n are positive real numbers, then:

$a^n > b^n$ and $a^{-n} < b^{-n}$

If $x > y$ and $q > p$, then $x + q > y + p$.

If $x > y > 0$ and $q > p > 0$, then $xq > yp$.

Inequalities that have the same solution set are called **equivalent inequalities**.

PROBLEM

Solve the inequality $2x + 5 > 9$.

SOLUTION

$$2x + 5 + (-5) > 9 + (-5). \qquad \text{Adding} - 5 \text{ to both sides.}$$
$$2x + 0 > 9 + (-5) \qquad \text{Additive inverse property}$$
$$2x > 9 + (-5) \qquad \text{Additive identity property}$$
$$2x > 4 \qquad \text{Combining terms}$$
$$\tfrac{1}{2}(2x) > \tfrac{1}{2} \cdot 4 \qquad \text{Multiplying both sides by } \tfrac{1}{2}.$$
$$x > 2$$

The solution set is

$$X = \{x \mid 2x + 5 > 9 \}$$
$$= \{x \mid x > 2\}$$

(that is all x, such that x is greater than 2).

PROBLEM

Solve the inequality $4x + 3 < 6x + 8$.

SOLUTION

In order to solve the inequality $4x + 3 < 6x + 8$, we must find all values of x which make it true. Thus, we wish to obtain x alone on one side of the inequality.

Add -3 to both sides:

$$
\begin{array}{r}
4x + 3 < 6x + 8 \\
-3 \qquad -3 \\
\hline
4x < 6x + 5
\end{array}
$$

Add $-6x$ to both sides:

$$
\begin{array}{r}
4x < \qquad 6x + 5 \\
-6x \qquad -6x \\
\hline
-2x < \qquad 5
\end{array}
$$

In order to obtain x alone we must divide both sides by (-2). Recall that dividing an inequality by a negative number reverses the inequality sign, hence

$$
\frac{-2x}{-2} > \frac{5}{-2}
$$

Cancelling $-2/_{-2}$ we obtain, $x > -5/2$.

Thus, our solution is $\{x : x > -5/2\}$ (the set of all x such that x is greater than $-5/2$).

☞ Drill: Inequalities

DIRECTIONS: Find the solution set for each inequality.

1. $3m + 2 < 7$

(A) $m \geq 5/3$ (B) $m \leq 2$ (C) $m < 2$

(D) $m > 2$ (E) $m < 5/3$

2. $\frac{1}{2}x - 3 \leq 1$

(A) $-4 \leq x \leq 8$ (B) $x \geq -8$ (C) $x \leq 8$

(D) $2 \leq x \leq 8$ (E) $x \geq 8$

3. $-3p + 1 \geq 16$

(A) $p \geq -5$ (B) $p \geq \dfrac{-17}{3}$ (C) $p \leq \dfrac{-17}{3}$

(D) $p \leq -5$ (E) $p \geq 5$

4.　　$-6 < \frac{2}{3} r + 6 \leq 2$

(A)　$-6 < r \leq -3$　　　　(B)　$-18 < r \leq -6$　　　(C)　$r \geq -6$

(D)　$-2 < r \leq -\frac{4}{3}$　　　　(E)　$r \leq -6$

5.　　$0 < 2 - y < 6$

(A)　$-4 < y < 2$　　　　(B)　$-4 < y < 0$　　　　(C)　$-4 < y < -2$

(D)　$-2 < y < 4$　　　　(E)　$0 < y < 4$

5.　RATIOS AND PROPORTIONS

The ratio of two numbers x and y written $x : y$ is the fraction x / y where $y \neq 0$. A ratio compares x to y by dividing one by the other. Therefore, in order to compare ratios, simply compare the fractions.

A proportion is an equality of two ratios. The laws of proportion are listed below:

If $a/b = c/d$, then

(A)　　$ad = bc$

(B)　　$b/a = d/c$

(C)　　$a/c = b/d$

(D)　　$(a + b)/b = (c + d)/d$

(E)　　$(a - b)/b = (c - d)/d$

Given a proportion $a : b = c : d$, then a and d are called extremes, b and c are called the means and d is called the fourth proportion to a, b, and c.

PROBLEM

Solve the proportion $\dfrac{x + 1}{4} = \dfrac{15}{12}$.

SOLUTION

Cross-multiply to determine x; that is, multiply the numerator of the first fraction by the denominator of the second, and equate this to the product of the numerator of the second and the denominator of the first.

$$(x + 1) 12 = 4 \cdot 15$$
$$12x + 12 = 60$$
$$x = 4.$$

PROBLEM

Find the ratios of $x : y : z$ from the equations

$$7x = 4y + 8z, \quad 3z = 12x + 11y.$$

SOLUTION

By transposition we have

$$7x - 4y - 8z = 0$$

$$12x + 11y - 3z = 0.$$

To obtain the ratio of $x : y$, we convert the given system into an equation in terms of just x and y. We may eliminate z as follows: Multiply each term of the first equation by 3, and each term of the second equation by 8, and then subtract the second equation from the first. We thus obtain:

$$21x - 12y - 24z = 0$$
$$- (96x + 88y - 24z = 0)$$
$$\overline{- 75x - 100y = 0}$$

Dividing each term of the last equation by 25 we obtain:

$$- 3x - 4y = 0$$

or, $\quad -3x = 4y.$

Dividing both sides of this equation by 4, and by $- 3$, we have the proportion:

$$\frac{x}{4} = \frac{y}{-3}$$

We are now interested in obtaining the ratio of $y : z$. To do this we convert the given system of equations into an equation in terms of just y and z, by eliminating x as follows: Multiply each term of the first equation by 12, and each term of the second equation by 7, and then subtract the second equation from the first. We thus obtain:

$$84x - 48y - 96z = 0$$
$$- (84x + 77y - 21z = 0)$$
$$\overline{- 125y - 75z = 0.}$$

Dividing each term of the last equation by 25 we obtain:

$$- 5y - 3z = 0$$

or, $\quad -3z = 5y.$

Dividing both sides of this equation by 5, and by $- 3$, we have the proportion:

$$\frac{z}{5} = \frac{y}{-3}.$$

From this result and our previous result we obtain:

$$\frac{x}{4} = \frac{y}{-3} = \frac{z}{5}$$

as the desired ratios.

☞ Drill: Ratios and Proportions

1. Solve for n : $\dfrac{4}{n} = \dfrac{8}{5}$.

(A) 10 (B) 8 (C) 6 (D) 2.5 (E) 2

2. Solve for n: $\dfrac{2}{3} = \dfrac{n}{72}$.

(A) 12 (B) 48 (C) 64 (D) 56 (E) 24

3. Solve for n: $n : 12 = 3 : 4$.

(A) 8 (B) 1 (C) 9 (D) 4 (E) 10

4. Four out of every five students at West High take a mathematics course. If the enrollment at West is 785, how many students take mathematics?

(A) 628 (B) 157 (C) 705 (D) 655 (E) 247

5. At a factory, three out of every 1,000 parts produced are defective. In a day, the factory can produce 25,000 parts. How many of these parts would be defective?

(A) 7 (B) 75 (C) 750 (D) 7,500 (E) 75,000

6. A summer league softball team won 28 out of the 32 games they played. What is the ratio of games won to games played?

(A) 4 : 5 (B) 3 : 4 (C) 7 : 8 (D) 2 : 3 (E) 1 : 8

7. A class of 24 students contains 16 males. What is the ratio of females to males?

(A) 1 : 2 (B) 2 : 1 (C) 2 : 3 (D) 3 : 1 (E) 3 : 2

8. A family has a monthly income of $1,250, but they spend $450 a month on rent. What is the ratio of the amount of income to the amount paid for rent?

(A) 16 : 25 (B) 25 : 9 (C) 25 : 16 (D) 9 : 25 (E) 36 : 100

9. A student attends classes 7.5 hours a day and works a part-time job for 3.5 hours a day. She knows she must get 7 hours of sleep a night. Write the ratio of the number of free hours in this student's day to the total number of hours in a day.

(A) 1 : 3 (B) 4 : 3 (C) 8 : 24 (D) 1 : 4 (E) 5 : 12

10. In a survey by mail, 30 out of 750 questionnaires were returned. Write the ratio of questionnaires returned to questionnaires mailed (write in simplest form).

(A) 30 : 750 (B) 24 : 25 (C) 3 : 75 (D) 1 : 4 (E) 1 : 25

ALGEBRA DRILLS

ANSWER KEY

Drill: Operations With Polynomials

1.	(B)	6.	(B)	11.	(C)	16.	(C)
2.	(C)	7.	(C)	12.	(B)	17.	(D)
3.	(C)	8.	(E)	13.	(E)	18.	(E)
4.	(D)	9.	(A)	14.	(A)	19.	(B)
5.	(A)	10.	(D)	15.	(D)	20.	(B)

Drill: Simplifying Algebraic Expressions

1.	(C)	4.	(A)	7.	(E)	10.	(E)
2.	(D)	5.	(D)	8.	(B)		
3.	(B)	6.	(B)	9.	(A)		

Drill: Linear Equations

1.	(C)	4.	(E)
2.	(A)	5.	(B)
3.	(E)		

Drill: Inequalities

1.	(E)	4.	(B)
2.	(D)	5.	(A)
3.	(C)		

Drill: Ratios and Proportions

1.	(D)	4.	(A)	7.	(A)	10.	(E)
2.	(B)	5.	(B)	8.	(B)		
3.	(C)	6.	(C)	9.	(D)		

IV. GEOMETRY

1. POINTS, LINES, AND ANGLES

Geometry is built upon a series of undefined terms. These terms are those which we accept as known in order to define other undefined terms.

A) **Point**: Although we represent points on paper with small dots, a point has no size, thickness, or width.

B) **Line**: A line is a series of adjacent points which extends indefinitely. A line can be either curved or straight; however, unless otherwise stated, the term "line" refers to a straight line.

C) **Plane**: A plane is a collection of points lying on a flat surface, which extends indefinitely in all directions.

If A and B are two points on a line, then the **line segment** AB is the set of points on that line between A and B and including A and B, which are endpoints. The line segment is referred to as AB.

A **ray** is a series of points that lie to one side of a single endpont.

PROBLEM

How many lines can be found that contain (a) one given point (B) two given points (c) three given points?

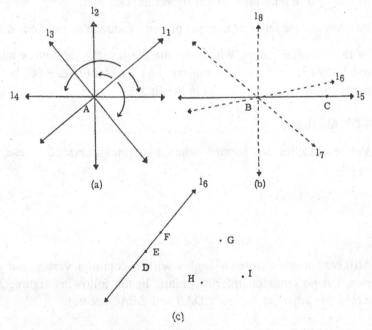

SOLUTION

(a)   *Given one point A*, there are an infinite number of distinct lines that contain the given point. To see this, consider line l_1 passing through point A. By rotating l_1 around A like the hands of a clock, we obtain different lines l_2, l_3, etc. Since we can rotate l_1 in infinitely many ways, there are infinitely many lines containing A.

(b)   *Given two distinct points B and C*, there is one and only one straight line passing through both. To see this, consider all the lines containing point B: l_5, l_6, l_7, and l_8. Only l_5 contains both points B and C. Thus, there is only one line containing both points B and C. Since there is always at least one line containing two distinct points and never more than one, the line passing through the two points is said to be determined by the two points.

(c)   *Given three distinct points*, there may be one line or none. If a line exists that contains the three points, such as D, E, and F, then the points are said to be **colinear**. If no such line exists (as in the case of points G, H, and I) then the points are said to be **noncolinear**.

INTERSECTION LINES AND ANGLES

An **angle** is a collection of points which is the union of two rays having the same endpoint. An angle such as the one illustrated below can be referred to in any of the following ways:

A)   by a capital letter which names its vertex, i.e., $\angle A$;

B)   by a lower-case letter or number placed inside the angle, i.e., $\angle x$;

C)   by three capital letters, where the middle letter is the vertex and the other two letters are not on the same ray, i.e., $\angle CAB$ or $\angle BAC$, both of which represent the angle illustrated in the figure.

TYPES OF ANGLES

A)   **Vertical angles** are formed when two lines intersect. These angles are equal.

$\angle a = \angle b$

B)   **Adjacent angles** are two angles with a common vertex and a common side, but no common interior points. In the following figure, $\angle DAC$ and $\angle BAC$ are adjacent angles. $\angle DAB$ and $\angle BAC$ are not.

C)   A **right angle** is an angle whose measure is 90°.

D)   An **acute angle** is an angle whose measure is larger than 0°, but less than 90°.

E)   An **obtuse angle** is an angle whose measure is larger than 90° but less than 180°.

F)   A **straight angle** is an angle whose measure is 180°. Such an angle is, in fact, a straight line.

G)   A **reflex angle** is an angle whose measure is greater than 180° but less than 360°.

H)   **Complimentary angles** are two angles whose measures total 90°.

I)   **Supplementary angles** are two angles whose measures total 180°.

J)   **Congruent angles** are angles of equal measure.

PROBLEM

In the figure, we are given $\overleftrightarrow{AB}$ and triangle *ABC*. We are told that the measure of ∠ 1 is five times the measure of ∠ 2. Determine the measures of ∠ 1 and ∠ 2.

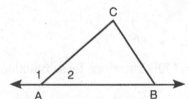

SOLUTION

Since ∠ 1 and ∠ 2 are adjacent angles whose non-common sides lie on a straight line, they are, by definition, supplementary. As supplements, their measures must total 180°.

If we let x = the measure of ∠2, then, $5x$ = the measure of ∠ 1.

To determine the respective angle measures, set $x + 5x = 180$ and solve for x. $6x = 180$. Therefore, $x = 30$ and $5x = 150$.

Therefore, the measure of ∠ 1 = 150 and the measure of ∠ 2 = 30.

PERPENDICULAR LINES

Two lines are said to be **perpendicular** if they intersect and form right angles. The symbol for perpendicular (or, is therefore perpendicular to) is ⊥;

$\overset{\leftrightarrow}{AB}$ is perpendicular to $\overset{\leftrightarrow}{CD}$ is written $\overset{\leftrightarrow}{AB} \perp \overset{\leftrightarrow}{CD}$.

PROBLEM

We are given straight lines $\overset{\leftrightarrow}{AB}$ and $\overset{\leftrightarrow}{CD}$ intersecting at point P. $\overset{\leftrightarrow}{PR} \perp \overset{\leftrightarrow}{AB}$ and the measure of $\angle APD$ is 170°. Find the measures of $\angle 1$, $\angle 2$, $\angle 3$, and $\angle 4$. (See figure below.)

SOLUTION

This problem will involve making use of several of the properties of supplementary and vertical angles, as well as perpendicular lines.

$\angle APD$ and $\angle 1$ are adjacent angles whose non-common sides lie on a straight line, $\overset{\leftrightarrow}{AB}$. Therefore, they are supplements and their measures total 180°.

$$m \angle APD + m \angle 1 = 180°.$$

We know $m \angle APD = 170°$. Therefore, by substitution, $170° + m \angle 1 = 180°$. This implies $m \angle 1 = 10°$.

$\angle 1$ and $\angle 4$ are vertical angles because they are formed by the intersection of two straight lines, $\overset{\leftrightarrow}{CD}$ and $\overset{\leftrightarrow}{AB}$, and their sides form two pairs of opposite rays. As vertical angles, they are, by theorem, of equal measure. Since $m \angle 1 = 10°$, then $m \angle 4 = 10°$.

Since $\overset{\leftrightarrow}{PR} \perp \overset{\leftrightarrow}{AB}$, at their intersection the angles formed must be right angles. Therefore, $\angle 3$ is a right angle and its measure is 90°. $m \angle 3 = 90°$.

The figure shows us that $\angle APD$ is composed of $\angle 3$ and $\angle 2$. Since the measure of the whole must be equal to the sum of the measures of its parts, $m \angle APD = m \angle 3 + m \angle 2$. We know the $m \angle APD = 170°$ and $m \angle 3 = 90°$, therefore, by substitution, we can solve for $m \angle 2$, our last unknown.

$$170° = 90° + m \angle 2$$

$$80° = m \angle 2$$

Therefore, $m \angle 1 = 10°$, $m \angle 2 = 80°$,

$m \angle 3 = 90°$, $m \angle 4 = 10°$.

PROBLEM

In the accompanying figure $\overline{SM}$ is the perpendicular bisector of $\overline{QR}$, and $\overline{SN}$ is the perpendicular bisector of $\overline{QP}$. Prove that $SR = SP$.

SOLUTION

Every point on the perpendicular bisector of a segment is equidistant from the endpoints of the segment.

Since point S is on the perpendicular bisector of $\overline{QR}$,

$$SR = SQ \qquad\qquad\qquad\qquad\qquad\qquad\qquad \text{(I)}$$

Also, since point S is on the perpendicular bisector of $\overline{QP}$,

$$SQ = SP \qquad\qquad\qquad\qquad\qquad\qquad\qquad \text{(II)}$$

By the transitive property (quantities equal to the same quantity are equal), we have:

$$SR = SP. \qquad\qquad\qquad\qquad\qquad\qquad\qquad \text{(III)}$$

PARALLEL LINES

Two lines are called **parallel lines** if, and only if, they are in the same plane (coplanar) and do not intersect. The symbol for parallel, or is parallel to, is $\|$; $\overleftrightarrow{AB}$ is parallel to $\overleftrightarrow{CD}$ is written $\overleftrightarrow{AB} \parallel \overleftrightarrow{CD}$.

The distance between two parallel lines is the length of the perpendicular segment from any point on one line to the other line.

$l_1 \parallel l_2$

Given a line l and a point P not on line l, there is one and only one line through point P that is parallel to line l.

Two coplanar lines are either intersecting lines or parallel lines.

If two (or more) lines are perpendicular to the same line, then they are parallel to each other.

If $l_1 \perp l_0$ and $l_2 \perp l_0$, then $l_1 \parallel l_2$

If two lines are cut by a transversal so that alternate interior angles are equal, the lines are parallel.

If $\angle \alpha = \angle \beta$ then $l_1 \parallel l_2$

If two lines are parallel to the same line, then they are parallel to each other.

If $l_1 \parallel l_0$ and $l_2 \parallel l_0$, then $l_1 \parallel l_2$

If a line is perpendicular to one of two parallel lines, then it is perpendicular to the other line, too.

If $l_1 \parallel l_2$ and $l_1 \perp l_0$, then $l_0 \perp l_2$

If two lines being cut by a transversal form congruent corresponding angles, then the two lines are parallel.

if $\angle \alpha = \angle \beta$, then $l_1 \parallel l_2$

If two lines being cut by a transversal form interior angles on the same side of the transversal that are supplementary, then the two lines are parallel.

If $m \angle \alpha + m \angle \beta = 180°$, then $l_1 \parallel l_2$

If a line is parallel to one of two parallel lines, it is also parallel to the other line.

If $l_1 \parallel l_2$ and $l_0 \parallel l_1$ then $l_0 \parallel l_2$

If two parallel lines are cut by a transversal, then:

A) The alternate interior angles are congruent.

B) The corresponding angles are congruent.

C) The consecutive interior angles are supplementary.

D) The alternate exterior angles are congruent.

PROBLEM

Given: $\angle 2$ is supplementary to $\angle 3$.

Prove: $l_1 \parallel l_2$.

SOLUTION

Given two lines intercepted by a transversal, if a pair of corresponding angles are congruent, then the two lines are parallel. In this problem, we will show that since $\angle 1$ and $\angle 2$ are supplementary and $\angle 2$ and $\angle 3$ are supplementary, $\angle 1$ and $\angle 3$ are congruent. Since corresponding angles $\angle 1$ and $\angle 3$ are congruent, it follows $l_1 \parallel l_2$.

	Statement		Reason
1.	$\angle 2$ is supplementary to $\angle 3$.	1.	Given.
2.	$\angle 1$ is supplementary to $\angle 2$.	2.	Two angles that form a linear pair are supplementary.
3.	$\angle 1 \cong \angle 3$	3.	Angles supplementary to the same angle are congruent.
4.	$l_1 \parallel l_2$.	4.	Given two lines intercepted by a transversal, if a pair of corresponding angles are congruent, then the two lines are parallel.

PROBLEM

If line $\overleftrightarrow{AB}$ is parallel to line $\overleftrightarrow{CD}$ and line $\overleftrightarrow{EF}$ is parallel to line $\overleftrightarrow{GH}$, prove that $m \angle 1 = m \angle 2$.

SOLUTION

To show $\angle 1 \cong \angle 2$, we relate both to $\angle 3$. Because $\overleftrightarrow{EF} \parallel \overleftrightarrow{GH}$, corresponding angles 1 and 3 are congruent. Since $\overleftrightarrow{AB} \parallel \overleftrightarrow{CD}$, corresponding angles 3 and 2 are congruent. Because both $\angle 1$ and $\angle 2$ are congruent to the same angle, it follows that $\angle 1 \cong \angle 2$.

	Statement		Reason
1.	$\overleftrightarrow{EF} \parallel \overleftrightarrow{GH}$	1.	Given.
2.	$m \angle 1 = m \angle 3$	2.	If two parallel lines are cut by a trans-

versal, corresponding angles are of equal measure.

3. $AB \| CD$
3. Given.

4. $m \angle 2 = m \angle 3$
4. If two parallel lines are cut by a transversal, corresponding angles are equal in measure.

5. $m \angle 1 = m \angle 2$
5. If two quantities are equal to the same quantity, they are equal to each other.

☞ Drill: Lines and Angles

Intersection Lines

1. Find *a*.

(A) 38°   (B) 68°   (C) 78°

(D) 90°   (E) 112°

2. Find *c*.

(A) 32°   (B) 48°   (C) 58°

(D) 82°   (E) 148°

3. Determine *x*.

(A) 21°   (B) 23°   (C) 51°

(D) 102°   (E) 153°

4. Find *x*.

(A) 8   (B) 11.75   (C) 21

(D) 23   (E) 32

5. Find *z*.

(A) 29°   (B) 54°   (C) 61°

(D) 88°   (E) 92°

Perpendicular Lines

6. $\overrightarrow{BA} \perp \overrightarrow{BC}$ and $m \angle DBC = 53$. Find $m \angle ABD$.

(A) 27°   (B) 33°   (C) 37°

(D) 53°   (E) 90°

7. $m \angle 1 = 90°$. Find $m \angle 2$.

(A) 80°   (B) 90°   (C) 100°

(D) 135°   (E) 180°

8. If $n \perp p$, which of the following statements is true?

(A) $\angle 1 \cong \angle 2$

(B) $\angle 4 \cong \angle 5$

(C) $m\angle 4 + m \angle 5 > m \angle 1 + m \angle 2$

(D) $m \angle 3 > m \angle 2$

(E) $m \angle 4 = 90°$

9. $\overleftrightarrow{CD} \perp \overleftrightarrow{EF}$. If $m \angle 1 = 2x$, $m \angle 2 = 30$, and $m \angle 3 = x$, find x.

(A) 5°   (B) 10°   (C) 12°

(D) 20°   (E) 25°

10. In the figure, $p \perp t$ and $q \perp t$. Which of the following statements is false?

(A) $\angle 1 \cong \angle 4$

(B) $\angle 2 \cong \angle 3$

(C) $m\angle 2 + m \angle 3 = m \angle 4 + m \angle 6$

(D) $m \angle 5 + m \angle 6 = 180°$

(E) $m \angle 2 > m \angle 5$

458

Parallel Lines

11. If $a \parallel b$, find z.

(A) 26°   (B) 32°   (C) 64°

(D) 86°   (E) 116°

12. In the figure, $p \parallel q \parallel r$. Find $m \angle 7$.

(A) 27°   (B) 33°   (C) 47°

(D) 57°   (E) 64°

13. If $m \parallel n$, which of the following statements is false?

(A) $\angle 2 \cong \angle 5$

(B) $\angle 3 \cong \angle 6$

(C) $m\angle 4 + m \angle 5 = 180°$

(D) $\angle 1 \cong \angle 8$

(E) $m \angle 7 + m \angle 1 = 180°$

14. If $r \parallel s$, find $m \angle 2$.

(A) 17°   (B) 27°   (C) 43°

(D) 67°   (E) 73°

15. If $a \parallel b$ and $c \parallel d$, find $m \angle 5$.

(A) 55°   (B) 65°   (C) 75°

(D) 95°   (E) 125°

2. POLYGONS (CONVEX)

A **polygon** is a figure with the same number of sides as angles.

An **equilateral polygon** is a polygon all of whose sides are of equal measure.

An **equiangular polygon** is a polygon all of whose angles are of equal measure.

A **regular polygon** is a polygon that is both equilateral and equiangular.

PROBLEM

Each interior angle of a regular polygon contains 120°. How many sides does the polygon have?

SOLUTION

At each vertex of a polygon, the exterior angle is supplementary to the interior angle, as shown in the diagram.

Since we are told that the interior angles measure 120 degrees, we can deduce that the exterior angle measures 60°.

Each exterior angle of a regular polygon of n sides measure $360°/_n$ degrees. We know that each exterior angle measures 60°, and, therefore, by setting $360°/_n$ equal to 60°, we can determine the number of sides in the polygon. The calculation is as follows:

$$360°/_n = 60°$$

$$60°n = 360°$$

$$n = 6.$$

Therefore, the regular polygon, with interior angles of 120°, has 6 sides and is called a hexagon.

The area of a regular polygon can be determined by using the **apothem** and **radius** of the polygon. The apothem (*a*) of a regular polygon is the segment from the center of the polygon perpendicular to a side of the polygon. The radius (*r*) of a regular polygon is the segment joining any vertex of a regular polygon with the center of that polygon.

(1) All radii of a regular polygon are congruent.

(2) The radius of a regular polygon is congruent to a side.

(3) All apothems of a regular polygon are congruent.

The **area** of a regular polygon equals one-half the product of the length of the apothem and the perimeter.

Area = $\frac{1}{2} a \cdot p$

PROBLEM

Find area of the regular pentagon whose radius is 8 and whose apothem is 6.

SOLUTION

If the radius is 8, the length of a side is also 8. Therefore, the perimeter of the polygon is 40.

$A = \frac{1}{2} a \cdot p$

$A = \frac{1}{2} (6) (40)$

$A = 120.$

PROBLEM

Find the area of a regular hexagon if one side has length 6.

SOLUTION

Since the length of a side equals 6, the radius also equals 6 and the perimeter equals 36. The base of the right triangle, formed by the radius and apothem, is half the length of a side, or 3. Using the Pythagorean Theorem, you can find the length of the apothem.

$a^2 + b^2 = c^2$

$a^2 + (3)^2 = (6)^2$

$a^2 = 36 - 9$

$a^2 = 27$

$a = 3\sqrt{3}$

The apothem equals $3\sqrt{3}$. Therefore, the area of the hexagon

$$= \frac{1}{2}\,a \cdot p$$
$$= \frac{1}{2}\,(3\sqrt{3})\,(36)$$
$$= 54\sqrt{3}$$

☞ Drill: Regular Polygons

1. Find the measure of an interior angle of a regular pentagon.

(A) 55   (B) 72   (C) 90   (D) 108   (E) 540

2. Find the measure of an exterior angle of a regular octagon.

(A) 40   (B) 45   (C) 135   (D) 540   (E) 1080

3. Find the sum of the measures of the exterior angles of a regular triangle.

(A) 90   (B) 115   (C) 180   (D) 250   (E) 360

4. Find the area of a square with a perimeter of 12 cm.

(A) $9\,\text{cm}^2$ (B) $12\,\text{cm}^2$ (C) $48\,\text{cm}^2$ (D) $96\,\text{cm}^2$ (E) $144\,\text{cm}^2$

5. A regular triangle has sides of 24 mm. If the apothem is $4\sqrt{3}$ mm, find the area of the triangle.

(A) $72\,\text{mm}^2$ (B) $96\sqrt{3}\,\text{mm}^2$ (C) $144\,\text{mm}^2$

(D) $144\sqrt{3}\,\text{mm}^2$ (E) $576\,\text{mm}^2$

6. Find the area of a regular hexagon with sides of 4 cm.

(A) $12\sqrt{3}\,\text{cm}^2$ (B) $24\,\text{cm}^2$ (C) $24\sqrt{3}\,\text{cm}^2$

(D) $48\,\text{cm}^2$ (E) $48\sqrt{3}\,\text{cm}^2$

7. Find the area of a regular decagon with sides of length 6 cm and an apothem of length 9.2 cm.

(A) $55.2\,\text{cm}^2$ (B) $60\,\text{cm}^2$ (C) $138\,\text{cm}^2$

(D) $138.3\,\text{cm}^2$ (E) $276\,\text{cm}^2$

8. The perimeter of a regular heptagon (7-gon) is 36.4 cm. Find the length of each side.

(A) 4.8 cm   (B) 5.2 cm   (C) 6.7 cm   (D) 7 cm   (E) 10.4 cm

9.   The apothem of a regular quadrilateral is 4 in. Find the perimeter.

(A)   12 in.   (B)   16 in.   (C)   24 in.   (D)   32 in.   (E)   64 in.

10.   A regular triangle has a perimeter of 18 cm; a regular pentagon has a perimeter of 30 cm; a regular hexagon has a perimeter of 33 cm. Which figure (or figures) have sides with the longest measure?

(A)   regular triangle

(B)   regular triangle and regular pentagon

(C)   regular pentagon

(D)   regular pentagon and regular hexagon

(E)   regular hexagon

3. TRIANGLES

A closed three-sided geometric figure is called a **triangle**. The points of the intersection of the sides of a triangle are called the **vertices** of the triangle.

The **perimeter** of a triangle is the sum of the measures of the sides of the triangle.

A triangle with no equal sides is called a **scalene** triangle.

A triangle having at least two equal sides is called an **isosceles** triangle. The third side is called the **base** of the triangle. AB = AC, AC is the base.

A side of a triangle is a line segment whose endpoints are the vertices of two angles of the triangle.

An interior angle of a triangle is an angle formed by two sides and includes the third side within its collection of points.

An **equilateral triangle** is a triangle having three equal sides. $AB = AC = BC$

$AB = AC = BC$

A triangle with one obtuse angle greater than 90° is called an **obtuse triangle**.

An **acute triangle** is a triangle with three acute angles (less than 90°).

A triangle with a right angle is called a **right triangle**. The side opposite the right angle in a right triangle is called the hypotenuse of the right triangle. The other two sides are called arms or legs of the right triangle.

An **altitude** of a triangle is a line segment from a vertex of the triangle perpendicular to the opposite side.

an altitude

an altitude

A line segment connecting a vertex of a triangle and the midpoint of the opposite side is called a **median** of the triangle.

A line that bisects and is perpendicular to a side of a triangle is called a **perpendicular bisector** of that side.

An **angle bisector** of a triangle is a line that bisects an angle and extends to the opposite side of the triangle.

The line segment that joins the midpoints of two sides of a triangle is called a **midline** of the triangle.

An **exterior angle** of a triangle is an angle formed outside a triangle by one side of the triangle and the extension of an adjacent side.

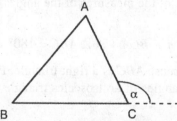

A triangle whose three interior angles have equal measure (60° each) is said to be **equiangular**.

Three or more lines (or rays or segments) are concurrent if there exists one point common to all of them, that is, if they all intersect at the same point.

PROBLEM

The measure of the vertex angle of an isosceles triangle exceeds the measurement of each base angle by 30°. Find the value of each angle of the triangle.

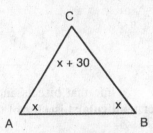

SOLUTION

We know that the sum of the values of the angles of a triangle is 180°. In an isosceles triangle, the angles opposite the congruent sides (the base angles) are, themselves, congruent and of equal value.

Therefore,

(1)   Let x = the measure of each base angle.

(2)   Then $x + 30$ = the measure of the vertex angle.

We can solve for x algebraically by keeping in mind the sum of all the measures will be 180°.

$$x + x + (x + 30) = 180$$
$$3x + 30 = 180$$
$$3x = 150$$
$$x = 50$$

Therefore, the base angles each measure 50°, and the vertex angle measures 80°.

PROBLEM

Prove that the base angles of an isosceles right triangle have measure 45°.

SOLUTION

As drawn in the figure, $\triangle ABC$ is an isosceles right triangle with base angles BAC and BCA. The sum of the measures of the angles of any triangle is 180°. For $\triangle ABC$, this means

$$m \angle BAC + m \angle BCA + m \angle ABC = 180° \qquad (1)$$

But $m \angle ABC = 90°$ because ABC is a right triangle. Furthermore, $m \angle BCA = m \angle BAC$, since the base angles of an isosceles triangle are congruent. Using these facts in equation (1)

$$m \angle BAC + m \angle BCA + 90° = 180°$$

or $2m \angle BAC = 2m \angle BCA = 90°$

or $m \angle BAC = m \angle BCA = 45°$.

Therefore, the base angles of an isosceles right triangle have measure 45°.

The area of a triangle is given by the formula $A = \frac{1}{2} bh$, where b is the length of a base, which can be any side of the triangle and h is the corresponding height of the triangle, which is the perpendicular line segment that is drawn from the vertex opposite the base to the base itself.

$A = \frac{1}{2} bh$

$A = \frac{1}{2} (10) (3)$

$A = 15$

The area of a right triangle is found by taking $\frac{1}{2}$ the product of the lengths of its two arms.

$A = \frac{1}{2} (5) (12)$
$A = 30$

☞ Drill: Triangles

Angle Measures

1. In $\triangle PQR$, $\angle Q$ is a right angle. Find $m \angle R$.

(A) 27°   (B) 33°   (C) 54°

(D) 67°   (E) 157°

2. $\triangle MNO$ is isosceles. If the vertex angle, $\angle N$, has a measure of 96, find the measure of $\angle M$.

(A) 21°   (B) 42°   (C) 64°

(D) 84°   (E) 96°

3. Find x.

(A) 15°   (B) 25°   (C) 30°

(D) 45°   (E) 90°

4. Find $m \angle 1$.

(A) 40   (B) 66   (C) 74

(D) 114   (E) 140

5. $\triangle ABC$ is a right triangle with a right angle at B. $\triangle BDC$ is a right triangle with right angle $\angle BDC$. If $m \angle C = 36$. Find $m \angle A$.

(A) 18   (B) 36   (C) 54

(D) 72   (E) 180

Similar Triangles

6. The two triangles shown are similar. Find b.

(A) 2 2/3   (B) 3   (C) 4

(D) 16   (E) 24

7. The two triangles shown are similar. Find $m \angle 1$.

(A) 48   (B) 53   (C) 74

(D) 127   (E) 180

8. The two triangles shown are similar. Find a and b.

(A) 5 and 10   (B) 4 and 8

(C) 4 2/3 and 7 1/3   (D) 5 and 8

(E) 5 1/3 and 8

9. The perimeter of $\triangle LXR$ is 45 and the perimeter of $\triangle ABC$ is 27. If $LX = 15$, find the length of AB.

(A) 9   (B) 15   (C) 27

(D) 45   (E) 72

10. Find b.

(A) 9   (B) 15   (C) 20

(D) 45   (E) 60

Area

11. Find the area of △ *MNO*.

(A) 22   (B) 49   (C) 56

(D) 84   (E) 112

12. Find the area of △ *PQR*.

(A) 31.5   (B) 38.5   (C) 53

(D) 77   (E) 82.5

13. Find the area of △ *STU*.

(A) $4\sqrt{2}$ (B) $8\sqrt{2}$ (C) $12\sqrt{2}$

(D) $16\sqrt{2}$ (E) $32\sqrt{2}$

14. Find the area of △ *ABC*.

(A) 54 cm²   (B) 81 cm²   (C) 108 cm²

(D) 135 cm²   (E) 180 cm²

15. Find the area of △ *XYZ*.

(A) 20 cm²   (B) 50 cm²   (C) $50\sqrt{2}$ cm²

(D) 100 cm²   (E) 200 cm²

4. QUADRILATERALS

A **quadrilateral** is a polygon with four sides.

PARALLELOGRAMS

A **parallelogram** is a quadrilateral whose opposite sides are parallel.

Two angles that have their vertices at the endpoints of the same side of a parallelogram are called **consecutive angles**.

The perpendicular segment connecting any point of a line containing one side of the parallelogram to the line containing the opposite side of the parallelogram is called the **altitude** of the parallelogram.

A diagonal of a polygon is a line segment joining any two non-consecutive vertices.

The area of a parallelogram is given by the formula $A = bh$ where b is the base and h is the height drawn perpendicular to that base. Note that the height equals the altitude of the parallelogram.

$A = bh$

$A = (10)(3)$

$A = 30$

RECTANGLES

A rectangle is a parallelogram with right angles.

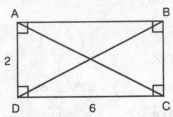

The diagonals of a rectangle are equal.

If the diagonals of a parallelogram are equal, the parallelogram is a rectangle.

If a quadrilateral has four right angles, then it is a rectangle.

The area of a rectangle is given by the formula $A = lw$ where l is the length and w is the width.

$A = lw$

$A = (3)(10)$

$A = 30$

RHOMBI

A rhombus is a parallelogram.

All sides of a rhombus are equal.

The diagonals of a rhombus are perpendicular to each other.

The diagonals of a rhombus bisect the angles of the rhombus.

If the diagonals of a parallelogram are perpendicular, the parallelogram is a rhombus.

If a quadrilateral has four equal sides, then it is a rhombus.

A parallelogram is a rhombus if either diagonal of the parallelogram bisects the angles of the vertices it joins.

SQUARES

A square is a rhombus with a right angle.

A square is an equilateral quadrilateral.

A square has all the properties of parallelograms and rectangles.

A rhombus is a square if one of its interior angles is a right angle.

In a square, the measure of either diagonal can be calculated by multiplying the length of any side by the square root of 2.

$$AD = AB\sqrt{2}$$

The area of a square is given by the formula $A = s^2$ where s is the side of the square. Since all sides of a square are equal, it does not matter which side is used.

$A = s^2$

$A = 6^2$

$A = 36$

The area of a square can also be found by taking $^1/_2$ the product of the length of the diagonal squared.

$$A = ^1/_2\, d^2$$
$$A = ^1/_2\, (8)^2$$
$$A = 32$$

TRAPEZOIDS

A **trapezoid** is a quadrilateral with two and only two sides parallel. The parallel sides of a trapezoid are called **bases**.

The **median** of a trapezoid is the line joining the midpoints of the non-parallel sides.

median of trapezoid

The perpendicular segment connecting any point in the line containing one base of the trapezoid to the line containing the other base is the **altitude** of the trapezoid.

altitude

An **isosceles trapezoid** is a trapezoid whose non-parallel sides are equal. A pair of angles including only one of the parallel sides is called **a pair of base angles**.

Pairs of base angles

The median of a trapezoid is parallel to the bases and equal to one-half their sum.

The base angles of an isosceles trapezoid are equal.
The diagonals of an isosceles trapezoid are equal.
The opposite angles of an isosceles trapezoid are supplementary.

PROBLEM

Prove that all pairs of consecutive angles of a parallelogram are supplementary. (See figure.)

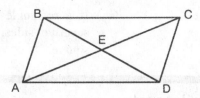

SOLUTION

We must prove that the pairs of angles ∠ *BAD* and ∠ *ADC*, ∠ *ADC* and ∠ *DCB*, ∠ *DCB* and ∠ *CBA*, and ∠ *CBA* and ∠ *BAD* are supplementary. (This means that the sum of their measures is 180°.)

Because *ABCD* is a parallelogram, $\overline{AB} \parallel \overline{CD}$. Angles *BAD* and *ADC* are consecutive interior angles, as are ∠ *CBA* and ∠ *DCB*. Since the consecutive interior angles formed by 2 parallel lines and a transversal are supplementary, ∠ *BAD* and ∠ *ADC* are supplementary, as are ∠ *CBA* and ∠ *DCB*.

Similarly, $\overline{AD} \parallel \overline{BC}$. Angles *ADC* and *DCB* are consecutive interior angles, as are ∠ *CBA* and ∠ *BAD*. Since the consecutive interior angles formed by 2 parallel lines and a transversal are supplementary, ∠ *CBA* and ∠ *BAD* are supplementary, as are ∠ *ADC* and ∠ *DCB*.

PROBLEM

In the accompanying figure, Δ *ABC* is given to be an isosceles right triangle with ∠ *ABC* a right angle and $\overline{AB} \cong \overline{BC}$. Line segment $\overline{BD}$, which bisects $\overline{CA}$, is extended to *E*, so that $\overline{BD} \cong \overline{DE}$. Prove *BAEC* is a square.

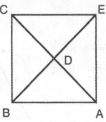

SOLUTION

A square is a rectangle in which two consecutive sides are congruent. This definition will provide the framework for the proof in this problem. We will prove that *BAEC* is a parallelogram that is specifically a rectangle with consecutive sides congruent, namely a square.

Statement		Reason
1.	$\overline{BD} \cong \overline{DE}$ and $\overline{AD} \cong \overline{DC}$	1.	Given ($\overline{BD}$ bisects $\overline{CA}$).
2.	*BAEC* is a parallelogram	2.	If diagonals of a quadrilateral bisect each other, then the quadrilateral is a parallelogram.
3.	∠ *ABC* is a right angle	3.	Given.
4.	*BAEC* is a rectangle	4.	A parallelogram, one of whose angles is a right angle, is a rectangle.
5.	$\overline{AB} \cong \overline{BC}$	5.	Given.

6.   *BAEC* is a square

6.   If a rectangle has two congruent con-
     secutive sides, then the rectangle is a
     square.

☞ Drill: Quadrilaterals

Parallelograms, Rectangles, Rhombuses, Squares, Trapezoids

1.   In parallelogram *WXYZ*, $\overline{WX} = 14$, $\overline{WZ} = 6$,
     $ZY = 3x + 5$, and $XY = 2y - 4$. Find *x* and *y*.

(A)   3 and 5   (B)   4 and 5   (C)   4 and 6

(D)   6 and 10   (E)   6 and 14

2.   Quadrilateral *ABCD* is a parellelogram. If
     $m \angle B = 6x + 2$ and $m \angle D = 98$, find *x*.

(A)   12   (B)   16   (C)   16 2/3

(D)   18   (E)   20

3.   Find the area of parallelogram *STUV*.

(A)   56   (B)   90   (C)   108

(D)   162   (E)   180

4.   Find the area of parallelogram *MNOP*.

(A)   19   (B)   32   (C) $32\sqrt{3}$

(D)   44   (E) $44\sqrt{3}$

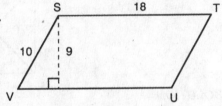

5.   Find the perimeter of rectangle *PQRS*.

(A)   31 in.   (B)   38 in.

(C)   40 in.   (D)   44 in.

(E)   121 in.

6. In rectangle *ABCD*, *AD* = 6 cm and $\overline{DC}$ = 8 cm. Find the length of the diagonal $\overline{AC}$.

(A) 10 cm (B) 12 cm (C) 20 cm

(D) 28 cm (E) 48 cm

7. Find the area of rectangle *UVXY*.

(A) 17 cm² (B) 34 cm² (C) 35 cm²

(D) 70 cm² (E) 140 cm²

8. Find *x* in rectangle *BCDE* if the diagonal $\overline{EC}$ is 17 mm.

(A) 6.55 mm (B) 8 mm (C) 8.5 mm

(D) 17 mm (E) 34 mm

9. In rhombus *DEFG*, $\overline{DE}$ = 7 cm. Find the perimeter of the rhombus.

(A) 14 cm (B) 28 cm (C) 42 cm

(D) 49 cm (E) 56 cm

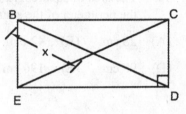

10. In rhombus *RHOM*, the diagonal $\overline{RO}$ is 8 cm and the diagonal $\overline{HM}$ is 12 cm. Find the area of the rhombus.

(A) 20 cm² (B) 40 cm² (C) 48 cm²

(D) 68 cm² (E) 96 cm²

11. In rhombus *GHIJ*, $\overline{GI}$ = 6 cm and $\overline{HJ}$ = 8 cm. Find the length of $\overline{GH}$.

(A) 3 cm (B) 4 cm (C) 5 cm

(D) $4\sqrt{3}$ cm (E) 14 cm

12. In rhombus *CDEF*, $\overline{CD}$ is 13 mm and $\overline{DX}$ is 5 mm. Find the area of the rhombus.

(A) 31 mm² (B) 60 mm² (C) 78 mm²

(D) 120 mm² (E) 260 mm²

13. Quadrilateral *ATUV* is a square. If the perimeter of the square is 44 cm, find the length of $\overline{AT}$.

(A) 4 cm (B) 11 cm (C) 22 cm (D) 30 cm (E) 40 cm

14. The area of square *XYZW* is 196 cm². Find the perimeter of the square.

(A) 28 cm (B) 42 cm (C) 56 cm

(D) 98 cm (E) 196 cm

15. In square *MNOP*, $\overline{MN}$ is 6 cm. Find the length of diagonal $\overline{MO}$.

(A) 6 cm (B) $6\sqrt{2}$ cm (C) $6\sqrt{3}$ cm

(D) $6\sqrt{6}$ cm (E) 12 cm

16. In square *ABCD*, *AB* = 3 cm. Find the area of the square.

(A) 9 cm² (B) 12 cm² (C) 15 cm²

(D) 18 cm² (D) 21 cm²

17. Find the area of trapezoid *RSTU*.

(A) 80 (B) 87.5 (C) 140

(D) 147 (E) 175

18. *ABCD* is an isosceles trapezoid. Find the perimeter.

(A) 21 cm (B) 27 cm (C) 30 cm

(D) 50 cm (E) 54 cm

19. Find the area of trapezoid *MNOP*.

(A) $(17 + 3\sqrt{3})$ mm^2

(B) 33/2 mm^2

(C) $33\sqrt{3}/2$ mm^2

(D) 33 mm^2

(E) $33\sqrt{3}$ mm^2

20. Trapezoid *XYZW* is isosceles. If $m \angle W = 58$ and $m \angle Z = 4x - 6$, find x.

(A) 8 (B) 12 (C) 13

(D) 16 (E) 58

5. CIRCLES

A **circle** is a set of points in the same plane equidistant from a fixed point, called its center.

A **radius** of a circle is a line segment drawn from the center of the circle to any point on the circle.

A portion of a circle is called an **arc** of the circle.

A line that intersects a circle in two points is called a **secant.**

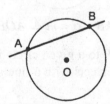

A line segment joining two points on a circle is called a **chord** of the circle.

A chord that passes through the center of the circle is called a **diameter** of the circle.

The line passing through the centers of two (or more) circles is called the **line of centers.**

An angle whose vertex is on the circle and whose sides are chords of the circle is called an **inscribed angle.**

An angle whose vertex is at the center of a circle and whose sides are radii is called a **central angle.**

The measure of a minor arc is the measure of the central angle that intercepts that arc.

$$m \overset{\frown}{AB} = \alpha = m \angle AOB$$

The distance from a point P to a given circle is the distance from that point to the point where the circle intersects with a line segment with endpoints at the center of the circle and point P.

The distance of point P to the diagrammed circle with center O is the line segment $\overline{PB}$ of line segment PO.

A line that has one and only one point of intersection with a circle is called a tangent to that circle, while their common point is called a **point of tangency.**

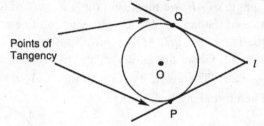

Points of Tangency

Congruent circles are circles whose radii are congruent.

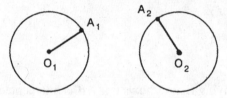

If $O_1A_1 \cong O_2A_2$, then $O_1 \cong O_2$.

The measure of a semicircle is 180°.

A **circumscribed circle** is a circle passing through all the vertices of a polygon.

Circles that have the same center and unequal radii are called **concentric circles**.

Concentric Circles

PROBLEM

A and B are points on circle Q such that
ΔAQB is equilateral. If length of side $\overline{AB}$ =
12, find the length of arc $\overset{\frown}{AB}$.

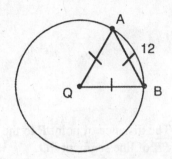

SOLUTION

To find the arc length of $\overset{\frown}{AB}$, we must find the measure of the central angle
∠AQB and the measure of the radius $\overline{QA}$. ∠AQB is an interior angle of the equi-
lateral triangle Δ AQB. Therefore, m∠ AQB = 60°. Similarly, in the equilateral Δ
AQB, AQ = AB = QB = 12. Given the radius, r, and the central angle, n, the arc
length is given by $n/_{360} \cdot 2\pi r$. Therefore, by substitution, ∠ AQB = $60/_{360} \cdot 2\pi \cdot 12$
= $^1/_6 \cdot 2\pi \cdot 12 = 4\pi$. Therefore, length of arc $\overset{\frown}{AB} = 4\pi$.

PROBLEM

In circle O, the measure of $\overset{\frown}{AB}$ is 80°. Find
the measure of ∠ A.

SOLUTION

The accompanying figure shows that $\overset{\frown}{AB}$ is intercepted by central angle AOB.
By definition, we know that the measure of the central angle is the measure of its
intercepted arc. In this case,

$$m\overset{\frown}{AB} = m \angle AOB = 80°.$$

Radius $\overline{OA}$ and radius $\overline{OB}$ are congruent and form two sides of ΔOAB. By a
theorem, the angles opposite these two congruent sides must, themselves, be
congruent. Therefore, m ∠ A = m ∠ B.

The sum of the measures of the angles of a triangle is 180°. Therefore,

$$m \angle A + m \angle B + m \angle AOB = 180°.$$

Since m ∠ A = m ∠ B, we can write

$$m \angle A + m \angle A + 80° = 180°$$

or $2m\angle A = 100°$

or m ∠ A = 50°.

Therefore, the measure of ∠ A is 50°.

☞ Drill: Circles

Circumference, Area, Concentric Circles

1. Find the circumference of circle A if its radius is 3 mm.

    (A) 3π mm   (B) 6π mm   (C) 9π mm   (D) 12π mm   (E) 15π mm

2. The circumference of circle H is 20π cm Find the length of the radius.

    (A) 10 cm   (B) 20 cm   (C) 10π cm   (D) 15π cm   (E) 20π cm

3. The circumference of circle A is how many millimeters larger than the circumference of circle B?

    (A) 3   (B) 6   (C) 3π

    (D) 6π (E) 7π

4. If the diameter of circle X is 9 cm and if $\pi = 3.14$, find the circumference of the circle to the nearest tenth.

    (A) 9 cm   (B) 14.1 cm   (C) 21.1 cm   (D) 24.6 cm   (E) 28.3 cm

5. Find the area of circle I.

    (A) 22 mm²   (B) 121 mm²

    (C) 12π mm²   (D) 132 mm²

    (E) 132π mm²

6. The diameter of circle Z is 27 mm. Find the area of the circle.

    (A) 91.125 mm²   (B) 182.25 mm²   (C) 191.5π mm²

    (D) 182.25π mm²   (E) 729 mm²

7. The area of circle B is 225π cm². Find the length of the diameter of the circle.

    (A) 15 cm   (B) 20 cm   (C) 30 cm   (D) 20π cm   (E) 25π cm

8. The area of circle X is 144π mm² while the area of circle Y is 81π mm². Write the ratio of the radius of circle X to that of circle Y.

    (A) $3:4$ (B) $4:3$ (D) $9:12$ (D) $27:12$ (E) $18:24$

9. The circumference of circle M is 18π cm. Find the area of the circle.

    (A) 18π cm²   (B) 81 cm²   (C) 36 cm²   (D) 36π cm²   (E) 81π cm²

10. In two concentric circles, the smaller circle
    has a radius of 3 mm while the larger circle
    has a radius of 5 mm. Find the area of the
    shaded region.

(A) 2π mm^2 (B) 8π mm^2

(C) 13π mm^2 (D) 16π mm^2

(E) 26π mm^2

11. The radius of the smaller of two concen-
    tric circles is 5 cm while the radius of the
    larger circle is 7 cm. Determine the area of
    the shaded region.

(A) 7π cm^2 (B) 24π cm2

(C) 25π cm^2 (D) 36π cm^2

(E) 49π cm^2

12. Find the measure of arc MN if $m \angle MON = 62$.

(A) 16°   (B) 32°   (C) 59°

(D) 62°   (E) 124°

13. Find the measure of arc AXC.

(A) 150°   (B) 160°   (C) 180°

(D) 270°   (E) 360°

14. If arc $MXP = 236°$, find the measure of arc MP.

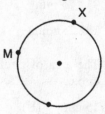

(A) 62°   (B) 124°   (C) 236°

(D) 270°   (E) 360°

15. In circle S, major arc PQR has a measure of
    298°. Find the measure of the central angle
    $\angle PSR$.

(A) 62°   (B) 124°   (C) 149°

(D) 298°   (E) 360°

16. Find the measure of arc *XY* in circle *W*.

(A) 40°   (B) 120°   (C) 140°

(D) 180°   (E) 220°

17. Find the area of the sector shown.

(A) 4 cm²   (B) 2π cm²   (C) 16 cm²

(D) 8π cm²   (E) 16π cm²

18. Find the area of the shaded region.

(A) 10   (B) 5π   (C) 25

(D) 20π   (E) 25π

19. Find the area of the shaded sector shown.

(A) $\dfrac{9\pi \text{ mm}^2}{4}$ (B) $\dfrac{9\pi \text{ mm}^2}{2}$ (C) 18 mm²

(D) 6π mm²   (E) 9π mm²

20. If the area of the square is 100 cm², find the area of the shaded sector.

(A) 10π cm²   (B) 25 cm²   (C) 25π cm²

(D) 100 cm²   (E) 100π cm²

---

6. SOLIDS

Solid geometry is the study of figures which consist of points not all in the same plane.

RECTANGULAR SOLIDS

A solid with lateral faces and bases that are rectangles is called a **rectangular solid**.

The surface area of a rectangular solid is the sum of the areas of all the faces.

The volume of a rectangular solid is equal to the product of its length, width, and height.

$$V = lwh$$

PROBLEM

What are the dimensions of a solid cube whose surface area is numerically equal to its volume?

SOLUTION

The surface area of a cube of edge length a is equal to the sum of the areas of its 6 faces. Since a cube is a regular polygon, all 6 faces are congruent. Each face of a cube is a square of edge length a. Hence, the surface area of a cube of edge length a is

$$S = 6a^2.$$

The volume of a cube of edge length a is

$$V = a^3.$$

We require that $A = V$, or that

$$6a^2 = a^3 \quad \text{or} \quad a = 6$$

Hence, if a cube has edge length 6, its surface area will be numerically equal to its volume.

☞ Drill: Solids

1. Find the total area of the rectangular prism shown.

(A) 138 cm² (B) 336 cm² (C) 381 cm²

(D) 426 cm² (D) 540 cm²

12 cm

5 cm

9 cm

2. Find the volume of the rectangular storage tank shown.

1.5 m

4 m

6 m

(A) 24 m³ (B) 36 m³ (C) 38 m³ (D) 42 m³ (E) 45 m³

3. The lateral area of a cube is 100 cm². Find the length of an edge of the cube.

(A) 4 cm   (B)   5 cm   (C)   10 cm (D)   12 cm (E)   15 cm

7. COORDINATE GEOMETRY

Coordinate geometry refers to the study of geometric figures using algebraic principles.

The graph shown is called the Cartesian coordinate plane. The graph consists of a pair of perpendicular lines called **coordinate axes**. The **vertical axis** is the **y**-axis and the **horizontal axis** is the *x*-axis. The point of intersection of these two axes is called the **origin**; it is the zero point of both axes. Furthermore, points to the right of the origin on the *x*-axis and above the origin on the *y*-axis represent positive real numbers. Points to the left of the origin on the *x*-axis or below the origin on the *y*-axis represent negative real numbers.

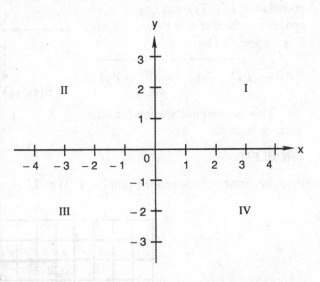

The four regions cut off by the coordinate axes are, in counterclockwise direction from the top right, called the first, second, third, and fourth quadrant, respectively. The first quadrant contains all points with two positive coordinates.

In the graph shown, two points are identified by the ordered pair, (*x*, *y*) of numbers. The *x*-coordinate is the first number and the *y*-coordinate is the second number.

To plot a point on the graph when given the coordinates, draw perpendicular lines from the number-line coordinates to the point where the two lines intersect.

To find the coordinates of a given point on the graph, draw perpendicular lines from the point to the coordinates on the number line. The *x*-coordinate is written before the *y*-coordinate and a comma is used to separate the two.

In this case, point *A* has the co-ordinates (4, 2) and the coordinates of point *B* are (− 3, − 5).

For any two points *A* and *B* with coordinates (X_A, Y_A) and (X_B, Y_B), respectively, the distance between *A* and *B* is represented by:

$$AB = \sqrt{(X_A - X_B)^2 + (Y_A - Y_B)^2}$$

This is commonly known as the distance formula.

PROBLEM

Find the distance between the point *A*(1, 3) and *B*(5, 3).

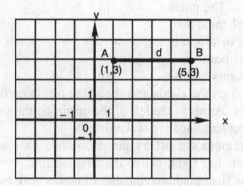

SOLUTION

In this case, where the ordinate of both points is the same, the distance between the two points is given by the absolute value of the difference between the two abscissas. In fact, this case reduces to merely counting boxes as the figure shows.

Let, x_1 = abscissa of *A* $\qquad$ y_1 = ordinate of *A*

$\qquad$ x_2 = abscissa of *B* $\qquad$ y_2 = ordinate of *B*

$\qquad$ d = the distance.

Therefore, $d = |x_1 - x_2|$. By substitution, $d = |1 - 5| = |-4| = 4$. This answer can also be obtained by applying the general formula for distance between any two points

$$d = \sqrt{(x_1 - x_2)^2 + (y_1 - y_2)^2}$$

By substitution,

$$d = \sqrt{(1-5)^2 + (3-3)^2} = \sqrt{(-4)^2 + (0)^2} = \sqrt{16} = 4.$$

The distance is 4.

To find the midpoint of a segment between the two given endpoints, use the formula

$$MP = \left(\frac{x_1 + x_2}{2}, \frac{y_1 + y_2}{2}\right)$$

where x_1 and y_1 are the coordinates of one point; x_2 and y_2 are the coordinates of the other point.

☞ Drill: Coordinate Geometry

1. Which point shown has the coordinates (−3, 2)?

(A) A   (B) B   (C) C

(D) D   (E) E

2. Name the coordinates of point A.

(A) (4, 3)   (B) (3, −4)   (C) (3, 4)

(D) (−4, 3)   (E) (4, −3)

3. Which point shown has the coordinates (2.5, −1)?

(A) M   (B) N   (C) P

(D) Q   (E) R

4. The correct *x*-coordinate for point *H* is what number?

(A) 3   (B) 4   (C) – 3

(D) – 4   (E) – 5

5. The correct *y*–coordinate for point *R* is what number?

(A) –7   (B) 2   (C) – 2

(D) 7   (E) . 8

6. Find the distance between (4, – 7) and (– 2, – 7).

(A) 4   (B) 6   (C) 7   (D) 14   (E) 15

7. Find the distance between (3, 8) and (5, 11).

(A) 2   (B) 3   (C) $\sqrt{13}$ (D) $\sqrt{15}$ (E) $3\sqrt{3}$

8. How far from the origin is the point (3, 4)?

(A) 3   (B) 4   (C) 5   (D) $5\sqrt{3}$ (E) $4\sqrt{5}$

9. Find the distance between the point (– 4, 2) and (3, – 5).

(A) 3   (B) $3\sqrt{3}$ (C) 7   (D) $7\sqrt{2}$ (E) $7\sqrt{3}$

10. The distance between points *A* and *B* is 10 units. If *A* has coordinates (4, – 6) and *B* has coordinates (– 2, *y*), determine the value of *y*.

(A) – 6   (B) – 2   (C) 0   (D) 1   (E) 2

11. Find the midpoint between the points (– 2, 6) and (4, 8).

(A) (3, 7)   (B) (1, 7)   (C) (3, 1)   (D) (1, 1)   (E) (– 3, 7)

12. Find the coordinates of the midpoint between the points (– 5, 7) and (3, – 1).

(A) (– 4, 4) (B) (3, – 1) (C) (1, – 3) (D) (– 1, 3) (E) (4, – 4).

13. The y-coordinate of the midpoint of segment $\overline{AB}$ if A has coordinates (– 3, 7) and B has coordinates (– 3, – 2) is what value?

(A) 5/2 (B) 3 (C) 7/2 (D) 5 (E) 15/2

14. One endpoint of a line segment is (5, – 3). The midpoint is (– 1, 6). What is the other endpoint?

(A) (7, 3) (B) (2, 1.5) (C) (– 7, 15)

(D) (– 2, 1.5) (E) (– 7, 12)

15. The point (– 2, 6) is the midpoint for which of the following pair of points?

(A) (1, 4) and (– 3, 8) (B) (– 1, – 3) and (5, 9)

(C) (1, 4) and (5, 9) (D) (– 1, 4) and (3, – 8)

(E) (1, 3) and (– 5, 9)

GEOMETRY DRILLS

ANSWER KEY

Drill: Lines and Angles

1.	(B)	5.	(D)	9.	(D)	13.	(B)
2.	(A)	6.	(C)	10.	(E)	14.	(E)
3.	(C)	7.	(B)	11.	(C)	15.	(A)
4.	(D)	8.	(A)	12.	(D)		

Drill: Regular Polygons

1.	(D)	4.	(A)	7.	(E)	10.	(B)
2.	(B)	5.	(D)	8.	(B)		
3.	(E)	6.	(C)	9.	(D)		

Drill: Triangles

1.	(D)	5.	(C)	9.	(A)	13.	(D)
2.	(B)	6.	(A)	10.	(C)	14.	(A)
3.	(C)	7.	(B)	11.	(C)	15.	(B)
4.	(E)	8.	(E)	12.	(B)		

Drill: Quadrilaterals

1.	(A)	6.	(A)	11.	(C)	16.	(A)
2.	(B)	7.	(D)	12.	(D)	17.	(E)
3.	(D)	8.	(C)	13.	(B)	18.	(B)
4.	(E)	9.	(B)	14.	(C)	19.	(C)
5.	(C)	10.	(C)	15.	(B)	20.	(D)

Drill: Circles

1.	(B)	6.	(D)	11.	(B)	16.	(C)
2.	(A)	7.	(C)	12.	(D)	17.	(B)
3.	(D)	8.	(B)	13.	(C)	18.	(D)
4.	(E)	9.	(E)	14.	(B)	19.	(A)
5.	(C)	10.	(D)	15.	(A)	20.	(C)

Drill: Solids

1. (D)   2. (B)   3. (C)

Drill: Coordinate Geometry

1. (C)   5. (A)   9. (D)   13. (A)
2. (E)   6. (B)   10. (E)   14. (C)
3. (B)   7. (C)   11. (B)   15. (E)
4. (D)   8. (C)   12. (D)

PRACTICE
EXAM I

EXAM I

TEST 1: LANGUAGE ARTS: WRITING, PART I
Tests of General Educational Development

Directions

The Language Arts: Writing Test is intended to measure your ability to use clear and effective English. It is a test of English as it should be written, not as it might be spoken. This test includes both multiple-choice questions and an essay. These directions apply only to the multiple-choice section; a separate set of directions is given for the essay.

The multiple-choice section consists of paragraphs with numbered sentences. Some of the sentences contain errors in sentence structure, usage, or mechanics (spelling, punctuation, and capitalization). After reading the numbered sentences, answer the multiple-choice questions that follow. Some questions refer to sentences that are correct as written. The best answer for these questions is the one that leaves the sentence as originally written. The best answer for some questions is the one that produces a sentence that is consistent with the verb tense and point of view used throughout the paragraph.

You should spend no more than 75 minutes on the multiple-choice questions and 45 minutes on your essay. Work carefully, but do not spend too much time on any one question. You may begin working on the essay part of this test as soon as you complete the multiple-choice section.

Do not mark in this test booklet. Record your answers on the separate answer sheet provided. Be sure that all requested information is properly recorded on the answer sheet.

To record your answers, mark one numbered space on the answer sheet beside the number that corresponds to the question in the test booklet.

FOR EXAMPLE:

Sentence I: **We were all honored to meet governor Phillips.**

What correction should be made to this sentence?

(1)   insert a comma after <u>honored</u>

(2)   change the spelling of <u>honored</u> to <u>honered</u>

(3)   change <u>governor</u> to <u>Governor</u>

(4)   replace <u>were</u> with <u>was</u>   ① ② ● ④ ⑤

(5)   no correction is necessary

In this example, the word "governor" should be capitalized; therefore, answer space 3 would be marked on the answer sheet.

Do not rest the point of your pencil on the answer sheet while you are considering your answer. Make no stray or unnecessary marks. If you change an answer, erase your first mark completely. Mark only one answer space for each question; multiple answers will be scored as incorrect. Do not fold or crease your answer sheet. All test materials must be returned to the test administrator.

Reprinted with permission of the General Educational Development Testing Service of the American Council on Education.

Directions: Choose the <u>one best answer</u> to each item.

<u>Items 1 to 5</u> refer to the following paragraph.

(1) Auto Striping Pro's is having a special on pin stripes for all vehicles. (2) This extraordinary sale is for today only. (3) Cars brought in today will get special attention from the owner and his son. (4) Cars done by he and his son always get a lot of special touches. (5) In fact, there the best in the business.

1. Sentence 1: **Auto Striping Pro's is having a special on pinstripes for all vehicles.**

    What correction should be made to this sentence?

    (1) change the spelling of <u>Pro's</u> to <u>Pros</u>
    (2) change <u>is having</u> to <u>will be having</u>
    (3) change <u>is</u> to <u>be</u>
    (4) change <u>pinstripes</u> to <u>pinstrips</u>
    (5) no correction is necessary

2. Sentence 2: **This extraordinary sale is for today only.**

    What correction is necessary?

    (1) change <u>this</u> to <u>these</u>
    (2) change <u>extraordinary</u> to <u>extra ordinary</u>
    (3) change <u>is</u> to <u>are</u>
    (4) change <u>for</u> to <u>four</u>
    (5) no correction is necessary

3. Sentence 3: **Cars brought in today will get special attention from the owner and his son.**

    What correction should be made?

    (1) change <u>get</u> to <u>got</u>
    (2) change <u>from</u> to <u>with</u>
    (3) change <u>owner</u> to <u>owner's</u>
    (4) change <u>Cars</u> to <u>cars</u>
    (5) no correction is necessary

4.   Sentence 4: **Cars done by he and his son always get a lot of special touches.**

What correction should be made?

(1)   change he to him

(2)   change a lot to alot

(3)   place a period after and his son

(4)   change always to all ways

(5)   no correction is necessary

5.   Sentence 5: **In fact, there the best in the business.**

What correction is necessary?

(1)   remove the comma after In fact

(2)   change there to their

(3)   change there to their are

(4)   change there to they're

(5)   no correction is necessary

Items 6 to 10 refer to the following paragraph.

(1) Preparing for a job interview is all ways a hard thing to do. (2) If you know whats going to be asked, it is easier. (3) Its easier to answer questions when you know what to expect. (4) To often, it is not possible to be prepared. (5) When I go on an interview, me and my friends talk first about what we think we will be asked.

6.   Sentence 1: **Preparing for a job interview is all ways a hard thing to do.**

What correction is necessary?

(1)   change a to on

(2)   change all ways to always

(3)   place a period between interview and is

(4)   change is to are

(5)   no correction is necessary

7.   Sentence 2: **If you know whats going to be asked, it is easier.**

What correction is necessary?

(1)   remove the comma after asked

(2)   change it is to its

(3)   change it is to its'

(4)   change what to what's

(5)   no correction is necessary

8.   Sentence 3: **Its easier to answer questions when you know what to expect.**

What correction is necessary?

(1)   begin a new sentence with the word when

(2)   replace Its with It's

(3)   replace to with too

(4)   change to to two

(5)   no correction is necessary

9.   Sentence 4: **To often, it is not possible to be prepared.**

What correction is necessary?

(1)   replace To with Too

(2)   replace To with Two

(3)   remove the comma after often

(4)   replace it is with its'

(5)   no correction is necessary

10.   Sentence 5: **When I go on an interview, me and my friends talk first about what we think we will be asked.**

What correction is necessary?

(1)   remove the comma after interview

(2)   change me and my friends to my friends and me

(3)   change me and my friends to my friends and I

(4)   change me and my friends to I and my friends

(5)   no correction is necessary

Items 11 to 18 refer to the following paragraphs.

(1) The Middle Ages in England went from the end of the Roman empire to the 1500s. (2) Barbaric tribes of German's swept into Britain. (3) There they excepted the Christian religion of the retreating Romans. (4) Chiefs governed these tribes.

(5) The strong system of the Romans were replaced by barbaric laws. (6) The invaders lacked the knowledge to carry on the Roman achievements. (7) Few people could read Latin the language of the well-educated. (8) All of these skills were soon to be forgotten.

11. Sentence 1: **The Middle Ages in England went from the end of the Roman empire to the 1500s.**

    What correction is necessary?

    (1) change 1500s to 1500's
    (2) change end of the to end to the
    (3) change empire to Empire
    (4) change in England to of England
    (5) no correction is necessary

12. Sentence 2: **Barbaric tribes of German's swept into Britain.**

    What correction is necessary?

    (1) change swept to sweeped
    (2) change into to in to
    (3) change swept to are swept
    (4) change German's to Germans
    (5) no correction is necessary

13. Sentence 3: **There they excepted the Christian religion of the retreating Romans.**

    What correction is necessary?

    (1) change There to Their
    (2) change There to They're
    (3) change excepted to accepted
    (4) change Romans to Roman's
    (5) no correction is necessary

14. Sentence 4: **Chiefs governed these tribes.**

    What correction is necessary?

    (1) change Chiefs to chiefs
    (2) change these to this
    (3) change tribes to tribes'

(4)   change <u>these</u> to <u>them</u>

(5)   no correction is necessary

15. Sentence 5: **The strong system,of the Romans were replaced by barbaric laws.**

What correction is necessary?

(1)   place a comma after <u>system</u>

(2)   change <u>Romans</u> to <u>romans</u>

(3)   change <u>were</u> to <u>was</u>

(4)   change <u>Romans</u> to <u>Roman</u>

(5)   no correction is necessary

16. Sentence 6: **The invaders lacked the knowledge to carry on the Roman achievements.**

What correction is necessary?

(1)   change <u>invaders</u> to <u>Invaders</u>

(2)   change <u>the Roman achievements</u> to <u>the Roman's achievements</u>

(3)   change <u>invaders</u> to <u>invader's</u>

(4)   change <u>to carry on</u> to <u>to carry</u>

(5)   no correction is necessary

17.   Sentence 7: **Few people could read Latin,the language of the well-educated.**

What correction is necessary?

(1)   change <u>Latin</u> to <u>latin</u>

(2)   change <u>educated</u> to <u>educated's</u>

(3)   change <u>well-educated</u> to <u>well educated</u>

(4)   place a comma after <u>Latin</u>

(5)   no correction is necessary

18.   Sentence 8: **All of these skills were soon to be forgotten.**

What correction is necessary?

(1)   replace <u>these</u> with <u>they're</u>

(2)   replace <u>were</u> with <u>was</u>

(3)   replace <u>forgotten</u> with <u>for got</u>

(4)   replace <u>forgotten</u> with <u>forgot</u>

(5) no correction is necessary

<u>Items 19 to 29</u> refer to the following paragraph.

(1) Much of what we watch on television is really more boring. (2) Several times a week, shows are on which, in my opinion are stupid. (3) Why do we even watch shows that make us board? (4) On the other hand there are good and informative serials that can teach and entertain us at the same time. (5) The programmers at television stations must think that were awfully stupid to put on some of the programs that they do. (6) How often do you wish that you could run a television station, or at least all of the programs selection? (7) It can be embarrassing to watch television with new friends. (8) when advertisements about private things come on. (9) I know were we could send stupid programmers. (10) We could send them to live with Bart Simpson, then they could have a cow, too. (11) What we really need is someone who asks you and I what we want to see.

19. Sentence 1: **Much of what we watch on television is really more boring.**

    What correction should be made?

    (1) change <u>Much</u> to <u>Many</u>
    (2) change <u>television</u> to <u>Television</u>
    (3) place a comma between <u>watch</u> and <u>on</u>
     (4) change <u>more boring</u> to <u>boring</u>
    (5) no correction is necessary

20. Sentence 2: **Several times a week, shows are on which, in my opinion are stupid.**

    What correction should be made?

    (1) change <u>week</u> to <u>weak</u>
    (2) remove the comma before <u>in</u>
    (3) add a comma after <u>opinion</u>
    (4) place a period after <u>opinion</u>
    (5) no correction is necessary

21. Sentence 3: **Why do we even watch shows that make us board?**

    What correction should be made?

    (1) change <u>that</u> to <u>which</u>
     (2) change <u>board</u> to <u>bored</u>

(3)   replace the question mark with a period

(4)   change the question mark to an exclamation point

(5)   no correction is necessary

22.   Sentence 4: **On the other hand, there are good and informative serials that can teach and entertain us at the same time.**

What correction should be made?

(1)   place a comma after hand

(2)   change serials to cereals

(3)   place a comma after teach

(4)   place a comma after us

(5)   no correction is necessary

23.   Sentence 5: **The programmers at television stations must think that were awfully stupid to put on some of the programs that they do.**

What correction should be made?

(1)   place a comma after programmers

(2)   place a comma after stupid

(3)   replace were with we're

(4)   place a period after stupid

(5)   no correction is necessary

24.   Sentence 6: **How often do you wish that you could run a television station, or at least all of the program selections?**

What correction should be made?

(1)   remove the comma after station

(2)   replace the question mark with a period

(3)   replace program with program's

(4)   place a comma after least

(5)   no correction is necessary

25.   Sentence 7: **It can be embarrassing to watch television with new friends.**

What correction should be made?

(1)   place a comma after embarrassing

    (2)   replace <u>new</u> with <u>knew</u>

    (3)   replace <u>television</u> with <u>Television</u>

    (4)   place a period after <u>embarrassing</u>

    (5)   no correction is necessary

26.   Sentence 8: **when advertisements about private things come on.**

    What correction should be made?

    (1)   replace <u>when</u> to <u>When</u>

    (2)   place a comma after <u>advertisements</u>

    (3)   let stand but connect with previous sentence

    (4)   change <u>when</u> to <u>win</u>

    (5)   no correction is necessary

27.   Sentence 9: **I know were we could send stupid programmers.**

    What correction should be made?

    (1)   change <u>were</u> to <u>we're</u>

    (2)   change <u>were</u> to <u>where</u>

    (3)   change <u>were</u> to <u>wear</u>

    (4)   change <u>know were</u> to <u>no where</u>

    (5)   no correction is necessary

28.   Sentence 10: **We could send them to live with Bart Simpson, then they could have a cow, too.**

    What correction should be made?

    (1)   remove the comma after <u>Simpson</u>

    (2)   change the comma after <u>Simpson</u> to a semi-colon

    (3)   replace <u>too</u> with <u>two</u>

    (4)   replace <u>too</u> with <u>to</u>

    (5)   no correction is necessary

29.   Sentence 11: **What we really need is someone who asks you and I what we want to see.**

    What correction should be made?

    (1)   place a comma after <u>need</u>

    (2)   place a comma after <u>I</u>

(3) replace <u>you and I</u> with <u>me and you</u>

_____(4) replace <u>you and I</u> with <u>you and me</u>

(5) no correction is necessary

<u>Items 30 to 38</u> refer to the following paragraph.

(1) I don't hardly ever get to talk about my favorite summer vacations. (2) The beach is most unique of all the places we visit. (3) I really like going there often. (4) Who's going to want to go any place else in the summer? (5) I guess I should of told you about the best beaches in Texas, Florida, and Alabama. (6) Whether you go or not, you still will know what they look like. (7) Its always fun to talk about the white beaches of Alabama. (8) When we drive threw Alabama, I'm always happy to spend some time on the beach. (9) Me and my family always spend some time on some beach each summer. (10) When we are at the beach, we wear very few clothes and use a lot of sunscreen. (11) If you think i like swimming, you are wrong. (12) My favorite thing to do is to lay on the beach and get a tan. (13) Thats why sunscreen is so important.

30. Sentence 1: **I don't hardly ever get to talk about my favorite summer vacations.**

What correction must be made?

(1) change <u>don't</u> to <u>do not</u>

(2) change <u>vacations</u> to <u>vacation</u>

(3) delete <u>don't</u>

(4) delete <u>hardly</u>

(5) no correction is necessary

31. Sentence 2: **The beach is most unique of all the places we visit.**

What correction needs to be made?

(1) place a comma after <u>unique</u>

(2) replace <u>is</u> with <u>are</u>

(3) replace <u>beach</u> with <u>beaches</u>

(4) remove <u>most</u>

(5) no correction is necessary

32. Sentence 5: **I guess I should of told you about the best beaches in Texas, Florida, and Alabama.**

What correction is necessary?

(1) insert <u>that</u> after <u>guess</u>

     (2)   replace <u>beaches</u> with <u>beach</u>

     (3)   replace <u>should of</u> with <u>should have</u>

     (4)   delete the comma after <u>Florida</u>

     (5)   no correction is necessary

33.   Sentence 7: **Its always fun to talk about the white beaches of Alabama.**

     What correction needs to be made?

     (1)   replace <u>Its</u> with <u>It's</u>

     (2)   replace <u>always</u> with <u>all ways</u>

     (3)   place a comma after <u>beaches</u>

     (4)   replace <u>to</u> with <u>too</u>

     (5)   no correction is necessary

34.   Sentence 8: **When we drive threw Alabama, I'm always happy to spend some time on the beach.**

     What correction needs to be made?

     (1)   remove the comma after <u>Alabama</u>

     (2)   replace <u>when</u> with <u>win</u>

     (3)   replace <u>always</u> with <u>all ways</u>

     (4)   replace <u>threw</u> with <u>through</u>

     (5)   no correction is necessary

35.   Sentence 9: **Me and my family always spend some time on some beach each summer.**

     What correction needs to be made?

     (1)   change <u>spend</u> to <u>spends</u>

     (2)   change <u>me and my family</u> to <u>I and my family</u>

     (3)   change <u>Me and my family</u> to <u>My family and I</u>

     (4)   change <u>Me and my family</u> to <u>My family and me</u>

     (5)   no correction is necessary

36.   Sentence 11: **If you think i like swimming, you are wrong.**

     What correction is necessary?

     (1)   place a comma after <u>think</u>

     (2)   remove the comma after <u>swimming</u>

(3) replace i with I

(4) end the sentence with an exclamation mark

(5) no correction is necessary

37. Sentence 12: **My favorite thing to do is to lay on the beach and get a tan.**

What correction needs to be made?

(1) place a comma after beach

(2) place a comma after is

(3) replace lay with lay out

(4) replace lay with lie

(5) no correction is necessary

38. Sentence 13: **Thats why sunscreens are so important.**

What correction needs to be made?

(1) place a comma after why

(2) replace sunscreens with sunscreen

(3) replace is with are

(4) replace Thats with That's

(5) no correction is necessary

Items 39 to 42 refer to the following paragraphs.

Dear Ms. Wells:

(A)

(1) I am writing in response to your advertisement in the Scotch Plains-Fanwood Reader for the salesperson/window dresser position at Lady Linda. (2) I believe I am an ideal candidate for this position.

(B)

(3) I am very familiar with your store my mother has shopped there for years. (4) I am familiar with the type of customer who shops at your store, and would be very eager to assist them in making their purchases. (5) In addition, I have experience in retail. (6) I worked last summer at the A & P.

(C)

(7) I would also love to be able to use my art skills to help decorate your windows. (8) I am an avid artist, and have taken several classes in art design. (9) I already have great ideas for some of your seasonal windows.

(D)

(10) I am a more responsible and hard working person. (11) I also have experience with money, as treasurer for both the French Club and the Freshman Class.

(E)

(12) Enclosed please find a resume for your review. (13) Feel free to call if you have any questions or if you would like to arrange an interview. (14) I look forward to hearing from you.

Sincerely,

Julia Bennett

39. Sentence 2: **I believe I am an ideal candidate for this position.**

   Of the following sentence fragments, which would be the most effective if added to the end of this sentence?

   (1) because of my relevant experience and qualifications
   (2) because I really want this job
   (3) because this job would mean so much to me
   (4) because my parents are friends with the store manager
   (5) because I'm the best person around for it

40. Sentence 3: **I am very familiar with your store my mother has shopped there for years.**

   What is wrong with this sentence?

   (1) It is a sentence fragment.
   (2) There is an incorrect pronoun use.
   (3) It is a run-on sentence.
   (4) There is a problem with the tense.
   (5) The sentence is correct.

41. **What would be the most effective arrangement of sentences for paragraph B?**

   (1) exactly as it is
   (2) 5, 6, 3, 4
   (3) 6, 5, 3, 4

    (4)   5, 3, 4, 6

    (5)   6, 5, 4, 3

42.   Sentence 10: **I am a more responsible and hard working person.**

       What word should be eliminated?

    (1)   I

    (2)   responsible

    (3)   working

    (4)   more

    (5)   and

Items 43 to 47 refer to the following paragraphs.

(A)

(1) Choosing the right college can be one of the most important decisions you will ever make. (2) This is a decision can shape the rest of your life. (3) With careful preparation, you can ensure that you will make the right choice for you

(B)

(4) The first step is to decide how important location is to you. (5) Do you want to stay in the area where you live now, or do you want to go someplace different? (6) Do you want to live in a rural area, or would you prefer to go to school in a big city like boston or Los Angeles? (7) Once you've decided what type of area in which you like to go to school, you can start to narrow your search by looking for schools in that area.

(C)

(8) Now that you've got a narrow selection of schools within a certain area, you can start concentrating on which of those schools will best serve your academic interests you will also want to think about some practical issues, like which school offers the best job placement program. (9) If you haven't yet decided on a major, that's alright, but you should try to at least have a sense of whether you are more oriented toward the humanities, the fine arts, the sciences, or business-oriented majors.

(D)

(10) Cost will of course be a crucial issue. (11) What schools in your target area can you afford? (12) You'll need to sit down with your parents and your financial aid counselor at school to figure this out. (13) It can be. (14) Very complicated and you will need to go over all the possibilities very carefully.

43. Sentence 2: **This is a decision can shape the rest of your life.**

    What correction is necessary?

    (1) a comma between decision and can

    (2) change life to live

    (3) place that after decision

    (4) capitalize shape

    (5) no correction is necessary

44. Sentence 5: **Do you want to stay in the area where you live now, or do you want to go someplace different.**

    What correction is necessary?

    (1) change the period after different to a question mark

    (2) place a comma after someplace

    (3) change do to does

    (4) change some to sum

    (5) no correction is necessary

45. Sentence 6: **Do you want to live in a rural area, or would you prefer to go to school in a big city like boston or Los Angeles?**

    What correction is necessary?

    (1) place a comma after big

    (2) capitalize boston

    (3) capitalize city

    (4) change Los Angeles to los angeles

    (5) no correction is necessary

46. Sentence 8: **Now that you've got a narrow selection of schools within a certain area, you can start concentrating on which of those schools will best serve your academic interests you will also want to think about some practical issues, like which school offers the best job placement program.**

    What correction should be made to this sentence?

    (1) start a new sentence after interests

    (2) remove the comma after area

    (3) start a new sentence after issues

(4)   place a comma after <u>interests</u>

(5)   no correction is necessary

47.   The last two sentences in paragraph D should be

(1)   deleted.

(2)   moved to paragraph A.

(3)   combined to correct a sentence-fragment error.

(4)   moved to the beginning of the paragraph.

(5)   left alone.

<u>Items 48 to 50</u> refer to the following paragraphs.

(A)

(1) The report found that obese people have on average nearly twice the chronic health troubles of people of normal weight. (2) The study also found that smoking harms the health of women more than men, with female smokers having about 43 percent more chronic health problems than nonsmokers. (3) The figure was 27 percent for men. (4) Obese adults have more chronic health problems than smokers, heavy drinkers or the poor, according to a newly available study. (5) The study depends on a figure called Body Mass Index, or BMI. (6) The study had a 2 percent margin of error.

(B)

(7) People of normal weight have a BMI between 18.5 and 24.9; those considered overweight score between 25 and 29.9; obese people are between 30 and 34.9 and very obese people are over 35. (8) Obesity was determined by finding a respondent's Body Mass Index, a figure derived by multiplying a person's weight in pounds by 703 and dividing that result by height in inches squared.

(C)

(9) The survey found that 52 percent of Americans are at least over-weight — a figure that is in line with other recent studies. (10) The study found that people of normal weight had an average of 1.1 chronic condi-tions. (11) Overweight people had an average of an additional 0.2 chronic conditions, obese people had an additional 0.6 chronic conditions, and the very obese had 0.9 more conditions. (12) Obesity tends to be looked down upon in our culture. (13) The study showed the obese tend to have slightly more health problems than people living in poverty and far more than daily smokers or heavy drinkers.

48. Which sentence in paragraph A should be the topic sentence?

    (1) sentence 1
    (2) sentence 2
    (3) sentence 3
    (4) sentence 4
    (5) sentence 5

49. Which sentence from paragraph A would make a better transition to paragraph B than sentence 6?

    (1) sentence 1
    (2) sentence 2
    (3) sentence 3
    (4) sentence 4
    (5) sentence 5

50. Which sentence in paragraph C disrupts the unity and coherence of the passage?

    (1) sentence 9
    (2) sentence 10
    (3) sentence 11
    (4) sentence 12
    (5) sentence 13

TEST 1: LANGUAGE ARTS: WRITING, PART II
Tests of General Educational Development

Directions

This part of the Language Arts: Writing Test is intended to determine how well you write. You are asked to write an essay that explains something or presents an opinion on an issue. In preparing your essay, you should take the following steps.

1. Read carefully the directions and the essay topic given below.

2. Plan your essay carefully before you write.

3. Use scratch paper to make any notes.

4. Write your essay on the lined pages of the separate answer sheet.

5. Read carefully what you have written and make any changes that will improve your essay.

6. Check your paragraphs, sentence structure, spelling, punctuation, capitalization, and usage, and make any necessary corrections.

Be sure you write the <u>letter</u> of the essay topic (given below) on your answer sheet. Write the letter in the box at the upper right-hand corner of the page where you write your essay.

You will have 45 minutes to write on the topic below. Write legibly and use a ballpoint pen so the evaluators will be able to read your writing.

Write your essay on the lined pages of the separate answer sheet. The notes you make on scratch paper will not be scored.

Your essay will be scored by at least two trained evaluators who will judge it according to its <u>overall effectiveness</u>. They will judge how clearly you make the main point of your composition, how thoroughly you support your ideas, and how clearly and correctly you write throughout the essay.

Topic A

Some state legislatures are considering making 18 years of age the legal age to get a driver's license. In an essay of approximately 250 words, tell why you think this is or is not a good idea.

TEST 2: SOCIAL STUDIES

Tests of General Educational Development

Directions

The Social Studies Test consists of multiple-choice questions intended to measure your knowledge of general social studies concepts. The questions are based on short readings which often include a graph, chart, or figure. Study the information given and then answer the question(s) following it. Refer to the information as often as necessary in answering the questions.

You should spend no more than 70 minutes answering the questions in this booklet. Work carefully, but do not spend too much time on any one question. Be sure you answer every question. You will not be penalized for incorrect answers.

Do not mark in this test booklet. Record your answers to the questions on the separate answer sheet provided. Be sure all requested information is properly recorded on the answer sheet.

To record your answers, mark the numbered space on the answer sheet beside the number that corresponds to the question in the test booklet.

FOR EXAMPLE:

Early colonists of North America looked for settlement sites that had adequate water supplies and were accessible by ship. For this reason, many early towns were built near

(1) mountains.   (4) glaciers.
(2) prairies.   (5) plateaus.
(3) rivers.   ① ② ● ④ ⑤

The correct answer is "rivers"; therefore, answer space 3 would be marked on the answer sheet.

Do not rest the point of your pencil on the answer sheet while you are considering your answer. Make no stray or unnecessary marks. If you change an answer, erase your first mark completely. Mark only one answer space for each question; multiple answers will be scored as incorrect. Do not fold or crease your answer sheet. Return all test materials to the test administrator.

Reprinted with permission of the General Educational Development Testing Service of the American Council on Education.

Directions: Choose the one best answer to each item.

Items 1 to 3 refer to the following passage.

Along about April 1, 1913, we first tried the experiment of an assembly line. We tried it on assembling the fly-wheel *magneto* ....

I believe that this was the first moving line ever installed. The idea came in a general way from the overhead trolley that the Chicago packers use in dressing beef. We had previously assembled the fly-wheel mag-neto in the usual method. With one workman doing a complete job he could turn out from thirty-five to forty pieces in a nine-hour day, or about twenty minutes to an assembly. What he did alone was then spread into twenty-nine operations; that cut down the assembly time to thirteen minutes, ten seconds. Then we raised the height of the line eight inches—this was in 1914—and cut the time to seven minutes. Further experimenting with the speed that the work should move at cut the time down to five minutes. In short, the result is this: by the aid of scientific study one man is now able to do somewhat more than four did only a comparatively few years ago. That line established the efficiency of the method and we now use it everywhere. The assembling of the motor, formerly done by one man, is now divided into eighty-four operations—those men do the work that three times their number formerly did. In a short time we tried out the plan on the *chassis* ....

It must not be imagined, however, that all this worked out as quickly as it sounds. The speed of the moving work had to be carefully tried out .... The chassis assembling line, for example, goes at a pace of six feet per minute; the front axle assembly line goes at one hundred eighty-nine inches per minute. In the chassis assembling are forty-five separate operations or stations.... Some men do only one or two small operations, others do more. The man who places a part does not fasten it—the part may not be fully in place until after several operations later. The man who puts in a bolt does not put on the nut; the man who puts on the nut does not tighten it. On operation number thirty-four the budding motor gets its gasoline; it has previously received lubrication; on operation number forty-four the radiator is filled with water, and on operation number forty-five the car drives out....

1. Which famous American, quoted above, pioneered the modern indus-trial assembly line?

    (1) John D. Rockefeller   (4) Henry Ford
    (2) J.P. Morgan   (5) Leland Stanford
    (3) Andrew Carnegie

2. The main reason for creating an assembly line, according to the
    was

    (1) to make a better product.
    (2) to make better use of skilled labor.
    (3) to make a product more quickly.
    (4) to increase employment.
    (5) to cut down the work day and week.

3. Which was not a factor in making Detroit the "Motor City"?

    (1) Home to early automotive inventors
    (2) Location central to major raw materials
    (3) Access to cheap water transportation
    (4) Availability of a large immigrant labor force
    (5) The crossroads for most of the major east-west railroads

Item 4 refers to the tables below.

Grain Producers				Grain Importers			
Grain	1st	2nd	3rd	Grain	1st	2nd	3rd
Corn	USA	China	Brazil	Corn	Russia	Japan	Spain
Wheat	Russia	USA	China	Wheat	China	Russia	Japan
Rice	China	India	Indonesia	Rice	Indonesia	Iran	Russia

4. Which nation seems to have the least efficient agricultural system?

    (1) Brazil
    (2) Indonesia
    (3) Russia
    (4) India
    (5) China

RECORD OF GALLUP POLL ACCURACY

Year	Final Gallup Poll		Election Result		Deviation
1980	47.0%	Reagan	50.8%	Reagan	-3.8
1978	55.0	Democratic	54.6	Democratic	+0.4
1976	48.0	Carter	50.0	Carter	-2.0
1974	60.0	Democratic	58.9	Democratic	+1.1
1972	62.0	Nixon	61.8	Nixon	+0.2
1970	53.0	Democratic	54.3	Democratic	-1.3
1968	43.0	Nixon	43.5	Nixon	-0.5
1966	52.5	Democratic	51.9	Democratic	+0.6
1964	64.0	Johnson	61.3	Johnson	+2.7
1962	55.5	Democratic	52.7	Democratic	+2.8
1960	51.0	Kennedy	50.1	Kennedy	+0.9
1958	57.0	Democratic	56.5	Democratic	+0.5
1956	59.5	Eisenhower	57.8	Eisenhower	+1.7
1954	51.5	Democratic	52.7	Democratic	-1.2
1952	51.0	Eisenhower	55.4	Eisenhower	-4.4
1950	51.0	Democratic	50.3	Democratic	+0.7
1948	44.5	Truman	49.9	Truman	-5.4
1946	58.0	Republican	54.3	Republican	+3.7
1944	51.5	Roosevelt	53.3	Roosevelt	-1.8
1942	52.0	Democratic	48.0	Democratic	+4.0
1940	52.0	Roosevelt	55.0	Roosevelt	-3.0
1938	54.0	Democratic	50.8	Democratic	+3.2
1936	55.7	Roosevelt	62.5	Roosevelt	-6.8

TREND IN DEVIATION

Elections	Avg. Error
1936–1950	3.6
1952–1960	1.7
1962–1970	1.6
1972–1980	1.5

Average deviation for 23 national elections: 2.3 percentage points

Average deviation for 16 national elections since 1950 inclusive: 1.6 percentage points

Items 5 to 7 refer to the chart above

5. Which is not shown by the chart?

    (1) The average error rate decreased in recent decades.
    (2) Every second poll was a presidential election year.
    (3) There were more negative deviations than positive.
    (4) Non-presidential polls favored the Democrats.
    (5) There were presidents elected by less than 50%.

6. According to the chart, who won the presidency with the lowest vote?

    (1) Carter   (4) Johnson
    (2) Reagan   (5) Kennedy
    (3) Nixon

7. Why was President Gerald Ford (1974-77) **not** shown in the poll?

    (1) He chose not to run for re-election.
    (2) He died in office.
    (3) He took over while vice-president, and was not elected.

(4)   He was impeached.
(5)   He resigned.

Items 8 and 9 refer to the following graph.

UNITED STATES 25.4

CANADA 24.5

JAPAN 14.8

GERMANY 13.5

ITALY 12.3

FRANCE 12.1

BRITAIN 11.1

U.S. Oil Consumption

Transportation

63

Manufacturing

25

Heating

8

Electricity

4

8.   Which is not a conclusion that can be drawn from the graphs?

(1)   Transportation takes up too high a portion of U.S. oil usage.
(2)   U.S. per capita consumption is over twice that of most European nations.
(3)   North American oil demands are the highest.
(4)   Manufacturing is a major consumer of oil.
(5)   Heating needs take less than 10% of oil use.

9.   Which would be least likely to explain the statistics above?

(1)   The area size of a nation has a relationship to oil usage.
(2)   The European nations consume large quantities of oil.
(3)   The larger the population, the greater the usage.
(4)   Japan is the largest industrial power in Asia.
(5)   Industrial nations' people have lifestyles that use more oil.

Items 10 to 13 refer to the following passage.

Do you support the collection of sales tax on purchases made through the internet? **YES** or **NO**

PRO: Supporters of this proposal say it is only fair to collect the sales tax since traditional "brick and mortar" stores have to collect sales tax and they face unfair competition from internet stores who do not collect sales tax. Michigan consumers purchased an estimated $7.3 billion in 1999 through remote sales and this figure is only expected to climb. It is estimated that Michigan lost an estimated $173 million in sales tax from these remote purchases. And, state law already states that a consumer is responsible for paying sales tax on purchases made through a catalog or out-of-state business. This "use tax" money has to be reported on an individual's state income tax form.

CON: Opponents claim that requiring sales tax on purchases made through the internet will slow the growth of the internet and cause many dot.com businesses to fail. The states, however, cannot force internet retailers to collect and pay the taxes nationwide without action by Congress since that is a matter of interstate commerce, and until that happens, the states should leave collecting internet sales tax alone.

10. These "Pro and Con" statements deal with the issue of

    (1) collection of a state sales tax on all purchases.
    (2) collection of a state sales tax on internet purchases.
    (3) collection of a state sales tax on mail order purchases.
    (4) collection of a state tax on internet use.
    (5) establishment of state regulation of internet use.

11. Which of the following is *not* an argument used in the "Pro" statement?

    (1) State law already requires payment of a sales tax on purchases made through catalogs or out-of-state businesses.
    (2) Lack of taxes on internet purchases constitutes unfair competition with "real" stores.
    (3) Michigan is losing a large amount of money because of internet purchases.
    (4) It will be easy for the state to collect sales taxes on internet purchases.
    (5) Individuals are required to report remote purchases on their state income tax form.

12. The "Con" position includes all of the following *except*

    (1) sales taxes on internet purchases will slow the growth of the internet.
    (2) internet retailers can be forced to collect sales taxes only by an act of Congress.
    (3) internet retailing is part of interstate commerce.
    (4) many dot.com companies will fail if sales taxes are instituted.
    (5) only an act of Congress can require purchasers to pay a sales tax on out-of-state internet purchases.

13. The term "use tax" in the "Pro" position refers to

    (1) a sales tax on purchases made from a catalog or other out-of-state business.
    (2) a sales tax on purchases made in traditional brick and mortar stores.
    (3) a tax collected by internet retailers and payed nationwide.
    (4) a tax paid by the consumer on purchases made from a Michigan internet retailer.
    (5) a tax paid by the consumer only on catalog purchases.

Items 14 to 16 refer to the following speech.

Slavery! How much misery is comprehended in that single word. No one [person] has more right to the full enjoyment of freedom than another. In every man's mind the good seeds of liberty are planted, and he who brings his fellow man down so low, as to make him contented with a condition of slavery, commits the highest crime against God and man. Brethren, your oppressors aim to do this. They endeavor to make you as much like beasts as possible. Then, and not till then, has American slavery done its perfect work.

If you would be free in this generation, here is your only hope. However much you and all of us may desire it, there is not much hope of redemption without the shedding of blood. If you must bleed, let it come all at once—rather die free men than live to be slaves.

In the name of the merciful God, and by all that life is worth, let it no longer be a debatable question, whether it is better to choose liberty or death.

In 1822, Denmark Vesey of South Carolina formed a plan for the liberation of his fellowmen. He was betrayed by the treachery of his own people, and died a martyr to freedom. The patriotic Nathaniel Turner followed Denmark Vesey. He was goaded to desperation by wrong and injustice. Next arose the immortal Joseph Cinque, the hero of the Amistad. He was a native African, and by the help of God he emancipated a whole shipload of his fellowmen on the high seas. Next arose Madison Washington, that bright star of freedom, and took his station in the constellation of true heroism. He was a slave on board the Brig Creole, of Richmond, bound to New Orleans with a hundred and four others. Nineteen struck for liberty or death. Only one life was taken, and the whole party was emancipated.

Brethren, arise, arise! Strike for your lives and liberty. Now is the day and the hour. Let every slave thoughout the land do this, and the days of slavery are numbered. You cannot be more oppressed than you have been—you cannot suffer greater cruelties than you have already. Rather die free men than live to be slaves. Remember that you are FOUR MILLION!

14. Which anti-slavery leader didn't succeed because of his own people?

    (1) Denmark Vesey   (4) Madison Washington
    (2) Nathaniel Turner   (5) Amistad
    (3) Joseph Cinque

15. Which statement is most true about the pre-Civil War South?

    (1) Only whites who owned slaves supported the system.
    (2) Opposition to slavery was nonexistent.
    (3) Strict controls prevented any slave revolts from occurring.
    (4) Blacks had many ways of resisting slavery.
    (5) The economic system could not exist without slavery.

16. Which would be considered a victory for civil rights over slavery or segregation?

    (1) Three-fifths Compromise in the Constitution
    (2) Dred Scott Decision
    (3) Plessy v. Ferguson
    (4) 15th Amendment
    (5) Missouri Compromise

Items 17 to 19 refer to the following graph.

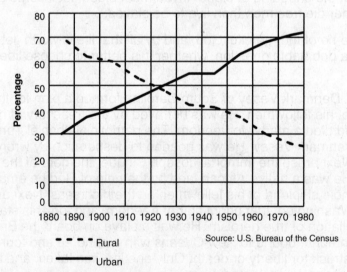

Source: U.S. Bureau of the Census

17. Which would be the best title for the graph?

    (1) Trends in Rural Settlements
    (2) Trends in Urban Settlements
    (3) 20th Century Population Trends
    (4) Population Growth Trends
    (5). A Century of Population Trends

18. Which would the graph be most useful in studying?

    (1) The growth of suburbia
    (2) The decline in farm production
    (3) Preferences for urban living
    (4) Urban problems
    (5) Non-farming rural residents

19. Which best describes the population trend?

    (1) Both rural and urban area population increased.
    (2) Rural area population increased while urban area population decreased.
    (3) Rural area population decreased while urban area population increased.
    (4) Both rural and urban area population decreased.
    (5) Both rural and urban area population remained the same.

Items 20 to 21 refer to the following table.

Educational Statistics, 1870-1910

	Total enrollment, public, elementary, and secondary schools	Enrollment, grades 9-12 and postgraduates (public schools)	Percent of population 17 years old graduating from high school	Bachelor's or first professional degrees awarded by institutions of higher education
1870-71	6,871,522	80,277	2.0%	9,371
1880	9,867,505	110,277	2.5%	12,896
1890	12,722,581	202,963	3.5%	15,539
1900	15,503,110	519,251	6.4%	27,410
1910	17,813,852	915,061	8.8%	37,199

20. Which statement is not true?

    (1) Public school enrollment increased over 10 times in a forty-year period.
    (2) There were more people graduating from college in 1910 than had enrolled in high school in 1870.
    (3) High school graduates increased fourfold during the period.
    (4) In 1880, less than ten times as many students enrolled in public schools as graduated from college.
    (5) Public education was becoming more important during this time.

21. Which statement is the most logical conclusion from the statistics?

    (1) School statistics were heavily impacted by the Civil War.
    (2) Many students graduating from high school were younger than 17.
    (3) High school enrollment and graduation rates slumped between 1890 and 1900.

(4) Most students never made it to high school.
(5) A high school education was not valued in 1910.

Items 22 to 24 refer to the following information.

Facts about Central America: Culturally, the region is part of Latin America, which refers to the colonial influence of the Spanish "Latin" rulers from the 1500s until almost the 20th century in some areas. Geographically, it is part of North America. Historically, this was the site of one of the great empires of the Mayas. The variety of experiences have created a people with a rich mixture of ethnic and cultural heritage. Today, Central American nations strive to keep their national independence and to raise their standard of living.

22. Central America includes all except

(1) Columbia.   (4) Costa Rica.
(2) Nicaragua.   (5) Guatemala.
(3) Panama.

23. Which is not a characteristic of Central America?

(1) It is part of North America.
(2) It has access to two oceans.
(3) Its heritage is modeled solely on the Spanish influence.
(4) It has strategic importance as a major trade artery.
(5) It contains nations that need economic assistance.

24. In what direction is Guatemala in relation to Costa Rica?

(1) Southwest   (4) West
(2) Northeast   (5) Northwest
(3) Southeast

Items 25 to 28 refer to the following passage.

DECLARATION OF INDEPENDENCE

We hold these truths to be self-evident, that all men are created equal; that they are endowed by their Creator with certain unalienable rights; that among these are life, liberty, and the pursuit of happiness. That, to secure these rights, governments are instituted among men, deriving their just powers from the consent of the governed; that, whenever any form of government becomes destructive of these ends, it is the right of the people to alter or to abolish it, and to institute a new government, laying its foundation on such principles, and organizing its powers in such form, as to them shall seem most likely to effect their safety and happiness. Prudence, indeed, will dictate that governments long established, should not be changed for light and transient causes; and, accordingly, all experience hath shown, that mankind are more disposed to suffer, while evils are sufferable, than to right themselves by abolishing the forms to which they are accustomed. But, when a long train of abuses and usurpations, pursuing invariably the same object, evinces a design to reduce them under absolute despotism, it is their right, it is their duty, to throw off such government and to provide new guards for their future security. Such has been the patient sufferance of these colonies, and such is now the necessity which constrains them to alter their former systems of government. The history of the present King of Great Britain is a history of repeated injuries and usurpations, all having, in direct object, the establishment of an absolute tyranny over these States.

25. According to the Declaration of Independence, the primary purpose of government is to

    (1) promote economic prosperity.
    (2) provide military security.
    (3) preserve fundamental human rights.
    (4) establish economic equality.
    (5) maintain democracy.

26. According to the Declaration of Independence, when a government prevents its citizens from enjoying inalienable rights, the people

    (1) have the right to elect new leaders.
    (2) must accept whatever the government does.
    (3) should move to another country.
    (4) can only call on leaders to change their practices.
    (5) have the right to abolish the existing government and establish a new one.

27. Which of the following terms best describes the Declaration's view of recent actions by the British government toward the American colonies?

    (1) conspiracy
    (2) benign neglect
    (3) incompetence
    (4) disinterest
    (5) ignorance

28. Which of the following ideas does *not* appear in this passage from the Declaration of Independence?

    (1) All men are created equal.
    (2) The people are normally reluctant to abolish their government.
    (3) The king has sought to establish an absolute tyranny.
    (4) All men have the right to property.
    (5) Human rights come from the Creator.

Item 29 refers to the following article.

[Ernesto] Miranda's case reached the U.S. Supreme Court in 1966. In a majority opinion, Chief Justice Earl Warren referred to the Court's decision in the case of Danny Escobedo and pointed out its importance in providing protection for individuals against overzealous police practices. Chief Justice Warren wrote: "The constitutional issue we decide… is the admissibility of statements obtained from a defendant questioned while in custody and deprived of his freedom of action."

The case that Chief Justice Warren was writing about was certainly a difficult one. On the one hand, there was the important question of the rights of a person under the protection of the Constitution. On the other hand, there was the equally important issue of interfering with the work of the police and preventing them from arresting criminals and bringing them to trial. Members of the Supreme Court were deeply divided on how the Court should rule.

The smallest possible majority of five justices made the historic ruling: "… it is clear that Miranda was not in any way apprised of his right to consult with an attorney and to have one present during the interrogation, nor was his right not to be compelled to incriminate himself effectively protected in any other manner. Without these warnings the statements were inadmissible. The mere fact that he signed a statement which contained a typed-in clause stating that he had 'full knowledge' of his 'legal rights' does not approach the knowing and intelligent waiver required to relinquish constitutional rights."

Source: *Great Trials in American History*, L. Arbetman, R. Roe, West Publishing, 1984.

29. Which instance would violate Miranda rights?

    (1) A non-English speaking person is told his rights in English.
    (2) A suspect understands his rights but refuses to sign a statement to that effect.
    (3) A person is questioned by police without having been read the Miranda rights, but is not arrested.
    (4) A suspect decides to confess without consulting an attorney after getting his Miranda rights explained.
    (5) An attorney advises his client to accept plea bargaining.

Items 30 to 32 refer to the following article.

"All men have the right to an environment capable of sustaining life and promoting happiness. If the accumulated actions of the past become destructive of this right, men now living have the further right to repudiate the past for the benefit of the future. And it is manifest that centuries of careless neglect of the environment have brought mankind to a final crossroads. The quality of our lives is eroded and our very existence threatened by our abuse of the natural world....

"Recognizing that the ultimate remedy for these fundamental problems is found in man's mind, not his machines, we call on societies and their governments to recognize and implement the following principles:

- We need an ecological consciousness that recognizes man as member, not master, of the community of living things sharing his environment.

- We must extend ethics beyond social relations to govern man's contact with all life forms and with the environment itself.

- We need a renewed idea of community which will shape urban environments that serve the full range of human needs.

- We must find the courage to take upon ourselves as individuals responsibility for the welfare of the whole environment, treating our own back yards as if they were the world and the world as if it were our back yard.

- We must develop the vision to see that in regard to the natural world private and corporate ownership should be so limited as to preserve the interest of society and the integrity of the environment.

- We need greater awareness of our enormous powers, the fragility of the earth, and the consequent responsibility of men and governments for its preservation.

- We must redefine 'progress' toward an emphasis on long-term quality rather than immediate quantity.

"We, therefore, resolve to act. We propose a revolution in conduct toward an environment which is rising in revolt against us. Granted that ideas and institutions long established are not easily changed; yet today is the first day of the rest of our life on this planet. We will begin anew."

Source: U.S. Government statistics

30. Which group is not called upon to act in the statement?

    (1) Private and corporate ownership   (4) Society
    (2) Government   (5) Communities
    (3) Individuals

31. What makes this quote relevant to economics?

    (1) Ethical use of the environment
    (2) Man as a member of the "community of all living things"
    (3) Need for individual responsibility
    (4) References to man's machines and past abuses
    (5) Progress, in terms of quality of life

32. Which is not an example of how environmental concerns can become economic priorities?

    (1) Recycling
    (2) Reforestation
    (3) Strip mining restoration
    (4) Greenhouse effect
    (5) Coal-generated electricity to replace imported oil

Items 33 to 35 refer to the diagram below.

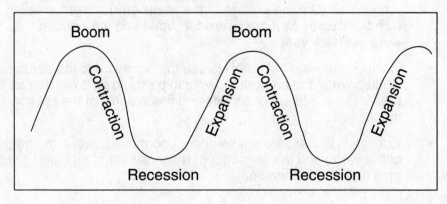

33. Which is the best title for the diagram above?

    (1) Boom and Bust
    (2) Causes of Economic Change
    (3) The Business Cycle
    (4) Causes of Recession
    (5) The History of Business Activity

34. In referring to the stages of the cycle above, on the previous page, which would not be a factor considered by economists?

    (1) Unemployment figures
    (2) Manufacturing production
    (3) Income levels
    (4) War or peace
    (5) Retail sales

35. Which is not a method used to encourage expansion during a recession?

    (1) Political crisis, such as war
    (2) Increased government spending
    (3) Increased taxation
    (4) Deregulation of industry
    (5) Restriction of imports

Items 36 to 39 refer to the following passage.

Business functions by public consent, and its basic purpose is to serve constructively the needs of society—to the satisfaction of society.

"Historically, business has discharged this obligation mainly by supplying the needs and wants of people for goods and services, by providing jobs and purchasing power, and by producing most of the wealth of the nation. This has been what American society required of business, and business on the whole has done its job remarkably well....

"In generating... economic growth, American business has provided increasing employment, rising wages and salaries, employee benefit plans, and expanding career opportunities for a labor force....

"Most important, the rising standard of living of the average American family has enabled more and more citizens to develop their lives as they wish with less and less constraint imposed on them by economic need. Thus, most Americans have been able to afford better health, food, clothing, shelter, and education than the citizens of any other nation have ever achieved on such a large scale....

Source: U.S. Government report

36. Which statement best summarizes the attitude of the quote?

    (1) Business has successfully met all the needs of society.
    (2) Business has done a good job supplying the economic needs of society.
    (3) Americans are best off with the least government.
    (4) All Americans have benefited from the rising living standard.
    (5) Government and business, in partnership, have created prosperity.

37. Which organization would be most likely to endorse this quote?

    (1) Chamber of Commerce   (4) Socialist Labor Party
    (2) Department of Labor   (5) AFL/CIO
    (3) General Accounting Office

38. Which of the following economic goals is not addressed by the quote?

    (1) Economic growth   (4) Economic justice
    (2) Economic stability   (5) Economic freedom
    (3) Economic security

39. Which is not one of the four basic economic activities of capitalism?

    (1) Production   (4) Service
    (2) Distribution   (5) Labor
    (3) Manufacturing

Item 40 refers to the following graph.

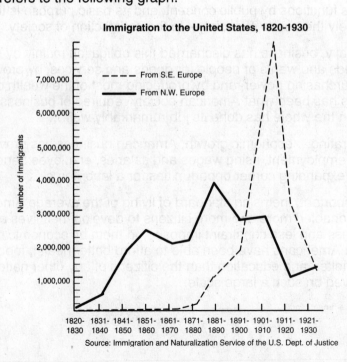

Immigration to the United States, 1820-1930

Source: Immigration and Naturalization Service of the U.S. Dept. of Justice

40. Northern and Western European immigration patterns were

    (1)   highest from 1851-60.
    (2)   lowest during the Civil War.
    (3)   peaking just before the turn of the century.
    (4)   declining as Southern and Eastern European immigration increased.
    (5)   the highest ever seen in U.S. history in 1841.

Items 41 and 42 refer to the following climate graphs.

Climate Graphs of 5 Canadian Cities,
showing Temperature (left scale) and Precipitation (right scale)

41. Which city experiences the highest rainfall in July?

    (1)   Vancouver   (4)   Winnipeg
    (2)   St. John's   (5)   Regina
    (3)   Fredericton

42. Which city is coldest in January?

    (1)   Vancouver   (4)   Winnipeg
    (2)   St. John's   (5)   Regina
    (3)   Fredericton

Items 43 to 45 refer to the following article.

The idea of a global shortage seems incredible when 70 percent of the Earth's surface is covered by H_2O. But 98 percent of that water is salty, making it unusable for drinking or agriculture. Desalinization is technically feasible, but it is far too expensive to use anywhere except in an ultra-rich, sparsely populated country like Saudi Arabia. Other options, like towing icebergs from the poles, are also beyond the means of poor nations.

The scarcity of fresh water for agriculture makes famines more likely every year. The world consumes more food than it produces, and yet there are few places to turn for additional cropland. Only by drawing on international stockpiles of grain have poorer countries averted widespread starvation. But those supplies are being depleted. From 1987 to 1989, the world's stock of grain fell from a 101-day surplus to a 54-day one. A drought in the U.S. bread-basket could rapidly lead to a global food calamity.

Even if rainfall stays at normal levels, current world food production will be difficult to maintain, much less increase. The food supply has kept pace with population growth only because the amount of land under irrigation has doubled in the past three decades. Now, however, agriculture is losing millions of acres of this land to the effects of improper watering.

From *Time Magazine*, August 20, 1990.

43. The best title for the article would be

  (1)   Alternative Water Supplies.
  (2)   Problems for Poor Nations.
  (3)   Famine Around the World.
  (4)   World Grain Supplies.
  (5)   Possible Water Problems.

44. World food supply is in danger because

  (1)   individual people are eating more.
  (2)   grain-growing nations have been unwilling to share surpluses.
  (3)   population is growing faster than the surplus of world grain.
  (4)   irrigated farmland is now being lost.
  (5)   poor nations waste money on desalinization projects.

45. According to the article, which country is a major supplier of grain to the world?

    (1) Saudi Arabia   (4) Soviet Union
    (2) Canada   (5) Brazil
    (3) United States

Items 46 to 48 refer to the following poll.

PRESIDENTIAL PREFERENCES OF DIFFERENT GROUPS

	Reagan	Carter
Total Sample	37	30
Democrats (29%)	18	56
Independents (43%)	32	24
Republicans (24%)	72	9
Detroit (15%)	24	57
Rest of tri-county area (25%)	40	28
Remainder of state (59%)	40	24
Liberal (22%)	26	37
Middle of the road (30%)	33	31
Conservative(42%)	50	25
Labor union households (37%)	30	34
Nonunion households (52%)	42	27
Black (10%)	4	73
White (87%)	41	25
Men (44%)	39	27
Women (56%)	36	32

46. Which conclusion can be made from the chart?

    (1) Reagan was most popular in Detroit.
    (2) There were more liberals than conservatives.
    (3) Republicans felt stronger about Reagan than Democrats felt about Carter.
    (4) Reagan was more popular with women than with men.
    (5) More people were independents than party members.

47. If you wanted Carter to campaign in his strongest areas, which would you avoid?

    (1) Detroit   (4) Black voters
    (2) Remainder of the state   (5) Liberals
    (3) Union households

48. Who wins the Presidential elections?

   (1) The winner of a majority of the Electoral College in December
   (2) The winner of a majority of the popular vote in November
   (3) The winner of the Electoral College in November
   (4) The candidate with the largest vote total in November
   (5) The party with the greatest popular vote

Items 49 and 50 refer to the following paragraph.

I will venture to say [declared Volney] that if a prize were proposed for the scheme of a regimen most calculated to injure the stomach, the teeth, and the health in general, no better could be invented than that of the Americans. In the morning at breakfast they deluge their stomach with a quart of hot water, impregnated with tea, or so slightly with coffee that it is mere colored water; and they swallow, almost without chewing, hot bread, half baked, toast soaked in butter, cheese of the fattest kind, slices of salt or hung beef, ham, etc., all which are nearly insoluble. At dinner they have boiled pastes under the name of puddings, and the fattest are esteemed the most delicious; all their sauces, even for roast beef, are melted butter; their turnips and potatoes swim in hog's lard, butter, or fat; under the name of pie or pumpkin, their pastry is nothing but a greasy paste, never sufficiently baked. To digest these viscous substances they take tea almost instantly after dinner, making it so strong that it is absolutely bitter to the taste, in which state it affects the nerves so powerfully that even the English find it brings on a more obstinate restlessness than coffee. Supper again introduces salt meats or oysters. As Chastellux says, the whole day passes in heaping indigestions on one another; and to give tone to the poor, relaxed, and wearied stomach, they drink Madeira, rum, French brandy, gin, or malt spirits, which complete the ruin of the nervous system.

The excerpt is from *A History of the United States During the Administrations of Jefferson and Madison* by Henry Adams, 1889.

49. Which was not part of the American diet in the early 1800s, according to this passage?

   (1) Dairy products   (4) Strong coffee
   (2) Pork products   (5) Alcoholic beverages
   (3) Vegetables

50. Which statement best expresses the author's opinion of the American
     diet?

     (1) Very unhealthy
     (2) Designed to keep the digestion calm
     (3) Necessarily based on what was available on farms
     (4) Cuisine that was fatty, but delicious
     (5) A product of the English colonial heritage

TEST 3: SCIENCE

Tests of General Educational Development

Directions

The Science Test consists of multiple-choice questions intended to measure your knowledge of the general concepts in science. The questions are based on short readings which often include a graph, chart, or figure. Study the information given and then answer the question(s) following it. Refer to the information as often as necessary in answering the questions.

You should spend no more than 80 minutes answering the questions in this booklet. Work carefully, but do not spend too much time on any one question. Be sure you answer every question. You will not be penalized for incorrect answers.

Do not mark in this test booklet. Record your answers to the questions on the separate answer sheet provided. Be sure all requested information is properly recorded on the answer sheet.

To record your answers, mark the numbered space on the answer sheet beside the number that corresponds to the question in the test booklet.

FOR EXAMPLE:

Which of the following is the smallest unit in a living thing?

(1) Tissue   (4) Muscle
(2) Organ   (5) Capillary
(3) Cell

① ② ● ④ ⑤

The correct answer is "cell"; therefore, answer space 3 would be marked on the answer sheet.

Do not rest the point of your pencil on the answer sheet while you are considering your answer. Make no stray or unnecessary marks. If you change an answer, erase your first mark completely. Mark only one answer space for each question; multiple answers will be scored as incorrect. Do not fold or crease your answer sheet. Return all test materials to the test administrator.

Directions: Choose the one best answer to each item.

Items 1 to 4 refer to the following passage.

An easy method of experimentally determining the acceleration due to gravity "g" is by measuring the period of one complete vibration of a simple pendulum of known length. If all the mass of the pendulum can be considered to be concentrated in the bob at the bottom, and if the amplitude of the vibration is kept small (less than a 5° arc), then "g" will be proportional to the length of the pendulum and inversely proportional to the square of the period. For example, on the Earth's surface where "g" is about 9.8 meters/sec², a 1-meter long pendulum has a vibrational period of 2.0 seconds and a 2-meter long pendulum has a vibrational period of 2.84 seconds.

1. If the acceleration due to gravity "g" on the Earth is determined by using a pendulum with a period of 4 seconds, then its length must be about

    (1)   1 meter.
    (2)   2 meters.
    (3)   3 meters.
    (4)   4 meters.
    (5)   5 meters.

2. On the moon the acceleration due to gravity is about one-sixth what it is here on the Earth. If a simple pendulum is to have a two-second period on the moon, its length must be close to

    (1)   1/2 meter.   (4)   1/5 meter.
    (2)   1/3 meter.   (5)   1/6 meter.
    (3)   1/4 meter.

3. Which of the following does not seem to affect the period of a simple pendulum?

    (1)   The acceleration due to gravity
    (2)   The mass of the bob
    (3)   The amplitude of the swing
    (4)   The length of the pendulum
    (5)   All of the above.

4. The units used to express the acceleration due to gravity express a measure of

   (1) velocity over time. (4) velocity over distance.
   (2) distance over time. (5) force over distance.
   (3) weight over time.

Items 5 to 9 refer to the following passage.

Ants are insects with two body parts, a thorax and abdomen, plus a head. Antennae protrude from the head. These antennae serve in communicating with other ants and examining food, and possess several other purposes. Ants have fixed compound eyes, which are made of many small lenses. Ants leave a trail when they travel; they never seem to get lost. Ants that have been trapped in resin and preserved for millions of years seem to be very similar to the ants of today.

5. The relationship between human eyelashes and the human eye is similar to the relationship between comblike hooks found on antennae and antennae themselves. What is this relationship?

   (1) The comblike hooks blink periodically to moisten the antennae.
   (2) The comblike hooks keep the antennae free from dust and dirt.
   (3) The comblike hooks are attractive to male ants when female ants move their antennae in a blinking manner.
   (4) The length of the comblike hooks and the antennae determine the age of the ants.
   (5) The comblike hooks help an ant find its way, similar to the function of eyelashes.

6. When an ant finds food, it leaves a trail behind it that has a different odor than the trail left by any other ant colony. This trail is most likely made of

   (1) food.
   (2) broken pieces of antennae.
   (3) drops of liquid from the abdomen.
   (4) lenses of compound eyes.
   (5) tiny pebbles.

7. How is a compound eye advantageous to an ant?

   (1) The ant sees multiple images of everything.
   (2) If one lens breaks, the ant still can see.
   (3) The eye can rotate and gives the ant better vision.
   (4) The ant can see moving objects more easily than objects that stand still.
   (5) Like a compound microscope, a compound eye magnifies objects a thousand times.

8.   Ants are considered to be most related to

(1) bees.   (4) fleas.
(2) spiders.   (5) crabs.
(3) fungus.

Item 9 refers to the following graph.

A microbiologist conducts an experiment involving the growth pattern of a bacterial population. The stages observed for the population are the Start phase, phase A, phase B, stationary, and death. The results of the growth are graphed. Study the accompanying graph of the growth of a bacterial population.

9.   From this pattern, the population is most likely to incorporate the most nutrients into its cells during the _____ phase.

(1) start
(2) A
(3) B
(4) stationary
(5) death

Items 10 to 11 refer to the following passage.

All matter can be divided into two categories: pure substances and mixtures. The pure substances can be further subdivided into elements and compounds, while mixtures can either be homogeneous or heterogeneous.

10.   According to the paragraph, which one of the following statements is true?

(1) A homogeneous mixture is a pure substance.
(2) Pure substances and mixtures are equivalent terms for the same type of matter.

(3)   A compound can be a pure substance.

(4)   A heterogeneous mixture is only composed of one type of element.

(5)   All matter is one lump that cannot be categorized.

11.   If a homogeneous mixture is combined with a heterogeneous mixture, what type of matter will result?

(1)   A homogeneous mixture
(2)   A heterogeneous mixture
(3)   A pure substance
(4)   The two mixtures will not combine because they are too different.
(5)   A new type of matter will result that has not yet been classified.

Item 12 refers to the following figure.

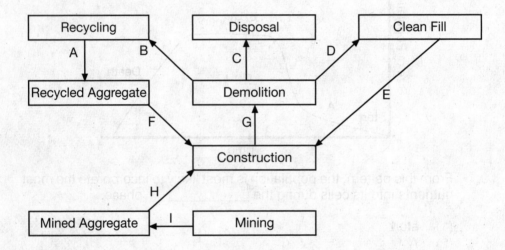

Aggregate is crushed stone or gravel that is used to make concrete. The stone and gravel are non-renewable resources. The U.S. Geological Survey works with different agencies to address sustainability issues. They have developed materials flow cycles for different materials. Above is the cycle for aggregates.

12.   In order to increase construction using concrete and reduce the amount of material mined, which of the following pathways would be required?

(1)   decrease A
(2)   increase B
(3)   increase C
(4)   decrease G
(5)   decrease I

Item 13 refers to the following passage.

The root is a region of active growth in a flowering plant. The root cap covers the tip of the root and protects the root as it grows into the soil. It shields the actively dividing cells that can be found in the meristematic region. The meristem consists of actively dividing cells from which all the other tissues of the root are formed. Immediately behind the meristem is the region of elongation. Here cells stop dividing and begin to grow and elongate by taking in large amounts of water. In the region of maturation, the root cells differentiate into the permanent tissues of the root, for example, the xylem and the phloem tissues. Root cells eventually specialize, carrying out different roles.

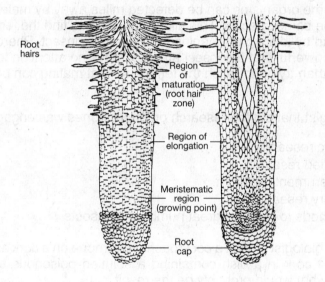

Root hairs

Region of maturation (root hair zone)

Region of elongation

Meristematic region (growing point)

Root cap

13. Out of the choices provided, where can the most specialized cells be found?

   (1)   root cap
   (2)   meristematic region
   (3)   region of elongation
   (4)   region of maturation
   (5)   none of the above

Items 14 to 16 refer to the following passage.

Scientific investigation involves two areas: pure science and applied science. Pure science is basic research, or the attempt to answer questions simply for the sake of knowledge itself. Applied science uses the knowledge gained from pure science to solve practical problems. Consider the following example: A biologist wants to know how insects attract mates. After much research, observation, and experimentation she discovers a substance called a pheromone, which is produced by the female insect and released into the air as an invisible gas, much like perfume. Pheromones are chemicals that are given off by organisms and affect or influence the behavior or the development of an individual organism. Pheromones are also known as "sex attractants" and are specific according to the type of organism. She found that pheromones produced by some organisms can be detected miles away by male organisms of the same species. This allows the male to find the female much faster than by looking or listening for the female insect. Pheromones are so powerful that the insect attracted pays no attention to anything other than trying to reach the female so that mating can begin.

14. The biologist that did the research on pheromones was engaged in

(1) basic research.
(2) applied research.
(3) government research.
(4) library research.
(5) methods to produce great numbers of insects.

15. If another biologist placed a cockroach pheromone on a cork and then placed the cork in a dish containing a solution poisonous to cockroaches, what would probably be the result?

(1) No cockroaches would be affected.
(2) Over a period of time, the dish would gradually be filled with dead cockroaches that crawled through the poison in an attempt to mate with the cork.
(3) Moths would be attracted to the pheromone impregnated cork.
(4) Cockroaches would surround the dish but not cross the poison.
(5) Not enough data has been given.

16. If a biologist used pheromones to attract male cockroaches to a cork containing a contact poison in hopes of ridding his home of cockroaches, what would this be an example of?

(1) Pure science   (4) Government research
(2) Basic research   (5) The scientific method
(3) Applied science

Item 17 refers to the following passage.

The exhaust from automobiles includes nitrogen oxides and hydrocarbons. At the surface of the earth solar radiation initiates a series of chemical reactions with nitrogen oxides and hydrocarbons that produce ozone. Because these reactions are initiated by solar radiation, the more intense the solar radiation, the more ozone that is produced. Ozone is the main component of photochemical smog. It is an eye and respiratory irritant and can damage the growth of plants.

17. At which of the following times would the ozone concentration in cities with many automobiles be the greatest?

    (1)   in the morning during the summer
    (2)   in the morning during the winter
    (3)   at night in the summer
    (4)   at night in the winter
    (5)   in the afternoon during the summer

Item 18 refers to the following passage.

A zygote is the fertilized egg. Early in animal development, the zygote divides by mitosis. Through the first cell division, the zygote forms two daughter cells. Each of these cells divides. By this pattern of cell division, an early animal embryo with more cells is produced.

18. After five cycles of cell division, _____ cells will exist in the early embryo produced from the zygote.

    (1)   sixteen
    (2)   twenty-four
    (3)   thirty-two
    (4)   forty-eight
    (5)   sixty-four

Item 19 refers to the following table.

ERA	PERIOD	EVENTS	BEGAN MILIONS OF YEARS AGO
CENOZOIC	Quaternary	Age of humans. Four major glacial advances.	2
	Tertiary	Increase in mammals. Appearance of primates. Mountain building in Europe and Asia.	65
MESOZOIC	Cretaceous	Extinction of dinosaurs. Increase in flowering plants and reptiles.	140
	Jurassic	Birds. Mammals. Dominance of dinosaurs. Mountain building in western North America.	195
	Triassic	Beginning of dinosaurs and primitive mammals.	230
PALEOZOIC	Permian	Reptiles spread and develop. Evaporate deposits. Glaciation in Southern Hemisphere.	280
	Carboniferous	Abundant amphibians. Reptiles appear.	345
	Devonian	Age of fishes. First amphibians. First abundant forests on land.	395
	Silurian	First land plants. Mountain building in Europe.	435
	Ordovician	First fishes and vertebrates.	500
	Cambrian	Age of marine invertebrates.	600
PRECAMBRIAN TIME		Beginning of life. At least five times longer than all geologic time following.	

Table from *Introduction to Oceanography*, fourth edition, 1988 by David A. Ross, Prentice Hall.

19. Which sequence of life is correct?

(1) Invertebrates, Fish, Reptiles, Mammals
(2) Fish, Invertebrates, Mammals, Birds
(3) Plants, Invertebrates, Forests, Fish
(4) Invertebrates, Mammals, Birds, Plants
(5) Mammals, Plants, Birds, Reptiles

Item 20 refers to the following passage.

Chromosomes occur in the body cells of most plants and animals in homologous (matched) pairs. For example, there are twenty-three pairs of chromosomes in the body cells of humans. In the fruit fly there are four pairs of chromosomes in a body cell. Cells with paired chromosomes are diploid. Mitosis is cell division that produces diploid cells. Cells with one chromosome of each kind are haploid. Haploid cells are produced by meiosis.

20. The chromosomes pictured above are single-stranded. They have not duplicated. Select the correct statement about the cell featured in the accompanying drawing.

    (1)   A haploid cell produced from this cell will have ten chromosomes.
    (2)   A haploid cell produced from this cell will have five chromosomes.
    (3)   This cell is haploid.
    (4)   This cell is not a body cell.
    (5)   This cell was produced by meiosis.

Items 21 to 22 refer to the following passage.

Over three hundred years ago, a British scientist named Robert Hooke was looking through a microscope at thin sections of cork. He noticed that there were many cavities in the cork. He coined the term "cells" to refer to these cavities. In 1835, Felix Dujardin was able to view living cells through a microscope. In 1838, Matthias Schleiden proposed that all plants are composed of cells, and in 1840 Theodor Schwann stated that all animals are made of cells. Approximately twenty years later, Rudolf Virchow published his observations that disease affected only living things. Today, we know that the information gained by these men is summed up in what is known as "The Cell Theory." The Cell Theory states that: 1) all living things are composed of cells; 2) cells carry on the life processes such as using energy, taking in nutrients, organizing protoplasm, having a life span, reproduction, adapting, and having irritability; and 3) all cells are produced from pre-existing cells.

21. Which of the following would not be considered to be a living thing?

    (1)   a rose   (4)   an amoeba
    (2)   a fungus   (5)   a sponge
    (3)   a virus

22.   According to the Cell Theory, an icicle is

   (1)   alive because it grows by the addition of more water.
   (2)   alive because it has a life span that involves a beginning, growth, a period of maturity, a period of decline, and finally, death.
   (3)   alive because it can reproduce.
   (4)   not alive because it is composed of cells.
   (5)   not alive because it is not composed of cells, it cannot reproduce, and it does not carry out any of the life functions.

Item 23 refers to the following passage.

   The top part of the soil is the active soil. Plant roots and animals are active in this area. Between the active soil and the bedrock is the parent material. The parent material may be weathered bedrock or it may be material deposited by water, glaciers, wind, and gravity. Parent materials that are transported from other areas and deposited are called surficial deposits. Surficial deposits differ with respect to particle size, shape, and depth. These characteristics depend on how the materials were transported. Therefore, the surficial deposits have names that relate to how the materials were transported. The main types of surficial deposits and their transporting agents are summarized in the following table. In many cases combinations of the names are used to more precisely identify the surficial deposits.

Transporting Agent	Type of Surficial Deposit
Glacial ice	glacial till
Rivers	fluvial
Wind	eolian
Gravity (landslides, etc.)	colluvial
Lakes	lacustrine
Ocean deposits	marine

23.   Surficial deposits from running meltwater under or at the ice margin of glaciers are most appropriately called

   (1)   till.
   (2)   fluvial.
   (3)   glaciomarine.
   (4)   fluvioglacial.
   (5)   glaciolacustrine.

Items 24 to 27 refer to the following information.

Isaac Newton was the first to point out that every mass in the universe attracts every other mass. This statement is known as the Law of Universal Gravitation. This attraction between bodies is proportional to the mass of each and is inversely proportional to the square of the distance between their centers. Also, by Newton's Third Law of Motion, this attraction must be the same on each pair of masses but in an opposite direction. For example, it is known that the Earth pulls on the moon with an average force of 2×10^{20} N and the moon pulls on the Earth with an average force of 2×10^{20} N.

**Relative Masses and Average Separations
Moon, Earth and Sun**

24. Newton's Universal Law of Gravitation implies that

    (1)   the attraction between the moon and the sun is the same as that between the moon and the Earth.
    (2)   the attraction between the Earth and the sun is the same as that between the moon and the Earth.
    (3)   the pull of the sun on the Earth is the same as the pull of the Earth on the sun.
    (4)   the pull of the sun on the moon must be 3×10^{19} N.
    (5)   the pull of the Earth on the sun must be 8×10^{24} N.

25. The pull of the sun on the Earth is

    (1)   about 82 times stronger than the pull of the sun on the moon.
    (2)   about 82 times weaker than the pull of the sun on the moon.
    (3)   about 393 times stronger than the pull of the sun on the moon.
    (4)   about 393 times weaker than the pull of the sun on the moon.
    (5)   about the same as the pull of the sun on the moon.

26. If the distance between the moon and the Earth was doubled, then the gravitational pull of the Earth on the moon would be

   (1) 8×10^{20} N.   (4) 5×10^{19} N.
   (2) 4×10^{20} N.   (5) 1×10^{19} N.
   (3) 2×10^{20} N.

27. If the Earth and the sun had the same mass, then the pull of the moon on the Earth would be about

   (1)   the same as the pull of the moon on the sun.
   (2)   393 times greater than the pull of the moon on the sun.
   (3)   393 times weaker than the pull of the moon on the sun.
   (4)   154,450 times greater than the pull of the moon on the sun.
   (5)   154,450 times weaker than the pull of the moon on the sun.

Items 28 and 29 refer to the following passage.

   Matter is found in three states: solid, liquid, and gas. Gases are both compressible and expandable. The liquid state and the solid state are both condensed phases since molecules "stick" together by attractive forces.

28. Why do two Br_2 molecules "stick" together at low temperatures?

   (1)   Ice forms between the molecules and prevents their separation.
   (2)   An increase in thermal energy causes the molecules to approach each other.
   (3)   The attraction between the molecules is stronger than the thermal energy pushing them apart, causing them to "stick."
   (4)   The Br_2 molecules expand quickly and bump into one another.
   (5) Br_2 molecules cannot "stick" together because Br_2 is a gas at all temperatures.

29. If the states of matter were organized in terms of randomness of the molecular arrangements, from most random to least random, the order would be

   (1)   solid, liquid, gas.   (4)   gas, liquid, solid.
   (2)   liquid, solid, gas.   (5)   liquid, gas, solid.
   (3)   gas, solid, liquid.

Items 30 to 31 refer to the following passage.

   When an Earthquake occurs, some of the energy released travels through the ground as waves. Two general types of waves are generated. One type, called the P wave, is a compression wave that alternately compresses and stretches the rock layers as it travels. A second type is a

Shear wave, called the S wave, which moves the rocks in an up and down manner.

A graph can be made of the travel times of these waves.

Distance from Epicenter (kilometers)

30. The main reason that a Time-Travel graph can be used to determine distance to an Earthquake's point of occurrence is that

    (1) S waves move up and down.
    (2) P waves are compressional.
    (3) P waves travel faster than S waves.
    (4) S waves travel faster than P waves.
    (5) P and S waves travel together.

31. Approximately how many minutes does it take a P wave to travel 8000 km?

    (1) 6 minutes   (4) 15 minutes
    (2) 12 minutes   (5) 18 minutes
    (3) 3 minutes

Items 32 to 35 refer to the following paragraph.

Cells contain chromosomes. The number of chromosomes that are in a cell varies. In sexually reproducing organisms, the cells usually have two sets of chromosomes. Cells like these are said to be "diploid." In organisms that reproduce asexually, the cells are usually "haploid," or having one set of chromosomes. Cells reproduce themselves by means of a process called mitosis. Some organisms can reproduce themselves by budding, or breaking, when there is no sexual reproduction. Sexually reproducing organisms undergo a process whereby they produce haploid cells from diploid cells. These haploid cells are called sperms or eggs. When a sperm and an egg are united, they fuse to form a single cell called a zygote. The zygote of a human has 46 chromosomes. A zygote is a diploid cell and will undergo mitosis to produce a mature organism.

32. There are 46 chromosomes found in the cheek cell of a human male. If this cell were to undergo mitosis, how many chromosomes would be found in each resulting daughter cell?

(1) 2   (4) 46
(2) 10   (5) 92
(3) 24

33. Humans have 46 chromosomes in their body cells. How many chromosomes are found in the zygote?

(1) 2   (4) 46
(2) 10   (5) 92
(3) 23

34. If mitosis were not to occur in both a male and a female human and their sperm and egg were to unite to form a zygote, how many chromosomes would the zygote have?

(1) 2   (4) 92
(2) 23   (5) 184
(3) 46

35. Which of the following relates to a sperm?

(1) A single organism composed of two cells
(2) Haploid
(3) Undergoes meiosis to produce four zygotes
(4) Diploid
(5) Undergoes meiosis to produce four eggs

Items 36 and 37 refer to the following passage.

The following represents a food chain in a South American rain forest:

banana tree → butterfly → tree frog → snake → predatory bird

The tree is the producer in this food chain. The butterfly is a herbivore and primary consumer of the chain. All remaining links are successive consumers in the food chain. The tree frog is the first carnivore, a meat-eater, in this food chain.

36. The predatory bird in this food chain is a

(1) carnivore and secondary consumer.
(2) carnivore and tertiary consumer.
(3) carnivore and fourth-level consumer.
(4) herbivore and secondary consumer.
(5) herbivore and tertiary consumer.

37. At each successive link of this food chain, only ten-percent usable energy remains for the consumer at that link. If 500,000 kilocalories are available in the banana tree, how many kilocalories are available for the snake in the chain?

    (1)   50,000   (2)   5,000
    (3)   500   (4)   50
    (5)   5

Items 38 to 40 refer to the following information.

Scaling is used by scientists and engineers to make predictions about what will happen if the size of a structure is increased or decreased dramatically. For example, model airplanes are built and studied under different conditions, and then predictions based on scaling arguments are used for understanding how a full-sized airplane will behave under similar circumstances.

For simple objects, the surface area is proportional to the square of its linear dimension. The volume is proportional to the cube of its linear dimension, and the strength is proportional to the cross-sectional area. For like materials, weight is proportional to volume.

38. Tripling the linear size of a bowling ball will increase its weight by

    (1)   twenty-seven and its surface area by nine.
    (2)   nine and its surface area by three.
    (3)   three and its surface area by nine.
    (4)   nine and its surface area by twenty-seven.
    (5)   twenty-seven and its surface area by three.

39. A small wood chair can support 25 lbs. Another wood chair is built with the same design but scaled up four times. Its strength will increase by

    (1)   four and its weight by sixteen.
    (2)   eight and its weight by thirty-two.
    (3)   four and its weight by thirty-two.

    (4)   sixteen and its weight by eight.

    (5)   sixteen and its weight by sixty-four.

40.   Suppose apples came in four sizes: A (6 cm), B (7cm), C (8 cm), and D (9 cm). Assuming each has the same density, a kilogram of what sized apples will produce the most skin when peeled?

    (1)   A   (4)   D

    (2)   B   (5)   They all produce the same amount of skin.

    (3)   C

Item 41 is based on the following passage.

Every living thing contains proteins. A protein molecule is composed of molecules called amino acids. These amino acids are chemically bonded together to form a chain (the protein molecule). Amino acids are generally composed of carbon, hydrogen, oxygen, and nitrogen. Every amino acid is basically alike except for one molecular component. That component, called the "R" factor, makes the amino acid unique. There are 20 different amino acids that make up hundreds of thousands of different kinds of proteins. Proteins are what make up our skin, our hair, our muscles, our cartilage, and many other components of our body. There is very little that is found in a living organism that is not composed, in part, of protein molecules. Protein molecules are specific to the organism of which they are a part. Therefore cow muscle protein cannot be found in the muscles of humans, and neither can chicken muscle protein be found in the muscles of hawks.

41.   If a chain of amino acids makes up a protein molecule, then one protein can be different from another protein by

    (1)   only the length of the protein molecule.

    (2)   the length of the protein molecule, and the order and type of amino acids in the protein molecule.

    (3)   only the type of amino acids found in the protein molecule.

    (4)   only the number of chemical bonds found in the protein molecule.

    (5)   only the order of amino acids in the protein.

Items 42 and 43 refer to the following information.

Substance	Length of Molecules
gasoline	short
tar	long
lubricating oil	medium

A liquid that flows with ease has molecules that do not tend to tangle. Tangles occur easily when long chains of atoms flow by one another. Viscosity is the resistance of liquids to flow.

42. According to the above information, which substance is most viscous?

    (1) Tar
    (2) Gasoline
    (3) Lubricating oil
    (4) Tar and lubricating oil are equally viscous
    (5) Gasoline and tar have equal viscosity

43. Why does the viscosity of most substances decrease as the temperature rises?

    (1) Chains join to form much longer chains.
    (2) Thermal energy rises and chains vibrate more, which causes more tangling.
    (3) The chains vaporize and less are present to tangle.
    (4) Most chains circularize.
    (5) Long chains break to form shorter chains.

Items 44 to 46 refer to the following paragraph.

   A flower is composed of several different modified leaves. The sepals are modified leaves that encircle the flower when it is in "bud." Sepals are green and protect the bud while it is developing into a flower. Just inside the sepals are the petals. The petals are usually large, showy, and brightly colored. They serve as a means of advertisement for animal pollinators that are attracted to bright patterns. Inside the petals are the stamens. The stamens are a two-part structure made up of the anther and the filament. The filament supports the anther. The anther is a structure that houses the developing pollen grains. In the very center of the flower is the pistil. The pistil is a series of modified leaves (the carpels) that contain the ovules. A pistil is composed of three basic parts: the stigma, the style, and the ovary/ovaries. The stigma is a sticky knob that receives the pollen. The pollen germinate and grow downward into the filamentous style and into the ovary and ultimately fertilize the egg that is contained within the ovary.

44. The modified leaves that produce the ovules are the

    (1) sepals.
    (2) petals.
    (3) carpels.
    (4) stigmas.
    (5) styles.

45. Some children pass by a bunch of flowers. After this interaction, bees are no longer attracted to the flowers. What did the children do?

    (1) They separated the sepals from the rest of the bud.
    (2) They crushed the pollen.
    (3) They crushed the stigma, which receives the pollen.
    (4) They plucked off all of the petals.
    (5) They separated the anther from the filament.

46. If a bug invades a flower that has not yet budded and causes damage to the petals, the bug must also have the ability to damage the

(1) sepals.   (4) style.
(2) stamens.   (5) ovary.
(3) pistil.

Items 47 and 48 refer to the following passage.

The boiling point of a liquid in an open system is the temperature where atmospheric pressure is equivalent to the vapor pressure of the liquid. Additionally, the boiling point of a liquid is the highest temperature at which there can be liquid as a component of a system.

47. Bubbles form in a boiling liquid because

(1) air from the atmosphere is entering the liquid.
(2) the liquid is condensing to form a gas.
(3) helium gas, which is lighter than any liquid, is rising.
(4) the liquid is vaporizing.
(5) microorganisms in the liquid are carrying out respiration.

48. A kettle containing water is heated to a boil. If the water is allowed to boil for fifteen minutes, what effect will this have on the volume of the water?

(1) The volume will increase as water molecules are created in the hot air over the kettle.
(2) The volume will remain constant.
(3) The volume will occasionally increase and decrease due to the effects of atmospheric pressure.
(4) The volume will decrease.
(5) The volume will remain constant only if the kettle is uncovered.

Item 49 refers to the following passage.

Energy is required for almost all aspects of life. Renewable resources are those that are replaced within a reasonable period of time (less than 50 to 100 years). Non-renewable resources are those that take thousands or millions of years to be replaced.

The five major sources of energy used in the USA in 1994 are shown in the following figure. Natural gas, coal, and oil are produced by the decomposition of organic matter and the chemical and physical changes within the earth over millions of years. Energy is obtained from burning the natural gas, coal, or oil. Hydroelectric energy is produced from the energy contained in falling water. A dam is built on a river, which creates a reservoir. The water falling over the dam is used to drive turbines to create energy. Nuclear energy is obtained from the fission of uranium which releases heat energy. Uranium is found in small amounts in the earth's crust. The heat energy is used to convert water to steam which drive turbines, creating usable energy.

Percentage of Different Types of Energy Used in the USA in 1994

Hydroelectric 3.5%

Nuclear 8.0%

Natural gas 24.9%

Coal 22.9%

Oil 40.7%

49. What percent of the energy used in the USA in 1994 was obtained from non-renewable resources?

    (1)   3.5 %
    (2)   8.0 %
    (3)   11.5 %
    (4)   88.5 %
    (5)   96.5%

Item 50 refers to the passage below.

Meiosis is cell division that produces sex cells called gametes. During meiosis these gametes receive genes on chromosomes from a dividing parent cell. As the parent cell divides, the genes and chromosomes sort independently. A gamete receives one gene from each gene pair in the parent cell. For example, if a parent cell has the genes Aa and Bb on different chromosome pairs, it can produce four genetically different kinds of sex cells by meiosis: AB, Ab, aB, and ab. The greater the number of different kinds of cells, the greater the variation.

50. Select the genotype that produces the greatest genetic variation in the sex cells produced by meiosis. Assume that the gene pairs are on different chromosome pairs.

    (1)   AABBcc
    (2)   aabbCC
    (3)   AaBbCc
    (4)   AaBbCC
    (5)   AaBBCC

TEST 4: LANGUAGE ARTS: READING

Tests of General Educational Development

Directions

The Language Arts: Reading Test consists of excerpts from classical and popular literature and articles about literature or the arts. Each excerpt is followed by multiple-choice questions about the reading material.

Read each excerpt first and then answer the questions following it. Refer back to the reading material as often as necessary in answering the questions.

Each excerpt is preceded by a "purpose question." The purpose question gives a reason for reading the material. Use these purpose questions to help focus your reading. You are not required to answer these purpose questions. They are given only to help you concentrate on the ideas presented in the reading materials.

You should spend no more than 65 minutes answering the questions in this booklet. Work carefully, but do not spend too much time on any one question. Be sure you answer every question. You will not be penalized for incorrect answers.

Do not mark in this test booklet. Record your answers on the separate answer sheet provided. Be sure all requested information is properly recorded on the answer sheet. To record your answers, mark the numbered space on the answer sheet beside the number that corresponds to the question in the test booklet.

FOR EXAMPLE:

It was Susan's dream machine. The metallic blue paint gleamed, and the sporty wheels were highly polished. Under the hood, the engine was no less carefully cleaned. Inside, flashy lights illuminated the instruments on the dashboard, and the seats were covered by rich leather upholstery.

The subject ("It") of this excerpt is most likely

(1)   an airplane.   (4)   a boat.
(2)   a stereo system.   (5)   a motorcycle.
(3)   an automobile.

① ② ● ④ ⑤

The correct answer is "an automobile"; therefore, answer space 3 would be marked on the answer sheet.

Do not rest the point of your pencil on the answer sheet while you are considering your answer. Make no stray or unnecessary marks. If you change an answer, erase your first mark completely. Mark only one answer space for each question; multiple answers will be scored as incorrect. Do not fold or crease your answer sheet. Return all test materials to the test administrator.

Reprinted with permission of the General Educational Development Testing Service of the American Council on Education.

Directions: Choose the <u>one best answer</u> to each item.

<u>Items 1 to 3</u> refer to the following selection.

WHY IS THIS WOMAN SO FEARLESS?

CREON: (*slowly, dangerously*) And you, Antigone,
    you with your head hanging,—do you confess this thing?

ANTIGONE: I do. I deny nothing.

CREON: (*to Sentry*): You may go.

    Exit Sentry.

    (*To Antigone*) Tell me, tell me briefly:
    Had you heard my proclamation touching this matter?

ANTIGONE: It was public. Could I help hearing it?

CREON: And yet you dared defy the law.

ANTIGONE: I dared.
    It was not God's proclamation. That final Justice
    That rules the world below makes no such laws.
    Your edict, King, was strong,
    But all your strength is weakness itself against
    The immortal unrecorded laws of God.
    They are not merely now: they were, and shall be,
    Operative for ever, beyond man utterly.
    I knew I must die, even without your decree:
    I am only mortal. And if I must die
    Now, before it is my time to die,
    Surely this is no hardship: can anyone
    Living, as I live, with evil all about me,
    Think Death less than a friend? This death of mine
    Is of no importance; but if I had left my brother
    Lying in death unburied, I should have suffered.
    Now I do not.
    You smile at me. Ah Creon,
    Think me a fool, if you like; but it may well be
    That a fool convicts me of folly.

CHORUS: Like father, like daughter: both headstrong, deaf to reason!
    She has never learned to yield.

CREON: She has much to learn.
    The inflexible heart breaks first, the toughest iron
    Cracks first, and the wildest horses bend their necks
    At the pull of the smallest curb.
    Pride? In a slave?
    This girl is guilty of double insolence,

Breaking the given laws and boasting of it.
Who is the man here,
She or I, if this crime goes unpunished?

From *Antigone* by Sophocles

1.   What is the conflict between Creon and Antigone?

     (1)   Antigone wants to marry a man whom Creon does not approve of.
     (2)   Antigone is deaf.
     (3)   Antigone has broken one of Creon's laws.
     (4)   Antigone's brother has just died.
     (5)   Creon is jealous of Antigone's independence.

2.   Why is Antigone not afraid to die?

     (1)   Because she is old.
     (2)   Because she has obeyed the laws of God.
     (3)   Because she is a slave.
     (4)   Because she has disobeyed the king.
     (5)   Because she is immortal.

3.   What does Creon seem to be concerned with in the last two lines?

     (1)   Punishment
     (2)   Antigone's virtue
     (3)   Antigone's morality
     (4)   Burial rituals
     (5)   His manhood

Items 4 to 6 refer to the following excerpt from a story.

WHAT DISILLUSIONMENTS DOES DEXTER EXPERIENCE?

1   "About Judy Jones."
        Devlin looked at him helplessly.
        "Well, that's—I told you all there is to it. He treats her like the
        devil. Oh, they're not going to get divorced or anything. When he's
5   particularly outrageous she forgives him. In fact, I'm inclined to
        think she loves him. She was a pretty girl when she first came to
        Detroit."
        A pretty girl! The phrase struck Dexter as ludicrous. "Isn't she a
        pretty girl, any more?"
10   "Oh, she's all right."
        "Look here," said Dexter, sitting down suddenly. "I don't under-
        stand. You say she was a 'pretty girl' and now she's 'all right.' I
        don't understand what you mean—Judy Jones wasn't a pretty girl,
        at all. She was a great beauty. Why, I knew her. I knew her. She
15   was—"

Devlin laughed pleasantly.

"I'm not trying to start a row," he said. "I think Judy's a nice girl and I like her. I can't understand how a man like Lud Simms could fall madly in love with her, but he did." Then he added: "Most of

20 the women like her."

Dexter looked closely at Devlin, thinking wildly that there must be a reason for this, some insensitivity in the man or some private malice.

"Lots of women fade just like that," Devlin snapped his fingers.

25 "You must have seen it happen. Perhaps I've forgotten how pretty she was at her wedding. I've seen her so much since then, you see. She has nice eyes."

A sort of dullness settled down upon Dexter. For the first time in his life he felt like getting very drunk. He knew that he was laugh-

30 ing loudly at something Devlin had said, but he did not know what it was or why it was funny. When, in a few minutes, Devlin went he lay down on his lounge and looked out the window at the New York skyline into which the sun was sinking in dull lovely shades of pink and gold.

35 He had thought that having nothing else to lose he was invulnerable at last—but he knew that he had just lost something more, as surely as if he had married Judy Jones and seen her fade before his eyes.

F. Scott Fitzgerald, *All the Sad Young Men*, New York, Charles Scribner's Sons, copyright 1922, 1950.

4. The underlying meaning of lines 35-38 is

   (1) Dexter is saddened but relieved that he never married Judy.
   (2) Judy was never meant for Dexter.
   (3) even though they never married, Dexter is still touched by Judy's life.
   (4) nothing can hurt Dexter any more than Judy did.
   (5) he still wishes that he and Judy could be united.

5. Which of the following quotations does not apply to Dexter's situation concerning Judy?

   (1) It is impossible to love and be wise. —Francis Bacon, *Of Love*
   (2) Love is blind. —Geoffrey Chaucer, "The Merchant," from *The Canterbury Tales*
   (3) Love comforteth like sunshine after rain. —Shakespeare, *Venus and Adonis*
   (4) Speak of me as I am, one that loved not wisely but too well. —Shakespeare, *Othello*
   (5) Love blinds all men alike, both the reasonable, and the foolish. —Meander, *Andria*

6.   From this dialogue, we can conclude that Devlin is being

    (1)   argumentative and harsh.   (4)   optimistic and charitable.
    (2)   realistic but kind.   (5)   rude but accurate.
    (3)   pessimistic and unforgiving.

<u>Items 7 to 10</u> refer to the following passage.

A SALES CONTRACT

THIS AGREEMENT is made and entered into this 31st day of January, 2002, between Richard Pojman, hereinafter referred to as the Seller, and Emily Barnes, hereinafter referred to as the Buyer.

Sale of Business. The Seller shall sell and the Buyer shall buy, free from all liabilities, the men's clothing store owned and conducted by the Seller under the name "Regal Men's Store" at the premises known as 120 North Main Street, Central City, Illinois.

Method of Payment. The purchase price for "Regal Men's Store" shall be $42,000. The Buyer shall pay to the Seller the purchase price in the following manner: (a) $5,000 by certified or cashier's check upon execution of this agreement; (b) $20,000 by certified or cashier's check at the date of closing; (c) the balance of $17,000 by a promissory note payable in consecutive monthly installments of $200, with interest at 8% per annum.

Seller's warranties. The Seller warrants and represents the following:

1. He is the owner of Regal Men's Store.

2. The financial statements about Regal Men's Store and its profits are true and accurate.

3. The Seller has no knowledge of any developments or future developments that would be adverse to the business of Regal Men's Store.

4. No litigation, governmental proceeding, or investigation is pending against or relating to said business.

Arbitration of disputes. All controversies arising under or in connection with, or relating to any alleged breach of this agreement, shall be submitted to a panel of three arbitrators. This panel shall be composed of two members chosen by the Seller and Buyer respectively and one additional member, to be chosen by the arbitrators. The findings of such arbitrators shall be conclusive and binding.

7.   According to the document, what does the term "Seller's warranties" mean?

    (1)   What the seller demands from the buyer

(2)   What the buyer demands from the seller

(3)   What the seller feels is likely to happen to the buyer

(4)   What the seller certifies as true and accurate to the buyer

(5)   Conditions that the buyer demands from the seller

8.   Which of the following is one of the Seller's warranties?

(1)   That the buyer will earn a profit from the business in the first three years

(2)   That any other parties who come forward with claims to ownership will not have any rights to the business

(3)   That all of the clothes are in good condition

(4)   That the financial statements about Regal Men's Store are generally accepted to be true and accurate

(5)   That the buyer will be happy with his purchase

9.   Which of the following is NOT a part of the "Method of Payment" agreement section of this document?

(1)   That the buyer shall pay to the seller $5,000 by certified or cashier's check upon execution of this agreement

(2)   That the buyer shall pay to the seller $40,000 by certified or cashier's check at the date of closing

(3)   That the buyer shall pay to the seller the balance of $17,000 by a promissory note

(4)   That the promissory note will be payable in consecutive monthly installments of $200

(5)   That the monthly installments will accrue at an 8% interest rate per annum

10.   According to the document, how will disputes be arbitrated?

(1)   The two lawyers will sit down and discuss any disputes.

(2)   The buyer and the seller will have to resolve their own disputes.

(3)   The buyer and the seller should go on a televised talk show and air their grievances in public.

(4)   The buyer and seller will take their grievances to a court of law, where the judge will arbitrate. The judge's findings will be the final ruling on the subject.

(5)   All controversies shall be submitted to a panel of three arbitrators.

Items 11 to 14 refer to the following excerpt from a story.

CAN DEATH UNITE LOVED ONES?

1   "It is coming, Maggie!" Tom said, in a deep hoarse voice, loosing the oars, and clasping her. The next instant the boat was no longer seen upon the water—and the huge mass was hurrying on in hideous triumph.

5   But soon the keel of the boat reappeared, a black speck on the golden water.

The boat reappeared—but brother and sister had gone down in an embrace never to be parted: living through again in one supreme moment the days when they had clasped their little hands in love and roamed the daisied fields together.

10   Nature repairs her ravages—repairs them with her sunshine, and with human labor. The desolation wrought by that flood had left little visible trace on the face of the earth, five years after. The fifth autumn was rich in golden corn-stacks, rising in thick clusters among the distant hedgerows: with echoes of eager voices, with hopeful lading and unlading.

15   And every man and woman mentioned in this history was still living—except those whose end we know.

Nature repairs her ravages—but not all. The uptorn trees are not rooted again; the parted hills are left scarred: if there is new growth, the trees are not the same as the old, and the hills underneath their green vesture bear the marks of the past rending. To the eyes that have dwelt on the past, there is no thorough repair....

20

25   Near the brick grave there was a tomb erected, very soon after the flood, for two bodies that were found in close embrace: and it was visited at different moments by two men who both felt that their keenest joy and keenest sorrow were forever buried there....

The tomb bore the names of Tom and Maggie Tulliver, and

30   below the names it was written:

"In their death, they were not divided."

George Eliot, *The Mill on the Floss* (abridged excerpt), N.Y., Doubleday Page and Co., 1901.

11. The tone of lines 11-16 is

    (1)   optimistic.   (4)   forboding.
    (2)   pessimistic.   (5)   None of the above.
    (3)   realistic.

12. The tone of lines 19-24 is

    (1)   optimistic.   (4)   sarcastic.
    (2)   encouraging.   (5)   compassionate.
    (3)   realistic.

13. Lines 19-24 reveal the meaning of the passage:

    (1)   nature, like a good doctor, can heal.
    (2)   not everything, once damaged, can be repaired.
    (3)   nothing can be permanently damaged.
    (4)   birth and death are a part of nature's plan.
    (5)   in time, all things can be replaced.

14. The sentence in lines 22-24, "To the eyes that have dwelt on the past, there is no thorough repair..." can be restated as

    (1) once you have known and loved something, you can never completely replace it.
    (2) some things are taken away from us prematurely.
    (3) people who dwell on the past can never be totally happy.
    (4) never "look back."
    (5) None of the above.

Items 15 to 19 refer to the following excerpt from a story.

1   Dear Fred—I try to find heart and life to tell you that it is all over with dear old Nolan. I have been with him on this voyage more than I ever was, and I can understand wholly now the way in which you used to speak of the dear old fellow. I could see that he
5 was not strong, but I had no idea the end was so near....
    "O Danforth," he said, "I know I am dying. I cannot get home. Surely, you will tell me something now?—stop! stop! Do not speak till I say what I am sure you know, that there is not in this ship, that there is not in America—God bless her!—a more loyal man than I
10 am. There cannot be a man who loves the flag as I do, prays for it as I do, or hopes for it as I do...."
    "Mr. Nolan," said I, "I will tell you everything you ask about. Only, where shall I begin?"...
    And he drank it in, and enjoyed it as I cannot tell you. He grew
15 more and more silent, yet I never thought he was tired or faint....
    But in an hour, when the doctor went in gently, he found Nolan had breathed his life away with a smile....
    We looked in his Bible, and there was a slip of paper, at the place where he had marked the text:
20   "They desire a country, even a heaven: wherefore God is not ashamed to be called their God: for he hath prepared for them a city."
    On this slip of paper he had written:
    "Bury me in the sea; it has been my home, and I love it... But
25 will not someone set up a stone for my memory at Fort Adams or at Orleans, that my disgrace may not be more than I ought to say on it

    'In memory of
    Phillip Nolan,
30   Lieutenant in the Army of the United States.

    He loved his country as no other man has loved her; but no man deserved less at her hands.' "

15. From lines 1-5, you can tell that Danforth now regards Nolan

    (1) with compassion.   (4) as a traitor.
    (2) with mixed feelings.   (5) indifferently.
    (3) with suspicion.

16. Nolan protests in lines 6-11 that

    (1) he wishes to go home.
    (2) he wants to live.
    (3) he has been treated unfairly.
    (4) nobody loves his country more than he.
    (5) no one understands him.

17. From lines 12-17, we can infer that Danforth related to Nolan information

    (1) that was classified.   (4) that was incorrect.
    (2) that gave his spirit peace. (5) reluctantly.
    (3) that caused him further unrest.

18. From a close reading of lines 6-17, we can form this analogy: Danforth's news to Nolan was as

    (1) exercise is to an athlete.
    (2) money is to a wealthy man's wallet.
    (3) peace is to a tormented spirit.
    (4) a toy is to a small child.
    (5) food is to a hungry man.

19. From the text Nolan had marked in his Bible, we can conclude that his burning desire was to have

    (1) a burial at sea.   (4) a country of his own.
    (2) an elaborate funeral.   (5) fame and fortune.
    (3) a medal of honor.

Items 20 to 25 refer to the following excerpt from an article.

VAN GOGH WAS A GENIUS, BUT WAS HE ALSO MAD?

     It has been almost exactly 100 years since Vincent van Gogh
1   propped his easel against a haystack near the Château d'Auvers
in France and fired a bullet into his chest. He managed to crawl
back to the house of a family named Ravoux, with whom he was
living. Doctors were summoned and the artist's younger brother,
5   Theo, rushed by train from Paris as soon as he heard the news.
     "I wish I could pass away like this," Vincent said as he lay
beside his brother, shortly before dying in the early morning of July
29, 1890, leaving behind hundreds of paintings and drawings no

10   one wanted. Theo had tried for years to sell them, not least in the
hope of recouping a fraction of the money he had shelled out to
support his hapless brother over the course of more than a decade. He had no luck, and neither did the Paris dealer, Julien
François (Pére) Tanguy, who had agreed to keep some of
15   Vincent's paintings in the attic of his shop.

     Was Vincent addicted to absinthe? Did he really chase Paul
Gauguin with a razor, or was that a story embroidered by Gauguin
to justify abandoning van Gogh in Arles? Did Theo die—six
months after his brother, at the age of 33, in an asylum near
20   Utrecht—from grief over Vincent's suicide? Was the artist epileptic
or manic depressive or did he suffer, as a recent article in the
Journal of the American Medical Association suggests, from an
inner-ear disorder that finally drove him in the winter of 1888 to lop
off part of his left ear in a desperate attempt to alleviate the pain?
25   An earlier generation of van Gogh biographers wove such
fanciful tales of the pathetic starving painter driven to drink and
lunacy that the latest crop of historians and writers has found it
necessary to undo, at least in part, the myth that has obscured the
man. As David Sweetman, author of the engaging new "Van
30   Gogh: His Life and His Art," says of the old biographies: "The one
significant conclusion that can be reached from them is that
whatever he was suffering from cannot be directly 'read' into his
art... the image of Vincent as an isolated Holy Fool, artist-sage or
whatever, has finally been exposed as the nonsense it always
35   was...."

Michael Kimmelman, "Vincent Obsessed," from *The New York Times Book Review*, August 12, 1990,
New York: copyright 1990, pp. 1, 22, 23.

20.   According to this review, the notion of Vincent van Gogh being a "mad
genius" is best explained as

    (1)   substantiated by incidents in his life.
    (2)   just a myth.
    (3)   created by his brother.
    (4)   proven by his suicide.
    (5)   challenged by recent historians and writers.

21.   The series of questions posed in lines 16-24 is used by the reviewer as
a literary device to

    (1)   prove his point that van Gogh was mad.
    (2)   give the reader insight into the controversial stories about van
Gogh's life.
    (3)   baffle the reader.
    (4)   amuse the reader.
    (5)   prove that van Gogh was not mad, but physically ill.

22. In lines 25-35 one new biographer

    (1)   questions old theories about van Gogh.
    (2)   accepts the "old" biographers' and writers' statements.
    (3)   rejects past and present theories.
    (4)   is uncertain about "old" and "new" reviews.
    (5)   None of the above.

23. The tone of this review is generally

    (1)   serious and informative.   (4)   derogatory and inflammatory.
    (2)   humorous and entertaining. (5)   None of the above.
    (3)   slanted and one-sided.

24. You can readily determine in lines 29-35 that van Gogh as the genius and madman

    (1)   has no basis in truth.
    (2)   has finally been exposed as the truth.
    (3)   is still debatable.
    (4)   has yet to be resolved.
    (5)   is best left for future biographers.

25. In lines 32 and 33, the word "read" as used in the sentence means

    (1)   summarized.   (4)   interpreted.
    (2)   questioned.   (5)   removed from.
    (3)   painted.

Items 26 to 28 refer to the following excerpt of an article.

WAS THIS MUSICIAN REALLY THE GREATEST BLUES SINGER-GUITARIST-SONGWRITER?

1   What we have in *Robert Johnson: The Complete Recordings* are solid facts in Stephen C. LaVere's meticulously researched liner notes, brief appreciations of Johnson by Keith Richards ("He was like a comet or meteor that came along and, BOOM, suddenly
5   he raised the ante, suddenly you just had to aim that much higher") and Eric Clapton ("I have never found anything more deeply soulful than Robert Johnson. His music remains the most powerful cry that I think you can find in the human voice, really"), lyrics and photos. And, of course, we have the songs—digitally
10   clarified and, as expected, at least as powerful and affecting as ever.
       The Robert Johnson recordings are musical art of the highest order, as rich and transcendent as anything produced by an American musician in this century—surely only a racist or classist
15   would argue otherwise. Was he really the greatest blues singer-guitarist-songwriter of all? Listening to Johnson in Frank Abbey's

lovingly restored and remastered new versions, the question
seems almost irrelevant. Johnson was a great one, all right, and
bluesman to the bottom of his soul. But at his most original, when
20   he is almost chilling, Johnson blows genre considerations and
invidious comparisons right out of the window.
Technically, Johnson the guitarist was an anomaly. He could
sing and play crossrhythms on the guitar, relating the parts in such
complex syncopations that, as Richards notes, "You think, 'This
25   guy must have three brains!' "... The music has a power that age
cannot dim. Familiarity with his work, even over many years,
breeds only a finer appreciation and a more acute sense of awe....

26.   In lines 4 and 5, "... suddenly he raised the ante..." most closely means:

    (1)   The musician raised the salary of musicians.
    (2)   Johnson raised the standards of excellence for musicians.
    (3)   The guitarist created a problem between musicians and the general public.
    (4)   He raised the risk of becoming obscure.
    (5)   Johnson aimed too high to actually achieve his goals.

27.   The reviewer answers the question in lines 15 and 16 ("Was he really the greatest...?")

    (1)   affirmatively by saying *yes*.
    (2)   negatively with a firm *no*.
    (3)   evasively by *avoiding* the question.
    (4)   *neither* affirmatively nor negatively by saying the question is of little importance.
    (5)   by *first affirming* then *denying* the question of Johnson's greatness.

28.   In a close reading of lines 22 through 27, we can conclude that Robert Johnson's music

    (1)   will soon become outdated.
    (2)   has no popular appeal.
    (3)   will survive the test of time.
    (4)   cannot endure the test of time.
    (5)   is the greatest of all time.

Items 29 to 33 refer to the following excerpt from a story.

WHAT DID THE NARRATOR LEARN DURING HER VISIT?

1   "Have a seat, Marguerite. Over there by the table."
    She carried a platter covered with a tea towel. Although she
warned that she hadn't tried her hand at baking sweets for some
time, I was certain that like everything else about her the cookies
5   would be perfect.
    As I ate she began the first of what we later called my "lessons
in living." She said that I must always be intolerant of ignorance
but understanding of illiteracy. That some people, unable to go to
school, were more educated and even more intelligent than
10   college professors. She encouraged me to listen carefully to what
country people called mother wit. That in those homely sayings
was couched the collective wisdom of generations.
    When I finished the cookies she brushed off the table and
brought a thick, small book from the bookcase. I had read *A Tale*
15   *of Two Cities* and found it up to my standards as a romantic novel.
She opened the first page and I heard poetry for the first time in
my life.
    "It was the best of times and the worst of times…"
    Her voice slid in and curved down through and over the words.
20   She was nearly singing. I wanted to look at the pages. Were they
the same that I had read? Or were there notes, music, lines on the
pages, as in a hymn book? Her sounds began cascading gently. I
knew from listening to a thousand preachers that she was nearing
the end of her reading, and I hadn't really heard, heard to under-
25   stand, a single word.
    "How do you like that?"
    It occurred to me that she expected a response. The sweet
vanilla flavor was still on my tongue and her reading was a wonder
in my ears. I had to speak.
30   I said, "Yes ma'am." It was the least I could do, but it was the
most also.
    "There's one more thing. Take this book of poems and memo-
rize one for me. Next time you pay me a visit, I want you to recite."

Maya Angelou, from *I Know Why the Caged Bird Sings*, copyright 1969 by Maya Angelou, New York, New York: Bantam Books, Feb., 1980.

29. From the beginning, we can judge that Marguerite's regard for her hostess is one of

    (1)   cool reserve.   (4)   awe and respect.
    (2)   fear.   (5)   no consequence.
    (3)   distrust.

30. You can equate the writer's "lessons in living," lines 6-12, with

    (1) wisdom.
    (2) unintelligence.
    (3) charm.
    (4) native intelligence.
    (5) "book" learning.

31. To be "intolerant of ignorance but understanding of illiteracy" implies

    (1) uneducated people are always intelligent.
    (2) illiterate people are always ignorant.
    (3) intolerance always means ignorance.
    (4) ignorant people are always educated.
    (5) educated people can sometimes be ignorant.

32. The author intended lines 16 and 17, "I heard poetry for the first time," to be interpreted

    (1) literally.
    (2) figuratively.
    (3) socially.
    (4) with "tongue in cheek."
    (5) None of the above.

33. After the poetic reading, lines 29 and 30, the writer reveals that she was

    (1) uneasy.
    (2) offended.
    (3) unable to express her feelings.
    (4) unimpressed.
    (5) eloquent in her praises.

Items 34 to 37 refer to the following poem.

WHY DOES THE SPEAKER STOP, THEN GO ON?

1   Whose woods these are I think I know
    His house is in the village though;
    He will not see me stopping here
    To watch his woods fill up with snow.

5   My little horse thinks it queer
    To stop without a farmhouse near
    Between the woods and frozen lake
    The darkest evening of the year.

    He gives his harness bells a shake
10 To ask if there is some mistake.
    The only other sound's the sweep
    Of easy wind and downy flake.

    The woods are lovely, dark and deep,
    But I have promises to keep,

15   And miles to go before I sleep,
           And miles to go before I sleep.

Robert Frost, "Stopping by Woods on a Snowy Evening," in *An Anthology of the New England Poets,* Ed. by Louis Untermeyer, New York: Random House, 1948.

34.   In the first stanza, the speaker stops by the woods because

     (1)   his horse is weary.
     (2)   he decides to visit a neighbor.
     (3)   he enjoys the silent beauty of the woodland.
     (4)   it's getting too dark to travel.
     (5)   some neighbor beckons him to stop.

35.   Stanzas two and three tell us that the horse

     (1)   knows this is the wrong path home.
     (2)   stops since he is weary.
     (3)   has lost the way.
     (4)   signals there is no farmhouse here.
     (5)   moves along stubbornly.

36.   The final stanza reveals that the woods are inviting, but the speaker

     (1)   decides not to stay since he has obligations.
     (2)   is confused.
     (3)   must go home to sleep.
     (4)   will return soon.
     (5)   None of the above.

37.   Symbolically, the poem presents a struggle between

     (1)   good and evil.   (4)   sickness and health.
     (2)   wealth and poverty.   (5)   past and present.
     (3)   life and death.

Items 38 to 40 refer to the following excerpt from an article.

HOW CAN TIME BE IMPRISONED IN A RECTANGLE?

1   Balzac had a "vague dread" of being photographed. Like some primitive peoples, he thought the camera stole something of the soul—that, as he told a friend, "every body in its natural state is made up of a series of ghostly images superimposed in layers to
5   infinity, wrapped in infinitesimal films." Each time a photograph was made, he believed, another thin layer of the subject's being would be stripped off to become not life as before but a membrane of memory in a sort of translucent anti-world.
      If that is what photography is up to, then the onion of the world
10 is being peeled away, layer by layer—lenses like black holes

gobbling up life's emanations. Mere images proliferate, while history pares down to a phosphorescence of itself.

15   The pictures made by photojournalists have the legitimacy of being news, fresh information. They slice along the hard edge of the present. Photojournalism is not self-conscious, since it first enters the room (the brain) as a battle report from the far-flung Now. It is only later that the artifacts of photojournalism sink into the textures of the civilization and tincture its memory.

20   If journalism—the kind done with words—is the first draft of history, what is photojournalism? Is it the first impression of history, the first graphic flash? Yes, but it is also (and this is the disturbing thing) history's lasting visual impression. The service that the pictures perform is splendid, and so powerful as to seem preternatural. But sometimes the power they possess is more than

25 they deserve.

    All great photographs have lives of their own, but they can be as false as dreams. Somehow the mind knows that and sorts out the matter, and permits itself to enjoy the pictures without getting sunk in the really mysterious business that they involve.

Lance Morrow, "Imprisoning Time in a Rectangle," Special Collector's Edition of *Time: 150 Years of Photo Journalism*, Fall, 1989, New York: New York, Time Inc. Magazine Company.

38. The author believes that, at times, photojournalism

    (1)   is not powerful enough.
    (2)   is not "good" journalism.
    (3)   can be more powerful than it is thought to be.
    (4)   is simply entertainment.
    (5)   is underestimated as a news media.

39. The writer implies that we should regard photojournalism

    (1)   casually.   (4)   tolerantly.
    (2)   cautiously.   (5)   disrespectfully.
    (3)   suspiciously.

40. According to the essayist, time can be "imprisoned in a rectangle" by

    (1)   revealing criminal misuse of photojournalism.
    (2)   capturing historic moments in photographs.
    (3)   accepting Balzac's dread of photographs.
    (4)   discontinuing the use of photojournalism.
    (5)   None of the above.

TEST 5: MATHEMATICS

Tests of General Educational Development

Directions

The Mathematics Test consists of multiple-choice and free-response questions intended to measure general mathematics skills and problem-solving ability. The questions are based on short readings which often include a graph, chart, or figure.

There are two separate sections of the Mathematics Test: Part 1 and Part 2. Part 1 allows the use of a calculator, Part 2 does not. You should spend no more than 45 minutes answering the questions in each part of the math test. Work carefully, but do not spend too much time on any one question. Be sure you answer every question. You will not be penalized for incorrect answers.

Formulas you may need are given on the following page. Only some of the questions will require you to use a formula. Not all the formulas given will be needed.

Some questions contain more information than you will need to solve the problem. Other questions do not give enough information to solve the problem. If the question does not give enough information to solve the problem, the correct answer choice is "Not enough information is given."

Do not mark in this test booklet. The test administrator will give you blank paper for your calculations. Record your answers on the separate answer sheet provided. Be sure all requested information is properly recorded on the answer sheet.

To record your answers, mark the numbered space on the answer sheet beside the number that corresponds to the question in the test booklet.

FOR EXAMPLE:

If a grocery bill totaling $15.75 is paid with a $20.00 bill, how much change should be returned?

(1)	$5.26	(4)	$3.75
(2)	$4.75	(5)	$3.25
(3)	$4.25		

①　②　●　④　⑤

The correct answer is "$4.25"; therefore, answer space 3 would be marked on the answer sheet.

Do not rest the point of your pencil on the answer sheet while you are considering your answer. Make no stray or unnecessary marks. If you change an answer, erase your first mark completely. Mark only one answer space for each question; multiple answers will be scored as incorrect. Do not fold or crease your answer sheet. Return all test materials to the test administrator.

Reprinted with permission of the General Educational Development Testing Service of the American Council on Education.

REFERENCE TABLE

SYMBOLS AND THEIR MEANINGS

=	is equal to	≤	is less than or equal to
≠	is unequal to	≥	is greater than or equal to
<	is less than	∥	is parallel to
>	is greater than	⊥	is perpendicular to

FORMULAS

DESCRIPTION	FORMULA
AREA (A) of a:	
square	$A = s^2$; where s = side
rectangle	$A = lw$; where l = length, w = width
parallelogram	$A = bh$; where b = base, h = height
triangle	$A = \frac{1}{2} bh$; where b = base, h = height
circle	$A = \pi r^2$; where π = 3.14, r = radius
PERIMETER (P) of a:	
square	$P = 4s$; where s = side
rectangle	$P = 2l + 2w$; where l = length, w = width
triangle	$P = a + b + c$; where a, b, and c are the sides
circumference (C) of a circle	$C = \pi d$, where π = 3.14, d = diameter
VOLUME (V) of a:	
cube	$V = s^2$; where s = side
rectangular container	$V = lwh$; where l = length, w = width, h = height
Pythagorean relationship	$c^2 = a^2 + b^2$; where c = hypotenuse, a and b are legs of a right triangle
distance (d) between two points in a plane	$d = \sqrt{(x_2 - x_1)^2 + (y_2 - y_1)^2}$ where (x_1, y_1) and (x_2, y_2) are two points in a plane
mean	$\text{mean} = \dfrac{x_1 + x_2 + \ldots x_n}{n}$ where the x's are the values for which a mean is desired, and n = number of values in the series
median	**median** = the point in an ordered set of numbers at which half of the numbers are above and half of the numbers are below this value
simple interest (i)	$i = prt$; where p = principal, r = rate, t = time
distance (d) as function of rate and time	$d = rt$; where r = rate, t = time
total cost (c)	$c = nr$; where n = number of units, r = *cost per unit*

PART 1

Calculator Use Permitted

Directions: Choose the <u>one best answer</u> to each item.

1. Triangles ABC and A'B'C' are similar right triangles. Find the length of side AC.

    (1)   10   (4)   16
    (2)   12   (5)   26
    (3)   13

2. A restaurant buys cans of corn in bulk. If 3 cans of corn sell for $8.00, how much will one gross cost the restaurant?

    (1) $24   (4) $384
    (2) $80   (5) $1,152
    (3) $246

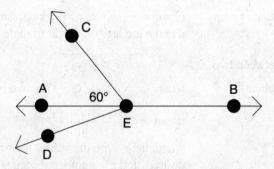

3. Line AB is a straight line. The measure of angle CEB is 8 times the measure of angle AED. Find the degree measure of angle DEB.

    (1)   15   (4)   165
    (2)   60   (5)   175
    (3)   120

4. Two cards are drawn from a standard deck of cards, one at a time, without replacement. What is the probability of drawing two queens?

    (1) $\dfrac{1}{221}$ (4) $\dfrac{1}{156}$

    (2) $\dfrac{1}{200}$ (5) $\dfrac{1}{144}$

    (3) $\dfrac{1}{169}$

5. The weight capacity of an elevator is 3,100 pounds. In a group of 10 women and 8 men, the average weight of the women is 138 pounds. What would be the maximum allowable average weight (in pounds) for the men in order for all 18 people to ride the elevator safely?

    (1) 225   (4) 195
    (2) 215   (5) 185
    (3) 205

6. A cylindrical can measures 4.2 inches in height. Its circular bases of 1 1/2 inch radii are removed, and the cylinder is cut open from top to bottom. What is the surface area of the cylinder?

    (1) $9\dfrac{3}{7}$ sq. in.   (4) $1\dfrac{4}{7}$ sq. in.
    (2) 6.3 sq. in.   (5) 66 sq. in.
    (3) 39.6 sq. in.

7. What is 1/2 of 4/5 divided into 2/3 of 60%?

    (1) 4/5   (4) 1
    (2) 4/25   (5) 3/2
    (3) 2/5

8. Given the population 7, 12, 9, 9, 5, 23, 15, 16, what is the value of the median?

    (1) 7   (4) 12
    (2) 9   (5) 13.5
    (3) 10.5

9. A case of cereal boxes measures 1 foot high, 2 feet wide, and 2.5 feet long. Each box of cereal has a volume of 288 cubic inches. How many boxes of cereal are in each case?

    (1) 5
    (2) 15
    (3) 25
    (4) 30
    (5) 40

10. Solve for x: $2x - 7 = 3x + 2$

    (1) −14
    (2) −9
    (3) 1
    (4) 9/5
    (5) 14/5

Item 11 refers to the following table.

The following table shows the rainfall, in inches, over a 5-day period in August for Hilo, Hawaii. It also includes the total rainfall for the year and the average rainfall for a typical year.

	Rainfall	Year	Normal
Monday	0.08	90.88	79.15
Tuesday	0.09	90.97	79.16
Wednesday	0.70	91.67	79.17
Thursday	0.19	91.86	79.17
Friday	0.32	92.18	79.50

11. Find the average rainfall for the week in August.

    (1) 1.38
    (2) 0.276
    (3) 0.32
    (4) 0.237
    (5) 0.138

12. A group of children share a package of cookies, each having six. If two more children join the group, they can each have four cookies. How many cookies were in the package, assuming none are left over?

    (1) 8
    (2) 10
    (3) 16
    (4) 24
    (5) 36

13. A floor that measures 10 feet by 20 feet is to be tiled with square tiles that are 36 square inches in area. How many tiles are needed to cover the entire floor?

    (1) 200
    (2) 360
    (3) 600
    (4) 800
    (5) 1,200

14. Pearl's bowling average after 15 games was 162. Her next three games were 187, 175, and 160. Her new average was increased by how much?

    (1) 2   (4) 8
    (2) 5   (5) 12
    (3) 6

15. A bike wheel has a radius of 12 inches. How many revolutions will it take to cover 1 mile? (Use 1 mile = 5,280 feet, and $\pi = 22/7$.)

    (1) 70   (4) 840
    (2) 84   (5) 1,020
    (3) 120

16. Mike is 8-1/2 times older than his son, Derek. The sum of their ages is 38. How old is Mike?

    (1) 32   (4) 38
    (2) 34   (5) 40
    (3) 36

17. Evaluate the following: $48 - 24 \div 3 + 5 \times 2$

    (1) 6   (4) 26
    (2) 12   (5) 50
    (3) 18

18. A board 3 feet long is to be cut into 3 pieces such that the first piece is one-third the length of the second and the third piece is five times the length of the first. Find the length of the longest piece.

    (1) 1/3 foot   (4) 1-2/3 foot
    (2) 1 foot   (5) 1-3/4 foot
    (3) 1-1/2 foot

Directions: Solve each problem. Write the answer on the answer sheet provided.

19. Twenty-five students rented a bus to attend a play. At the last moment, five students decided not to go. The others were each assessed an additional $1.00 to their share of the fare to cover the total cost of the bus rental. How much was the bus rental?

20. A family earned $40,000 last year. Twenty-five percent of it paid the mortgage. Twenty-five percent of the remainder paid for their food and clothing. After the food and clothing, twenty percent of the remaining

balance was saved for a vacation. What percent of the total earnings was saved for the vacation?

21. Lance traveled 90 miles in 2 hours. How much faster does he need to go in order to return in 1.5 hours?

22. The formula to convert Fahrenheit temperature to Celsius is

$$C = \frac{5}{9}(F - 32)$$

Convert 98.6°F to Celsius.

23. Sam has $1,000 to invest. He would like to invest 3/5 of it at 6% simple interest. The remainder would be invested at 8% simple interest. How much interest would he have earned after one year?

24. The angles of a triangle are in a ratio of 3 : 5 : 10. How many degrees is the largest angle?

Directions: Solve the problem below. On the answer sheet, mark the circle on the graph that designates the solution's coordinates.

25. Locate the point on the graph whose coordinates are $x = 6$, $y = x - 2$.

PART 2

Calculator Use **Not** Permitted

26. Sandy was *x* years old four years ago. What expression represents how old she will be four years from now?

    (1)   *x*   (4)   *x* + 8
    (2)   *x* + 4   (5)   16*x*
    (3)   4*x* + 4

27. There are 25 students in a chemistry class and 23 students taking physics. Seven students are in both classes. How many individuals are enrolled in either of the classes or both?

    (1)   24   (4)   41
    (2)   34   (5)   48
    (3)   38

28. Let *a* − *b* represent a real number. Which of the following must be true?

    I. $a > b$
    II. $a - b < a + b$
    III. $a - b < a$

    (1)   I only   (4)   I and III
    (2)   II only   (5)   none
    (3)   III only

29. A swimming pool measures 160 feet long and 80 feet wide. What is the perimeter of the pool in yards?

    (1)   40   (4)   280
    (2)   160   (5)   320
    (3)   240

30. Scott can pot 100 plants in 30 minutes. Henri can do the same job in 60 minutes. If they worked together, how many minutes would it take them to pot 200 plants?

    (1)   20   (4)   60
    (2)   30   (5)   90
    (3)   40

31. Find the area of the polygon.

   (1) 8   (4) 24
   (2) 12   (5) 30
   (3) 20

32. If $4x - 3 = 2y + 7$, find the value of $2x - y$.

   (1) −21   (4) 5
   (2) 21   (5) 10
   (3) 1

Items 33 and 34 refer to the following coordinate plane.

33. Find the equation for the line AC.

   (1) $x = 4$ (4) $x - y = 4$
   (2) $y = 4$ (5) not enough information
   (3) $x + y = 4$

34. What is the midpoint of segment AB?

    (1) (−1, 2)   (4) (−1, 1/2)
    (2) (0, 0)   (5) (−1, −1/2)
    (3) (−1/2, 1)

35. A jar contains ten marbles. Five are red, three are blue, and two are green. Two marbles are randomly selected, one at a time and without replacement. What is the probability that both marbles are red?

    (1) 1/5   (4) 7/10
    (2) 2/9   (5) 17/18
    (3) 1/2

36. A jar contains twelve marbles. Five are white, four are black, and three are yellow. Two marbles are randomly selected, one at a time and with replacement. What is the probability that one of these is white and the other is yellow?

    (1) 5/48   (4) 5/22
    (2) 5/44   (5) 5/12
    (3) 5/24

37. Which of the following samples has a *mode* of 8 and a range of 3?

    (1) 3, 4, 5, 6, 7, 8, 8, 9   (4) 6, 6, 7, 7, 8, 8, 8, 9
    (2) 7, 7, 7, 8, 8, 9, 9, 10   (5) 5, 5, 6, 6, 7, 7, 8
    (3) −1, 2, 5, 8, 11, 14, 17

Item 38 refers to the following chart.

Kristen's Growth Chart

Age in months:	Birth	6	12	18
Length in inches:	20	27-1/2	30-3/4	33
Weight in lbs./oz.:	7/4	19/15	24/8	30/2

38. By what percent did Kristen's height increase from birth to 18 months of age?

    (1) 13   (4) 65
    (2) 22   (5) 75
    (3) 42

39. Simplify the following:

$$\frac{\dfrac{1}{3}}{1+\dfrac{2}{4+5}}$$

   (1) 7/24   (4) 1
   (2) 3/11   (5) 1/3
   (3) 8/21

40. Neal spent 3/4 of his money for a shirt. If he was left with $20.00, how much did he have originally?

   (1) $15   (4) $80
   (2) $25   (5) $100
   (3) $60

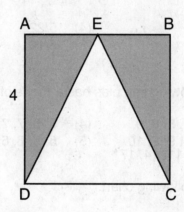

41. ABCD is a square and E is the midpoint of segment AB. Find the area of the shaded region.

   (1) 4   (4) 12
   (2) 6   (5) 16
   (3) 8

42. Solve for all possible values of b: $b^2 - 121 > 0$.

   (1) $b = 11$ (4) $b < -11$ or $b > 11$
   (2) $b = -11$ or $b = 11$ (5) $b > -11$ or $b > 11$
   (3) $b > -11$ or $b < 11$

43. Tracey has 13 more dimes than nickels. In terms of *n* (for nickels), find an expression for the value of Tracey's coins.

    (1)   2*n* + 13   (4)   5*n* + 130
    (2)   2*n* + 130   (5)   15*n* + 130
    (3)   15*n* + 13

44. A recipe for Chicken Divan will serve 8 people. Jann has invited 17 friends over for dinner. By how much does she need to increase the recipe in order to have enough servings?

    (1)   1-3/4 times   (4)   3-1/2 times
    (2)   2 times   (5)   9 times
    (3)   2-1/4 times

45. Estimate to the nearest hundred:

    $$\frac{(7,592)(4,892)}{(3,810)(70)}$$

    (1)   98   (4)   1,000
    (2)   100   (5)   4,900
    (3)   980

46. In rolling three ordinary dice, what is the probability of getting exactly 3 even numbers?

    (1)   1/10   (4)   1/6
    (2)   1/9   (5)   1/3
    (3)   1/8

47. What is the minimum amount that 534 may be increased by to be a multiple of 7?

    (1)   2   (4)   76-2/7
    (2)   5   (5)   3,738
    (3)   44

Directions: Solve each problem. Write the answer on the answer sheet provided.

48. The denominator of a fraction is four more than the numerator. If the numerator is doubled and the denominator is increased by five, the resulting fraction is equal to 1/2. What is the original fraction?

49. In a certain Algebra class, a student's grade is based on a midterm, three quizzes, and a final exam. The midterm counts for 25% of the final grade, each quiz counts for 15%, and the final exam counts for 30%. If Melissa's quiz average is 80, and her midterm grade is 88, what grade does she need on the final exam in order to earn a grade of 85 for the course?

Directions: Solve the problem below. On the answer sheet, mark the circle on the graph that designates the solution's coordinates.

50. Locate the point that lies two units to the right of (−2, 5).

EXAM I

ANSWER KEY

Test 1—Language Arts: Writing

1. (1)	14. (5)	27. (2)	40. (3)
2. (5)	15. (3)	28. (2)	41. (2)
3. (5)	16. (5)	29. (4)	42. (4)
4. (1)	17. (4)	30. (3)	43. (3)
5. (4)	18. (5)	31. (4)	44. (1)
6. (2)	19. (4)	32. (3)	45. (2)
7. (4)	20. (3)	33. (1)	46. (1)
8. (2)	21. (2)	34. (4)	47. (3)
9. (1)	22. (1)	35. (3)	48. (4)
10. (3)	23. (3)	36. (3)	49. (5)
11. (3)	24. (5)	37. (4)	50. (4)
12. (4)	25. (5)	38. (4)	
13. (3)	26. (3)	39. (1)	

Test 2—Social Studies

1. (4)	14. (1)	27. (1)	40. (4)
2. (3)	15. (4)	28. (4)	41. (3)
3. (5)	16. (4)	29. (1)	42. (4)
4. (3)	17. (5)	30. (1)	43. (5)
5. (3)	18. (3)	31. (4)	44. (4)
6. (3)	19. (3)	32. (5)	45. (3)
7. (3)	20. (2)	33. (3)	46. (3)
8. (1)	21. (4)	34. (4)	47. (2)
9. (3)	22. (1)	35. (3)	48. (1)
10. (2)	23. (3)	36. (2)	49. (4)
11. (4)	24. (5)	37. (1)	50. (1)
12. (5)	25. (3)	38. (4)	
13. (1)	26. (5)	39. (5)	

Test 3—Science

1. (4)	14. (1)	27. (4)	40. (1)
2. (5)	15. (2)	28. (3)	41. (2)
3. (2)	16. (3)	29. (4)	42. (1)
4. (1)	17. (5)	30. (3)	43. (5)
5. (2)	18. (3)	31. (2)	44. (3)
6. (3)	19. (1)	32. (4)	45. (4)
7. (4)	20. (2)	33. (4)	46. (1)
8. (1)	21. (3)	34. (4)	47. (4)
9. (3)	22. (5)	35. (2)	48. (4)
10. (3)	23. (4)	36. (3)	49. (5)
11. (2)	24. (3)	37. (3)	50. (3)
12. (2)	25. (1)	38. (1)	
13. (4)	26. (4)	39. (5)	

Test 4—Language Arts: Reading

1. (3)	11. (1)	21. (2)	31. (5)
2. (2)	12. (3)	22. (1)	32. (2)
3. (5)	13. (2)	23. (1)	33. (3)
4. (3)	14. (1)	24. (1)	34. (3)
5. (3)	15. (1)	25. (4)	35. (4)
6. (2)	16. (4)	26. (2)	36. (1)
7. (4)	17. (2)	27. (4)	37. (3)
8. (4)	18. (3)	28. (3)	38. (3)
9. (2)	19. (4)	29. (4)	39. (2)
10. (5)	20. (5)	30. (1)	40. (2)

Test 5—Math

Part 1

1.	(5)	13.	(4)	25.	(6, 4)
2.	(4)	14.	(1)		
3.	(4)	15.	(4)		
4.	(1)	16.	(2)		
5.	(2)	17.	(5)		
6.	(3)	18.	(4)		
7.	(4)	19.	$100.00		
8.	(3)	20.	11.25%		
9.	(4)	21.	15 mph		
10.	(2)	22.	37°		
11.	(2)	23.	68		
12.	(4)	24.	100		

Part 2

26.	(4)	38.	(4)	50.	(0, 5)
27.	(4)	39.	(2)		
28.	(5)	40.	(4)		
29.	(2)	41.	(3)		
30.	(3)	42.	(4)		
31.	(4)	43.	(5)		
32.	(4)	44.	(3)		
33.	(2)	45.	(2)		
34.	(3)	46.	(3)		
35.	(2)	47.	(5)		
36.	(3)	48.	3/7		
37.	(4)	49.	90		

DETAILED EXPLANATIONS
OF ANSWERS

TEST 1: LANGUAGE ARTS:
WRITING, PART I

1.   **(1) Sentence 1   Pros**, the plural of the word **Pro**, is the correct answer. **Pro's** is possessive, showing that Pro owns the business. Since Auto Striping Pros is a single business, the singular "is" is the correct verb form to use. The phrase "will be having" would imply that the sale will occur in the future, whereas the phrase "is having" implies that the sale is going on right now. **Pinstripes** is the correct spelling. The "e" at the end of the word makes the "i" a long "i".

2.   **(5) Sentence 2**   The sentence is correct.

3.   **(5) Sentence 3**   The sentence is correct. **From** is the correct word choice, the car owners will receive attention **from** the owner of the shop. **Cars** must be capitalized because this word begins the sentence. The possessive form of **owner** is not needed.

4.   **(1) Sentence 4**   Cars are done by **him**, not by **he**. **Him** is the correct word choice because **him** is the direct object. **A lot** is always **two words**. A period placed after **and his son** would make two fragments and no complete sentence. **Always** is an adverb and is always one word.

5.   **(4) Sentence 5**   **They're** is the contraction of **they are**, and is the correct answer to this sentence. **There** indicates place. **In fact** needs the comma following it to make the sentence clear. **Their** is a possessive and is not appropriate.

6.   **(2) Sentence 1**   **Always**, the adverb modifying the verb is, is the correct answer. **All ways** is the word "ways" modified by all, meaning every kind of way. The indefinite article **a** should remain. **An** is used before words that begin with vowel sounds. **A** is used before words beginning with consonant sounds. A period should not be placed after interview, since "is all ways a hard thing to do" is not a complete sentence. Do not use the plural **are** with the singular **preparing**.

7. **(4) Sentence 2** Change **whats** to the contraction **what's**, meaning **what is. Its'** is not a word. **Its** is possessive. The comma should remain, as it separates two clauses.

8. **(2) Sentence 3** **Its** is possessive. **It's** means **it is**, the contraction, and is the correct answer. The homonym **two** (2) should not replace **to** because the number does not make sense in the sentence. **Too** is an adverb meaning "excessively" or "also". A new sentence can not be started with **When** as "When you know what to expect" is an incomplete sentence.

9. **(1) Sentence 4** **Too** means more than enough and is the correct answer. **To** means direction, or is used as a preposition, when followed by a noun (to the top). **Two** means the number 2.

10. **(3) Sentence 5** When confused, drop everything but the pronoun referring to yourself; you would not say **me talk**. Also, always list others before yourself.

11. **(3) Sentence 1** **Roman Empire** is a term and both words must be capitalized. The accepted form is 1500s—not 1500's. The other two choices are weaker sentence forms.

12. **(4) Sentence 2** **German's** infers that one German owned barbaric tribes that swept into Britain. The plural form of German, **Germans**, should be used here, making (4) correct. The past form of **sweep** is not **sweeped**. Do not use **are swept**, which changes from the past tense of the rest of the paragraph.

13. **(3) Sentence 3** **Except** means to exclude, to not include. **Accept** means to approve of, to receive. Do not use the possessive pronoun **their**, the contraction **they're**, or the possessive **Roman's** in the sentence.

14. **(5) Sentence 4** The sentence is correct. The possessive forms are not needed. Neither the singular **this** nor the objective pronoun **them** fits.

15. **(3) Sentence 5** The subject of this sentence is **system**; thus the verb must be the singular form **was**. The spelling and punctuation are correct.

16. **(5) Sentence 6** The sentence is correct.

17. **(4) Sentence 7** A comma is necessary after **Latin** to make the sentence read clearly. The words following **Latin** modify **Latin**. **Well-educated** is correct. Puntuation and capitalization are correct. No possession is needed.

18. **(5) Sentence 8** The sentence is correct.

19. **(4) Sentence 1**   **Boring** is the correct answer. **To bore** is to be dull and uninteresting. **More boring** implies a comparison and there is no comparison in this sentence. **Many** must be followed by a noun. The word **television** is not capitalized unless it is the beginning of a sentence or is part of a title. **On** is a preposition and it is bad form to separate a preopositional phrase from the clause it is modifying.

20. **(3) Sentence 2**   The homonym **week** is correct. A comma (not a period) is needed after **opinion**.

21. **(2) Sentence 3**   A **board** is a piece of wood. To be **bored** is to be uninterested, or to find something dull. No punctuation changes or additions are necessary. **Which** should not be substituted for **that**. **That** introduces restrictive clauses. **Which** generally introduces nonrestrictive clauses and is usually preceded by a comma.

22. **(1) Sentence 4**   **On the other hand** is an introductory phrase and must be set off from the main sentence by a comma.

23. **(3) Sentence 5**   **Were** is the plural of was. The correct choice, **we're**, means **we are**. No additional punctuation is needed.

24. **(5) Sentence 6**   The sentence is correct.

25. **(5) Sentence 7**   The sentence is correct.

26. **(3) Sentence 8**   This item is a fragment and not a sentence. It must be attached to the previous sentence in order to be correct. It does not fit with sentence 9. **Win** (achieve) should not replace **when**.

27. **(2) Sentence 9**   **Were** is the plural of **was**. The word **where** refers to place and is the correct answer for this sentence. **Wear** means to put on clothing or to over-use something. The negative **no** should not replace **know**.

28. **(2) Sentence 10**   **Too** means also. **To** means direction or is a preposition. **Two** is the number. The word **too** is correct. Joining two sentences with a comma is wrong. Change the comma to a semicolon.

29. **(4) Sentence 11**   Remember to drop all but reference to yourself, when in doubt about correct pronoun choice. You would not say "Someone who asks I." Also remember to place yourself at the end of a listing of people.

30. **(3) Sentence 1**   You cannot have two negative words together. **Don't** and **hardly** are both negative words. If you delete **hardly**, you are saying that you **don't ever get to talk**. If you delete **don't** you mean that you rarely get the chance to talk. **Don't** is the contraction of **do not**, and is acceptable.

Vacations or **vacation** is acceptable in this sentence, and so is not the best answer here.

31. **(4) Sentence 2**   **Unique** means that something is one of a kind or has no equal. Adding **most** to **unique** is redundant. Therefore, **most** must be dropped. The other choices are incorrect spelling, punctuation, or verb choice. The plural **beaches** will not fit the singular verb "is."

32. **(3) Sentence 5**   **Should** is part of the verb phrase here and must be attached to another verb. **Of** is a preposition, not a verb. **Should have** is the correct answer.

33. **(1) Sentence 7**   **Its** is the possessive form of "it." **It's** means "it is," and is the correct answer. The other choices are all incorrect.

34. **(4) Sentence 8**   **Threw** is the past tense of **throw**, to pitch or hurl something. **Through** means between things. **Win** is to come in first. **Always** is the correct adverb form in this sentence.

35. **(3) Sentence 9**   Dropping "my family," you can see that the correct choice is clearly **my family and I**; these words are in the subject position in this sentence.

36. **(3) Sentence 11**   When the letter "i" is used as a pronoun referring to yourself, "I" is always capitalized. No correction is necessary in punctuation.

37. **(4) Sentence 12**   People **lie** when they recline. You **lay** things down, such as books. Hens **lay** eggs. No commas are necessary in this sentence.

38. **(4) Sentence 13**   **That's** means "that is" and is what is meant in this sentence. "**Thats**" could not be correct because it isn't a word. Everything else in the sentence is correct.

39. **(1)**   The answer is (1). Unlike (1), the other choices do not make a case for consideration of this application on the grounds of merit, but rather on grounds of need or personal connection. The addition in (1) sets up the material that will follow, and directs the prospective employee to look more closely at the applicant's resume. In terms of tone, this is the obvious answer choice. The others are too informal or inappropriately familiar, without giving the impression of responsibility.

40. **(3)**   The first sentence in paragraph B is a run-on, choice (3). There is something missing between "store," and "my," a joining word such as "because," or "as," or even a period that would break this into two sentences.

41. **(2)** The best arrangement is choice (2). In that configuration, the topic sentence is a strong and direct statement of qualification that leads into some specific examples.

42. **(4)** All the words are necessary to this sentence except "more," choice (4), which is neither necessary, nor grammatically correct.

43. **(3)** The answer is (3). None of the other sentences correct the fact that the sentence is missing a joining word between "decision" and "can."

44. **(1)** The answer is (1). The sentence is asking a question. All questions must end with a question mark.

45. **(2)** The name of a city, such as Boston (2), must always be capitalized.

46. **(1)** By just looking at this sentence you can see it is too long, and will probably be a run-on. When you read it carefully, you will notice that there are in fact two separate thoughts here that need to be made into two separate sentences. The answer, then, is choice (1).

47. **(3)** The answer is (3). The short sentence "It can be" is clearly an error because it does not make clear what it is that it can be. It is an incomplete thought, a sentence fragment, and needs to be combined with the following sentence.

48. **(4)** The answer is choice (4). This sentence introduces the topic and sets up the following sentences. The other sentences do not have a clear significance because the referent, the study as described in sentence 4, has not yet been introduced.

49. **(5)** Paragraph B begins by explaining how the Body Mass Index is calculated. Sentence 5 in paragraph A introduces the term BMI, and would make a better transition than sentence 6. The answer, then, is (5).

50. **(4)** Sentence 12, choice (4), is relevant to the discussion, but does not fit in at this moment, when statistical analysis is being worked through.

TEST 1: LANGUAGE ARTS: WRITING, PART II

Sample Essay — Possible Score of 4

Making eighteen years the minimum age for people to receive their drivers' licenses would be unfair to young people. Many younger than eighteen have regular jobs away from their homes. It would be hard for these people to reach their job sites, and they could not continue to hold down those jobs.

Some families depend upon under-eighteen family members to help with family finances. The loss of one person's pay could put an entire family in a serious financial position.

Lots of high school students work toward their college education costs. Being unable to legally drive could put them in a position of not being able to work or attend college later.

The state lawmakers say that accident rates would go down if young people were taken off of the roads. They seem to believe all young people ride around, causing problems. In fact, many accidents are caused by the elderly and those under the influence of drugs or alcohol.

Controlled substances aren't solely used by high school students. What percentage of drug abuse and drinking is done by teenagers? Do they control the statistics on these abuses? What percentage of accidents is caused by and involves teenagers? If statistics are fairly collected and presented, then the public could vote on whether or not people under eighteen should be able to drive.

Why this essay scores a 4

A superior essay goes below the surface. This essay is thoughfully organized and presents adequate support for the main idea that states that it is not a good idea to make eighteen years of age the legal age to obtain a driver's license. It is also very well structured, with no obvious problems with the use of standard written English.

This essay addresses both sides of the argument and proposes that the reader is intelligent and can make decisions from the information offered. The essayist begins by presenting his argument. He then proceeds to explain the rationale behind each side of the argument, so as to give the reader the complete picture. His conclusion is nicely developed by suggesting possible solutions to the argument.

Sample Essay — Possible Score of 3

Eighteen year olds are not responsible. Any state legislature that makes eighteen the legal age for a driver's license is not doing enough. It should be twenty-one.

Statistics show that most accidents are caused by or involve drivers under the age of twenty-one, especially male drivers. Maybe male drivers should not be able to be licensed to drive until they are twenty-five.

Fatalities are reaching world war proportions. Only major, twentieth century wars have higher fatality statistics.

Somehow, if legislatures could tie alcohol and driving, perhaps our highways could and would be safer.

In Canada, if someone causes an accident while intoxicated, his or her driver's license is taken away permanently. This rule seems to have affected the behavior of Canadians. Their driving statistics are certainly better then those of this country. We only slap drunk or irrational drivers on the wrist when they take the lives of others.

Maybe legislators should make driving a privilege, only earned by a special few who prove themselves worthy.

Why this essay scores a 3

This essay is not extensively organized. Errors in sentence structure appear and detract somewhat from the essay. Many of the points presented are repetitive and most of the paragraphs are underdeveloped.

Some of the supporting details are effective, but many contain weaknesses. The essayist presents support for the argument in the form of statistics that show that male drivers under the age of twenty-one cause a great many automobile accidents. However, he then strays from the topic to suggest that since male drivers under the age of twenty-one cause most accidents, they should therefore not be licensed to drive until they are twenty-five years of age. The essayist writes about driving while intoxicated, but does not tie this point into the argument. Standing alone, this point has absolutely nothing to do with the essay topic.

Sample Essay — Possible Score of 2

State legislatures get into the darndest things. Why should they worry themselves over the driving age when there are so many greater problems to be faced.

I am reminded of the old saying: "If it ain't broke, dont fix it!" As a general rule, driving stats seem to reflect a pretty good record, considering the population of this country.

Today, our states are faced with high crime rates and overcrowded jails. The drug problem is getting bigger. In large cities, gangs are a threat to the safety of everyone. State legislators should be trying to figure out ways to improve these situations, and to correct these problems.

Drivers buy gasoline. They pay auto taxes. And pay license taxes. All of this help to pave our highways and to raise revenues. The boys at the state capitol need to remember this when they are figuring ways to raise the driving age. What they are doing is reducing the number of drivers on the highways. In the long run, this hurts us all in our pocketbooks, the greatest hurt of all.

Why this essay scores 2

This essay has very little structure and does not address the topic. The topic of raising the driving age is mentioned in passing in the first paragraph and then is not mentioned again until the fifth sentence of the last paragraph. Ideas are basically unorganized and do not sufficiently support the essay.

The paragraphs in this essay are not well developed and the essayist does not go into enough detail to support his statements. The essayist begins one sentence with, "As a general rule"; however, he does not cite whose rule it is, therefore giving it no credence. He cites that, "our states are faced with high crime rates and overcrowded jails," but he does not attribute this information to anyone to support his claim. He says the drug problem in this country is getting bigger, but provides no evidence that this is the case. Another unsupported claim is that, "in large cities, gangs seem to be a threat to the safety of everyone." He does not tell us how he knows this to be true.

Yet, there are still other problems. He uses poor word choice. The cliché, "If it ain't broke, dont fix it!" is employed, but does not work well here. Also, the conclusion is poor, in that it touches upon ideas not discussed in the writing and does not really sum up the essay.

Sample Essay — Possible Score of 1

Eighteen is not a good age. Lots of kids are ready before that. Its dumb to give them a permit and let them drive at sixteen and not give them a license until 18 their doing it anyway. Kids have to go to school and work, they can't always get rides everywhere.

This stuff just gets me mad. Politishians are always telling us what to do and I'm sick of it! I need to drive but I cant yet, there's a car I think I could buy but it doesn't matter because I couldn't drive it anyway. Why? Because there's a law that says I can't! I've never heard a very good reason why.

Maybe some kids isn't responsible enough or something. People want to be safe but the fact is that teenagers should be trusted we're not all the same. You have to give a person a chance, its only fair.

Why this essay scores a 1

This essay does not adequately support its thesis that minors should be allowed to drive. The essay makes many claims that are awkward, confusing, and poorly supported. As it stands now, the essayist's analysis of this issue is too simplistic to warrant a score above a one.

This essay is full of grammatical and syntactic errors that cause a great deal of difficulty for the reader. Spelling errors abound, and the writer experiences real difficulty in attempting to write complex sentences. Problems with verb tenses are evident. Due to the serious weaknesses in the essay's organization and development, as well as its problems with grammar and syntax, the essay writer receives a score of 1.

TEST 2: SOCIAL STUDIES

1. **(4)** Henry Ford is considered the father of assembly line techniques for the manufacture of complex products. (1) Rockefeller created Standard Oil, one of the most efficient monopolies. (2) Morgan was the premier financier of his day, controlling banking and Wall Street. (3) Carnegie created the first billion dollar corporation, which became U.S. Steel. (5) Stanford was one of several railroad millionaires.

2. **(3)** is correct. The stress was on saving time, building a product faster and thus more of them. (1) The improving of quality was never mentioned. (2) The job descriptions make it clear that less, not more, skill is needed in this type of operation. (4) The article states that four workers can be replaced by one. (5) The work day is mentioned, but not in terms of shortening it.

3. **(5)** Chicago was the recognized rail center of the nation. (1) Ford, Dodge, Durant and many others lived in or near Detroit. (2) The Great Lakes make Detroit highly accessible for iron ore and coal shipments. (3) The Detroit River is the connecting link between the upper and lower Great Lakes. (4) Michigan, like the rest of the Midwest, had access to a large immigrant influx whenever jobs were available.

4. **(3)** is correct. Despite the fact that Russia is the leading wheat-producing nation, the former Soviet Union and current Commonwealth of Independent States (CIS) member is the only country which is one of the top three *importers* of each grain (corn, wheat, and rice).

5. **(3)** is correct. There were 13 positive deviations and only 10 negative. (1) is shown by the Trend in Deviation table to be decreasing. (2) Non-presidential elections are indicated by listing only party names. These so-called "off-year" elections are for Congress only. (4) The non-presidential years, beginning with 1938, show the Democrats winning every year except 1946. (5) In both 1948 (Truman) and 1968 (Nixon), presidents were elected with less than 50% of the popular vote, largely because of strong third-party candidates.

6. **(3)** is correct. In 1968, Nixon won with only 43.5% of the popular vote. (1) Carter won with 50% of the vote in 1976. (2) Reagan won with 50.8% in 1980. (4) Johnson won with 61.3% in 1964. (5) Kennedy won with 50.1% in 1960.

7. **(3)** is correct. When Nixon's vice-president, Spiro Agnew, resigned, Ford was chosen by Congress to replace him. When Nixon resigned over the Watergate scandal, Ford became president, but failed in his only election bid in 1976, losing to Carter. (1) He could not run for re-election since he was

never elected. (2) He did not die in office. (4) Only Andrew Johnson (1865–69) and Bill Clinton (1992–2000) were impeached, which means to bring to trial, and they were not removed from office. (5) He did not resign. Only Richard Nixon has ever resigned while in office.

8. **(1)** is not a proper conclusion because it is an opinion. The facts from the graph may be used to try to prove the need to cut transportation oil consumption, but the graph itself makes no conclusions. (2) This is true if the average of Germany, Italy, France, and Great Britain is used. (3) Since the U.S. and Canada top the chart, this is true. (4) This is true, with 25%. (5) True, about 8%.

9. **(3)** This cannot be a conclusion from the graphs, which are per person. Also, Canada, ranking second, has the smallest population on the list. (1) This could be a conclusion because the two largest nations are also the top two consumers. (2) Since four of the top seven consumers are European, this is true. (4) Japan is the only Asian nation listed. (5) This is a probable conclusion, especially when the quantity used for manufacturing in the U.S. is used as an indicator.

10. **(2)** The document asks, "Do you support the collection of sales tax on purchases made through the internet?" Although other types of purchases are mentioned in the course of the argument, only internet purchases are at issue. The document refers specifically to the state of Michigan and uses the phrase "state sales tax" in four different ways.

11. **(4)** The "Pro" position says nothing about the ease or difficulty of collecting an internet sales tax. All of the other arguments listed are specifically stated.

12. **(5)** Because of its control over interstate commerce, given by the Constitution, an act of Congress is necessary if *retailers* are to be required to collect sales taxes on out-of-state internet purchases (2). But this power has nothing to do with a state requiring *individuals* to pay a tax on their internet purchases (5). Although the "Con" position does not explicitly state that internet retailing is part of interstate commerce, its comments regarding the power of Congress over such commerce strongly implies that view. The other points are explicitly stated in the "Con" position.

13. **(1)** The key element here is the phrase "catalog or out-of-state business," which suggests other types of "remote" purchases in addition to those from a catalog, and therefore includes internet purchases. Furthermore, "out of state" refers to retailers other than those located in Michigan; the latter are required by the state to collect sales taxes on sales to Michigan residents, although this is not mentioned in the statement. The "use tax" is paid by the purchaser on his or her income tax form rather than being collected by the retailer.

14. **(1)**   The speech states that Vesey was "betrayed by the treachery of his fellowmen." None of the others (2), (3) or (4) were cited for failure because of their own people. (5) The *Amistad* was the ship that Joseph Cinque was on.

15. **(4)**   Blacks could and did resist slavery, using revolts, escape, passive resistance, and social customs. (1) This is not correct. Many poor whites supported the slave system as a means of keeping a class beneath them. (2) This is a direct contradiction of both (4) and the quoted revolts above. (3) Again, slave revolts did occur despite terrible penalties. Nat Turner's revolt, referred to in the speech, was one of the most famous. (5) This was a myth perpetuated by the supporters of slavery. Obviously, the same agricultural products are grown today without slavery.

16. **(4)**   This is one of the three Civil War Amendments (13–15) that moved the black population from slavery to citizenship. The 15th Amendment specifically gave the ex-slaves and all other black males the right to vote. (1) This counted the slaves of a state as only three-fifths of a person for the purposes of gaining votes in the House of Representatives. (2) This Supreme Court decision ruled that slaves remained property even when their masters took them into free territory. (3) This 1886 Supreme Court decision declared that segregation was legal as long as it was "separate but equal." (5) This 1820 deal in Congress drew a line across the U.S., allowing slavery in any new states south of the line.

17. **(5)**   is most accurate. The graph covers over 100 years and shows total population trends. (1) and (2) are not complete enough. Each is only a partial description. (3) is not accurate because the graph also includes the 1880s and 1890s. (4) is wrong because the graph shows percentages, not growth.

18. **(3)**   is most correct because the graph definitely shows a constant increase in urban population. (1) may be assumed as one part of urban increases, but is not specifically shown on the chart. (2) is incorrect. Farm production has not declined, rather fewer farmers are needed to grow more food. (4) is not referred to by the graph. (5) Occupations are not singled out, so there is no way to know anything about this category from the graph.

19. **(3)**   is the correct answer. As the 20th century approached, the population began leaving the rural areas of the country to inhabit the cities. The trend of moving into urban areas from rural areas continued steadily over the next hundred years. (1) and (2) are incorrect. Rural area population decreased over time. (4) is wrong because urban area population increased. (5) The population trend didn't remain the same between 1880 and 1980.

20. **(2)**   is the untrue statement; 80,277 were enrolled in grades 9–12, while only 37,199 got higher degrees. (1) Enrollment went to 915,061 by 1910, well over ten times the 80,277 of 1870. (3) High school graduate percentages went from 2% to 8.8%. (4) 12,896 graduated from college, over

one-tenth of the 110,277 in grades 9–12. (5) This conclusion can be drawn by the rapid increases in enrollments and graduations.

21. **(4)** is the most logical, because comparing any year's total enrollment to the high school total shows how few were enrolled in grades 9–12. (1) All the years are post-war and there is no reference to the war. (2) There are no statistics that deal with this. (3) Just the opposite, the rate of increase was highest that decade. (5) The increase in graduation rates over 40 years implies an increasing value placed on getting a degree.

22. **(1)** is not in Central America. It is part of Latin America, but its location south of the isthmus of Panama puts it in South America, not North America. (2), (3), (4), and (5) are all part of the region south of Mexico and north of the isthmus.

23. **(3)** is incorrect because both the Spanish and Mayan influence are discussed. (1) This is stated in the text. (2) This is clear from the map. (4) The Panama Canal is a major shipping artery and any land trade between northern North America and South America must go through Central America. (5) The need to raise the standard of living is stated above.

24. **(5)** The information you need to answer correctly is contained in the map's compass, which points north but which requires you to extrapolate to determine which way is south, east, or west.

25. **(3)** The Declaration states "That, to secure these rights, governments are instituted among men." It says nothing regarding economic prosperity or military security; there is a reference to "safety," but whether that involves the military is unclear. Although it mentions "that all men are created equal," there is no reference to economic equality. "Democracy" appears nowhere in the document.

26. **(5)** The Declaration states that when "any form of government becomes destructive of these ends, it is the right of the people to alter or abolish it, and to institute a new government." Although altering the government might involve electing new leaders, the Declaration says nothing specifically about elections. It also takes a more activist stance than simply calling on leaders to change. The option of moving to another country nowhere appears in the document and accepting whatever the government does is directly opposite of the Declaration's intent.

27. **(1)** The Declaration speaks of "a long train of abuses and usurpations… [that] evinces a design to reduce them under absolute despotism." In other words, the government has followed a careful plan, or conspiracy, to deprive the colonists of their rights. "Benign neglect," "disinterest," and "ignorance" all suggest inactivity on England's part, whereas the Declaration charges the contrary. "Incompetence" implies that English actions have been accidental or unintended, but the Declaration states that there has been a "design."

28. **(4)** The Declaration refers to "life, liberty and the pursuit of happiness" rather than "Life, liberty, and property," as John Locke phrases it. The first sentence of the passage states "that all men are created equal" and "that they are endowed by their Creator with certain unalienable rights." The middle of the passages states that "mankind are more disposed to suffer . . . than to right themselves by abolishing [the government]." And the final sentence speaks of the king "having, in direct object, the establishment of an absolute tyranny over the states."

29. **(1)** is correct. The Court ruling stated that a person must be told his rights so he understands them. (2) Miranda does not insist that a suspect sign anything, but merely that he has been informed of his rights and given a chance to exercise them. (3) The Court referred to questioning "while in custody," so Miranda rights apply at the time of arrest, but police are free to ask questions to try to determine if a person is a suspect. (4) The Court did not mandate legal counsel, only the suspect's right to have it if he so chooses. (5) Miranda is being obeyed because the suspect is getting legal counsel and it is the suspect's choice whether or not to follow it.

30. **(1)** is taken to task and it is stated that they should be limited. All other groups are called upon to band together to help the environment.

31. **(4)** These are obvious references to the past use of the environment for economic purposes rather than environmental concerns. (1) and (2) are moral statements, not economic ones. (3) This is a call to action. (5) This tries to redefine society's values.

32. **(5)** This is a political, cost concern. Coal is more polluting than oil. (1) This is now used to sell products, changing packaging, and is becoming profitable. (2) This is an attempt to replace trees as a renewable resource. (3) Repair and replacement of topsoil, erosion control, and replanting are attempts to reuse mined areas for agriculture. (4) Concern over this has changed products' chemical contents and created new laws to reduce airborn pollution.

33. **(3)** Although the chart can be used for several of the choices, it is a simplified version of the Business Cycle. (1) The chart does not refer to "bust" or depression. (2) and (4) Changes are shown, but not causes. (5) If you added data, such as dates, it could be used to track historical fluctuations, but doesn't in this form.

34. **(4)** This may influence the other factors, but can have a variety of effects and is not part of the purely economic picture. (1) The number of people employed is used to define whether we are in a recession or not. (2) Obviously directly related to (1), it also shows prosperity, if products are in demand. (3) Personal earnings rise with an economic boom and help sustain it with spending. (5) This is an important indicator of income, production, and consumer confidence in the economy.

35. **(3)** is the most counterproductive to economic growth because it takes money out of spending circulation and reduces sales. (1) is usually not planned, but has been credited with helping the economy as a side effect because of the increased need for services and products. (2) Keynesian economics calls for "pump-priming" of the economy through government spending to employ people and increase production. (4) Supply-side economics contends that reducing government regulation frees up capital to create products and jobs. (5) This is often used as a short term solution to help specific industries, such as the auto industry in the early 1980s. Long term use may trigger international retaliation and create worse problems.

36. **(2)** is the most specific statement because, although the first paragraph refers to the "needs of society," those needs are specified as economic in the rest of the quote. (1) Many of society's needs—legal rights, social needs, poverty—are not addressed. (3) This is not discussed. (4) The terms "average," "more and more," and "most" are used, not "all." (5) The government role is not discussed.

37. **(1)** The Chamber of Commerce represents U.S. business people and this is definitely a pro-business statement. (2) The federal Department of Labor is not anti-business, but it is not its major concern to advocate pro-business stands. (3) The GAO is the auditing branch of the government and doesn't take a stand on pro- or anti-business statements. (4) The Socialist belief would probably be the opposite of the quote. (5) The union position would probably credit workers more and business less.

38. **(4)** Justice means fair treatment for all, sometimes enforced by government regulation. (1) This is specifically referred to in relation to employment, wages, etc. (2) This is indirectly referred to through rising living standards and growth, which also provides security (3). (5) This is implied throughout and referred to as "less constraint."

39. **(5)** Labor is a factor in creating all of the others, which are the basic activities.

40. **(4)** is most correct, the N.W. line declined as the S.E. line increased. (1) was the second-highest period, after 1881–90. (2) Immigration slowed during 1861-70, but it was lower in 1911–20. (3) It peaked 10 years before 1900, then increased slightly from 1891–1900. (5) The 1901–1910 peak of the S.E. line was much higher.

41. **(3)** Fredericton experiences about 90 mm of precipitation in July. (1) Vancouver experiences 38 mm, (2) St. John's = 83 mm, (4) Winnipeg = 83 mm, and (5) Regina = 60 mm.

42. **(4)** Winnipeg is correct at –18C. The incorrect choices are (1) Vancouver, at +5C; (2) St. John's, at –2C; (3) Fredericton, at –10C; and (5) Regina, at –13C.

43. **(5)** is correct. The lead sentence in each paragraph deals with projected water shortage. All the other topics such as (1) alternative water supplies, (2) poor nations, (3) famine, and (4) grain supplies are focused on fresh water shortages. (1) is mentioned only in the first paragraph as options to a global water shortage. (2) is incorrect because water problems in both rich and poor nations are discussed. (3) is not correct because starvation is a sub-topic in the main discussion of fresh water for farming. (4) The statistics on world grain supplies are related back to lack of water. So, although all topics are mentioned, water resources is the one common main topic; the others are examples.

44. **(4)** is correct. The article states that irrigated land is being lost to improper watering. (1) is incorrect because the article does not discuss individual food consumption. (2) and (3) are wrong because, even though the producing nations are sharing their surpluses, the population growth has reduced the world surplus from a 101-day to a 54-day supply. (5) is wrong because only rich nations, like Saudi Arabia, can afford such projects.

45. **(3)** is correct because the passage states that if the U.S. bread-basket were to receive a drought, the whole world would suffer. One can infer that the U.S. is a major supplier of grain if its problem could affect the whole planet. Saudi Arabia (1) is mentioned in the passage but not as a worldwide supplier. (2), (4), and (5) are not mentioned at all.

46. **(3)** is correct. The chart shows a 72% to 56% margin. (1) is the opposite, with Carter holding a 40% to 24% edge. (2) Conservatives outnumbered liberals, 42% to 22%. (4) Women preferred Reagan by 36% while 39% of men preferred him. (5) Adding together the Democrats (29%) and the Republicans (24%) creates 53% with party membership and only 43% independents.

47. **(2)** is correct; at 24% support, it is his weakest area. (1) Carter (57%) had over twice the support that Reagan had. (3) Carter was favored in union households by a 34% to 30% margin. (4) Black voters gave Carter his strongest margin, 73% to 4%. (5) Liberals gave Carter a 37% to 26% edge over Reagan.

48. **(1)** is correct. The popular vote determines who gets a state's entire Electoral College vote. Those delegates convene in Washington in December of the election year and officially elect the next president. (2) is not correct. It is even possible for the popular vote winner to lose the presidency if the other candidate wins in enough key states to get a majority of Electoral College votes. (3) The Electoral College meets in December, not November. (4) is not correct because either the situation described in (2) could happen or, with more than two candidates, no one may receive a majority of either the popular or Electoral votes. In that case, the House of Representatives would

elect a president. (5) Americans vote for candidates, not parties, and the same rules about the popular vote referred to in (2) and (4) apply.

49. **(4)** is correct because of the reference to coffee as "mere colored water." (1) Several dairy products are mentioned, such as butter and cheese. (2) is wrong because lard and ham are referred to. (3) is not correct because turnips and potatoes are among the mentioned vegetables. (4) At least 5 different alcoholic beverages are referred to at the end.

50. **(1)** is correct. It is described as winning the "prize" for most injurious. (2) is wrong. The result of the day's meals was "heaping indigestions on one another." (3) is not correct because this topic is never mentioned. (4) is wrong because the author is very critical of the food's taste. (5) is not complete because only the tea is referred to as an English habit.

TEST 3: SCIENCE

1.   **(4)**   The longer the pendulum, the greater the time for one complete vibrational period. Since the acceleration due to gravity is constant, the length of the pendulum must be directly proportional to the square of the period. Here on the Earth a 2-second pendulum is one meter long. Doubling the period to 4 seconds implies a quadrupling of the length to 4 meters. Tripling the period to 6 seconds implies increasing the pendulum's length 9 times.

2.   **(5)**   If the period of a pendulum is to remain constant while it is moved to a different position in space, then the length is directly proportional to the acceleration due to gravity "g". On the moon the acceleration due to gravity is one-sixth what it is here on the Earth, so that to have the same-period pendulum on the moon means its length must also be one-sixth what it is here on Earth. Similarly, on Jupiter the acceleration due to gravity at its cloud tops is over 2.3 times what it is here on Earth, so that there the same pendulum would have to be over 2.3 times longer.

3.   **(2)**   From the information given, it is apparent that the period depends on "g" (1), on the fact that the amplitude must be less than 5 degrees (3), and on the length (4). No mention of the mass (2) was made. Hence, we can assume it makes no difference for what we need here. The only difference a greater mass could make is increasing the effective length of the pendulum by taking up more space. The length of the pendulum is defined to be from the pivot point at the top to the bob's center of mass.

4.   **(1)**   The units of "g" were given as meters/sec^2. This is distance divided by (time × time). This can be rearranged to read distance (divided by time) divided by time. This is speed divided by time. And that is exactly what acceleration means: how fast the speed is changing in time. Weight (3) and force (5) are concepts that require mass. Distance over time (2) is speed. Velocity over distance (4) is the inverse of time.

5.   **(2)**   Human eyelashes help keep dust and dirt out of the eye. Similarly, the hooks have tiny comblike ridges on them and they keep the antennae free from dust and dirt. Thus, (2) is correct. (1) is wrong because hooks are structures on the antennae that do not blink. (3) is wrong because the hooks are not involved in attraction between male and female ants. (4) is incorrect because the length of these structures is not indicative of the age of the ant. (5) is wrong because eyelashes do not help people find their way.

6.   **(3)**   For the trail to be different from any other trail of another ant colony, the trail must have a unique composition. The trail is drops of liquid from the abdomen. Each ant colony has its own odor. Thus, (3) is correct. Ants do not

use food (1), broken pieces of antennae (2), lenses of compound eyes (4), or tiny pebbles (5) to mark their trail.

7. **(4)** The compound eye permits the ant to see moving objects more easily than objects that stand still. Thus, (4) is correct. If an ant saw multiple images (1), its perception would be distorted. The same would be true if images were highly magnified (5). (3) is wrong because a compound eye is fixed and cannot rotate. (2) is wrong because the whole compound eye works together in vision; all parts of it are needed for good vision.

8. **(1)** Ants are most closely related to bees. Ants, bees, and wasps are all classified in the order called Hymenoptera. These insects are social and live in communities rather than living alone. The body is similar to that of a bee. (2), spiders, are different from ants in body structure and number of legs. Fungus (3) is very different from ants since fungus is a simple plantlike organism. Fleas (4) have a different body structure and do not live in communities. Crabs (5) are ten-legged crustaceans and are very different from ants.

9. **(3)** The population grows at the most rapid rate during the B phase. The slope of the B phase is greatest among all of the phases shown on the graph. During the B phase, cells are dividing rapidly. This is their most active time metabolically. They require nutrients to grow rapidly during this active period. The start and A phases are not active phases. Although the population size is greatest during the stationary phase, the population is not actively growing. During the death phase, the population is declining.

10. **(3)** The answer to question 1 is (3)—a compound can be a pure substance. The passage states that pure substances are either elements or compounds. It is easier to see the relationships posed in the answer choices by this simple chart:

By studying this chart, which shows the relationships described in the passage, it becomes possible to eliminate the incorrect answer choices. (1) is wrong because a homogeneous mixture is a mixture, not a pure substance. (2) is incorrect since pure substances and mixtures are two distinctly different types of matter. (4) is wrong because the term "heterogeneous" implies being composed of parts with visibly different properties. Since one type of element, such as a lump of lead, is consistent with respect to its physical properties, this one element cannot simultaneously possess visibly different properties. (5) is wrong because matter can be categorized, as shown in the above diagram.

11. **(2)**   The right answer is (2). This can be proven by visualizing a homogeneous mixture to be water (which has the same properties through-out) and a heterogeneous mixture to be water with rocks in it (since this combination would be composed of parts with visibly different properties). If the water is combined with water plus rocks, the resulting mixture will be water plus rocks, which is a heterogeneous mixture. (1) is wrong because the mixture will not be homogeneous; rocks have very different properties in comparison to water. (3) is wrong since a pure substance is entirely a different branch of matter from mixtures. (4) is wrong because these two mixtures will indeed be miscible, and (5) is incorrect because the resulting solution can be classified as a heterogeneous mixture.

12. **(2)**   Choice (2) is correct. This would increase the supply of aggregate and thus make more available for construction without increasing the amount mined. If A (1) was decreased, more aggregate would have to be mined in order to increase construction. Increasing C (3), the amount lost to disposal areas, would reduce the amount that could be recycled and thus increase the amount that had to be mined in order to increase construction. Decreasing G (4) would reduce the amount of construction required and the question stipulated that construction increased. Decreasing I (5) would increase the amount mined, not decrease it.

13. **(4)**   Cells are pushed from the tip of the root toward the interior of this structure. Cells in the region of maturation are the oldest cells in the root. As cells increase in number by mitosis in the zone of cell division, they are pushed into the region of maturation. As cells mature, they develop more specialized roles to function in the root.

14. **(1)**   Answer choice (1), "basic research," is the correct answer since the biologist wanted to gain the knowledge simply for the sake of curiosity or knowledge itself. "Applied research" (2) cannot be the correct answer since it involves using knowledge that has been gained from basic research or pure research and used to solve a problem. "Government research" (3) cannot be the correct answer since it may be either basic research or applied research, and in the paragraph there is no mention of who is funding the research. "Library research" (4) cannot be the correct answer even though in scientific research there is work done in the library; the paragraph deals with the major theme of a biologist doing "basic research." "Methods to produce great numbers of insects" (5) cannot be the correct answer since nothing is mentioned in the paragraph concerning a reason for producing large num-bers of insects.

15. **(2)**   Answer choice (2), "over a period of time, the dish would gradually be filled with dead cockroaches that crawled through the poison in an attempt

to mate with the cork," is the correct answer since they would attempt to crawl to the cork thinking that it is a female. "No cockroaches would be affected" (1) cannot be the correct answer since the pheromone would definitely affect the insect. "Moths would be attracted to the pheromone impregnated cork" (3) cannot be the correct answer since the biologist in the question was not using a moth pheromone and pheromones are specific. "Cockroaches would surround the dish but not cross the poison" (4) cannot be the correct answer since the cockroach would not notice what it is crawling through. "Not enough data has been given" (5) cannot be the correct answer since it is mentioned that the pheromone is so powerful that the insect does not pay attention to its own safety.

16. **(3)** Answer choice (3), "Applied science," would be the correct answer since the biologist is solving a problem by applying the information gained from the basic research or pure science. "Pure science" (1) cannot be the correct answer since the biologist is not experimenting out of curiosity or for only the sake of knowledge. "Basic research" (2) cannot be the correct answer since it is the same thing as "pure science." "Government research" (4) cannot be the correct answer since "government" would imply who is sponsoring the research, and not whether it is pure science/basic research or applied science/research. "The scientific method" (5) cannot be the correct answer since there is no mention of the methodology of a controlled experiment.

17. **(5)** In the afternoon during the summer (5) is the correct choice. The highest concentration has been found to be in the afternoon during summer months when the solar radiation is the most intense. At night during both summer (3) and winter (4) there is the lowest solar radiation. The intensity of the solar radiation increases after the sun rises in both summer (1) and winter (2), but the solar radiation is not as intense in the morning as in the afternoon.

18. **(3)** The total production of cells after five cycles of cell division is 1 – 2 – 4 – 8 – 16 – 32. The structure doubles its total cell number after each division cycle. After a sixth division, the total cell number is 64. After seven cycles, the total cell number is 128 and so forth.

19. **(1)** The sequence of life listed is correct, so answer choice (1) should be chosen. (2) is incorrect because invertebrates evolved before fish. (3) is incorrect because the first fish appeared much earlier than the first forests. Plants were present before birds, so (4) is wrong, and (5) is incorrect because reptiles had evolved before mammals.

20. **(2)** The cell in the drawing has five homologous pairs of chromosomes. It is diploid with a total chromosome number of ten. Mitosis produces diploid cells. If the cell produces a haploid cell, the chromosome number is halved, from ten to five. This occurs by meiosis.

21. **(3)** Answer choice (3), "a virus" would be the correct answer since a virus is not composed of cells, nor does it organize protoplasm into cells, and it does not come from pre-existing cells. "A rose" (1) cannot be the correct answer since it is a living thing composed of cells; it came from a cell; it carries on all of the life processes. "A fungus" (2) cannot be the correct answer since it is a living thing composed of cells; it came from a cell; it carries on all of the life processes. "An amoeba" (4) cannot be the correct answer since it is a living thing composed of cells; it came from a cell; it carries on all of the life processes. "A sponge" (5) cannot be the correct answer since it is a living thing composed of cells; it came from a cell; it carries on all of the life processes.

22. **(5)** Answer choice (5), "not alive because it is not composed of cells, it cannot reproduce, and it does not carry out any of the life functions," is correct since icicles are made of only water and not cells. "Alive because it grows by the addition of more water" (1) cannot be the correct answer since icicle growth is by accumulation of water freezing to the outside, and not by assimilation where food is chemically broken down, absorbed, and incorporated into the body of the organism. "Alive because it has a life span that involves a beginning, growth, a period of maturity, a period of decline and finally, death" (2) is wrong because there is no proper beginning (from a pre-existing cell); growth is not of the right kind; no "maturity" is exhibited; no decline (breaking down of cells due to age) is exhibited; no death is exhibited. "Alive because it can reproduce" (3) cannot be the correct answer since icicles cannot reproduce. Not "live because it is composed of cells" (4) cannot be the correct answer since icicles are composed of water, not cells.

23. **(4)** Fluvioglacial (4) is correct. The material deposited from running water (fluvial) and it is under or at the end of a glacier (glacial); the terms are combined as fluvioglacial. Till (1) is deposited by glacial ice, not running water. The deposits are fluvial (2) because running water transports them but as they are associated with glaciers the most appropriate name is fluvioglacial, not fluvial. Glaciomarine (3) and glaciolacustrine (5) deposits are not only associated with glaciers, but also with ocean deposits (3) and lakes (5).

24. **(3)** By Newton's Third Law of Motion, the gravitational pull of a first body on a second must be equal and opposite to the pull of the second back on the first, no matter what the mass of each body is or what the motion of each body is. Therefore, I pull back on the (1) with the same force the Earth pulls on me, but in the opposite direction. But, because my mass is so small, I accelerate downward a great deal (9.8 m/s^2) while the mass of the Earth is so large that it accelerates minutely.

25. **(1)** The gravitational pull between two masses is proportional to the product of their masses. Hence, doubling the two masses would increase the pull by 4 times. Since the Earth is 82 times more massive than the moon, the pull between the sun and Earth must be 82 times greater than the pull between the Earth and moon if their separations were the same. Actually, the

smaller distance between the Earth and moon makes the pull between the sun and Earth only 175 times the pull between the Earth and moon.

26. **(4)**   The gravitational pull between any two masses is inversely proportional to the square of the distance between them. The pull between the moon and Earth was given as 2×10^{20} N. If their separation was increased by two, then the force between them would have to decrease by four. A force of 2×10^{20} N divided by four is 5×10^{19} N.

27. **(4)**   Since each answer given involves the pull between the moon and sun, the key factor is the relative distances between the bodies. The distance between the sun and moon is on the average 393 times greater than the distance between the moon and Earth. Remembering that the pull is inversely proportional to the square of the distance, the pull between the moon and Earth must be 393^2 or 154,449 times the pull between the sun and moon.

28. **(3)**   The Br_2 molecules "stick" together at low temperatures because attractive forces between the molecules become stronger than the thermal energy, which tends to cause separation of molecules. Thus, choice (3) is correct. Choice (1) does not apply because the electrostatic forces of attraction are what cause the molecules to "stick." Ice is not involved. (2) is incorrect because molecules at low temperatures have decreased thermal energy, not increased thermal energy. (4) is wrong because gases tend to condense at low temperatures, not expand. (5) is wrong because Br_2 molecules, and most elements in general, will compress at low temperatures and go into a liquid phase.

29. **(4)**   The correct answer is (4). Gases contain molecules that move freely in space. Gases are thus the most random. Liquids still move but attractive forces between molecules prevent totally random motion. The solid state contains molecules that are ordered and close together. Thus, the rigid state of a solid renders it least random. The correct order is gas, liquid, solid.

30. **(3)**   is correct, because of the difference between the P and S waves, the P wave travels faster. It can be seen on the graph that the P wave covers a greater distance in less time. (1) and (2) are incorrect as they are descriptions of the waves rather than an explanation. (4) is incorrect as an examination of the graph reveals the S wave to be slower. (5) is incorrect; if the P and S wave traveled together they would both occupy the same line.

31. **(2)**   is correct. Locate the position labeled 8,000 km and look up until you reach the P wave line and read across to the time. (1) is incorrect, it would be 3,000 km. (3) is incorrect, it would be 1,000 km. (4) is incorrect, it would be > 10,000 km. (5) is incorrect, it would be > 10,000 km.

32. **(4)**   Answer choice (4), "46," is the correct answer since a cell undergoing mitosis will first double its chromosome number and then divide and

during that division the chromosomes will be evenly and correctly divided between the two daughter cells. "2" (1) cannot be the correct answer since the information in the question states that a cell starts out with 46 chromosomes. "10" (2) cannot be the correct answer since this number is still too small to make up even one set of chromosomes, much less "2." "24" (3) cannot be the correct answer since humans are sexually reproducing organisms and in a body cell there are two sets of chromosomes; therefore, 24 would be more than a single set but less than two sets. "92" (5) cannot be the correct answer since this number would indicate a doubling of the chromosome number without a cell division taking place.

33. **(4)**   Answer choice (4), "46," is the correct answer since the zygote of a human is a cell derived from a sperm containing 23 chromosomes and an egg containing 23 chromosomes. "2" (1) cannot be the correct answer since it represents too few chromosomes for either a haploid sex cell or a diploid body cell. "10" (2) cannot be the correct answer since it also represents too few chromosomes for either a haploid sex cell or a diploid body cell. "23" (3) cannot be the correct answer since it represents the number of chromosomes in a sperm or an egg. "92" (5) cannot be the correct answer since it represents the number of chromosomes in a diploid cell that has doubled its chromosome number without dividing.

34. **(4)**   Answer choice (4), "92," is the correct answer since the egg and the sperm, in this case, would have the diploid number of chromosomes (46), and if they were to unite, then the number of chromosomes would be doubled. "2" (1) cannot be the correct answer since this number represents too few chromosomes for even a human sex cell. "23" (2) cannot be the correct answer since this is the haploid chromosome number of a normal human sex cell. "46" (3) cannot be the correct answer since this is the diploid chromosome number of a normal zygote. "184" (5) cannot be the correct answer since this number is greater than a zygote with twice the normal number of chromosomes.

35. **(2)**   Answer choice (2), "haploid," is the correct answer since a sperm is a product of meiosis and has only one set of chromosomes. "A single organism composed of two cells" (1) cannot be the correct answer since a sperm is a single cell that has only one set of chromosomes. "Undergoes meiosis to produce four zygotes" (3) cannot be the correct answer since sperm do not undergo meiosis, and zygotes are not produced by meiosis. "Diploid" (4) cannot be the correct answer since sperm contain only one set of chromosomes and are haploid. "Undergoes meiosis to produce "four" eggs" (5) cannot be the correct answer since sperm do not undergo meiosis and they do not produce eggs.

36. **(3)**   All succeeding links of the food chain after the herbivore (the butterfly) are carnivores. If the butterfly is the primary (first) consumer in the food chain, the tree frog is the secondary consumer (1). Therefore, the snake

is the tertiary (third) level of consumer in the food chain. The predatory bird is the fourth-level consumer (3).

37. **(3)** Fifty thousand kilocalories remain for the butterfly population (1). Five thousand kilocalories remain for the tree frog population (2). Reduced to 10 percent for the next link of the food chain, snakes, 500 kilocalories remain available (5,000 × 0.1).

38. **(1)** Weight is proportional to size cubed. Surface area is proportional to size squared. Tripling the size of the ball means the weight goes up by 3^3 and the surface area up by 3^2. The weight then is 27 times larger and the surface area is 9 times larger.

39. **(5)** Strength is proportional to size squared while weight is proportional to size cubed. Having the size increase by a factor of four means the strength increases by 4^2 and the weight increases by 4^3. The strength is 16 times greater and the weight is 64 times greater.

40. **(1)** The amount of apple skin is proportional to the surface area of the apples. If we take a cube and slice it into eighths as shown below, it is apparent that the total surface area of the eight little cubes is greater than that of the large cube since the inside dotted surfaces of the small cubes are not available to the larger cube as surface area.

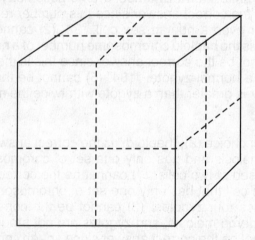

For the same mass, the smaller apples will provide the greater skin area. Since the A apples are the smallest, they will generate the most skin.

41. **(2)** Answer choice (2), "the length of the protein molecule, and the order and type of amino acids in the protein molecule" is the correct answer since proteins can be of different lengths; they can contain different types of amino acids; the amino acids can be in different orders in the protein. "Only

the length of the protein molecule" (1) cannot be the correct answer since proteins can also differ by the order of their amino acids and/or by the types of amino acids they contain. "Only the type of amino acids found in the protein molecule" (3) cannot be the correct answer since proteins can also differ in length and/or by the order of their amino acids. "Only the number of chemical bonds found in the protein molecule" (4) cannot be the correct answer since it is not mentioned as being one of the factors by which proteins can be different. "Only the order of amino acids in the protein" (5) cannot be the correct answer since proteins can differ by the length of the protein and/or the type of amino acids found in the protein.

42. **(1)** The correct response is (1). Tar is the most viscous because the molecules composing tar are long and thus tangle easily. Lubricating oil (3) and gasoline (2) are composed of shorter molecules and thus flow easier, or are less viscous. (4) is wrong because tar and lubricating oil, or gasoline and tar (5) have molecules of different lengths and thus different viscosities.

43. **(5)** is correct. Long chains breaking to form shorter chains will help the substance to flow better, and viscosity will be reduced. (1) is wrong because the formation of long chains will result in increased viscosity. (2) is wrong because although thermal energy does increase, it will cause chain break-age, not increased tangling. (3) is wrong because chain vaporization has never been observed. (4) is wrong for the same reason.

44. **(3)** Answer choice (3), "carpels," is the correct answer since these are the modified leaves that produced the ovules. "Sepals" (1) cannot be the correct answer since the sepals are the modified leaves that surround the flower while it is in bud. "Petals" (2) cannot be the correct answer since these are the modified showy leaves used to attract insects to aid in pollination. "Stigmas" (4) cannot be the correct answer since they are the portions of the pistil that are sticky and receive the pollen. "Styles" (5) cannot be the correct answer since they are the portions of the pistil that are beneath the stigmas.

45. **(4)** The reason why bees are attracted to flowers is because of the bright and showy petals. If these are removed, the bees will not notice the flowers. Thus, (4) is correct. In (1), separating the sepals from the bud will still put the petals in a prominent position to be viewed by the bees. (2) is wrong because the pollen does not affect the bees' attraction for the flowers. (3) is incorrect because crushing the stigma will affect pollination but not bee attraction. (5), separating the anther from the filament, will break structures within the flower but will not affect the ability of the petals to attract bees.

46. **(1)** Since the sepal is the protective covering over the petals, the sepal must have been invaded if the petals are to be reached. Stamens (2), the pistil (3), the style (4), and the ovary (5) are all reproductive portions of the flower and are not involved in protecting the petals from damage.

47. **(4)** The correct answer is (4). The liquid is vaporizing to form a gas at the boiling point. Air does not enter from the atmosphere (1) because the atmospheric pressure is equivalent to the vapor pressure; there is not a higher external pressure forcing air into the liquid. (2) is wrong because although liquid does form a gas at the boiling point, it does so by expanding, not by condensing. (3) is incorrect because the passage does not mention helium gas in the liquid as the cause of the bubbles. Helium gas is rare on Earth. (5) is wrong because microorganisms do not cause bubbles in boiling liquid. In fact, most microorganisms would not thrive at the boiling points of most naturally occurring liquids, such as water.

48. **(4)** Choice (4) is correct. As water boils, the liquid water evaporates. Water loss occurs in the form of steam, and the volume of water decreases. Choice (1) is incorrect because water molecules are not created over the hot steam. Choice (2) is wrong because the volume decreases rather than remains constant. Atmospheric pressure will not cause the volume to increase and decrease as statement (3) describes, and statement (5) is also incorrect.

49. **(5)** The answer 96.5% is correct. Natural gas (24.9%), coal (22.9%), oil (40.7%) and uranium (8%) are materials within the earth that formed over millions of years. Choice (2) is the percent from hydroelectric energy. Hydroelectricity is derived from moving water in rivers and although the dams may fill or require maintenance, the rivers continue to flow. Choice (3) is 8%, the amount obtained from nuclear fission of uranium. Uranium is a component of the earth's crust and thus it is not readily replaced. Choice (3) is the total hydroelectric and nuclear energy. Choice (4) is the total for fossil fuels. Fossil fuels are a non-renewable resource but this total does not include uranium.

50. **(3)** Genotype AaBbCc has three, heterozygous gene pairs. A heterozygous gene pair has a dominant allele (form of the gene) and a recessive allele. A heterozygous gene pair produces more variety than a homozygous gene pair. In a homozygous gene pair, both genes are either dominant or recessive. For example, a dividing cell with the gene pair Aa can produce a sex cell with the gene A or a. If the genotype is AA, meiosis will produce a sex cell with the dominant gene A. If the genotype is aa, meiosis will produce a sex cell with the recessive gene a. Although the other listed genotypes among the answers have three gene pairs (AABBcc, aabbCC, AaBbCC, and AaBBCC), all three gene pairs are not heterozygous. Therefore, they will not produce as much gene variation as the genotype AaBbCc.

TEST 4: LANGUAGE ARTS: READING

1. **(3)** Creon wants Antigone to obey his laws, but she has already broken his law forbidding the burial of her brother, Polyneices. She believes that she must obey the laws of the gods rather than the laws of man. Creon cannot accept this; he is outraged not only that she dared to break his law but that she does not repent.

2. **(2)** Antigone is not afraid to die because she has obeyed the laws of God.

3. **(5)** Creon seems to be concerned with his manhood. He is afraid that if he does not punish Antigone, he will be less of a man.

4. **(3)** Still affected by her life, Dexter loses Judy twice, proving he is still emotionally vulnerable, overreacting to Devlin's account of her fading beauty and unhappy marriage. (1) and (2) are not correct since Dexter wanted to marry Judy, never hinting that it was not meant to be. (4) is not the best choice since he is still being hurt by Judy, long after her rejection. Nothing suggests that Dexter still wished they could be united (5).

5. **(3)** Attention should be brought to the question that asks which of the following does <u>not</u> apply to Dexter's dilemma. Answers (1) and (4) <u>do</u> apply since they concern the lack of wisdom concerning love. Also, (2) and (5) do apply, since they state that love is blind.

6. **(2)** Here the emphasis is on Devlin and his account of Judy Jones. He "tells it like it is," but tempers his description with kindness, speaking of her "nice eyes," mentioning "most of the women like her." No other answers apply.

7. **(4)** The answer is (4). The word "warrants" means to promise. The three conditions in this section are the guarantees that the seller is making to the buyer.

8. **(4)** The correct answer is (4). Answers (3) and (5) have no place in a business document; answers (1) and (2) are not at all mentioned in the seller's warranties.

9. **(2)** The answer is (2). The amount included in the document is $20,000, not, as listed in (2), $40,000. The other answers are in fact part of the "method of payment" section of the business document.

10. **(5)** The correct answer is (5). Answers (1), (2), and (4) are not mentioned in the document. The same is true of answer (3), which is very unlikely to be included in any business document.

11. **(1)** Adjectives such as rich, golden, thick, eager, and hopeful abound through this passage, giving hope and promise and negating pessimistic (2) and foreboding (4) as possible answers. Realistic (3) is not the best choice because of the poetic promise within the passage.

12. **(3)** Realistic is the best choice even though the passage begins with the same phrase as the optimistic paragraph before it. This time, "but not all" is added with adjectives such as "scarred" and such phrases as "no thorough repair." Therefore, positive possible answers such as (1) optimistic, (2) encouraging, and (5) compassionate are not good choices. There is no hint of (4) sarcasm in the paragraph.

13. **(2)** By the use of contrast and the words "no" and "not," the author shows that not all devastation can be repaired. Answers (1), (3), and (5) are incorrect since they speak of healing, restoration, and replacement. (4) is also not a correct choice since the passage does not give the reader any reason to draw that conclusion.

14. **(1)** is the best answer since the writer's intended meaning transcends the notion of just looking back on the past. Although (2) and (3) are astute observations of life in general, they have very little to do with the passage. (4) does not apply.

15. **(1)** "Now" is the key word for choosing the answer, since we discover that Nolan had initially been received with (2) mixed feelings and accepted with reluctance. (4) and (5) are not answers that are supported by the passage.

16. **(4)** Nolan's message is explicit that "not in America" is there one more loyal, nor is there one who loves and prays for its flag more. No other answer approaches Nolan's heartfelt protests.

17. **(2)** The feeling that Nolan died in peace is substantiated and is apparent by the smile he had with his last breath. This eliminates further unrest (3) as a possible choice. There is no hint that this information is classified, thus (1) is also incorrect as well as (5), given reluctantly, since Danforth declares he will tell Nolan "everything you asked about it."

18. **(3)** Danforth's news transcends the material and physical since we witnessed that Nolan's death is made easier by it. Therefore all the following are incorrect since they appeal to material or physical gratification: (1) exercise-athlete, (2) money-wallet, (4) toy-child, (5) food-man.

19. **(4)** Although burial at sea (1) is mentioned, the biblical text alludes to desiring a country and excludes the more materialistic desires such as (2) an elaborate funeral, (3) a medal of honor, and (5) fame and fortune.

20. **(5)** Challenged by recent historians and writers is the best answer. Even though "myth" is used in line 28, it is qualified by the phrase "to undo, at least in part." Only alleged incidents about the artist's life appear and cannot be presumed to be substantiated, therefore (1) is incorrect. Van Gogh's brother, Theo, was close to him and van Gogh's suicide is still not understood.

21. **(2)** The literary technique of stringing critical questions is most effective here, capsulizing the controversy. (1) and (5) are poor choices since the writer takes no specific stand; likewise, (3) and (4) are poor choices, since it is the writer's intent to inform and not to amuse or baffle the reader.

22. **(1)** Descriptives such as "fanciful tales" and "Holy Fool" are quoted from a new biographer who questions old van Gogh stories. Sweetman does not (2) accept these nor does he (3) reject past and present theories. He is quite clear in his endorsement, negating any uncertainty (4).

23. **(1)** The informative nature of this review is immediately apparent from the onset. It chronicles important information in reverse order, beginning with van Gogh's self-inflicted wound. (2) Humor is nowhere introduced. (3) is a poor choice since the review presents both "old" and "new" schools of thought. Derogatory and inflammatory (4) is inaccurate because the writer presents his information with little bias.

24. **(1)** Sweetman leaves no doubt as to his conviction that van Gogh (as "Holy Fool") is nonsense. Therefore, his madness is neither (2) true nor (3) debatable. Since he so emphatically believes it is true, it cannot be resolved (4) or left for future biographers (5).

25. **(4)** "Read" in this context means interpreted. The writer feels that whatever maladies may have been present in van Gogh's life, they cannot be found in his art. Since (5) removed from would mean the opposite, it is incorrect. Contextually, (1) summarized, (2) questioned, and (3) painted are not precise.

26. **(2)** Line 5 clarifies this informally used poker term to mean that musicians' standards of excellence were raised. Neither salary (1) nor public problems (3) were mentioned nor implied. Obscurity (4) is incorrect since lines 24–25 reveal that his music will not be outdated with time. Line 11 negates that (5) Johnson "aimed too high" since his music is called "art of the highest order."

27. **(4)** The reviewer answers his question neither affirmatively (1) nor negatively (2) in lines 15–17—"comparisons seem almost irrelevant." Evasively (3) is incorrect in lines 20–21—"blows… comparisons right out of the window."

28. **(3)** Implicit in lines 25–26 is the message of surviving time—"has a power that age cannot dim." Therefore (4) is wrong as is (1): see lines 26 and 27—"over many years… finer appreciation." This entire review is a tribute to the artist excluding (2) no popular appeal. (5) is neither affirmed nor negated (see explanation to preceding question).

29. **(4)** From the first paragraph of this excerpt, the writer tells us that she knows everything about her hostess's cookies would be as "perfect" as her hostess is; "perfect," therefore, suggests awe and respect, which logically excludes (1) cool reserve, as well as fear (2) and distrust (3). (5) is a poor choice of answers since it suggests there is no regard for her hostess at all.

30. **(1)** Wisdom is suggested here since the author mentions such things as "mother wit" emanating from "country people"; people more educated than college professors. Unintelligence (2) as well as book learning (5) are polar opposites and incorrect. Neither charm (3) nor native intelligence (4) are implied.

31. **(5)** Buried beneath this statement is the lesson, "some people, unable to go to school, were more educated and even more intelligent than college professors." Therefore, numbers (1), (2), (3), and (4) are incorrect because they contain the absolute "always," but miss the entire point—"sometimes."

32. **(2)** Since Marguerite had read the novel and "found it up to my standards," we can disregard (1) a literal meaning. Socially (3) is incorrect since the visit was not social, but scholarly, in its intent. Marguerite was too much in awe of her hostess for "tongue in cheek" (4) comments.

33. **(3)** Lines 29–30 reveal that all Marguerite could manage was, "Yes ma'am." Uneasy (1) might have been an appropriate answer, if she had not earlier compared her hostess's recitation to music, to which she had listened mesmerized. Therefore offended (2), unimpressed (4) as well as eloquent (5) in her praises are entirely incorrect.

34. **(3)** The best answer, "enjoy the silent beauty," is suggested in line 4. Since he admits the neighbor "will not see me," (2) is incorrect. There is no neighbor about to beckon him, so (5) is incorrect. No mention is made here of his horse (1) or of darkness (4).

35. **(4)** Lines 5, 9, and 10 tell us that his "little horse" stops and signals to the poet that there is no farmhouse so there must be a mistake in stopping. Wrong path (1) and lost the way (3) are immediate poor choices since we know there is a rapport and friendship between the man and his horse. No mention is made of weariness (2) or of stubbornness (5).

36. **(1)** The key word in the last stanza is "promises," and the idea that the poet goes on, which suggests that he has made his choice by resuming to meet his obligations. Although we might infer that (4) he will return soon, there

is no hint of that possibility in the last stanza. Confused (2) is a poor choice because we sense determination. The effect of repeating lines 15 and 16 rule out (3) as a possible answer.

37. **(3)** If this poem is read on the symbolic level, "sleep" in the final two lines of the last stanza can be equated with death. Therefore the serenity and peace of the winter scene can be interpreted as the lure of death, while the "miles to go" can be read as the obligations of life. There is nothing literal or figurative that would suggest any of the other answers as appropriate choices.

38. **(3)** The power of photojournalism is prevalent throughout this essay, but lines 24 and 25 are the most explicit. Line 24 speaks of its "power" which makes not powerful (1) a very poor choice. (2) is incorrect since photojournalism is called "splendid" in line 23. Simply entertainment (4) is negated throughout the entire piece; likewise (5), underestimated, is incorrect since its power is called "preternatural" in line 24.

39. **(2)** Implicit within the message of the essay with its emphasis on the power of photojournalism is a precautionary note that the power of pictures may be "more than they deserve." Casually (1) implies the opposite, so it is incorrect. Suspiciously (3) presents an averse connotation, not found within the essay's context. Both tolerantly (4) and disrespectfully (5) are poor choices for answers since neither is suggested by the author.

40. **(2)** The author has cleverly entitled his essay, "Imprisoning Time in a Rectangle," and equated it with photojournalism's method of capturing history in a rectangular-shaped mode. Although permeating the piece is a caution concerning the media's power, there is no mention of (1) criminal misuse or (4) discontinuing its use. Balzac's dread of photography is presented in the opening paragraph only to emphasize the power of photography itself; therefore, (3) is incorrect.

TEST 5: MATHEMATICS

PART 1

1.   **(5)**   The sides of similar triangles are in proportion. Using the Pythagorean Theorem the length of B'C' is:

$$5^2 + (B'C')^2 = 13^2$$
$$25 + (B'C')^2 = 169$$
$$(B'C')^2 = 144$$
$$B'C' = 12$$

BC and B'C' are corresponding sides of similar triangles in a ratio of 24 : 12 or 2 : 1. Similarly side AC and A'C' have the same ratio; AC must be twice as long as A'C'. In other words, AC = 2(13) = 26.

2.   **(4)**   One gross amounts to 144 cans. Since each set of 3 cans will cost $8.00, and there are 144/3 = 48 sets, (48 sets)($8) = $384.

3.   **(4)**   Line AB is a straight line and also a straight angle measuring 180°. ∠CEA = 60°, therefore ∠CEB = 120. Because ∠CEB is 8 times ∠AED, ∠AED must be 120/8 = 15°. ∠AED and ∠DEB form another straight angle: ∠AED + ∠DEB = 180° or 15° + ∠DEB = 180°. Therefore, ∠DEB = 165°.

4.   **(1)**   For the 1st queen, the probability is 4/52. For the second queen, the probability is now 3/51 (no replacement). Then, $\left(\dfrac{4}{52}\right)\left(\dfrac{3}{51}\right) = \dfrac{1}{221}$.

5.   **(2)**   The total weight of the women = (10)(138) = 1,380 pounds. 3,100 − 1,380 = 1,720. Then 1,720 ÷ 8 = 215 pounds.

6.   **(3)**   When the can is cut open and flattened out, its shape will be a rectangle.

$\frac{66}{7}$ in.

4.2 in.

The length, which is the circumference of the circular base, is:

$$C = 2\pi \text{ (radius)}$$

$$C = 2\pi \left(\frac{3}{2} \text{inches} \right)$$

$$C = 3\pi$$

$$C = 3\left(\frac{22}{7} \right) = \frac{66}{7} \text{in.}$$

The area of the rectangle is (length)(width):

$$A = \left(\frac{66}{7} \right)(4.2)$$

$$A = (9.42)\,(4.2) = 39.6 \text{ sq. in.}$$
$$\text{(rounded to the nearest tenth)}$$

7. **(4)** 1/2 of 4/5 is interpreted as:

$$\frac{1}{2} \times \frac{4}{5} = \frac{2}{5}$$

2/3 of 60% is translated into:

$$\frac{2}{3} \times \frac{60}{100} = \frac{2}{3} \times \frac{3}{5} = \frac{2}{5}$$

Following the problem then:

$$\frac{2}{5} \div \frac{2}{5} = 1$$

8. **(3)** Rearrange the data as 5, 7, 9, 9, 12, 15, 16, 20. The median is the

average of the fourth and fifth numbers: $\frac{9+12}{2} = 10.5$

9. **(4)** Because the volume of the cereal boxes is in cubic inches, convert the measure of the case to inches also.

$$1 \text{ ft.} = 12 \text{ in.}$$
$$2 \text{ ft.} = 24 \text{ in.}$$
$$2\text{-}1/2 \text{ ft.} = 30 \text{ in.}$$

The volume of the case is calculated by using the volume formula:

$$V = (\text{length})(\text{width})(\text{height})$$
$$= (30)(24)(12)$$
$$= 8{,}649 \text{ cubic in.}$$

Now find how many boxes of cereal are needed:

$$\frac{8{,}640}{288} = 30 \text{ boxes}$$

10. **(2)** To solve any equation, use some simple rules of algebra. First, get the like terms on one side of the equation, then simplify to solve for the variable.

$$2x - 7 = 3x + 2 \text{ becomes}$$
$$2x - 3x = 2 + 7$$
$$-x = 9 \text{ or}$$
$$x = -9$$

11. **(2)** To find the average rainfall for the week, add the five amounts in the "rainfall" column, then divide by five.

$$\frac{0.08 + 0.09 + 0.70 + 0.19 + 0.32}{5} =$$
$$\frac{1.38}{5} = 0.276 \text{ in.}$$

12. **(4)** Using some algebraic expressions to represent the unknown should help here. Let:

$x =$ the number of children in the original group
$6x =$ the number of cookies in the package.

When two more children join the group, the expressions are:

$x + 2 =$ the number of children
$4(x + 2) =$ the number of cookies in the package.

Notice that there are two expressions for "the number of cookies in the package." These are equivalent expressions so set up an equation and solve for *x*.

$$6x = 4(x + 2)$$
$$6x = 4x + 8$$
$$2x = 8$$
$$x = 4$$

There were four children in the original group, and therefore, $6x = 6(4) = 24$ cookies in the package.

13. **(4)** The floor that measures 10 ft. by 20 ft. has an area of $10 \times 20 = 200$ sq. ft. The tiles with 36 sq. in. of area must measure 6 in. by 6 in. or 1/2 ft. by 1/2 ft. for 1/4 sq. ft. of area. Because it would take 4 tiles to cover 1 sq. ft., 4(200 sq. ft.) = 800 tiles would be needed to cover the entire floor.

14. **(1)** Any average score is calculated by adding all the scores and dividing the sum by the number of games. An average of 162 out of 15 games came from a total pin count of (162)(15 games) = 2,430 pins. Adding the last three scores to the total will yield $187 + 175 + 160 + 2430 = 2,952$ pins for 18 games. Pearl's new average is:

$$2,952 \div 18 = 164$$

and so her average increased by 2 pins.

Method 2: The number of pins that an average is increased (or decreased) by can also be calculated by finding the differences between the scores and the 162 average, adding the differences together, then dividing by the total number of games.

$$187 - 162 = 25$$
$$175 - 162 = 13$$
$$160 - 162 = -2$$
Now, $25 + 13 - 2 = 36$
Therefore: $36 \div 18 = 2$

15. **(4)** The circumference of the wheel is:

$$C = 2\pi \ (1 \text{ ft.})$$

$$C = 2\left(\frac{22}{7}\right) = \frac{44}{7} \text{ ft.}$$

To find the number of revolutions the wheel takes, calculate:

$$5,280 \div \frac{44}{7} =$$

$$5,280 \times \frac{7}{44} =$$

$$120 \times 7 = 840 \text{ revolutions}$$

16. **(2)** Because the indicated operation in this problem is addition, find the two expressions that are to be added together. Let:

$$x = \text{Derek's age}$$
$$(17/2)x = \text{Mike's age}$$

Now add the expressions for a sum of 38.

$$\frac{17}{2}x + x = 38$$
$$17x + 2x = 76$$
$$19x = 78$$
$$x = 4$$

Derek is 4 years old, and Mike is 38 − 4 = 34 years old.

17. **(5)** When evaluating an expression without grouping symbols to indicate what operation should be done first, always do all multiplication and division first as they appear from left to right, then do any addition or subtraction, again as they appear from left to right. Therefore,

$$48 - 24 \div 3 + 5 \times 2 =$$
$$48 - 8 + 10 =$$
$$40 + 10 = 50$$

18. **(4)** To make the problem easier to understand, first translate the phrase "the first piece is one-third the length of the second" into "the second piece is three times the first." Because the third piece is five times the first, the pieces are in a ratio of 1 : 3 : 5. The board must be divided into 9 equal parts of 1/3 ft. which equals 4 inches. The longest piece takes 5 parts or 20 inches, which is:

$$\frac{20 \text{ inches}}{12 \text{ inches}} = 1\frac{2}{3} \text{ ft.}$$

19. **$100.00** The twenty students that actually went to the play were assessed an additional $20.00 total to cover the remaining cost of the bus when the other 5 students decided not to go. Therefore, each of the 5 students were paying $4.00 for their share of the bus rental along with the other 20 students.

$$(\$4.00)(25 \text{ students}) = \$100.00$$
was the cost of the bus rental.

20. **11.25%** 25% or 1/4 of $40,000 = $10,000 was for the mortgage, leaving $30,000. 25% or 1/4 of $30,000 = $7,500 was used for food and clothing, leaving a $22,500 balance. 20% or 1/5 of $22,500 = $4,500 was

saved for a vacation. The problem, then, can be restated as: $4,500 is what percent of $40,000? Using proportions:

$$\frac{?}{100} = \frac{4,500}{40,000}$$

or

$$\frac{?}{100} = \frac{9}{80}$$

$$? = \frac{900}{80} = \frac{90}{8} = 11.25\%$$

Method 2: Although $40,000 was used as a base figure, in a problem like this one, any number would have worked. If $100 was used instead, the figures would have yielded the same results; in fact, it would have eliminated one step.

25% or 1/4 of $100 = $25, leaving $75
25% or 1/4 of $75 = $18.75, leaving $56.25
20% or 1/5 of $56.25 = $11.25
$11.25 of $100 is 11.25% of $100

21. **15 mph** Ninety miles in 2 hours is equivalent to 45 miles in 1 hour (60 minutes) or 45 mph. If Lance has only 1.5 hours or 90 minutes to cover the same 90 miles when he returns, he needs to travel 1 mile a minute, which translates into 60 mph, 15 mph faster than his original speed.

22. **37°** Substitute 98.6°F into the formula for F:

$$C = \frac{5}{9}(F - 32)$$

$$C = \frac{5}{9}(98.6 - 32)$$

$$C = \frac{5}{9}(66.6)$$

$$C = 5(7.4)$$

$$C = 37°$$

23. **68** Because Sam is making 2 investments, first find 3/5 of $1,000. Divide $1,000 into 5 equal parts ($1,000/5 = $200) and take 3 parts ($600). $600 is invested at 6% simple interest, which yields:

$$\$600 (6\%) = \$600 (0.06) = \$36$$

The remaining $400 is invested at 8% simple interest, which yields:

$$\$400 (8\%) = \$400 (0.08) = \$32$$

The total interest earned is $36 + $32 = $68

24. **100** The ratio 3 : 5 : 10 indicates that the 180 degrees of the triangle must be divided into 3 + 5 + 10 = 18 equal parts or 10 degrees for each part. The largest angle is made up of ten 10 degree parts or 100 degrees.

25. If x = 6, then y = 6 − 2.

   y = 4

Therefore, the coordinates for this point are (6,4).

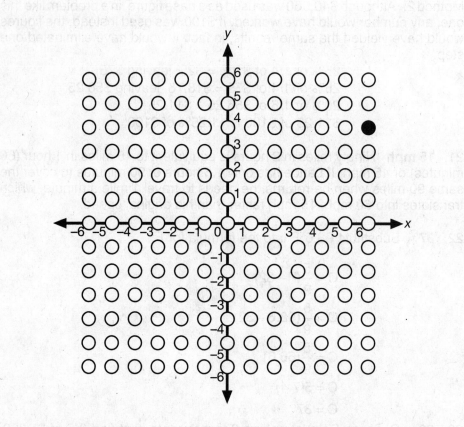

PART 2

26. **(4)** x represents Sandy's age 4 years ago. Therefore, she is now $x + 4$ years old. Adding another 4 years to $x + 4$, in other words, $(x + 4) + 4$, will yield $x + 8$ as Sandy's age 4 years from now.

27. **(4)** Of the 25 chemistry students, 7 are also in physics. There are $23 - 7 = 16$ remaining students taking only physics. Therefore, $25 + 16 = 41$ individual students are enrolled in the two science classes.

28. **(5)** Although it may seem time consuming, if numbers are substituted in for the variables, the problem may not be so difficult. In this case, try to find contradictions to the statements to find the true statements, if any.

Case I.   For $a - b$, $a > b$ is not always true.

$2 - 3 = -1$, which is a real number.

Case II. $a - b > a + b$ will be false when a and b are both negative numbers.

$(-2) - (-3) < (-2) + (-3)$ yields $1 < -5$ which is not true.

Case III. $a - b < a$ is also nullified by this example:

$(-2) - (-3) < -2$ which yields

$$1 < -2$$

All three statements in this problem are false.

29. **(2)** The perimeter or measure around the pool will use the formula:
2(lengths) + 2(widths) = perimeter
$2(160) + 2(80) = 320 + 160 = 480$ feet

Because the question asks for the answer in terms of yards,

$$\frac{480 \text{ ft.}}{3 \text{ ft.}} = 160 \text{ yards}$$

30. **(3)** Because this is a rate of work problem, consider what fraction of the job would get done in one minute. Scott would get 1/30th of the job done while Henri would get 1/60th of the job done in one minute. Together, they would get:

$$\frac{1}{30} + \frac{1}{60} = \frac{2}{60} + \frac{1}{60} = \frac{3}{60} = \frac{1}{20}$$

of the job done in one minute. Therefore, 20 minutes would be needed to pot 100 plants, and 40 minutes to pot all 200 pants.

31. **(4)**   The polygon can be divided into three rectangles whose areas are easy to calculate by using the formula: area = (length)(width).

Rectangle A = 2(2) = 4
Rectangle B = 2(4) = 8
Rectangle C = 2(6) = 12

The sum 4 + 8 + 12 = 24 is the area of the polygon.

32. **(4)**   Using some rules of algebra,

$$4x - 3 = 2y + 7 \text{ becomes}$$
$$4x - 2y = 7 + 3 \text{ or}$$
$$4x - 2y = 10$$

Dividing by 2: $2x - y = 5$

33. **(2)**   Identify several ordered pairs that are on Line A such as (0,4), (1,4), (2,4), and (3,4) . Notice that the y-term or second term of the ordered pairs is always 4. Therefore, the equation is $y = 4$.

34. **(3)** The ordered pairs for points A and B, respectively, are (–3,4) and (2,–2). The midpoint is calculated by finding the averages of the x and y coordinates. In other words, the midpoint is:

$$\left(\frac{-3+2}{2}, \frac{4+(-2)}{2}\right) = \left(\frac{-1}{2}, 1\right)$$

35. **(2)** The probability is $\frac{5}{10} \times \frac{4}{9} = \frac{2}{9}$, since the drawing is done without replacement.

36. **(3)** With replacement, the probability is $\frac{5}{12} \times \frac{3}{12}$ (if the sequence is white-yellow) added to $\frac{3}{12} \times \frac{5}{12}$ (if the sequence is yellow-white).

$$\frac{5}{12} \times \frac{3}{12} + \frac{3}{12} \times \frac{5}{12} = \frac{5}{24}$$

37. **(4)** 6, 6, 7, 7, 7, 8, 8, 8, 9. Since the mode is the most common number, only choices (1) and (4) qualify. In choice (4), the range is $9 - 6 = 3$, whereas the range in choice (1) is 6.

38. **(4)** Kristen grew 13 inches in 18 months. Setting up a proportion yields the following:

$$\frac{\text{percent}}{100} = \frac{13}{20}$$

$$\text{percent} = \frac{13}{20}(100)$$

$$\text{percent} = 65$$

39. **(2)** Complex fractions such as this one can be solved one of two ways. The first method would be to work on the numerator and denominator separately so they are each simplified to simple fractions, then treat them as a quotient of two fractions. Therefore,

$$\frac{\dfrac{1}{3}}{1+\dfrac{2}{4+5}} =$$

$$\frac{\dfrac{1}{3}}{1+\dfrac{2}{9}} = \frac{\dfrac{1}{3}}{\dfrac{11}{9}} =$$

$$\frac{1}{3} \times \frac{9}{11} = \frac{3}{11}$$

In the second method, multiply every term by the common denominator (g) to cancel all of the denominators of the complex fraction, then work to simplify what is left:

$$\frac{\dfrac{1}{3}}{1+\dfrac{2}{4+5}} = \frac{\dfrac{1}{3}}{1+\dfrac{2}{9}} =$$

$$= \frac{9 \times \dfrac{1}{3}}{(9 \times 1) + \left(9 \times \dfrac{2}{9}\right)}$$

$$= \frac{3}{9+2} = \frac{3}{11}$$

40. (4) Since Neal was left with only $20.00 or 1/4 of what he had originally, he must have spent 3($20.00) = $60.00 for his shirt. The cost of the shirt added to the $20.00 equals $80.00.

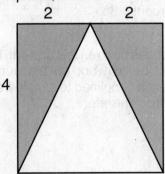

41. **(3)** The shaded regions of the square are two right triangles with heights of 4 and bases of 2. Each region has an area of (1/2)(base)(height) = (1/2)(4)(2) = 4. Two of the areas will equal 8 sq. units.

42. **(4)** The interpretation of the sign "> 0" means that all the answers derived from the inequality $b^2 - 121 > 0$ must be of positive value. Therefore, the values of b when it is squared must be greater than 121 in order for the difference to be positive. Because the product of two negative numbers is positive, negative values less than −11 must be considered, as well as all the positive values greater than +11.

43. **(5)** Let n = the number of nickels and $n + 13$ = the number of dimes. Then let $5n$ = the value of the n nickels and $10(n + 13)$ = the value of the dimes. The total value of Tracey's coins may now be represented by the expression:

$$5n + 10(n + 13) =$$
$$5n + 10n + 130 =$$
$$15n + 130$$

44. **(3)** There will be a total of 18 people for dinner, Jann and her 17 guests. Doubling her recipe will serve only 16 people, so another 1/4 of the recipe must be included to feed the remaining 2 people. Jann needs to increase her recipe to 2-1/4 times the original.

45. **(2)** In estimating an answer to the nearest hundred, round off to the nearest hundred all the numbers of the expression. This will create a much easier problem to simplify with less chance of a mistake.

$$\frac{(7,592)(4,892)}{(3,810)(70)}$$

is rounded off to:

$$\frac{(7,600)(4,900)}{(3,800)(100)} =$$
$$(2)(49) = 98$$

98 rounded off to the nearest hundred is 100.

46. **(3)** The probability is $\frac{1}{2} \times \frac{1}{2} \times \frac{1}{2} = \frac{1}{8}$, since there are 3 even numbers out of a total of 6 numbers $\left(\frac{3}{6} = \frac{1}{2}\right)$.

47. **(5)** In order for 534 to be a multiple of 7, it must be divisible by 7 with no remainder. Doing some long division gives:

$$
\begin{array}{r}
76 \\
7\overline{)534} \\
\underline{49} \\
44 \\
\underline{42} \\
2
\end{array}
$$

If the remainder 2 is increased by 5, then 534 + 5 = 539 will be a multiple of 7.

48. **(3/7)** Let x = the numerator and $x + 4$ = the denominator. Therefore, the fraction is expressed as:

$$\frac{x}{x+4}$$

When the numerator is doubled and the denominator is increased by five, the expression for the new fraction is:

$$\frac{2x}{(x+4)+5}$$

Now set up the equation and solve for x:

$$\frac{2x}{x+9} = \frac{1}{2}$$
$$4x = x + 9$$
$$3x = 9$$
$$x = 3$$
$$x + 4 = 7$$

The original fraction is 3/7.

49. Let x = required score. Then $(88)(0.25) + (80)(0.45) + (x)(0.30) = 85$. Solving $x = 90$.

50. (0,5)

To move the point two units to the right, you must move the point two units towards right on the *x*-axis only.

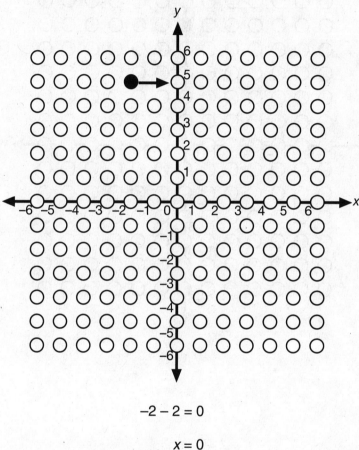

$$-2 - 2 = 0$$

$$x = 0$$

The new point will now be located at (0,5).

PRACTICE
EXAM II

EXAM II

TEST 1: LANGUAGE ARTS: WRITING, PART I

Tests of General Educational Development

Directions

The Language Arts: Writing Test is intended to measure your ability to use clear and effective English. It is a test of English as it should be written, not as it might be spoken. This test includes both multiple-choice questions and an essay. These directions apply only to the multiple-choice section; a separate set of directions is given for the essay.

The multiple-choice section consists of paragraphs with numbered sentences. Some of the sentences contain errors in sentence structure, usage, or mechanics (spelling, punctuation, and capitalization). After reading the numbered sentences, answer the multiple-choice questions that follow. Some questions refer to sentences that are correct as written. The best answer for these questions is the one that leaves the sentence as originally written. The best answer for some questions is the one that produces a sentence that is consistent with the verb tense and point of view used throughout the paragraph.

You should spend no more than 75 minutes on the multiple-choice questions and 45 minutes on your essay. Work carefully, but do not spend too much time on any one question. You may begin working on the essay part of this test as soon as you complete the multiple-choice section.

Do not mark in this test booklet. Record your answers on the separate answer sheet provided. Be sure that all requested information is properly recorded on the answer sheet.

To record your answers, mark one numbered space on the answer sheet beside the number that corresponds to the question in the test booklet.

FOR EXAMPLE:

Sentence 1: **We were all honored to meet governor Phillips.**

What correction should be made to this sentence?

    (1)   insert a comma after honored

    (2)   change the spelling of honored to honered

    (3)   change governor to Governor

    (4)   replace were with was

    (5)   no correction is necessary.   ① ② ● ④ ⑤

In this example, the word "governor" should be capitalized; therefore, answer space 3 would be marked on the answer sheet.

Do not rest the point of your pencil on the answer sheet while you are considering your answer. Make no stray or unnecessary marks. If you change an answer, erase your first mark completely. Mark only one answer space for each question; multiple answers will be scored as incorrect. Do not fold or crease your answer sheet. All test materials must be returned to the test administrator.

Reprinted with permission of the General Educational Development Testing Service of the American Council on Education.

Directions: Choose the <u>one best answer</u> to each item.

<u>Items 1 to 5</u> refer to the following paragraph.

(1) The word "home" may be considered in many ways but, each will always be a positive one. (2) For instance home is where a child goes after a neighborhood quarrel. (3) Mother would bandage any wounds and serve milk and cookies. (4) But whatever she might do you would feel safe and secure. (5) Home is where they should receive a great deal of comfort and support.

1. Sentence 1: **The word "home" may be considered in many ways but, each will always be a positive one.**

    Which correction should be made to this sentence?

    (1) place the word <u>way</u> after <u>each</u>
    (2) put the comma before <u>but</u>
    (3) place a comma after <u>home</u>
    (4) replace <u>each</u> with <u>home</u>
    (5) no correction is necessary

2. Sentence 2: **For instance home is where a child goes after a neighborhood quarrel.**

    Which correction should be made to this sentence?

    (1) place a comma after <u>goes</u>
    (2) change <u>where</u> to <u>we're</u>
    (3) place a comma after <u>instance</u>
    (4) change <u>where</u> to <u>were</u>
    (5) no correction is necessary

3. Sentence 3: **Mother would bandage any wounds and serve milk and cookies.**

    Which correction should be made to this sentence?

    (1) change <u>would</u> to <u>wood</u>
    (2) place a comma after <u>wounds</u>
    (3) place a comma after <u>milk</u>
    (4) place a comma after <u>bandage</u>
    (5) no correction is necessary

4. Sentence 4: **But whatever she might do you would feel safe and secure.**

Which correction should be made to this sentence?

   (1) change <u>whatever</u> to <u>what ever</u>
   (2) place a comma after <u>safe</u>
   (3) place a comma after <u>do</u>
   (4) place a comma after <u>But</u>
   (5) no correction is necessary

5. Sentence 5: **Home is where they should receive a great deal of comfort and support.**

Which correction should be made to this sentence?

   (1) change <u>they</u> to <u>one</u>
   (2) change <u>where</u> to <u>we're</u>
   (3) place a comma after <u>where</u>
   (4) place a comma after <u>receive</u>
   (5) no correction is necessary

<u>Items 6 to 10</u> refer to the following passage.

To: All Deli Employees

From: Deli Department manager

(A)

(1) The following rules and regulations are in effect immediately, and failure to uphold them will result in disciplinary action. (2) There have been several complaints from customers about bad service in this department.

(B)

(3) Thank you for your attention to these rules.

(C)

(4) Employees cannot smoke while made sandwiches. (5) It is against the law in this state to smoke anywhere but in designated areas in the store. (6) This is not sanitary or appetizing. (7) You must waited until your regularly scheduled break to smoke.

(D)

(8) Employees cannot swear or use obscene language in front of customers. (9) Employees especially should not direct such abuse at

customers. (10) Using foul language does not create a friendly or inviting atmosphere. (11) I also don't like it when I watch TV and see people use such language.

(E)

(12) Employees do not has the authority to change the price of a product if a customer is annoying, or is deemed "funny looking." (13) Employees can only charge what is listed on the board behind the counter. (14) Violation of this rule could lead to serious legal conse-quences for the store, including lawsuits, or police action to shut the store down.

6. Paragraph A will be most effective if

   (1) the sentence order is reversed.
   (2) the first sentence is eliminated.
   (3) several is deleted from the second sentence.
   (4) it is combined with paragraph B.
   (5) it is left as is.

7. Paragraph B should appear

   (1) exactly where it is.
   (2) at the end of the memo.
   (3) where it is now and at the end of the memo.
   (4) after paragraph C and before paragraph D.
   (5) nowhere in this memo. It should be deleted.

8. In paragraph C there are two major tense problems. Which words are in the wrong tense?

   (1) smoke and break
   (2) sandwiches and employees
   (3) waited and break
   (4) made and sanitary
   (5) made and waited

9. For the sake of clarity and conciseness, which sentence should be eliminated from paragraph D?

    (1) sentence 8

    (2) sentence 9

    (3) sentence 10

    (4) sentence 11

    (5) no change is necessary

10. There is a subject-verb disagreement in paragraph E. How can you fix it?

    (1) In sentence 12, change Employees to Employee

    (2) In sentence 13, change charge to charges

    (3) In sentence 12, change do to does

    (4) In sentence 13, change counter to counters

    (5) In sentence 12, change has to have

Items 11 to 14 refer to the paragraphs below.

(A)

(1) In 1947 Jackie Robinson became the first black player in the modern major leagues. (2) He was called to the Brooklyn Dodgers from its Montreal Royals farm club by Dodger president Branch Rickey. (3) Robinson, who helped his team win a pennant in his first year and was named most valuable player in his league after his third year. (4) He was elected to the Baseball Hall of Fame in 1962, the first year he was eligible. (5) Robinson played infield for the Brooklyn Dodgers of the National League from 1947 through 1956.

(B)

(6) Reared in Pasadena, California, Robinson became an outstanding all-around athlete at Pasadena Junior College and the University of California at Los Angeles. (7) He would later become a baseball legend. (8) He excelled in football, basketball, and track as well as baseball. (9) Robinson withdrew from U.C.L.A. in his third year to help his mother care for the family.

(C)

(10) In 1942 he entered the U.S. Army, attended officer candidate school, was commissioned a second lieutenant in 1943, and received a medical discharge in 1945. (11) He then played professional football in Hawaii and baseball with the Kansas City Monarchs of the Negro National League.

(D)

(12) His career average was .311. (13) On October 23, 1945, Robinson was signed by Branch Rickey, president of the Brooklyn club, to play on a Dodger farm team, the Montreal Royals of the International League. (14) Robinson led that league in batting average in 1946 and was brought up to play for Brooklyn in 1947. (15) He was an immediate success. (16) Leading the National League in stolen bases, he was chosen rookie of the year. (17) In 1949 he won the batting championship with a .342 average and was voted the league's most valuable player. (18) As a base runner, Robinson unnerved opposing pitchers and terrorized infielders who had to try to prevent his stealing bases.

(E)

(19) After retiring from baseball early in 1957, Robinson engaged in business. (20) He was a civil rights advocate, and worked on many campaigns and issues to heighten awareness of racial inequality in the United States. (21) He died in 1972.

11.   There is some repetition in this passage. How would you fix it?

   (1)   Eliminate the mention of the Montreal Royals and the signing of Robinson in paragraph A.

   (2)   Remove the reference to the Hall of Fame.

   (3)   Delete paragraph E.

   (4)   Take out all reference to Robinson's statistics.

   (5)   Combine paragraph A with paragraph B.

12.   Which sentence in paragraph D should be the topic sentence?

   (1)   sentence 12

   (2)   sentence 13

   (3)   sentence 14

   (4)   sentence 15

   (5)   sentence 16

13.   Which of the following sentences would be the best transition between paragraphs D and E?

   (1)   Pee-wee Reese was the Dodger shortstop.

   (2)   The Dodgers played at Ebbets Field in Brooklyn.

   (3)   Ebbets Field no longer stands.

(4)   The Dodgers finally won a World Series in 1955, and Robinson
       began to contemplate leaving baseball.

(5)   There are still many people in Brooklyn who are mad that the
       Dodgers left.

14.   Which sentence in paragraph B disrupts the unity and coherence of the
       paragraph?

(1)   sentence 6

(2)   sentence 7

(3)   sentence 8

(4)   sentence 9

(5)   none of the above

Items 15 to 20 refer to the following paragraphs.

(A)

(1) To plan an effective party, you need to think ahead. (2) Dont wait
until the last minute to plan the event. (3) With advanced preparation you
will have a greater chance of putting on a successful party.

(B)

(4) First, you need to decide on the size of the party. (5) If it's going to
be very big, you might have to hold it at a banquet hall. (6) If its going to
be small, you can probably hold it in your house. (7) When you've decided
on an approximate size, you can begin to plan your food and beverage
needs.

(C)

(8) You will also need to decide whether you want to hire musicians,
clowns, magicians, or other entertainers for your party. (9) At this point,
you will be ready to draw up a budget. (10) You can use a budget to
compare how much the party will cost versus how much you have to
spending. (11) You may find you'll have to cut corners a bit to stay within
your budget.

(D)

(12) Now that you have a sense of what you need to buy and how
much you have to spend, you can start making the appropriate purchases. (13) Do as much as you can in advance so that you won't have
too much to do at the last minute. (14) When calculating your budget, you
should make sure some extra money is available in case certain items
end up being more expensive than you think. (15) By following these
simple rules, you can be assured of having a fiscally responsible and well-
organized party. .

15. Sentence 2: **Dont wait until the last minute to plan the event.**

    What correction is necessary?

    (1) change <u>wait</u> to <u>weight</u>

    (2) change the period to a question mark

    (3) change <u>dont</u> to <u>don't</u>

    (4) place a semi-colon after <u>minute</u>

    (5) no correction is necessary

16. Sentence 5: **If it's going to be very big, you might have to hold it at a banquet hall.**

    What correction is necessary?

    (1) change <u>it's</u> to <u>its</u>

    (2) remove the comma after <u>big</u>

    (3) place a comma after <u>it</u>

    (4) capitalize <u>banquet</u>

    (5) no correction is necessary

17. Sentence 6: **If its going to be small, you can probably hold it in your house.**

    What correction is necessary?

    (1) change <u>its</u> to <u>it's</u>

    (2) change <u>your</u> to <u>you're</u>

    (3) remove the comma after <u>small</u>

    (4) start a new sentence after <u>small</u>

    (5) no correction is necessary

18. How can paragraph C can be fixed?

    (1) Change the period in sentence 11 to a colon.

    (2) Change <u>spending</u> in the third sentence to <u>spend</u>

    (3) Delete the comma after <u>point</u> in sentence 9

    (4) Reverse the order of the first two sentences

    (5) Make sentence 11 the first sentence

19. Which of the following sentences from paragraph D should be moved to paragraph C?

 (1) sentence 12

 (2) sentence 13

 (3) sentence 14

 (4) sentence 15

 (5) no change is necessary

20. Paragraph D contains which of the following bad sentences?

 (1) a fragment

 (2) a run-on

 (3) a fused sentence

 (4) a sentence that is not parallel

 (5) none of the above

Items 21 to 27 refer to the following paragraph.

   (1) In todays society people are always asking about where you went to school. (2) Education is getting more and more important, especially concerning employment. (3) Often potential employers ask more about education than they do about skills abilities. (4) Major companies find that they have to teach basic educational skills to new employees before they can train these employees to work. (5) What is happening in the public school system that is not preparing young people to enter the work world? (6) Are we passing students, letting them move on from one grade to the next without really making sure that they have learned? (7) How do people get out of school without learning how to read or do simple arithmetic? (8) Do these same young people fool teachers, or do teachers except poor papers and bad work, just letting these students graduate without proving themselves academically? (9) What can we all do to improve the national educational system? (10) We certainly do not want our children to go through twelve years of school and not be able to read. (11) Companies certainly should not have to step in after people have graduated high school. (12) We should of learned academic skills in high school and elementary classes. (13) I know that I would like to be hired for any job I wanted, and be able to do it when I was hired. (14) Me and my family want to live comfortably and have enough money. (15) With good reading and math skills I should be able to get a good job. (16) Its not being prepared for the work market that makes getting a good job hard to do.

21. Sentence 1: **In todays society people are always asking about where you went to school.**

    Which correction should be made to this sentence?

    (1) add a comma after society

    (2) place a comma after where

    (3) change todays to today's

    (4) add a comma after asking

    (5) no change is necessary

22. Sentence 7: **How do people get out of school without learning how to read or do simple arithmetic?**

    Which correction should be made to this sentence?

    (1) place a comma after school

    (2) place a comma after learning

    (3) place a period after school

    (4) change simple to simply

    (5) no correction is necessary

23. Sentence 8: **Do these same young people fool teachers, or do teachers except poor papers and bad work...?**

    Which correction should be made to this sentence?

    (1) remove the comma after teachers

    (2) place a comma after papers

    (3) place a period after teachers

    (4) change except to accept

    (5) no correction is necessary

24. Sentence 12: **We should of learned academic skills in high school and elementary classes.**

    Which correction should be made to this sentence?

    (1) change high school to High School

    (2) change of to have

    (3) place a comma after skills

    (4) place a comma after high school

    (5) no correction is necessary

25. Sentence 14: **Me and my family want to live comfortably and have enough money.**

    Which correction should be made to this sentence?

    (1) place commas before and after comfortably

    (2) place a comma after comfortably

    (3) change Me and my family to I and my family

    (4) change Me and my family to My family and I

    (5) no correction is necessary

26. Sentence 15: **With good reading and math skills I should be able to get a good job.**

    Which correction should be made to this sentence?

    (1) place a comma after reading

    (2) place a comma after skills

    (3) place a comma after able

    (4) place a period after able

    (5) no correction is necessary

27. Sentence 16: **Its not being prepared for the work market that makes getting a good job hard to do.**

    Which correction should be made to this sentence?

    (1) change work market to work-market

    (2) change Its to It's

    (3) place a comma after prepared

    (4) place a comma after market

    (5) no correction is necessary

Items 28 to 34 refer to the following paragraph.

   (1) This country is football-crazy to a extreme. (2) Every weekend people all over the United States root for teams. (3) Their is no way that every team can win every game. (4) High school ball players are the town heros when they win. (5) Whole families plan the weekend around the local game. (6) My favorite team has had a winning season this year and it has been lots of fun. (7) It is gonna be lots of fun having a winning season. (8) Our special team always runs the ball back on kick-offs. (9) They seem to break tackels right and left. (10) Last week, we were the receiving team first and ran the first play for a touchdown. (11) Boy! Was that a fun night—creaming the other team.

28. Sentence 1: **This country is football-crazy to a extreme.**

    Which correction should be made to this sentence?

    (1) change football to foot ball
    (2) place a period after crazy
    (3) change a extreme to an extreme
    (4) place a comma after crazy
    (5) no correction is necessary

29. Sentence 2: **Every weekend people all over the United States root for teams.**

    Which correction should be made to this sentence?

    (1) change weekend to week end
    (2) change root to rote
    (3) place a comma after weekend
    (4) place a comma after United States
    (5) no correction is necessary

30. Sentence 3: **Their is no way that every team can win every game.**

    Which correction should be made to this sentence?

    (1) place a comma after way
    (2) place a comma after team
    (3) change Their to There
    (4) change Their to They're
    (5) no correction is necessary

31. Sentence 4: **High school ball players are the town heros when they win.**

    Which correction should be made to this sentence?

    (1) change High school to High School
    (2) change ball players to ball-players
    (3) change heros to heroes
    (4) place a comma after heros
    (5) no correction is necessary

32. Sentence 6: **My favorite team has had a winning season this year and it has been lots of fun.**

    Which correction should be made to this sentence?

    (1) omit <u>had</u>

    (2) place a comma after <u>season</u>

    (3) place a comma after <u>year</u>

    (4) place a period after <u>year</u>

    (5) no correction is necessary

33. Sentence 7: **It is gonna be lots of fun having a winning season.**

    Which correction should be made to this sentence?

    (1) change <u>It is</u> to <u>Its</u>

    (2) change <u>gonna</u> to <u>going to</u>

    (3) place a comma after <u>lots</u>

    (4) place a comma after <u>fun</u>

    (5) no correction is necessary

34. Sentence 9: **They seem to break tackels right and left.**

    Which correction should be made to this sentence?

    (1) change <u>break</u> to <u>brake</u>

    (2) change <u>tackels</u> to <u>tackles</u>

    (3) place a comma after <u>right</u>

    (4) place a comma after <u>tackels</u>

    (5) no correction is necessary

<u>Items 35 to 41</u> refer to the following passage.

(1) During America's encounter with Iraq in the Persian Gulf War, anti-war protests springed up throughout the country. (2) From this many people were reminded of the violent protests associated with the Vietnam War. (3) Many people attributed these similar incidents to a sign of progressive change in the country's attitude toward piece. (4) The fact is however that anti-war protest has been a feature of this country through every major war, excluding World War II. (5) The reason being the attack on Pearl Harbor. (6) Moreover, many have tried to argue that Roosevelt engineered the attack on Pearl Harbor to stem America's anti-war sentiments. (7) While this is a rather extreme proof of America's anti-war history, the fact remains that the last two wars have indicated nothing new about this country's attitude, yet they have shown that the roots of America's war philosophy have remained unchanged.

35. Sentence 1: **During America's encounter with Iraq in the Persian Gulf War, anti-war protests springed up throughout the country.**

    Which correction should be made to this sentence?

    (1) change America's to Americas

    (2) change anti-war to anti war

    (3) change Gulf to gulf

    (4) change springed to sprung

    (5) no correction is necessary

36. Sentence 2: **From this many people were reminded of the violent protests associated with the Vietnam War.**

    Which correction should be made to this sentence?

    (1) insert a comma after this

    (2) insert a comma after people

    (3) change were to was

    (4) change associated to associates

    (5) no correction is necessary

37. Sentence 3: **Many people attributed these similar incidents to a sign of progressive change in the country's attitude toward piece.**

    Which correction should be made to this sentence?

    (1) insert a comma after incidents

    (2) place a comma after change

    (3) change country's to countries

    (4) change piece to peace

    (5) no correction is necessary

38. Sentence 4: **The fact is however that anti-war protest has been a feature of this country through every major war, excluding World War II.**

    Which correction should be made to this sentence?

    (1) change is to being

    (2) insert commas before and after however

    (3) change has to have

(4)   omit excluding World War II

(5)   no correction is necessary

39.   Sentence 5: **The reason being the attack on Pearl Harbor.**

Which rewrite of Sentence 5 is correct?

(1)   The reason not being the attack on Pearl Harbor.

(2)   The reason for this was the attack on Pearl Harbor.

(3)   The reason for this being the attack on Pearl Harbor.

(4)   The reason for this were the attack on Pearl Harbor.

(5)   The sentence is correct as it stands.

40.   Sentence 6: **Moreover, many have tried to argue that Roosevelt engineered the attack on Pearl Harbor to stem America's anti-war sentiments.**

Which correction should be made to this sentence?

(1)   change Moreover to More over

(2)   change many to much

(3)   change Roosevelt to Roosevelt's

(4)   place a comma after Harbor

(5)   no correction is necessary

41.   Sentence 7: **While this is a rather extreme proof of America's anti-war history, the fact remains that the last two wars have indicated nothing new about this country's attitude, yet they have shown that the roots of America's war philosophy have remained un-changed.**

Which of the following is the best way to write the underlined portion of this sentence? If you think the original is the best way, choose option (1).

(1)   attitude, yet   (4)   attitude, as yet

(2)   attitude, as   (5)   attitude. As

(3)   attitude. Yet

Items 42 to 45 refer to the following passage.

   (1) The past decade saw a rising interest, mostly negative, in the role-playing game, Dungeons & Dragons. (2) Complaints ranged from calling it a devil worshipers' game, hold it responsible for witchcraft use, and, worst of all, blaming it for teenage suicide. (3) Talk shows have even invited practically evangelical speakers denounce players of the game as being

in league with Satan. (4) Crater Gary Gygax disagrees. (5) He says that the purpose of the game is merely to broaden the imaginations of those who play, without influencing their every day lives at least not in a negative sense. (6) However, one might see why others could misconstrue his game's purposes. (7) The game allows characters to encounter demons such as Mephistopheles and Baalzebul, traditional names in Biblical texts. (8) In fact, despite the denial of demonic worship as part of the game, there has been a flurry of activity by its makers. (9) A whole new edition of the game has been produced; it excludes the demons and disallows players to be of an evil code of ethics.

42. Sentence 2: **Complaints ranged from calling it a devil worshipers' game, hold it responsible for witchcraft use, and, worst of all, blaming it for teenage suicide.**

Which correction should be made to this sentence?

(1) change <u>ranged</u> to <u>ranges</u>

(2) change <u>worshipers'</u> to <u>worshiper's</u>

(3) change <u>hold</u> to <u>holding</u>

(4) insert <u>by</u> before <u>worst</u>

(5) no corrections are necessary

43. Sentence 3: **Talk shows have even <u>invited</u> practically evangelical speakers <u>denounce</u> players of the game as being in league with Satan.**

Which of the following is the best way to write the underlined portions of this sentence? If you think the original is the best way, choose option (1).

(1) invited… denounce

(2) invited… to denounce

(3) inviting… to denounce

(4) inviting… denounce

(5) been invited… denounce

44. Sentence 8: **In fact, despite the denial of demonic worship as part of the game, there has been a flurry of activity by its makers.**

Which correction should be made to this sentence?

(1) change <u>has</u> to <u>have</u>

(2) change <u>denial</u> to <u>denied</u>

(3) insert a comma after <u>worship</u>

     (4)   change <u>its</u> to <u>it's</u>

     (5)   no correction is necessary

45.   Sentence 9: **A whole new edition of the game has been produced; it excludes the demons and disallows players to be of an evil code of ethics.**

     Which correction should be made to this sentence?

     (1)   change <u>has</u> to <u>have</u>

     (2)   change <u>produced</u> to <u>produce</u>

     (3)   change <u>disallows</u> to <u>unallows</u>

     (4)   change <u>of</u> to <u>have</u>

     (5)   no correction is necessary

<u>Items 46 to 50</u> refer to the following passage.

(1) Many movie critics complain that there has been a literary glut in the films produced within the past decade. (2) They attribute this to the rise of the "Hollywood genre." (3) That is, the recurrence of certain movie plots. (4) Examples of this so-called "Hollywood genre" include movies about intergalactic wars, visits by cute aliens from space, and an intelligent pet. (5) The cause of these genres, say critics, stem from an original movie that has been a box office success. (6) For example, the movie *Gremlins* motivated a whole slew of movies involving miniature creatures who were cute but deadly; such as *Critters* and *Ghoulies*. (7) Hollywood producers, however, counter these critiques, and say that audiences are pleased with recurring plots that appear more than once. (8) They argue that movies are too expensive to produce to be risking new ideas.

46.   Sentences 2 and 3: **They attribute this to the rise of the "Hollywood <u>genre". That is, the recurrence</u> of certain movie plots.**

     Which of the following is the best way to write the underlined portion of this sentence? If you think the original is the best way, choose option (1).

     (1)   genre". That is, the recurrence

     (2)   genre. That is," the recurrence

     (3)   genre." In other words, the recurrence

     (4)   genre," or the recurrence

     (5)   genre." Rather, the recurrence

47. Sentence 4: **Examples of this so-called "Hollywood genre" include movies about intergalactic wars, visits by cute aliens from space, <u>and an intelligent pet.</u>**

    Which of the following is the best way to write the underlined portion of this sentence? If you think the original is the best way, choose option (1).

    (1) and an intelligent pet.
    (2) and also an intelligent pet.
    (3) and intelligent pets.
    (4) or an intelligent pet.
    (5) but an intelligent pet.

48. Sentence 5: **The cause of these genres, say critics, stem from an original movie that has been a box office success.**

    Which correction should be made to this sentence?

    (1) change <u>say</u> to <u>says</u>
    (2) change <u>critics</u> to <u>critic</u>
    (3) change <u>stem</u> to <u>stems</u>
    (4) change <u>has</u> to <u>have</u>
    (5) no correction is necessary

49. Sentence 6: **For example, the movie *Gremlins* motivated a whole slew of movies involving miniature creatures who were cute but deadly; such as *Critters* and *Ghoulies*.**

    Which correction should be made to this sentence?

    (1) remove the comma after <u>example</u>
    (2) change <u>motivated</u> to <u>motivating</u>
    (3) insert a comma after <u>slew of movies</u>
    (4) replace the semi-colon with a comma
    (5) no correction is necessary

50. Sentence 7: **Hollywood producers, however, counter these critiques, and say that audiences are pleased with recurring plots that appear more than once.**

    Which correction should be made to this sentence?

    (1) remove the commas around <u>however</u>
    (2) remove the comma after <u>critiques</u>

(3) remove <u>recurring</u>

(4) insert a comma after <u>plots</u>

(5) no correction is necessary

TEST 1: LANGUAGE ARTS: WRITING, PART II

Tests of General Educational Development

Directions

This part of the Language Arts: Writing Test is intended to determine how well you write. You are asked to write an essay that explains something or presents an opinion on an issue. In preparing your essay, you should take the following steps.

1. Read carefully the directions and the essay topic given below.

2. Plan your essay carefully before you write.

3. Use scratch paper to make any notes.

4. Write your essay on the lined pages of the separate answer sheet.

5. Read carefully what you have written and make any changes that will improve your essay.

6. Check your paragraphs, sentence structure, spelling, punctuation, capitalization, and usage, and make any necessary corrections.

Be sure you write the <u>letter</u> of the essay topic (given below) on your answer sheet. Write the letter in the box at the upper right-hand corner of the page where you write your essay.

You will have 45 minutes to write on the topic below. Write legibly and use a ballpoint pen so that the evaluators will be able to read your writing.

Write your essay on the lined pages of the separate answer sheet. The notes you make on scratch paper will not be scored.

Your essay will be scored by at least two trained evaluators who will judge it according to its <u>overall effectiveness</u>. They will judge how clearly you make the main point of your composition, how thoroughly you support your ideas, and how clearly and correctly you write throughout the essay.

Reprinted with permission of the General Educational Development Testing Service of the American Council on Education.

Topic A

This country is faced with crime, health problems, a possibility of war, financial problems, and a lessening of world respect.

Is this true? If so, what can we do about it? If not, why do people say it is true? What can we do to improve our image internationally? Respond to this statement in an essay of approximately 250 words.

TEST 2: SOCIAL STUDIES

Tests of General Educational Development

Directions

The Social Studies Test consists of multiple-choice questions intended to measure your knowledge of general social studies concepts. The questions are based on short readings which often include a graph, chart, or figure. Study the information given and then answer the question(s) following it. Refer to the information as often as necessary in answering the questions.

You should spend no more than 70 minutes answering the questions in this booklet. Work carefully, but do not spend too much time on any one question. Be sure you answer every question. You will not be penalized for incorrect answers.

Do not mark in this test booklet. Record your answers to the questions on the separate answer sheet provided. Be sure all requested information is properly recorded on the answer sheet.

To record your answers, mark the numbered space on the answer sheet beside the number that corresponds to the question in the test booklet.

FOR EXAMPLE:

Early colonists of North America looked for settlement sites that had adequate water supplies and were accessible by ship. For this reason, many early towns were built near

(1)	mountains.	(4)	glaciers.
(2)	prairies.	(5)	plateaus.
(3)	rivers.		

① ② ● ④ ⑤

The correct answer is "rivers"; therefore, answer space 3 would be marked on the answer sheet.

Do not rest the point of your pencil on the answer sheet while you are considering your answer. Make no stray or unnecessary marks. If you change an answer, erase your first mark completely. Mark only one answer space for each question; multiple answers will be scored as incorrect. Do not fold or crease your answer sheet. Return all test materials to the test administrator.

Directions: Choose the one best answer to each item.

Items 1 to 5 refer to the following letter.

Department of State,
Washington, May 13, 1915

To Ambassador Gerard:

Please call on the Minister of Foreign Affairs and after reading to him this communication leave with him a copy.

In view of recent acts of the German authorities in violation of American rights on the high seas which culminated in the torpedoing and sinking of the British steamship *Lusitania* on May 7, 1915, by which over 100 American citizens lost their lives, it is clearly wise and desirable that the Government of the United States and the Imperial German Government should come to a clear and full understanding as to the grave situation which has resulted.

The sinking of the British passenger steamer *Falaba* by a German submarine on March 28, through which Leon C. Thrasher, an American citizen, was drowned; the attack on April 28 on the American vessel *Cushing* by a German aeroplane; the torpedoing on May 1 of the American vessel *Gulflight* by a German submarine, as a result of which two or more Americans citizens met their death; and finally, the torpedoing and sinking of the steamship *Lusitania*, constitute a series of events which the Government of the United States has observed with growing concern, distress, and amazement....

The Government of the United States has been apprised that the Imperial German Government considered themselves to be obliged by the extraordinary circumstances of the present war and the measures adopted by their adversaries in seeking to cut Germany off from all commerce, to adopt methods of retaliation which go much beyond the ordinary methods of warfare at sea, in the proclamation of a war zone from which they have warned neutral ships to keep away. This Government has already taken occasion to inform the Imperial German Government that it cannot admit the adoption of such measures or such a warning of danger to operate as in any degree an abbreviation of the rights of American shipmasters or of American citizens bound on lawful errands as passengers on merchant ships of belligerent nationality; and that it must hold the Imperial German Government to a strict accountability for any infringement of those rights, intentional or incidental.

1.   The stated purpose of the letter was to

   (1)   declare war.
   (2)   demand payment for all damages.
   (3)   create an alliance.

(4)   make sure no American ships were attacked.

(5)   issue a warning.

2.   From the quote, the war going on was

(1)   the American Civil War.   (4)   World War II.

(2)   the Spanish-American War. (5)   the Vietnam War.

(3)   World War I.

3.   The letter acknowledges that the Germans have done all except what?

(1)   Used submarines to attack ships

(2)   Bombed ships from planes

(3)   Used poison gas

(4)   Created a war zone to stop shipping

(5)   Warned neutral nations away from war zones

4.   Which is not stated in the letter?

(1)   Germany is being cut off from trade by her enemies.

(2)   Americans claim the right to safely sail on merchant ships of warring nations.

(3)   American ships will observe war zones.

(4)   Neutral nations have rights.

(5)   The war circumstances are extraordinary.

5.   The President who sent this letter and eventually led the U.S. to declare war was

(1)   T. Roosevelt.   (4)   H. Hoover.

(2)   W. Wilson.   (5)   F. Roosevelt.

(3)   W. Harding.

Items 6 to 10 refer to the following table.

Parliamentary	Restricted Parliamentary	One Party
Canada	Brazil	Eritrea
United States	Colombia	Algeria
Venezuela	Turkey	Sudan
India	Egypt	Kenya
Spain	Indonesia	Ivory Coast

6.   What would be the best title tor the table?

(1)   World government forms

(2)   Sample government organization

    (3)   Capitalism v. communism
    (4)   First World v. Third World government
    (5)   Poor v. rich governments

7.   The term parliamentary refers to

    (1)   a representative form of government.
    (2)   the name of the governing body.
    (3)   an ex-British colony.
    (4)   the lack of an elected leader.
    (5)   a written constitution.

8.   One pattern of the one-party system is that

    (1)   all are ex-British colonies.
    (2)   all have kings.
    (3)   all are Arabic.
    (4)   all are on the Mediterranean Sea.
    (5)   all are from the same continent.

9.   Which is the most likely definition of restricted parliamentary rule?

    (1)   Elected for short terms
    (2)   Only allowed to veto laws
    (3)   Countered by a strong executive
    (4)   Only meets for limited sessions
    (5)   Limited to one term

10.   Which would not be a government that would fit under a one-party system?

    (1)   Fascist   (4)   Dictatorship
    (2)   Militarist   (5)   Republic
    (3)   Monarchy

Items 11 to 15 refer to the graphs below.

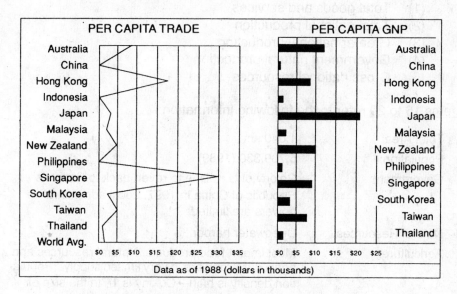

Data as of 1988 (dollars in thousands)

11. Comparing the two charts, the best conclusion is that

    (1)   there is a direct relationship between GNP and trade.
    (2)   the nations all have increased their GNP.
    (3)   they all exceeded the world average in trade.
    (4)   Japan is the leader in both GNP and trade.
    (5)   China ranks lowest in both categories.

12. Which is not true about both charts?

    (1)   Both are figured per person.
    (2)   Both are in thousands of dollars.
    (3)   Both compare the same nations.
    (4)   Both are the same type of graph.
    (5)   Both use the same year's data.

13. Which economic region of the world is reflected in the graphs?

    (1)   East Asia   (4)   All Pacific
    (2)   All Asia   (5)   All ex-British colonies
    (3)   North West Asia

14. The nation that is increasing its prosperity the most is probably

    (1)   Australia.   (4)   Singapore.
    (2)   Hong Kong.   (5)   Taiwan.
    (3)   Japan.

15. Which is the best way to describe the GNP?

    (1) Total goods and services
    (2) Total national production
    (3) Greater national production
    (4) Government natural production
    (5) Gross national resources

Items 16 to 20 refer to the following information.

Total Area:	1,040 km^2
Population:	5,709,330 (1989)
Government:	Colony of U.K. Due to revert back to People's Republic of China in 1997. Local administrative powers are limited.
Natural Resources:	Deepwater harbor
Agriculture:	Must import food products. Natural resources and agricultural land are in very limited supply. (Population density is high—Colony is 1/7th the size of Ireland with twice the population.)
GNP:	$45 billion
Per Capita GNP:	$9,220
Major Industries:	Textiles, electronics, manufacturing, finance, and distribution services
Industrial Output:	+16.4% (1988)
Merchandise Trade:	(1988) Exports = $48.5 billion; Imports = $48.5 billion
Per Capita Trade:	$17,017
Foreign Debt:	$9.6 billion (1988)
Inflation (CPI): 1980-88	6.7%

16. The area being described is

    (1) Australia.   (4) Gibraltar.
    (2) Northern Ireland.   (5) Singapore.
    (3) Hong Kong.

17. Which occupation is particularly suited to this area?

    (1) Farmer   (4) Teacher
    (2) Merchant   (5) Tourist guide
    (3) Autoworker

18. Statistics would indicate which of the choices below about population patterns?

    (1)   High density   (4)   Uneven distribution
    (2)   Low density   (5)   Heavily rural
    (3)   Even distribution

19. The statistics contained in the list above would lead to what conclusion?

    (1)   This is a poor nation.
    (2)   This is a rich nation.
    (3)   The nation is industrially efficient.
    (4)   The nation is weak industrially.
    (5)   The nation has a one-product economy.

20. The statistics indicate what kind of trade balance?

    (1)   Favorable   (4)   Reasonable debt
    (2)   Unfavorable   (5)   Balanced
    (3)   Excessive debt

Items 21 to 24 refer to the following passage.

THE CONSTITUTION

ARTICLE II

Section 2. The President shall be Commander in Chief of the Army and Navy of the United States, and of the Militia of the several States, when called into the actual Service of the United States; he may require the Opinion, in writing, of the principal Officer in each of the executive Departments, upon any subject relating to the Duties of their respective Offices, and he shall have Power to Grant Reprieves and Pardons for Offences against the United States, except in Cases of Impeachment.

He shall have Power, by and with the Advice and Consent of the Senate, to make Treaties, provided two thirds of the Senators present concur; and he shall nominate, and by and with the Advice and Consent of the Senate, shall appoint Ambassadors, other public Ministers and Consuls, Judges of the Supreme Court, and all other Officers of the United States, whose Appointments are not herein otherwise provided for, and which shall be established by Law: but the Congress may by Law vest the Appointment of such inferior Officers, as they think proper, in the President alone, in the Courts of Law, or in the Heads of Departments.

The President shall have Power to fill up all Vacancies that may happen during the Recess of the Senate, by granting Commissions which shall expire at the End of their next Session.

Section 3. He shall from time to time give to the Congress information of the State of the Union, and recommend to their Consideration such Measures as he shall judge necessary and expedient; he may, on extraordinary occasions, convene both Houses, or either of them, and in Case of Disagreement between them, with respect to the Time of Adjournment, he may adjourn them to such Time as he shall think proper; he shall receive Ambassadors and other public Ministers; he shall take Care that the laws be faithfully executed, and shall Commission all the Officers of the United States.

Section 4. The President, Vice President and all civil Officers of the United States, shall be removed from Office on Impeachment for, and Conviction of, Treason, Bribery, or other high Crimes and Misdemeanors.

21. What fraction of the senators must approve a treaty proposed by the President?

    (1) one-third
    (2) one-half
    (3) three-fifths
    (4) two-thirds
    (5) four-fifths

22. Which of the following is *not* given in Article II: *Section 4* as a reason for removing a president from office?

    (1) Incapacity
    (2) Treason
    (3) Bribery
    (4) High Crimes
    (5) Misdemeanors

23. Which of the following is *not* a power granted to the President in Article II: *Section 2?*

    (1) Appointment of ambassadors
    (2) Commander in Chief of Army and Navy
    (3) Appointment of Supreme Court judges
    (4) Granting of pardons for offenses against the United States
    (5) Declaring of war

24. Article II: *Section 3* prescribes that the President shall do all of the following *except*

    (1) receive ambassadors.
    (2) commission all of the officers of the United States.
    (3) convene on extraordinary occasions the House and Senate.
    (4) dissolve the House and Senate.
    (5) provide Congress with information on the State of the Union.

Items 25 to 29 refer to the following information.

Caucus Standing Rules

1. This caucus shall be governed by Robert's Rules of Order (newly revised), unless the caucus rules provide otherwise.
2. Membership in this caucus is based on both of the following criteria:
    a. ...being either a member in good standing of the Party or a precinct delegate of the Party (in accordance with the rules of the state convention).
    b. ...being an active member, a retired member, or a professional staff member.
3. Voting privileges shall be extended to all qualified caucus members as defined in Section 2.
4. Officers of the caucus shall be the chairperson, vice-chairperson, and secretary.
    a. The officers shall be elected by the majority of those persons present and voting.
    b. The officers shall be elected for a two-year term in accordance with the election of the State Party officers at the spring convention held in February of the odd-numbered years.
    c. The chairperson shall fill vacancies by appointment, subject to the approval of the Executive Committee.
    d. In the event the chairperson can no longer serve, the secretary shall call an Executive Committee meeting within 30 days. At the meeting, the Executive Committee shall appoint a chairperson to serve until the next regularly scheduled election, at which point, the caucus will elect a chairperson to fill the unexpired term.
5. Each congressional district will elect one coordinator and one alternate at the spring convention.

---

25. The presiding officer of the organization is the

    (1) president.
    (2) caucus leader.
    (3) chairperson.
    (4) chief executive.
    (5) chief executive officer.

26. A caucus is part of a

    (1)   political party.
    (2)   local government.
    (3)   state government.
    (4)   national government.
    (5)   corporation.

27. Who could not vote in the caucus?

    (1)   A party member
    (2)   A precinct delegate
    (3)   A staff member
    (4)   A retired member
    (5)   All can vote.

28. The caucus is organized by

    (1)   cities.
    (2)   states.
    (3)   counties.
    (4)   congressional districts.
    (5)   age.

29. The caucus meets

    (1)   every spring.
    (2)   annually.
    (3)   every two years.
    (4)   quarterly.
    (5)   monthly.

Items 30 to 34 refer to the following graphs.

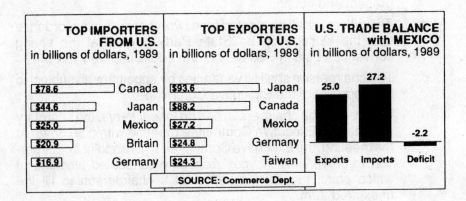

TOP IMPORTERS FROM U.S. in billions of dollars, 1989	TOP EXPORTERS TO U.S. in billions of dollars, 1989	U.S. TRADE BALANCE with MEXICO in billions of dollars, 1989
$78.6 Canada	$93.6 Japan	25.0 Exports
$44.6 Japan	$88.2 Canada	27.2 Imports
$25.0 Mexico	$27.2 Mexico	-2.2 Deficit
$20.9 Britain	$24.8 Germany	
$16.9 Germany	$24.3 Taiwan	

SOURCE: Commerce Dept.

30. Which nation is a top importer, but not a top exporter?

    (1)   Britain
    (2)   Canada
    (3)   Germany
    (4)   Japan
    (5)   Mexico

31. Taken together, which area imports the most from the U.S.?

    (1)   Canada   (4)   Africa
    (2)   Latin America   (5)   Europe
    (3)   Asia

32. Taken together, which area exports the most to the U.S.?

    (1)   Canada   (4)   Africa
    (2)   Latin America   (5)   Europe
    (3)   Asia

33. Who has the most favorable trade balance with the U.S.?

    (1)   Britain   (4)   Japan
    (2)   Canada   (5)   Mexico
    (3)   Germany

34. If exports exceed imports, it is called

    (1)   favorable balance of payments.
    (2)   unfavorable balance of payments.
    (3)   favorable balance of trade.
    (4)   unfavorable balance of trade.
    (5)   deficit spending.

Item 35 refers to the following paragraphs.

The account of the physical condition of the manufacturing population in the large towns in the northeastern District of England is less favourable. It is of this district that the Commissioners state, "We have found undoubted instances of children five years old sent to work thirteen hours a day; and frequently of children nine, ten, and eleven consigned to labour for fourteen and fifteen hours." The effects ascertained by the Commissioners in many cases are, "deformity," and in still more "stunted growth, relaxed muscles, and slender conformation": "twisting of the ends of the long bones, relaxation of the ligaments of the knees, ankles, and the like." "The representation that these effects are so common and universal as to enable some persons invariably to distinguish factory children from other children is, I have no hesitation in saying, an exaggerated and unfaithful picture of their general condition; at the same time it must be said, that the individual instances in which some one or other of those effects of severe labour are discernible are rather frequent than rare....

"In conclusion, I think it has been clearly proved that children have been worked a most unreasonable and cruel length of time daily, and that even adults have been expected to do a certain quantity of labour which scarcely any human being is able to endure. I am of opinion no child under fourteen years of age should work in a factory of any description for more than eight hours a day. From fourteen upwards I would recommend that no individual should, under any circumstances, work more than twelve hours a day; although if practicable, as a physician, I would prefer the limitation of ten hours, for all persons who earn their bread by their industry."

Source: Commission for Inquiry into the Employment of Children in Factories, *Second Report, with Minutes of Evidence and Reports by the Medical Commissioners*, Vol. V, Session 29 January-20 August, 1833 (London: His Majesty's Printing Office, 1833), pp. 5, 26-28.

35. The type of conditions described in the article were created as a result of what historical event?

(1) The Age of Revolution
(2) The creation of capitalism
(3) The rise of communism
(4) The rise of fascism
(5) The Industrial Revolution

Items 36 to 39 refer to the following form.

a Control number			Void ☐	For Official Use Only OMB No. 1545-0008			
b Employer identification number					1 Wages, tips, other compensation $		2 Federal income tax withheld $
c Employer's name, address, and ZIP code					3 Social security wages $		4 Social security tax withheld $
					5 Medicare wages and tips $		6 Medicare tax withheld $
					7 Social security tips $		8 Allocated tips
d Employee's social security number					9 Advance EIC payment $		10 Dependent care benefits $
e Employee's first name and initial		Last name			11 Nonqualified plans $		12a See instructions for box 12 $
					13 Statutory employee ☐ Retirement plan ☐ Third-party sick pay ☐		12b $
					14 Other		12c $
							12d $
f Employee's address and ZIP code							
15 State Employer's state ID number		16 State wages, tips, etc. $		17 State income tax $	18 Local wages, tips, etc. $	19 Local income tax $	20 Locality name
		$		$	$	$	

Form W-2 Wage and Tax Statement

Copy A For Social Security Administration—Send this entire page with Form W-3 to the Social Security Administration; photocopies are **not** acceptable.

Cat. No. 10134D

Department of the Treasury — Internal Revenue Service
For Privacy Act and Paperwork Reduction Act Notice, see separate instructions.

36. Which box indicates the amount of federal income tax withheld from an employee's paycheck?

(1) Box one
(2) Box two
(3) Box three
(4) Box four
(5) Box six

37. Which of the following types of information is *not* included on the W-2 form?

    (1) Name of employee
    (2) Name of employer
    (3) Identification number of employer
    (4) Name of employee's spouse
    (5) Address of employee

38. In which box is the employee's state income tax withholding listed?

    (1) Box two
    (2) Box three
    (3) Box sixteen
    (4) Box seventeen
    (5) Box nineteen

39. The W-2 Form states that the information on the form is being furnished to the Internal Revenue Service, which is part of what branch of the Federal Government?

    (1) Department of State
    (2) Department of Interior
    (3) Department of the Treasury
    (4) Department of Justice
    (5) Department of Commerce

Items 40 and 41 refer to the following passage.

It is an ugly, elusive war, fought with all the clever stunts in the guerrilla's handbook, not all of them deadly. Gangs disguised as official mosquito-spray teams walk into villages to confiscate farm equipment in the name of the government; sometimes they tear up peasants' identity cards to disrupt local administration; the Communists even managed to sabotage the national census by substituting falsified lists in some areas. The Viet Cong, which is what the Communist Vietnamese are called, are everywhere: tossing grenades into isolated villages in the rice fields in the south, sowing unrest among the border tribesmen in the thickly wooded Annamese highlands to the north. By day Saigon, a city of 2,000,000, is safe enough. But no one willingly sets his foot outside town after dark.

Fueled by Communist North Viet Nam with supplies and men smuggled through Laos over the clandestine Ho Chi Minh Trail, this wasting war has been going on for seven years. Its object is the destruction of South Viet Nam's stubby, stubborn President Ngo Dinh Diem, 60, who runs the war, the government, and everything else in South Viet Nam from a massive desk in his yellow stucco Freedom Palace in Saigon. President Diem had fought the Communists in his country long before World War II. At war's end, he was arrested by them; his brother was shot by them. He has stood in their way ever since.

Faced with this Communist challenge, the U.S. has made a major decision: South Viet Nam must be defended at all costs. While all Asia watched, the U.S., by fumbling unpreparedness and the lack of a dependable local fighting force to attach itself to, last spring abandoned Laos to its fate. South Viet Nam has been U.S.-sponsored from the start; its government is militantly anti-Communist, and its soldiers are willing to fight. If the U.S. cannot or will not save South Viet Nam from the Communist assault, no Asian nation can ever again feel safe in putting its faith in the U.S.—and the fall of all of Southeast Asia would only be a matter of time.

40. At the time of the quote, the Viet Nam War

 (1) was winding down.
 (2) was just beginning the U.S. involvement.
 (3) was at its height.
 (4) had become a UN police action.
 (5) had just been lost by the French.

41. Which of the following was a U.S. ally in the conflict?

 (1) Laos   (4) Ngo Dinh Diem
 (2) Viet Cong   (5) Southeast Asia
 (3) Ho Chi Minh

Items 42 to 45 refer to the following table.

Nation	Chemical Fertilizers	Oil Spills	Acid Rain
United States	moderate	moderate	severe
France	severe	severe	moderate
Japan	severe	small	moderate
Australia	small	small	small
Russia	small	small	moderate

42. The best title for this graph is

 (1) "Pollution Problems."   (4) "Leading Polluters."
 (2) "Modern Industry."   (5) "Western Pollution Problems."
 (3) "National Problems."

43. The chart reflects

    (1)   all major polluters.
    (2)   the major world polluters.
    (3)   land, sea, and air problems.
    (4)   similar national problems.
    (5)   problems of heavy industrialization.

44. According to the chart, the nation with the least problems is

    (1)   United States.   (4)   Australia.
    (2)   France.   (5)   Russia.
    (3)   Japan.

45. According to many scientists, the end result of continuing pollutions will be all except

    (1)   greenhouse effect.   (4)   more rain forests.
    (2)   health problems.   (5)   water shortages.
    (3)   depleted resources.

<u>Items 46 to 50</u> refer to the following passage.

Hoover had been in office less than a year, stocks had been falling for over a month; they had lost, on the average, about 1/6 of their quoted value, and looked "cheap" according to the opinion of important bankers, economists, and government officials. Business was still good—the economic position of the country was "sound" and technically the stock market itself had been improved by a "healthy reaction." Almost everyone thought a rally must be close at hand.

The market opened steady with prices little changed from the previous day, though some rather large blocks, of 20,000 to 25,000 shares, came out at the start. It sagged easily for the first half hour, and then around eleven o'clock the deluge broke.

It came with a speed and ferocity that left men dazed. The bottom simply fell out of the market. From all over the country a torrent of selling orders poured onto the floor of the Stock Exchange and there were no buying orders to meet it. Quotations of representative active issues, like Steel, Telephone, and Anaconda, began to fall two, three, five, and even ten points between sales. Less active stocks became unmarketable. Within a few moments the ticker service was hopelessly swamped and from then on no one knew what was really happening. By 1:30 the ticker tape was nearly two hours late; by 2:30 it was 147 minutes late. The last quotation was not printed on the tape until 7:08:05 P.M., four hours, eight and one-half minutes after the close. In the meantime, Wall Street had lived through an incredible nightmare.

46. What is the event the quote describes?

    (1) The Panic of 1837
    (2) The Great Depression
    (3) The Crash of 1929
    (4) Pearl Harbor Day
    (5) The assassination of John Kennedy

47. What compounded the problems of the day?

    (1) The ticker tape was running slow.
    (2) Business leaders were pessimistic.
    (3) Government leaders were pessimistic.
    (4) Major issues were not affected.
    (5) There was a lack of selling orders.

48. The stock prices were driven down by

    (1) lack of activity.
    (2) massive activity at the open of the market.
    (3) the market's rising trend over several months.
    (4) the general collapsing of businesses nationwide.
    (5) sell orders overwhelming buy orders.

49. The results of the Crash were partially blamed on the administration of

    (1) Woodrow Wilson.   (4) Herbert Hoover.
    (2) Warren Harding.   (5) Franklin Roosevelt.
    (3) Calvin Coolidge.

50. Which was not a reform created to try to prevent a repetition of 1929?

    (1) SEC
    (2) Margin restrictions
    (3) FDIC
    (4) Restrictions on corporation issuing stocks
    (5) Restrictions on insider trading

TEST 3: SCIENCE

Tests of General Educational Development

Directions

The Science Test consists of multiple-choice questions intended to measure your knowledge of the general concepts in science. The questions are based on short readings that often include a graph, chart, or figure. Study the information given and then answer the question(s) following it. Refer to the information as often as necessary in answering the questions.

You should spend no more than 80 minutes answering the questions in this booklet. Work carefully, but do not spend too much time on any one question. Be sure you answer every question. You will not be penalized for incorrect answers.

Do not mark in this test booklet. Record your answers to the questions on the separate answer sheet provided. Be sure all requested information is properly recorded on the answer sheet.

To record your answers, mark the numbered space on the answer sheet beside the number that corresponds to the question in the test booklet.

FOR EXAMPLE:

Which of the following is the smallest unit in a living thing?

(1) Tissue   (4) Muscle
(2) Organ   (5) Capillary
(3) Cell

① ② ● ④ ⑤

The correct answer is "cell"; therefore, answer space 3 would be marked on the answer sheet.

Do not rest the point of your pencil on the answer sheet while you are considering your answer. Make no stray or unnecessary marks. If you change an answer, erase your first mark completely. Mark only one answer space for each question; multiple answers will be scored as incorrect. Do not fold or crease your answer sheet. Return all test materials to the test administrator.

Directions: Choose the <u>one best answer</u> to each item.

<u>Item 1</u> refers to the following diagram.

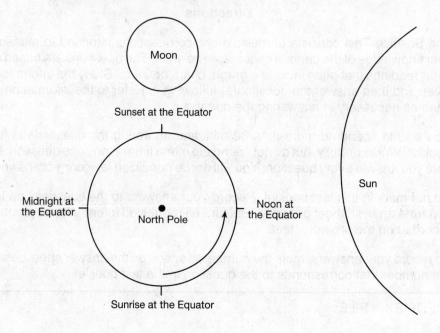

1. At what time(s) would a person standing on the equator see the moon in the position it is shown?

    (1) Midnight to noon
    (2) Noon to midnight
    (3) Sunrise to sunset
    (4) Sunset to sunrise
    (5) Only at sunset

<u>Item 2</u> refers to the following passage.

   Plants are photosynthetic organisms. Photosynthesis is the process by which plants use light energy to build sugars. Photosynthetic organisms can produce their needed nutrients by using carbon dioxide, water, and minerals. Plants give off oxygen.

2. A potted plant will have good growth indoors by

    (1) locating it away from a window and placing sugar and water in its soil.
    (2) locating it away from a window and placing water and fertilizer in its soil.
    (3) locating it near a window and placing sugar and water in its soil.

(4)   locating it near a window and placing water and fertilizer in its soil.

(5)   locating it anywhere and oxygenating its soil.

Items 3 and 4 refer to the following passage.

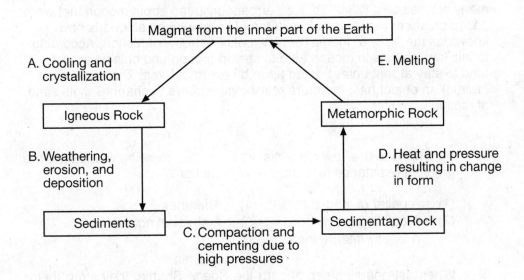

One process that occurs within the rock cycle is the formation of the rock we know as marble. Marble is limestone that has undergone a change in form due to extreme heat and pressure. Limestone is a form of sedimentary rock that is composed mostly of calcium carbonate.

3.   Given what is shown above, what type of rock is marble?

    (1)   magma
    (2)   igneous rock
    (3)   sediments
    (4)   sedimentary rock
    (5)   metamorphic rock

4.   What part(s) of the cycle represent(s) the above given process for the conversion of limestone into marble?

    (1)   A
    (2)   B
    (3)   C
    (4)   D
    (5)   E

<u>Items 5 to 7</u> refer to the following information.

The discoveries of Galileo Galilei (1564–1642) and Isaac Newton (1642–1727) precipitated the scientific revolution of the 17th century. Stressing the use of detailed measurements during experimentation enabled them to frame several universal laws of nature and to overthrow many of Aristotle's (384–322 B.C.) erroneous ideas about motion that were based on sheer reasoning alone. One of these universal laws is now known as the "Law of Inertia" or Newton's First Law of Motion. According to this law, objects in motion tend to stay in motion and objects at rest tend to stay at rest unless acted upon by external force. The more mass (inertia) an object has, the more resistance it offers to changes in its state of motion.

5. According to the Law of Inertia, which of the following would offer the greatest resistance to a change in its motion?

(1) A pellet of lead shot   (4) A feather
(2) A golf ball   (5) A sheet of notepaper
(3) A large watermelon

6. When astronauts sleep aboard the Space Shuttle, they strap themselves to a wall or bunk. If one of the thruster rockets was fired, resulting in a change of Shuttle velocity, any unstrapped, sleeping astronauts would be injured by slamming into a Shuttle wall. The sleeping astronauts need to be strapped down because

(1) their bodies have inertia.
(2) gravity is not strong enough to keep them touching their beds.
(3) their body functions need to be constantly monitored.
(4) astronauts cannot sleep while floating free in space.
(5) their bodies need a reaction force.

7. In Einstein's famous equation, $E = mc^2$, which of the following is most closely associated with a body's inertia?

(1) The energy $= E$
(2) The mass $= m$
(3) The speed of light $= c$
(4) The speed of light squared $= c^2$
(5) The momentum $= mc$

<u>Items 8 to 10</u> refer to the following paragraphs.

Carolus Linnaeus introduced a scientific system of naming organisms. He developed this because there were so many names for the same organism. For example, a mountain lion could be called a puma, mountain lion, panther, cougar, red lion, etc. In order to avoid this confusion, he set up what is known as the binomial system of nomenclature. This means that for the name of the animal, one would use two names. Carolus used Latin names because Latin is a dead language that is not spoken by anyone; therefore, it is not subject to change. In a two-word name, the first name refers to the animal's genus and the second name to its species.

Carolus Linnaeus also set up a system of grouping organisms. He began by dividing up all living things into two groups. These he named kingdoms. Today there are five kingdoms: Animalia, Plantae, Monera, Protista, and Fungi. The classification (grouping) hierarchy of today is: kingdom, phylum, class, order, family, genus, species. Note that members of a genus group can have a special name like *Felis* (cat), or *Canis* (dog). Every type of animal has a unique species name, which also places them in a single grouping. For example, *Canis lupis* (wolf) and *Canis latrans* (coyote) are two different species of the dog family. *Canis* is the genus name; *lupis* and *latrans* are species names. *Felis domesticus* and *Canis familiaris* are not the same and their genus names tell us so.

8. The panda bear, *Aleropoda melanoleuca*, is not a bear like the black bear, *Ursus americanus*, or the grizzly bear, *Ursus horribilis*. How can this distinction be shown?

    (1)   Panda bears live only in China.
    (2)   Pandas are not bears, and their genus name, *Aleropoda*, indicates this.
    (3)   Pandas are not bears, and their species name, *melanoleuca*, indicates this.
    (4)   Pandas are on the endangered list and have black and white fur.
    (5)   Pandas are not bears because they are really called "pandas."

9. Given: 2 animals. Animal #1 is called *Linius alba*, and animal #2 is called *Canis alba*. Which of the following is true?

    (1)   The species name indicates that there is a close genetic relationship.
    (2)   The species name indicates a filial relationship.
    (3)   The genus names indicate that there is no relationship.
    (4)   The genus name indicates there is a filial relationship.
    (5)   Both animals are totally black.

10. The first name of a scientific name, such as *Happlopappus gracilis*, is the

    (1)   kingdom name.   (4)   order name.
    (2)   phylum name.   (5)   genus name.
    (3)   class name.

Items 11 to 13 refer to the following graph.

In the graph below, the dark black line represents the growth in a ranch's population of mule deer. The shaded line represents the growth of a population of whitetail deer in the same area. In both cases, sufficient food is supplied, and no other outside influences or diseases affect either populations.

11. According to the graph, two species with the same living requirements cannot live long together in the same environment. Competition will eliminate one of the two.

(1) This conclusion is supported by the data.
(2) This conclusion is not supported by the data.
(3) This conclusion includes the effect of hunting and is supported by the data.
(4) This conclusion includes the effect caused by a drought and is supported by the data.
(5) This conclusion is right, but the data is wrong.

12. If one comes to the conclusion that the idea of survival of the fittest is supported by this graph, then

(1) the conclusion is supported by the data.
(2) the conclusion is refuted by the data.
(3) the conclusion is refuted because only one kind of deer survived.
(4) the conclusion is refuted because the two kinds of deer do not compete with each other, and the data supports this.
(5) the conclusion is right, but the data is wrong.

13. If one comes to the conclusion that the mule deer are better adapted to the environment than are the whitetail deer, then

    (1) the conclusion is supported by the data.
    (2) the conclusion is refuted by the data.
    (3) the conclusion is neither supported nor refuted by the data.
    (4) the data gives plenty of information concerning the mule deer's adaptability, which supports the conclusion.
    (5) the data gives plenty of information concerning the type of terrain, which supports the conclusion.

Item 14 refers to the following table.

The following table gives the mean monthly temperature (°C) and precipitation (mm). (Data from Environment Canada, 1900).

Month	Mean Temperature (°C)	Mean Precipitation (mm)
January	2.5	153.8
February	4.6	114.7
March	5.8	101.0
April	8.8	59.6
May	12.2	51.6
June	15.1	45.2
July	17.3	32.0
August	17.1	41.1
September	14.2	67.1
October	10.0	114.0
November	5.9	150.1
December	3.9	182.4

14. In which month would precipitation in the form of snow be most likely?

    (1) January
    (2) October
    (3) November
    (4) December
    (5) April

Items 15 and 16 refer to the following diagram.

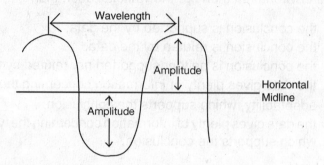

15. The wavelength is

    (1) the distance between any two peaks.
    (2) the distance between two adjacent peaks.
    (3) the distance between the height of a wave and the low point of a
         wave.
    (4) the rate of motion of the peak.
    (5) the length of the horizontal midline.

16. A wave does not carry along the medium through which it travels. Thus,
    it follows that

    (1) molecules of water in the ocean are pushed to shore by waves.
    (2) the ocean's water molecules are thoroughly mixed each day by
         waves.
    (3) debris in the ocean is washed ashore by waves.
    (4) individual water molecules do not travel toward shore, but wave
         peaks do.
    (5) waves move water, not swimmers.

Items 17 and 18 refer to the following paragraph.

   Protein synthesis is very important in living things. All cells contain
protein and the making of protein is controlled by DNA (deoxyribonucleic
acid), which is a major constituent of the chromosomes. DNA molecules
contain information in the form of 64 chemical "code words." This information is also known as the "genetic code." Since DNA is only found in the
nucleus of cells, the information that is needed for protein synthesis must
be carried to the portion of the cell involved with protein synthesis, the
endoplasmic reticulum (ER) and the ribosomes. This is done by a molecule called messenger ribonucleic acid (mRNA), which is made by DNA.
Once the mRNA is in the ER, the ribosomes begin to "read" the instructions on the mRNA. As the instructions are read, transfer ribonucleic acid
(tRNA) brings to the ribosomes, from the cytoplasm, the proper amino
acids. The ribosomes then bond these amino acids together in the proper
order until a long chain of amino acids (the protein) is formed.

17. Imagine that a cosmic ray obliterates a "code word" in a single DNA molecule. What happens when the DNA molecule is read so that mRNA can be built?

    (1)   Nothing happens.
    (2)   The message of the mRNA is different from the DNA before the event.
    (3)   mRNA cannot be made.
    (4)   Triplets can no longer be produced, so doublets are used.
    (5)   DNA repairs itself perfectly.

18. DNA nucleotides are found in what part of the cell?

    (1)   The lysosomes
    (2)   The endoplasmic reticulum
    (3)   The cytoplasmic matrix
    (4)   The nucleus
    (5)   The ribosomes

Items 19 to 22 refer to the following information.

When assigning oxidation numbers, simple rules can be followed: (1) The sum of all oxidation numbers of the atoms in an electrically neutral chemical substance is zero. (2) The sum of the oxidation numbers must equal the charge on the ion for polyatomic ions. (3) The oxidation number of an atom in a monatomic ion is its charge. (4) Hydrogen always has the oxidation number +1 when combined with nonmetals and -1 when combined with metals.

19. Which rule(s) must be applied to find the oxidation number of H_2S?

    (1)   1   (4)   1, 4
    (2)   4   (5)   2, 4
    (3)   1, 2

20. What is the oxidation number of the Mn in the neutral compound $KMnO_4$ if the oxidation number of K is +1 and the oxidation number for one oxygen atom (O) is -2?

    (1)   +1   (4)   +3
    (2)   +7   (5)   -3
    (3)   0

21. Calculate the oxidation number of the P atom in HPO_4^{2-} if the oxidation number of one oxygen atom is -2?

    (1) +1
    (2) +7
    (3) +5

    (4) 0
    (5) +2

22. Which rule(s) is/are used to find the oxidation numbers of HPO_4^{2-} and the oxidation numbers of the atoms comprising this compound?

    (1) 2
    (2) 3, 4
    (3) 4

    (4) 2, 4
    (5) 1, 2, 4

Items 23 and 24 refer to the following diagram.

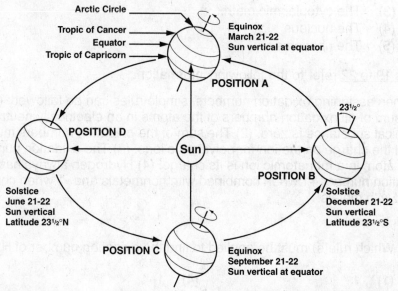

From *The Atmosphere: An Introduction to Meteorology*, 1989, Fourth Edition, Fredrick K. Lutgens, Edward J. Tarbuck. Prentice Hall.

23. Which position(s) in the above diagram result(s) in the North Polar regions being referred to as the Land of the Midnight Sun?

    (1) Position A
    (2) Position B
    (3) Position C

    (4) Position D
    (5) Positions B and D

24. The Earth's seasons are caused by the

    (1) tilt of the Earth's axis.
    (2) distance from the sun to the planet.
    (3) rotation of the sun.

(4) rotation of the Earth.

(5) effects of the moon's position.

Item 25 refers to the following passage.

X-linked genetic traits are controlled by genes on the X chromosome. In humans, color blindness is an X-linked trait. It is produced by the recessive allele of a gene. An allele is an alternative form of a gene. A lower-case letter indicates a recessive allele. A dominant allele is indicated by a capital letter. In females, the sex chromosome pair is written as XX. In males the sex chromosome pair is XY. The Y chromosome does not contain the gene for color blindness.

25. In females, color blindness will develop if the genotype is

(1) $X^B X^B$.
(2) $X^B X^b$.
(3) $X^b X^b$.
(4) $X^B Y$.
(5) $X^b Y$.

Item 26 refers to the following passage.

The heart of a mammal is a four-chambered pump. A wall seals off the right and left sides of the heart from one another. As blood flows through the chambers on the right side of this structure, it has a low concentration of oxygen. This side of the heart pumps blood to the lungs where it acquires more oxygen. From the lungs, blood flows through the left side of the heart and out through the aorta. The aorta is an artery.

26. In which area of the heart is oxygen-rich blood found?

(1) The aorta
(2) The right atrium
(3) The lungs
(4) The right side of the heart
(5) The left side of the heart

Items 27 and 28 refer to the following paragraph.

Chameleons are lizards found mainly in Africa. The popular belief that chameleons change color to match their environment is largely false. Temperature, sunlight, and emotion affect the chameleon more than the color of its surroundings. A chameleon can swiftly shoot out its sticky tongue to a distance longer than the length of its body. In this way, it can catch its food.

27. A chameleon sitting on a black rock turns black in color. This color change is most likely because

    (1) the chameleon is hiding from a predator.
    (2) the chameleon is attempting to blend into its surroundings.
    (3) the chameleon is most likely dying.
    (4) the chameleon is cold, causing the animal to darken.
    (5) the animal is preparing to extend its long tongue.

28. The chameleon's tongue catches prey because

    (1) prey will stick to the sticky substance covering the tongue.
    (2) the fork on the end of the tongue spears the prey.
    (3) the tongue wraps around the prey in the same way that a snake will squeeze its prey to death.
    (4) the tongue contains poisonous glands that kill their prey.
    (5) the prey is stunned to see the chameleon change color.

Items 29 and 30 refer to the following information.

   The solubility of a substance is the maximum amount of that substance that can dissolve in a given quantity of solvent. A like substance can dissolve a like substance. A solution containing the maximum amount of solute is saturated.

29. If a solid substance is added to a solution but will not dissolve, one can hypothesize that

    (1) the solution is unsaturated.
    (2) the substance is insoluble in that solvent.
    (3) the solution is saturated.
    (4) one solution may never contain more than one type of solute.
    (5) both choices (2) or (3) may be correct.

30. A solute dissolves in a solvent because

    (1) like substances dissolve in like substances, such as oil dissolving in water.
    (2) like substances do not dissolve in like substances.
    (3) like substances dissolve in unlike substances.
    (4) like substances do not dissolve in unlike substances, such as NaCl not dissolving in water.
    (5) like substances dissolve like substances.

Item 31 refers to the following information.

The graph below shows how the relative light energy given off by a tungsten lamp (3000 K) and a fluorescent lamp compared with that of average sunlight at the earth's surface. The wavelength of 4000 A is at the blue end of the spectrum, and 7000 A is at the red end.

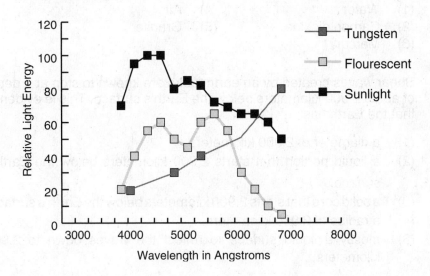

31. Which source tends to be the reddest?

   (1) Tungsten filament lamp
   (2) Fluorescent lamp
   (3) Sunlight
   (4) Sunlight and fluorescent lamp
   (5) Each lamp has the same amount of red

Items 32 to 34 refer to the following information.

Surface water waves are fundamentally different from sound waves in that the vibration of the former is perpendicular to the direction of motion, while that of sound is always parallel to the direction of motion. If a large disturbance in a material is created by a strong external blow, then it is possible for shear or transverse waves (like water waves) to propagate through the material. However, it is impossible for these shear waves to travel through the inside of a liquid or gas; the attractive forces between the molecules are so weak that there is little restoring force to cause displaced sections of the liquid or gas to return to their original positions, which is required for a continuous wave. These shear or S-waves are known to travel through the earth at about 4.25 kilometers/sec.

32. Shear (transverse) waves, set up by a strong blow to the material, are able to travel through which of the following at room temperature?

    (1) Water
    (2) Carbon dioxide
    (3) Mercury
    (4) Air
    (5) Granite

33. Shear waves created by an earthquake are known to stop at a depth of about 2,900 kilometers below the Earth's surface. This is evidence that the Earth has

    (1) a diameter of 2,900 kilometers.
    (2) a liquid portion that starts 2,900 kilometers below the Earth's surface.
    (3) a solid core that starts 2,900 kilometers below the Earth's surface.
    (4) a radius of 2,900 kilometers.
    (5) mostly a liquid surface to reflect the waves down to 2,900 kilometers.

34. Earthquakes cause pressure-type waves (P-waves), which travel about twice as fast as the associated S-waves. If a seismographic station records an Earthquake's P-waves arriving 4 minutes after the earthquake occurs, its distance away from the station must be about

    (1) 500 kilometers.
    (2) 1,000 kilometers.
    (3) 2,000 kilometers.
    (4) 3,000 kilometers.
    (5) 4,000 kilometers.

Item 35 refers to the following passage.

During each year of development in a woody plant, layers of xylem and phloem are added to the stem. Xylem and phloem are vascular tissue. The meristem is one growth layer in the wall of the stem. Each year this single growth layer adds a layer of phloem to the outside and a layer of xylem to the inside. The layers of xylem add significantly to the thickness of the stem each year.

35.   A botanist cuts through the stem of a woody plant that has seven layers of xylem.

   (1)   The plant has seven layers of phloem and has an age of fourteen years.
   (2)   The plant has seven layers of phloem and has an age of fifteen years.
   (3)   The plant has fourteen layers of vascular tissue and has an age of seven years.
   (4)   The plant has fourteen layers of vascular tissue and has an age of fourteen years.
   (5)   The plant has fifteen layers of meristem and vascular tissue and has an age of fourteen years.

Item 36 refers to the following passage.

   One type of experiment that a biologist might do is compare two variables. In the simplest type of experiment, the two main variables studied are the independent variable and the dependent variable. The independent variable is a characteristic that is manipulated by the researcher. This manipulation causes different responses in a dependent variable. For example, a biologist studies the effect of antibiotic dosage on the immune system in frogs. Identical populations of frogs, located in the same environment, are subjected to different amounts of an antibiotic over three months. The health and body weights of the frogs are studied and recorded every two weeks.

36.   In this experiment, the independent variable is

   (1)   antibiotic dosage.
   (2)   biological sex.
   (3)   body weight.
   (4)   health.
   (5)   time.

Items 37 and 38 refer to the following map.

WORLD MEAN SEA-LEVEL TEMPERATURES IN JANUARY IN °C

From *The Atmosphere: An Introduction to Meteorology*, 1989, Fourth Edition, Fredrick K. Lutgens, Edward J. Tarbuck. Prentice Hall.

37. Which mean sea-level temperature line passes through central Florida?

    (1)   5°C
    (2) 10°C
    (3) 15°C
    (4) 20°C
    (5) 25°C

38. At approximately what latitude is the warmest sea-level temperature?

    (1) 0°
    (2) 20°N
    (3) 20°S
    (4) 40°N
    (5) 40°S

Items 39 and 40 refer to the following passage.

For five years Charles Darwin traveled around the world aboard the *H.M.S. Beagle*. During that time he observed many things, especially the plants and animals of South America and the Galapagos Islands. Later, he published his famous book *On the Origin of Species*, which made sense of what he saw. His theory may be summarized by the following four observations: (1) individuals vary genetically; (2) generally, organisms will produce more offspring than the environment can support; (3) even though there are large numbers of offspring, the population remains fairly constant; and (4) the environment all over the planet is in a constant state of change. From these four observations Darwin concluded that: (1) in every population there is competition for available resources, (2) those organisms that have favorable genetic variation will be able to live and reproduce, and (3) those genetic variations that allowed the parents to survive will be handed down to offspring through generations and will accumulate in the population until the whole population will have these favorable genes. In this way, Darwin could see how things change or evolve.

39. It is a well-known fact that clams release millions of eggs and sperm. If 50% of all eggs were fertilized, would this be consistent with Darwin's conclusions?

    (1)   Yes, because favorable variations occur.
    (2)   Yes, because there are more offspring produced than the environment could support, and only some of the clams would survive.
    (3)   Yes, because the environment is constantly changing.
    (4)   No, because individual sperm and egg are different genetically.
    (5)   No, because genetic variation does not allow for natural selection.

40. It is estimated that a single fern can produce upwards of 50 million spores in a single year. It is easy to realize that all of the spores do not grow into a mature adult fern, because if they did, whole continents would be covered with ferns. What did Darwin observe that would explain this?

    (1)   Organisms produce more offspring than the environment can support, so a population will remain constant because there are not enough resources for all offspring.
    (2)   The environment is slowly changing all over the world, which prevents all of the offspring from maturing.
    (3)   Genetic variation is allowing the ferns to keep the same level of population.
    (4)   Genetic variation, which allows for survival, will increase.
    (5)   Individuals vary genetically.

Items 41 and 42 refer to the following information.

One way of describing animals is to describe how their body parts are arranged. The arrangement of body parts is called symmetry. If an organism has no definite shape, then it is said to be asymmetrical. No matter which way the organism is sliced, no two halves will look similar. If an organism is shaped like a ball, then it is said to have spherical symmetry. No matter how you slice it, both halves will look similar. If an organism is bilaterally symmetrical, then it will have a right and a left side. If an organism has radial symmetry, then it will have the general shape of a cylinder, with its body parts extending outward from the middle of the cylinder (radiating). However, one must be careful when considering radial symmetry. Sometimes the cylindrical shape will be flattened.

41. What type of symmetry is exhibited by the organism shown to the right?

    (1)   Asymmetry
    (2)   Radial symmetry
    (3)   Spherical symmetry
    (4)   Bilateral symmetry
    (5)   Longitudinal symmetry

42. The organism to the right exhibits what type of symmetry?

    (1)   Asymmetry
    (2)   Radial symmetry
    (3)   Bilateral symmetry
    (4)   Spherical symmetry
    (5)   Triradial symmetry

Item 43 refers to the passage below.

Most substances are denser during the solid phase than during the liquid phase. Water is an exception to this rule. Additionally, water has a very high boiling point compared to other hydrides of nonmetals. Water has several other unusual properties that are related to the structure and composition of the water molecules.

43. The unusually high boiling and melting points of water result from

    (1)   a great amount of intermolecular attraction in water.
    (2)   low surface tension.
    (3)   low amount of hydrogen bonding between water molecules.
    (4)   the low heat capacity of water.
    (5)   strong covalent bonds between water molecules.

Item 44 refers to the following passage.

Skin is the flexible outer covering on the bodies of vertebrate animals. The thickness varies on different body areas. Human skin is composed of an outer layer called the epidermis and an inner layer called the dermis. The epidermis has several layers. Near the outside is the stratum corneum. Under it is the layer of Malpighi, which quickly grows to replace the cells of the stratum corneum, which wears away quickly. Human skin protects the body from injury, helps get rid of waste products, regulates water and regulates temperature.

44. Since the stratum corneum is constantly wearing away, structures such as blood vessels, nerve endings, and sweat glands must be found in

    (1)   the layer of Malpighi.
    (2)   the stratum corneum.
    (3)   the epidermis.
    (4)   the dermis.
    (5)   the muscle tissue.

Items 45 to 48 refer to the following graphs.

Assume you have grown some bacterial cultures in a test tube. You carefully keep track of how they grow. The graphs below represent some possible growth curves. Use the following graphs to answer the next four questions.

45. Which of the statements would be best represented by graph (a)?

    (1) The number of bacteria being produced by mitosis is equal to the number of bacteria dying.
    (2) Nothing was done to the culture of bacteria at first, but after a while some of the waste products were removed.
    (3) Bacteria "love" this growth curve because it represents ideal conditions.
    (4) The growth of the bacteria is represented by a normal growth curve.
    (5) While growing the bacteria, the test tube was inoculated with poison.

46. Which of the statements would be best represented by graph (b)?

    (1) The number of bacteria being produced by mitosis is equal to the number of bacteria dying.
    (2) Nothing was done to the culture of bacteria at first, but after a while some of the waste products were removed.
    (3) Bacteria "love" this growth curve because it represents ideal conditions.
    (4) The growth of the bacteria is represented by a normal growth curve.
    (5) While growing the bacteria, the test tube was inoculated with poison.

47. Which of the statements would be best represented by graph (c)?

    (1) The number of bacteria being produced by mitosis is equal to the number of bacteria dying.
    (2) Nothing was done to the culture of bacteria at first, but after a while some of the waste products were removed.
    (3) Bacteria "love" this growth curve because it represents ideal conditions.
    (4) The growth of the bacteria is represented by a normal growth curve.
    (5) While growing the bacteria, the test tube was inoculated with poison.

48. Which of the statements would be best represented by graph (d)?

    (1) The number of bacteria being produced by mitosis is equal to the number of bacteria dying.
    (2) Nothing was done to the culture of bacteria at first, but after a while some of the waste products were removed.
    (3) Bacteria "love" this growth curve because it represents ideal conditions.

(4)   The growth of the bacteria is represented by a normal growth curve.

(5)   While growing the bacteria, the test tube was inoculated with poison.

Items 49 and 50 refer to the following information.

The average home use of electricity in the United States as compared to a developing country like Brazil is shown in the table below. The amount of electrical energy used is given in kilowatt-hours (KWH) per household per year. (October 1990, *Scientific American*, p. 113)

Use	United States	Brazil
Lighting	1,000	350
Cooking	635	15
Water Heating	1,540	380
Air-Conditioning	1,180	45
Refrigeration	1,810	470
Other	1,180	200

49.   Which of the statements below is the best conclusion based on the data provided?

(1)   The total electrical consumption by the average U.S. household is about twice that of the typical Brazilian home wired for electricity.

(2)   Because it is warmer in Brazil, the percentage of electricity used in air-conditioning is greater than that used in the United States.

(3)   The greatest amount of electricity use in both countries is for lighting.

(4)   United States households use more electricity for water heating than lighting, while Brazilian households use more electricity for lighting than water heating.

(5)   Both countries have a somewhat similar pattern of electricity consumption.

50.   How much more electrical energy per household does the United States consume than developing Brazil?

(1)   3 times   (4)   6 times
(2)   4 times   (5)   7 times
(3)   5 times

TEST 4: LANGUAGE ARTS: READING

Tests of General Educational Development

Directions

The Language Arts: Reading Test consists of excerpts from classical and popular literature and articles about literature or the arts. Each excerpt is followed by multiple-choice questions about the reading material.

Read each excerpt first and then answer the questions following it. Refer back to the reading material as often as necessary in answering the questions.

Each excerpt is preceded by a "purpose question." The purpose question gives a reason for reading the material. Use these purpose questions to help focus your reading. You are not required to answer these purpose questions. They are given only to help you concentrate on the ideas presented in the reading materials.

You should spend no more than 65 minutes answering the questions in this booklet. Work carefully, but do not spend too much time on any one question. Be sure you answer every question. You will not be penalized for incorrect answers.

Do not mark in this test booklet. Record your answers on the separate answer sheet provided. Be sure all requested information is properly recorded on the answer sheet. To record your answers, mark the numbered space on the answer sheet beside the number that corresponds to the question in the test booklet.

FOR EXAMPLE:

It was Susan's dream machine. The metallic blue paint gleamed, and the sporty wheels were highly polished. Under the hood, the engine was no less carefully cleaned. Inside, flashy lights illuminated the instruments on the dashboard, and the seats were covered by rich leather upholstery.

The subject ("It") of this excerpt is most likely

(1) an airplane.   (4) a boat.
(2) a stereo system.   (5) a motorcycle.
(3) an automobile.

① ② ● ④ ⑤

The correct answer is "an automobile"; therefore, answer space 3 would be marked on the answer sheet.

Do not rest the point of your pencil on the answer sheet while you are considering your answer. Make no stray or unnecessary marks. If you change an answer, erase your first mark completely. Mark only one answer space for each question; multiple answers will be scored as incorrect. Do not fold or crease your answer sheet. Return all test materials to the test administrator.

Reprinted with permission of the General Educational Development Testing Service of the American Council on Education.

Directions: Choose the <u>one best answer</u> to each item.

Items 1 to 8 refer to the following conversation.

WHAT IS THE RELATIONSHIP BETWEEN THESE MEN?

1   George still stared morosely at the fire. "When I think of the swell time I could have without you, I go nuts. I never get no peace."

       Lennie still knelt. He looked off into the darkness across the

5   river. "George, you want I should go away and leave you alone?"

       "Where the hell could you go?"

       "Well, I could go off in the hills there. Some place I'd find a cave."

       "Yeah? How'd you eat? You ain't got sense enough to find

10   nothing to eat."

       "I'd find things, George. I don't need no nice food with ketchup. I'd lay out in the sun and nobody'd hurt me. An' if I foun' a mouse, I could keep it. Nobody'd take it away from me."

       George looked quickly and searchingly at him. "I been mean,

15   ain't I?"

       "If you don' want me I can go off in the hills and find a cave. I can go away any time."

       "No—look! I was jus' foolin', Lennie. 'Cause I want you to stay with me. Trouble with mice is you always kill 'em." He paused.

20   "Tell you what I'll do, Lennie. First chance I get I'll give you a pup. Maybe you wouldn't kill it. That'd be better than mice. And you could pet it harder."

       Lennie avoided the bait. He had sensed his advantage. "If you don't want me, you only jus' got to say so, and I'll go off in those

25   hills right there—right up in those hills and live by myself. An' I won't get no mice stole from me."

       George said, "I want you to stay with me, Lennie, Jesus Christ, somebody'd shoot you for a coyote if you was by yourself. No, you stay with me. Your Aunt Clara wouldn't like you running off by

30   yourself, even if she is dead."

       Lennie spoke craftily, "Tell me—like you done before."

       "Tell you what?"

       "About the rabbits."

       George snapped, "You ain't gonna put nothing over on me."

35   Lennie pleaded, "Come on, George. Tell me, please George. Like you done before."

       "You get a kick outta that, don't you? Awright, I'll tell you, and then we'll eat our supper...." George's voice became deeper. He repeated his words rhythmically as though he had said them many

40   times before....

       Lennie was delighted. "That's it—that's it. Now tell how it is with us."

       George went on. "With us it ain't like that. We got a future. We

got somebody to talk to that gives a damn about us. We don't
45   have to sit in no barroom blowin' our jack jus because we
got no place to go....
      "O.K. Someday—we're gonna get the jack together and we're
gonna have a little house and a couple of acres an' a cow and
some pigs and—"
50   "An' live off the fatta the lan'!," Lennie shouted.

John Steinbeck, *Of Mice and Men*, New York, New York: Bantam Books, copyright 1965 by John Steinbeck, pp. 15–17.

1.   You can tell from the dialogue that

      (1)   each man is bonded in friendship with the other.
      (2)   neither one really cares what happens to the other.
      (3)   George will stay angry with Lennie this time.
      (4)   Lennie sincerely intends to leave.
      (5)   George intends to abandon Lennie soon.

2.   It becomes clear when studying the conversation that

      (1)   George has little compassion for Lennie.
      (2)   Lennie has learned to manipulate George.
      (3)   George has the "upper hand" at all times.
      (4)   Lennie intends to hurt George.
      (5)   Lennie is a survivor.

3. You can best compare the relationship of George and Lennie with one of

      (1)   best friends.   (4)   feuding neighbors.
      (2)   father and son.   (5)   complete strangers.
      (3)   casual acquaintances.

4.   Lines 18-22 provide insight into

      (1)   George's inner conflict.
      (2)   George's intelligence.
      (3)   Lennie's attitude.
      (4)   both men's devotion to each other.
      (5)   George's impatience.

5.   The fact that Lennie accidentally kills mice while he pets them indicates

      (1)   he is careless.   (4)   he is kind.
      (2)   he is cruel.   (5)   he is stubborn.
      (3)   he is not aware of his own strength.

6.   The conflict within George appears to be one concerning

    (1)   his relationship with Lennie.
    (2)   his lack of money.
    (3)   his lack of education.
    (4)   his job.
    (5)   his bad luck.

7.   The fact that Lennie knows George's story by heart means

    (1)   Lennie created it.
    (2)   he has heard it many times.
    (3)   it is probably untrue.
    (4)   there is cause for concern.
    (5)   nothing in particular.

8.   Essentially the story gives each man

    (1)   something to talk about.   (4)   cause for concern.
    (2)   hope for the future.   (5)   nothing in particular.
    (3)   reason to leave town.

Items 9 to 13 are based on the following excerpt.

WHY AREN'T THESE TWO MEN CONTENT?

BIFF: I tell ya, Hap, I don't know what the future is. I don't know—what I'm supposed to want.

HAPPY: What do you mean?

BIFF: (*with rising agitation*): Hap, I've had twenty or thirty different kinds of jobs since I left home before the war, and it always turns out the same. I just realized it lately. In Nebraska, when I herded cattle, and the Dakotas, and Arizona, and now in Texas. It's why I came home now, I guess, because I realized it. This farm I work on, it's spring there now, see? And they've got about fifteen new colts. There's nothing more inspiring or—beautiful than the sight of a mare and a new colt. And it's cool there now, see? Texas is cool now, and it's spring. And whenever spring comes to where I am, I suddenly get the feeling, my God, I'm not gettin' anywhere! What the hell am I doing, playing around with horses, twenty-eight dollars a week! I'm thirty-four years old, I oughta be makin' my future. That's when I come running home. And now, I get here, and I don't know what to do with myself. (*After a pause.*) I've always made a point of not wasting my life, and every time I come back here I know that all I've done is to waste my life.

HAPPY: You're a poet, you know that, Biff? You're a—you're an ideal-ist!

BIFF: No, I'm mixed up very bad. Maybe I oughta get married. Maybe I oughta get stuck into something. Maybe that's my trouble. I'm like a boy. I'm not married, I'm not in business, I just—I'm like a boy. Are you content, Hap? You're a success, aren't you? Are you content?

HAPPY: Hell, no!

BIFF: Why? You're making money, aren't you?

HAPPY: (*moving about with energy, expressiveness*) All I can do now is wait for the merchandise manager to die. And suppose I get to be merchandise manager? He's a good friend of mine, and he just built a terrific estate on Long Island. And he lived there about two months and sold it, and now he's building another one. He can't enjoy it once it's finished. And I know that's just what I would do. I don't know what the hell I'm workin' for. Sometimes I sit in my apartment—all alone. And I think of the rent I'm paying. And it's crazy. But then, it's what I always wanted. My own apartment, a car, and plenty of women. And still, goddammit, I'm lonely.

From *Death of a Salesman* by Arthur Miller (1949)

9. Biff is home because

    (1) he is making money.
    (2) he only gets $28 a week.
    (3) he isn't getting anywhere in life.
    (4) he's lonely.
    (5) he doesn't like horses.

10. Biff thinks that Happy is content because

    (1) he has a successful job.
    (2) he has a lot of girlfriends.
    (3) he has an apartment.
    (4) he has a car.
    (5) he has friends.

11. Happy can best be described by which sentence?

    (1) You can't run away from yourself.
    (2) Money can't buy you happiness.
    (3) What goes around comes around.
    (4) People who live in glass houses shouldn't throw stones.
    (5) The early bird gets the worm.

12. Why isn't the merchandise manager happy?

    (1) He doesn't have enough money.
    (2) Happy is after his job.
    (3) He doesn't have a home.
    (4) He's friends with Happy.
    (5) The more he has, the more he wants.

13. We can conclude from this passage that Happy's name is

    (1) not his real name.
    (2) symbolic.
    (3) ironic.
    (4) metaphorical.
    (5) A pun.

Items 14 to 16 refer to the following conversation.

WHAT CODE OF MANHOOD DOES THE OLD MAN PORTRAY?

1   "Santiago," the boy said.

"Yes," the old man said. He was holding his glass and thinking of many years ago.

"Can I go out to get sardines for you for tomorrow?"

5   "No. Go and play baseball. I can still row and Rogelio will throw the net."

"I would like to go. If I cannot fish with you, I would like to serve in some way."

"You bought me a beer," the old man said. "You are already a
10   man."

"How old was I when you first took me in a boat?"

"Five and you nearly were killed when I brought the fish in too green and he nearly tore the boat to pieces. Can you remember?"

"I can remember the tail slapping and banging and the thwart
15   breaking and the noise of the clubbing. I can remember you throwing me into the bow where the wet coiled lines were and feeling the whole boat shiver and the noise of you clubbing him like chopping a tree down and the sweet blood smell all over me."

"Can you really remember that or did I just tell it to you?"
20   "I remember everything from when we first went together."

The old man looked at him with his sun-burned confident loving eyes.

"If you were my boy I'd take you out and gamble," he said. "But you are your father's and your mother's and you are in a lucky
25   boat."

"May I get the sardines? I know where I can get four baits, too."

14. From the preceding selection, what can be concluded about the old man and the boy?

    (1) They are father and son.
    (2) They have a deep, bonding friendship.
    (3) They are merely casual acquaintances.
    (4) They care very little for one another.
    (5) They most likely have just met.

15. In lines 12-13 "fish in too green" means

    (1) the fish was spoiled.
    (2) the fish was brought aboard too soon.
    (3) the fisherman was only a novice.
    (4) the boy was careless.
    (5) the incident happened by chance.

16. This passage is most likely from a story primarily concerned with

    (1) mystery and intrigue.   (4) character portrayal.
    (2) geographical location.   (5) science fiction.
    (3) humor.

Items 17 to 21 refer to the following passage.

1   "How do you feel, fish?" he asked aloud. "I feel good and my left hand is better and I have food for a night and a day. Pull the boat, fish."

       He did not truly feel good because the pain from the cord
5   across his back had almost passed pain and gone into a dullness that he mistrusted. But I have had worse things than that, he thought. My hand is only cut a little and the cramp is gone from the other. My legs are all right. Also now I have gained on him in the question of sustenance.
10   It was dark now as it becomes dark quickly after the sun sets in September. He lay against the worn wood of the bow and rested all that he could. The first stars were out. He did not know the name of Rigel but he saw it and knew soon they would all be out and he would have all his distant friends.
15   "The fish is my friend too," he said aloud. "I have never seen or heard of such a fish. But I must kill him. I am glad we do not have to try to kill the stars."

       Imagine if each day a man must try to kill the moon, he thought. The moon runs away. But imagine if a man each day should have
20   to try to kill the sun? We were born lucky, he thought.

       Then he was sorry for the great fish that had nothing to eat and his determination to kill him never relaxed in his sorrow for him.

25

How many people will he feed, he thought. But are they worthy to eat him? No, of course not. There is no one worthy of eating him from the manner of his behaviour and his great dignity.

I do not understand these things, he thought. But it is good that we do not have to try to kill the sun or the moon or the stars. It is enough to live on the sea and kill our true brothers.

Ernest Hemingway, selections from *The Old Man and the Sea*, New York, New York: Charles Scribner's Sons (p.b.), copyright 1952 by Ernest Hemingway, pp. 12, 13, 74, 75.

17. The preceding selection reveals that the story primarily emphasizes which of the following aspects of the old man's character?

    (1)   Determination and endurance
    (2)   Wit and humor
    (3)   Intelligence and formal schooling
    (4)   Irrational stubbornness
    (5)   Blind hatred

18. In lines 16–17, Santiago reveals that he must

    (1)   kill the fish with no remorse.
    (2)   kill the fish with deep regret.
    (3)   let the fish go.
    (4)   soon give up.
    (5)   find someone worthy of eating this fish.

19. Which of Santiago's personality traits are evident in his self-dialogue?

    (1)   Appreciation and compassion for all creation
    (2)   Self-centered interest in achieving this goal
    (3)   Pride in his fishing ability
    (4)   Blind hatred of losing
    (5)   Total disregard for danger

20. On a literal level, lines 23–25 refer to the "great fish"; on a deeper level, they convey what universal idea?

    (1)   Honor and dignity once earned should not be carelessly cast away.
    (2)   Youth should respect old age.
    (3)   The fish should be fed to the poor of the village.
    (4)   The fisherman himself would eat the fish.
    (5)   None of the above.

21. Lines 26-28 suggest that Santiago considers the fish his "true brothers"

    (1) literally.
    (2) figuratively.
    (3) paradoxically.
    (4) humorously.
    (5) satirically.

Items 22 to 25 refer to the following passage.

XYZ COMPANY POLICY

All organizations seek to adopt a set of standards and practices that define "the rules of the road," bind their members together in a common venture, promote efficiency and, in the case of businesses, profitability. XYZ Company, Inc., is no exception.

Every point of our policy has been instituted with a view toward sound judgment, fairness, the standards of our industry, and logic.

We at XYZ Company are committed to exercising the greatest care in producing our products. Furthermore, we are pledged to conducting business within the strictest ethical guidelines and with total integrity and good will.

Following is a summary of our "General Office Procedures and Policy."

(1) **Use proper documentation when sub-contracting work.** No non-employee may engage in the production of any work for XYZ except as specifically contracted under terms spelled out in XYZ contractual agreements known as forms 1054A (Authors), 1054E (Editors/Proofreaders), 1054P (Printers), and 1054T (Typesetters).

(2) **Prevent conflicts of interest.** No employee may accept gratuities, payment for services other than those specifically contracted and payable through XYZ Company, Inc., or gifts of any substantial value from any person or entity that might benefit—in even the smallest way—from the employee's connection with XYZ. To ensure that no conflict of interest exists, you and your department may be audited on occasion. Please give the auditors your full cooperation; their interest lies only in keeping XYZ operating strictly within federal, state, and local law and regulatory guidelines.

(3) **Report to work on time.** Regular company hours are from 9 to 5. If you are more than 30 minutes late to work, or will be taking a sick day, we ask that you please call before 9:30 AM and inform your manager that you will be late. Employees who wish to take more than three vacation days in a row must inform their manager in writing at least two weeks in advance. Employees who wish to take up to three vacation days in a row must inform their manager in writing at least one week in advance.

(4) **Present yourself professionally.** We depend on you to exercise sound professional judgment and integrity in decisions you make in all business transactions on behalf of XYZ Company. This includes the way

you present yourself in person, on the telephone, and via any electronic means. Remember that every word you speak or write reflects on how your colleagues, vendors, and customers view you.

(5) **Consult your manager.** Ask your manager for clarification of any XYZ policy point.

22. Company XYZ's contractual agreements concern work performed for the company by which of the following groups?

    (1)   Authors, Editors/Proofreaders, Printers, and Typesetters
    (2)   Authors, Editors/Proofreaders, Plumbers, and Typographers
    (3)   Authors, Engineers, Security Officers, and Photographers
    (4)   Teachers, Printers, Writers, and Scuba Divers
    (5)   Authors, Editors/Proofreaders, and Printers

23. According to the document, what does the XYZ Company promise to do?

    (1)   Produce the finest-quality products and services, and serve the public to the best of its ability
    (2)   Exercise the greatest care in producing its products, and to conduct business within the strictest ethical guidelines
    (3)   Lead its industry in innovation and attention to detail
    (4)   Increase its profits in every conceivable fashion
    (5)   None of the above

24. According to the passage, why is XYZ company audited on occasion?

    (1)   Because employees should not engage in the production of any work without using the proper forms, or other documentation
    (2)   To ensure that the employees are not doing anything, or receiving any gifts, that might place them in a position of obligation
    (3)   Because it is important that employees are using good judgment in the dealings in person, on the telephone, and via electronic means
    (4)   Because the managers need training
    (5)   To improve employee morale

25. Stephen, an employee of XYZ Company, wants to take five days off for vacation. If Stephen wants to comply with company policy he must

    (1)   call before 9:30 AM on the first day of his vacation and inform his manager.
    (2)   tell management at least one week in advance.
    (3)   tell management at least two weeks in advance.

    (4)   inform his manager in writing of his planned vacation at least two weeks in advance.

    (5)   inform his manager at least one day in advance.

<u>Items 26 to 31</u> refer to the following story.

WHAT HARDSHIPS DID THIS YOUNG, MODERN WRITER ENDURE IN CHILDHOOD?

1   She was born in 1949 into tropical poverty. Her father was a carpenter and her mother kept house. They had no electricity, no bathroom, no running water. Every Wednesday she registered their outhouse at the Public Works Department so that the "night

5   soil men," as they were called, would take away their full tub and replace it with a clean one. And every morning she went to a public pipe and drew four pails of water for her mother—more if it was a wash day. After school, she went to the pipe for more water. At night she had to wipe the soot from the lampshade and trim the

10   wick. If the lamp was out of oil she would buy more kerosene. Those were her duties.

        As a young child, the only child in the family, she was happy and deeply connected to her mother. But when she was nine the first of her three brothers was born, and life became complicated.

15   Not only did her mother's focus shift from her to the new baby, but an enlarged family caused a keener sense of their poverty. Around this time she entered adolescence, with its attendant emotional storms. For the first time, her intelligence demanded its own realm, but on a 10-by-12-mile outpost of British rule, the intellectual

20   needs of a gifted, indeed brilliant, child could find no organized outlet. That was when she began to steal books, hide them under the house and read in secret.

        Her formal education was at Government schools, where she was considered bright but troublesome. "I was sullen," she says. "I

25   was always accused of being rude, because I gave some back chat. I moved very slowly. I was never where I should be. I wasn't really angry yet. I was just incredibly unhappy."

        I ask her if any teachers in her school recognized her talent, and she says, with a tight smile: "Absolutely not. Everyone thought

30   I had a way with words, but it came out as a sharp tongue. No one expected anything from me at all. Had I just sunk in the cracks it would not have been noted. I would have been lucky to be a secretary somewhere."

Leslie Garis, "Through West Indian Eyes," *The New York Times Magazine*, 7 October 1990, Section 6, pp. 44, 70.

26.   The first paragraph suggests that the woman lived

    (1)   in a small town.   (4)   in an apartment complex.
    (2)   in a large city.   (5)   on a houseboat.
    (3)   on an island.

27. Her life first became complicated by

    (1) family poverty.   (4) catastrophic events.
    (2) bad luck.   (5) poor schooling.
    (3) her mother's emotional abandonment and poverty.

28. The passage infers that the woman was

    (1) intellectually undemanding, until adolescence.
    (2) a demanding child.
    (3) unintellectual.
    (4) unhappy.
    (5) uneducated.

29. In the phrase "attendant adolescent storms," attendant most closely means

    (1) uncontrolled.   (4) severe.
    (2) accompanying.   (5) mild.
    (3) numerous.

30. The woman admits that she stole books because

    (1) she was bored.
    (2) she was revengeful.
    (3) she needed to use her gifted mind.
    (4) she was intimidated by her friends.
    (5) None of the above.

31. From the woman's viewpoint, memories of her childhood could be described most appropriately as

    (1) happy.   (4) normal.
    (2) unexamined.   (5) abnormal.
    (3) misunderstood.

Items 32 to 40 refer to the following poem.

WHAT OR WHO IS THIS MYSTERIOUS BIRD?

1   Once upon a midnight dreary, while I pondered, weak and weary,
        Over many a quaint and curious volume of forgotten lore—
    While I nodded nearly napping, suddenly there came a tapping
        As of someone gently rapping, rapping at my chamber door.
5   "Tis some visitor," I muttered, "tapping at my chamber door—
            Only this and nothing more."
        Ah, distinctly I remember it was in the bleak December,
    And each separate dying ember wrought its ghost upon the floor.

Eagerly I wished the morrow, vainly I had sought to borrow
10   From my books surcease of sorrow—sorrow for the lost Lenore—
For the rare and radiant maiden whom the angels named Lenore—
Nameless here for evermore.
.....
Open here I flung the shutter, when, with many a flirt and flutter,
In there stepped a stately Raven of the saintly days of yore.
15 Not the least obeisance made he; not a minute stopped or stayed he;
But, with mien of lord or lady, perched above my chamber door,
Perched upon a bust of Pallas just above my chamber door—
Perched and sat, and nothing more.
Then this ebony bird beguiling my sad fancy into smiling,
20   By the grave and stern decorum of the countenance it wore,
"Though thy crest be shorn and shaven, thou," I said, "art sure no craven;
Ghastly, grim, and ancient raven, wandering from the nightly shore,
Tell me what thy lordly name is on the night's Plutonian shore?"
Quoth the raven, "Nevermore!"
.....
25   "Prophet!" said I, "thing of evil—prophet still, if bird or devil!
By that heaven that bends above us, by that God we both adore,
Tell this soul with sorrow laden, if within the distant Aidenne,
It shall clasp a sainted maiden, whom the angels name Lenore,
Clasp a fair and radiant maiden, whom the angels name Lenore!"
30   Quoth the raven, "Nevermore!"
.....
And the raven, never flitting, still is sitting, still is sitting
On the pallid bust of Pallas, just above my chamber door;
And his eyes have all the seeming of a demon that is dreaming,
And the lamplight o'er him streaming throws his shadow on the floor;
35 And my soul from out that shadow that lies floating on the floor shall be
lifted—nevermore!

Edgar Allan Poe, "The Raven" *The Best Loved Poems of the American People*, selected by Hazel
Felleman, Garden City, New York: Doubleday and Company, copyright, 1936, pp. 209-11.

32. The setting of the poem as revealed in the first stanza presents

(1)   the narrator in his study, browsing sleepily over old books.
(2)   the narrator writing in his diary.
(3)   the narrator, daydreaming.
(4)   the narrator, working at his business.
(5)   the narrator, ill.

33. In the second stanza, the narrator's thoughts are preoccupied by

(1)   concern about the stormy weather.
(2)   involvement in some business venture.
(3)   mourning over a loved one who has died.

    (4)   mulling over ghostly memories.

    (5)   the supernatural.

34.   Imagery of the bird perching above the chamber door suggests

    (1)   pearls and diamonds.

    (2)   feathers arrayed on silk.

    (3)   red emblazoned on gold.

    (4)   ebony on alabaster.

    (5)   marble.

35.   What does the narrator ask the raven in lines 25–29?

    (1)   What do you want?

    (2)   Where do you live?

    (3)   Are you of this world or of a spiritual world?

    (4)   Are you sincere?

    (5)   Is there a maiden by the name of Lenore, in Paradise?

36.   The narrator in his setting is presented as

    (1)   a poet deeply involved in his work.

    (2)   an involved reporter.

    (3)   a bereft lover.

    (4)   a businessman at his desk.

    (5)   a student.

37.   In the third paragraph, the raven appears with "mien of lord or lady," which is the same as one who is

    (1)   acting savagely.

    (2)   acting as a person with position or royal birth.

    (3)   acting harshly or "mean."

    (4)   acting haughty or superior.

    (5)   acting in a benevolent manner.

38.   The mood of the poem is

    (1)   happy.   (4)   angry.

    (2)   optimistic.   (5)   morose.

    (3)   indecisive.

39.   Lines 35–36 mean

    (1)   the raven will return no more.

    (2)   the poet's soul will never be free.

(3) there is another life after death.
(4) Lenore will return once more.
(5) the raven will remain forever.

40. What is the poem's theme?

(1) Death is final and hopeless.
(2) Love is fleeting.
(3) There is hope for those who have loved and lost.
(4) Love is fickle.
(5) Loved ones lost are soon replaced.

TEST 5: MATHEMATICS

Tests of General Educational Development

Directions

The Mathematics Test consists of multiple-choice questions and free-response questions intended to measure general mathematics skills and problem-solving ability. The questions are based on short readings which often include a graph, chart, or figure.

There are two separate sections of the Mathematics Test: Part 1 and Part 2. Part 1 allows the use of a calculator. Part 2 does not. You should spend no more than 45 minutes answering the questions in each part of the math test. Work carefully, but do not spend too much time on any one question. Be sure you answer every question. You will not be penalized for incorrect answers.

Formulas you may need are given on the following page. Only some of the questions will require you to use a formula. Not all the formulas given will be needed.

Some questions contain more information than you will need to solve the problem. Other questions do not give enough information to solve the problem. If the question does not give enough information to solve the problem, the correct answer choice is "Not enough information is given."

Do not mark in this test booklet. The test administrator will give you blank paper for your calculations. Record your answers on the separate answer sheet provided. Be sure all requested information is properly recorded on the answer sheet.

To record your answers, mark the numbered space on the answer sheet beside the number that corresponds to the question in the test booklet.

FOR EXAMPLE:

If a grocery bill totaling $15.75 is paid with a $20.00 bill, how much change should be returned?

(1) $5.26
(2) $4.75
(3) $4.25
(4) $3.75
(5) $3.25

(1) (2) ● (4) (5)

The correct answer is "$4.25"; therefore, answer space 3 would be marked on the answer sheet.

Do not rest the point of your pencil on the answer sheet while you are considering your answer. Make no stray or unnecessary marks. If you change an answer, erase your first mark completely. Mark only one answer space for each question; multiple answers will be scored as incorrect. Do not fold or crease your answer sheet. Return all test materials to the test administrator.

Reprinted with permission of the General Educational Development Testing Service of the American Council on Education.

REFERENCE TABLE

SYMBOLS AND THEIR MEANINGS

=	is equal to		≤	is less than or equal to
≠	is unequal to		≥	is greater than or equal to
<	is less than		‖	is parallel to
>	is greater than		⊥	is perpendicular to

FORMULAS

DESCRIPTION	FORMULA
AREA (A) of a:	
square	$A = s^2$; where s = side
rectangle	$A = lw$; where l = length, w = width
parallelogram	$A = bh$; where b = base, h = height
triangle	$A = \frac{1}{2}bh$; where b = base, h = height
circle	$A = \pi r^2$; where π = 3.14, r = radius
PERIMETER (P) of a:	
square	$P = 4s$; where s = side
rectangle	$P = 2l + 2w$; where l = length, w = width
triangle	$P = a + b + c$; where a, b, and c are the sides
circumference (C) of a circle	$C = \pi d$, where π = 3.14, d = diameter
VOLUME (V) of a:	
cube	$V = s^2$; where s = side
rectangular container	$V = lwh$; where l = length, w = width, h = height
Pythagorean relationship	$c^2 = a^2 + b^2$; where c = hypotenuse, a and b are legs of a right triangle
distance (d) between two points in a plane	$d = \sqrt{(x_2 - x_1)^2 + (y_2 - y_1)^2}$ where (x_1, y_1) and (x_2, y_2) are two points in a plane
mean	$\textbf{mean} = \dfrac{x_1 + x_2 + \ldots x_n}{n}$; where the x's are the values for which a mean is desired, and n = number of values in the series
median	**median** = the point in an ordered set of numbers at which half of the numbers are above and half of the numbers are below this value
simple interest (i)	$i = prt$; where p = principal, r = rate, t = time
distance (d) as function of rate and time	$d = rt$; where r = rate, t = time
total cost (c)	$c = nr$; where n = number of units, r = cost per unit

PART 1

Calculator Use Permitted

Directions Choose the <u>one best answer</u> to each item.

1.   About how much is 75% of $9.89?

    (1) $75.00   (4) $2.50
    (2) $7.50   (5) $6.00
    (3) $5.00

2.   What is the volume, in cubic centimeters, of this cylinder?

20 cm

20 cm

    (1)   6,280 cu. cm.   (4)   200 cu. cm.
    (2)   25,120 cu. cm.   (5)   628 cu. cm.
    (3)   400 cu. cm.

3.   George took his dog for 3 long walks Saturday. First they walked 1 mile, then they walked 720 yards, and for the last walk they walked 3,500 feet. How many feet did they walk?

    (1)   4,221 ft.   (4)   10,940 ft.
    (2)   9,500 ft.   (5)   10,660 ft.
    (3)   3,780 ft.

4.   Bowling Balls Unlimited wants to know how much to sell their new shipment of bowling balls for if they bought them for $68.00 each?

    $S = (p \times 1.6) + \$4.00$ where S = selling price and p = purchase price

    (1) $73.60   (4) $112.80
    (2) $108.80   (5) $272.00
    (3) $278.40

5. Kelly has $15,000 in a checking account, to be used exclusively for making her down payment and monthly payments on a car she just bought. Her down payment is $3,000 and she will make 48 monthly payments to pay off the balance. Let x dollars represent her monthly payment. If after making all monthly payments she still has $960 left in her checking account, which equation represents the correct solution?

(1) $48 + x + 960 = 12,000$
(2) $48x + 960 = 12,000$
(3) $48x + 960 = 3,000$
(4) $48 + x + 960 = 3,000$
(5) $48x + 960 = 15,000$

6. A group of students rents a van for $1,120 in order to attend a play. This cost will be split equally among all class members. When 8 students become ill on the day of the play (and could not attend), the remaining students have to each pay an additional $16 for the van. If x represents the number of students in the group, which equation represents the correct solution?

(1) $\dfrac{1,120}{x} + 8 = \dfrac{1,120}{x - 16}$

(2) $\dfrac{1,120}{x} - 8 = \dfrac{1,120}{x - 16}$

(3) $\dfrac{1,120}{x} - 16 = \dfrac{1,120}{x - 8}$

(4) $\dfrac{1,120}{x} + 16 = \dfrac{x - 8}{1,120}$

(5) $\dfrac{1,120}{x} + 16 = \dfrac{1,120}{x - 8}$

7.

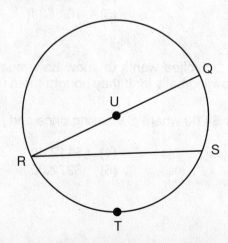

For this circle, U is the center, $\overline{QR}$ is the diameter and T is equally distant from R and S. If ∠R = 20°, how many degrees are there in arc RT?

(1) 85
(2) 80
(3) 75

(4) 70
(5) 65

8. A cylindrical can has a lateral surface area of 251.2 square inches and a height of 16 inches. Using π = 3.14 and assuming that the circular bases are equal in area, what is the diameter, in inches, of either base?

(1) 2.5
(2) 4.0
(3) 5.0

(4) 6.0
(5) 7.5

9. Mary wants to cover a small chest with contact paper. The chest is 24" × 12" × 10". How much contact paper is needed?

24"

10"

12"

(1) 5 sq. ft.
(2) 4 sq. ft.
(3) 9 sq. ft.

(4) 1-2/3 sq. ft.
(5) 720 sq. ft.

10. In triangle ABC, ∠A is four times as large as ∠B, and ∠B is 10° less than ∠C. If x represents the number of degrees in ∠B, which equation represents the correct solution?

(1) $x + 4 + x + x - 10 = 180$
(2) $4x + x + x - 10 = 180$
(3) $4x - x - x + 10 = 180$
(4) $x + 4 + x + x + 10 = 180$
(5) $4x + x + x + 10 = 180$

11. In triangle ABC, AB = AC = 4. BCED is a rectangle in which BD = 5 and its perimeter is 22. What is the area of triangle ABC?

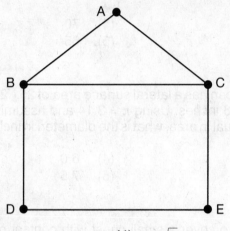

(1) $2\sqrt{7}$

(2) $3\sqrt{7}$

(3) $5\sqrt{7}$

(4) $8\sqrt{7}$

(5) $12\sqrt{7}$

12. Harry bought a sofa priced at $995 and a chair priced at $149. The sales tax is 8%. How much must he pay for the sofa and chair and tax?

(1) $1,144.00

(2) $91.52

(3) $1,134.00

(4) $1,224.72

(5) $1,235.52

13. A list of seven numbers is given: 4, 7, 8, 12, 14, 18, 25. Which one of the following numbers could be joined with this list so that the median of the new list of eight numbers would equal 10?

(1) 20

(2) 16

(3) 10

(4) 9

(5) 3

14. How many degrees in angle X?

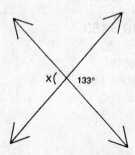

(1) 47°   (4) 223°
(2) 360°   (5) 133°
(3) 180°

15. The stopping distance of a car varies directly as the square of its speed. If a car requires 75 feet to stop when its speed is 30 miles per hour, what is the stopping distance, in feet, when the car's speed is 40 miles per hour?

(1) 133-1/3   (4) 100
(2) 125   (5) 85
(3) 112-1/2

Items 16 and 17 are based on the following graph.

16. The total area of our world's oceans is about 140,000,000 square miles. What is the area of the Pacific Ocean?

(1) 46,000,000 sq. mi.   (4) 86,000,000 sq. mi.
(2) 64,400,000 sq. mi.   (5) 6,440,000 sq. mi.
(3) 94,000,000 sq. mi.

17. The total area of our world is about 200,000,000 square miles. What percent of our world's surface is covered with water?

(1) 7%   (4) 28%
(2) 70%   (5) 60%
(3) 14%

18. Jerry wanted to buy a new pickup truck. In his home town he found one he liked for $11,558, but the sales tax in his state is 6% on vehicles. He lived near another state with lower sales tax. He found a truck there for $11,599. How much would it cost him to buy it in the next state?

(1) $12,251.48   (4) $12,062.95
(2) $12,294.94   (5)   Not enough information is given.
(3) $12,178.95

Directions: Solve each problem. Write the answer on the answer sheet provided.

19.   Going with the current, a boat can travel 60 miles in 4 hours. Going against the current, this boat would require 5 hours to travel 45 miles. In miles per hour, what is the speed of this boat in still water?

20.   What is the slope of the equation of a line perpendicular to the line described by the equation $7x + 3y = 10$?

21.   A jar contains one red marble, two blue marbles, and three white marbles. If two marbles are taken, one at a time without replacement, what is the probability that both marbles are white?

22.   Simplify: $38 + (-17) + 91 + (-58)$

23.   Mary's new car got the following gas mileage during the first five months she had the car: 35.5 mpg, 37 mpg, 34.25 mpg, 40.5 mpg, and 39.25 mpg. What was her average mpg (miles per gallon)?

24.   What would Sammy's score on the next algebra test have to be to have an average of 95? His grades so far are 93, 100, 92, and 100.

Directions: Solve the problem below. On the answer sheet, mark the circle on the graph that designates the solution's coordinates.

25.   On the graph on your answer sheet, locate the point which represents the solution to the following system of equations:

$$2x - 3y = -7$$
$$-5x - 4y = 29$$

PART 2

Calculator Use **Not** Permitted

26. Juan found a portable TV that normally costs $225, but now it is on sale at 30% off. What is the sale price?

    (1) $157.50
    (2) $67.50
    (3) $199.95

    (4) $195.00
    (5) Not enough information is given.

27. Joan won at tennis 4 out of 6 matches. What percentage did she win?

    (1) 33-1/3%
    (2) 66-2/3%
    (3) 40%

    (4) 60%
    (5) 80%

28. John was looking for the smallest wrench in his tool box. If he has 5 wrenches, and the sizes are 1/2 inch, 3/8 inch, 7/8 inch, 3/4 inch, and 9/16 inch, then which is smallest?

    (1) 1/2 in.
    (2) 3/8 in.
    (3) 7/8 in.

    (4) 3/4 in.
    (5) 9/16 in.

29. The planet Jupiter is said to be about 480 million miles from the sun. How is that distance written in scientific notation?

    (1) 4.8×10^8
    (2) 48×10^8
    (3) 4.8×10^6

    (4) 480×10^2
    (5) 48×10

30. Robert is doing a population study and needs to find 36.59% of 11,356. He should multiply 11,356 by

    (1) 36.59
    (2) 3.659
    (3) 0.3659

    (4) 0.03659
    (5) 365.9

31. Solve for *x:* $(1/4)x + 3 = 15$

    (1) 15-1/4
    (2) 12-1/4
    (3) 3

    (4) 12
    (5) 48

32. Toby runs track. Last week she ran 8 miles on Monday, 3 miles on Tuesday, 9 miles on Wednesday, 5 miles on Thursday, and 10 miles on Friday. Find the mean.

(1)   7 miles   (4)   5 miles
(2)   35 miles   (5)   There is no mean.
(3)   8 miles

33. What is the measure of angle Q?

(1)   58°   (4)   32°
(2)   100°   (5)   180°
(3)   122°

34. Evaluate the expression $x^2 + 2x - y + 3$ when $x = -2$ and $y = 3$.

(1)   -5   (4)   -3
(2)   3   (5)   5
(3)   0

35. Joey has seven marbles in his pocket. Two are red, four are blue, and one is white. What is the probability he will not pull out a red marble, if he picks one at random?

(1)   2/7   (4)   3/7
(2)   1/7   (5)   5/7
(3)   4/7

36. What is the measure of angle A?

(1) 43°   (4) 137°
(2) 47°   (5) 57°
(3) 90°

37. Simplify: $15 - 4(x + 2) + (6x + 2)$

(1) $2x + 7$ (4) $10x + 9$
(2) $2x + 9$ (5) $2x + 25$
(3) $10x + 25$

38. Laura went cruising in her motor boat. She cruised for 2 hours and 20 minutes and found she had traveled 21 nautical miles. What was her speed to the nearest knot? (One knot = one nautical mile in one hour.)

(1) 7 knots   (4) 9 knots
(2) 2-1/3 knots   (5) 49 knots
(3) 21 knots

39. Factor: $x^2 - 6x + 9$

(1) $x(x + 6)$ (4) $(x + 3)^2$
(2) $(x + 3)(x + 3)$ (5) $(x + 3)(x - 3)$
(3) $(x - 3)^2$

40. Line a is parallel to line b. Angle BFE measures 80°. What is the measure of angle CGF?

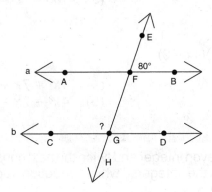

(1) 100°   (4) 120°
(2) 40°   (5) 80°
(3) 180°

41. What is the probability of the spinner stopping on "5"?

    (1)   1/5   (4)   1/6
    (2)   1/2   (5)   5/6
    (3)   1/3

42. In triangle ABC what is the measure of angle B?

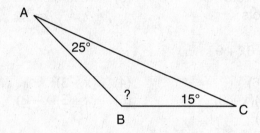

    (1)   140°   (4)   40°
    (2)   25°   (5)   100°
    (3)   15°

43. Multiply: $(x + 1)(4x + 3)$

    (1) $4x^2 + 4$ (4) $4x^2 + 7x + 3$
    (2) $4x^2 + 3$ (5) $4x^2 - 7x - 4$
    (3) $4x^2 + 4x + 3$

44. The sum of an even integer and twice the next consecutive even integer is 40. To find the integers, which equation represents the correct solution?

    (1) $x \cdot x = 40$ (4) $x(x + 2) = 40$
    (2) $x(x + 1) = 40$ (5) $x + 2(x + 2) = 40$
    (3) $x + 2(x + 1) = 40$

45. Out of a 52-card deck, what is the probability of drawing one of the four kings?

    (1) 1/12   (4) 52/4
    (2) 1/4   (5) 1/13
    (3) 4/1

46. Multiply: $10(-3w + 2)$

    (1) $30w + 2$ (4) $-30w - 20$
    (2) $-30w + 2$ (5) $-30w + 20$
    (3) $-30w - 2$

47. Johnny is 6 feet tall and casts a shadow of 3 feet. At the same time, a tree next to Johnny casts a shadow of 35 feet. How tall is the tree?

    (1) 30 ft.   (4) 75 ft.
    (2) 60 ft.   (5) 100 ft.
    (3) 70 ft.

Directions: Solve each problem. Write the answer on the answer sheet provided.

48. There are 650 seniors at Warm Weather High School. What percentage of the seniors are girls if 351 of the seniors are boys?

49. At a local bank, an employee ID badge consists of two letters followed by two digits. The letters must be vowels (not including "y"), with no repetition. The digits must be non-zero, but repetition is allowed. How many different badges are possible?

Directions: Solve the problem below. On the answer sheet, mark the circle on the graph that designates the solution's coordinates.

50. On the graph on your answer sheet, locate the point which lies 3 units directly above the midpoint of the line segment joining (−2, −9) and (6, 1).

EXAM II

ANSWER KEY

Test 1—Language Arts: Writing

1.	(2)	14.	(2)	27.	(2)	40.	(5)
2.	(3)	15.	(3)	28.	(3)	41.	(3)
3.	(5)	16.	(5)	29.	(5)	42.	(3)
4.	(3)	17.	(1)	30.	(3)	43.	(2)
5.	(5)	18.	(2)	31.	(3)	44.	(5)
6.	(1)	19.	(3)	32.	(3)	45.	(5)
7.	(2)	20.	(5)	33.	(2)	46.	(4)
8.	(5)	21.	(3)	34.	(2)	47.	(3)
9.	(4)	22.	(5)	35.	(4)	48.	(3)
10.	(5)	23.	(4)	36.	(1)	49.	(4)
11.	(1)	24.	(2)	37.	(4)	50.	(3)
12.	(2)	25.	(4)	38.	(2)		
13.	(4)	26.	(2)	39.	(2)		

Test 2—Social Studies

1.	(5)	14.	(4)	27.	(5)	40.	(2)
2.	(3)	15.	(1)	28.	(4)	41.	(4)
3.	(3)	16.	(3)	29.	(3)	42.	(1)
4.	(3)	17.	(2)	30.	(1)	43.	(3)
5.	(2)	18.	(1)	31.	(1)	44.	(4)
6.	(2)	19.	(3)	32.	(3)	45.	(4)
7.	(1)	20.	(5)	33.	(4)	46.	(3)
8.	(5)	21.	(4)	34.	(3)	47.	(1)
9.	(3)	22.	(1)	35.	(5)	48.	(5)
10.	(5)	23.	(5)	36.	(2)	49.	(4)
11.	(5)	24.	(4)	37.	(4)	50.	(3)
12.	(4)	25.	(3)	38.	(4)		
13.	(1)	26.	(1)	39.	(3)		

Test 3—Science

1.	(2)	14.	(1)	27.	(4)	40.	(1)
2.	(4)	15.	(2)	28.	(1)	41.	(4)
3.	(5)	16.	(4)	29.	(5)	42.	(1)
4.	(4)	17.	(2)	30.	(5)	43.	(1)
5.	(3)	18.	(4)	31.	(1)	44.	(4)
6.	(1)	19.	(4)	32.	(5)	45.	(5)
7.	(2)	20.	(2)	33.	(2)	46.	(4)
8.	(2)	21.	(3)	34.	(3)	47.	(1)
9.	(3)	22.	(4)	35.	(3)	48.	(3)
10.	(5)	23.	(4)	36.	(1)	49.	(5)
11.	(1)	24.	(1)	37.	(3)	50.	(3)
12.	(1)	25.	(3)	38.	(3)		
13.	(3)	26.	(5)	39.	(2)		

Test 4—Language Arts: Reading

1.	(1)	11.	(2)	21.	(2)	31.	(3)
2.	(2)	12.	(5)	22.	(1)	32.	(1)
3.	(2)	13.	(3)	23.	(2)	33.	(3)
4.	(1)	14.	(2)	24.	(2)	34.	(4)
5.	(3)	15.	(2)	25.	(4)	35.	(5)
6.	(1)	16.	(4)	26.	(3)	36.	(3)
7.	(2)	17.	(1)	27.	(3)	37.	(2)
8.	(2)	18.	(2)	28.	(1)	38.	(5)
9.	(3)	19.	(1)	29.	(2)	39.	(2)
10.	(1)	20.	(1)	30.	(3)	40.	(1)

Test 5—Math

Part 1

1.	(2)	13.	(5)
2.	(1)	14.	(5)
3.	(4)	15.	(1)
4.	(4)	16.	(2)
5.	(2)	17.	(2)
6.	(5)	18.	(5)
7.	(4)	19.	12
8.	(3)	20.	3/7
9.	(3)	21.	1/5
10.	(5)	22.	54
11.	(2)	23.	37.3
12.	(5)	24.	90

25. (−5, −1)

Part 2

26.	(1)	38.	(4)
27.	(2)	39.	(3)
28.	(2)	40.	(1)
29.	(1)	41.	(4)
30.	(3)	42.	(1)
31.	(5)	43.	(4)
32.	(1)	44.	(5)
33.	(3)	45.	(5)
34.	(3)	46.	(5)
35.	(5)	47.	(3)
36.	(2)	48.	46
37.	(2)	49.	1,620

50. (2, −1)

DETAILED EXPLANATIONS OF ANSWERS

TEST 1: LANGUAGE ARTS: WRITING, PART I

1. **(2) Sentence 1** When "but" is used in a sentence to join two compound sentences, the comma always goes before it. The word choices in the sentence are good, and the punctuation is correct as it is.

2. **(3) Sentence 2** A comma is needed after "For instance" for clarity. The reader needs to be clear, and "For instance" is an introductory phrase in this sentence. Spelling is correct, and no other punctuation is needed.

3. **(5) Sentence 3** The sentence is correct.

4. **(3) Sentence 4** **Whatever** is a correctly spelled word. A comma after **whatever** would break up the sentence incorrectly. A comma should be after the dependent, introductory clause ending with the word **do**.

5. **(5) Sentence 5** All punctuation and all spelling are correct. No changes are needed.

6. **(1)** Reversing the order of the sentences introduces the topic of the memo and ensures that the purpose of the memo is clear from the start.

7. **(2)** Paragraph B should be moved to the end of the memo choice (2). This sentence is an appropriate closing sentiment, and does not make as much sense in its current position.

8. **(5)** The answer is choice (5). "Made" and "waited" should each be in the present tense—"making" and "wait."

9. **(4)** Sentence 11 is on the same subject as the rest of the paragraph, foul language, but it is not relevant to the context of this memo. It is a distraction and impedes the clarity and directness of the memo. The answer is therefore choice (4).

10. **(5)** "Employees" is plural, so the verb "have" must agree with this—in this case, "has" should be "have," choice (5).

11. **(1)** The answer is choice (1). All of the other options would take information of the passage that is only mentioned once.

12. **(2)** The answer is choice (2), sentence 13, which is a coherent starting point. The present topic sentence begins in the middle of a thought, and the "he" is not clearly established.

13. **(4)** Choice (4) is the best transition. The others do not follow the general focus on Robinson that the passage creates, and choice (4) sets up the first sentence in paragraph E.

14. **(2)** Sentence 7 is out of place, and does not build on the previous sentence or set up the following sentence. Therefore, choice (2) is the correct answer.

15. **(3)** The answer is (3). This should jump out as an obvious mistake when reading the sentences, but the other choices can also be eliminated because they would result in more serious mechanical errors for the sentence.

16. **(5)** No correction is necessary. The correct contraction of "it is" is "it's." "Its" is the possessive of "it." The comma is correctly placed after big. A comma should not be placed after it (3), because it, the object, and the preposition, should not be separated. The sentence refers to any banquet hall, therefore it is not a proper noun and does not need to be capitalized.

17. **(1)** The answer is (1). "Its" is the possessive of "it," while "it's" is the contraction for "it is." In this case, the sentence is not assigning a possession to "it," but rather using "its" to express "it is."

18. **(2)** The answer is (2). This is a major grammatical error, and should stand out as a problem when reading this paragraph. The other suggestions would worsen the paragraph's mechanics and organization.

19. **(3)** The answer is (3). This sentence clearly is out of place in paragraph D—it logically fits into paragraph C.

20. **(5)** A careful look at the paragraph will reveal that none of the problems represented in choices (1), (2), (3), and (4) are evident in the sentence. The answer is (5).

21. **(3) Sentence 1** **Today's** is the possessive form, meaning "the society of today." This is the correct answer in this sentence. Spelling and punctuation are all correct.

22. **(5) Sentence 7** No changes are needed.

23. **(4) Sentence 8   Accept** means to take in, allow to happen. **Except** means everything but that. All other spelling and punctuation is correct.

24. **(2) Sentence 12** "Of" is incorrect; it is not a verb. The choice must be **should have**. Spelling and punctuation are correct.

25. **(4) Sentence 14** When confused on what pronoun to use to refer to yourself, drop the other part of that phrase. You would not say, "Me want to live." Also, remember to list others before yourself.

26. **(2) Sentence 15   With good reading and math skills** is the introductory statement and must be set off by a comma.

27. **(2) Sentence 16   It's** means "it is" and is the correct choice for this sentence. Work market is correct. No commas are necessary.

28. **(3) Sentence 1** The indefinite article **an** should be used with **extreme**.

29. **(5) Sentence 2** The sentence is correct.

30. **(3) Sentence 3   There**, meaning in that place, is the correct answer in this sentence. **They're** means they are and would be incorrect here. No commas are necessary in this sentence.

31. **(3) Sentence 4** The correct spelling is **heroes. Ball players** is correctly spelled as two words. **High School** is not capitalized unless following a proper noun. No commas are necessary.

32. **(3) Sentence 6** Place a comma after **year**. This is a compound sentence, and the comma gives clarity to the sentence.

33. **(2) Sentence 7   Going to** is the correct answer choice. **Gonna** is not a word and not standard English. **It is** would have to be replaced by **It's**. No commas are needed.

34. **(2) Sentence 9   Tackles** is the correct spelling. **Brake** means to stop. No commas are needed.

35. **(4) Sentence 1** The past of **spring** is **sprung; springed** is not a word. **America's** is obviously possessive, and there are no spelling or capitalization errors.

36. **(1) Sentence 2** Without the comma after **this**, its role would be changed from that of demonstrative pronoun to demonstrative adjective modifying **people**. Because this makes no syntactic sense, there is likewise

no comma placed after **people**. **People** is the subject, which agrees with **were**. Changing to associates makes no syntactic sense.

37. **(4) Sentence 3**   **Piece** means a portion of, not an opposite to war. There are no other spelling or structural errors.

38. **(2) Sentence 4**   When used in this way, **however** must be surrounded by commas. There is no reason to omit **excluding World War II**, as this hardly constitutes Sentence 4 as a run-on sentence.

39. **(2) Sentence 5**   All the sentences listed are fragments except (2) and (4). Sentence (2) is the only one that contains a main verb that agrees with the subject **reason**. Sentence (4) has a verb that does not agree with the subject.

40. **(5) Sentence 6**   There are no errors in this sentence. When used in this context, **moreover** is always a single word.

41. **(3) Sentence 7**   This run-on sentence would best be broken up into two sentences. **As** is not suitable; it introduces a subordinate clause that would accompany no main clause.

42. **(3) Sentence 2**   Verbs in a series must be of the same tense and form. There are no spelling or structural errors. The passive noun is correct as written.

43. **(2) Sentence 3**   **Invited** in this use calls for an infinitive verb. **Inviting** is not suitable with the auxiliary have. **Been invited** would only have been usable if **denounce** was in the infinitive.

44. **(5) Sentence 8**   The sentence is correct as written.

45. **(5) Sentence 9**   There are no corrections necessary. **Unallows** is not a word.

46. **(4) Sentences 2 and 3**   Sentence 3 is a fragment, and incorporating it into Sentence 2 excuses its verbal deficiency without forming a run-on sentence from the two single-clause sentences.

47. **(3) Sentence 4**   **Wars** and **visits** both agree in number with the word **movies**, which they elaborate, but **pet** stands out in its singular number. The other selections all retained this flaw in number agreement.

48. **(3) Sentence 5**   **Stem** does not agree with the subject, **cause**, but this is difficult to spot due to the structural intervention of the plural noun **genres** and the plural noun **critics** (which is spelled correctly). **Say** agrees with **critics**; **says** would agree with a singular noun.

49. **(4) Sentence 6** The semi-colon indicates a complete sentence follows. Therefore, the semi-colon should be changed to a comma. No comma is required after **slew of movies** because this would create an unnatural break that would separate **movies** from **involving**, whose clause modifies **movies**.

50. **(3) Sentence 7** Using **recurring** and **appear more than once** is redundant; therefore, one of them must be omitted. **However** in this context must retain its commas.

TEST 1: LANGUAGE ARTS: WRITING, PART II

Sample Essay — Possible Score of 4

Crime rates are rising alarmingly. Newspapers and television news-casts report frightening situations in all of our major cities. Young people form gangs, doing illegal activities and atrocities that were unheard of only a few years ago.

HIV and AIDS are common terms, when we had never heard of this national health threat twenty years ago. Many diseases are growing out of control, and overtaking the health of our country.

War in the Middle East is not something that we wanted to become involved in, yet our young American troops were in that area, in great numbers. Were we defending oil fields or were we taking a stand against world aggression? Was this all to the greater benefit of the greater number of people, or were we jeopardizing the credibility of the United States in the eyes of the world?

Could we afford to take such a step? Not only was the cost in human lives great, but the cost in money was great. Our nation was already running "in the red." Preparing a defense in the Middle East was certainly going to increase the deficit in America's finances.

Is involvement in the Middle East going to enhance our image in the eyes of the world or is it only going to further tarnish us? Who can answer these questions? Not I.

Why this essay scores a 4

This essay is thoughtfully organized and is well structured. The topic states that the U.S. is faced with crime, health problems, a possibility of war, financial problems, and a lessening of world respect. The essayist uses this as an outline for his essay by writing on each point in the order in which it is presented.

The essayist's thoughts flow together nicely, which makes the essay easy to read. There are, also, no obvious errors in use of standard written English. In addition, adequate support for the main idea has been presented, and is drawn upon and tied together in the conclusion.

Sample Essay — Possible Score of 3

The United States of America is the greatest country in the world, today or at any other time in history. We have more to offer, more freedoms, more goods, more opportunities than any other country in the world has, ever.

When people criticize us, they make me angry. When our own citizens do not stand for "The Pledge of Allegiance" and "The Star Spangled Banner," I am furious. These people should have to spend time as "guests" in Iraq. That might clarify for them what is great in this country.

Few countries allow people the freedom to publically state their beliefs, if these are against State doctrine. Few countries have so many opportunities available to the general populace.

Granted, we have homeless who would argue about opportunities. This is a fact which must be faced. But, the homeless situation is not one which is strictly to be found in America. Homeless are found in all parts of the world. Maybe, the public cry over the plight of the homeless in America is yet another example of how free we are in our rights to criticize, as well as to praise what is America.

For the most part, praise is what America deserves.

Why this essay scores a 3

This essay is not well organized. It attacks the essay topic in a rather roundabout manner. Support presented in this essay is only partially related to the topic of the problems this country faces. This essay only deals with a lessening of respect for our country, although the essay topic deals with "a lessening of world respect."

Support for the main idea is very weak and is made worse by the use of poor sentence structure and the misspelling of words, such as "publicly" in the third paragraph, which is spelled "publically." To say that the conclusion of this essay is not well developed would be an understatement—it is not developed at all. One sentence is presented that does not tie together any of the points in the essay.

Sample Essay — Possible Score of 2

Yes. It is true that our country has a lot of problems.

Our country's problem can be traced back to money. People commit crimes because they dont have anything. And because poor people dont have money, they often dont have health insurence. Also, when your poor your less likely to have the time or money to have a personal trainer to be healthy and more likely to smoke. Because we live in a society based on advertising and materialism people go into debt trying to buy all the stupid junk that rich corporations tell us we have to have if we want to be some body.

If you ask me, the rich are the ones who are the real problem. They dont want to give health insurance benefits to people so they can save money. But they do want everyone in the whole country to go out and buy, buy, buy.

If you want to talk about other problems no matter what the answer is the same. Pollution, same. Sickness, same. No one cares about the pollution in places where the poor live, even if it makes them sick. The government make laws that favor the rich because its the rich corporations that have money to "donate" to campains. Protecting the rich—this is what kills justice. Everybody knows it. And that's why other nations are losing respect for us.

Why this essay scores a 2

This essay attempts to answer the questions in presented in the essay topic. It presents a main idea clearly in the second sentence. The essayist presents examples that back up his opinion. These examples clearly illustrate some of the many problems that can be found in America. However, the essayist does not answer the final question presented in the writing topic. He does not give any ways in which the nation's image might be improved.

This essay also has a moderate amount of spelling and grammatical errors. The essayist does not have full control over the use of contractions, such as the use of "dont" for "don't." There are also many places where punctuation, such as commas, are missing. Many of the more complex sentences become confusing because of grammar mistakes.

Sample Essay — Possible Score of 1

Can you imagin a wall goin cross this country? In reality, there seem to be an imaginary wall running from east to west, across America's middle.

This wall separates north from south. Why do people in Boston think a Texan is bein "smart" when he uses what he been raised to know as good maners? Why is it that North Carolinians think a New Yorker is being rude when he says Sure instead of Yes, sir to a question?

Do Americans speak diferent languages? Absolutely. In our familes, we speak languages that we do not share with strangers. This does not make us weker; it makes us stronger. We accept other Americans outside of our own smaller cultures. This, in turn, makes us a good. This may be the gratest strength we have.

The United States of America is faced with problems only because this country continually tries to improve itself to grow and to be a better nation. The rest of this planet should know this.

Why this essay scores a 1

This essay has one main problem—it does not address the topic. The only mention of the problems faced by the U.S. appears in the last paragraph and this point is not developed. Even if this point was developed, it would appear too late in the essay to mean anything.

In addition, there is no organization of ideas. Apparently, not a great deal of planning was put into this essay. As it stands, the essay is wordy and has no purpose whatsoever. This essay also has many problems with spelling and grammar.

TEST 2: SOCIAL STUDIES

1. **(5)**   is most correct. The German government is being warned that a "grave situation…has resulted…" from the loss of American lives. (1) There is no statement declaring war by the U.S. (2) No mention of payments or compensation is made. (3) The U.S. is claiming to be neutral in the conflict. (4) It is stated that American ships have already been attacked.

2. **(3)**   World War I began in Europe in 1915, and incidents like the *Lusitania*'s sinking helped bring the U.S. into the war in 1917.

3. **(3)**   is most correct. Although the Germans do introduce poison gas in the trench warfare in France, this is not discussed in the letter. All the other tactics are discussed in the letter.

4. **(3)**   is the opposite of the letter's intent, which is to insist on the right of the U.S. to trade anywhere. The other points are stated in the letter, (1) and (2) being disagreed with.

5. **(2)**   is correct. Woodrow Wilson finally had to ask for a declaration of war because of increasing German attacks on Atlantic shipping.

6. **(2)**   is most correct. There is a sampling of both government types and nations with those types. A sampling means it is not an all-inclusive list. (1) is partially correct, but not all government forms are included. Others include despotic, military, and colonial rule. (3) refers to economic, not political, systems, and would not be a good title. (4) and (5) describe living standards, and the first column contains a mix of these.

7. **(1)**   is correct, because a representative form of government is where elected officials represent the people in a legislature. (2) The legislative body may take other names, such as the U.S. Congress. (3) Most ex-British colonies have parliaments, but not all. (4) All governments have leaders, most parliamentary forms have elected ones. (5) Most modern governments have a written constitution like the U.S., but the oldest parliamentary government, Britain, has no written constitution.

8. **(5)**   is correct, all are African states. All are ex-colonies of various European powers, not just Britain (1). Most have some form of military rule, with or without kings (2). Algeria is Arab and on the Mediterranean, the others are in northeast or sub-Saharan Africa ((3) and (4)).

9. **(3)**   is the most correct pattern; usually the legislature has become a rubber-stamp for a strong leader. For answers (1), (4), and (5), length of term or limits may exist, but these do not deal with the power of the parliament, which is what "restricted" refers to.

10. **(5)** is correct. A republic is a government of elected representatives that debates issues, which implies several factions or parties. The other choices are all versions of one-person or single-action rule.

11. **(5)** is correct. (1) is not correct, because there are some variances between nations high in GNP while not so high in trade. (2) is incorrect because there is no data comparing previous years. (3) is incorrect. Thailand, the Philippines, and Indonesia did not exceed the world average in trade. (4) is incorrect; Japan was not the leader in trade.

12. **(4)** is not true, the trade graph is a line graph, and the GNP is a bar graph. All the others are true. (1) per capita means per person.

13. **(1)** is most accurate; all are on the eastern edge of Asia. (2) is incorrect because all of Asia is not represented, for example, India or the Persian Gulf. (3) is wrong; North West Asia would be either the Persian Gulf area or Asian USSR. (4) is incorrect; Malaysia and Thailand are as close to the Indian Ocean as to the Pacific. (5) is wrong; only Australia, Hong Kong, Malaysia, New Zealand, and Singapore were ever British colonies. Japan and Thailand were never colonized by foreigners.

14. **(4)** Singapore shows the greatest growth rate because its per capita trade is not only highest, but exceeds its GNP, which means its people are producing exportable products that bring money back into the nation. Hong Kong is second.

15. **(1)** GNP is the gross national product and is defined as the total goods and services produced by the nation in a given year. (2) is only partially correct because services are not specified. The others are not correct.

16. **(3)** is correct, the key fact being the proximity to China.

17. **(2)** is most correct, with the key data being on the importance of trade. (1) is not correct because of the statistic on scarcity of agricultural area. (3), (4), and (5) have no supporting data from which a conclusion may be drawn.

18. **(1)** is correct. Density means the number of people per set area. The high population and small area would indicate high density. (3) and (4) have no data to come to a conclusion about how the population is scattered or distributed. (5) The data indicating little farming area and high manufacturing and trade would indicate an urban population.

19. **(3)** is most correct, again with data to support good manufacturing and trade, which must be efficient to compete on the world market as well as they do. The statistics show a 16% increase, which is very high.

20. **(5)** is most correct, with the export and import figures exactly tied. (3) and (4) have no supporting data.

21. **(4)** *Section 2* states that the President has the power to make treaties "provided two thirds of the Senators present concur." None of the other fractions is applicable.

22. **(1)** Although the terms "high crimes" and "misdemeanors" are notoriously vague, they refer to illegal acts, as do the terms "Treason" and "Bribery." Nothing in this section provides for removal of a president because of incapacity, although Article II: *Section 1* (not quoted here) gives the vice president the power to discharge the powers of the president in the case of the latter's incapacity but says nothing about removal from office.

23. **(5)** Article II: *Section 2* specifically gives the President the power to appoint ambassadors, serve as Commander and Chief, appoint Supreme Court judges, and grant pardons for offense against the United States. It says nothing about the power to declare war. Article I: *Section 8* (not quoted here), however, gives Congress the power to declare war.

24. **(4)** Although Article II: *Section 3* gives the President the power to adjourn the House and Senate when they cannot agree on the time of adjournment, the President does not have the power to dissolve these bodies or even a general power to adjourn them. All of the other duties and powers listed as answers are explicitly stated in this section.

25. **(3)** is correct. Section 4 describes the officers, with chairperson listed first and with the most power. None of the other choices are mentioned.

26. **(1)** is correct, as the rules refer to the "Party" several times. (2), (3), and (4) are not correct, although political parties obviously exist to control these governments. (5) is not mentioned anywhere.

27. **(5)** is correct. All are mentioned specifically in section 2 as eligible to vote.

28. **(4)** is correct, as mentioned in section 5.

29. **(3)** is correct, as mentioned in section 4b. Other groups, like the Executive Board, meet more frequently.

30. **(1)** is correct. Britain is the only top importing nation that does not appear among the top five exporters.

31. **(1)** is correct. Canada is the largest importer. Even the two European nations combined, Britain and Germany, imported less.

32. **(3)** is correct. Japan was the largest single exporter, and combining with Taiwan made it even larger. No other region had two exporters listed.

33. **(4)** is correct, with the difference between exports and imports being the greatest in Japan's favor. The others are relatively close, with no comparisons available for Britain.

34. **(3)** is correct. If your nation sells more exports than it buys imports, it creates a surplus of capital coming in or a profit. (1) and (2) refer to the payments made for many things, including trade. So they may reflect on trade balances, but are not the same. (4) is the opposite. In the graph, the U.S.'s imports from Japan reflect a balance of trade unfavorable for the U.S. and favorable for Japan. (5) This can result from unfavorable trade balances, but reflects many other spending and revenue factors.

35. **(5)** The early years of mass-production and the factory system saw many abuses of laborers until attitudes and laws balanced the needs of owners and workers. (1) is a political era rather than economic. (2) is incorrect because capitalism existed before the Industrial Revolution, although its free market theories were used to justify poor working conditions. (3) is wrong because Karl Marx observed the abuses of capitalism and envisioned communism as a solution with workers in control. (4) is incorrect because fascism was a 20th Century political/economic dictatorship, but did not advocate these conditions.

36. **(2)** This box states, "Federal income tax withheld." Only two other boxes– box four and box six– are for tax withholding, but they are for Social Security and Medicare. Box one is a place to list the amount of money made from working and box three is a place to list the amount of money a person has received from Social Security (if any).

37. **(4)** The W-2 form concerns only the employer and the employee and therefore lists no personal information regarding the employee's family.

38. **(4)** Although it does not use the term "withholding," box seventeen lists the amount withheld for state income tax. Box two is for federal income tax withholding. Box three is for wages subject to Social Security. Box sixteen is for wages subject to state income tax, and box nineteen is for local income tax withholding.

39. **(3)** At the bottom of the form on the lower right hand corner are the words "Department of Treasury–Internal Revenue Service." On the lower left hand corner is the statement, "This information is being furnished to the Internal Revenue Service."

40. **(2)** is correct. The statement is that the "U.S. has made a decision— defend at all costs." (1) is incorrect; all the statements point to an ongoing war, with no end in sight. (3) is incorrect because there is no statement to support this. (4) is incorrect because all the discussions revolve around U.S., not UN,

involvement. (5) is incorrect; although this had already happened in the past, there is nothing to indicate when.

41. **(4)** is correct, as the second paragraph discusses his anti-communist feelings. The U.S. support for his government is clear in the last paragraph. (1) is not a correct choice, because Laos is cited as part of the communist supply line. Viet Cong, (2), is wrong because they were the South Vietnamese branch of the Communist party. (3) is incorrect; he was the legendary leader of Vietnamese communists, who opposed the U.S.. (5) is wrong because this would include North Viet Nam and Laos, areas already communist.

42. **(1)** This is the only one that fits specifically. (2) is a poor choice, because the problems come from industry, and the title is too general. There are other national problems besides pollution, so (3) is wrong. (4) Several of the nations listed have small pollution problems in these areas. (5) is wrong because the table includes both "western" and "eastern" nations. Therefore, the table could not be accurately titled "Western Pollution Problems."

43. **(3)** is most accurate, with one pollution problem from each area represented. (1) and (2) have no data to say whether either all or the major ones are all represented. The variety of problems, from small to severe, suggests they are not similar to all nations, so (4) is incorrect. (5) is wrong because the category of fertilizers is an agricultural problem.

44. **(4)** is correct, with small classification in all areas.

45. **(4)** is the opposite of what is predicted, with air pollution destroying the rain forests. All the others are predicted results.

46. **(3)** is correct because the event was obviously a stock market crash, with no outside event cited as a cause. Historical references, such as ticker tape and Anaconda, help pinpoint the era. (1) is incorrect, because modern references, such as telephone, eliminate this era. (2) is incorrect. This will be a partial result of the crash, but no references to it are made. Pearl Harbor Day (4) is also incorrect. No reference to this is made, plus historically the attack occurred on a weekend when the market is closed. (5) is incorrect because there is no reference to point to this event, which occurred in the afternoon while the crash began in the morning.

47. **(1)** The quote says that once the tape lost track no one knew what was happening. This lack of information would increase the panic. (2) and (3) are cited as being the opposite, with a sound economy waiting for a stock market rally. (4) is incorrect, because three major issues, steel, telephone, and anaconda (copper), were listed. (5) is incorrect. This is the opposite of what happened, there were "no buying orders...."

48. **(5)** is most correct as cited, with sell orders coming in from all over the country, with no buy orders to meet them. (1) is wrong. The passage states that there was so much activity that the ticker tape was overwhelmed. (2) is

incorrect. The quote says that the market opened "steady." (3) is incorrect. The opening sentence discusses the general falling market recently. (4) is incorrect. There is no evidence of this in the quote.

49. **(4)** is correct, even though he had been in office for less than a year, and the economic conditions were already in place. (1), (2), and (3) were the three presidents before Hoover, and (5) was elected after Hoover to try to solve the depression that followed.

50. **(3)** is most correct. The Federal Deposit Insurance Corporation was created as part of the New Deal to restore confidence in banks, not stocks. (1) is incorrect; the Securities and Exchange Commission was created to regulate the stock market after the crash. Among its reforms were (2), which reduced the percentage of stock that could be bought on credit (margin), tighter checks on the economic soundness of businesses issuing stocks (4), and checks on how people inside a company can buy and sell their own stocks (5).

TEST 3: SCIENCE

1. **(2)** The earth is rotating counterclockwise as shown and thus a person on the circumference of the circle, which is the equator, would first see the moon at noon and lose sight of the moon at midnight (2). Although the person would see the moon at midnight and at noon, the person would not see it between midnight and noon and thus (1) is not a correct answer. At sunrise the moon is on the other side of the earth from the person on the equator and thus not visible. Therefore (3) and (4) are not possible answers. The person would see the moon at sunset but not only at sunset (5).

2. **(4)** A plant needs water to build its nutrients. It will acquire carbon dioxide from the atmosphere. Locating the plant close to the window makes it available to the light energy necessary to carry out photosynthesis. Placing sugar in the soil is not necessary. The plant will make its sugar by photosynthesis. Oxygenating the soil is not necessary. The plant produces oxygen by photosynthesis.

3. **(5)** Marble is a type of metamorphic rock (5). It is formed from limestone, a type of sedimentary rock (4) when it is exposed to intense heat and pressure. Magma (1) is molten rock that can be found below the earth's crust. When it cools, it becomes igneous rock (2). Igneous rock breaks into sediment, small pieces of weathered rock, due to erosion. Sedimentary rock forms when sediments and small parts of organic matter such as bones are compacted due to pressure.

4. **(4)** is correct. If limestone is exposed to extreme heat and pressure (D), marble can form. Igneous rock is formed through the solidification and crystallization of the magma (A). Sediments, not marble, are formed when igneous rock is exposed to weathering, erosion, or deposition (B). The formation of sedimentary rock from sediments (C) forms limestone, marble's precursor. Melting of metamorphic rocks (E) produces molten magma not rock.

5. **(3)** The property of an object which determines the object's resistance to motion is its mass. A large watermelon (3) has a far greater mass than the pellet of lead shot, golf ball, feather, or notepaper. The mass of an object never changes. It is equal to an object's weight divided by the acceleration due to gravity "g" at its current position in space.

6. **(1)** The sleeping astronauts would continue their motion in a straight line if the Shuttle suddenly changed velocity due to the firing of its thrusters. If the Shuttle slowed down, the astronauts would move forward relative to the walls. This is all due to the fact that the astronauts have mass, or inertia. Gravity is so weak that it is negligible on the astronauts. They can be monitored by battery driven devices that allow them to move around, and they

can certainly sleep without being strapped. Bodies do not need a reaction force to sleep.

7. **(2)**   Inertia is measured by mass, m, which is choice (2). Choices (1) and (5) do contain mass but also involve other complicating factors like the speed of light, c, which invalidate the choice. There are two ways to measure mass: gravitationally through an object's weight, and inertially through an object's resistance to motion. Both measures, gravitational mass and inertial mass, have always been found to be the same for a given object.

8. **(2)**   Answer choice (2), "pandas are not bears, and their genus name, *Aleropoda*, indicates this," is the correct answer. Since *Ursus* is the genus name of bears, *Aleropoda* would indicate that the panda is not a bear. "Panda bears live only in China" (1) cannot be the correct answer since where a panda lives does not indicate that it is a bear. "Pandas are not bears, and their species name, *melanoleuca*, indicates this" (3) cannot be the correct answer since species names are not used to designate the grouping. "Pandas are on the endangered list and have black and white fur" (4) cannot be the correct answer since being on the endangered list and the color of fur does not make the panda a bear. "Pandas are not bears because they are really called 'pandas'"(5) cannot be the correct answer since the only way to tell what pandas are is to compare the genus name of the bear *Ursus* and the genus name of the panda, *Aleropoda*, and, if they are the same, then the panda is a bear. Simply calling it a "panda" is using its common name which tells one nothing about its classification.

9. **(3)**   Answer choice (3), "the genus names indicate that there is no relationship," is the correct answer since the genus names of the two animals are different. "The species name indicates that there is a close genetic relationship" (1) cannot be the correct answer since the species name does not show genetic relationships. "The species name indicates a filial relationship" (2) cannot be the correct answer since the species name is not used to show a genetic relationship. "The genus name indicates there is a filial relationship" (4) cannot be the correct answer since the two names are different. "Both animals are totally black" (5) cannot be the correct answer since not enough information is given.

10. **(5)**   Answer choice (5), "genus name," is the correct answer since all scientific names begin with the genus name. "Kingdom name" (1) cannot be the correct answer since a kingdom name is never used in an organism's scientific name. "Phylum name" (2) cannot be the correct answer since a phylum name is never used in an organism's scientific name. "Class name" (3) cannot be the correct answer since a class name is never used in an organism's scientific name. "Order name" (4) cannot be the correct answer since an order name is never used in an organism's scientific name.

11. **(1)**   Answer choice (1), "this conclusion is supported by the data," is the correct answer since the gray line representing the whitetail deer population

drops over a period of time, and the mule deer (black line) stays the same or shows an increase in population. "This conclusion is not supported by the data" (2) cannot be the correct answer since one can determine that there are fewer whitetail deer over a period of time. "This conclusion includes the effect of hunting and is supported by the data" (3) cannot be the correct answer since it is stated in the paragraph that hunting was not allowed. "This conclusion includes the effect caused by drought and is supported by the data" (4) cannot be the correct answer since no drought was mentioned in the data. "The conclusion is right but the data is wrong" (5) cannot be the correct answer since a proper conclusion can only be based on the data, and if that data is incorrect, then the conclusion must also be incorrect.

12. **(1)** Answer choice (1), "the conclusion is supported by the data," is the correct answer since the mule deer survived and the whitetail deer did not survive. "The conclusion is refuted by the data" (2) cannot be the correct answer since the fittest, in this case, were the mule deer. "The conclusion is refuted because only one kind of deer survived" (3) cannot be the correct answer since there is no data indicating that any of the whitetail deer survived. "The conclusion is refuted because the two kinds of deer do not compete with each other, and the data supports this" (4) cannot be the correct answer since both animals had the same food and opportunities. "The conclusion is right, but the data is wrong" (5) cannot be the correct answer since a conclusion is based on data and if the data is wrong, then the conclusion must also be wrong, and there is no evidence of that.

13. **(3)** Answer choice (3), "the conclusion is neither supported nor refuted by the data," is correct since there is no data concerning any special adaptations to the environment. "The conclusion is supported by the data" (1) cannot be the correct answer since there is no data concerning any special adaptations to the environment. "The conclusion is refuted by the data" (2) cannot be the correct answer since environmental adaptations are not addressed by the graph. "The data gives plenty of information concerning the mule deer's adaptability, which supports the conclusion" (4) cannot be the correct answer since there are no data about adaptability. "The data gives plenty of information concerning the type of terrain, which supports the conclusion" (5) cannot be the correct answer since no information is given about the terrain.

14. **(1)** January has a low mean temperature and high precipitation, making snow highly likely.

15. **(2)** is correct since, as the diagram shows, the distance between the two adjacent peaks is labelled as the wavelength. If the peaks are not adjacent, more than one wavelength will be measured, as in (1). (3) is wrong because the distance described is twice the wave amplitude, not wavelength. (4) is describing velocity, not wavelength. (5) is incorrect because the horizontal midline is only an imaginary line to divide the height of a wave from a trough.

16. **(4)** is correct. The water molecules, which is the medium, is not carried, but the wave peaks do move toward shore. (1) states the opposite of what is mentioned in the question. (2) is wrong because although the ocean is somewhat mixed each day, this mixing is due to currents and turbulence, not by waves. (3) is wrong because debris washes ashore by currents and turbulence, not by waves. (5) is incorrect because waves move neither water nor swimmers. The waves travel through the water and the swimmer will bob up and down but will not be carried by the wave. Again, currents and turbulence are responsible for moving both water and swimmers.

17. **(2)** Answer choice (2), "the message of the mRNA is different from the DNA before the event," is the correct answer. Since the DNA contains the information for the mRNA, the mRNA made after the event will be different because the DNA will be changed. Since DNA makes mRNA, the mRNA will be changed whenever the DNA is changed. "Nothing happens" (1) cannot be the correct answer since the removal of a "code word" is at least considered a point mutation, and the resulting mRNA will be changed. "mRNA cannot be made" (3) cannot be the correct answer since many of the DNA "code words" would have to be destroyed before this would happen. "Triplets can no longer be produced, so doublets are used" (4) cannot be the correct answer since "code words" are always "read" by threes (triplets). "DNA repairs itself perfectly" (5) cannot be the correct answer since although DNA can repair itself, the mechanism for repair is often flawed.

18. **(4)** Answer choice (4), the nucleus, is the correct answer since the nucleus contains the chromosomes, which are composed of DNA nucleotides and some protein. The lysosomes (1) cannot be the correct answer since lysosomes contain digestive enzymes. The endoplasmic reticulum (2) cannot be the correct answer since it is a series of membranes found in the cytoplasm and it serves as a site of protein synthesis. "Cytoplasmic matrix" (3) cannot be the correct answer since DNA nucleotides are not found outside of the nucleus. Ribosomes (5) cannot be the correct answer since ribosomes are found in the cytoplasm and are in the endoplasmic reticulum.

19. **(4)** is correct. To find the oxidation number of H_2S, rule 1 says that the sum of the oxidation numbers of the atoms must be zero. Rule 1 is important here, so choices (2) and (5) can be disqualified from being correct. Also rule 4 states that hydrogen has a charge of +1 when combined with nonmetals (such as sulfur). Rule 2 concerns polyatomic ions. H_2S, however, is not an ion. It is not monatomic, but polyatomic, so rule 3 does not apply.

20. **(2)** is correct. The sum of all of the oxidation numbers must equal zero. O_4 must be $4 \times 2 = -8$. K is +1. $-8 + 1 = 7$. To equal zero, then, Mn must equal +7.

21. **(3)** is correct. Since H is combined with a nonmetal (P), H must have a charge of +1. The four oxygen atoms have a combined charge of −8 since $4x - 2 = -8$. The charge on the ion is −2. Thus, P must have a charge of +5 since $5 + 1 - 8 = -2$.

22. **(4)** is correct since rules 2 and 4 are necessary to find the charges of H, P, O_4, and the combined ion. Specifically, rule 2 states that HPO_4^{2-} must have a net charge of −2. Rule 4 helps in determining the charge of the hydrogen. Rule 1 is not applicable since HPO_4^{2-} is not a neutral substance. Rule 3 does not apply because HPO_4^{2-} is polyatomic, not monatomic.

23. **(4)** (4) is correct, because at this location, the North Pole is tilted toward the sun, resulting in continual daylight. (1) and (3) are incorrect, because in this position the pole is neither pointing toward nor from the sun, and equal hours of night and day would occur. (2) is not the right answer because the North Pole is pointing away from the sun and is in continual darkness. (5) is incorrect; these two positions are so very different.

24. **(1)** It is the varying angle of the sunrays in relationship to the poles that causes the change in seasons, therefore answer (1) is correct. (2) is incorrect, because the changes in distance as the Earth revolves around the sun are not great enough to account for the changes in the seasons. (3), (4), and (5) have no bearing on the seasons.

25. **(3)** Genotypes X^BY and X^bY represent males. In humans, a female has two copies of the gene for an X-linked trait, as she has two X chromosomes. Genotypes X^BX^B and X^BX^b cannot produce color blindness. Color blindness is caused by a recessive allele. In the genotype X^BX^b, the dominant allele B masks the effect of the recessive allele b. In the genotype X^bX^b, both alleles of the gene cause color blindness.

26. **(5)** Blood is oxygenated in the lungs, and then moves into the left side of the heart. Although the aorta (1) is connected to the heart and is a part of the circulatory system, it is not a part of the heart, which is composed of four chambers. The right atrium (2) and right side of the heart (4) receive blood that has passed through the body already, and therefore is lacking in oxygen. The lungs (3) are a part of the respiratory system and not a part of the heart.

27. **(4)** A chameleon changes color mostly due to temperature, sunlight, and emotion. Thus, a black chameleon is probably black because it is cold. Thus, (4) is correct. It is a false belief that chameleons change color to match their environment. Thus, (2) is wrong. (1) is wrong because hiding is a possibility for a color change but not a main reason why a color change occurs. (3) is wrong because color changes are normal occurrences for chameleons and do not signify that the animal is dying. (5) is incorrect because extending the tongue is not necessarily preceded by a color change.

28. **(1)** The sticky substance on the tongue aids in catching prey. Thus, (1) is correct. (2) is incorrect because the fork on the end of a tongue is too soft to spear prey. (3) is wrong because the tongue flicks the prey into the chameleon's mouth; the tongue does not squeeze the prey. In this case, the length of the tongue is helpful for catching prey at a distance. (4) is wrong because the chameleon does not have poisonous glands. (5) is wrong because the color change of a chameleon will not distract the prey.

29. **(5)** is correct because either the added substance may be insoluble in the solvent, or the solution may already be saturated, or both may be true. (1) is wrong because the substance would dissolve in an unsaturated solution. (4) is wrong because a solution often does contain more than one type of solute.

30. **(5)** is correct. The rule is that like substances dissolve in like substances. Here, "like" means that both substances are polar or both are nonpolar. (1) is wrong because oil will dissolve in water. (2) is incorrect because like does dissolve in like. (3) is wrong for the same reason. (4) is incorrect because again, the example states incorrect information. NaCl does, in fact, dissolve in water.

31. **(1)** Visible light consists of waves which have wavelengths from blue at 4000 angstroms to red at 7000 angstroms. For the three sources plotted in the displayed graph, the tungsten filament lamp has the greatest relative energy output at the red end, with a reading of slightly greater than 80. This compares with the lower red readings of about 57 for daylight and about 7 for the fluorescent lamp. Note average daylight is far brighter than the other two sources, explaining why camera exposures inside under artificial lights need to be longer than those for outside on a normal day.

32. **(5)** Liquid substances and gases are unable to transmit transverse shear waves. Each of the choices provided are liquids or gases at standard conditions except the igneous rock, granite (5). Mountains of granite on the earth transmit the three types of waves generated by earthquakes: P-, S-, and L-waves.

33. **(2)** If the S-waves are stopped at 2,900 kilometers below the surface, then there must be liquid present there. The radius of the Earth is about 6,400 kilometers, or 3,960 miles. This implies that this liquid outer core must have a radius of about 3,500 kilometers, or about 2,170 miles.

34. **(3)** For this problem, S-waves travel at 4.25 km/sec and the P-waves at about 8.5 km/sec. Using the equation that distance equals rate multiplied by time, we see that the distance must be equal to 8.5 km/sec times 4 minutes (240 seconds) to get 2,040 kilometers. This is closest to the 2,000 km of choice (3). The associated S-waves would arrive about 4 minutes after the P-waves.

35. **(3)** The layer of cambium is not added each year and is not added to the age of the plant. Each year the stem adds one layer of xylem and phloem. Therefore in seven years the plant stem will have fourteen layers of vascular tissue, seven layers of xylem and seven layers of phloem.

36. **(1)** The researcher is manipulating the amount of the antibiotic administered to the two populations of frogs. Time and biological sex are not manipulated. Life span and body weight are dependent variables.

37. **(3)** Answer choice (3) is the correct answer. If you trace the line going through central Florida in either direction, you will see it is 15° Celsius.

38. **(3)** is the correct answer. The numbers along the left and right edges of the map represent latitude. The warmest sea-level temperature shown on this map is 30°C which is located at approximately 20°S. Answer choice (2) is incorrect because 20°N is in the Northern Hemisphere which is located above the 0° latitude line, also known as the Equator.

39. **(2)** Answer choice (2), "yes, because there are more offspring produced than the environment could support, and only some of the clams would survive," would be the correct answer since it is consistent with the second of Darwin's observations and the first of his conclusions. "Yes, because favorable variations occur" (1) cannot be the correct answer since the question has nothing to do with the variation. "Yes, because the environment is constantly changing" (3) cannot be the correct answer since even though the environment is constantly changing, the change is not fast enough to affect the single release of clams' sex cells. "No, because individual sperm and egg are different genetically" (4) cannot be the correct answer since this is not consistent with any of Darwin's observations nor with any of his conclusions. "No, because genetic variation does not allow for natural selection" (5) cannot be the correct answer since it is not consistent with any of Darwin's observations or conclusions.

40. **(1)** Answer choice (1), "organisms produce more offspring than the environment can support so a population will remain constant because there are not enough resources for all offspring," is the correct answer because it is consistent with Darwin's observations and conclusions. "The environment is slowly changing all over the world, which prevents all of the offspring from maturing" (2) cannot be the correct answer since the environment does not change that quickly. "Genetic variation is allowing the ferns to keep the same level of population" (3) cannot be the correct answer since genetic variation has nothing to do with the leveling of the population of ferns. "Genetic variation, which allows for survival, will increase" (4) cannot be the correct answer since the survival characteristics, which can accumulate, do not do so quickly enough for this to occur in a single year. "Individuals vary genetically" (5) cannot be the correct answer since this is not a source that would prevent all of the spores from maturing.

41. **(4)** Answer choice (4), "bilateral symmetry," is the correct answer since the bird has a right and a left side. "Asymmetry" (1) cannot be the correct answer since asymmetry refers to something that has no definite shape. "Radial symmetry" (2) cannot be the correct answer since radial symmetry refers to organisms that have their parts radiating outward as in a cylindrical shape or a flattened cylindrical shape. "Spherical symmetry" (3) cannot be the correct answer since the bird is not shaped like a sphere. "Longitudinal symmetry" (5) cannot be the correct answer since there is no such terminology.

42. **(1)** Answer choice (1), "asymmetry," is the correct answer since the amoeba is constantly changing shape. "Radial symmetry" (2) cannot be the correct answer since radial symmetry refers to organisms that have their parts radiating outward as in a cylindrical shape or a flattened cylindrical shape. "Bilateral symmetry" (3) cannot be the correct answer since the figure has no right or left side. "Spherical symmetry" (4) cannot be the correct answer since the amoeba is not shaped like a sphere. "Triradial symmetry" (5) cannot be the correct answer since there is no such terminology.

43. **(1)** is correct. Intermolecular attraction, namely, hydrogen bonding, leads to the high boiling and melting point. (2) is wrong because water has high surface tension. (3) is wrong because there is a great deal of hydrogen bonding between water molecules. (4) is wrong because water has a high heat capacity. (5) is wrong because hydrogen bonds, not covalent bonds, are present between the oxygen and hydrogen of one water molecule.

44. **(4)** The nerve endings, blood vessels, and sweat glands are found in the dermis. They are not in the layer of Malpighi, since this layer's main function is to replace the stratum corneum that quickly wears away. Thus, (1) is wrong. It would not be beneficial to have these important structures in a layer that wears away; thus, they are not found in the stratum corneum. Choice (2) must be wrong. Since the layer of Malpighi and the stratum corneum are the two layers of epidermis, (3) must be wrong. Since it is known that nerve endings and sweat glands are in the skin, they could not be contained in the muscle tissue, or (5). Therefore, (4) must be the correct answer.

45. **(5)** Answer choice (5), "While growing the bacteria, the test tube was inoculated with poison," is the correct answer since the graph indicates that the bacteria increase their population and then as the poison was assimilated the population decreased, and then all of the bacteria died. "The number of bacteria being produced by mitosis is equal to the number of bacteria dying" (1) cannot be the correct answer since this answer is best represented by graph (c). "Nothing was done to the culture of bacteria at first, but after a while some of the waste products were removed" (2) cannot be the correct answer since this answer is best represented by graph (e). "Bacteria 'love' this growth curve because it represents ideal conditions" (3) cannot be the correct answer since this statement is best represented by graph (d). "The growth of

the bacteria is represented by a normal growth curve" (4) cannot be the correct answer since this statement is best represented by graph (a).

46. **(4)** Answer choice (4), "The growth of the bacteria is represented by a normal growth curve," is the correct answer since the graph indicates that the bacteria increase their population and then the population decreases when waste products accumulate or the population becomes too dense. "The number of bacteria being produced by mitosis is equal to the number of bacteria dying" (1) cannot be the correct answer since this statement is best represented by graph (c). "Nothing was done to the culture of bacteria at first, but after a while some of the waste products were removed" (2) cannot be the correct answer since this statement is best represented by graph (e). "Bacteria 'love' this growth curve because it represents ideal conditions" (3) cannot be the correct answer since this statement is best represented by graph (d). "While growing the bacteria, the test tube was inoculated with poison" (5) cannot be the correct answer since this answer is best represented by graph (b).

47. **(1)** Answer choice (1), "The number of bacteria being produced by mitosis is equal to the number of bacteria dying," is the correct answer since the population line is horizontal. "Nothing was done to the culture of bacteria at first, but after a while some of the waste products were removed" (2) cannot be the correct answer since this answer is best represented by graph (e). "Bacteria 'love' this growth curve because it represents ideal conditions" (3) cannot be the correct answer since this answer is best represented by graph (d). "The growth of the bacteria is represented by a normal growth curve" (4) cannot be the correct answer since this statement is best represented by graph (a). "While growing the bacteria, the test tube was inoculated with poison" (5) cannot be the correct answer since this answer is best represented by graph (b).

48. **(3)** Answer choice (3), "Bacteria 'love' this growth curve because it represents ideal conditions," is the correct answer since there is nothing preventing the growth of the bacteria. "The number of bacteria being produced by mitosis is equal to the number of bacteria dying" (1) cannot be the correct answer since this answer is best represented by graph (c). "Nothing was done to the culture of bacteria at first, but after a while some of the waste products were removed" (2) cannot be the correct answer since this statement is best represented by graph (e). "The growth of the bacteria is represented by a normal growth curve" (4) cannot be the correct answer since this answer is best represented by graph (a). "While growing the bacteria, the test tube was inoculated with poison" (5) cannot be the correct answer since this answer is best represented by graph (b).

49. **(5)** Choice (1) is unacceptable because in each area of use, the U.S. household utilizes far more than twice the electrical energy of the Brazilian household. Choice (2) is incorrect because the percent used in air-conditioning is greater in the U.S. than in Brazil. Choice (3) is invalid since the greatest

use in both countries is for refrigeration. Choice (4) is incorrect since in Brazil more electrical energy is used for water heating than for lighting. By the process of elimination, choice (5) is left and supported by the observations that both countries use the least for cooking and the most for refrigeration.

50. **(3)** Both columns of electrical energy in KWH must be totaled. The U.S. household consumes 7,345 KWH while the Brazilian household consumes 1,460 KWH per year. This is a ratio of 5 to 1.

TEST 4: LANGUAGE ARTS: READING

1. **(1)** It is evident that this friendship is deeply rooted since each man threatens to leave the other but will not. Neither one cares (2) is incorrect since George shows his remorse with, "I been mean, ain't I?" in line 14. Lennie intends to leave (4) and George intends to abandon him (5) are not good choices since Lennie "senses his advantage" in line 23 and George says he is "jus' foolin" in line 18. (3) is a poor choice since George is no longer angry at the end of his speech.

2. **(2)** The author states clearly in line 23 that Lennie, despite his limited intellect, has learned to manipulate George: "Lennie avoided the bait. He had sensed his advantage." These lines make (3), George has the "upper hand" at all times, a poor choice. (1) is incorrect since George demonstrates compassion in lines 27–29 by asking Lennie to stay with him. This paragraph also makes (4), "Lennie intends to hurt George," and (5), "Lennie is a survivor," incorrect.

3. **(2)** Because of Lennie's dependence on George and his childlike nature, father and son is the best choice. It is not a reciprocal relationship as in most cases with best friends, so (1) is incorrect. Their bonding is too apparent throughout their dialogue to consider them (3) casual acquaintances, (4) feuding neighbors, or (5) complete strangers.

4. **(1)** First, George entertains himself with thoughts of "the swell time" he could have without Lennie, but lines 18 to 21, however, reverse this idea and reveal his inner conflict. There is no intellect demonstrated by George (2); neither is impatience (5) apparent. This dialogue does not reveal devotion (4), but rather appeasement when George offers Lennie a pup.

5. **(3)** It is evident that the childlike Lennie is totally unaware of his brute strength when George offers him a pup so he can "pet it harder." When he threatens to leave George, Lennie says, "An' if I foun' a mouse, I could keep it. Nobody'd take it away from me." This fondness suggests Lennie is neither careless (1) nor cruel (2). Neither (4) kindness nor (5) stubbornness have anything to do with the reason Lennie kills mice.

6. **(1)** George's ambivalence, his inner conflict, has to do with his relationship with Lennie. The dialogue introducing conflict begins with his expressed desire to leave Lennie; a few paragraphs on, he daydreams of the farm they will buy, living "off the fatta the lan'!"

7. **(2)** George's story about buying a farm and prospering have been memorized word for word by Lennie. Lennie is not intelligent enough to create it (1), and he appears to be too childlike to fabricate it (3). Since it is the story which seems to delight both men, it apparently is not cause for concern (4) or nothing in particular (5).

8. **(2)** George's voice deepens and his words are repeated rhythmically. Lennie "is delighted" with the story of their hope and future. Although it does give them something to talk about (1), it is more than casual conversation (5); it's a dream, not cause for concern (4). (3) is incorrect, since they must earn their money in this town.

9. **(3)** Biff is home because (3), he isn't getting anywhere in life. He tells his brother that "whenever spring comes to where I am, I suddenly get the feeling, my God, I'm not gettin' anywhere!…That's when I come running home." He also says that "every time I come back here I know that all I've done is to waste my life."

10. **(1)** Biff thinks Happy is content because Happy has a successful job. Biff doesn't understand how Happy could not be content, since Happy is "making money."

11. **(2)** Happy can best be described by sentence (2), "Money can't buy you happiness." Even though Happy has money, he tells Biff that he is not happy (see explanation for question 12, above).

12. **(5)** The merchandise manager isn't happy because (5), "the more he has, the more he wants." Happy tells us that the manager "just built a terrific estate on Long Island" but that he only lived there for two months because "He can't enjoy it once it's finished." He wants something more, so "he's building another one." We know that the manager has money, so (1) isn't the answer, and there is no indication in the passage that the merchandise manager knows that (2), "Happy is after his job."

13. **(3)** We can conclude from this passage that Happy's name is (3), "ironic." Happy, the passage reveals, is not happy, so his name is the opposite of its reality. This is irony.

14. **(2)** The only accurate conclusion is that there is a deep bond between the two. (1) is a poor choice because Santiago says in line 23, "If you were my boy." The boy himself wants to be of service to the old man in every possible way, even if his fishing is "unlucky." This rules out (3) casual acquaintances, (4) little care for one another, or (5) just met as correct answers.

15. **(2)** Santiago remembers the incident when the fish was "too green" and the boy, five years old, was "nearly killed," obviously from the thrashings of the still strong fish. There is no suggestion of the fish being (1) spoiled or

of (4) the boy being careless. Neither is there mention of the incident being a "chance" happening (5). Santiago admits he brought it in too green, too soon.

16. **(4)** The old fisherman's gentleness, wisdom, and endurance are evident throughout the selection; therefore character is the focus. Mystery and intrigue (1) as well as humor (3) are never evident. Even though the sea is important to the plot, there is no preoccupation by the author with geography (2).

17. **(1)** Determination and endurance is the correct answer since, despite the pain, his injured hand, and his weakened condition, the old man struggles on, determined. There is no hint of wit and humor (2) or of blind hatred (5)— Santiago feels sorry for the fish. Although the old man demonstrates intelligence in philosophic musing (3), there is no hint of formal schooling, except that Santiago apparently reads baseball scores. (4) is incorrect since Santiago is stubborn, but quite rational in his thought process.

18. **(2)** Santiago reveals that he must kill him, but he is glad that he does not have to "kill the stars." This statement negates (1), no remorse, as well as (3) let the fish go, and (4) soon give up.

19. **(1)** Santiago declares that the fish "is my friend, too." He then goes on to say that he is glad that he does not have to try and kill the stars, then, the sun, the moon, thus displaying appreciation and compassion for all of mankind. Never once, through this dialogue, has Santiago demonstrated (2) self-centered interest in achieving his goal, or (3) pride in fishing, or (4) hatred. Although Santiago demonstrates bravery, there is no disregard of danger (5).

20. **(1)** A more universal idea is honor and dignity, earned, should not be carelessly cast away. Santiago is explicit, "There is no one worthy of eating him from the manner of his behaviour and his great dignity."

21. **(2)** Figuratively is correct since "true brothers" is used out of literal (1) or ordinary use. Paradoxically (3) is incorrect since the passage does not involve two opposite statements. It is evident that humor (4) is missing from Santiago's statement, as well as satire (5), since there is no use of wit or ridicule.

22. **(1)** The correct answer is (1). The answer can be found in the first of the five summarized company policies.

23. **(2)** The answer is (2). The answer is located in the third paragraph of the document.

24. **(2)**   The correct answer is choice (2). While all of the five policies are clearly important, only (2) involves an outside audit, which is a serious business procedure.

25. **(4)**   The policy specifies that any employee who wishes to take more than three days off must inform his or her manager of this request in writing at least two weeks in advance.

26. **(3)**   No electricity, no bathroom, no running water and "night soil men," in addition to "tropical poverty," suggest that island (3) is the best answer. A small town (1), a large city (2), and apartment complex (4) are all incorrect since they would provide the subject with necessary utilities and facilities. A houseboat (5) might be a possible answer were it not for the "outhouse" mentioned.

27. **(3)**   Since the author is explicit that her mother's focus on the new baby came at a period of adolescent "storm" when she needed her the most, (3) is correct. She suggests that family poverty (1) was always there, and more children compounded the problem. There was no mention of (2) bad luck, nor was there mention of (4) catastrophic events. Although schooling was not a pleasant experience, there is no basis for concluding that her education was a poor one (5).

28. **(1)**   The article reveals that it is in early adolescence that the gifted intellect of the writer interviewed began expanding. (2) is incorrect since there is no hint of overt demands, just intellectual queries, which also makes answer (3) a very poor choice. Unhappy (4) is a possible answer although it does not specify that she was a happy child up until her turbulent adolescent days. If even in a basic sense, the reader is led to infer that she was educated; therefore (5) is incorrect.

29. **(2)**   Contextual clues within the sentence leads the reader to choose "accompanying" as the best synonym for "attendant." None of the others are as suitable in context.

30. **(3)**   Quite candidly the gifted author admits in lines 18–22 that she stole books because the intellectual demands of her gifted mind were not met. Bored (1) might have been a good choice if lines 18–22 were not as explicit, since boredom can be a natural consequence of not fulfilling intellectual demands. Never is there a hint of the subject being revengeful (2), even though she does confess to giving teachers "back chat." (4) is a poor choice for an answer, since in these selected excerpts friends are not mentioned.

31. **(3)**   Lines 28–33 strongly suggest that, all in all, her strongest memories of her childhood are of being "misunderstood." Neither (1) happy nor (2) unexamined fit appropriately since she admits, "Had I just sunk in the cracks, it would not have been noticed," and that her facility with words was interpreted as "a sharp tongue." For those reasons, we should not assume

that her adolescence was neither (4) normal nor (5) abnormal, however misunderstood it might have been.

32. **(1)** The first three lines lead us to infer that the narrator is in his study since he "pondered" over quaint and curious volumes; he also tells us that he was "nearly napping." There is no mention of a diary (2). Daydreaming (3) might have been a viable alternative, except that it would exclude the presence of books. Since he is apparently at leisure, we cannot presume that he is (4) working or (5) ill.

33. **(3)** The narrator explains that he seeks "surcease of sorrow," of the lost Lenore, named by angels—now nameless. (4) is not correct; although the mourner is musing over memories of Lenore, we must not assume that they are ghostly, or that he is in this stanza preoccupied with (5) the supernatural world. Weather (1) and business (2) are too mundane to select and make no appearance in stanza two.

34. **(4)** The provocative imagery of an ebony bird in lines 19 and 20 suggests the ebony of the raven upon alabaster marble.

35. **(5)** The narrator addresses the raven as if it were nonhuman in line 25: "'Prophet!' said I, 'thing of evil.'" Essentially the question is, "Is there a maiden by the name of Lenore in paradise (Aidenne)?"

36. **(3)** Bereft, lamenting the death of the beautiful lost maiden, the poet/lover bares his soul in every stanza although stanza one finds him trying to forget his lost Lenore by occupying himself with volumes (1). Reporter (2) is an inappropriate answer since there is no suggestion that the speaker is one; nor is businessman (4) a substantiated answer. If the poet happens to be a student (5), there is no hint of this, although through his allusions to Greek mythology we can infer he is a scholar.

37. **(2)** The raven's appearance with royal "mien" tells us that he is of stately and regal birth; it further suggests that he might be a harbinger of some distant shore, or world beyond. Haughty or superior (4) might seem to be a viable alternative, but the term "mien" presents an image of demeanor and suggests stateliness.

38. **(5)** Images of the poet, alone, pondering, mourning and lamenting his lost love, abound throughout the poem; therefore, morose or sullen is the best choice. Happy (1) and optimistic (2) are completely inappropriate answers, while indecisive (3) and angry (4) are also weak choices since there is little, if anything, to substantiate them.

39. **(2)** The poet is emphatic in his declaration, "And my soul from out that shadow… shall be lifted—nevermore!" We can infer with finality that there is no hope; therefore, (3) another life and (4) Lenore will return are clearly poor

choices. Since his statement transcends the mortal presence of a bird, (1) and (5), both of which have to do with the raven, are not correct.

40. **(1)** The poem leaves us with a hopeless, morose message in which the poet reiterates the finality of death. Therefore (3) and (5), which speak of hope and replacement, are poor choices. Love is fleeting (2) might be a choice to consider, but it really is too weak when one investigates the poem's bleak imagery.

TEST 5: MATHEMATICS

PART 1

1.   **(2)**   This is another estimation problem. $9.89 is about $10.00, and 75% of $10.00 is $7.50. Answer (1) has a misplaced decimal point.

2.   **(1)**   The volume of any solid is the area of the base multiplied by the height. The base of a cylinder is a circle. The formula for the area of a circle is $A = \pi r^2$. The diameter is marked 20 cm on the figure, so the radius is 10 cm. $10 \times 10 = 100$ and $100 \times 3.14 = 314$. This is the area of the base. Now multiply by the height, 20, and the answer is 6,280 cubic cm.

3.   **(4)**   First convert all measurements to **feet**, since the answers are in feet. One mile is 5,280 ft. and 720 yds. is 2,160 ft. The sum is 10,940 ft. Answer (1) is obtained by adding all numbers without converting them to the same measure. Answer (2) is obtained by converting 1 mile to 5,280 ft. and then adding 720 and 3,500. Answer (5) mistakenly converts 1 mile to 5,000 ft.

4.   **(4)**   Substitute the values given into the formula: $s = (68 \times 1.6) + 4$, then $108.8 + 4 = \$112.80$.

5.   **(2)** $48x + 960 = 12,000$. Kelly's 48 monthly payments result in $48x$. Since she already made a down payment of $3,000, her remaining obligation is $12,000. Her account still showed $960 after all 48 payments, which means $12,000 - 48x = 960$.

6.   **(5)**   The ratio $1,120/x$ represents each student's cost for the van. When 8 students can't go on the trip, each student's cost increases to $1,120/(x-8)$ and this amount is $16 more than the initial cost of $1,120/x$.

7.   **(4)**   Arc QS = (2)(R) = 40°. Arc RTS must be 180° − 40° = 140° (because arc RTSQ = 180°). Finally, $\overset{\frown}{RT} = \overset{\frown}{TS} = (1/2)(140°) = 70°$.

8.   **(3)**   The lateral surface area $= 2\pi Rh = 251.2$. Using $\pi = 3.14$ and given $h = 16$, we can solve for $R = 2.5$. The diameter is twice the radius = 5.

9.   **(3)**   The problem is really to find the surface area of the rectangular solid. This is done by finding the sum of the areas of every side, including the top and bottom. This problem is complicated by the fact that the measurements in the problem are given in inches, and the answers are given in square feet. We must convert to the same unit of measure. If we convert the inches to feet, the dimensions of the chest are 1' × 2' × 5/6'. A formula to find the lateral area (area of all the sides, but not the top and bottom) is $L = ph$, where

p = perimeter of the base and h = the height. The perimeter of the base is 1 + 2 + 1 + 2 or 6. Then $6 \times 5/6 = 5$ sq. ft. for the sides. Now find the area of the top and bottom and add it to the sides. The bottom is a rectangle and the area = lw, where l = length and w = width. So the area is 2×1 or 2 sq. ft. This is the bottom, but the top is the same. Finally add the area of the sides and the top and the bottom: $5 + 2 + 2 = 9$ sq. ft.

10. **(5)** $4x + x + x + 10 = 180$. Since $\angle B = x$, $\angle A = 4x$. Now $\angle C$ is 10° less than $\angle B$, which is $x - 10°$. The sum of all three angles is 180°.

11. **(2)** $(BC)(2) + (BD)(2) = 22$. Solving with $\overline{BD} = 5$, yields $\overline{BC} = 6$. Draw a perpendicular from A to $\overline{BC}$. Using the Pythagorean Theorem on either of the resulting right triangles, $3^2 + x^2 = 5^2$. where x is the height in triangle ABC.

Solving, $x = \sqrt{7}$. Finally, the area of triangle ABC = $\dfrac{1}{2} \times 6 \times \sqrt{7} = 3\sqrt{7}$

12. **(5)** $995 + 149 = 1{,}144$ and $1{,}144 \times .08 = \$91.52$ tax. $\$1{,}144 + \$91.52 = \$1{,}235.52$. Answer (1) is the cost of the sofa and chair without tax. Answer (2) is the tax. Answer (3) results from an addition error, and answer (4) results from adding tax to the incorrect answer (3).

13. **(5)** The new list is 3, 4, 7, 8, 12, 14, 18, 25 and the median is the average of 8 and 12, which is 10.

14. **(5)** Vertical angles are formed when two lines intersect. These angles are equal. Therefore, angle X is 133°.

15. **(1)** $133\dfrac{1}{3}$. Let x = stopping distance. Then we get the proportion

$\dfrac{75}{x} = \dfrac{30^2}{40^2}$. This simplifies to $\dfrac{75}{x} = \dfrac{900}{1{,}600}$. Solving $x = 133\dfrac{1}{3}$.

16. **(2)** The Pacific is 46% of the 140 million square miles, or $0.46 \times 140{,}000{,}000$. Answer (5) has a misplaced decimal point, answer (2) is the 46 written as 46 million, and answer (3) subtracts 46 million from 140 million.

17. **(2)** In problem 16 you were told that about 140 million square miles of our Earth's surface are covered with oceans. This problem adds the information that the total surface of our Earth is about 200 million square miles. The percentage is 140 divided by 200, or about 70%. Answer (1) has a misplaced decimal point, and answer (5) is $200 - 140$.

18. **(5)** There is not enough information given to find the cost in the next state. The tax rate in that state is needed. Answer (1) is the cost in his state, and the other answers are costs with tax rates of 6%, 5%, and 4% respectively.

19. **12**   Let x = speed of the boat in still water and let y = speed of the current. Then we have $(4)(x+y) = 60$ and $5(x-y) = 45$, since $x + y$ = speed of the boat with the current and $x - y$ = speed of the boat against the current. These equations simplify to $x + y = 15$ and $x - y = 9$. Solving, $x = 12$. (The current = 3.)

20. **3/7**   The slope of $7x + 3y = 10$ would be $-\dfrac{7}{3}$, which can be determined by rewriting as $y = -\dfrac{7}{3}x + \dfrac{10}{3}$. Any line which is perpendicular would have a slope equal to the negative reciprocal of $-\dfrac{7}{3}$, which is $\dfrac{3}{7}$.

21. **1/5**   The number of combinations of two white balls is $_3C_2 = 3$. The total number of combinations for any two balls is $_6C_2 = 15$. The probability required is $\dfrac{3}{15} = \dfrac{1}{5}$.

22. **54**   You may either combine each two terms as you get to them, $38 - 17 = 21$ and $21 + 91 = 112$ and $112 - 58 = 54$, or you may combine all of the positive numbers and then combine all of the negative numbers and then combine the two answers. This gives $38 + 91 = 129$ and $-17 + -58 = -75$, which gives you the equation $129 - 75 = 54$.

23. **37.3** To find the average, add the five figures and divide by 5. $186.5 \div 5 = 37.3$.

24. **90**   All of his grades added together and divided by 5 must equal 95. Multiply both sides of that equation by 5 and $93 + 100 + 92 + 100 + x = 475$. Then $385 + x = 475$ and $x = 90$.

25. **(–5, –1)** Multiply the first equation by 4 and the second equation by –3. This yields $8x - 12y = -28$ and $15x + 12y = -87$. Adding these equations, $23x = -115$, so $x = -5$. Substitute this value into the original first equation: $(2)(-5) - 3y = -7$, so $y = -1$.

PART 2

26. **(1)** An easy way to work this is to think that if the TV set is 30% OFF, then it is 70% ON, and 70% of $225 is $157.50. The traditional way to work this is to take 30% of $225, which is $67.50, and subtract this from $225, giving $157.50. Answer (2) is the 30% discount. Answer (4) is obtained by simply subtracting $30.00 from $225.

27. **(2)** 4 divided by 6 is 4/6 and reduces to 2/3, or use long division to divide 6 into 4. Either way, this is 66-2/3%. Answer (1) is the percent she **lost**.

28. **(2)** Answers (3), (4), and (5) are each more than 1/2. Answer (1) is 1/2. Only answer (2) is less than 1/2.

29. **(1)** Scientific notation writes numbers as a product of numbers from 1 to 10 and a power of 10. Only two answers have numbers less than 10, they are answers (1) and (3). 480 million is 480,000,000, that is 4.8×10^8, moving the decimal point eight places.

30. **(3)** To change 36.59% to a decimal, divide by 100, or move the decimal point two places to the left.

31. **(5)** First subtract 3 from both sides of the equation, then multiply both sides by 4. This gives $x = 48$. Answer (3) is the result if 12 is mistakenly multiplied by 1/4 rather than by 4.

32. **(1)** The mean is the average obtained by adding each day's miles and dividing by the number of days. For the week, she ran a total of 35 miles. Divide this by 5 days, and the mean is 7 miles. Answer (2) is the total miles she ran. Answer (3) is the median.

33. **(3)** The two angles pictured form a linear pair, and together they form a straight angle. The sum of the measures of angle Q and 58 is 180°, the number of degrees in a straight angle. To obtain the correct answer, subtract 58 from 180.

34. **(3)** To evaluate an expression, simply replace the **x** or **y** with the equivalent number, $(-2)^2 + 2(-2) - 3 + 3 = 4 - 4 - 3 + 3 = 0$.

35. **(5)** To find the probability, make a fraction with the total number of possibilities on the bottom (as the denominator) and the number of ways to fulfill the given condition on top (as the numerator). There are seven marbles, so 7 is the denominator. Joey will be successful and will not pull out a red one if he pulls out any of the 5 that are not red. So 5/7 is the correct answer.

36. **(2)** The sum of the measures of the angles of a triangle is 180 degrees. Angle D is marked as a right angle, which is 90 degrees. This leaves the other two angles to make up the other 90 degrees. So the correct answer is obtained by subtracting 43 from 90. Also you could add 90 and 43 to get 133 and subtract 133 from 180. The answer is the same.

37. **(2)** To simplify, remove parentheses and collect like terms. $15 - 4x - 8 + 6x + 2 = 2x + 9$. The most common error is failure to distribute the minus sign with the 4.

38. **(4)** The formula $D = rt$ is the one to use for this problem. $21 = r \times 2\text{-}1/3$ and $r = 9$ knots. Answer (2) is the time, answer (3) is the distance, and answer (5) is obtained by multiplying 21 by 2 rather than by dividing.

39. **(3)** This expression is of the form $A^2 - 2AB + B^2$, which is the square of a binomial $(A - B)^2$. So the answer is $(x - 3)^2$. Answer (1) ignores the third term. When answer (4) is squared, the middle term is positive. Answer (2) is the same as answer (4) only in a different form. When the factors of answer (5) are multiplied together, the last term of the trinomial formed is negative.

40. **(1)** $\angle$BFG and $\angle$CGF are alternate interior angles and are therefore congruent, or equal in measure. If we can find the measure of either one, we will know the measure of $\angle$CGF. We know that $\angle$BFG and $\angle$BFE form a linear pair, and are supplementary, and we know $\angle$BFE measures 80 degrees. Subtracting 80 from 180 we find that $\angle$BFG is 100 degrees. Since $\angle$CGF is an alternate interior angle and congruent to $\angle$BFG, the measure of $\angle$CGF is 100 degrees.

41. **(4)** There is the same chance or probability that the spinner will stop on any one of the numbers. This is 1 out of 6 or 1/6.

42. **(1)** The sum of the measures of the angles of a triangle equals 180°. $25 + 15 = 40$ and $180 - 40 = 140$.

43. **(4)** Multiplying x and $4x$ gives $4x^2$. Multiplying x and 3 gives $3x$. Multiplying 1 and $4x$ gives $4x$. Multiplying 1 and 3 gives 3, collecting like terms gives $4x^2 + 7x + 3$. Answer (1) is incorrect because 1 and 3 were added, and the middle term is missing. Answer (2) is incorrect because the middle term is missing. Answer (3) is incorrect because the middle term is incorrect. Answer (5) is incorrect because the sign of the middle term is incorrect and the last term is incorrect.

44. **(5)** If one integer is represented by x, then the next consecutive **even** integer is $(x + 2)$. The product of one even integer and twice the next even integer is represented by $x + 2(x + 2)$. This is set equal to 40 to form the equation. Answer (1) is simply an integer times itself. Answer (2) represents the product of any two consecutive integers. Answer (3) represents the sum

of one integer and twice the next consecutive integer. Finally answer (4) represents the product of two even or odd integers.

45. **(5)** There are 4 kings in the 52 card deck, so the probability is 4/52, this fraction reduces to 1/13. Answer (4) uses the two numbers in a fraction but in the wrong positions.

46. **(5)** Distribute the 10 to both terms inside the parenthesis. Answer (5) is correct because 10 times (−3*w*) is (−30*w*) and 10 times 2 is 20. Answer (1) is incorrect because the negative sign was omitted from the first term, and the second term was not multiplied by 10. Answer (2) is incorrect because the second term was not multiplied by 10. In answer (3), the second term was not multiplied by 10, but the sign was changed. Answer (4) is incorrect because the sign of the second term was erroneously changed.

47. **(3)** Draw two right triangles, a small one to represent Johnny and his shadow and a larger one to represent the tree and its shadow. These triangles are similar. A proportion can be set up between Johnny's height and the length of his shadow and the tree's height and the length of its shadow.

$$\frac{6}{3} = \frac{x}{35} \qquad 3x = 210 \text{ and } x = 70.$$

You may have noticed that Johnny is twice as tall as his shadow and realized that the tree is twice as tall as its shadow.

48. **46** You may either find the percent of boys (351 divided by 650) and then subtract from 100% to find the percent of girls, or you may subtract 351 from 650 and find that there are 299 girls and divide this by 650 to get 46% girls.

49. **1,620** The number of ways to select the two vowels is (5)(4) = 20, since there is no repetition. The two digits may be selected in (9)(9) = 81 ways, since only zero is excluded and repetition is allowed. Finally, the number of different badges is (20)(81) = 1,620.

50. **(2, −1)** The midpoint is $\left(\dfrac{2+6}{2}, \dfrac{-9+1}{2}\right) = (2, -4)$. Three units above (2, −4) is (2, −1).

PRACTICE EXAM III

EXAM III

TEST 1: LANGUAGE ARTS: WRITING, PART I

Tests of General Educational Development

Directions

The Language Arts: Writing Test is intended to measure your ability to use clear and effective English. It is a test of English as it should be written, not as it might be spoken. This test includes both multiple-choice questions and an essay. These directions apply only to the multiple-choice section; a separate set of directions is given for the essay.

The multiple-choice section consists of paragraphs with numbered sentences. Some of the sentences contain errors in sentence structure, usage, or mechanics (spelling, punctuation, and capitalization). After reading the numbered sentences, answer the multiple-choice questions that follow. Some questions refer to sentences that are correct as written. The best answer for these questions is the one that leaves the sentence as originally written. The best answer for some questions is the one that produces a sentence that is consistent with the verb tense and point of view used throughout the paragraph. You should spend no more than 75 minutes on the multiple-choice questions and 45 minutes on your essay. Work carefully, but do not spend too much time on any one question. You may begin working on the essay part of this test as soon as you complete the multiple-choice section.

Do not mark in this test booklet. Record your answers on the separate answer sheet provided. Be sure that all requested information is properly recorded on the answer sheet.

To record your answers, mark one numbered space on the answer sheet beside the number that corresponds to the question in the test booklet.

FOR EXAMPLE:

Sentence 1: **We were all honored to meet governor Phillips.**

What correction should be made to this sentence?

   (1)   insert a comma after <u>honored</u>

   (2)   change the spelling of <u>honored</u> to <u>honered</u>

   (3)   change <u>governor</u> to <u>Governor</u>

   (4)   replace <u>were</u> with <u>was</u>

   (5)   no correction is necessary

In this example, the word "governor" should be capitalized; therefore, answer space 3 would be marked on the answer sheet.

Do not rest the point of your pencil on the answer sheet while you are considering your answer. Make no stray or unnecessary marks. If you change an answer, erase your first mark completely. Mark only one answer space for each question; multiple answers will be scored as incorrect. Do not fold or crease your answer sheet. All test materials must be returned to the test administrator.

Reprinted with permission of the General Educational Development Testing Service of the American Council on Education.

Directions: Choose the <u>one best answer</u> to each item.

<u>Items 1 to 5</u> refer to the following paragraphs.

(A)

(1) Our company has been seeking to expand to offer more services. (2) In this proposal, I will outline some of the ways we might accomplish this. (3) First, we need to decide exactly which services we can expect to profitably add to our current offerings. (4) This is very important. (5) Because if we add several new services without first deciding which is most likely to succeed, the whole enterprise could fail.

(B)

(6) Currently, we offer two key services pet grooming and flea baths for cats and dogs. (7) Possible additional services that would be in line with what we do include: providing kenneling for dogs and cats; providing dog walking services for people who work during the day and cannot let their dogs out; providing a full line of pet food products; and a full line of pet toy products.

(C)

(8) After careful investigation, I have concluded that while all of these services could be very profitable for us, only the first two are feasible. (9) As is clear, then, we can expand our company, but not as ambitiously as some of us have hoped.

(D)

(10) By the way, I have also found out that the soda machine we wanted to install in front of the store is not available in this area. (11) We need to start developing a plan for finding a more appropriate vending machine option.

(E)

(12) This report is only preliminary. (13) I welcome any suggestions or feedback. (14) I will be away from the office for the next two weeks on another company research project you must contact me before Friday if you wish to comment on this report.

1.   There is a sentence fragment in paragraph A. It can be fixed by

    (1)   combining sentences 1 and 2.
    (2)   combining sentences 2 and 3.
    (3)   combining sentences 3 and 4.
    (4)   combining sentences 4 and 5.
    (5)   eliminating sentence 3.

2. Sentence 6: **Currently, we offer two key services pet grooming and flea baths for cats and dogs.**

   What correction is necessary?

   (1)   add a comma after <u>services</u>

   (2)   replace <u>flea</u> with <u>flee</u>

   (3)   replace <u>two</u> with <u>too</u>

   (4)   add a colon after <u>services</u>

   (5)   no correction is necessary

3. Paragraph C would be more effective if which sentence or sentences from the choices were inserted between sentences 8 and 9?

   (1)   Although we do not have enough space to stock our store with supplies or toys, we do have enough space in the back of the store to kennel pets. We also have enough employees with their own cars who we can send out to walk dogs.

   (2)   There is no substitute for excellence.

   (3)   We must all strive to work smarter, not harder.

   (4)   The kennels will be a lot of work.

   (5)   No one here knows how to perform animal surgery.

4. Sentence 14: **I will be away from the office for the next two weeks on another company research project you must contact me before Friday if you wish to comment on this report.**

   What correction is necessary?

   (1)   begin a new sentence after the word <u>weeks</u>

   (2)   capitalize <u>company</u>

   (3)   place a comma after <u>office</u>

   (4)   begin a new sentence after the word <u>project</u>

   (5)   no correction is necessary

5. Which paragraph would you eliminate to make this report more direct, focused, and effective?

   (1)   paragraph (A)

   (2)   paragraph (B)

   (3)   paragraph (C)

   (4)   paragraph (D)

   (5)   paragraph (E)

Items 6 to 9 refer to the following paragraphs.

(A)

(1) First, be sure you understand leasing. (2) If you lease, you have no obligation to keep the car after the end of the lease term (on a closed lease), as long as you have observed the mileage and wear-and-tear stipulations. (3) But when the lease expires, you'll have to find another car and basically, a lease is a long-term rental agreement.

(B)

(4) As with any contract, read the small print. (5) Make sure you look for the car that is right for you. (6) Don't settle for a good deal on something you don't want. (7) An incredibly low monthly payment should send up warning signs: there may be hidden charges.

(C)

(8) Go into the showroom pretending to buy, and negotiate the purchase price first. (9) This way you'll have a firm assessment of the car's value from the start. (10) At this point, you can ask about leasing. (11) Once you've know the car's selling price, get the residual value of the car after the lease expires. (12) Ask for a residual value estimate in dollars, not at "market price." (13) That will protect you if the car's value is lower than expected at the end of the lease.

(D)

(14) Having a car is essential to living in the world today. (15) The advantages of leasing soon fade if you have to pay an early termination fee if your car is stolen, or if you just change your mind about the car. (16) Sometimes these fees can be equal to the total of your remaining monthly payments.

(E)

(17) A closed-end lease is desirable. (18) That means your residual value is set, and not dependent on the market when you return the car.

6. Sentence 3: **But when the lease expires, you'll have to find another car and basically, a lease is a long-term rental agreement.**

What correction is necessary?

(1) delete <u>and</u>

(2) put a period after <u>expires</u>

(3) delete <u>and</u>, and start a new sentence after <u>car</u>

(4) delete the comma after <u>expires</u>

(5) no correction is necessary

7. To improve the organization of paragraph B you should

   (1) delete the first sentence.
   (2) move the first sentence so that it immediately precedes the last sentence.
   (3) delete the last sentence.
   (4) combine it with paragraph E.
   (5) Make the paragraph one long sentence.

8. There is an error in paragraph C. How can you fix it?

   (1) change you'll in sentence 9 to they'll
   (2) change you in sentence 13 to us
   (3) change you in sentence 10 to I
   (4) change you've in sentence 11 to you
   (5) none of the above.

9. How could you improve the clarity of paragraph D?

   (1) combine it with paragraph A
   (2) delete sentence 16
   (3) insert sentence 1 at the end of paragraph D
   (4) combine sentences 15 and 16
   (5) delete sentence 14

Items 10 to 16 refer to the following two paragraphs.

(1) In most organizations, the employees can be divided into two groups, one of which is the doers. (2) Often the doers, an integral part of the organization, is industrious. (3) They take on any task; even if they have to learn the process after making some mistakes. (4) Because they are self-driving, they cannot be deterred by criticism or temporary failure.

(5) Their counterparts, the critics, are always ready to tell the doers how to perform, however, more of this group's advice is offered as the result of hindsight than of foresight. (6) Usually appearing disgruntled, the critics possess the answers to all questions, at least in their own opinions. (7) This group often rationalizes when an error is made; in addition, to claim credit, these people are quick when a job is done well. (8) Most organizations need less critics than doers because the doers perform most of the tasks.

10. Sentence 1: **In most organizations, the employees can be divided into two groups, one of which is the doers.**

    What correction should be made to this sentence?

    (1) change employees to employs
    (2) change two to too
    (3) change into to to
    (4) change is to are
    (5) no correction is necessary

11. Sentence 2: **Often the doers, an integral part of the organization, is industrious.**

    What correction should be made to this sentence?

    (1) place a comma after often
    (2) change integral to intregrated
    (3) change is to are
    (4) remove the commas
    (5) no correction is necessary

12. Sentence 3: **They take on any task; even if they have to learn the process after making some mistakes.**

    What correction should be made to this sentence?

    (1) change take to took
    (2) change the semicolon after task to a comma
    (3) change some to sum
    (4) place a comma after process
    (5) no correction is necessary

13. Sentence 5: **Their counterparts, the critics, are always ready to tell the doers how to perform, however, more of this group's advice is offered as a result of hindsight than of foresight.**

    What correction should be made to this sentence?

    (1) insert the word and after counterparts
    (2) change group's to groups
    (3) change the comma after perform to a semicolon

(4)   change <u>foresight</u> to <u>for sight</u>

(5)   no correction is necessary

14.   Sentence 6: **Usually appearing disgruntled, the critics possess the answers to all questions, at least in their own opinions.**

What correction should be made to this sentence?

(1)   place a period after <u>disgruntled</u>

(2)   change <u>disgruntled</u> to <u>disgruntle</u>

(3)   change <u>possess</u> to <u>poses</u>

(4)   move the comma after <u>questions</u> to after <u>at least</u>

(5)   no correction is necessary

15.   Sentence 7: **This group often rationalizes when an error is made; in addition, to claim credit, these people are quick when a job is done well.**

What correction should be made to this sentence?

(1)   move <u>often</u> from after <u>group</u> to after <u>rationalizes</u>

(2)   place a comma after <u>rationalizes</u>

(3)   change the semicolon after <u>made</u> to a comma

(4)   change <u>in addition, to claim credit, these people are quick when a job is done well.</u> to <u>in addition, these people are quick to claim credit when a job is done well.</u>

(5)   no correction is necessary

16.   Sentence 8: **Most organizations need less critics than doers because the doers perform most of the tasks.**

What correction should be made to this sentence?

(1)   change <u>less</u> to <u>fewer</u>

(2)   place a comma after <u>critics</u>

(3)   place a comma after <u>doers</u>

(4)   change <u>because the doers perform most of the tasks</u> to <u>because most of the tasks are performed by the doers</u>

(5)   no correction is necessary

Items 17 to 23 refer to the following paragraph.

(1) Sitting on the bank of the Mississippi River and watching the sun set is a breathe-taking experience for anyone. (2) The observer has a double treat, since he sees not only the beauty of the sky but the reflection also on the river. (3) No artist can realistically capture first the brilliance and then the softening hews against the gradually darkening blue canvas. (4) First, a giant ball spreads its fieriness in different directions. (5) Next, the striated pinks and purples that follow the oranges, reds, and yellows inspire a feeling of inner peace. (6) As these pastels finally were absorbed by the indigo, the onlooker alternately feels a calmness and disappoint-ment that the experience has ended so quickly. (7) He realizes, though, just how sensational watching the sun set is.

17. Sentence 1: **Sitting on the bank of the Mississippi River and watching the sun set is a breathe-taking experience for anyone.**

    What correction should be made to this sentence?

    (1) change Mississippi River to Missippi river
    (2) place a comma after River
    (3) change breathe-taking to breath-taking
    (4) change anyone to any one
    (5) no correction is necessary

18. Sentence 2: **The observer has a double treat, since he sees not only the beauty of the sky but the reflection also on the river.**

    What correction should be made to this sentence?

    (1) change double treat to doubletreat
    (2) remove the comma after treat
    (3) change he to they
    (4) change but the reflection also on the river to but also the reflection on the river
    (5) no change is necessary

19. Sentence 3: **No artist can realistically capture first the brilliance and then the softening hews against the gradually darkening blue canvas.**

    What correction should be made to this sentence?

    (1) change hews to hues
    (2) move first after the brilliance

(3) move gradually to after can

(4) change brilliance to brilliant

(5) no change is necessary

20. Sentence 4: **First, a giant ball spreads its fieriness in different directions.**

What correction should be made to this sentence?

(1) remove the comma after First

(2) change its to it's

(3) change its to it is

(4) change its to its'

(5) no correction is necessary

21. Sentence 5: **Next, the striated pinks and purples that follow the oranges, reds, and yellows inspire a feeling of inner peace.**

What correction should be made to this sentence?

(1) remove the comma after Next

(2) change striated to straight

(3) place a comma after purples

(4) place a comma after yellows

(5) no correction is necessary

22. Sentence 6: **As these pastels finally were absorbed by the indigo, the onlooker alternately feels a calmness and disappointment that the experience has ended so quickly.**

What correction should be made to this sentence?

(1) change were to are

(2) change were to was

(3) place a comma after calmness

(4) place a comma after disappointment

(5) no correction is necessary

23. Sentence 7: **He realizes, though, just how sensational watching the sun set is.**

    What correction should be made to this sentence?

    (1) change <u>though</u> to <u>through</u>
    (2) remove the commas after <u>realizes</u> and after <u>though</u>
    (3) change <u>just how sensational watching the sun set is</u> to <u>just how sensational is watching the sun set</u>
    (4) change <u>sun set</u> to <u>sunset</u>
    (5) no correction is necessary

<u>Items 24 to 28</u> refer to the following paragraphs.

(A)

(1) If you are purchasing a home, saving for your children's education, or funding your retirement, you need to develop a solid investment foundation, that is, an accumulation of funds. (2) A good investment strategy can help finance your needs—today and tomorrow. (3) Learning to invest can be a great help to people who want to have enough money for their priorities. (4) It is important that you assess your current financial picture before you invest. (5) Once you've measured your financial situation, you're ready to determine how much you can invest reasonably.

(B)

(6) The first step in evaluating your finances is figuring out your net worth. (7) To find your net worth, you need to assess what you have and what you owe. (8) Calculating the total amount of your assets and debts will enable you to determine how much you have to invest.

(C)

(9) Assets are your possessions, including money in bank accounts, stocks and bonds, or real estate. (10) The first step in finding your net worth is to determine the total amount of your assets. (11) Once you've calculated your assets, determine the total amount of your liabilities. (12) Liabilities are financial obligations, or debts. (13) Most people want to get rich quick. (14) These include credit card balances, personal or car and boat loans, mortgages, education loans, or outstanding lawsuits.

(D)

(15) Once you've figured out the amount of your assets and debts, subtract the total amount of liabilities from the total amount of assets. (16) There is a long tradition of investment in this country. (17) Obviously, you'll want to have more assets than debt. (18) If your assets are more than your liabilities, your net worth is "positive." (19) If your liabilities are greater than your assets, your net worth is "negative." (20) If you have a

negative net worth, it's a bad idea to think about investing for now. (21) You should re-evaluate your finances and determine how you can decrease debt, and then later you can start again to plan an investment strategy. (22) If you have a positive net worth and cash flow, you're probably ready to start an investment plan.

24. Which sentence in paragraph A should be the topic sentence?

    (1) sentence 1
    (2) sentence 2
    (3) sentence 3
    (4) sentence 4
    (5) sentence 5

25. Which sentence in paragraph C should be placed at the beginning of paragraph C?

    (1) sentence 9
    (2) sentence 10
    (3) sentence 11
    (4) sentence 12
    (5) sentence 13

26. Which sentence in paragraph C disrupts the unity and coherence of the passage?

    (1) sentence 9
    (2) sentence 10
    (3) sentence 11
    (4) sentence 12
    (5) sentence 13

27. Which sentence in paragraph D disrupts the unity and coherence of the passage?

    (1) sentence 15
    (2) sentence 16
    (3) sentence 17
    (4) sentence 18
    (5) sentence 19

28. Which paragraph is off topic and should be deleted?

    (1) paragraph A
    (2) paragraph B
    (3) paragraph C

    (4)   paragraph D

    (5)   none of the above

Items 29 to 34 refer to the following paragraph.

    (1) To enjoy many different activities in the summer, a person kneads to be knowledgeable and to exercise caution. (2) One danger that he may encounter, especially if he is outside for long periods of time, is heat stroke. (3) He certainly needs to avoid prolonged direct exposure to the sun. (4) Seeking shade when he has the opportunity. (5) Drinking water or some liquid can help him to retain necessary fluids. (6) At work or at play, a person needs to pace himself so he don't become too hot. (7) By being aware of potential problems and by dealing with them wisely, you can enjoy summer activities.

29.   Sentence 1: **To enjoy many different activities in the summer, a person kneads to be knowledgeable and to exercise caution.**

    What correction should be made to this sentence?

    (1)   place a comma after activities

    (2)   remove the comma after summer

    (3)   change kneads to needs

    (4)   place a comma after knowledgeable

    (5)   no correction is necessary

30.   Sentence 2: **One danger that he may encounter, especially if he is outside for long periods of time, is heat stroke.**

    What correction should be made to this sentence?

    (1)   place a comma after danger

    (2)   remove the comma after encounter

    (3)   change outside to out side

    (4)   change heat stroke to heatstroke

    (5)   no correction is necessary

31.   Sentences 3 and 4: **He certainly needs to avoid prolonged direct exposure to the sun. Seeking shade when he has the opportunity.**

    Which of the following is the best way to write the underlined portion of these sentences? If you think the original is the best way, choose option (1).

    (1)   sun. Seeking shade   (4)   sun—seeking shade

    (2)   sun. Seek shade   (5)   sun; seeking shade

    (3)   sun by seeking shade

32. Sentence 5: **Drinking water or some liquid can help him to retain necessary fluids.**

    What correction should be made to this sentence?

    (1)　place a comma after water
    (2)　change some liquid to some other liquid
    (3)　change him to you
    (4)　change necessary to neccessary
    (5)　no correction is necessary

33. Sentence 6: **At work or at play, a person needs to pace himself so that he don't become too hot.**

    What correction should be made to this sentence?

    (1)　remove the comma after play
    (2)　change himself to hisself
    (3)　change don't to does'nt
    (4)　change don't to does not
    (5)　no correction is necessary

34. Sentence 7: **By being aware of potential problems and by dealing with them wisely, you can enjoy summer activities.**

    What correction should be made to this sentence?

    (1)　change being aware to awareness
    (2)　place a comma after problems
    (3)　change them to it
    (4)　change you to a person
    (5)　no correction is necessary

Items 35 to 40 refer to the following paragraph.

(1) A person who likes to be outside during the winter may encounter problems resulting from exposure to the elements, frostbite and hypothermia, for example. (2) A person can become too cold without realizing their condition. (3) Because sometimes the cold numbs not only one's body but also his brain. (4) When one knows that he is going to be outside, he can take certain preventive measures: dressing warmly, avoid getting wet, and generally just use common sense. (5) If, for example, he feels that his extremities are becoming too cold, he can engage his arms and legs in vigorous exercise to stimulate circulation. (6) In addition, avoiding the intake of much alcohol which affects the circulation of the blood and gives

a person the feeling of being warmer than he is. (7) Simply by exercising good judgment, a person can enjoy winter activities safe.

35. Sentence 1: **A person who likes to be outside during the winter may encounter problems resulting from exposure to the elements, frostbite and hypothermia, for example.**

    What correction should be made to this sentence?

    (1) remove the comma after hypothermia

    (2) place a comma after winter

    (3) place a comma after person

    (4) change the comma after elements to a dash

    (5) no correction is necessary

36. Sentence 2: **A person can become too cold without realizing their condition.**

    What correction should be made to this sentence?

    (1) change can become to became

    (2) change too to to

    (3) place a comma after cold

    (4) change their to his

    (5) no correction is necessary

37. Sentences 2 and 3: **A person can become too cold without realizing their condition. Because sometimes the cold numbs not only one's body but also his brain.**

    Which of the following is the best way to write the underlined portion of these sentences? If you think that the original is the best way, choose option (1).

    (1) condition. Because sometimes

    (2) condition; because sometimes

    (3) condition: because sometimes

    (4) condition, because sometimes

    (5) condition—because sometimes

38. Sentence 4: **When one knows that he is going to be outside, he can take certain preventive measures: dressing warmly, avoid getting wet, and generally just use common sense.**

What correction should be made to this sentence?

(1) place a comma after knows

(2) change he to they

(3) change the colon after measures to a comma

(4) change dressing warmly, avoid getting wet, and generally just use common sense to dressing warmly, avoiding getting wet, and generally just using common sense

(5) no correction is necessary

39. Sentence 5: **If, for example, he feels that his extremities are becoming too cold, he can engage his arms and legs in vigorous exercise to stimulate circulation.**

What correction should be made to this sentence?

(1) remove the comma after If

(2) change extremities to extremity

(3) change engage to engaged

(4) change stimulate to simulate

(5) no correction is necessary

40. Sentences 5 and 6: **If, for example, he feels that his extremities are becoming too cold, he can engage his arms and legs in vigorous exercise to stimulate circulation. In addition, avoiding the intake of much alcohol which affects the circulation of the blood and gives a person the feeling of being warmer than he is.**

Which of the following is the best way to write the underlined portion of these sentences? If you think that the original is the best way, choose option (1).

(1) circulation. In addition, avoiding

(2) circulation; in addition, avoiding

(3) circulation; in addition, he can avoid

(4) circulation, in addition, avoiding

(5) circulation, in addition; avoiding

41. Sentence 7: **Simply by exercising good judgment, a person can enjoy winter activities safe.**

    What correction should be made to this sentence?

    (1) place a period after judgment

    (2) place a comma after Simply

    (3) remove the comma after judgment

    (4) change a person can enjoy winter activities safe to a person can safely enjoy winter activities

    (5) no correction is necessary

Items 42 to 47 refer to the following paragraph.

(1) Reminding us of an icicle, the young girl came to our school along with the chilling temperatures. (2) Though she created a chill of her own, she possesses a special beauty. (3) Soft tints—the semitransparent blue of her eyes and the pale pink of her lips—highlighted her creamy complexion. (4) Lending to the atmosphere of mystery about her was her eyes—sometimes with a faraway look. (5) And sometimes with an almost mischievous sparkle, as if she knew something that the rest of us did not. (6) When we showed any warmth toward her, she disappeared, no one could touch her in any way.

42. Sentence 1: **Reminding us of an icicle, the young girl came to our school along with the chilling temperatures.**

    What correction should be made to this sentence?

    (1) place a period after icicle

    (2) remove the comma after icicle

    (3) place a comma after school

    (4) change came to come

    (5) no correction is necessary

43. Sentence 2: **Though she created a chill of her own, she possesses a special beauty.**

    What correction should be made to this sentence?

    (1) change though to tho

    (2) change created to creates

    (3) remove the comma after own

    (4) change possesses to possessed

    (5) no correction is necessary

44. Sentence 3: **Soft tints—the semitransparent blue of her eyes and the pale pink of her lips—highlighted her creamy complexion.**

    What correction should be made to this sentence?

    (1) change the dash after tints to a comma

    (2) change semitransparent to semi-transparent

    (3) change highlighted to highlight

    (4) change the dash after lips to a comma

    (5) no correction is necessary

45. Sentence 4: **Lending to the atmosphere of mystery about her was her eyes—sometimes with a faraway look.**

    What correction should be made to this sentence?

    (1) change Lending to Loaning

    (2) change atmosphere to environment

    (3) place a comma after about her

    (4) change faraway to far away

    (5) no correction is necessary

46. Sentences 4 and 5: **Lending to the atmosphere of mystery about her was her eyes—sometimes with a faraway <u>look. And some-times</u> with an almost mischievous sparkle, as if she knew something that the rest of us did not.**
    Which of the following is the best way to write the underlined portion of these sentences? If you think that the original is the best way, choose option (1).

    (1) look. And sometimes

    (2) look, and sometimes

    (3) look; and sometimes

    (4) look and sometimes

    (5) look—sometimes

47. Sentence 6: **When we showed any warmth toward her, she disappeared, no one could touch her in any way.**

    What correction should be made to this sentence?

    (1) change showed to show

    (2) change disappeared to dissappeared

    (3) change the comma after disappeared to a semicolon

    (4) change no one to noone

    (5) no correction is necessary

Items 48 to 50 refer to the following paragraph.

(1) After deciding to observe the drivers in my city on three successive Friday afternoons, I precluded that these vehicle operators had to be the worst in the world. (2) Evidently some of these drivers could not read street signs, they thought that yield meant to speed up before another car approached or to play "dodge 'em" if one was already there. (3) Some impatient people passed on the shoulder of the road while others pulled out of driveways, seemingly daring anyone to hit them, in fact, one driver actually held up his hand for everyone to stop while he pulled out into heavy traffic. (4) One lady traveling in the inside lane of a boulevard suddenly makes a right turn across the path of a car in the right lane. (5) Some drivers crept along, posing as great a problem as some speeders did, still others impeded the flow of traffic in different ways. (6) On one street with two narrow lanes edged by deep ditches; for example, a man picking up goods for a charitable organization stopped the truck right in the middle of the road, causing all traffic to come to a standstill. (7) At one stop sign, two different drivers hardly decreased their speed and ran up into a yard, one driver hitting the porch of a house. (8) The drivers in my city certainly proved, in my opinion, that they are some of the worst in the world.

48. Sentence 1: **After deciding to observe the drivers in my city on three successive Friday afternoons, I precluded that these vehicle operators had to be the worst in the world.**

    What correction should be made to this sentence?

    (1) place a comma after <u>drivers</u>
    (2) place a comma after <u>city</u>
    (3) change <u>drivers</u> to <u>driver's</u>
    (4) change <u>precluded</u> to <u>concluded</u>
    (5) no correction is necessary

49. Sentence 2: **Evidently some of these drivers could not read street signs, they thought that yield meant to speed up before another car approached or to play "dodge 'em" if one was already there.**

    What correction should be made to this sentence?

    (1) Add a comma after <u>Evidently</u>
    (2) change the comma after <u>signs</u> to a semicolon
    (3) change <u>there</u> to <u>their</u>
    (4) place a comma after <u>approached</u>
    (5) no correction is necessary

50. Sentence 6: **On one street with two narrow lanes edged by deep ditches; for example, a man picking up goods for a charitable organization stopped the truck right in the middle of the road, causing all traffic to come to a standstill.**

What correction should be made to this sentence?

(1) place a comma after <u>lanes</u>

(2) change <u>On one street with two narrow lanes edged by deep ditches; for example, a man picking up goods for a charitable organization stopped the truck right in the middle of the road, causing all traffic to come to a standstill to In the middle of one narrow street, a man picking up goods for a charitable organization parked his truck, causing all traffic to come to a standstill.</u>

(3) place a semicolon after <u>ditches</u>

(4) change <u>road, causing all traffic</u> to <u>road, and caused all traffic</u>

(5) no correction is necessary

TEST 1: LANGUAGE ARTS: WRITING, PART II
Tests of General Educational Development
Directions

This part of the Language Arts: Writing Test is intended to determine how well you write. You are asked to write an essay that explains something or presents an opinion on an issue. In preparing your essay, you should take the following steps.

1. Read carefully the directions and the essay topic given below.

2. Plan your essay carefully before you write.

3. Use scratch paper to make any notes.

4. Write your essay on the lined pages of the separate answer sheet.

5. Read carefully what you have written and make any changes that will improve your essay.

6. Check your paragraphs, sentence structure, spelling, punctuation, capitalization, and usage, and make any necessary corrections.

Be sure you write the letter of the essay topic (given below) on your answer sheet. Write the letter in the box at the upper right-hand corner of the page where you write your essay.

You will have 45 minutes to write on the topic below. Write legibly and use a ballpoint pen so that the evaluators will be able to read your writing.

Write your essay on the lined pages of the separate answer sheet. The notes you make on scratch paper will not be scored.

Your essay will be scored by at least two trained evaluators who will judge it according to its overall effectiveness. They will judge how clearly you make the main point of your composition, how thoroughly you support your ideas, and how clearly and correctly you write throughout the essay.

Reprinted with permission of the General Educational Development Testing Service of the American Council on Education.

TOPIC A

Many experts agree that the influence of high technology in the workplace has created stressful working conditions. Experts also agree that in order to be more productive, such job-related pressures must be relieved. In a composition of about 250 words, explain how you relieve job-related pressures.

TEST 2: SOCIAL STUDIES

Tests of General Educational Development

Directions

The Social Studies Test consists of multiple-choice questions intended to measure your knowledge of general social studies concepts. The questions are based on short readings which often include a graph, chart, or figure. Study the information given and then answer the question(s) following it. Refer to the information as often as necessary in answering the questions.

You should spend no more than 70 minutes answering the questions in this booklet. Work carefully, but do not spend too much time on any one question. Be sure you answer every question. You will not be penalized for incorrect answers.

Do not mark in this test booklet. Record your answers to the questions on the separate answer sheet provided. Be sure all requested information is properly recorded on the answer sheet.

To record your answers, mark the numbered space on the answer sheet beside the number that corresponds to the question in the test booklet.

FOR EXAMPLE:

Early colonists of North America looked for settlement sites that had adequate water supplies and were accessible by ship. For this reason, many early towns were built near

(1)	mountains.	(4)	glaciers.
(2)	prairies.	(5)	plateaus.
(3)	rivers.			

The correct answer is "rivers"; therefore, answer space 3 would be marked on the answer sheet.

Do not rest the point of your pencil on the answer sheet while you are considering your answer. Make no stray or unnecessary marks. If you change an answer, erase your first mark completely. Mark only one answer space for each question; multiple answers will be scored as incorrect. Do not fold or crease your answer sheet. Return all test materials to the test administrator.

Reprinted with permission of the General Educational Development Testing Service of the American Council on Education.

Directions: Choose the one best answer to each item.

Items 1 to 4 refer to the following form.

**Print clearly in Ink-
Use ball-point pen or
marker**

76

**State of New Jersey
County Commissioners of Registration**

**Qualifications of an
Eligible Applicant**

You must be a citizen of the
United States and, by the date
of the next election, at least 18
years old and a resident of New
Jersey and your county for at
least 30 days.

The Commissioner of Registration
will notify you upon receipt of this
form.

The Registration deadline to
vote at the next election is 29
days prior to election day.

Check if you wish to be
a board worker/poll clerk
in future elections. ❑

Check if you are permanently
disabled, unable to go to the
polls to vote, and wish to
receive information on an
Absentee Ballot. ❑

Sign or Mark ➡

If applicant is unable to complete
this form, print name and address
of individual who completed
this form.

Voter Registration Application

1 Check one:

❑ New Registration ❑ Address Change ❑ Name Change

2 Last Name | First Name | Middle Initial | Jr. Sr.
II III

3 Street Address Where You Live | Apt. #

4 City or Town | County | Zip Code

5 Address Where You Get Your Mail (if different from above)

6 Date of Birth- Month, Day, Year | **7** Telephone Number (optional)

8 Name And Address Of Your Last Voter Registration

County

9 Declaration - I swear or affirm that:

- I am a U.S. citizen
- I live at the above address
- I will be at least 18 years old on or before the next election
- I am not on parole, probation or serving sentence due to
  a conviction for an indictable offense under any federal
  or state laws.
- I understand that any false or fraudulent registration
  may subject me to a fine up to $1,000, imprisonment
  up to 5 years or both pursuant to R.S. 19:34-1.

For Office Use Only

Clerk

Registration No.

Office Time Stamp

Signature or Mark | Date

10 Name

Address

---

1. The voter registration deadline in New Jersey is how many days prior
   to an election?

   (1) 5 days
   (2) 18 days
   (3) 20 days
   (4) 29 days
   (5) 30 days

2. The registrant in New Jersey must swear to all of the following *except*

    (1) that he/she is a U.S. citizen.
    (2) that he/she will be 21 years old on or before the next election.
    (3) that he/she recognizes that a fraudulent registration is subject to a fine and/or imprisonment.
    (4) that he/she is not on parole, probation, or serving a sentence for an indictable offense.
    (5) that he/she lives at the address indicated.

3. Which of the following is not mandatory information that must be provided?

    (1) date of birth
    (2) street address
    (3) name and address of last voter registration
    (4) first and last name
    (5) telephone number

4. How long must one have been a resident of New Jersey and the county to qualify for voter registration?

    (1) 10 days
    (2) 30 days
    (3) 60 days
    (4) 90 days
    (5) 180 days

Items 5 and 6 refer to the following paragraph.

In the Confederate states, as in the Union states, the opening of the Civil War on April 12, 1861 was marked by enthusiasm and unity of sentiment of a high degree. The capture of Fort Sumter and Lincoln's subsequent call for troops had the effect of solidifying public opinion in the seven seceded states of the lower South. In addition, these events touched off a second secession movement in the border slaveholding states of Virginia, North Carolina, Tennessee, and Arkansas. The governors of these states indignantly rejected Lincoln's appeal for soldiers, and, within a few weeks, the four states seceded and joined the Confederacy. Thus was effected a political union of upper and lower South, and in this enlarged Confederacy (outside of a few pro-Union areas, primarily in the hill country) there was firm popular approval of the war policy in the early months of the conflict. Charleston, Montgomery, and New Orleans witnessed similar scenes of excited crowds ardently voicing their support of the government. "The South is now united to a man," wrote the sister-in-law of Salmon P. Chase (Lincoln's Secretary of the Treasury) from New

Orleans; her phrases were strikingly like those used by George Ticknor to describe the prevailing mood in the Union states.

Pressly, *Americans Interpret their Civil War*, The Free Press, New York, 1962.

5. Which best describes the public opinion about the beginning of the Civil War?

   (1) The South was enthusiastic, the North fearful.
   (2) The North was enthusiastic, the South fearful.
   (3) Both sides were enthusiastic.
   (4) Both sides were fearful.
   (5) Neither side was excited.

6. Which is most true about the causes of the Civil War?

   (1) It was fought in the 1850s over secession and slavery.
   (2) It was fought in the 1860s over secession and slavery.
   (3) It was fought in the 1870s over secession and slavery.
   (4) The main issue was Lincoln's plan to outlaw all slavery.
   (5) The main cause was the federal government's refusal to allow Southern cotton to be sold overseas.

Items 7 to 9 refer to the following passage.

   The struggle of socialism against capitalism is part of the historic rhythm in the concentration and dispersion of wealth. The capitalist, of course, has fulfilled a creative function in history: he has gathered the savings of the people into productive capital by the promise of dividends or interest; he has financed the mechanization of industry and agriculture, and the rationalization of distribution; and the result has been such a flow of goods from producer to consumer as history has never seen before. He has put the liberal gospel of liberty to his use by arguing that business-men left relatively free from transportation tolls and legislative regulation can give the public a greater abundance of food, homes, comfort, and leisure than has ever come from industries managed by politicians, manned by governmental employees, and supposedly immune to the laws of supply and demand. In free enterprise the spur of competition and the zeal and zest of ownership arouse the productiveness and inventive-ness of men; nearly every economic ability sooner or later finds its niche and reward in the shuffle of talents and the natural selection of skills; and a basic democracy rules the process insofar as most of the articles to be produced, and the services to be rendered, are determined by public demand rather than by governmental decree. Meanwhile competition compels the capitalist to exhaustive labor, and his products to ever-rising excellence.

Will and Ariel Durant, *The Lessons of History*, Simon and Schuster, New York, 1968.

7. Capitalism is seen as a positive influence because of all except

    (1) its immunity from the laws of supply and demand.
    (2) creating capital from savings.
    (3) creating more consumer goods.
    (4) rewarding ability and skills.
    (5) meeting consumer demands.

8. The best conclusion on the author's feelings about capitalism is

    (1) it is a useful system with some serious flaws.
    (2) it is best used in partnership with socialism.
    (3) it fits into the basic ideals of democracy.
    (4) it functions best in partnership with government.
    (5) it is a new concept that did not influence history.

9. Which saying best describes capitalism?

    (1) The greatest good for the greatest number
    (2) Ask not what you can do for yourself, ask what you can do for your country
    (3) To each according to his needs
    (4) No work, no eat
    (5) Man does not live by bread alone

Items 10 to 13 refer to the following map.

10. Which best describes the chart's arrangement?

    (1) From South to North   (4) From West to East
    (2) From North to South   (5) Random
    (3) From East to West

11. Lakes Erie and Ontario are mostly in which region?

    (1) Maritimes
    (2) Canadian Shield/Northern Territories
    (3) St. Lawrence Lowlands
    (4) Prairies
    (5) Mountain/Coastal

12. Alberta, Manitoba, and Saskatchewan are in

    (1) Maritimes.
    (2) Canadian Shield/Northern Territories.
    (3) St. Lawrence Lowlands.
    (4) Prairies.
    (5) Mountain/Coastal.

13. Which is not true about Canada?

    (1) Part of it is above the Arctic Circle.
    (2) Most of the population is close to the U.S. border.
    (3) All the Great Lakes are partially in Canada.
    (4) Quebec is a French-culture province.
    (5) Canada adapted its government system from Britain.

Items 14 to 15 refer to the following passage.

What became known as the Watergate crisis began during the 1972 presidential campaign. Early on the morning of June 17, James McCord, a security officer with the Committee for the Re-election of the President, and four other men broke into Democratic headquarters at the Watergate apartment complex in Washington, D.C., and were caught while going through files and installing electronic eavesdropping devices, or bugs. On June 22, Nixon announced that the administration was in no way involved in the burglary attempt. Ultimately, however, the intrepid reporting of Bob Woodward and Carl Bernstein of the *Washington Post* would lay bare the scandal for what it was. CBS News and *The New York Times* also contributed distinguished investigative reporting on the matter.

The trial of the burglars began in early 1973, with all but McCord, who was convicted, pleading guilty. Before sentencing, McCord wrote a letter to U.S. District Judge John J. Sirica arguing that high Republican officials had known in advance about the burglary and that perjury had been committed at the trial.

Soon Jeb Stuart Magruder, head of the re-election committee, and John W. Dean, Nixon's attorney, stated that they had been involved. Dean testified before a Senate Watergate investigating committee that Nixon had been involved in covering up the incident. Over the next several months, extensive involvement of the administration, including payment of "silence" money to the burglars, destruction of FBI records, forgery of documents, and wiretapping, was revealed. Dean was fired and H.R. Haldeman and John Ehrlichman, who headed the White House Staff, and Attorney General Richard Kleindienst, resigned. Nixon claimed that he had not personally been involved in the cover-up but refused, on the grounds of executive privilege, to allow investigation of White House documents.

Under considerable pressure, Nixon agreed to the appointment of a special prosecutor, Archibald Cox of Harvard Law School. When Cox obtained a subpoena for tape recordings of White House conversations (whose existence had been revealed during the Senate hearings)—and the administration lost an appeal in the appellate court—Nixon ordered Elliot Richardson, now the attorney general, to fire Cox. Both Richardson and his subordinate, William Ruckelshaus, resigned, leaving Robert Bork, the solicitor general, to carry out the order. This "Saturday Night Massacre," which took place on October 20, 1973, aroused a storm of controversy. The House Judiciary Committee, headed by Peter Rodino of New Jersey, began looking into the possibilities of impeachment. Nixon agreed to turn the tapes over to Judge Sirica and named Leon Jaworski as the new special prosecutor. But it soon became known that some of the tapes were missing and that a portion of another had been erased.

14. The Saturday Night Massacre refers to

    (1)   Nixon's firing of Watergate special prosecutor, Archibald Cox, and his staff, in October 1973.

    (2)   the bombing of the Marine Corps barracks in Lebanon by a suicide truck bomber in October 1983.

    (3)   Reagan's bombing of military bases in Libya in April 1986.

    (4)   Oliver North's destruction of files related to the Iran-Contra scandal, the day before his office was searched by the FBI.

    (5)   the slaughter of Vietnamese villagers in My Lai by American soldiers under the command of Lt. William Calley.

15. The two reporters who broke the story of the Watergate scandal in the *Washington Post* were

    (1)   Cronkite-Rather.   (4)   Woodward-Bernstein.
    (2)   Hearst-Pulitzer.   (5)   Liddy-Dean.
    (3)   Ervin-Baker.

<u>Items 16 to 18</u> refer to the following paragraph.

At the time of the Crusades, most of Western Europe was a decentralized feudal society, living a self-sufficient hand-to-mouth existence. A few scholars, chiefly in the monasteries, kept alive some learning. In the city states of northern Italy, a surviving merchant class carried on limited commerce, chiefly with the Byzantine Empire, and so had some contact with the slightly higher Byzantine civilization. For the most part, though, the cultural achievements of the Greeks and Romans had been lost. All of the peasants and most of the nobles were entirely illiterate. At that same time, Moslems generally, and especially the Moors in Spain and the Saracens in the Near East, enjoyed a much higher culture. They lived better, had more commerce, and had kept alive the learning of the classical Greeks and of the Hellenistic age. They traded indirectly, through caravans to Persia, with India and China, and so had contact with those civilizations.

Samuel A. Johnson, *An Interpretation of American History*, Barron's Inc., Woodbury, New York, 1968.

16. Western Europe was backward because

   (1) the advancements of Greek and Roman civilizations had not been kept up.
   (2) Moslems ruled them and lived better.
   (3) Europe had no trade with others.
   (4) there were no nearby civilizations to imitate.
   (5) no one could read or write.

17. Which of the western civilizations in existence during the Crusades was the most advanced?

   (1) Western Europe   (4) The Roman Empire
   (2) The Byzantine Empire   (5) Moors and Saracens
   (3) Classical Greece

18. The Crusades were an attempt to do all except

   (1) free the Holy Land from Moslem control.
   (2) increase trade with the rest of the world.
   (3) destroy all Moslems.
   (4) protect Christian pilgrims.
   (5) expand wealth and territory.

Items 19 to 22 refer to the following graph.

The Growth of Nonfarm Activities, 1810–1980

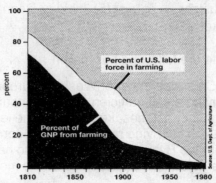

19. The graph most clearly shows that

 (1)   the economic impact of farming was always more important than the number of people working in the field.
 (2)   GNP and labor force maintained a constant relationship to each other.
 (3)   farming remained the most important economic activity until about 1900.
 (4)   the decline in farming importance finally reversed itself in the 1970's.
 (5)   recently, the farming GNP and the farm labor force have more accurately matched each other.

20. Which statement is most true about American agriculture and the graph?

 (1)   Farming is no longer an important occupation.
 (2)   It is not possible to make a good living from farming.
 (3)   Farming is becoming more automated.
 (4)   American agriculture's production is now possible with fewer workers.
 (5)   There was never a time when either GNP or labor force actually increased.

21. Which does not apply to American agriculture?

 (1)   Farmers usually have to borrow money to operate.
 (2)   The U.S. farmer almost always creates a surplus.
 (3)   Farming is one of the last areas to resist big corporations.
 (4)   Modern farming still depends on weather conditions.
 (5)   Modern farmers have depended heavily on government aid.

22. The best description of American agricultural problems in the future is

 (1)   increasing numbers of Americans will return to agriculture.
 (2)   world food supplies will increase and need for U.S. exports will diminish.
 (3)   efficiency will increase and production will need fewer workers.
 (4)   water supplies and chemical fertilizers will both increase.
 (5)   Third World food growing needs will diminish.

Items 23 to 25 refer to the following information.

   The words of the Fourth Amendment recognize that, while individuals have a right to privacy, the government has a need to gather information. The police, for example, need to collect evidence against criminals in order to protect society against crime. The amendment considers the interests of both the public and the government.

The Fourth Amendment does not give an absolute right to privacy. It does not prohibit all searches and seizures—only those that are unreasonable. In deciding if a search is reasonable, the courts look at the facts and circumstances of each case. As a general rule, courts usually rule that searches and seizures are unreasonable unless authorized by a valid warrant or justified by special situations. In these special situations, police have a lawful or justifiable reason to discover the evidence. For instance, a person may consent to a search. The evidence, such as a gun on a seat of a car, may be in plain view of the officer. When a lawful arrest is being made, police may search a suspect for their own protection. Also, when an emergency situation arises, such as a bomb threat or house fire, police may find evidence of crime in the course of doing their duty.

L. Arbetman, R. Roe, *Great Trials in American History*, West Publishing, p. 100.

23. The best title for this reading would be

    (1)   Citizen's Rights under the Fourth Amendment.
    (2)   Search and Seizure—What's Legal.
    (3)   Limits on the Fourth Amendment.
    (4)   How to Search for Evidence.
    (5)   Court Rulings on the Fourth Amendment.

24. Which would be an illegal search?

    (1)   Any search without a warrant
    (2)   Searching for weapons while arresting a person
    (3)   A suspect voluntarily allows a search
    (4)   Illegal drugs are found while investigating a shooting
    (5)   Searching a house without a warrant

25. Which is not part of the Bill of Rights?

    (1)   The right to a jury trial
    (2)   Freedom of religion
    (3)   Freedom from quartering of troops in private quarters
    (4)   The freedom from slavery
    (5)   The right to bear arms

Items 26 to 29 refer to the following passage.

BROWN V. BOARD OF EDUCATION OF TOPEKA

Today, education is perhaps the most important function of state and local governments. Compulsory school attendance laws and the great expenditures for education both demonstrate our recognition of the importance of education to our democratic society. It is required in the performance of our most basic public responsibilities, even service in the armed forces. It is the very foundation of good citizenship. Today it is a principal instrument in awakening the child to cultural values, in preparing him for later professional training, and in helping him to adjust normally to his environment. In these days, it is doubtful that any child may reasonably be expected to succeed in life if he is denied the opportunity of an education. Such an opportunity, where the state has undertaken to provide it, is a right which must be made available to all on equal terms.

We come then to the question presented: Does segregation of children in public schools solely on the basis of race, even though the physical facilities and other "tangible" factors may be equal, deprive the children of the minority group of equal education opportunities? We believe that it does.

...To separate them [minority children] from others of similar age and qualifications solely because of their race generates a feeling of inferiority as to their status in the community that may affect their hearts and minds in a way unlikely ever to be undone ....

We conclude that in the field of public education the doctrine of "separate but equal" has no place. Separate educational facilities are inherently unequal. Therefore, we hold that the plaintiffs and others similarly situated for whom the actions have been brought are, by reasons of the segregation complained of, deprived of the equal protection of the laws guaranteed by the Fourteenth Amendment....

26. According to the Supreme Court in its *Brown v. Board of Education* decision, education contributes all of the following to our democratic society *except*

    (1) helps children adjust normally to their environment.
    (2) preserves a diversity of social classes.
    (3) awakens children to cultural values.
    (4) prepares children for later professional training.
    (5) provides the foundation for good citizenship.

27. In *Brown v. Board of Education*, the Supreme Court declared that separate educational facilities for the races

    (1) can provide equal education if equally funded.
    (2) is constitutional in certain circumstances.
    (3) is supported by the 14th amendment.
    (4) is inherently unequal.
    (5) is a matter of states' rights.

28. In *Brown v. Board of Education*, the Supreme Court identified which of the following as a right?

    (1)   opportunity of education
    (2)   success in life
    (3)   compulsory school attendance
    (4)   great expenditures for education
    (5)   service in the armed forces

29. According to the Supreme Court in *Brown v. Board of Education*, separation on the basis of race necessarily produces which of the following?

    (1)   unequal educational facilities
    (2)   potential physical violence between the races
    (3)   new opportunities for minorities
    (4)   social harmony
    (5)   a feeling of inferiority among the minority group

<u>Items 30 to 33</u> refer to the following list.

    Department of State
    Department of the Treasury
    Department of Defense
    Department of Justice
    Department of the Interior
    Department of Agriculture
    Department of Commerce
    Department of Labor
    Department of Housing and Urban Development
    Department of Transportation
    Department of Energy
    Department of Health and Human Services
    Department of Education
    Department of Veterans Affairs

30. Which department is responsible for foreign policy?

    (1)   State   (4)   Commerce
    (2)   Defense   (5)   Transportation
    (3)   Justice

31. Which department supervises the FBI?

    (1) State
    (2) Treasury
    (3) Defense
    (4) Justice
    (5) Interior

32. Which is not a role of the Department of Health and Human Services?

    (1) Social Security
    (2) Medicare
    (3) National Parks
    (4) Food and Drug Administration
    (5) Disease research

33. Which is not part of the Executive Branch?

    (1) Secret Service
    (2) Pentagon
    (3) National Security Council
    (4) Securities and Exchange Commission
    (5) Council of Economic Advisors

Item 34 refers to the following chart.

Parliamentary Government

Voters

elect ↓

Legislature

elects ↓

Prime Minister or Premier

proposes ↓

Laws

enacts

34. In a parliamentary system

    (1) there is no popular election of the government leader.
    (2) the voters directly create laws.
    (3) the legislature has less power than our Congress.
    (4) only the prime minister or premier can enact laws.
    (5) only the legislature is responsible for law-making.

Items 35 to 37 refer to the following map.

35. What geographic features have created the "Ring of Fire"?

    (1) Geothermics   (4) Tectonics
    (2) Oceanography   (5) Landforms
    (3) Ecosystems

36. Which would not be a characteristic of the area?

    (1) Volcanoes   (4) Island Formations
    (2) Earthquakes   (5) Fault Lines
    (3) Tornadoes

37. Partly as a result of volcanic activity, many Asian nations are on chains
    of islands known as

    (1) atolls.   (4) lagoons.
    (2) archipelagoes.   (5) continental shelves.
    (3) barrier reefs.

Items 38 to 40 refer to the following table.

New York Stock Exchange Companies With Largest Number of Stockholders, 1985	
Company	**Stockholders**
American Tel & Tel (AT&T)	2,927,000
General Motors	1,990,000
Bell South Corp.	1,685,000
Bell Atlantic	1,413,000
American Information Tech.	1,382,000
NYNEX Corp.	1,348,000
Southwestern Bell	1,320,000
Pacific Telesis Group	1,242,000
US WEST	1,156,000
International Business Machines	798,000
Exxon Corp.	785,000
General Electric	490,000
GTE Corp.	442,000
Bell Canada Enterprises	332,000
Sears Roebuck	326,000

From *1986 Fact Book*, copyright New York Stock Exchange, Inc., 1986.

38. Which is most true about the table?

   (1) Telephone companies have the largest number of stockholders.
   (2) Manufacturing companies have more stockholders than service companies.
   (3) Retail merchandise companies have the largest number of stock-holders.
   (4) Only domestic companies are represented.
   (5) Oil companies do not have large numbers of stockholders.

39. Which company would you buy if you wanted the greatest voice in its management?

   (1) American Tel & Tel   (4) GTE
   (2) Southwestern Bell   (5) Sears Roebuck
   (3) Exxon

40. Stockholders control a company through

(1) the chief executive officer.
(2) the chairperson of the board.
(3) the president of the company.
(4) the elected board of directors.
(5) stock options.

Items 41 to 43 refer to the following graph.

41. Under a unified Germany,

(1) the U.S. continues to be the leading exporter.
(2) Britain will export about 60% of Germany's total.
(3) the East will increase Germany's exports by nearly 10%.
(4) the U.S. and Germany will almost be tied in exports.
(5) British and German exports together will total nearly $600 billion.

42. The best indicator of people's standard of living is the

(1) per capita gross national product.
(2) the population divided into the annual exports.
(3) the annual exports.
(4) the per capita gross national product divided into the exports.
(5) the per capita national product multiplied by the population.

43. Which statement would be most true?

(1) The U.S. leads in productivity and GNP.
(2) Germany will go from 4th to 2nd in GNP by unifying.
(3) For its population, the U.S. produced the fewest exports.
(4) For its population, Britain produced the most exports.
(5) Unified Germany's per capita income will surpass the U.S.

Item 44 refers to the following paragraph.

The exploitation of the beasts took hunter and trader to the west, Mormons went west to escape persecution, the exploitation of the grasses took the rancher west, and the exploitation of the virgin soil of the river valleys and prairies attracted the farmer. Good soils have been the most continuous attraction to the farmer's frontier. The land hunger of the Virginians drew them down the rivers into Carolina, in early colonial days; the search for soils took the Massachusetts men to Pennsylvania and to New York. As the eastern lands were taken up migration flowed across them to the west. Daniel Boone, the great backwoodsman, who combined the occupations of hunter, trader, cattle-raiser, farmer, and surveyor— learning probably from the traders of the fertility of the lands on the upper Yadkin, where the traders were wont to rest as they tool their way to the Indians, left his Pennsylvania home with his father, and passed down the Great Valley road to that stream. Learning from a trader whose posts were on the Red River in Kentucky of its game and rich pastures, he pioneered the way for the farmers to that region.

From "The Significance of the Frontier in American History," by Fredrick Jackson Turner

44. Which of the reasons given for moving West is strongest?

   (1) Better hunting   (4) Owning land
   (2) Good soils   (5) Trade
   (3) River valleys

Item 45 refers to the following passage.

Although the Thirteen States lacked a great political leader to call forth a spirit of sacrifice, Washington did his best to fill the political as well as the military role. He was more than a general: the embodiment of every-thing fine in American character. With no illusions about his own gran-deur, no thought of the future except an intense longing to return to Mount Vernon, he assumed every responsibility thrust upon him, and fulfilled it. He not only had to lead an army but constantly to write letters to Con-gress, state leaders, and state governments, begging them for the where-withal to maintain his army. He had to compose quarrels among his officers and placate cold, hungry, unpaid troops. Intrigues against his authority he ignored, and the intriguers came to grief. In his relations with French officers he proved to be a diplomat second only to Franklin. Refusing to accept a salary, he dipped into his modest fortune to buy comforts for the soldiers and to help destitute families of his companions in battle. Thus Washington brought something more important to the cause than military ability and statesmanship: the priceless gift of charac-ter.

Although Washington was scrupulous in his respect for the civil power, there was a certain jealousy of him in Congress and the state governments, largely from fear that he would be too successful and become a dictator. Yet, inconsistently, several members, especially Richard Henry Lee of his own state, and James Lovell of Massachusetts, thought he was not successful enough and played with the idea of relieving him by Charles Lee, or Gates, or the French Duc de Broglie. Just how far the "Conway cabal" of 1777 intended to go; whether it was an officer's plot to supersede Washington, or mere grumbling by ambitious malcontents, is still a mystery. But it is certain that the commander in chief was regarded by the rank and file, and by the people in all parts of the country, with deep respect and affection. He did not have the personality of a Napoleon, a Nelson, or a Stonewall Jackson to arouse men to fanatical loyalty; but the soldiers knew that they could depend on him for valor, for military wisdom, and for justice.

Reprinted from *The Oxford History of the American People*, Samuel Eliot Morison, Oxford University Press, NY, 1965.

45.   Among the problems Washington faced was

    (1)   lack of confidence by his troops.
    (2)   accusations of dishonesty.
    (3)   opposition by the commander-in-chief.
    (4)   lack of popular support.
    (5)   fear that he was either too successful or not successful enough.

Items 46 to 48 refer to the following article.

The idea of a global shortage seems incredible when 70% of the Earth's surface is covered by H_2O. But 98% of that water is salty, making it unusable for drinking or agriculture. Desalinization is technically feasible, but it is far too expensive to use anywhere except in an ultra-rich, sparsely populated country like Saudi Arabia. Other options, like towing icebergs from the poles, are also beyond the means of poor nations.

The scarcity of fresh water for agriculture makes famines more likely every year. The world consumes more food than it produces, and yet there are few places to turn for additional cropland. Only by drawing on international stockpiles of grain have poorer countries averted widespread starvation. But those supplies are being depleted. From 1987 to 1989, the world's stock of grain fell from a 101-day surplus to a 54-day one. A drought in the U.S. bread-basket could rapidly lead to a global food calamity.

Even if rainfall stays at normal levels, current world food production will be difficult to maintain, much less increase. The food supply has kept pace with population growth only because the amount of land under irrigation has doubled in the past three decades. Now, however, agriculture is losing millions of hectares of this land to the effects of improper watering.

Reprinted from *Time Magazine*, August 20, 1990.

46. The best title for the article would be

    (1)   Alternative Water Supplies.   (2)   Problems for Poor Nations.
    (3)   Famine Around the World.   (4)   World Grain Supplies.
    (5)   Possible Water Problems.

47. World food supply is in danger because

    (1)   individual people are eating more.
    (2)   grain-growing nations have been unwilling to share surpluses.
    (3)   population is growing faster than the surplus of world grain.
    (4)   irrigated farmland is now being lost.
    (5)   poor nations waste money on desalination projects.

48. Which of the following would least influence fresh water supplies?

    (1)   Annual rainfall   (4)   Soil drainage types
    (2)   Temperature patterns   (5)   Greenhouse effect
    (3)   Hydrologic cycle

Items 49 to 50 refer to the following cartoon.

Reprinted with permission of Bill Day; *Detroit Free Press*, Tribune Media Services

49. Which problem in the cartoon would be found in an underdeveloped nation?

    (1) Acid rain
    (2) Nuclear waste
    (3) Toxic waste
    (4) Ozone layer depletion
    (5) Destroyed rain forests

50. According to scientists, which would not be a major result of the greenhouse effect?

    (1) Average temperature rising
    (2) Higher sea levels
    (3) Higher disease rates
    (4) Polar ice caps receding
    (5) Lowered sun radiation levels

TEST 3: SCIENCE

Tests of General Educational Development

Directions

The Science Test consists of multiple-choice questions intended to measure your knowledge of the general concepts in science. The questions are based on short readings, which often include a graph, chart, or figure. Study the information given and then answer the question(s) following it. Refer to the information as often as necessary in answering the questions.

You should spend no more than 80 minutes answering the questions in this booklet. Work carefully, but do not spend too much time on any one question. Be sure you answer every question. You will not be penalized for incorrect answers.

Do not mark in this test booklet. Record your answers to the questions on the separate answer sheet provided. Be sure all requested information is properly recorded on the answer sheet.

To record your answers, mark the numbered space on the answer sheet beside the number that corresponds to the question in the test booklet.

FOR EXAMPLE:

Which of the following is the smallest unit in a living thing?

(1)	Tissue	(4)	Muscle	
(2)	Organ	(5)	Capillary	
(3)	Cell			① ② ● ④ ⑤

The correct answer is "cell"; therefore, answer space 3 would be marked on the answer sheet.

Do not rest the point of your pencil on the answer sheet while you are considering your answer. Make no stray or unnecessary marks. If you change an answer, erase your first mark completely. Mark only one answer space for each question; multiple answers will be scored as incorrect. Do not fold or crease your answer sheet. Return all test materials to the test administrator.

Directions: Choose the one best answer to each item.

Items 1 and 2 refer to the following graph.

THERMAL STRUCTURE OF THE ATMOSPHERE
TO A HEIGHT OF ABOUT 110 KILOMETERS

The Atmosphere: An Introduction to Meteorology, 1989, Fourth Edition, Frederick K. Lutgens, Edward J. Tarbuck, Prentice Hall.

1. The warmest place in the atmosphere is near the ground because

    (1) the ground is under the ozone layer.
    (2) the ground can store heat.
    (3) the ground is covered by ice in some regions.
    (4) the Earth is both land and water.
    (5) All of the above.

2. Which would be a reason for temperature changes as you travel up through the atmosphere?

    (1) Distance from the sun decreases.
    (2) Weather disruptions cause mixing of the temperatures.
    (3) Presence of ozone.
    (4) Presence of man.
    (5) Changes in composition.

Item 3 refers to the following figure showing the geological layers where oil and gas reserves are found.

Earth's Surface

B and E are impermeable material.

C and D are porous material.

Oil and gas are important sources of energy that are found below the ground. Geologists must know the conditions under which they are formed and the locations where they may be found in large quantities. They are formed after the death and burial of organisms followed by chemical changes to the buried organism. The locations where they are found have two important characteristics. First, the oils and gas must be in permeable material rock, where water is present, so the oil and gas, which are less dense than water, can move up and above the water. Second, the oil and gas must be trapped below an impermeable layer. This trap can take several forms but it must contain the oil and gas re-serves, preventing them from migrating away and thus dispersing.

3. Which letter represents the layer containing the oils and gas?

   (1) A
   (2) B
   (3) C
   (4) D
   (5) E

Item 4 refers to the following passage.

Salinity is a measure of dissolved solids in water. On the average, 1,000 grams of typical sea water contains 35 grams of salts. The level of salinity is below average in areas where large amounts of fresh water enter the ocean, and above average in hot, arid climates.

4. The Mediterranean Sea and the Red Sea are adjacent to deserts. The water in these two seas would be expected to have

    (1) above-average salinity.
    (2) below-average salinity.
    (3) average salinity.
    (4) no salt content whatsoever.
    (5) cold temperatures.

Items 5 to 8 refer to the following paragraph.

Most of the land plants that one observes have vascular tissue. This tissue transports substances between various regions of the plant. There are two types of vascular tissue: phloem and xylem. The phloem transports or conducts organic materials, mainly food, from where they are made to various storage sites or regions of use. Xylem transports water and minerals from the roots to the stems and leaves and flowers. Another function of the xylem is that of support. To prevent drying out, the surface of a plant is covered with a waxy cuticle. The cuticle is impermeable to gases such as carbon dioxide and oxygen, and to water. Since the plant needs carbon dioxide and oxygen to carry on photosynthesis, these gases are exchanged through tiny pores in the leaf called stomata. Each stomata is surrounded by two guard cells, which regulate the size of the opening of the pore.

5. The tissue that is able to conduct food to specialized areas in the plant is the

    (1) xylem.   (4) stomata.
    (2) phloem.   (5) cuticle.
    (3) precambrium.

6. The tissue that is able to prevent the plant from drying out is the

    (1) xylem.   (4) stomata.
    (2) phloem.   (5) cuticle.
    (3) precambrium.

7. Guard cells make up the

    (1) xylem.   (4) stomata.
    (2) phloem.   (5) cuticle.
    (3) precambrium.

8. The amount of carbon dioxide and oxygen is regulated by the

   (1) xylem.
   (2) phloem.
   (3) precambrium.
   (4) stomata.
   (5) cuticle.

Items 9 and 10 refer to the following information.

   An electroscope is a device used to detect the presence of electric charge. One such device consists of a pair of gold foil leaves suspended from a metal rod that is electrically connected to the outside of a metal and glass enclosure as shown below. An insulator prevents charge from leaking from the leaves and metal rod to the enclosure.

ELECTROSCOPE

   If a piece of vinyl is rubbed with a wool cloth and then brought near the top metal knob, the gold leaves separate, indicating that the vinyl has acquired a certain amount of charge, either positive or negative. Only electrons (negatively charged particles) are allowed to move on the surface of the metal rod and gold leaves. The amount of spread in the gold leaves indicates the strength of the charge. Touching the top knob with your finger immediately makes the leaves come together, indicating that electrons are either added to or taken away from the electroscope to neutralize it.

9. Suppose a positively charged vinyl rod is brought near the top knob of a neutral electroscope.

   (1) The gold leaves will not spread.
   (2) The gold leaves spread because they become positively charged and they repel each other.
   (3) The gold leaves become negatively charged.
   (4) The top knob becomes positively charged.
   (5) The top knob remains neutral.

10. Suppose a negatively charged vinyl rod is brought near the top knob of an electroscope with its gold leaves separated because they both are negatively charged and repel each other.

    (1) The top knob will become more negative.
    (2) The gold leaves will tend to separate even more.
    (3) The gold leaf separation will remain the same.
    (4) The gold leaves will tend to come together.
    (5) Both (1) and (4) are true.

Items 11 refers to the following passage.

In an ionic bond, the entities bonded together are ions of opposite charge. Electrons must be transferred to form an ionic bond. In a covalent bond, which is a strong bond, electrons are shared between two neutral atoms. Hard substances, such as diamonds, consist of covalently bonded atoms.

11. An example of a substance joined by one or several covalent bonds would be

    (1) H_2.
    (2) Cl_2.
    (3) NaCl.
    (4) a diamond.
    (5) choices (1), (2), and (4).

Items 12 and 13 refer to the following map.

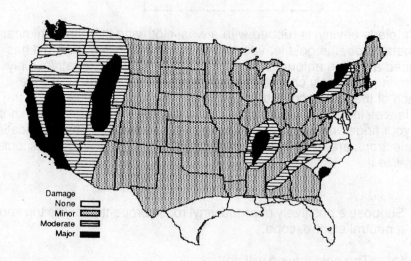

Damage
None
Minor
Moderate
Major

Seismic risk map for the U. S. issued January 1969, showing earthquake damage areas of reasonable expectancy in the next 100 years. (Derived from U. S. Coast and Geodetic Survey, ESSA Rel. ES-1, January 14, 1969.)

12. People living in which state have little need for earthquake insurance?

    (1) Rhode Island   (4) California
    (2) Wyoming   (5) Washington
    (3) Illinois

13. Data from the map indicates that

    (1) a major earthquake will definitely occur within 100 years.
    (2) a major earthquake will definitely occur in California within 100 years.
    (3) an earthquake can never occur in Texas.
    (4) nothing can be concluded from this map concerning the location of earthquakes.
    (5) few states are safe from earthquakes.

Items 14 to 16 refer to the following passage.

The term "volcanic activity" can mean erupting volcanoes complete with lava and pyroclastic display, or it can mean a simple gaseous emission. It is believed that volcanic activity formed the early Earth's atmosphere. Volcanic gases typically include water vapor, carbon dioxide, hydrogen sulfide, sulfur dioxide, chlorine, and fluorine.

14. Which statement can be drawn in conclusion from the above information?

    (1) Volcanic gases can be more dangerous than lava.
    (2) Erupting volcanoes always emit both lava and gas.
    (3) The term "volcanic activity" is always clear in its meaning.
    (4) Erupting volcanoes emit lava only.
    (5) Erupting volcanoes emit gases only.

15. Which statement is false?

    (1) The early Earth's atmosphere contained no free oxygen.
    (2) The early Earth's atmosphere was poisonous to present day life forms.
    (3) Current Earth's atmosphere must be formed by factors other than volcanic activity.
    (4) Volcanic activity today emits oxygen to the atmosphere.
    (5) None of the above.

16. "Pyroclastic display" is best defined as

    (1)   a fallout of ice and snow.   (4)   a hot, green vapor.
    (2)   trees that fall near the volcano.   (5)   fire and rock particles.
    (3)   a mushroom-type cloud.

Items 17 to 20 refer to the following information.

    Pressure is a concept in physics that has a very precise definition. It is the force acting divided by the area upon which it acts. Air pressure at the Earth's surface is 14.7 lbs/in^2 or 1.013 x 105 N/m^2. (1.0 lb/in^2 is known as a PSI.) This pressure is enough to support a 34-foot high, 1-inch square column of water in a vacuum or a 2.5-foot high, 1-inch square column of mercury in a vacuum. Water weighs 62.4 lbs per cubic foot or 9797 N per cubic meter.

17. Comparing identical volumes of liquid, mercury weighs

    (1)   157 times more than water.
    (2)   68.1 times more than water.
    (3)   13.6 times more than water.
    (4)   2.3 times more than water.
    (5)   the same as water.

18. A 200 lb man standing on snow with boots each having a bottom area of 35 square inches will exert a downward pressure due to his weight equal to

    (1)   200 PSI   (4)   2.86 PSI
    (2)   100 PSI   (5)   1.93 PSI
    (3)   5.71 PSI

19. A young girl wearing snow skis weighs 110 lbs. If the total area of the skis touching the snow is 330 square inches, then the air pressure on the snow is about

    (1)   11 times that of the girl.   (4)   44 times that of the girl.
    (2)   22 times that of the girl.   (5)   55 times that of the girl.
    (3)   33 times that of the girl.

20. An air pressure of 14.7 PSI can support a one square foot column of water in a vacuum that is

    (1)   34 feet high.   (4)   2.83 inches high.
    (2)   17 feet high.   (5)   less than an inch high.
    (3)   2.83 feet high.

Item 21 refers to the following chart.

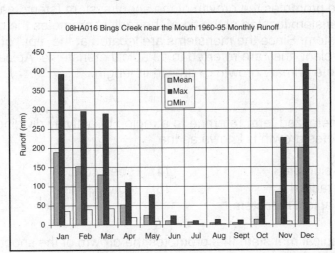

08HA016 Bings Creek near the Mouth 1960-95 Monthly Runoff

Weathering, erosion, and deposition are three important processes that re-shape the surface of the earth. Weathering is the breaking up of rocks. It results from changes in temperature, pressure, and biological and chemical activity. Erosion is the picking up and transport of weathered material. The agents of erosion are glaciers, gravity, moving water, and wind. The greater the energy (rate of movement) of the eroding agents, the greater the extent of erosion. Deposition is the falling out of eroded materials. It occurs when the erosion agents can no longer hold the weathered material.

21. When would the greatest erosion occur?

    (1)   December and January
    (2)   February and March
    (3)   April and May
    (4)   July and August
    (5)   September and October

Items 22 to 25 refer to the following paragraph.

A bean seed is a reproductive structure produced by a flower. It contains a plant embryo that is in an arrested stage of development. It also contains the food supply that nourishes the embryo as it begins to grow. The outer covering of the bean is its protective seed coat. Inside of the seed coat is the embryonic plant and two large "seed leaves" or cotyledons. The seed leaves contain nutrients that help the embryo grow until the plant can depend on photosynthesis to make its own food. The embryo has two meristems. Meristems are growth points where the dividing cells promote growth in length or diameter. One of the meristems is located in the plumule which is found between the first foliage leaves. The other meristem is found at the tip of the radical. The meristem located in the plumule promotes the growth of the shoot system (stem, leaves, etc.), and the meristem located at the tip of the radical promotes the growth of the root system. Since the meristems are located at the "tips" of the embryonic plant, they are referred to as apical meristems. Apical meristems promote primary growth or growth in length.

22. A generalized term referring to a region of actively dividing cells that promotes growth is known as the

    (1) plumule.   (4) seed coat.
    (2) radical.   (5) cotyledon.
    (3) apical meristem.

23. The apical meristem that promotes the growth of the shoot system of a plant is the

    (1) plumule.   (4) seed coat.
    (2) radical.   (5) cotyledon.
    (3) meristem.

24. The apical meristem that promotes the growth of the root system of a plant is the

    (1) plumule.   (4) seed coat.
    (2) radical.   (5) cotyledon.
    (3) meristem.

25. The embryonic plant receives nourishment from the

    (1) plumule.   (4) seed coat.
    (2) radical.   (5) cotyledons.
    (3) apical meristem.

Items 26 to 29 refer to the following paragraph.

Life in the sea has its advantages and its disadvantages. Most of the food is found near the surface. The fish, which are vertebrates, have the advantage of being able to maintain position while cruising through the sea looking for food. Few invertebrates are powerful enough swimmers to do this. However, invertebrates have become adapted to remain small enough to float. These zooplankton are subject to the whims of the currents. An alternate adaptation that is exhibited by some invertebrates is to remain firmly anchored (sessile) to the sea floor or some solid object in the sea. Some of these animals, such as oysters and clams, are filter feeders, and filter the water for microscopic animals and plants, which are their food. Since they are sessile, they must also have a means of protection from the mobile predators of the sea. That is why many of these animals have either a passive protection such as a thick, hard, outer shell, or an active protection such as stinging cells, or an unappetizing, toxic mucus covering their body.

26. Fish are

    (1) filter feeders.   (4) zooplankton.
    (2) invertebrates.   (5) phytoplankton.
    (3) vertebrates.

27. Zooplankton are

    (1) invertebrates.   (4) toxic mucus.
    (2) vertebrates.   (5) mobile predators.
    (3) fish.

28. Sessile means to

    (1) move around.   (4) float on the surface.
    (2) swim freely.   (5) be firmly attached.
    (3) crawl along the sea floor.

29. Invertebrates such as zooplankton are

    (1) voracious predators.
    (2) powerful swimmers.
    (3) fish.
    (4) voluntarily able to move from one ocean current to another.
    (5) tiny enough to float near the surface.

Item 30 refers to the following passage.

The body of an animal consists of several levels of organization. Atoms, such as hydrogen and oxygen, build the molecules, such as water, in the organism. These chemicals provide the framework for the organelles in a cell. The cell is the minimal unit in an organism that displays the properties of life. A tissue is a group of similar cells carrying out a common function. Two or more tissues compose an organ. Related organs belong to the same organ system.

30. A student is handed a model of a brain and is asked to identify the level-of-organization it represents. This model represents a(n)

    (1) cell
    (2) organ

(3)   organ system
(4)   organelle
(5)   tissue

31.   Carbon dioxide is a major contributor to global warming. It is released
into the atmosphere when the organic matter contained in fossil fuels
is burned. Which of the following is an effective means of reducing the
production of carbon dioxide?

(1)   recycling paper produced from trees
(2)   cutting trees for wood
(3)   reducing the amount of livestock
(4)   burning more fossil fuels
(5)   burning wood

Items 32 to 38 refer to the following paragraph.

An animal cell is composed of many parts. The outside of the cell is
surrounded by a membrane. The cell membrane is selective, which
means that it only allows certain things in or out of the cell. The inside of
the cell is composed of various cell organelles (little organs) and the
matrix in which they are suspended. The matrix is called the cytoplasm.
One of the most conspicuous objects in the cytoplasm is the nucleus. The
nucleus is a large spherical structure. It is composed of a nuclear membrane which, like the cell membrane, is selective. Inside the nucleus is a
viscous matrix, the nucleoplasm. Suspended in the nucleoplasm are the
chromosomes and the nucleoli. The nucleoli are dark staining spherical
structures that are thought to function in the production of ribosomes,
structures that are involved in protein synthesis. The chromosomes, the
number of which may vary from organism to organism, are elongated
threadlike structures that cannot be seen with a normal microscope.
However, during cell division, the chromosomes coil up and become
visible. Some other cell organelles include the mitochondria and the
vacuoles. The mitochondria produce energy for the cell. The vacuoles are
used as storage centers. They may store food, water, or waste products.

32.   Which of the following is the first barrier of defense that a foreign
molecule must face upon entering an animal cell?

(1)   Nucleoplasm   (4)   Chromosomes
(2)   Cytoplasm   (5)   Cell membrane
(3)   Nuclear membrane

33. The number of elongated threadlike chromosomes that can be visualized during cell division

   (1) depends on the random manner in which the chromosomes reassemble during coiling.
   (2) varies among the different types of somatic cells within one organism.
   (3) depends on the strength of the microscope.
   (4) is the same for somatic cells within one individual.
   (5) is influenced by the presence of the nucleoli, which are also suspended in the nucleoplasm.

34. Since nucleoli are involved in the formation of ribosomes, it follows that

   (1) ribosomes must be located in the nucleus so as not to be far from their origin.
   (2) ribosomes must be transferred from the nucleus to the cytoplasm in order to function in protein synthesis.
   (3) ribosomes must be transferred to the area where they can produce energy for the cell.
   (4) the coiling of the chromosomes always hinders the formation of the ribosomes.
   (5) ribosomes must also be dark staining.

35. Since the cell membrane and nuclear membrane are selective in nature, they can be considered

   (1) totally permeable.   (4) opaque.
   (2) nonpermeable.   (5) translucent.
   (3) semipermeable.

36. Dark staining spherical structures in the nucleus are

   (1) nucleoplasm.   (4) chromosomes.
   (2) cytoplasm.   (5) mitochondria.
   (3) nucleoli.

37. Which of the following are used as storage structures in a cell?

   (1) Ribosomes   (4) Nucleoli
   (2) Mitochondria   (5) Chromosomes
   (3) Vacuoles

38. Which structures are thought to be involved in making ribosomes?

   (1) Chromosomes   (4) Mitochondria
   (2) Nucleoli   (5) Cytoplasm
   (3) Vacuoles

Items 39 to 41 refer to the following information.

Ernest Rutherford's (1871-1937) experiment provided the basis for the description of an atom's structure. In his experiment, alpha particles were directed toward a thin gold foil. Most particles went through the foil in a fairly straight line, but a few particles were deflected at sharp angles. A diagram of the experiment is shown below.

RUTHERFORD'S APPARATUS FOR OBSERVING THE SCATTERING OF ALPHA PARTICLES BY A METAL FOIL (within a vacuum chamber)

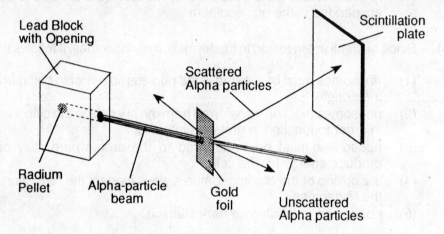

39. Why were some alpha particles deflected at sharp angles?

    (1) The particles did not have enough velocity to penetrate the gold foil, which may have been too thick in some areas.
    (2) The alpha particles were hitting electrons.
    (3) The alpha particles were colliding with atomic nuclei.
    (4) The alpha particles were being repelled from the gold since both alpha particles and gold possess the the same charge.
    (5) The surrounding air pulled the alpha particles from the area where the gold foil was located.

40. Why do most alpha particles pass through the gold foil without being deflected?

    (1) Most of the atom is empty space which alpha particles can pass through unaffected.
    (2) The gold foil was mostly thin enough to allow alpha particles to pass through.
    (3) The electrons did not get in the way.
    (4) The atomic nuclei are semipermeable.
    (5) The alpha particles move so fast that they push the atomic nuclei out of the way.

41.   The symbol for gold is

(1)   Ga.   (4)   Na.
(2)   Hg.   (5)   Au.
(3)   He.

Item 42 refers to the following passage.

Fungi can produce a variety of human diseases. Spores cause many of these diseases, such as histoplasmosis, a respiratory disease. Spores are airborne reproductive bodies that are part of the life cycle of the fungi.

42.   A person most likely gets histoplasmosis via the

(1)   circulatory system.
(2)   digestive system.
(3)   nervous system.
(4)   reproductive system.
(5)   respiratory system.

Item 43 refers to the following figure.

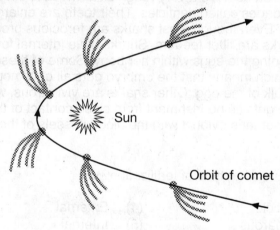

The tail of the comet consists of dust and ionized gases. When the tail is present the head glows and is called a coma.

43.   Which of the following is the best explanation of the above view of a comet orbiting about the sun?

(1)   The tail of the comet appears when the solar winds are blowing.
(2)   The tail of the comet appears when the comet moves away from the sun.
(3)   The tail of the comet is pushed away from the sun by the solar winds.

(4) The tail of the comet is attracted to the sun by the solar winds.
(5) Insufficient information provided.

44. A fossilized bone contains the radioactive isotope carbon fourteen. The half-life of this isotope is one million years. Every one million years, the isotope loses one-half of its radioactivity. An analysis of the isotope in this bone reveals that one-sixteenth of the radioactivity of the bone remains in this fossil. The age of the bone is _____ million years.

(1) two
(2) four
(3) eight
(4) sixteen
(5) thirty-two

Items 45 to 48 refer to the following paragraph.

Sharks are vertebrate animals and their skeleton is composed of cartilage. Sharks are not in the class Osteichthyes because sharks do not have bony skeletons. The shark is a member of the class Chondrichtheyes. Other members of this class included the rays, skates, and dogfishes. Sharks have a very rough skin, which is covered with little toothlike appendages called denticles. Their teeth are enlarged versions of the denticles. Even though most sharks are ferocious predators, the two largest sharks are filter feeders. Sharks have internal fertilization with the female retaining the eggs within her body. Some of these sharks are ovoviparous, which means that the embryo gets all of its nourishment or food from the yolk of the egg. Other sharks are viviparous, which means that the embryo gets its nourishment from close contact of the blood vessels of the mother's oviduct with the blood vessels of the yolk.

45. Sharks have what type of fertilization?

(1) Denticle
(2) Viviparous
(3) Ovoviparous
(4) External
(5) Internal

46. Sharks are members of the

(1) phylum Reptilia.
(2) class Aves.
(3) class Vertebrata.
(4) class Osteichthyes.
(5) class Chondrichthyes.

47. If a shark is said to be viviparous, then

(1) as an embryo it eats its brothers and sisters before they hatch.
(2) as an embryo it gets nourishment from the yolk.
(3) as an embryo it gets its nourishment directly from the mother's blood.
(4) as an embryo it gets its nourishment by eating the mother's oviduct.
(5) as an embryo it gets its nourishment from the yolk's blood vessels, which are close to the the oviduct's blood vessels.

48. The part of a whale most related to fish scales would be the

(1) denticles.   (4) embryos.
(2) yolks.   (5) internal fertilization.
(3) oviducts.

Items 49 to 50 refer to the following paragraph.

A plant contains organs arranged in what is known as the shoot system and the root system. The shoot system is that portion of the plant that is above the ground, and the root system is that portion of the plant that is usually under the ground. The root system functions as an anchor, and absorbs water and minerals from the ground. The stem supports the leaves and the flowers. The leaves function in photosynthesis while the flowers function as reproductive organs, which ultimately produce seeds.

49. That portion of the plant that is involved with the absorption of water and minerals is the

(1) flower.   (4) stomata.
(2) stem.   (5) leaves.
(3) root.

50. Seeds are produced from

(1) nodes.   (4) flowers.
(2) internodes.   (5) tubers.
(3) stomata.

TEST 4: LANGUAGE ARTS: READING

Tests of General Educational Development

Directions

The Language Arts: Reading Test consists of excerpts from classical and popular literature and articles about literature or the arts. Each excerpt is followed by multiple-choice questions about the reading material.

Read each excerpt first and then answer the questions following it. Refer back to the reading material as often as necessary in answering the questions.

Each excerpt is preceded by a "purpose question." The purpose question gives a reason for reading the material. Use these purpose questions to help focus your reading. You are not required to answer these purpose questions. They are given only to help you concentrate on the ideas presented in the reading materials.

You should spend no more than 65 minutes answering the questions in this booklet. Work carefully, but do not spend too much time on any one question. Be sure you answer every question. You will not be penalized for incorrect answers.

Do not mark in this test booklet. Record your answers on the separate answer sheet provided. Be sure all requested information is properly recorded on the answer sheet. To record your answers, mark the numbered space on the answer sheet beside the number that corresponds to the question in the test booklet.

FOR EXAMPLE:

It was Susan's dream machine. The metallic blue paint gleamed, and the sporty wheels were highly polished. Under the hood, the engine was no less carefully cleaned. Inside, flashy lights illuminated the instruments on the dashboard, and the seats were covered by rich leather upholstery.

The subject ("It") of this excerpt is most likely

(1)　an airplane.　　　　(4)　a boat.
(2)　a stereo system.　　(5)　a motorcycle.
(3)　an automobile.

The correct answer is "an automobile"; therefore, answer space 3 would be marked on the answer sheet.

Do not rest the point of your pencil on the answer sheet while you are considering your answer. Make no stray or unnecessary marks. If you change an answer, erase your first mark completely. Mark only one answer space for each question; multiple answers will be scored as incorrect. Do not fold or crease your answer sheet. Return all test materials to the test administrator.

Reprinted with permission of the General Educational Development Testing Service of the American Council on Education.

Directions: Choose the <u>one best answer</u> to each item.

<u>Items 1 to 5</u> are based on the following excerpt.

HOW DOES ADVENTURE FIT INTO LIFE?

TOM: —Oh.—Laura...

AMANDA: (*touching his sleeve*) You know how Laura is. So quiet but—still water runs deep! She notices things and I think she—broods about them. (*Tom looks up.*) A few days ago I came in and she was crying.

TOM: What about?

AMANDA: You.

TOM: Me?

AMANDA: She has an idea that you're not happy here.

TOM: What gave her that idea?

AMANDA: What gives her any idea? However, you do act strangely. I—I'm not criticizing, understand that! I know your ambitions do not lie in the warehouse, that like everybody in the whole wide world—you've had to—make sacrifices, but—Tom—Tom—life's not easy, it calls for—Spartan endurance! There's so many things in my heart that I cannot describe to you! I've never told you but I—loved your father....

TOM: (*gently*) I know that, Mother.

AMANDA: And you—when I see you taking after his ways! Staying out late—and—well, you had been drinking the night you were in that—terrifying condition! Laura says that you hate the apartment and that you go out nights to get away from it! Is that true, Tom?

TOM: No. You say there's so much in your heart that you can't describe to me. That's true of me, too. There's so much in my heart that I can't describe to you! So let's respect each other's—

AMANDA: But, why—why, Tom—are you always so restless? Where do you go to, nights?

TOM: I—go to the movies.

AMANDA: Why do you go to the movies so much, Tom?

TOM: I go to the movies because—I like adventure. Adventure is something I don't have much of at work, so I go to the movies.

AMANDA: But, Tom, you go to the movies entirely too much!

TOM: I like a lot of adventure.

Amanda looks baffled, then hurt. As the familiar inquisition resumes he becomes hard and impatient again. Amanda slips back into her querulous attitude toward him.

AMANDA: Most young men find adventure in their careers.

TOM: Then most young men are not employed in a warehouse.

AMANDA: The world is full of young men employed in warehouses and offices and factories.

TOM: Do all of them find adventure in their careers?

AMANDA: They do or they do without it! Not everybody has a craze for adventure.

TOM: Man is by instinct a lover, a hunter, a fighter, and none of those instincts are given much play at the warehouse!

AMANDA: Man is by instinct! Don't quote instinct to me! Instinct is something that people have got away from! It belongs to animals! Christian adults don't want it!

TOM: What do Christian adults want, then, Mother?

AMANDA: Superior things! Things of the mind and the spirit! Only animals have to satisfy instincts! Surely your aims are somewhat higher than theirs! Than monkeys—pigs—

TOM: I reckon they're not.

From "The Glass Menagerie," by Tennessee Williams

1.   Why is Laura upset?

    (1)   Tom has left home.
    (2)   Tom goes to the movies without her.
    (3)   She thinks Tom is unhappy.
    (4)   Tom cannot describe his feelings.
    (5)   Tom is happy with her.

2.   Tom goes to the movies

    (1)   because he wants to be an actor.
    (2)   because he likes to be alone.
    (3)   because he is Christian.
    (4)   because he is restless.
    (5)   because he wants to be away from Amanda.

3. Amanda is upset because

    (1)   Tom wants to quit his job.
    (2)   Tom is always out.
    (3)   Tom made Laura cry.
    (4)   Tom is a pig.
    (5)   Tom is unfaithful.

4. We can tell from this passage that Tom and Amanda

    (1)   are very open with each other.
    (2)   fight often.
    (3)   are adventurous.
    (4)   are happy.
    (5)   agree on everything.

5. Amanda thinks Tom

    (1)   should go out more.
    (2)   should get a better job.
    (3)   should apologize to his sister.
    (4)   should be satisfied with what he has.
    (5)   should take her to the movies.

Items 6 to 10 refer to the following passage.

A SALES CONTRACT

Richard Pojman is selling his clothing store, the Regal Men's Store, to Emily Barnes. Below is a part of the sales contract.

Seller's obligation pending closing. **The Seller promises and agrees with the Buyer as follows:**

(1) The Seller shall conduct the business up to the date of closing in a regular and normal manner and shall use his best efforts to keep available to the Buyer the services of its present employees and to preserve the goodwill of the Seller's suppliers and customers.

(2) The Seller shall keep and maintain an accurate record of all items of inventory sold during the ordinary course of business from January 31, 2005 up until the date of closing.

(3) The Seller shall give the Buyer or his representative full access during the normal business hours to the business premises, records, and properties, and shall furnish the Buyer with such information concerning operation of the business as the Buyer may reasonably request.

(4) The Seller shall deliver to the Buyer's attorney for examination and approval prior to the closing date such bills of sale and instruments of assignment as in the opinion of the Buyer's attorney shall be necessary to vest in the Buyer good and marketable title to the business, assets and goodwill of the Seller.

Risk of loss. The Seller assumes all risk of destruction, loss or damage due to fire or other casualty up to the date of closing. If any destruction, loss or damage occurs and is such that the business of the Seller is interrupted, curtailed or otherwise materially affected, the Buyer shall have the right to terminate this agreement. If any destruction, loss or damage occurs which does not interrupt, curtail or otherwise materially affect the business, the purchase price shall be adjusted at the closing to reflect such destruction, loss or damage.

Covenant not to compete. The Seller promises to the Buyer that for a period of five years after the closing date, he will not, directly or indirectly, either as principal, agent, manager, employee, owner, partner, stockholder, director or officer of a corporation, engage in any business similar to or in competition with the business hereby sold, within a fifty mile radius of Central City, Illinois.

6.   According to the document, which party assumes all risk of destruction, loss, or damage up to the date of closing?

    (1)   the Buyer   (4)   the customers
    (2)   the Seller   (5)   the suppliers
    (3)   the attorneys

7.   What will happen if there is any destruction, loss or damage that does not interrupt, curtail or otherwise materially affect the business?

    (1)   The contract will be cancelled.
    (2)   There will be no change in the contract.
    (3)   The purchase price shall be adjusted at the closing to reflect the cost of the damages.
    (4)   The Seller shall compensate the Buyer.
    (5)   The closing date will delayed.

8.   How many obligations does the seller agree to in this document?

    (1)   four   (4)   two
    (2)   five   (5)   three
    (3)   one

9. According to the Seller's obligations pending closing section of the document, the seller shall keep and maintain an accurate record of all items of inventory sold in the ordinary course of business from when until when?

    (1) From January 1, 2002 until the date of closing
    (2) From February 31, 2002 until the date of closing
    (3) From February 1, 2002 until the date of closing
    (4) From January 31, 2002 until the date of closing
    (5) For two years, until January 31, 2002

10. For how long a period of time does the Seller promise that he will not engage in any business similar to that of the business he is selling?

    (1) one year
    (2) three years
    (3) five years
    (4) seven years
    (5) ten years

Items 11 to 14 refer to the following passage.

IS THIS ARTIST "AMERICA'S FIRST MODERNIST PAINTER"?

1   The atmosphere is one of sunlit charm. Children ride merry-go-rounds. Tourists festively promenade up the Spanish steps in Rome. Parasol-toting weekenders buy balloons on the South Boston Pier. This is the turn-of-the century world brought to life in

5   Maurice Prendergast's paintings and watercolors. This world view is also, unfortunately, the main reason that Prendergast has remained a neglected artist. Ostensibly, such vibrant images were the product of an artist who has taken all the work out and left only the joy. Little wonder then that the modernist movement found

10   Prendergast's work too easy and tranquil and shouldered him to the sidelines. Now, it is startling to learn that some historians consider him America's first modernist painter: the first to journey to Paris, to become familiar with the new trends in art, and to spread the word back in America….

15   Boston was Prendergast's home for all but twelve years of his life, although his five trips to Europe and his many sojourns to New York City—where he became a member of the group known as "The Eight" and exhibited in the famous 1913 Armory Show— were the greatest influences on his work. His art, as with any true

20   pathfinder, resists easy classification. From the Impressionists he took his improvisational brushwork; from the Postimpressionists, his subjective, stylized view of reality; from the Nabis—Pierre Bonnard in particular—his decorative expression of color. This rich stew was then flavored with a gentle simplicity to create a uniquely

25   American mix.

Above all, his color—or rather, the amount he used—was new. He would have none of the "brown sauce" with which many Bostonian artists of the day served up their paintings. In fact, he used so many colors, one critic called his work "an explosion in a

30   color factory." To this spectrum, he added a sparklingly animated line that blocked out forms as fluidly as an abstractionist—forms he also used in more than two hundred masterful monotypes.

As this show reveals, Prendergast (1859–1924) was an important link between the masters of the nineteenth century and the

35   new ones of the twentieth....

Thoroughly Modern Maurice, AMERICAN PAINTER, "Exhibits," ed. Robert I. C. Fisher, October 1990, p. 12, Copyright 1990, by BPI Communications, Inc., a subsidiary of Affiliated Publications,1515 Broadway, New York.

11.   Which of the following statements best expresses the irony, or turn of events, involving the artist reviewed?

(1)   The modernist movement rejected him.
(2)   His art resists easy classification.
(3)   Although rejected by modernists, some historians consider him America's first modernist painter.
(4)   He is an important link between the 19th and 20th centuries.
(5)   He combines richness and simplicity.

12.   Lines 5–11 suggest that modernist critics felt that Prendergast's work was too

(1)   conservative.   (4)   ordinary.
(2)   careless.   (5)   suggestive.
(3)   carefree.

13.   In line 20, the description "pathfinder" most closely means

(1)   his work was unlike any of his predecessors.
(2)   his work was difficult to classify.
(3)   the artist was a hard worker.
(4)   the artist made it easier for his successors.
(5)   the artist was influenced by the Impressionists.

14.   Of all Prendergast's techniques, the most revolutionary was

(1)   his improvisational brushwork.
(2)   his stylized view of reality.
(3)   his decorative expression of color.
(4)   the amount of color he used.
(5)   All of the above.

Items 15 to 18 refer to the following passage.

WHAT ARE THE HUSBAND'S AND WIFE'S ATTITUDES TOWARD EACH OTHER?

1   "Father!"

"What is it?"

"What are them men diggin' over there in the field for?"

There was a sudden dropping and enlarging of the part of the

5   old man's face, as if some heavy weight had settled therein; he shut his mouth tight, and went on harnessing the bay mare. He hustled the collar on to her neck with a jerk.

"Father!"

The old man slapped the saddle upon the mare's back.

10   "Look here, father, I want to know what them men are diggin' over in the field for, an' I'm goin' to know."

"I wish you'd go into the house, mother, an' 'tend to your own affairs," the old man said then. He ran his words together, and his speech was almost as inarticulate as a growl.

15   But the woman understood; it was her most native tongue. "I ain't goin' into the house till you tell me what them men are doin' over there in the field," said she.

The old man glanced doggedly at his wife as he tightened the last buckles on the harness. She looked as immovable to him as

20   one of the rocks in his pasture-land, bound to the earth with generations of blackberry vines. He slapped the reins over the horse, and started forth from the barn.

"Father!" said she.

The old man pulled up. "What is it?"

25   "I want to know what them men are diggin' over there in that field for."

"They're digging a cellar, I s'pose, if you've got to know."

"A cellar for what?"

"A barn."

30   "A barn? You ain't goin' to build a barn over there where we was goin' to have a house, father?"

The old man said not another word. He hurried the horse into the farm wagon, and clattered out of the yard, jouncing as sturdily on his seat as a boy.

From "The Revolt of Mother," Mary Wilkins Freeman (c. 1892).

15. By saying, "I wish you'd go into the house, mother, an' 'tend to your own affairs," (line 12) father implies

    (1)   her work is not done.
    (2)   he has no time to talk.
    (3)   he will meet her inside.
    (4)   they will talk later.
    (5)   she has no business in the goings on outside the house.

16. This passage is a good example of

    (1) rhyme.   (4) dialect.
    (2) meter.   (5) exaggeration.
    (3) irony.

17. Mother can be best described as

    (1) quiet.   (4) humorous.
    (2) strong-willed.   (5) pleasant.
    (3) subservient.

18. Mother's question, "barn? You ain't goin' to build a barn over there where we was goin' to have a house, father?" (line 30) suggests that

    (1) father is going back on his promise to build her a house.
    (2) father changed the location of the barn.
    (3) mother is pleased with father's intentions.
    (4) mother wants to help with the construction.
    (5) mother doesn't think they can afford to build a barn.

Items 19 to 25 refer to the following poem.

IN EXCERPTS FROM HIS NARRATIVE POEM, WHAT TECHNIQUES
DOES THE POET USE TO TELL HIS STORY?

1   The wind was a torrent of darkness among the gusty trees,
       The moon was a ghostly galleon tossed upon cloudy seas,
       The road was a ribbon of moonlight over the purple moor,
       And the highwayman came riding—
5   Riding—riding—
       The highwayman came riding, up to the old inn-door.

       He'd a French cocked-hat on his forehead, a bunch of lace at his chin,
       A coat of the claret velvet, and breaches of brown doe-skin:
10   They fitted with never a wrinkle: his boots were up to the thigh!
       And he rode with a jewelled twinkle,
       His pistol butts a twinkle,
       His rapier hilt a-twinkle, under the jewelled sky.
       Over the cobbles he clattered and clashed in the dark inn-yard,
15   And he tapped with his whip on the shutters, but all was locked and barred;
       He whistled a tune to the window, and who should be waiting there
       But the landlord's black-eyed daughter,

20   Bess, the landlord's daughter,
        Plaiting a dark red love-knot into her long black hair.

        And dark in the dark old inn-yard a stable-wicket creaked
        Where Tim the ostler listened, his face was white and peaked;
        His eyes were hallows of madness, his hair like mouldy hay,
25   But he loved the landlord's daughter,
        The landlord's red-lipped daughter,
        Dumb as a dog he listened, and he heard the robber say—
        "One kiss, my bonny sweetheart, I'm after a prize to-night,
        But I shall be back with the yellow gold before the morning light;
30   Yet, if they press me sharply, and harry me through the day,
        Then look for me by moonlight,
        Watch for me by moonlight,
        I'll come to thee by moonlight, though hell should bar the way."

—passages from *The Highwayman*, by Alfred Noyes, *The Family Book of Verse*, selected and edited by Lewis Gannett, New York: Harper and Row, 1961, pp. 75–76.

19.   These stanzas tell a story and are excerpts from

    (1)   a sonnet.   (4)   a folk ballad.
    (2)   a narrative poem.   (5)   an epic poem.
    (3)   a limerick.

20.   Lines 1, 2, and 3 are examples of a poetic technique that

    (1)   explicitly compares two essentially unlike objects.
    (2)   implicitly compares two objects.
    (3)   rhymes.
    (4)   grossly exaggerates.
    (5)   entertains the reader.

21.   In lines 6–14, the highwayman is described as

    (1)   a villain.   (4)   a soldier in the king's army.
    (2)   a nondescript individual. (5)   a coward.
    (3)   a dashing and romantic figure.

22.   In line 21, the red ribbon is most likely a symbol of Bess's

    (1)   vanity.   (4)   availability.
    (2)   patriotism.   (5)   greed.
    (3)   love.

23. The one implicit comparison of two unlike objects, a metaphor, used in lines 23–27 is

   (1) "His face was white and peaked."
   (2) "His eyes were hallows of madness."
   (3) "His hair like mouldy hay."
   (4) "The landlord's red-lipped daughter."
   (5) "Dumb as a dog he listened."

24. A close reading of the dialogue in lines 28–33 suggest that the hero

   (1) has reformed.   (4) will join the king's army.
   (2) will marry Bess.   (5) None of the above.
   (3) has planned a robbery tonight.

25. The meter of the poem is somewhat suggestive of

   (1) a waterfall.   (4) horses' hoof beats.
   (2) a bugle call.   (5) a folk song.
   (3) a drumroll.

Items 26 to 32 refer to the following passage.

WHAT IS THE AUTHOR REVEALING TO YOU ABOUT THE NARRATOR'S STATE OF MIND?

1　　　True!—nervous—very, very dreadfully nervous I had been and am! but why will you say that I am mad? The disease had sharpened my senses—not destroyed—not dulled them. Above all was the sense of hearing acute. I heard all things in the heaven and in
5　　the earth. I heard many things in hell. How, then, am I mad? Hearken! and observe how healthily—how calmly I can tell you the whole story.
　　　It is impossible to say how first the idea entered my brain: but once conceived, it haunted me day and night. Object there was
10　　none. Passion there was none. I loved the old man. He had never wronged me. He had never given me insult. For his gold I had no desire. I think it was his eye! yes, it was this! One of his eyes whenever it fell upon me, my blood ran cold; and so by degrees— very gradually—I made up my mind to take the life of the old man,
15　　and thus rid myself of the eye forever.
　　　Now this is the point. You fancy me mad. Madmen know nothing. But you should have seen me. You should have seen how wisely I proceeded— with what caution—with what foresight—with what dissimilation I went to work!
20　　　I was never kinder to the old man than during the whole week

25   before I killed him. And every night, about midnight, I turned the
latch of his door and opened it—oh, so gently! And then, when I
had made an opening sufficient for my head, I put in a dark lantern, all closed, closed so that no light shone out, and then I thrust
in my head. Oh, you would nave laughed to see how cunningly I
thrust it in! I moved it slowly—very, very slowly, so that I might lay
upon his bed. Ha!—would a madman have been so wise as this?
And then, when my head was well in the room, I undid the lantern
cautiously—oh, so cautiously—cautiously (for the hinges

30   creaked)—I undid it just so much that a single ray fell upon the
vulture eye. And this I did for seven long nights—every night just
at midnight—but I found the eye always closed; and so it was
impossible to do the work; for it was not the old man who vexed
me, but his Evil Eye. And every morning, when the day broke, I

35   went boldly into the chamber, and spoke courageously to him,
calling him by name in a hearty tone, and inquiring how he had
passed the night. So you see he would have been a very profound
old man, indeed, to suspect that every night, just at twelve I looked
in upon him while he slept.

The Tell-Tale Heart, Edgar Allan Poe, *Collected Works of Edgar Allan Poe* (Tales and Sketches,
1843–1849), Edited by Thomas Olive Mabbott, Cambridge, Ma: The Belknap Press of Harvard
University Press, 1978, pp. 792–793.

26.   In lines 1–7, the reader can sense that the speaker is

    (1)   clever.   (4)   intelligent.
    (2)   angry.   (5)   suicidal.
    (3)   crazy.

27.   The statement, "For his gold I had no desire," (lines 11–12) suggests
that the old man

    (1)   is penniless.
    (2)   is financially well off.
    (3)   is charitable.
    (4)   hoards (or accumulates) all of his money.
    (5)   collects cans.

28.   The only motive mentioned in lines 9–15 is

    (1)   to find peace and tranquility without the old man.
    (2)   to gain wealth from old man's gold.
    (3)   to win power and respect.
    (4)   to rid himself of the eye.
    (5)   None of the above.

29. The statement "Ha! would a madman have been so wise as this?" proves that the speaker

   (1)   is mad.
   (2)   wishes us to believe he is not mad.
   (3)   is not mad.
   (4)   is very clever.
   (5)   is concerned about the old man.

30. On each of his seven attempts to kill the old man, the speaker finds

   (1)   the door locked.
   (2)   someone thwarting his plans.
   (3)   he has a change of heart.
   (4)   the old man's eye is closed.
   (5)   the old man has not fallen asleep.

31. The narrator's intentions in lines 34–39 are best described as

   (1)   proud and self-serving.   (4)   hesitant.
   (2)   sincere and honorable.   (5)   frivolous.
   (3)   charitable.

32. The general tone of the narration is

   (1)   tranquil.   (4)   hostile.
   (2)   fearful.   (5)   anxious.
   (3)   reverential.

Items 33 to 40 refer to the following passage.

WHAT IS THE SPEAKER'S VIEW OF LIFE AND NATURE AS REVEALED IN EXCERPTS FROM HIS ESSAYS BELOW?

Why should we be in such desperate haste to succeed, and in such desperate enterprises? If a man does not keep pace with his companions, perhaps it is because he hears a different drummer. Let him step to the music which he hears, however measured or
5   far away. It is not important that he should mature as soon as an apple-tree or an oak. Shall he turn his spring into summer? If the condition of things which we were made for is not yet, what were any reality which we can substitute? We will not be shipwrecked on a vain reality. Shall we with pains erect a heaven of blue glass
10   over ourselves, though when it is done we shall be sure to gaze still at the true ethereal heaven far above, as if the former were not?

However mean your life is, meet it and live it; do not shun it and call it hard names. It is not so bad as you are. It looks poorest

15   when you are richest. The fault-finder will find faults even in
paradise. Love your life, poor as it is. You may perhaps have
some pleasant, thrilling, glorious hours, even in a poorhouse. The
setting sun is reflected from the windows of the alms-house as
brightly as from the rich man's abode; the snow melts before its
20   door as early in the spring. I do not see but a quiet mind may live
as contentedly there, and have as cheering thoughts, as in a
palace.
      Rather than love, than money, than fame, give me truth. I sat at
a table where were rich food and wine in abundance and obsequi-
25   ous attendance, but sincerity and truth were not; and I went away
hungry from the inhospitable board. The hospitality was as cold as
the ices. I thought that there was no need of ice to freeze them.
They talked to me of the age of the wine and the fame of the
vintage; but I thought of an older, newer, and purer wine, of a
30   more glorious vintage, which they had not got, and could not buy.
The style, the house and the grounds and "entertainment" pass for
nothing with me. I called on the king, but he made me wait in his
hall, and conducted like a man incapacitated for hospitality. There
was a man in my neighborhood who lived in a hollow tree. His
35   manners were truly regal. I should have done better had I called
on him.

—Excerpts from *Walden* (XVIII, Conclusions), by Henry David Thoreau, ed. Walter Harding, New
York: Washington Square Press, a division of Simon and Schuster, Copyright 1962, 1967, pp. 247,
248, 250.

33. The essential message of lines 1–12 have to do mainly with

     (1)   salvation of souls.
     (2)   society's pressure for success.
     (3)   surviving in nature.
     (4)   economy.
     (5)   playing a musical instrument.

34. Lines 2 and 3, "If a man does not keep pace with his companions,
     perhaps it is because he hears a different drummer," are used

     (1)   as figures of speech.   (4)   as a paradox.
     (2)   in their literal sense.   (5)   as a touch of humor.
     (3)   as an overstatement.

35. The imagery used in the excerpt deals primarily with

     (1)   nature.   (4)   heaven.
     (2)   material wealth.   (5)   death.
     (3)   animals.

36. The term "mean," in line 13, most closely is a synonym for

    (1) unkind.   (4) humble.
    (2) benevolent.   (5) lonely.
    (3) wealthy.

37. Lines 13–17 suggest

    (1) material wealth and happiness are compatible.
    (2) wealthy people cannot attain true happiness.
    (3) people who are not wealthy are happy.
    (4) true happiness is not a result of material wealth.
    (5) true happiness is not attainable.

38. Which of the following best describes the author's attitude toward material wealth in the second paragraph?

    (1) Sympathetic   (4) Contemptuous
    (2) Accepting   (5) Nonappreciative
    (3) Envious

39. What is the general theme of the third paragraph?

    (1) Those who live with truth and sincerity are wealthy.
    (2) Material gain is the only truth.
    (3) Vintage wine and hospitality are solely for the rich.
    (4) Mankind is basically greedy.
    (5) Man has dominion over nature.

40. The "older, newer, and purer wine" referred to in line 29 is most probably

    (1) nature.   (4) a rare, vintage wine.
    (2) material wealth.   (5) heaven.
    (3) truth and sincerity.

TEST 5: MATHEMATICS

Tests of General Educational Development

Directions

The Mathematics Test consists of multiple-choice and free-response questions intended to measure general mathematics skills and problem-solving ability. The questions are based on short readings which often include a graph, chart, or figure.

There are two separate sections of the Mathematics Test: Part 1 and Part 2. Part 1 allows the use of a calculator. Part 2 does not. You should spend no more than 45 minutes answering the questions in each part of the math test. Work carefully, but do not spend too much time on any one question. Be sure you answer every question. You will not be penalized for incorrect answers.

Formulas you may need are given on the following page. Only some of the questions will require you to use a formula. Not all the formulas given will be needed.

Some questions contain more information than you will need to solve the problem. Other questions do not give enough information to solve the problem. If the question does not give enough information to solve the problem, the correct answer choice is "Not enough information is given."

Do not mark in this test booklet. The test administrator will give you blank paper for your calculations. Record your answers on the separate answer sheet provided. Be sure all requested information is properly recorded on the answer sheet.

To record your answers, mark the numbered space on the answer sheet beside the number that corresponds to the question in the test booklet.

FOR EXAMPLE:

If a grocery bill totaling $15.75 is paid with a $20.00 bill, how much change should be returned?

(1)	$5.26	(4)	$3.75
(2)	$4.75	(5)	$3.25
(3)	$4.25		

① ② ● ④ ⑤

The correct answer is "$4.25"; therefore, answer space 3 would be marked on the answer sheet.

Do not rest the point of your pencil on the answer sheet while you are considering your answer. Make no stray or unnecessary marks. If you change an answer, erase your first mark completely. Mark only one answer space for each question; multiple answers will be scored as incorrect. Do not fold or crease your answer sheet. Return all test materials to the test administrator.

Reprinted with permission of the General Educational Development Testing Service of the American Council on Education.

REFERENCE TABLE

SYMBOLS AND THEIR MEANINGS

=	is equal to	$\leq$	is less than or equal to
$\neq$	is unequal to	$\geq$	is greater than or equal to
<	is less than	$\parallel$	is parallel to
>	is greater than	$\perp$	is perpendicular to

FORMULAS

DESCRIPTION	FORMULA

AREA (A) of a:

square $A = s^2$; where s = side

rectangle $A = lw$; where l = length, w = width

parallelogram $A = bh$; where b = base, h = height

triangle $A = \frac{1}{2}\,bh$; where b = base, h = height

circle $A = \pi r^2$; where π = 3.14, r = radius

PERIMETER (P) of a:

square $P = 4s$; where s = side

rectangle $P = 2l + 2w$; where l = length, w = width

triangle $P = a + b + c$; where a, b, and c are the sides

circumference (C) of a circle $C = \pi d$, where π = 3.14, d = diameter

VOLUME (V) of a:

cube $V = s^2$; where s = side

rectangular container $V = lwh$; where l = length, w = width, h = height

Pythagorean relationship $c^2 = a^2 + b^2$; where c = hypotenuse, a and b are legs of a right triangle

distance (d) between two points in a plane $d = \sqrt{(x_2 - x_1)^2 + (y_2 - y_1)^2}$

where (x_1, y_1) and (x_2, y_2) are two points in a plane

mean $\text{mean} = \dfrac{x_1 + x_2 + \ldots + x_n}{n}$;

where the x's are the values for which a mean is desired, and n = number of values in the series

median   **median** = the point in an ordered set of numbers at which half of the numbers are above and half of the numbers are below this value

simple interest (i) $i = prt$; where p = principal, r = rate, t = time

distance (d) as function of rate and time $d = rt$; where r = rate, t = time

total cost (c) $c = nr$; where n = number of units, r = cost per unit

PART 1

Calculator Use Permitted

<u>Directions</u>: Choose the <u>one best answer</u> to each item.

1. Find the total cost of these items if the sales tax rate is 5%. Two bottles of aspirin at $4.19 each, two cans of shoe polish at $0.69 each, and three cans of hair spray at $1.15 each.

    (1) $8.38   (4) $13.87
    (2) $13.21   (5) $79.26
    (3) $66.05

2. In a class of 30 students, the mean score on an exam was 80 and the standard deviation was 4. Let *x* represent Peter's standard score. If his raw score was 86, which of the following equations represents the correct solution.

    (1) $86 = 50 + x/4$ (4) $80 = 86 + 4x$
    (2) $86 = 80 + x/4$ (5) $80 = 56 + 4x$
    (3) $86 = 80 + 4x$

3. Ruben tuned up his car. He bought

        spark plugs $ 9.96
        distributor cap $16.95 and
        rotor $ 6.45.

    What was his total cost if the tax rate on parts is 6%?

    (1) $33.36   (4) $34.36
    (2) $32.36   (5) $35.36
    (3) $2.00

4.

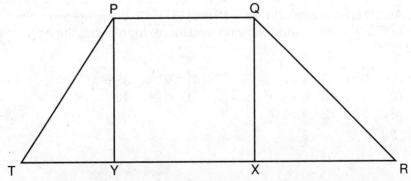

PQRT is a trapezoid and PQXY is a rectangle. TR = 30, PQ = 10, and the area of PQRT is 280. What is the perimeter of PQXY?

(1)   48   (4)   26
(2)   40   (5)   14
(3)   34

5.   Find the area of a circle with a diameter 10 inches. (Use pi = 3.14.)

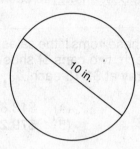

10 in.

(1)   31.4 sq. in.   (4)   78.5 sq. in.
(2)   15.7 sq. in.   (5)   85.25 sq. in.
(3)   31.4 sq. in.

6.

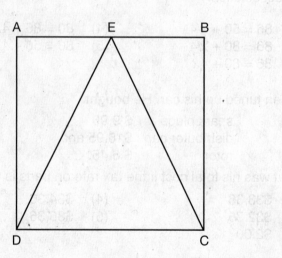

ABCD is a square with AB = 12 and ED = 13. Let x represent the length of EC. Which of the following equations represents the correct solution?

(1) $5^2 + 12^2 = x^2$ (4) $7^2 + 13^2 = x^2$
(2) $5^2 + 13^2 = x^2$ (5) $12^2 + 13^2 = x^2$
(3) $7^2 + 12^2 = x^2$

7. Juan's house is valued at $55,000. The property tax rate is $2.10 per $100 value. What is his property tax?

    (1) $210   (4) $115.50
    (2) $550   (5) $115,500
    (3) $1,155

8.

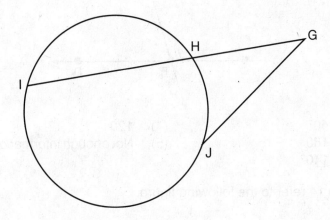

    GI is a secant and GJ is a tangent to the given circle. ∠G = 25° and arc IJ = 140°. How many degrees are there in arc IH?

    (1) 145   (4) 90
    (2) 130   (5) 75
    (3) 115

9. Apples are 2 pounds for $0.98. How much would 5 pounds cost?

    (1) $9.80   (4) $2.45
    (2) $4.90   (5) $0.49
    (3) $1.96

10. There were 350 tickets sold for a concert. Adult tickets were $5.00 each, and student tickets were $3.50 each. The total amount received for tickets sold was $1,306.00. How many of each kind of tickets were sold?

    (1) 296 students & 54 adults   (4) 54 students & 296 adults
    (2) 300 students & 50 adults   (5) 50 students & 300 adults
    (3) 175 students & 175 adults

11. The figure below shows two parallel lines *l* and *m*. Line *H* is intersecting both lines *l* and *m*. Angle *GEB* measures 40°. What is the measure of angle *CFE*?

(1) 40°
(2) 180°
(3) 140°

(4) 120°
(5) Not enough information is given.

Items 12 to 14 refer to the following figure.

High School Grade Point Average of Students Who Graduated from College

For the above chart, the grading is as follows: A = 4, B+ = 3.5, B = 3, C+ = 2.5, C = 2, D+ = 1.5, D = 1. Assume that 800 students were sampled.

12. How many students had grade point averages of at least a B?

(1) 136
(2) 282
(3) 350

(4) 568
(5) 704

13. What total percent scored lower than C+?

    (1) 1   (4) 4
    (2) 2   (5) 5
    (3) 3

14. If the top 1% of students received a monetary award, how many "A" students did not receive this award?

    (1) 448   (4) 296
    (2) 352   (5) 240
    (3) 344

15. A travel agent earns 10% commission on each ticket sold. If the agent sold one ticket for $210 and two for $400, how much would be his commission?

    (1) $18.60   (4) $80.00
    (2) $21.00   (5) $101.00
    (3) $40.00

16. One medical study says golfers consume 300 calories per hour. Jose Gonzalez played golf for 3-1/2 hours. How many calories did he use?

    (1) 100 calories   (4) 250 calories
    (2) 150 calories   (5) 1,050 calories
    (3) 85.71 calories

17.

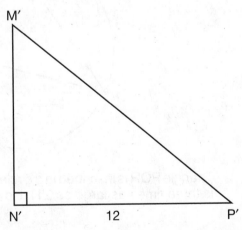

Triangle MNP is similar to triangle M'N'P', with right angles at N and N'. If the area of triangle M'N'P' is 96, what is the area of triangle MNP?

    (1) 90.76   (4) 69.36
    (2) 83.56   (5) 54.86
    (3) 75.46

18. Two water hoses being used simultaneously require two hours to fill up an outdoor pool. If only the larger hose were used, this task would take three hours. Let *x* represent the time needed if only the smaller hose were used to fill the pool. Which of the following equations represents the correct solution?

(1) $\dfrac{x}{2} + \dfrac{2}{3} = 1$ (4) $\dfrac{2}{3} + \dfrac{3}{x} = 1$

(2) $\dfrac{3}{2} - \dfrac{x}{2} = 1$ (5) $\dfrac{2}{3} + \dfrac{2}{x} = 1$

(3) $\dfrac{3}{2} - \dfrac{x}{3} = 1$

Directions: Solve each problem. Write the answer on the answer sheet provided.

19. Mary has some nickels and some quarters worth $4.65. She has three more nickels than quarters. How many coins does she have?

20.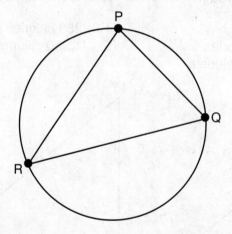

Triangle PQR is inscribed in a circle, as shown above. ∠P = 80° and ∠Q is three times as large as ∠R. How many degrees is arc PQ?

21. Colleen is driving between Harrisburg and Pittsburgh, a distance of 240 miles. For the first part of the trip, she averaged 55 miles per hour. For the remainder of the trip, she averaged only 40 miles per hour. If the entire trip took 4.8 hours, for how many hours did she travel an average of 55 miles per hour?

22. Johnny has 17 marbles. Mary has twice as many marbles as Johnny and half as many as Joe. How many marbles does Mary have?

23. Mike's Machine Repair pays repairmen $0.20 per mile for travel to and from repair jobs. Manny traveled an average of 367 miles per week last year for a 50-week work year. What was his annual travel benefit?

24. What is the value of the median for the following set of numbers?

    10, 18, 9, 22, 12, 30

Directions: Solve the problem below. On the answer sheet, mark the circle on the graph that designates the solution's coordinates.

25. Let $y = -3x - 16$. The domain is $-6 \leq x \leq 6$. On the graph on your answer sheet, locate the point on this line segment which has the highest y value.

PART 2

Calculator Use **Not** Permitted

26. What percent of 80 is 32?

    (1) 40%   (4) 25%
    (2) 0.4%   (5) 400%
    (3) 2.5%

27. Paul had to rent some tools for 3 days for a repair job. He rented a drill at $5 per day and a cement mixer for $20 per day. What was the total rental charge?

    (1) $75.00   (4) $25.00
    (2) $60.00   (5) $15.00
    (3) $35.00

28. Solve $D = rt$ for t.

    (1) $D = rt$ (4) $t = r/D$
    (2) $t = rD$ (5) $t = D/r$
    (3) $t = Dr$

29. Find the area of a regular hexagon with sides 8 inches long.

8 in

    (1) $16\sqrt{3}\,in^2$ (4) 128 in²

    (2) $96\sqrt{2}\,in^2$ (5) $96\sqrt{3}\,in^2$

    (3) 64 in²

30. Simplify: $3x^3 \cdot x^5$

    (1) $3x^{15}$ (4) $8x^3$
    (2) $9x^5$ (5) x^{14}
    (3) $3x^8$

31. Medical insurance costs Maria $26.03 per week. What is the annual cost?

    (1) $312.36   (4) $104.12
    (2) $1,301.50   (5) $1,367.60
    (3) $1,353.56

32. Simplify: $\left(\dfrac{x^2}{y}\right)^5$

    (1) $\dfrac{x^2}{y^5}$ (4) x^8

    (2) $\dfrac{x^7}{y}$ (5) $\dfrac{x^{10}}{y^5}$

    (3) $\dfrac{x^7}{y^5}$

33. What is the measure of exterior angle ACD as shown in the figure below?

    (1) 58°   (4) 108°
    (2) 50°   (5) 130°
    (3) 72°

34. A government fact sheet reveals that the average farmworker produces enough food for 76 people. Approximately how many farm workers are needed to feed a city of 4 million people?

    (1) 304   (4) 304,000,000
    (2) 50,000   (5) 40,000
    (3) 57,000

35. $7(-4y + 2) =$

    (1) $28y + 2$ (4) $-42y$
    (2) $28y + 14$ (5) $-28y + 14$
    (3) $-14y$

36. Which is the best buy for pencils:

    $0.10 each or
    2 dozen for $2.50 or
    10 for $0.99?

    (1) $0.10 each   (4) There is no difference.
    (2) 2 dozen for $2.50   (5) Not enough information is given.
    (3) 10 for $0.99

37. Factor: $x^2 + 6x + 9$

    (1) $x(x + 6)$ (4) $(x - 3)^2$
    (2) $(x - 3)(x - 3)$ (5) $(x - 3)(x + 3)$
    (3) $(x + 3)^2$

38. Sally entered a certain sweepstakes 8 times. There were 1,600 entries. What are her chances of winning?

    (1) 0.5%   (4) 12.8%
    (2) 5%   (5) 128%
    (3) 50%

39. Ira has enough seed to plant a garden of 220 square feet. He has a place 20 feet long to put the garden. How wide must it be to have exactly 220 square feet?

? | 220 sq. ft.

20 feet

    (1) 20 ft.   (4) 11 ft.
    (2) 10 ft.   (5) 9.5 ft.
    (3) 12 ft.

40. The product of two consecutive integers is 72. Which equation represents this?

    (1) $x + x = 72$
    (2) $x \cdot x = 72$
    (3) $x(x + 1) = 72$
    (4) $x(x + 2) = 72$
    (5) $x + (x + 1) = 72$

Items 41 and 42 refer to the following figure.

The bar graph shows the amount of real estate sold by the XYZ Company.

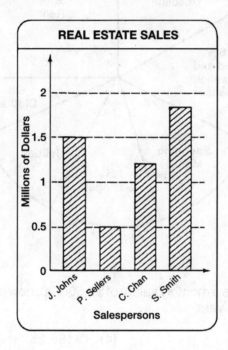

41. Which salesperson sold $1,500,000 worth of real estate?

    (1) J. Johns
    (2) P. Sellers
    (3) C. Chan
    (4) S. Smith
    (5) None of the above.

42. Which person sold about three times the amount of property as P. Sellers?

    (1) J. Johns
    (2) C. Chan
    (3) S. Smith
    (4) All of the above.
    (5) None of the above.

Items 43 to 45 refer to the following figure.

MYRNA'S MONTHLY BUDGET

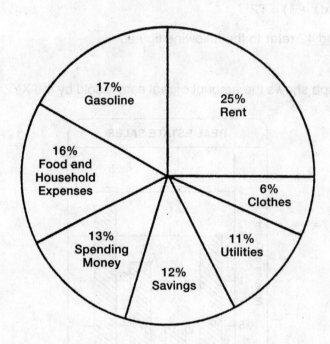

43. If Myrna makes a monthly salary of $2,500.00, how much will she spend on rent in one year?

(1) $7,500
(2) $625
(3) $32,500
(4) $156.25
(5) $2,500

44. What percentage does she spend for utilities?

(1) 275%
(2) 11%
(3) 132%
(4) 16%
(5) 13%

45. What amount does she save each month?

(1) $12
(2) $300
(3) $3,600
(4) $1,200
(5) $325

46. What is the height (altitude) of an equilateral triangle with a side the length of 6 centimeters?

6 cm

?

(1) $3\sqrt{2}$ cm.   (4)   9 cm.

(2) $3\sqrt{3}$ cm.   (5)   3 cm.

(3)   6 cm.

47. $f(x) = -x + 4$, find $f(-3)$.

(1)   −3   (4)   3
(2)   4   (5)   7
(3)   1

Directions: Solve each problem. Write the answer on the answer sheet provided.

48. Alfred and Joe ordered pizza. It was cut into 12 pieces. As they each were about to get 1/2 of it, Bobby came over. Now they want to divide it into thirds. How many pieces will Bobby get?

49. An airplane made a 6-hour trip with the wind which blew in the same direction as the airplane. The return flight against the wind took 8 hours. What was the speed of the airplane in still air?

Directions: Solve the problem below. On the answer sheet, mark the circle on the graph that designates the solution's coordinates.

50. On the graph on your answer sheet, locate the point on the line segment connecting (−5, 7) and (4, 1) which lies twice as far from (−5, 7) as it does from (4, 1).

EXAM III

ANSWER KEY

Test 1—Language Arts: Writing

1. (4)	14. (5)	27. (2)	40. (3)
2. (4)	15. (4)	28. (5)	41. (4)
3. (1)	16. (1)	29. (3)	42. (5)
4. (4)	17. (3)	30. (4)	43. (4)
5. (4)	18. (4)	31. (3)	44. (5)
6. (3)	19. (1)	32. (2)	45. (5)
7. (2)	20. (5)	33. (4)	46. (4)
8. (4)	21. (5)	34. (4)	47. (3)
9. (5)	22. (1)	35. (4)	48. (4)
10. (5)	23. (4)	36. (4)	49. (2)
11. (3)	24. (3)	37. (4)	50. (2)
12. (2)	25. (2)	38. (4)	
13. (3)	26. (5)	39. (5)	

Test 2—Social Studies

1. (4)	14. (1)	27. (4)	40. (4)
2. (2)	15. (4)	28. (1)	41. (3)
3. (5)	16. (1)	29. (5)	42. (1)
4. (2)	17. (5)	30. (1)	43. (3)
5. (3)	18. (3)	31. (4)	44. (2)
6. (2)	19. (5)	32. (3)	45. (5)
7. (1)	20. (4)	33. (4)	46. (5)
8. (3)	21. (3)	34. (1)	47. (4)
9. (4)	22. (3)	35. (4)	48. (2)
10. (1)	23. (2)	36. (3)	49. (5)
11. (3)	24. (5)	37. (2)	50. (5)
12. (4)	25. (4)	38. (1)	
13. (3)	26. (2)	39. (5)	

Test 3—Science

1. (2)	14. (1)	27. (1)	40. (1)
2. (5)	15. (4)	28. (5)	41. (5)
3. (3)	16. (5)	29. (5)	42. (5)
4. (1)	17. (3)	30. (2)	43. (3)
5. (2)	18. (4)	31. (1)	44. (2)
6. (5)	19. (4)	32. (5)	45. (5)
7. (4)	20. (1)	33. (4)	46. (5)
8. (4)	21. (1)	34. (2)	47. (5)
9. (2)	22. (3)	35. (3)	48. (1)
10. (2)	23. (1)	36. (3)	49. (3)
11. (5)	24. (2)	37. (3)	50. (4)
12. (2)	25. (5)	38. (2)	
13. (5)	26. (3)	39. (3)	

Test 4—Language Arts: Reading

1. (3)	11. (3)	21. (3)	31. (1)
2. (4)	12. (3)	22. (3)	32. (5)
3. (2)	13. (1)	23. (2)	33. (2)
4. (2)	14. (4)	24. (3)	34. (1)
5. (4)	15. (5)	25. (4)	35. (1)
6. (2)	16. (4)	26. (3)	36. (4)
7. (3)	17. (2)	27. (2)	37. (4)
8. (1)	18. (1)	28. (4)	38. (5)
9. (4)	19. (2)	29. (2)	39. (1)
10. (3)	20. (2)	30. (4)	40. (3)

Test 5—Math

Part 1

1. (4)	13. (4)	25. (−6, 2)
2. (3)	14. (3)	
3. (5)	15. (5)	
4. (1)	16. (5)	
5. (4)	17. (4)	
6. (3)	18. (5)	
7. (3)	19. 33	
8. (2)	20. 50	
9. (4)	21. 3.2	
10. (1)	22. 34	
11. (3)	23. 3,670	
12. (5)	24. 15	

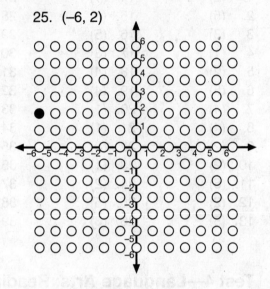

Part 2

26. (1)	38. (1)	50. (1, 3)
27. (1)	39. (4)	
28. (5)	40. (3)	
29. (5)	41. (1)	
30. (3)	42. (1)	
31. (3)	43. (1)	
32. (5)	44. (2)	
33. (4)	45. (2)	
34. (2)	46. (2)	
35. (5)	47. (5)	
36. (4)	48. 4	
37. (3)	49. 420	

DETAILED EXPLANATIONS
OF ANSWERS

TEST 1: LANGUAGE ARTS:
WRITING, PART I

1. **(4)** The answer is (4). The sentence starting with "Because" is a fragment, and needs to be added to the preceding sentence to be grammatically correct. Each of the other suggestions would cause grammatical and syntactical mistakes.

2. **(4)** Both flea (2) and two (3) are spelled correctly. Since the sentence is complete and is setting up to present information, a colon (4) needs to be inserted after the word services. A comma (1) would not introduce properly introduce additional information such as "pet grooming and flea baths for cats and dogs."

3. **(1)** Paragraph C makes a leap between a premise and a conclusion without any explanation of how the one leads to the other. Choice (1) provides an explanation, while the other choices are not relevant or sufficiently informative.

4. **(4)** Sentence 14 is a run-on sentence. The only choice that corrects this problem is choice (4).

5. **(4)** Paragraph D is off topic and detracts from the focus of the report. It should be eliminated.

6. **(3)** The correct choice is (3). This is the only option that fully addresses the run-on problem.

7. **(2)** Choice (2) is the correct choice. This guidance is specifically relevant to the advice in the last sentence.

8. **(4)** Since this passage is written in the second person, it would be inappropriate to change any form of "you" to a first or third person pronoun, as suggested in choices (1), (2), and (3). Choice (4) is the correct answer.

9. **(5)** The answer is choice (5). The first sentence is not clearly related to the rest of the paragraph. It is about cars, but not about leasing, and the

rest of the paragraph doesn't specifically build on the thought this first sentence expresses.

10. **(5) Sentence 1** The correct answer is choice (5). The sentence contains no error. Choices (1) and (2) are not correct because **employees** and **two** are spelled correctly. Choices (3) and (4) are wrong because **into** is the correct preposition and **is** is the verb that agrees with the subject **one**.

11. **(3) Sentence 2** The correct answer is choice (3). The subject **doers** needs the plural verb **are** instead of the singular verb **is**. Choice (1) is incorrect because **Often** is not parenthetical and should not be set off by a comma. **Integral** is spelled correctly. The commas belong in the sentence (4) and should not be removed. Commas should be used to set off elements that provide nonessential informaton. (5) is incorrect.

12. **(2) Sentence 3** The correct answer is choice (2). The sentence contains an independent and a dependent clause; a semicolon can be used to separate only parallel elements. A comma is needed to set off the parenthetical adverb clause. Choice (1) is incorrect, since **took** would constitute a tense shift. Choice (3) is wrong; **Some** is spelled correctly. No comma (4) is needed to set off the prepositional phrase. (5) is incorrect.

13. **(3) Sentence 5** The correct answer is choice (3). **However** is a conjunctive adverb that is not strong enough to link independent clauses; therefore, a semicolon is necessary to separate the clauses. Choices (2) and (4) are incorrect because **group's** and **foresight** are spelled correctly. The conjunction **and** is not needed after **counterparts** (1). (5) is incorrect.

14. **(5) Sentence 6** The sentence is correct.

15. **(4) Sentence 7** The correct answer is choice (4). The original sentence contains a misplaced modifier. **To claim credit** is an infinitive phrase, which modifies **quick**. The adverb clause **when a job is done well** modifies the infinitive **to claim**. The modifier **often** (1) is placed correctly. No comma is needed after **rationalizes** (2) because the adverb clause that follows is needed. The semicolon after **made** is needed to separate the independent clauses; the adverbial expression **in addition** is not strong enough to link independent clauses (3).

16. **(1) Sentence 8** The correct answer is choice (1). **Fewer** is used for things that can be counted and **less** for a fractional part of a whole. No comma is needed after **critics** (2). No comma is needed after **doers** (3). Choice (4) is incorrect because the change would constitute a shift in the voice of the verb—from active to passive. (5) is incorrect.

17. **(3) Sentence 1** The correct answer is choice (3). The correct form of the word is **breath-taking**. Choice (1) is incorrect because **Mississippi**

River is spelled correctly in the original sentence. Commas are not needed in compound parts (2). Choice (5) is incorrect.

18. **(4) Sentence 2**   The correct answer is choice (4). The correlative conjunction **not only… but also** is used to link **the beauty** and **the reflection. Double treat** (1) is the correct form. The comma after **treat** (2) is correct because it sets off the adverb clause beginning with **since** ("because"). The singular pronoun **he** (3) is needed to agree in number with its antecedent **observer**. (5) is incorrect.

19. **(1) Sentence 3**   The correct answer is choice (1). **Hews** means cuts or carves, **hues** refers to shades and tints of color. Changing the order of words changes the meaning; choices (2) and (3) are incorrect. **Brilliance** (4) is spelled correctly. (5) is incorrect.

20. **(5) Sentence 4**   The correct answer is choice (5). A comma is needed after **First** (1) because the word is clearly parenthetical. There are no misspelled words.

21. **(5) Sentence 5**   The correct answer is choice (5). The sentence contains no error. The comma after **Next** (1) is needed because the word is clearly parenthetical. **Striated** (2) is the correct spelling. No comma is needed after **purples** (3) or after **yellows** (4) because the adjective clause is essential.

22. **(1) Sentence 6**   The correct answer is choice (1). Because the paragraph is written in the present tense, **are** is the correct auxiliary verb; **were** is past tense. The plural **were** is used instead of the singular **was** (2). No comma is needed after calmness (3) to separate parallel parts. No comma is needed after disappointment (4) because the adjective clause which follows is essential. (5) is incorrect.

23. **(4) Sentence 7**   The correct answer is choice (5). **Sun set** should be **sunset. Though** (1) is spelled correctly in the original sentence. The commas are needed after **realizes** and after **though** to set off **though**, a parenthetical expression (2). The change in choice (3) is worded awkwardly. (5) is incorrect.

24. **(3)**   The correct answer is choice (3). This sentence opens up the topic of investing and helps set up the ideas this paragraph, and the entire passage, will explore.

25. **(2)**   The correct answer is (2), sentence 10, which takes off from the transition in the previous paragraph and sets up the rest of this paragraph.

26. **(5)**   Choice (5), sentence 13, is the best choice. This may be true, but it is not appropriate in this context.

27. **(2)** Choice (2), is the answer. This thought, as with sentence 13 in the previous paragraph, may be true, and may be tangentially relevant, but it does not work with the other sentences in this paragraph to create unity or coherence.

28. **(5)** The answer is (5)—there is no paragraph in this passage that is off-topic or digresses from the central idea of offering investment advice.

29. **(3) Sentence 1** The correct answer is choice (3). Change **kneads** (to mix) to **needs**. No comma is needed after **activities** because the introductory infinitive phrase also contains the following prepositional phrase (1); the comma is placed after summer (2), the word that ends the introductory infinitive phrase. No comma is placed after **knowledgeable** (4) in the compound parts. (5) is incorrect.

30. **(4) Sentence 2** The correct answer is choice (4). **Heatstroke** is written as one word. No comma goes after **danger** (1), since the adjective clause that follows is essential. A comma is needed after **encounter** (2) to set off the parenthetical phrase that follows. **Outside** (3) is written as one word. (5) is incorrect.

31. **(3) Sentences 3 and 4** The correct answer is choice (3). Sentence 4, a fragment, needs to be attached to sentence 3; the problem can be corrected by adding the word **by** and making the fragment a prepositional phrase modifying **to avoid** and telling **how**. Since sentence 4 is a fragment, choice (1) is incorrect. In choice (2), sentence 4 becomes imperative and causes both a person shift (with **you** as the understood subject) and a mood shift (from indicative to imperative). The dash (4) is not the correct punctuation mark for setting off a participial phrase that comes at the end of the sentence but modifies the subject; a comma can be used to set off that type of element. A semicolon (5) is used between elements that are parallel; a clause and a phrase do not rank equally.

32. **(2) Sentence 5** The correct answer is choice (2). Since **water** is a **liquid**, **water** has to be excluded from the group by saying **some other liquid**; otherwise, the writer is saying drinking **water** or **water** (part of the **liquid** group). No comma goes after **water** (1) in compound parts. The use of (3) is a shift in persons. **Necessary** (4) is the correct spelling. (5) is incorrect.

33. **(4) Sentence 6** The correct answer is choice (4). The informal contraction **don't** does not agree in number with the subject **he**. The comma is needed after **play** (1) to set off the two introductory prepositional phrases, as well as to prevent misreading. In choice (2), **hisself** is not a word. Though **doesn't** (3) agrees in number with the subject **he**, contractions are informal; the remainder of the paragraph is more formal. (5) is incorrect.

34. **(4) Sentence 7**   The correct answer is choice (4). Since the paragraph has been written in third person and **you** is second person, **a person** avoids a shift in voice. A change from **being aware** (1) to awareness would present a non-parallel construction with "by dealing." No comma is needed after **problems** (2) in compound parts. A plural pronoun, not the singular **it** (3), is needed. (5) is incorrect.

35. **(4) Sentence 1**   The correct answer is choice (4). A dash is needed after **elements** to set off the appositive which follows, since the appositive contains a comma. No comma is needed after **person** (1) because the adjective clause that follows is essential; no comma goes after **winter**, the last word in the essential adjective clause (2). (5) is incorrect.

36. **(4) Sentence 2**   The correct answer is choice (4). The pronoun **his** is needed to agree in number with its singular antecedent **person**. The use (1) of **became**, a past tense verb, causes a tense shift, since the paragraph is in present tense. The correct spelling of the adverb is **too** (2). No comma goes after **cold** (3) because the prepositional phrase that follows is essential to the sense of the sentence. (5) is incorrect.

37. **(4) Sentences 2 and 3**   The correct answer is choice (4). Sentence 3 is a dependent clause, which needs to be attached to sentence 2, an independent clause. Choices (1) and (2) are incorrect, since sentence 3 is a dependent clause and does not rank equally with sentence 2. Choice (3) is incorrect because sentence 3 is not an independent clause explaining the former clause (sentence 2). A dash is not the correct mark of punctuation to attach the dependent clause, which is not an abrupt break in thought or does not need particularly to be emphasized (5).

38. **(4) Sentence 4**   The correct answer is choice (4). The appositives following **measures** need to be parallel in structure: **dressing**, **avoiding**, and **using** are parallel. No comma goes after **knows** (1), since what follows is a noun clause used as the direct object. **He** (2) is the correct pronoun to agree with its antecedent **one**. In (3), the colon after **measures** is correct before a list of appositives (renaming or explaining **measures**). (5) is incorrect.

39. **(5) Sentence 5**   The correct answer is choice (5). The correct spelling is **extremities** (2). The comma after **If** (1) is needed to set off the parenthetical expression which follows. **Engage** (3) and **stimulate** (4) are spelled correctly.

40. **(3) Sentences 5 and 6**   The correct answer is choice (3). **In addition** is an adverbial expression serving somewhat as a link between parallel elements. Though the phrase is not strong enough to link two independent clauses and has to be preceded by a semicolon, it is conjunctive in nature. The material following **In addition** needs also to have an independent clause, since the material preceding the the expression does. Choices (1)

and (2) are incorrect because sentence 6 is only a fragment. Simply attaching sentence 6 (4) with a comma results in illogical construction. Choice (5) is wrong because the adverbial expression is preceded by a semicolon and usually followed by a comma.

41. **(4) Sentence 7** The correct answer is choice (4). The adjective **safe** should be changed to the adverb **safely**, which modifies **can enjoy** and tells **how**. The comma after **judgment** (3) should remain as it is separating an introductory element from a main clause. No comma goes after **Simply,** which modifies the introductory prepositional phrase (2). (5) is incorrect.

42. **(5) Sentence 1** The correct answer is choice (5). The comma after **icicle** is needed to set off the introductory participial phrase (2). No comma is needed after **school** because the element that follows is not parenthetical (3).

43. **(4) Sentence 2** The correct answer is choice (4). The past tense verb **possessed** is consistent with the tense in the paragraph. **Though** (1) is the correct spelling for the subordinate conjunction. **Created** (2) is consistent with the other past tense verbs in the paragraph. In (3), the comma after **own** is necessary to set off the introductory adverb clause. (5) is incorrect.

44. **(5) Sentence 3** The correct answer is choice (5). The sentence contains no error. The dashes after **tints** (1) and **lips** (4) are needed to set off the appositive, which contains material that needs to be emphasized. **Semitransparent** (2) is the correct form of the word, according to one current dictionary. **Highlighted** (3) is a correct spelling.

45. **(5) Sentence 4** The correct answer is choice (5). The sentence contains no error. **Lending** (1) and **atmosphere** (2) are the correct word choices for the context. No comma is needed after **about her** (3) in this inverted sentence. **Faraway** (4) is the correct form of the word.

46. **(4) Sentences 4 and 5** The correct answer is choice (4). Sentence 5 is a fragment which needs to be attached to sentence 4, an independent clause. Choices (1) and (3) are incorrect, since sentence 5 is a fragment. No comma (2) is needed in compound parts. Dashes (5), instead of a coordinate conjunction, are not used to separate parallel parts within a sentence.

47. **(3) Sentence 6** The correct answer is choice (3). A sentence containing two independent clauses and no coordinate conjunction needs a semicolon to separate the clauses. **Showed** (1) is the correct past tense verb. **Disappeared** (2) is the correct spelling. **No one** (4) is the correct form of the pronoun. (5) is incorrect.

48. **(4) Sentence 1** The correct answer is choice (4). **Precluded** is a malapropism (a ludicrous misuse of words, especially through confusion caused by resemblance in sound); **concluded** ("decided by reasoning") fits

the context. No commas are needed after **drivers** (1) or **city** (2), since both words are followed by essential prepositional phrases. **Drivers** (3) is correct. (5) is incorrect.

49. **(2) Sentence 2** The correct answer is choice (2). A semicolon needs to be placed after **signs** because the material before and after the punctuation mark contains an independent clause. The independent clauses have to be separated by a mark stronger than a comma (the error is a comma splice); a semicolon is used if the clauses are closely related. No comma is needed after **evidently** (1). **There** (3) is the correct spelling. No comma is needed after **approached** (4) in compound parts. (5) is incorrect.

50. **(2) Sentence 6** The correct answer is choice (2). The change in choice (2) is much more concise. The original sentence has redundancy ("needless repetition"), especially with the prepositional phrases that tell where the truck stopped—for instance, **On one street with two narrow lanes edged by deep ditches** and **right in the middle of the road**. No comma is needed after **lanes** (1) because the participial phrase that follows is essential. A semicolon cannot be used after **ditches** because the material before the punctuation mark does not rank equally with that after the mark (3). No change is needed in **road, causing all traffic** because the participial phrase coming at the end of the sentence is set off by a comma; the change cannot be accurate because no comma is used in compound parts (4). Choice (5) is incorrect.

TEST 1: LANGUAGE ARTS: WRITING, PART II

Sample Essay — Possible Score of 4

Occasionally, I feel that I need to escape the pressures of my job. The only way to relieve this stress is to go to a completely different location. My choice of site varies with the seasons and weather conditions.

Since I am not a lover of cold weather, the southern climate is better in late winter and early spring. Actually, the coastal beaches are my choice. There I can sit outside, listening to the waves while dreaming about faraway places. Usually in these reveries, the last thing I think about is my job.

In the summer I like to find a location where the weather is temperate. I like to feel a gentle breeze against my cheek, as well as to see lush foliage and flowers bin full blossom; observing the beauty of nature is very relaxing to me. Some of the foothills of the Ozark Mountains and of the Rocky Mountains provide the serenity that I need. Compared to that of the city, the pace of life there seems so deliberate. At least, in such a locale, I can clear my mind for a few days before returning to my job.

Actually, in the fall I have difficulty in choosing among the places of escape. The foliage is so beautiful in many areas. Still, though, I think that the mountains provide some of the prettiest scenes; some are breathtakingly beautiful. I am entranced by the sights and spend little time worrying about my work.

When the pressures of my job weigh heavily, I am never in a quandary about what to do. I know that I need to escape my work environment. The only problem I have is in deciding at which beach or in which mountain area I want to while away my time. Somehow, I usually manage to make a choice, though.

Why this essay scores a 4

This essay is very well developed. It thoroughly addresses the topic of explaining how the essayist relieves job-related pressures. He/she provides many examples to support the main idea which makes for a more believable essay. In addition, examples are presented in full detail.

There are no obvious errors in the use of standard written English, which shows that the author has a good command of the English language. The essay is easy to follow and read, and also draws the reader through to the end of the essay. The conclusion nicely ties together the ideas presented, without merely reiterating the essay.

Sample Essay — Possible Score of 3

To releive job-related pressure, I have to escape the hustle and bustle of the city. I can no longer be a part of the rat race if I want to maintain my sanity. I have to get away from it all.

My escape is not complete unless I can let my hair down. I try to find some place where I do not worry about my looks. If I want to be a slouch, I can. When I want to dress up, I do. I don't want anyone telling me how to act or look. I just do my own thing.

I want no one making any demands on me. Since I leave my alarm clock at home, I get up when I want to and sleep when I want to; I also eat when I get ready. Finally, I do no work—for myself or anyone else.

The main way I can escape stress asociated with my work is to do the opposite of what I usually do. My looks do not concern me. I want niether demands made or me nor a schedule to meet. To put it simply, I want to be free as a bird.

Why this essay scores a 3

Although this essay is not extensively organized, it does present some effective points. However, the effectiveness of these points is minimized by the fact that the essayist does not present supporting examples. The essay is wordy, somewhat repetitive, and not well developed. The ideas that the essayist relieves job-related stress through escaping work, going someplace where he does not have to worry about his looks, and having no demands made upon him are repeated throughout the essay. It is apparent that some thought was put into the creation of this essay, but not enough.

The writing style of this essay is a bit too informal. Poor sentence structure and some spelling errors detract from the overall writing. A quick proofreading would have caught the incorrect word "or" in the third sentence of the last paragraph. The sentence should have read "...demands made **on** me...." Consistent with the essay, the conclusion is weak. It basically reiterates the points previously mentioned and does not tie-up the ideas presented.

Sample Essay — Possible Score of 2

During the summer, most of us who work look forward to weekends when we can find relief from job-related presures. Some of my friends like to escape to the woods. Others trade the drudgery of their jobs for dangerous but exhilerating activities. Still others including me, prefer relaxing in front of the television or out by the pool. All of us escapees have one thing in common—to forget our Monday-Friday activities.

The people who flee to the woods sometimes rest but sometimes encounter other kinds of problems. Tents are not good shelters during a three-day rainstorm. Despite advertising claims, insect repellants for the deep woods are ineffective against texas-sized mosquitoes whose droning song lingers long after the lights have been snuffed out. Crawling things come to check you out. Someone tells a scarey story or reminds you that you can get leeches on you when you are in some damp places. In the woods is no place for me!

Other ways of relaxing include watching my favorite television shows and sitting out by the pool. Unless someone tells me to get up and get him a drink or a snack or something else. Then I go bananas! Anyway, back to my favorite escape. I like watching game shows—at least until I get depressed because I am not winning any money. I hate sports programs, especially boxing and wresling; because most of them are just incediary anyways. And who can relax under those conditions? The soap operas are sickning; all of the characters have facades. They get on my nerves! Maybe, I'd better relax by the pool instead of in front of the television. I like the pool when the water is clear. I hate it when that yucky green stuff is floating in the pool or attaches itself to the sides. I guess I don't like the pool, either.

Well, I've just about concluded that relaxation anywhere is just not for me. Though I have no escape, I certainly wont try to mess up or begrudge the lives of others. I'll remain envyous of those who blaze a path to the woods, leave old terra firma for excitement, or become couch potatoes or pool loungers every weekend. It would be a dull world if everyone was as unhappy as I am.

Why this essay scores a 2

This essay has a few very serious problems. First, it does not directly address the topic. The topic requires the essay writer to explain how he/she relieves job-related stress; however, this essayist puts more thought into describing how other people relieve their job-related stress. Less than one-third of the entire essay really deals with the topic.

Second, the essayist has a horrible habit of going off on a tangent. The second paragraph begins by going off the topic to describe how other people relax in the woods. Then, the essayist begins to describe some of the problems these people face such as rainstorms, which leads him to mention that tents are not good shelters during three-day rainstorms and that, "despite advertising claims, insect repellants for the deep woods are ineffective against texas-sized mosquitoes...." All of this has absolutely nothing to do with topic of relieving job-related stress.

Finally, this essay contains numerous errors in use of standard written English, such as incomplete sentences, "Unless someone tells me to get up and get him a drink or a snack or something else," and consistently employs bad sentence structure. All of the sentences are short and choppy, which is monotonous to read. This essay consistently has no real structure or organization.

Sample Essay — Possible Score of 1

I don't have alot of job-related stress so I don't know what to write. Sure some people maybe realy stressed, but I'm not. I don't want to live that way there are lots of good jobs that don't give you stress.

People should decide on there own not to be stressed. After all its up to you. you need to stick up for your self in this world. Thats pretty simple isn't it? People wine about stress but their the ones that are causing it, or letting it happen to them. You have to live your life, no one's going to do that for you. Take charge and cause some one else some stress for a change.

Why this essay scores a 1

This essay has little content in it. Although the essay question asks the essayist to discuss how he or she relieves job-related stress, the author fails to provide any real information on how he relaxes. The essayist spends most of this essay addressing how other people can avoid stress.

Poor spelling (e.g., "realy" instead of "really") and the many punctuation and grarnmatical errors contribute to a sloppy, illiterate appearance. The lack of proper punctuation often confuses the reader and causes the context of the essay to be unclear in its meaning. For these grave mistakes, this essay receives a score of 1.

TEST 2: SOCIAL STUDIES

1. **(4)** The third sentence under the section "Qualifications of an Eligible Applicant" indicates that the voter registration deadline is 29 days prior to election day.

2. **(2)** All of the choices appear in item 9, the list of the registrant's declarations, except minumum voting age is 21 (2). The legal voting age is 18.

3. **(5)** Item 7 indicates that one's phone number is optional. By implication, all other information listed in choices (1) through (4) is required.

4. **(2)** The first sentence under the section "Qualifications of an Eligible Applicant" states that the registrant must be a "resident of New Jersey and your county for at least 30 days." The other numbers are inapplicable.

5. **(3)** The article quotes Southern enthusiasm as being in the same mood as in the Union states. (1) and (2) are incorrect because the mood was similar in both areas. (4) is wrong because, although fear was a natural and secondary reaction, the article does not emphasize it. (5) is not a logical reaction to such dramatic and exciting events.

6. **(2)** The war was fought between 1861–65. (1) and (3) are the wrong decades. (4) Lincoln's well-known views on slavery stated that slavery should not be extended, but he would not attempt to eliminate it in the existing slave states. (5) The cotton export trade to Europe was not restricted.

7. **(1)** is the correct answer; the authors strongly imply the obvious: that the laws of supply and demand cannot be repealed. The rest are all part of pro-capitalist arguments: (2) is the very definition of capitalism, creating investment money, (3) is seen as creating a greater "flow of goods." (4) The article talks about how abilities, talents, and skills will be developed. (5) Several areas refer to consumers who will get more and determine the products and services.

8. **(3)** is correct. Several key terms, like liberty, free, and democracy, are used to describe a capitalistic society. (1) is incorrect because there is no reference to any flaws of capitalism. (2) is wrong. The first sentence refers to "the struggle of socialism against capitalism...." (4) is wrong because there are several references to keeping business free from government rules. (5) The author emphasizes the historical influence of capitalism.

9. **(4)** "No work, no eat" was the famous rule of early struggling colonists and it expresses the idea that a person's economic fate is directly related to

his or her own efforts. (1) is very socialistic, emphasizing the group rather than the individual. (2) President John Kennedy's famous appeal to patriotism has no relationship to capitalism. (3) This famous concept, tried in many socialist utopian experiments, is the opposite of capitalism. (5) This is also not an economic theory, but refers to emotional and spiritual needs.

10. **(1)** is most correct. Although the Canadian Shield and St. Lawrence Lowlands overlap north to south, the general trend is from the Atlantic Maritimes westward to the Rockies and Pacific.

11. **(3)** These two southern lakes empty the waters of the Great Lakes into the St. Lawrence River through Lake Ontario. (2) would be equally true if the question just said the Great Lakes in general, because they touch on Lakes Huron and Superior.

12. **(4)** All these are prairie provinces that are part of the same Great Plains ecosystem as the U.S. states to their south.

13. **(3)** is not correct. Lake Michigan is entirely within the U.S.

14. **(1)** When stories of White House involvement in the Watergate break-in began surfacing in 1973, President Richard Nixon came under increasing pressure to formally investigate the entire affair. Nixon denied any involvement in the Watergate caper, but during the trial of one of the Watergate burglars, a White House aide revealed that Nixon had a taping system that had recorded virtually all conversations in the oval office during the period in question. Investigators demanded the tapes. Nixon refused on the grounds of "executive privilege." Investigators smelled a coverup.

To quiet his critics, Nixon appointed a special prosecutor, Archibald Cox, to investigate any White House involvement in Watergate. Cox also requested the tapes. When Nixon refused, Cox went to court to obtain a court order forcing Nixon to relinquish the tapes. When Nixon realized what Cox had done and also realized that Cox might succeed in getting the court order, he ordered Cox to be fired. Nixon's attorney general and his assistant both refused to carry out the order. Instead, they resigned in protest. Nixon finally got another Justice Department official to carry out the order. Cox and his staff were duly fired on Saturday night, October 20, 1973, thus the name "Saturday Night Massacre."

The press, the public, and Nixon's political opposition (even some of his supporters) were outraged. The demand for continued investigation forced Nixon to name a new special prosecutor, Leon Jaworski. Jaworski also sought, and eventually got, custody of the complete tapes and those tapes proved to be the "smoking gun," which ruined the little credibility Nixon had left and finished his presidency.

15. **(4)** Bob Woodward and Carl Bernstein were the two *Washington Post* reporters who painstakingly tracked down the Watergate scandal for the

American public. Their investigative journalism eventually led to the resignation of President Nixon in 1974 and the criminal indictments for most of his top advisors owing to violations of various campaign laws and obstruction of justice charges. Gordon Liddy and John Dean (5) were two of Nixon's indicted aides, while Sam Ervin and Howard Baker (3) were the two U.S. Senators heading the Senate Investigative Hearings into the Watergate affair. William Randolph Hearst and Joseph Pulitzer (2) were New York newspaper editors in the late 19th century who created "yellow journalism." Walter Cronkite and Dan Rather (1) were television media reporters.

16. **(1)** is correct. The reading states that the cultural achievements had been lost. (2) is incorrect because, although the Moslems lived better, they did not control Western Europe. (3) is wrong because the article refers to merchants trading with the Byzantine Empire. (4) Several near civilizations are mentioned: the Moslems and Byzantium. (5) Some nobles and church scholars were learned, as stated.

17. **(5)** is correct. The article says that these two Moslem cultures were much higher than the others. (1) is wrong. The whole purpose of the reading was to show how inferior Western Europe was at the time. (2) lists Byzantine culture as only "slightly higher" than Europe's. (3) and (4) are incorrect because they are no longer in existence during the Crusades; their cultures are referred to as "lost."

18. **(3)** is correct. Only the Holy Land and the Eastern Mediterranean were attacked. Other, closer areas such as Spain and North Africa were left alone. (1) is the main official Church reason for calling for Crusades. (2) Demand had been increasing for the new spices and silks that merchants had bought from Moslem traders. (4) One of the reasons for demanding Christian control of the Holy Land was the poor treatment that some pilgrims had received. (5) As a feudal society, nobles always sought new land wealth, merchants wanted expanded trade, and the Catholic Church wanted control over the Jerusalem area.

19. **(5)** is most correct as the two line graphs have met in the 1970s. (1) The opposite has been true as the GNP line was almost always below that of the labor force. (2) is incorrect as the difference between the two lines widened and narrowed in different areas. (3) Farming had declined to below 50% well before 1900. (4) Even though the graphs' curves became more level in the 1970's, they still reflected a declining influence.

20. **(4)** is most correct. The closing of the gap between GNP and labor force reflect the increasing efficiency of each farmer. (1) is not an accurate conclusion because, with fewer farmers growing the food supply, their importance is great. (2) is not addressed by the graph. The range of farm incomes is wide. (3) Automation might be an explanation for the increased efficiency, but the graphs do not supply that information. (5) There was at least one period on each graph when the line went upward.

21. **(3)** is the correct answer. Farming has become increasingly agri-business and the family farm has decreased in influence and number. (1) is a traditional problem as farmers have to borrow until crops are harvested and hope income is good. (2) The U.S. is usually a food exporter, using its surpluses to sell crops abroad. (4) Several years of severe weather, such as drought, in the 1980s illustrated how dependent agriculture still is on nature. (5) Government farm programs have been very important for 70 years, helping by price supports, quotas, crop limits, and direct payments.

22. **(3)** is most correct. Efficiency is not necessarily a problem, but the reduction of workers reduces both the earning power of agricultural workers and the the political clout of agriculture as an occupation. (1) is the exact opposite of the trend, which had continued for most of the 20th century. (2) World food demands, not supplies, are increasing with population growth and all food exporters will be pressured to increase production. (4) Water supplies are decreasing in relation to the population worldwide. (5) Again, the world population growth will increase food needs.

23. **(2)** is the best choice because the excerpt limits itself to the topic of search law. (1) is not correct because the article refers to both citizen and police rights. (3) The article discusses how the Fourth Amendment works, not what limits it. (4) Evidence search is discussed, but other topics are also covered. (5) The article does not detail specific Court rulings on the Fourth Amendment.

24. **(5)** is correct. All of the other choices were listed as exceptions in the article. A person's property is protected from search unless probable cause convinces a court to issue a warrant. (1) The article uses several examples, such as a plain view car search, of non-warrant legal searches. (2) The article states that police may search a suspect during an arrest for their own protection. (3) That "a person may consent to a search" is stated in the article. (4) The search is legal to find evidence of a shooting but whether or not the drugs can be used in a criminal charge is up to court.

25. **(4)** is the correct answer. Slavery was made illegal as part of the Constitution after the Civil War (Thirteenth Amendment), which is not part of the original Bill of Rights, the first 10 amendments. (1) is guaranteed under the Seventh Amendment. (2) is part of the First Amendment. (3) is the Third Amendment. It is little known now, but that's because the abuse by the British Army against the colonists was eliminated by the American Revolution and then by the Bill of Rights. (5) is the Second Amendment.

26. **(2)** The underlying concern in this passage is "equality," the opposite of preservation of a class system that by its nature is unequal. The other points listed are explicitly stated in the first paragraph of this excerpt.

27. **(4)** The last paragraph of this selection states that "separate educational facilities are inherently unequal." For this reason, segregated schooling is unconstitutional. Therefore, there are no circumstances in which it is constitutional, including whether or not equal facilities are provided or a state argues that the issue is a matter of states' rights. The 14th Amendment guarantees equal protection of the laws, which again conflicts with segregated schooling because the latter is inherently unequal.

28. **(1)** The last sentence of the first paragraph states that opportunity of education "is a right which must be made available to all on equal terms." The only qualification is the phrase, "where the state has undertaken to provide it," but this has no effect on the ruling because public education is provided in all of the states of the union. References in the paragraph to compulsory attendance laws and expenditures are simply descriptions of what is being done, rather than being matters of rights, and are used to support the argument that education is important. The opinion also argues that education is important in preparing for service in the armed forces and for success in life, but identifies neither as a right.

29. **(5)** The statement in the third paragraph of this excerpt refers explicitly to a feeling of inferiority generated by segregation among the minority group. Elsewhere, the opinion argues that physical facilities might be equal but that they would still produce this feeling of inferiority. The remaining three options do not appear in the opinion in any form.

30. **(1)** is correct. The Department of State advises the President on foreign policy, maintains diplomatic relations with foreign nations, issues passports, and maintains embassies and consulates. (2) Defense may carry out a foreign policy goal, but does not make the policy. (3), (4) and (5) are not directly involved in foreign policy but may carry it out.

31. **(4)** The Justice Department is the federal law enforcement agency including the Federal Bureau of Investigation. The other agencies do not have any control over the FBI.

32. **(3)** is the correct answer. The parks are under the Interior Department. All the others are part of HHS.

33. **(4)** is correct. The SEC is one of many independent agencies that is not part of any branch of government. It has a specific non-partisan role. (1) The Secret Service is under the Treasury Department. (2) The Pentagon is the headquarters of the Armed Forces under the Defense Department. (3) and (5) are part of the Executive Branch offices that advise the President.

34. **(1)** As the chart indicates, the voters elect a legislature and the legislators then choose a prime minister or premier. (2) is not correct because the legislature enacts laws, not the people. (3) This type of government gives the legislature more power than ours because Congress does not get to choose the government leader. (4) As answered in (2), only the legislature can create laws; the leader may propose legislation for them to consider. (5) There is a dual function, with the leader proposing laws and the legislature either passing or rejecting them.

35. **(4)** The theory of plate tectonics explains the areas around the edge of the Pacific plate being geologically active. (1) Geothermics is the study of using the energy released by hot spots around the world and why it exists. It fits into the theory of tectonics. (2) This is the general study of all ocean behavior, not just the Ring of Fire. (3) Any climate and the natural life forms it supports is an ecosystem. (5) All physical features of the surface of the Earth are landforms.

36. **(3)** These cyclonic storms may occur but are not common to the region or caused by tectonic activity. (1) Volcanoes occur where the Earth's crust is thin, such as where two plates come together. The Ring of Fire takes its name from their eruptions. (2) and (5) go together when tension builds up as two plates rub against each other on fault lines and the eventual slippage creates earthquakes. (4) Many islands in this ring are volcanic in origin or have been reshaped by Earthquakes.

37. **(2)** An archipelago is a chain of islands. In Asia, many such as Japan and Indonesia are united into nations. (1) An atoll is a coral reef surrounding a lagoon. (3) A barrier reef is a coral formation offshore that protects the shore from wave action and storms. (4) A lagoon is a bay created by protective atolls. (5) The continental shelf is the shallow portion of the ocean offshore of a land mass.

38. **(1)** is most true. Besides AT&T, the various Bell companies are all on the list. (2) Obvious manufacturing companies, such as General Motors and General Electric, are outnumbered by service companies, such as utilities. (3) Retailers, such as Sears, appear toward the bottom of the list. (4) Bell Canada obviously does foreign business, as do most of the others with their international branches, such as IBM. (5) Exxon appears on the list, with over three-quarters of a million stockholders.

39. **(5)** is correct because it has the least number of stockholders on the list, so the fewest number of votes is required to make decisions. All of the others have more stockholders, so each share of stock is less important in a total vote. The reality is that the number of shares in any large company is so great that influence at the annual stockholders meeting is minimal for any one share of stock.

40. **(4)** is correct. The stockholders elect a board of directors and give them direction at the annual meeting. The board then directs the company for the rest of the year, appointing a chairperson and setting policy. (1) The chief executive officer (CEO) is appointed or elected by the board of directors. (2) The board elects a chair, but controls its power. (3) The president (often the CEO) directs the day-to-day operations under board direction. (5) Stock options are opportunities for top employees to invest in the company, but do not give control unless the employees buy a large portion of the outstanding stock, thus gaining control.

41. **(3)** is the correct answer because East Germany's $31 billion is 10% of West Germany's $323 billion. (1) is incorrect because the U.S. was not the leading exporter ($322 billion v. $323 billion for West Germany). (2) is wrong because Britain's $145 billion is less than half of Germany's total of $354 billion. (4) is not correct because with East Germany's $31 billion added to West Germany's $323 billion, the total gap will widen to $32 billion more than the U.S. (5) is wrong because the total will be almost $500 billion, not $600 billion.

42. **(1)** is correct. Per capita gross national product is one of the accepted economic figures to compare relative standards of living because it includes all (gross) goods and services produced by a nation. (2) relates to a nation's exporting production per capita only, not standard of living. (3) The annual exports alone do not show a relationship to the number of people who share those sales. (4) is incorrect because it compares an individual figure (per capita) with a total national figure. (5) creates the gross national product of a country, not individuals.

43. **(3)** is correct. The U.S., with a population of 248 million, produced $322 billion in exports. Not worrying about the zeroes, the 248 is less than double 322. West Germany produced over 5 times its population, East Germany nearly double, and the British nearly 3 times. (1) is incorrect because the graphs do not show total productivity, only the products exported. (2) is wrong. Britain was fourth. It will go to third and the unified Germany will be second behind the U.S. (4) is incorrect. As noted in explaining (3), the West Germans produced the most exports per capita. (5) is wrong. In a unified Germany, the East German lower GNP will temporarily create a figure for the total for the whole country somewhere between the two figures $12,480 and $14,260.

44. **(2)** is correct. It is mentioned the most often and called the "most continuous attraction." (1) is mentioned the second most often, but not in every example like soil. (3) is only mentioned in connection with its good soils. (4) is not specifically referred to. (5) is mentioned as one occupation that came from settlements by farmers and hunters/trappers.

45. **(5)** is correct. The example is given that some in government feared he would become a dictator while others (Lee, Lowell) talked about replacing him as unsuccessful. (1) is incorrect. The article gives several examples of officer discontent but only praise from the common troops. (2) There are several references to his character and justice. (3) Since he was the commander-in-chief this has to be incorrect. (4) The last part of the article discusses the "deep respect and affection" the people had for him.

46. **(5)** is correct. The lead sentence in each paragraph deals with projected water shortage. All the other topics such as (1) alternative water supplies, (2) poor nations, (3) famine, and (4) grain supplies are focused on fresh water shortages. (1) is mentioned only in the first paragraph as options to a global water shortage. (2) is incorrect because water problems in both rich and poor nations are discussed. (3) is not correct because starvation is a sub-topic in the main discussion of fresh water for farming. (4) The statistics on world grain supplies are related back to lack of water. So, although all topics are mentioned, water resources is the one common main topic; the others are examples.

47. **(4)** is correct. The article states that irrigated land is being lost to improper watering. (1) is incorrect because the article does not discuss individual food consumption. (2) and (3) are wrong because, even though the producing nations are sharing their surpluses, the population growth has reduced the world surplus from a 101-day to a 54-day supply. (5) is wrong because only rich nations, like Saudi Arabia, can afford such projects.

48. **(2)** is correct because fresh water precipitation occurs in all temperature ranges, from rain forest heat to arctic snow. (1) is incorrect because annual rainfall is the measure used to tell a dry climate from a wet one. (3) Hydrologic cycle is the name for the constant pattern of precipitation and evaporation between the earth and atmosphere. (4) is wrong because how the soil absorbs and holds water does influence the supply of water available through rivers and wells for example. (5) is the theory that the warming of the atmosphere will create new climate regions, including shifting rainfall patterns.

49. **(5)** is correct. All of the world's major rain forests are in less developed areas. (1) Acid rain is primarily caused by industrial pollution created by the industrialized nations. (2) Underdeveloped nations generally do not have the technological ability to have large-scale nuclear facilities. (3) Most toxic waste is generated by developed nations' industries. (4) Again, developed nations' products seem to be depleting the ozone.

50. **(5)** is correct because the greenhouse effect would have the opposite effect and would raise radiation levels by depleting the ozone layer protecting the Earth. (1) is a predicted result of ozone damage that would create a worldwide warming trend. (2) Sea levels would be expected to rise

as rising temperatures cause the melting of polar ice caps (4). (3) The increased radiation levels are predicted to increase the incidence of skin cancer.

TEST 3: SCIENCE

1. **(2)** is correct. The physical properties of the ground allow it to absorb heat. (1) is incorrect, because the troposphere is under the ozone layer. (3) is incorrect, because ice cover affects only the place it is covering, not the entire planet. (4) is incorrect, because land and water have different rates of heating and cooling.

2. **(5)** is correct. Changes in composition would cause different rates of heating. (1) is incorrect, because change in distance is insignificant. (2) is incorrect, because weather is only found in the lowest atmospheric layer. (3) is incorrect, because ozone is only found in one layer. (4) is incorrect, because man does not affect the atmosphere.

3. **(3)** Choice (3) is the correct answer. It is porous material through which the oil and gas move, but it is capped and thus trapped by the impermeable layer B (2). A (1) is the Earth's surface and the oil and gas are found below the ground. D (4) is also porous but it is below C and is the water above which the oil and gas would rise. E (5) is impermeable.

4. **(1)** Desert areas increase evaporation of the water that is present, causing a concentration of salts. Therefore, the remaining answers are incorrect.

5. **(2)** Answer choice (2), phloem, is the correct answer since phloem conducts food to the storage areas of the plant. Xylem (1) cannot be the correct answer since xylem conducts water from the roots throughout the plant. Precambrium (3) cannot be the correct answer since this is a geologic age. Stomata (4) cannot be the correct answer since stomata are the openings on the underside of leaves. Cuticle (5) cannot be the correct answer since the cuticle is a thin, waxy covering that waterproofs the leaf.

6. **(5)** Answer choice (5), cuticle, is the correct answer since the cuticle is a thin waxy covering that waterproofs the leaf. Xylem (1) cannot be the correct answer since xylem conducts water from the roots throughout the plant. Phloem (2) cannot be the correct answer since phloem conducts food to the storage areas of the plant. Precambrium (3) cannot be the correct answer since this is a geologic age. Stomata, (4) cannot be the correct answer since stomata are the openings on the underside of leaves.

7. **(4)** Answer choice (4), stomata, is the correct answer since stomata are the openings on the underside of leaves. Xylem (1) cannot be the correct answer since xylem conducts water from the roots throughout the plant. Phloem (2) cannot be the correct answer since phloem conducts food to the storage areas of the plant. Precambrium (3) cannot be the correct answer

since this is a geologic age. Cuticle (5) cannot be the correct answer since the cuticle is a thin, waxy covering that waterproofs the leaf.

8. **(4)** Answer choice (4), stomata, is the correct answer since stomata are the openings on the underside of leaves and the guard cells on either side of the opening swell and shrink to regulate the passage of air into and out of the leaf. Xylem (1) cannot be the correct answer since xylem conducts water from the roots throughout the plant. Phloem (2) cannot be the correct answer since phloem conducts food to the storage areas of the plant. Precambrium (3) cannot be the correct answer since this is a geologic age. Cuticle (5) cannot be the correct answer since the cuticle is a thin, waxy covering that waterproofs the leaf.

9. **(2)** When a positively charged rod is brought near the top, electrons will be drawn from the gold up the internal rod to the knob. This leaves the gold leaves positively charged. If they are close to the same mass, they both will give up the same number of electrons and will result in the same positive charge. They then repel each other and separate. The knob has become negative but the entire electroscope is still neutral since no charge has been added to it or taken away. All that has happened is that charge has been rearranged upon it due to the presence of an outside electrical field provided by the positively charged rod.

10. **(2)** If the gold leaves of an electroscope are separated before the vinyl is brought near, it must mean that some charge has been added to or taken from the electroscope. In this case electrons have been added to the electroscope so that it is charged negatively. When a negative vinyl is now brought near, electrons in the knob will be repelled down the internal rod to the gold leaves. They will now acquire a greater negative charge and tend to spread even further apart.

11. **(5)** is correct. The bonds in H_2 (1) and Cl_2 (2) are covalent because the two identical atoms share the electrons equally. Additionally, diamonds (4) are covalently bonded. To be so hard, a diamond cannot have any weak bonds. NaCl (3) is ionic because Na^+ and Cl^- are ions of opposite charge.

12. **(2)** is correct, because Wyoming is located in an area of predicted minor damage. (1), (3), (4), and (5) are all states that are predicted to have more serious earthquakes.

13. **(5)** is correct. The map indicates that earthquakes of varying degrees can occur in almost every state. (1) and (2) are incorrect because the map is making predictions about where earthquakes might occur, rather than where earthquakes will definitely occur. (3) is wrong because according to the map, Texas might suffer minor damage in the next 100 years. (4) is incorrect, because many theories and conclusions can be drawn from the information given.

14. **(1)** is correct, because all of the gases listed are dangerous to life. (2) is wrong because volcanoes, according to the passage, do not always emit both lava and gas. (3) is incorrect, because "volcanic activity" is a term that relates to different types of events. (4) and (5) are wrong, and sentence 1 confirms this.

15. **(4)** is correct. In the passage a list of gases emitted from volcanoes is given and oxygen is not listed. (1) and (2) are incorrect choices as stated in the paragraph. (3) is incorrect since the Earth's atmosphere contains oxygen, and volcanoes do not emit oxygen, some other factor must have been involved in the development of the atmosphere.

16. **(5)** is the only correct answer. "Pyroclastic" comes from the term "pyro," meaning fire. A "pyroclastic display" is a shower of fire and debris from a volcano.

17. **(3)** The water column is 34 feet high while the mercury column under the same conditions is only 2.5 feet high. Since the columns have the same cross-sectional area, the weight of the mercury must be 34/2.5 times that of water. This ratio is 13.6 to 1. Mercury is 13.6 times more dense than water. This is why air pressure was formerly measured with mercury barometers rather than water barometers. The latter would not fit in a normal classroom.

18. **(4)** The pressure is defined to be force per unit area. Weight is a force. The weight of the man divided by the area of the boots is 200 lb/70 square inches. This is a pressure of about 2.86 PSI. Notice that this is only about one-fifth of what the air applies to snow.

19. **(4)** The pressure is defined to be force per unit area. Weight is a force. The weight of the girl is 110 pounds. and the area of the skis is 330 square inches. This is a pressure of (110/330) 0.333 PSI. Since air applies a pressure of 14.7 PSI, it is greater by a factor of about 44. This explains why sleds and snowshoes are so useful in traveling great distances over snow-covered terrain.

20. **(1)** Since air exerts the same pressure whether it is viewed over one square inch or over one square mile, the one square foot column of water will be forced to the same 34-foot height. It is the total force that is greater on the larger area, but it is the ratio of force divided by area that is the same. The larger diameter column of fluid needs more force to reach the same height but the area is larger so that the pressure stays the same.

21. **(1)** Choice (1) is correct. Rivers are moving bodies of water and therefore can be considered agents of erosion. The faster the flow of water, the greater the rate of erosion. In December and January, the mean, maximum, and minimum flows are the highest. All of the other combinations of months: February and March (2), April and May (3), June and July (4), and August and September (5) have lower flow values.

22. **(3)** Answer choice (3), apical meristem, is the correct answer since it refers to an area where cells are actively dividing to produce growth. Plumule (1) cannot be the correct answer since it is a region of growth located between the first foliage leaves. Radical (2) cannot be the correct answer since it is a region of growth found at the opposite end of the plant from the plumule. Seed coat (4) cannot be the correct answer since it covers the seed and prevents mechanical injury. Cotyledon (5) cannot be the correct answer since it is a seed leaf that is found within the seed coat.

23. **(1)** Answer choice (1), plumule, is the correct answer since it is the growing region that is found between the first foliage leaves of the plant and will produce all of the shoot system. Radical (2) cannot be the correct answer since it is a region of growth found at the opposite end of the plant from the plumule. Meristem (3) cannot be the correct answer since it is a generalized term for a growing region of a plant. Seed coat (4) cannot be the correct answer since it covers the seed and prevents mechanical injury. Cotyledon (5) cannot be the correct answer since it is a seed leaf that is found within the seed coat.

24. **(2)** Answer choice (2), radical, is the correct answer since it is the region of growth found opposite the the plumule and will produce all of the root system. Plumule (1) cannot be the correct answer since it is a region of growth located between the first foliage leaves. Meristem (3) cannot be the correct answer since it is a generalized term for a growing region of a plant. Seed coat (4) cannot be the correct answer since it covers the seed and prevents mechanical injury. Cotyledon (5) cannot be the correct answer since it is a seed leaf that is found within the seed coat.

25. **(5)** Answer choice (5), cotyledons, is the correct answer since they are the leaves found inside the seed and the embryonic plant will use these for food until it can make its own food by photosynthesis. Plumule (1) cannot be the correct answer since it is a region of growth located between the first foliage leaves. Radical (2) cannot be the correct answer since it is a region of growth found at the opposite end of the plant from the radical. Apical meristem (3) cannot be the correct answer since it is a generalized term for a growing region of a plant. Seed coat (4) cannot be the correct answer since it covers the seed and prevents mechanical injury.

26. **(3)** Answer choice (3), vertebrates, is the correct answer since fish have a backbone (vertebrate). Filter feeders (1) cannot be the correct answer since these are animals like clams and oysters which have no backbones. Invertebrates (2) cannot be the correct answer since invertebrates do not have backbones. Zooplankton (4) are very small invertebrate animals that are carried by the currents and have no backbones. Phytoplankton (5) cannot be the correct answer since they are one- to few-celled plants and do not have backbones.

27. **(1)**   Answer choice (1), invertebrates, is the correct answer since zooplankton are very small animals without backbones. Vertebrates (2) cannot be the correct answer since vertebrates have backbones and zooplankton are not vertebrates. Phytoplankton (3) cannot be the correct answer since they are plant-like organisms. Toxic mucus (4) cannot be the correct answer since it is not mentioned in relation to being a type of organisms, but it is a protective device. Toxic mobile predators (5) cannot be the correct answer since zooplankton are carried by the currents, they are not extremely mobile, and they are not toxic.

28. **(5)**   Answer choice (5), be firmly attached, is the correct answer since being sessile is to be anchored or attached to something. Move around (1) cannot be the correct answer since sessile means to be attached or anchored to something. Swim freely (2) cannot be the correct answer since sessile means to be attached or anchored to something. Crawl along the sea floor (3) cannot be the correct answer since sessile means to be attached or anchored to something. Answer choice (4), float on the surface, is also wrong because something which floats is not sessile.

29. **(5)**   Answer choice (5), tiny enough to float near the surface, is the correct answer since zooplankton are very small and they are easily buoyed up by the water. Voracious predators (1) cannot be the correct answer since nothing of this nature is mentioned in the paragraph. Powerful swimmers (2) cannot be the correct answer since zooplankton are invertebrates and it is mentioned that invertebrates are not powerful swimmers. Fish (3) cannot be the correct answer since fish are not invertebrates. Able to move from one ocean current to another (4) cannot be the correct answer since this implies being able to be a powerful swimmer, which zooplankton are not.

30. **(2)**   The brain has several tissues working together. From this makeup it belongs to an organ in the levels-of-organization. Organelles are the parts in its cells. For example, mitochondria are organelles found in cells. The brain belongs to an organ system called the nervous system. For the student to identify an organ system, the brain must be presented with other organs of this system such as the spinal cord, cranial nerves, and spinal nerves.

31. **(1)**   Choice (1) is correct. Paper is made from trees and thus if paper is recycled instead of cutting down more trees, the trees can continue to use and store carbon dioxide and help remove it from the atmosphere. Removing trees (2) will reduce the uptake of carbon dioxide and leave more in the atmosphere. Reducing the amount of livestock (3) will decrease the transfer from plants to the animals and thus reduce the amount of carbon dioxide taken up by animals. Burning fossil fuels (4) will increase the amount of carbon dioxide in the atmosphere. Wood is organic matter and thus burning wood (5) will increase the production of carbon dioxide.

32. **(5)**   The cell membrane, which surrounds the outside of a cell, is the first barrier that a foreign molecule will meet. Nucleoplasm (1) is the

substance inside the nucleus and is far from the outside of a cell. Cytoplasm (2) is immediately inside the cell membrane, so the foreign molecule must pass the cell membrane first before reaching the cytoplasm. Both the nuclear membrane (3) and the chromosomes (4) are inside the cell and will not be the first structure reached by an approaching foreign molecule.

33. **(4)** There is a constant number of chromosomes for any somatic cell within an organism. Thus, choice (4) is correct. (1) is incorrect because the chromosomes do not assemble randomly. (2) is incorrect because it is the opposite of the correct answer. (3) is incorrect because the strength of the microscope will not change or affect the number of chromosomes. Also, during cell division, all of the chromosomes should be easily visible. (5) is incorrect because there is no evidence for nucleoli interfering with chromosome coiling.

34. **(2)** It is true that ribosomes function in protein synthesis, which occurs in the cytoplasm. Thus, the ribosomes must move from the site of their synthesis in the nucleus to the cytoplasm. Choice (2) is correct. (1) is incorrect because the ribosomes are located in the cytoplasm. (3) is incorrect because mitochondria, not ribosomes, produce the energy for a cell. (4) is wrong since there is no evidence that chromosome coiling interferes with ribosome formation. (5) is incorrect because one cannot assume that the product (the ribosome) of a dark staining organelle (the nucleolus) will also stain dark.

35. **(3)** A selective membrane is considered semipermeable (3) because some things pass through while others do not. Thus, (1) and (2) are wrong. The terms opaque (4) and translucent (5) refer to the ability of light to pass through. These terms are unrelated to selective membranes.

36. **(3)** Answer choice (3), nucleoli, is the correct answer since nucleoli are dark staining spherical bodies found suspended within the nucleoplasm. Nucleoplasm (1) cannot be the correct answer since the nucleoplasm is the viscous matrix inside of the nuclear membrane. Cytoplasm (2) cannot be the correct answer since it is the viscous matrix outside of the nuclear membrane. Chromosomes (4) cannot be the correct answer since they are rod-shaped bodies found suspended within the nucleoplasm. Mitochondria (5) cannot be the correct answer since they are found suspended in the cytoplasm.

37. **(3)** Answer choice (3), vacuoles, is the correct answer since vacuoles store either waste food, or water. Ribosomes (1) cannot be the correct answer since they are structures that function in protein synthesis and have nothing to do with storage. Mitochondria (2) cannot be the correct answer since they are the energy producers of the cell. Nucleoli (4) cannot be the correct answer since they are thought to produce the ribosomes. Chromosomes (5) cannot be the correct answer since they carry the genetic code.

38. **(2)** Answer choice (2), nucleoli, is the correct answer since nucleoli, which are composed of RNA, are thought to produce ribosomes which function in protein synthesis. Chromosomes (1) cannot be the correct answer since they carry the genetic code. Vacuoles (3) cannot be the correct answer since they are storage structures. Mitochondria (4) cannot be the correct answer since they are the energy producers of the cell. Cytoplasm (5) cannot be the correct answer since the cytoplasm is the viscous matrix in which many of the organelles are suspended.

39. **(3)** The right answer is (3). Rutherford concluded that the particles were colliding with the nucleus of the gold atom, which is where most of the mass of the atom is concentrated. (1) is incorrect because the particles do have enough velocity to pass through the empty space surrounding the nuclei. (2) is wrong because the electrons have a mass too small to repel alpha particles. (4) is wrong because although alpha rays and gold nuclei are both positively charged, this would not cause the large deflection. (5) is wrong because air cannot pull alpha particles in any way.

40. **(1)** is correct since it is true that most of the atom is empty space. (2) is wrong because the thickness of the gold foil does not affect the movement of the alpha particles. If a nucleus was in the path of the particle, the particle would then be deflected. (3) is wrong because the electrons are too small to influence the alpha particles. (4) is incorrect; atomic nuclei are not semi-permeable. They are dense and cause the alpha particles to be deflected. (5) is wrong because the nuclei will not be moved by the alpha particles. Instead, the alpha particles collide with the nuclei and bounce off at an angle.

41. **(5)** Choice (5), Au, is the correct answer. (4) Na is the chemical symbol for sodium. (3) He is the symbol for helium. Hg, answer choice (2), is mercury, and (1), Ga, is the symbol for Gallium.

42. **(5)** Spores are airborne bodies. These structures can be inhaled and enter the human body through the respiratory tract (5). Spores do not enter by the blood of the circulatory system (1). They do not enter by food passing through the digestive system (2). They do not attack the nervous system directly (3). Although spores are reproductive bodies for fungi, they do not attack the human reproductive system (4).

43. **(3)** As the comet approaches the sun, the materials in the head vaporize and are pushed away from the sun by the solar winds (3). The solar winds are always present and thus do not affect the formation of the comet's tail (1). The tail of the comet appears as the comet approaches the sun, not as it moves away from the sun (2). The tail is pushed away by the solar winds and is not attracted by the solar winds (4).

44. **(2)** The pattern of radioactivity loss is as follows: full amount to 1/2 after one million years; 1/2 to 1/4 after another one million years, bringing the

running total to two million; 1/4 to 1/8 after another one million years, bringing the running total to three million; and 1/8 to 1/16 after another one million years. Thus, the total time accumulation is four million years.

45. **(5)** Answer choice (5), internal, is the correct answer since sharks do not lay their eggs to be externally fertilized by the male shark. Denticle (1) cannot be the correct answer since denticles are the little toothlike append-ages found on the skin of a shark. Viviparous (2) cannot be the correct answer since this term refers to how the embryos of some kinds of shark get their nourishment. Ovoviparous (3) cannot be the correct answer since this term refers to how the embryos of some kinds of shark get their nourishment. External (4) cannot be the correct answer since sharks do not lay eggs to be externally fertilized by the male shark.

46. **(5)** Answer choice (5), class Chondrichthyes, is the correct answer since sharks, rays, skates, and dogfishes are members of this class. Phylum Reptilia (1) cannot be the correct answer since there is no phylum Reptilia, and it is not mentioned in the paragraph. Class Aves (2) cannot be the correct answer since this is a class/group of birds, and it is not mentioned in the paragraph. Class Vertebrata (3) cannot be the correct answer since there is no class Vertebrata, even though the shark is a vertebrate animal. Class Osteichthyes (4) cannot be the correct answer since this is the class of fish that have skeletons composed of bone.

47. **(5)** Answer choice (5), "as an embryo it gets its nourishment from the yolk's blood vessels, which are close to the oviduct's blood vessels," is correct because this is the correct term referring to viviparous. "As an embryo it eats its brothers and sisters before they hatch" (1) cannot be the correct answer since viviparous refers to an embryo that gets its nourishment from the mother's blood supply by having the yolk's blood vessels close to the oviduct's blood vessels. "As an embryo it gets nourishment from the yolk" (2) cannot be the correct answer since viviparous refers to an embryo that gets its nourishment from the mother's blood supply by having the yolk's blood vessels close the the oviduct's blood vessels. "As an embryo it gets its nourishment directly from the mother's blood" (3) cannot be the correct answer since viviparous refers to an embryo that gets its nourishment from the mother's blood supply by having the yolk's blood vessels close to the oviduct's blood vessels. "As an embryo it gets its nourishment by eating the mother's oviduct" (4) cannot be the correct answer since viviparous refers to an embryo that gets its nourishment from the mother's blood supply by having the yolk's blood vessels close to the oviduct's blood vessels.

48. **(1)** Answer choice (1), denticles is the correct answer since embed-ded in the shark's skin are little toothlike appendages called denticles. Yolks (2) cannot be the correct answer since yolks are not found in the skin. Oviducts (3) cannot be the correct answer since oviducts are part of the reproductive system and not a part of the skin. Embryos (4) cannot be the correct answer since embryos are, in this case, young sharks. Internal

fertilization (5) cannot be the correct answer since this is a process and not a structure.

49. **(3)**   Answer choice (3), roots, is the correct answer since the main function of the root system is to absorb water and minerals, and to firmly anchor the plant in the ground. Flower (1) cannot be the correct answer since the main function of a flower is reproduction. Stem (2) cannot be the correct answer since the main function of the stem is the support of the leaves and flowers. Stomata (4) cannot be the correct answer since stomata are openings on the underside of leaves that aid in transpiration. Leaves (5) cannot be the correct answer since the main function of leaves is in the process of photosynthesis.

50. **(4)**   Answer choice (4), flowers, is the correct answer since the seed is an embryonic plant that is produced by flowers. Nodes (1) cannot be the correct answer since nodes are regions from where leaves arise. Internodes (2) cannot be the correct answer since internodes are the regions between nodes. Stomata (3) cannot be the correct answer since stomata are openings on the underside of leaves that aid in transpiration. Tubers (5) cannot be the correct answer since tubers are formed in the roots of a plant.

TEST 4: LANGUAGE ARTS:
READING

1.   **(3)**   Laura is upset because (3), she thinks Tom is unhappy. This is revealed near the beginning of the passage when Amanda tells Torn that Laura "has an idea that you're not happy here." Although Tom does go to the movies without her (2) and although Tom cannot describe his feelings (4), neither of these are the reason Amanda expresses. Answer (1), Tom has left home, cannot be correct because Amanda specifically says Laura "has an idea that you're not happy here," where they are together, and we know that Tom is Amanda's son. We can safely assume that he is still living at home, so he cannot be happy without her (5).

2.   **(4)**   Tom goes to the movies because (4), he is restless. This is the best answer because when Amanda asks Tom why he's "always so restless" and where he goes at night, he replies that he goes to the movies. We also know that he's bored at work, so he goes to the movies for adventure. He doesn't go because he wants to be an actor (1)—there's no mention of this anywhere in the passage—or because he likes to be alone (2)—again, there's no mention of this, although it may indeed be true. There is also no evidence that he wants to be apart from Amanda (5). Finally, answer (3), because he is Christian, is not correct, because according to Amanda, Tom's movie-going is not Christian.

3.   **(2)**   Amanda is upset because Tom is always out (2). Amanda wants to know where Tom goes at night and why he's always at the movies. We learn from their conversation that he goes out because he's not happy, and Amanda becomes upset that he's not happy.

4.   **(2)**   We can tell from this passage that Tom and Amanda (2), fight often. We know they are not very open with each other (1) because Amanda says, "There's so many things in my heart that I cannot describe to you!" and Tom says the same ("There's so much in my heart that I can't describe to you!"). We can infer that Amanda is not adventurous since she tells Tom "Not everybody has a craze for adventure" and tries to tell him to control his instincts, so (3) cannot be correct. This passage shows us that Tom, at least, isn't happy, so (4) cannot be correct. Finally, we know they do not agree on everything so (5) cannot be correct.

5.   **(4)**   Amanda thinks Tom should be satisfied with what he has. She tells him that people who do not find adventure in their careers "do without it!" She tells him that life "calls for—Spartan endurance!" Furthermore, she is clearly upset by his restlessness and desire for adventure. We know that she wants him to stay home at night instead of going to the movies and that she wants

him to control his instinct for adventure, because instinct "belongs to animals!"

6.   **(2)**   The answer is (2). The answer can be found in the first sentence of the paragraph entitled "Risk of loss": "The Seller assumes all risk of destruction, loss or damage due to fire or other casualty up to the date of closing." The customers (4) and suppliers (5) are not responsible for the care and upkeep of the company. Neither are the attorneys (3) who are only aiding in the legal transaction of the sale of the company. The Buyer (1) is only responsible for damage after the closing date.

7.   **(3)**   The correct answer is (3). The answer can be found in the last sentence of the third paragraph. The contract can only be cancelled (1) if there is damage which curtails the ability of the business to continue.

8.   **(1)**   The answer is (1). The seller's obligations pending closing are in the paragraph entitled "Seller's obligations pending closing."

9.   **(4)**   The correct answer is (4). The answer can be found in the paragraph "Seller's obligation pending closing" which states that the Seller should maintain an accurate record of sales from January 31, 2002 until the closing date.

10. **(3)**   The answer is number (3). The answer is found in the last paragraph. Although the last paragraph includes supplemental details, it is in essence an agreement that the seller will not own or operate a business that competes with that of the buyer, within a radius of fifty miles, for a period of five years.

11. **(3)**   is correct when using guidelines from the question itself; the "turn of events" is that the artist was initially "neglected," now considered by some as "America's first." Choices (1) modernists rejected him and (2) art resists easy classification do not present a "turn of events." (4) is also incorrect since it does not contain an incongruity of what is expected and what actually happens. Combining richness and simplicity is simply a statement of style, not irony (5).

12. **(3)**   "Carefree" is the most accurate answer since lines 8 and 9 define him as an artist who has taken "all the work out and left only the joy." Conservative (1) is incorrect according to line 7, "vibrant images," and so is (4), ordinary, since lines 29 and 30 describe his work as "an explosion in a color factory." Suggestive (5) is a poor choice because nothing suggests that his work brings something else to mind.

13. **(1)**   The most apt and literal definition for pathfinder is "unlike any of his predecessors." All of the following are mentioned in the review, but they do not adequately define the term: (2) difficult to classify, (3) hard worker, (5)

influenced by Impressionists. (4) is incorrect since nothing in the review states or suggests that Pendergast's successors were affected by his success.

14. **(4)** Line 26 is clear as to what was revolutionary—"Above all, his color—or rather, the amount he used—was new." (1) Lines 20 and 21 state that he took his improvisational brushwork from the Impressionists, making it anything but new. His subjective, stylized view of reality (2) is not new either, but rather patterned after the Postimpressionists (lines 21 and 22). Additionally, (3) is incorrect since he borrowed his decorative expression of color from the Nabis.

15. **(5)** Clearly, father refuses to talk to his wife because in his opinion his farm business does not require his wife's opinion or deal with her sphere of the house to which he orders her to go back; the home is her affair, not the farm.

16. **(4)** Words like "diggin'," "an'," and "ain't" portray a non-standard form of speaking particular to a certain section of the country or a certain type of person. (1) and (2) are poetic terms. There is no hint of irony (5) or exaggeration (3).

17. **(2)** Mother's persistence and defiance make her quite strong-willed; certainly none of the other choices would justify the fact that father sees her as "immovable."

18. **(1)** Mother blatantly says, "we was goin' to have a house." (2) Geography and (5) economics do not factor into their discussion. Mother does not sound (3) pleased or (4) willing to help out with the barn since she questions the idea in the first place.

19. **(2)** The poem tells a story, so it is narrative. It is too long for (1) a sonnet or (3) a limerick and too short for (5) an epic poem. (4) Although folk ballad is narrative also, the missing element is that this poem is not designed to be sung.

20. **(2)** The poet effectively uses metaphor in the first three lines that implicitly compare two objects (road and ribbon). (1) If "like" or "as" were used then the poetic technique would be simile. There is more rhythmic beat than (3) rhyme; neither (4) gross exaggeration nor (5) entertainment are apparent.

21. **(3)** From his claret velvet coat to his French cocked hat, there is no doubt that he is a romantic and dashing figure. No hint of any other possible choice is apparent in lines 6 through 14.

22. **(3)** In line 21, Bess is braiding a dark red "love-knot" in her long black hair; the symbolism is explicitly love.

23. **(2)** Since a metaphor, unlike a simile, does not employ the use of "like" or "as," eyes were hollows of madness is the correct answer. (4) and (5) are similes.

24. **(3)** A close look at these lines reveal that he is "after a prize to-night," and he will be back with "the yellow gold" before daylight. Therefore, "planned a robbery" is the best answer.

25. **(4)** Since meter in poetry is its measure, a close look at these stanzas suggest horses' hoof beats due mainly to the number of monosyllable words.

26. **(3)** Although the narrator wishes us to believe that he is "nervous" we are led to believe that he is not "healthy" in mind, but crazy. He seems to be struggling to be (1) clever, and (4) intelligent, but he falls short. There is no hint of (2) anger or (5) suicidal tendencies.

27. **(2)** Since "gold" could be used synonymously with money, and since the old man has gold, it seems that the old man therefore has money.

28. **(4)** The speaker is quite clear that there was no passion, just the desire to be rid of "the eye."

29. **(2)** The desire to prove to the reader that he is not mad is evident when the speaker utters this phrase. To select (1) is mad or (3) is not mad would be too presumptive. He is too apparent in motive to be (4) clever; nor is he (5) concerned about the old man since he plans to kill him.

30. **(4)** Line 32, "but I found the eye always closed," excludes all other possible answers.

31. **(1)** Lines 34–39 include "spoke courageously" and calling in a "hearty tone" while all the while plotting his demise indicate that the speaker is proud and self-serving rather than (2) sincere and (3) charitable. Since we are considering the speaker's intentions, (4) hesitant and (5) frivolous are poor choices.

32. **(5)** The general tone of the narration from the onset is anxious, as witnessed by statements as "—nervous—very dreadfully nervous—." (1) Tranquil and (3) reverential are entirely inappropriate responses. The narrator is neither (2) afraid of his crime, since he is so calculating, and neither is he (4) hostile, since he tells us that he has no passion for the old man.

33. **(2)** "Desperate haste to succeed" as well as "keeping pace with companions" are but two of a number of phrases suggesting that society does pressure man in a quest for achievement and success, excluding all other choices.

34. **(1)** These often-quoted lines have far-reaching implications when taken as intended as figures of speech. "Keep pace" could mean trying to "keep up with," and "different drummer," as figurative language, could mean a man's inner drive or natural bent.

35. **(1)** Imagery of nature is present within this excerpt with references to apple and oak trees. By inference (2) material wealth is not held in high regard as suggested by such terms as "desperate enterprises."

36. **(4)** Humble is the closest synonym for mean in this particular context, since we are soon instructed not to "shun it and call it hard names," and that "It looks poorest when you are richest." There are no references to an (1) unkind, (2) benevolent, or (5) lonely life. Since (3) wealthy is an antonym for the intended meaning of the word, it is also incorrect.

37. **(4)** Mention is made of having "pleasant, thrilling glorious hours, even in a poorhouse," as well as other references suggesting that true happiness is not a result of material wealth. Since the question asks for the message of the excerpt, the reader must be careful not to make judgments based on personal beliefs concerning wealth and happiness as suggested in choices (1), (2), and (3). Since (5) does not include wealth or the lack of wealth, it is a poor choice.

38. **(5)** Nonappreciative is the best description of material wealth as revealed in the comparison of the "alms-house" and the "rich man's abode." Since (1) sympathetic and (2) accepting are entirely opposite of the author's intended attitude, they are poor choices. Both (3) envious and (4) contemptuous are unsubstantiated.

39. **(1)** The third passage concentrates on truth and mentions sincerity. (5) Nature is forgotten momentarily. (2) Material wealth is opposite in the inherent intent of the line as well as (3) a rare, vintage wine. (4) Mankind and greed is a value judgment and not part of the general theme.

40. **(3)** Since this entire passage endorses truth, "rather than love, than money, than fame…," then (3) truth and sincerity is your best choice. (1) Nature, as in the preceding passage, is momentarily put aside. (2) Material wealth is mentioned as lesser in importance than truth and sincerity; and since (4) a rare, vintage wine is symbolic of wealth, it is not endorsed. (5) Heaven is not referred to.

TEST 5: MATHEMATICS

PART 1

1.   **(4)**   This multi-step problem requires multiplication and then addition. Two times $4.19 is $8.38 plus two times $0.69 ($1.38) plus three times $1.15 ($3.45) equals $13.21. Multiplying $13.21 by 0.05 to find the tax is $0.66. Adding the tax to the total of merchandise gives $13.87.

2.   **(3)** $86 = 80 + 4x$. A standard score is found by taking the difference of a raw score and the mean, then dividing by the standard deviation. So $x = (86 - 80)/4$, which is equivalent to $86 = 80 + 4x$. (Note: The number 30 was *not* used.)

3.   **(5)**   The correct answer is found by adding together the costs of the items, which is $33.36, and multiplying this by 0.06 to find the tax of $2.00, and adding the two totals together.

4.   **(1)**   The formula for the area of a trapezoid is $280 = (1/2)(\overline{PY})(\overline{PQ} + \overline{TR})$. Since $(\overline{PQ}) = 10$ and $\overline{TR} = 30$, we can solve for $(\overline{PY})$ to get 14. The perimeter of PQXY = $2(14 + 10) = 48$.

5.   **(4)**   Completing the formula $A = 1/2 (4\sqrt{3})(48)$. The formula for the area of a circle is $A = \pi r^2$. Since the diameter is 10, the radius is 5. Completing the formula: $A = 3.14$ times $25 = 78.5$.

6.   **(3)** $AE = \sqrt{(ED)^2 - (AD)^2} = \sqrt{13^2 - 12^2} = 15$. (Note: AD = AB). Then $EB = 12 - 5 = 7$. EC is the hypotenuse of $\triangle EBC$, which has legs of 7 and 12, therefore the Pythagoreon theorem can be applied to $\triangle EBC$ to find the length of EC: $7^2 + 12^2 = x^2$.

7.   **(3)**   The tax rate is $2.10 for each $100 in value. There are 550 one hundred dollars in $55,000. Therefore the tax is $2.10 times 550, or $1,155.

8.   **(2)** $\angle G = 1/2 (\widehat{IJ} - \widehat{HJ})$, so $25° = 1/2 (140° - \widehat{HJ})$. Then $\widehat{HJ} = 90°$. $\widehat{IH} = 360° - \widehat{IJ} - \widehat{HJ} = 130°$.

9.   **(4)**   98 divided by 2 gives the cost of one pound, which is $0.49. Then $0.49 times 5 is $2.45.

10.   **(1)**   This problem requires a system of equations. Let *A* represent the number of adult tickets and *S* represent the number of student tickets, then $A + S = 350$. The value of the adult tickets is $5 a piece and the value of the student tickets is $3.50 a piece and the total value for all of the tickets is

$1,306. The equation for this is $5A + 3.5S = 1,306$. If $A + S = 350$, then $A = 350 - S$. This can be substituted in the second equation for A and get $5(350 - S) + 3.5S = 1,306$. Distribute the 5 and get $1,750 - 5S + 3.5S = 1,306$. Collect like terms and solve for S to find 54 is the number of adult tickets. Subtract this from 350 to get 296 student tickets.

11. **(3)**　Angle BEF and angle CFE are alternate interior angles and are therefore congruent, or equal in measure. If we can find the measure of either one, we will know the measure of angle CFE. We know that angle GEB and angle BEF form a linear pair, and we know angle GEB measures 40 degrees. Subtracting 40 from 180 we find that angle BEF is 140 degrees. Since CFE is an alternate interior angle and congruent to angle BEF, the measure of angle CFE is 140 degrees.

12. **(5)**　"At least a B" means a grade of B, B+, or A. Therefore, one adds the frequencies of these grades and then multiplies that sum by 800: $(0.17 + 0.27 + 0.44)(800) = 704$.

13. **(4)**　"Below C+" means C, D+, or D. One adds the relative frequencies of these grades and then converts the sum to a percentage. This corresponds to $0.02 + 0.01 + 0.01 = 0.04 = 4\%$.

14. **(3)**　The top 1% is $(0.01)(800) = 8$ students. Since $(0.44)(800) = 352$ students who received a grade of A, $352 - 8 = 344$ of them did *not* receive the monetary award.

15. **(5)**　Two tickets times $400 equals $800, plus $210 equals $1,010. Multiplying by 0.1 (for 10%), the answer is $101.

16. **(5)**　The correct answer is found by multiplying 300 by 3.5.

17. **(4)**　Area of $\triangle M'N'P' = 96 = (1/2)\,(N'P')\,(M'N') = (1/2)\,(12)\,(M'N')$, so $M'N' = 16$.

$$M'P' = \sqrt{12^2 + 16^2} = 20$$

The sides of $\triangle M'N'P'$ are 12, 16, and 20. Reduced, this gives us a ratio of 3:4:5. Since the two triangles are similar we can apply this same ratio to $\triangle MNP$. This would make sides $NP = 10.2$, $MN = 13.6$, and $MP = 17$. To find the area ($A = 1/2\ bh$), we use $1/2(10.2)(13.6) = 69.36$.

18. **(5)**　2/3 represents the amount of work done by the larger hose, whereas $2/x$ is the amount of work done by the smaller hose. In this context, amount of work equals the fraction of the pool being filled up. The total of 1 represents the complete filling of the pool by both hoses.

19. **33**　Let n represent the number of nickels and q represent the number of quarters, then $n = q + 3$. The value of the nickels is 5 cents and the value

of the quarters is 25 cents and the total value of the coins she has is 465 cents or $4.65. The equation for this is $5n + 25q = 465$. If $(q + 3)$ is substituted in the second equation for n, we get $5(q + 3) + 25q = 465$. Distribute the 5 and get $5q + 15 + 25q = 465$. Collect like terms $30q + 15 = 465$. Subtract 15 from both sides $30q = 450$, then divide both sides by 30 to find $q = 15$. She has three more nickels than that or $15 + 3 = 18$. She has 18 nickels and 15 quarters for a total of 33 coins.

20. **50** $\angle Q + \angle R = 180° - 80° = 100°$. Since $\angle Q = 3 \times \angle R$, $\angle R = 25°$ and $\angle Q = 75°$. Finally arc PQ must be 50°, or twice the amount of $\angle R$, since an inscribed angle is half its intercepted arc.

21. **3.2**   Let $x =$ the hours traveled at 55 miles per hour. Then $4.8 - x =$ the hours traveled at 40 miles per hour. We then get the equation $55x + 40(4.8 - x) = 240$, for which $x = 3.2$.

22. **34**   2 times 17 is 34. The number of marbles Joe has is not known and is not needed.

23. **3,670** The correct answer is obtained by multiplying 367 miles times 50 weeks times $0.20.

24. **15**   Arrange in order these numbers: 9, 10, 2, 18, 22, 30. The median

$$= \frac{12 + 18}{2} = 15.$$

25. **(−6, 2)** Since this line segment has a negative slope (−3), its highest y value corresponds to its lowest x value. The lowest x value is −6 and by substitution, $y = 2$.

PART 2

26. **(1)** This may be solved by "translating" the problem directly into algebraic symbols. "What" = x, percent = 0.01, "of" = multiply or times, and "in" = equals. Put this together and you have an equation, $x (0.01) (80) = 32$. Solve for x and x = 40. This is the percent. Another way to work this problem is to divide 32 by 80 and multiply by 100. A third way to work percent problems is by setting up a proportion, with the "parts" on top and the "wholes" on the bottom.

percent quantity

$$\frac{x}{100} = \frac{32}{80}$$

By solving the proportion, you find the answer to the problem. You may use a proportion to solve any percent problem by letting x fill in the unknown place in the proportion.

27. **(1)** The cost of the drill is $5; the cost of the mixer is $20, so it costs $25 for each day, and the real answer is $25 \times 3 = \$75$.

28. **(5)** To solve this, simply divide both sides of the equation by r.

29. **(5)** The formula usually used to find the area of any polygon is $A = 1/2\ ap$, where a is the apothem and p is the perimeter. Since the side is known and the number of sides is known, the perimeter can be found. It is 8 times 6 or 48. The apothem is the segment from the center of the figure perpendicular to one of the sides (see figure below). The radius (the segment from the center of the figure to a vertex) is 8, the same length as a side, and forms a triangle with the apothem and a side. This triangle is 30-60-90. The side opposite the 30 angle is 4, therefore the apothem is $4\sqrt{3}$.

30. **(3)** The rule for multiplying variables with exponents is $a^N \times a^M = a^{N+M}$. So the exponents are just added together.

31. **(3)**   There are 52 weeks in a year, therefore multiply the weekly cost of $26.03 by 52 = $1,353.56.

32. **(5)**   When a fraction is raised to a power, both the numerator and the denominator is raised to that power. So, x^2 taken as a factor 5 times is x^{10}, and y taken as a factor 5 times is y^5.

33. **(4)**   Angle ACD is called an exterior angle of the triangle, and it is equal to the sum of the two remote interior angles. This means you add the two opposite angles inside the triangle and the answer is the measure of angle ACD.

Another way to obtain the answer is to find the measure of the interior angle of the triangle at C, by adding the other two angles and then subtracting from 180. Angle C is 72 degrees. Then the two angles at point C form a linear pair whose sum is 180. So subtract 72 from 180 and you have the measure of angle ACD.

34. **(2)**   The best answer given is not exact, but it is an estimate. 76 rounds to 80, which goes into 4,000,000 exactly 50,000 times. Answer (1) is 76 times 4. Answer (3) is produced by incorrectly rounding 76 to 70 and dividing that into the 4,000,000. Answer (4) is 76 times 4, and answer (5) is 4,000,000 divided by 100.

35. **(5)**   Answer (5) is correct because 7 times $(-4y)$ is $(-28y)$, and 7 times 2 is 14.

36. **(4)**   The correct answer is found by finding the unit cost (cost for one pencil) in each of the three price structures. $0.10 each is $0.10 for one. 2 dozen is 24 and dividing that into $2.50 gives $0.10416666 as the cost for one. $0.99 divided by 10 makes this the best buy at $0.099 for one pencil. There is a slight difference in the costs, but still $0.099 is the smallest value. (The difference is evident if we buy in large quantity.)

37. **(3)**   This problem is in the form of $A^2 + 2AB + B^2$, which is the square of a binomial $(A + B)^2$. So the answer is $(x + 3)^2$.

38. **(1)**   Her chances are 8 out of 1,600 or 8/1,600. This is one out of 200 or 0.5%.

39. **(4)**   The problem is asking, "20 times what equals 220." You must know that the length times the width of a rectangle is the area, and then use algebra to solve for the unknown. $20x = 220$. Divide both sides by 20 to find $x = 11$. Also, for a problem like this, you may try each answer to find the one which gives 220.

40. **(3)**   If one integer is represented by x the the next consecutive integer is $(x + 1)$. The product is represented by $x(x + 1)$.

41. **(1)**   To read the graph properly, notice that the columns represent millions of dollars, so locate 1.5 for the $1,500,000. Then look down to the bottom of the column to read the name of the salesperson. It is J. Johns.

42. **(1)**   First find the amount sold by P. Sellers. Look to the top of the column above his name and read the amount to the left. It is 0.5 or one half of a million dollars. Three times that would be 1.5 million. The person selling 1.5 million is J. Johns. C. Chan did not sell that much, and S. Smith sold more.

43. **(1)**   This is found by taking 25%, or 1/4, of $2,500 and then multiplying by 12 months.

44. **(2)**   The correct answer is written on the graph.

45. **(2)**   She saves 12% of $2,500, or $300.

46. **(2)**   All sides of an equilateral triangle are congruent, or have the same measure. The altitude is the perpendicular bisector of the base and the bisector of the vertex angle. So the altitude divides the triangle into two triangles that have angles of 30°-60°-90°. The sides of this kind of triangle have the special relationship $1:\sqrt{3}:2$. This makes the length of the altitude of our triangle $3\sqrt{3}$.

47. **(5)**   To find the $f(-3)$ simply substitute (-3) for x. This gives $f(-3) = -(-3) + 4$, which is 7, because $-(-3) = +3$.

48. **4**   12 times 1/3 or 12 divided by 3 is 4. Each person would get 4 pieces.

49. **420** The easiest way to solve this is with a chart. The chart below represents the trip going and the trip returning. The distance is the same for both trips. The trip going has the speed of the airplane plus the tail wind. The trip returning has the speed of the airplane minus the tail wind. The times are as stated.

	D =	r	t
going ➡	D	r + 60	6
returning ⬅	D	r - 60	8

Since the distance equals the rate times the time and the distances are equal, set up an equation of representations of the equal distances and solve: $6(r + 60) = 8(r - 60)$. $6r + 360 = 8r - 480$. Then $r = 420$.

50. **(1,3)** Let (x,y) represent the required point. Then, $x - (-5) = 2(4 - x)$, which yields $x = 1$. Also $7 - y = 2(y - 1)$, which yields $y = 3$.

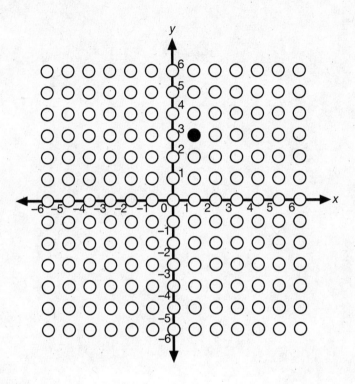

▼
APPENDIX

MATHEMATICS REFERENCE TABLE

SYMBOLS AND THEIR MEANINGS

$=$	is equal to	$\leq$	is less than or equal to
$\neq$	is unequal to	$\geq$	is greater than or equal to
$<$	is less than	$\parallel$	is parallel to
$>$	is greater than	$\perp$	is perpendicular to

FORMULAS

DESCRIPTION	FORMULA

AREA (A) of a:

    square $A = s^2$; where s = side

    rectangle $A = lw$; where l = length, w = width

    parallelogram $A = bh$; where b = base, h = height

    triangle $A = \frac{1}{2} bh$; where b = base, h = height

    circle $A = \pi r^2$; where π = 3.14, r = radius

PERIMETER (P) of a:

    square $P = 4s$; where s = side

    rectangle $P = 2l + 2w$; where l = length, w = width

    triangle $P = a + b + c$; where a, b, and c are the sides

    circumference (C) of a circle $C = \pi d$, where π = 3.14, d = diameter

VOLUME (V) of a:

    cube $V = s^2$; where s = side

    rectangular container $V = lwh$; where l = length, w = width, h = height

    Pythagorean relationship $c^2 = a^2 + b^2$; where c = hypotenuse, a and b are legs of a right triangle

    distance (d) between two points in a plane $d = \sqrt{(x_2 - x_1)^2 + (y_2 - y_1)^2}$

where (x_1, y_1) and (x_2, y_2) are two points in a plane

    mean $\text{mean} = \dfrac{x_1 + x_2 + \ldots + x_n}{n}$;

where the x's are the values for which a mean is desired, and n = number of values in the series

    median   **median** = the point in an ordered set of numbers at which half of the numbers are above and half of the numbers are below this value

    simple interest (i) $i = prt$; where p = principal, r = rate, t = time

    distance (d) as function of rate and time $d = rt$; where r = rate, t = time

    total cost (c) $c = nr$; where n = number of units, r = *cost per unit*

THE PERIODIC TABLE

METALS — NONMETALS

KEY

Atomic Number → 22
Symbol → Ti
Atomic Weight → 47.88
Group Classification → 4 / IVA / IVB

( ) indicates most stable or best known isotope

TRANSITIONAL METALS

Alkali Metals · Alkaline Earth Metals

1 IA	2 IIA	3 IIIB	4 IVB	5 VB	6 VIB	7 VIIB	8 VIII	9 VIII	10 VIII	11 IB	12 IIB	13 IIIA	14 IVA	15 VA	16 VIA	17 VIIA Halogens	18 VIII 0 Noble Gases
1 H 1.008																	2 He 4.003
3 Li 6.941	4 Be 9.012											5 B 10.811	6 C 12.011	7 N 14.007	8 O 15.999	9 F 18.998	10 Ne 20.180
11 Na 22.990	12 Mg 24.305											13 Al 26.982	14 Si 28.086	15 P 30.974	16 S 32.066	17 Cl 35.453	18 Ar 39.948
19 K 39.098	20 Ca 40.078	21 Sc 44.956	22 Ti 47.88	23 V 50.942	24 Cr 51.996	25 Mn 54.938	26 Fe 55.847	27 Co 58.933	28 Ni 58.693	29 Cu 63.546	30 Zn 65.39	31 Ga 69.723	32 Ge 72.61	33 As 74.922	34 Se 78.96	35 Br 79.904	36 Kr 83.8
37 Rb 85.468	38 Sr 87.62	39 Y 88.906	40 Zr 91.224	41 Nb 92.906	42 Mo 95.94	43 Tc (97.907)	44 Ru 101.07	45 Rh 102.906	46 Pd 106.4	47 Ag 107.868	48 Cd 112.411	49 In 114.818	50 Sn 118.710	51 Sb 121.757	52 Te 127.60	53 I 126.905	54 Xe 131.29
55 Cs 132.905	56 Ba 137.327	57 La 138.906	72 Hf 178.49	73 Ta 180.948	74 W 183.84	75 Re 186.207	76 Os 190.23	77 Ir 192.22	78 Pt 195.08	79 Au 196.967	80 Hg 200.59	81 Tl 204.383	82 Pb 207.2	83 Bi 208.980	84 Po (208.982)	85 At (209.982)	86 Rn (222.018)
87 Fr (223.020)	88 Ra (226.025)	89 Ac (227.028)	104 Rf (261.108)	105 Db (262.114)	106 Sg (266.121)	107 Bh (264.124)	108 Hs (269.134)	109 Mt (268.138)	110 Uun (271.146)	111 Uuu (272.153)	112 Uub (277)		114 Uuq (289)		116 Uuh (289)		118 Uuo (293)

LANTHANIDE SERIES

58 Ce 140.115	59 Pr 140.908	60 Nd 144.24	61 Pm (144.913)	62 Sm 150.36	63 Eu 151.965	64 Gd 157.25	65 Tb 158.925	66 Dy 162.50	67 Ho 164.930	68 Er 167.26	69 Tm 168.934	70 Yb 173.04	71 Lu 174.967

ACTINIDE SERIES

90 Th 232.038	91 Pa 231.036	92 U 238.029	93 Np (237.048)	94 Pu (244.064)	95 Am (243.061)	96 Cm (247.070)	97 Bk (247.070)	98 Cf (251.080)	99 Es (252.083)	100 Fm (257.095)	101 Md (258.1)	102 No (259.101)	103 Lr (262.11)

The Declaration of Independence

Drafted by Thomas Jefferson between June 11 and June 28, 1776, the Declaration of Independence is at once the nation's most cherished symbol of liberty and Jefferson's most enduring monument. Here, in exalted and unforgettable phrases, Jefferson expressed the convictions in the minds and hearts of the American people. The political philosophy of the Declaration was not new; its ideals of individual liberty had already been expressed by John Locke and the Continental philosophers. What Jefferson did was to summarize this philosophy in "self-evident truths" and set forth a list of grievances against the King in order to justify before the world the breaking of ties between the colonies and the mother country.

IN CONGRESS, July 4, 1776.

The unanimous Declaration of the thirteen United States of America,

When in the Course of human events, it becomes necessary for one people to dissolve the political bands which have connected them with another, and to assume among the powers of the earth, the separate and equal station to which the Laws of Nature and of Nature's God entitle them, a decent respect to the opinions of mankind requires that they should declare the causes which impel them to the separation.

We hold these truths to be self-evident, that all men are created equal, that they are endowed by their Creator with certain unalienable Rights, that among these are Life, Liberty and the pursuit of Happiness.—That to secure these rights, Governments are instituted among Men, deriving their just powers from the consent of the governed, —That whenever any Form of Government becomes destructive of these ends, it is the Right of the People to alter or to abolish it, and to institute new Government, laying its foundation on such principles and organizing its powers in such form, as to them shall seem most likely to effect their Safety and Happiness. Prudence, indeed, will dictate that Governments long established should not be changed for light and transient causes; and accordingly all experience hath shewn, that mankind are more disposed to suffer, while evils are sufferable, than to right themselves by abolishing the forms to which they are accustomed. But when a long train of abuses and usurpations, pursuing invariably the same Object evinces a design to reduce them under absolute Despotism, it is their right, it is their duty, to throw off such Government, and to provide new Guards for their future security.—Such has been the patient sufferance of these Colonies; and such is now the necessity which constrains them to alter their former Systems of Government. The history of the present King of Great

Britain is a history of repeated injuries and usurpations, all having in direct object the establishment of an absolute Tyranny over these States. To prove this, let Facts be submitted to a candid world.

He has refused his Assent to Laws, the most wholesome and necessary for the public good.

He has forbidden his Governors to pass Laws of immediate and pressing importance, unless suspended in their operation till his Assent should be obtained; and when so suspended, he has utterly neglected to attend to them.

He has refused to pass other Laws for the accommodation of large districts of people, unless those people would relinquish the right of Representation in the Legislature, a right inestimable to them and formidable to tyrants only.

He has called together legislative bodies at places unusual, uncomfortable, and distant from the depository of their public Records, for the sole purpose of fatiguing them into compliance with his measures.

He has dissolved Representative Houses repeatedly, for opposing with manly firmness his invasions on the rights of the people.

He has refused for a long time, after such dissolutions, to cause others to be elected; whereby the Legislative powers, incapable of Annihilation, have returned to the People at large for their exercise; the State remaining in the mean time exposed to all the dangers of invasion from without, and convulsions within.

He has endeavoured to prevent the population of these States; for that purpose obstructing the Laws for Naturalization of Foreigners; refusing to pass others to encourage their migrations hither, and raising the conditions of new Appropriations of Lands.

He has obstructed the Administration of Justice, by refusing his Assent to Laws for establishing Judiciary powers.

He has made Judges dependent on his Will alone, for the tenure of their offices, and the amount and payment of their salaries.

He has erected a multitude of New Offices, and sent hither swarms of Officers to harrass our people, and eat out their substance.

He has kept among us, in times of peace, Standing Armies without the Consent of our legislatures.

He has affected to render the Military independent of and superior to the Civil power.

He has combined with others to subject us to a jurisdiction foreign to our constitution, and unacknowledged by our laws; giving his Assent to their Acts of pretended Legislation:

For Quartering large bodies of armed troops among us:

For protecting them, by a mock Trial, from punishment for any Murders which they should commit on the Inhabitants of these States:

For cutting off our Trade with all parts of the world:

For imposing Taxes on us without our Consent:

For depriving us in many cases, of the benefits of Trial by Jury:

For transporting us beyond Seas to be tried for pretended offences

For abolishing the free System of English Laws in a neighbouring Province, establishing therein an Arbitrary government, and enlarging its Boundaries so as to render it at once an example and fit instrument for introducing the same absolute rule into these Colonies:

For taking away our Charters, abolishing our most valuable Laws, and altering fundamentally the Forms of our Governments:

For suspending our own Legislatures, and declaring themselves invested with power to legislate for us in all cases whatsoever.

He has abdicated Government here, by declaring us out of his Protection and waging War against us.

He has plundered our seas, ravaged our Coasts, burnt our towns, and destroyed the lives of our people.

He is at this time transporting large Armies of foreign Mercenaries to compleat the works of death, desolation and tyranny, already begun with circumstances of Cruelty & perfidy scarcely paralleled in the most barbarous ages, and totally unworthy the Head of a civilized nation.

He has constrained our fellow Citizens taken Captive on the high Seas to bear Arms against their Country, to become the executioners of their friends and Brethren, or to fall themselves by their Hands.

He has excited domestic insurrections amongst us, and has endeavoured to bring on the inhabitants of our frontiers, the merciless Indian Savages, whose known rule of warfare, is an undistinguished destruction of all ages, sexes and conditions.

In every stage of these Oppressions We have Petitioned for Redress in the most humble terms: Our repeated Petitions have been answered only by repeated injury. A Prince whose character is thus marked by every act which may define a Tyrant, is unfit to be the ruler of a free people.

Nor have We been wanting in attentions to our Brittish brethren. We have warned them from time to time of attempts by their legislature to extend an unwarrantable jurisdiction over us. We have reminded them of the circumstances of our emigration and settlement here. We have appealed to their native justice and magnanimity, and we have conjured them by the ties of our common kindred to disavow these usurpations, which, would inevitably interrupt our connections and correspondence. They too have been deaf to the voice of justice and of consanguinity. We must, therefore, acquiesce in the necessity, which denounces our Separation, and hold them, as we hold the rest of mankind, Enemies in War, in Peace Friends.

We, therefore, the Representatives of the united States of America, in General Congress, Assembled, appealing to the Supreme Judge of the world for the rectitude of our intentions, do, in the Name, and by Authority of the good People of these Colonies, solemnly publish and declare, That these United Colonies are, and of Right ought to be Free and Independent States; that they are Absolved from all Allegiance to the British Crown, and that all political connection between them and the State of Great Britain, is and ought to be totally dissolved; and that as Free and Independent States, they have full Power to levy War, conclude Peace, contract Alliances, establish Commerce, and to do all other Acts and Things which Independent States may of right do. And for the support of this Declaration, with a firm reliance on the protection of divine Providence, we mutually pledge to each other our Lives, our Fortunes and our sacred Honor.

Outline of the United States Constitution

Articles of the Constitution
Preamble

"We the People of the United States, in order to form a more perfect Union, establish justice, insure domestic tranquility, provide for the common defense, promote the general welfare, and secure the blessings of liberty to ourselves and our posterity, do ordain and establish this Constitution for the United States of America."

Article I – Legislature

The legislature is divided into two parts—the House of Representatives (435 members currently; determined by proportional representation of the population) and the Senate (100 members currently; two from each state).

The House of Representatives may bring impeachment charges. All bills which concern money must originate in the House. Because of the size of the body, debate is limited except in special cases, where all representatives may meet as the Committee of the Whole. The Speaker of the House presides over the proceedings. Terms of representatives are two years, re-electable without limit, to persons who are at least 25 years of age.

The Senate, originally elected by state legislatures but now by direct election (17th Amendment), approves or rejects presidential nominations and treaties, and serves as the court and jury in impeachment proceedings. Debate within the Senate is unlimited. The President pro tempore usually presides, but the Vice-President of the United States is the presiding officer, and may vote to break a tie. Senate elected terms are for six years, re-electable without limit, to persons who are at least 30 years of age.

Article II – Executive

The President of the United States is elected for a four-year term, originally electable without limit (the 22nd Amendment limits election to two terms), and must be at least 35 years old.

Responsibilities for the President as outlined in the Constitution include acting as the Chief of State, the Chief Executive, Commander-in-Chief of the Armed Forces, the Chief Diplomat, and Chief Legislature.

Article III – Judiciary

While the Constitution describes the Supreme Court in Article 111, the actual construction of the court system was accomplished by the Judiciary Act of 1789. The Supreme Court has jurisdiction for federal courts and appellate cases on appeal from lower courts.

Article IV – Interstate Relations

This article guarantees that court decisions and other legal actions (marriage, incorporation, etc.) valid in one state are valid in another. Extradition of criminals (and, originally, runaway slaves) and the exchange of citizenship benefits are likewise guaranteed. Article IV also provides for the admission of new states and guarantees federal protection against invasion and violence for each state. States admitted maintain the same status as the original states. All states are guaranteed a republican form of government.

Article V – Amendment Process

Amendments are proposed by a two-thirds vote of each house of Congress or by a special convention called by Congress upon the request of two-thirds of the state legislatures. Amendments are ratified by three-fourths of the state legislatures or state conventions.

Article VI – Supremacy Clause

Article VI sets up the hierarchy of laws in the United States. The Constitution is the "supreme law of the land," and supersedes treaties. Treaties supercede federal laws, federal laws (later to include federal regulatory agency directives) supercede state constitutions, state laws and local laws, respectively. All federal and state officials, including judges, must take an oath to support and defend the Constitution.

Article VII – Ratification

This article specified the ratification process necessary for the Constitution to take effect. Nine of the original thirteen states had to ratify the Constitution before it became operative.

Amendments to the Constitution

The Amendments to the Constitution guarantee certain individual rights and amend original dictates of the Constitution. The first ten amendments are known as the Bill of Rights, for which Thomas Jefferson provided the impetus.

1 – protects the freedom of religion, speech, press, assembly, as well as the right to petition the government for the redress of grievances (1791)

2 – protects the right to bear arms in a regulated militia (on a state basis; it was not intended to guarantee an individual's rights) (1791)

3 – ensures that troops will not be housed in private citizens' homes (1791)

4 – protects against unreasonable search and seizure (need for search warrant) (1791)

5 – protects the rights for the accused, including required indict-

ments, double jeopardy, self-incrimination, due process, and just compensation (1791)

6 – guarantees a speedy and public trial, the confrontation by witnesses, and the right to call witnesses on one's own behalf (1791)

7 – guarantees a jury trial (1791)

8 – protects against excessive bail and cruel and unusual punishment (1791)

9 – says that all rights not enumerated are nonetheless retained by the people (1791)

10 – says that all powers not specifically delegated to the federal government are retained by the states (1791)

11 – states may not be sued by individuals (1798)

12 – dictates that electors will cast separate ballots for President and Vice-President; in the event of no clear winner, the House will select the President and the Senate the Vice-President (1804)

13 – abolished slavery (1865)

14 – extends citizenship to all persons; made Confederate debt void and Confederate leaders ineligible for public office; states which denied voting rights to qualified citizens (blacks) would have their representation in Congress reduced; conferred "dual" citizenship (both of the United States and of a specific state) on all citizens. (1868)

15 – extends voting rights to blacks (1870)

16 – legalized the income tax (1913)

17 – provides for the direct election of senators (1913)

18 – prohibited the general manufacture, sale and use of alcoholic beverages (1919)

19 – extends voting rights to women (1920)

20 – changed inauguration date from March 4 to January 20; eliminated the "lame duck" session of Congress (after the November elections) (1933)

21 – repealed the 18th Amendment (1933)

22 – limits presidents to two terms (1951)

23 – gives presidential electoral votes to the District of Columbia (1961)

24 – prohibits poll taxes (1964)

25 – changed the order of the presidential line of succession and provides guidelines for presidential disability (1967)

26 – extends voting rights to eighteen-year-olds (1971)

27 – restricts the practice of congressional salary adjustment (1992)

GENERAL EDUCATIONAL DEVELOPMENT
PRACTICE EXAM I
ANSWER SHEET

Test 1—Language Arts: Writing

1. ① ② ③ ④ ⑤
2. ① ② ③ ④ ⑤
3. ① ② ③ ④ ⑤
4. ① ② ③ ④ ⑤
5. ① ② ③ ④ ⑤
6. ① ② ③ ④ ⑤
7. ① ② ③ ④ ⑤
8. ① ② ③ ④ ⑤
9. ① ② ③ ④ ⑤
10. ① ② ③ ④ ⑤
11. ① ② ③ ④ ⑤
12. ① ② ③ ④ ⑤
13. ① ② ③ ④ ⑤
14. ① ② ③ ④ ⑤
15. ① ② ③ ④ ⑤
16. ① ② ③ ④ ⑤
17. ① ② ③ ④ ⑤
18. ① ② ③ ④ ⑤
19. ① ② ③ ④ ⑤
20. ① ② ③ ④ ⑤
21. ① ② ③ ④ ⑤
22. ① ② ③ ④ ⑤
23. ① ② ③ ④ ⑤
24. ① ② ③ ④ ⑤
25. ① ② ③ ④ ⑤
26. ① ② ③ ④ ⑤
27. ① ② ③ ④ ⑤
28. ① ② ③ ④ ⑤
29. ① ② ③ ④ ⑤
30. ① ② ③ ④ ⑤
31. ① ② ③ ④ ⑤
32. ① ② ③ ④ ⑤
33. ① ② ③ ④ ⑤
34. ① ② ③ ④ ⑤
35. ① ② ③ ④ ⑤
36. ① ② ③ ④ ⑤
37. ① ② ③ ④ ⑤
38. ① ② ③ ④ ⑤
39. ① ② ③ ④ ⑤
40. ① ② ③ ④ ⑤
41. ① ② ③ ④ ⑤
42. ① ② ③ ④ ⑤
43. ① ② ③ ④ ⑤
44. ① ② ③ ④ ⑤
45. ① ② ③ ④ ⑤
46. ① ② ③ ④ ⑤
47. ① ② ③ ④ ⑤
48. ① ② ③ ④ ⑤
49. ① ② ③ ④ ⑤
50. ① ② ③ ④ ⑤

Test 2—Social Studies

1. ① ② ③ ④ ⑤
2. ① ② ③ ④ ⑤
3. ① ② ③ ④ ⑤
4. ① ② ③ ④ ⑤
5. ① ② ③ ④ ⑤
6. ① ② ③ ④ ⑤
7. ① ② ③ ④ ⑤
8. ① ② ③ ④ ⑤
9. ① ② ③ ④ ⑤
10. ① ② ③ ④ ⑤
11. ① ② ③ ④ ⑤
12. ① ② ③ ④ ⑤
13. ① ② ③ ④ ⑤
14. ① ② ③ ④ ⑤
15. ① ② ③ ④ ⑤
16. ① ② ③ ④ ⑤
17. ① ② ③ ④ ⑤
18. ① ② ③ ④ ⑤
19. ① ② ③ ④ ⑤
20. ① ② ③ ④ ⑤
21. ① ② ③ ④ ⑤
22. ① ② ③ ④ ⑤
23. ① ② ③ ④ ⑤
24. ① ② ③ ④ ⑤
25. ① ② ③ ④ ⑤
26. ① ② ③ ④ ⑤
27. ① ② ③ ④ ⑤
28. ① ② ③ ④ ⑤
29. ① ② ③ ④ ⑤
30. ① ② ③ ④ ⑤
31. ① ② ③ ④ ⑤
32. ① ② ③ ④ ⑤
33. ① ② ③ ④ ⑤
34. ① ② ③ ④ ⑤
35. ① ② ③ ④ ⑤
36. ① ② ③ ④ ⑤
37. ① ② ③ ④ ⑤
38. ① ② ③ ④ ⑤
39. ① ② ③ ④ ⑤
40. ① ② ③ ④ ⑤
41. ① ② ③ ④ ⑤
42. ① ② ③ ④ ⑤
43. ① ② ③ ④ ⑤
44. ① ② ③ ④ ⑤
45. ① ② ③ ④ ⑤
46. ① ② ③ ④ ⑤
47. ① ② ③ ④ ⑤
48. ① ② ③ ④ ⑤
49. ① ② ③ ④ ⑤
50. ① ② ③ ④ ⑤

Test 3—Science

1. ① ② ③ ④ ⑤
2. ① ② ③ ④ ⑤
3. ① ② ③ ④ ⑤
4. ① ② ③ ④ ⑤
5. ① ② ③ ④ ⑤
6. ① ② ③ ④ ⑤
7. ① ② ③ ④ ⑤
8. ① ② ③ ④ ⑤
9. ① ② ③ ④ ⑤
10. ① ② ③ ④ ⑤
11. ① ② ③ ④ ⑤
12. ① ② ③ ④ ⑤
13. ① ② ③ ④ ⑤
14. ① ② ③ ④ ⑤
15. ① ② ③ ④ ⑤
16. ① ② ③ ④ ⑤

17. ① ② ③ ④ ⑤
18. ① ② ③ ④ ⑤
19. ① ② ③ ④ ⑤
20. ① ② ③ ④ ⑤
21. ① ② ③ ④ ⑤
22. ① ② ③ ④ ⑤
23. ① ② ③ ④ ⑤
24. ① ② ③ ④ ⑤
25. ① ② ③ ④ ⑤
26. ① ② ③ ④ ⑤
27. ① ② ③ ④ ⑤
28. ① ② ③ ④ ⑤
29. ① ② ③ ④ ⑤
30. ① ② ③ ④ ⑤
31. ① ② ③ ④ ⑤
32. ① ② ③ ④ ⑤
33. ① ② ③ ④ ⑤

34. ① ② ③ ④ ⑤
35. ① ② ③ ④ ⑤
36. ① ② ③ ④ ⑤
37. ① ② ③ ④ ⑤
38. ① ② ③ ④ ⑤
39. ① ② ③ ④ ⑤
40. ① ② ③ ④ ⑤
41. ① ② ③ ④ ⑤
42. ① ② ③ ④ ⑤
43. ① ② ③ ④ ⑤
44. ① ② ③ ④ ⑤
45. ① ② ③ ④ ⑤
46. ① ② ③ ④ ⑤
47. ① ② ③ ④ ⑤
48. ① ② ③ ④ ⑤
49. ① ② ③ ④ ⑤
50. ① ② ③ ④ ⑤

Test 4—Language Arts: Reading

1. ① ② ③ ④ ⑤
2. ① ② ③ ④ ⑤
3. ① ② ③ ④ ⑤
4. ① ② ③ ④ ⑤
5. ① ② ③ ④ ⑤
6. ① ② ③ ④ ⑤
7. ① ② ③ ④ ⑤
8. ① ② ③ ④ ⑤
9. ① ② ③ ④ ⑤
10. ① ② ③ ④ ⑤
11. ① ② ③ ④ ⑤
12. ① ② ③ ④ ⑤

13. ① ② ③ ④ ⑤
14. ① ② ③ ④ ⑤
15. ① ② ③ ④ ⑤
16. ① ② ③ ④ ⑤
17. ① ② ③ ④ ⑤
18. ① ② ③ ④ ⑤
19. ① ② ③ ④ ⑤
20. ① ② ③ ④ ⑤
21. ① ② ③ ④ ⑤
22. ① ② ③ ④ ⑤
23. ① ② ③ ④ ⑤
24. ① ② ③ ④ ⑤
25. ① ② ③ ④ ⑤
26. ① ② ③ ④ ⑤

27. ① ② ③ ④ ⑤
28. ① ② ③ ④ ⑤
29. ① ② ③ ④ ⑤
30. ① ② ③ ④ ⑤
31. ① ② ③ ④ ⑤
32. ① ② ③ ④ ⑤
33. ① ② ③ ④ ⑤
34. ① ② ③ ④ ⑤
35. ① ② ③ ④ ⑤
36. ① ② ③ ④ ⑤
37. ① ② ③ ④ ⑤
38. ① ② ③ ④ ⑤
39. ① ② ③ ④ ⑤
40. ① ② ③ ④ ⑤

Test 5—Math: Part 1

1. ① ② ③ ④ ⑤
2. ① ② ③ ④ ⑤
3. ① ② ③ ④ ⑤
4. ① ② ③ ④ ⑤
5. ① ② ③ ④ ⑤
6. ① ② ③ ④ ⑤
7. ① ② ③ ④ ⑤
8. ① ② ③ ④ ⑤
9. ① ② ③ ④ ⑤
10. ① ② ③ ④ ⑤
11. ① ② ③ ④ ⑤
12. ① ② ③ ④ ⑤
13. ① ② ③ ④ ⑤
14. ① ② ③ ④ ⑤
15. ① ② ③ ④ ⑤
16. ① ② ③ ④ ⑤
17. ① ② ③ ④ ⑤
18. ① ② ③ ④ ⑤

19.

20.

21.

22.

23.

24.

Test 5—Math: Part 1 (cont.)

25.

Test 5—Math: Part 2

26. ① ② ③ ④ ⑤
27. ① ② ③ ④ ⑤
28. ① ② ③ ④ ⑤
29. ① ② ③ ④ ⑤
30. ① ② ③ ④ ⑤
31. ① ② ③ ④ ⑤
32. ① ② ③ ④ ⑤
33. ① ② ③ ④ ⑤
34. ① ② ③ ④ ⑤
35. ① ② ③ ④ ⑤
36. ① ② ③ ④ ⑤
37. ① ② ③ ④ ⑤
38. ① ② ③ ④ ⑤
39. ① ② ③ ④ ⑤
40. ① ② ③ ④ ⑤
41. ① ② ③ ④ ⑤
42. ① ② ③ ④ ⑤
43. ① ② ③ ④ ⑤
44. ① ② ③ ④ ⑤
45. ① ② ③ ④ ⑤
46. ① ② ③ ④ ⑤
47. ① ② ③ ④ ⑤

48.

	/	/	/	
⊙	⊙	⊙	⊙	⊙
⓪	⓪	⓪	⓪	⓪
①	①	①	①	①
②	②	②	②	②
③	③	③	③	③
④	④	④	④	④
⑤	⑤	⑤	⑤	⑤
⑥	⑥	⑥	⑥	⑥
⑦	⑦	⑦	⑦	⑦
⑧	⑧	⑧	⑧	⑧
⑨	⑨	⑨	⑨	⑨

49.

	/	/	/	
⊙	⊙	⊙	⊙	⊙
⓪	⓪	⓪	⓪	⓪
①	①	①	①	①
②	②	②	②	②
③	③	③	③	③
④	④	④	④	④
⑤	⑤	⑤	⑤	⑤
⑥	⑥	⑥	⑥	⑥
⑦	⑦	⑦	⑦	⑦
⑧	⑧	⑧	⑧	⑧
⑨	⑨	⑨	⑨	⑨

Test 5—Math: Part 2 (cont.)

50.

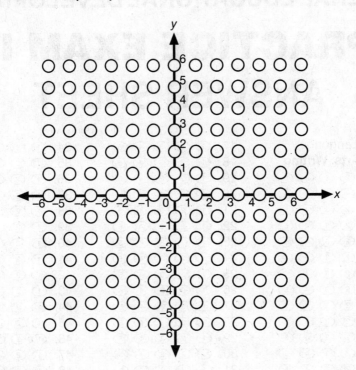

GENERAL EDUCATIONAL DEVELOPMENT
PRACTICE EXAM II
ANSWER SHEET

Test 1—Language Arts: Writing

1. ① ② ③ ④ ⑤
2. ① ② ③ ④ ⑤
3. ① ② ③ ④ ⑤
4. ① ② ③ ④ ⑤
5. ① ② ③ ④ ⑤
6. ① ② ③ ④ ⑤
7. ① ② ③ ④ ⑤
8. ① ② ③ ④ ⑤
9. ① ② ③ ④ ⑤
10. ① ② ③ ④ ⑤
11. ① ② ③ ④ ⑤
12. ① ② ③ ④ ⑤
13. ① ② ③ ④ ⑤
14. ① ② ③ ④ ⑤
15. ① ② ③ ④ ⑤
16. ① ② ③ ④ ⑤
17. ① ② ③ ④ ⑤
18. ① ② ③ ④ ⑤
19. ① ② ③ ④ ⑤
20. ① ② ③ ④ ⑤
21. ① ② ③ ④ ⑤
22. ① ② ③ ④ ⑤
23. ① ② ③ ④ ⑤
24. ① ② ③ ④ ⑤
25. ① ② ③ ④ ⑤
26. ① ② ③ ④ ⑤
27. ① ② ③ ④ ⑤
28. ① ② ③ ④ ⑤
29. ① ② ③ ④ ⑤
30. ① ② ③ ④ ⑤
31. ① ② ③ ④ ⑤
32. ① ② ③ ④ ⑤
33. ① ② ③ ④ ⑤
34. ① ② ③ ④ ⑤
35. ① ② ③ ④ ⑤
36. ① ② ③ ④ ⑤
37. ① ② ③ ④ ⑤
38. ① ② ③ ④ ⑤
39. ① ② ③ ④ ⑤
40. ① ② ③ ④ ⑤
41. ① ② ③ ④ ⑤
42. ① ② ③ ④ ⑤
43. ① ② ③ ④ ⑤
44. ① ② ③ ④ ⑤
45. ① ② ③ ④ ⑤
46. ① ② ③ ④ ⑤
47. ① ② ③ ④ ⑤
48. ① ② ③ ④ ⑤
49. ① ② ③ ④ ⑤
50. ① ② ③ ④ ⑤

Test 2—Social Studies

1. ① ② ③ ④ ⑤
2. ① ② ③ ④ ⑤
3. ① ② ③ ④ ⑤
4. ① ② ③ ④ ⑤
5. ① ② ③ ④ ⑤
6. ① ② ③ ④ ⑤
7. ① ② ③ ④ ⑤
8. ① ② ③ ④ ⑤
9. ① ② ③ ④ ⑤
10. ① ② ③ ④ ⑤
11. ① ② ③ ④ ⑤
12. ① ② ③ ④ ⑤
13. ① ② ③ ④ ⑤
14. ① ② ③ ④ ⑤
15. ① ② ③ ④ ⑤
16. ① ② ③ ④ ⑤
17. ① ② ③ ④ ⑤
18. ① ② ③ ④ ⑤
19. ① ② ③ ④ ⑤
20. ① ② ③ ④ ⑤
21. ① ② ③ ④ ⑤
22. ① ② ③ ④ ⑤
23. ① ② ③ ④ ⑤
24. ① ② ③ ④ ⑤
25. ① ② ③ ④ ⑤
26. ① ② ③ ④ ⑤
27. ① ② ③ ④ ⑤
28. ① ② ③ ④ ⑤
29. ① ② ③ ④ ⑤
30. ① ② ③ ④ ⑤
31. ① ② ③ ④ ⑤
32. ① ② ③ ④ ⑤
33. ① ② ③ ④ ⑤
34. ① ② ③ ④ ⑤
35. ① ② ③ ④ ⑤
36. ① ② ③ ④ ⑤
37. ① ② ③ ④ ⑤
38. ① ② ③ ④ ⑤
39. ① ② ③ ④ ⑤
40. ① ② ③ ④ ⑤
41. ① ② ③ ④ ⑤
42. ① ② ③ ④ ⑤
43. ① ② ③ ④ ⑤
44. ① ② ③ ④ ⑤
45. ① ② ③ ④ ⑤
46. ① ② ③ ④ ⑤
47. ① ② ③ ④ ⑤
48. ① ② ③ ④ ⑤
49. ① ② ③ ④ ⑤
50. ① ② ③ ④ ⑤

Test 3—Science

1. ① ② ③ ④ ⑤
2. ① ② ③ ④ ⑤
3. ① ② ③ ④ ⑤
4. ① ② ③ ④ ⑤
5. ① ② ③ ④ ⑤
6. ① ② ③ ④ ⑤
7. ① ② ③ ④ ⑤
8. ① ② ③ ④ ⑤
9. ① ② ③ ④ ⑤
10. ① ② ③ ④ ⑤
11. ① ② ③ ④ ⑤
12. ① ② ③ ④ ⑤
13. ① ② ③ ④ ⑤
14. ① ② ③ ④ ⑤
15. ① ② ③ ④ ⑤
16. ① ② ③ ④ ⑤
17. ① ② ③ ④ ⑤
18. ① ② ③ ④ ⑤
19. ① ② ③ ④ ⑤
20. ① ② ③ ④ ⑤
21. ① ② ③ ④ ⑤
22. ① ② ③ ④ ⑤
23. ① ② ③ ④ ⑤
24. ① ② ③ ④ ⑤
25. ① ② ③ ④ ⑤
26. ① ② ③ ④ ⑤
27. ① ② ③ ④ ⑤
28. ① ② ③ ④ ⑤
29. ① ② ③ ④ ⑤
30. ① ② ③ ④ ⑤
31. ① ② ③ ④ ⑤
32. ① ② ③ ④ ⑤
33. ① ② ③ ④ ⑤
34. ① ② ③ ④ ⑤
35. ① ② ③ ④ ⑤
36. ① ② ③ ④ ⑤
37. ① ② ③ ④ ⑤
38. ① ② ③ ④ ⑤
39. ① ② ③ ④ ⑤
40. ① ② ③ ④ ⑤
41. ① ② ③ ④ ⑤
42. ① ② ③ ④ ⑤
43. ① ② ③ ④ ⑤
44. ① ② ③ ④ ⑤
45. ① ② ③ ④ ⑤
46. ① ② ③ ④ ⑤
47. ① ② ③ ④ ⑤
48. ① ② ③ ④ ⑤
49. ① ② ③ ④ ⑤
50. ① ② ③ ④ ⑤

Test 4—Language Arts: Reading

1. ① ② ③ ④ ⑤
2. ① ② ③ ④ ⑤
3. ① ② ③ ④ ⑤
4. ① ② ③ ④ ⑤
5. ① ② ③ ④ ⑤
6. ① ② ③ ④ ⑤
7. ① ② ③ ④ ⑤
8. ① ② ③ ④ ⑤
9. ① ② ③ ④ ⑤
10. ① ② ③ ④ ⑤
11. ① ② ③ ④ ⑤
12. ① ② ③ ④ ⑤
13. ① ② ③ ④ ⑤
14. ① ② ③ ④ ⑤
15. ① ② ③ ④ ⑤
16. ① ② ③ ④ ⑤
17. ① ② ③ ④ ⑤
18. ① ② ③ ④ ⑤
19. ① ② ③ ④ ⑤
20. ① ② ③ ④ ⑤
21. ① ② ③ ④ ⑤
22. ① ② ③ ④ ⑤
23. ① ② ③ ④ ⑤
24. ① ② ③ ④ ⑤
25. ① ② ③ ④ ⑤
26. ① ② ③ ④ ⑤
27. ① ② ③ ④ ⑤
28. ① ② ③ ④ ⑤
29. ① ② ③ ④ ⑤
30. ① ② ③ ④ ⑤
31. ① ② ③ ④ ⑤
32. ① ② ③ ④ ⑤
33. ① ② ③ ④ ⑤
34. ① ② ③ ④ ⑤
35. ① ② ③ ④ ⑤
36. ① ② ③ ④ ⑤
37. ① ② ③ ④ ⑤
38. ① ② ③ ④ ⑤
39. ① ② ③ ④ ⑤
40. ① ② ③ ④ ⑤

Test 5—Math: Part 1

1. ① ② ③ ④ ⑤
2. ① ② ③ ④ ⑤
3. ① ② ③ ④ ⑤
4. ① ② ③ ④ ⑤
5. ① ② ③ ④ ⑤
6. ① ② ③ ④ ⑤
7. ① ② ③ ④ ⑤
8. ① ② ③ ④ ⑤
9. ① ② ③ ④ ⑤
10. ① ② ③ ④ ⑤
11. ① ② ③ ④ ⑤
12. ① ② ③ ④ ⑤
13. ① ② ③ ④ ⑤
14. ① ② ③ ④ ⑤
15. ① ② ③ ④ ⑤
16. ① ② ③ ④ ⑤
17. ① ② ③ ④ ⑤
18. ① ② ③ ④ ⑤

19.

20.

21.

22.

23.

24.

Test 5—Math: Part 1 (cont.)

25.

Test 5—Math: Part 2

26. ① ② ③ ④ ⑤
27. ① ② ③ ④ ⑤
28. ① ② ③ ④ ⑤
29. ① ② ③ ④ ⑤
30. ① ② ③ ④ ⑤
31. ① ② ③ ④ ⑤
32. ① ② ③ ④ ⑤
33. ① ② ③ ④ ⑤
34. ① ② ③ ④ ⑤
35. ① ② ③ ④ ⑤
36. ① ② ③ ④ ⑤
37. ① ② ③ ④ ⑤
38. ① ② ③ ④ ⑤
39. ① ② ③ ④ ⑤
40. ① ② ③ ④ ⑤
41. ① ② ③ ④ ⑤
42. ① ② ③ ④ ⑤
43. ① ② ③ ④ ⑤
44. ① ② ③ ④ ⑤
45. ① ② ③ ④ ⑤
46. ① ② ③ ④ ⑤
47. ① ② ③ ④ ⑤

48.

	⊘	⊘	⊘	
⊙	⊙	⊙	⊙	⊙
⓪	⓪	⓪	⓪	⓪
①	①	①	①	①
②	②	②	②	②
③	③	③	③	③
④	④	④	④	④
⑤	⑤	⑤	⑤	⑤
⑥	⑥	⑥	⑥	⑥
⑦	⑦	⑦	⑦	⑦
⑧	⑧	⑧	⑧	⑧
⑨	⑨	⑨	⑨	⑨

49.

	⊘	⊘	⊘	
⊙	⊙	⊙	⊙	⊙
⓪	⓪	⓪	⓪	⓪
①	①	①	①	①
②	②	②	②	②
③	③	③	③	③
④	④	④	④	④
⑤	⑤	⑤	⑤	⑤
⑥	⑥	⑥	⑥	⑥
⑦	⑦	⑦	⑦	⑦
⑧	⑧	⑧	⑧	⑧
⑨	⑨	⑨	⑨	⑨

Test 5—Math: Part 2 (cont.)

50.

GENERAL EDUCATIONAL DEVELOPMENT
PRACTICE EXAM III
ANSWER SHEET

Test 1—Language Arts: Writing

1. ① ② ③ ④ ⑤
2. ① ② ③ ④ ⑤
3. ① ② ③ ④ ⑤
4. ① ② ③ ④ ⑤
5. ① ② ③ ④ ⑤
6. ① ② ③ ④ ⑤
7. ① ② ③ ④ ⑤
8. ① ② ③ ④ ⑤
9. ① ② ③ ④ ⑤
10. ① ② ③ ④ ⑤
11. ① ② ③ ④ ⑤
12. ① ② ③ ④ ⑤
13. ① ② ③ ④ ⑤
14. ① ② ③ ④ ⑤
15. ① ② ③ ④ ⑤
16. ① ② ③ ④ ⑤

17. ① ② ③ ④ ⑤
18. ① ② ③ ④ ⑤
19. ① ② ③ ④ ⑤
20. ① ② ③ ④ ⑤
21. ① ② ③ ④ ⑤
22. ① ② ③ ④ ⑤
23. ① ② ③ ④ ⑤
24. ① ② ③ ④ ⑤
25. ① ② ③ ④ ⑤
26. ① ② ③ ④ ⑤
27. ① ② ③ ④ ⑤
28. ① ② ③ ④ ⑤
29. ① ② ③ ④ ⑤
30. ① ② ③ ④ ⑤
31. ① ② ③ ④ ⑤
32. ① ② ③ ④ ⑤
33. ① ② ③ ④ ⑤

34. ① ② ③ ④ ⑤
35. ① ② ③ ④ ⑤
36. ① ② ③ ④ ⑤
37. ① ② ③ ④ ⑤
38. ① ② ③ ④ ⑤
39. ① ② ③ ④ ⑤
40. ① ② ③ ④ ⑤
41. ① ② ③ ④ ⑤
42. ① ② ③ ④ ⑤
43. ① ② ③ ④ ⑤
44. ① ② ③ ④ ⑤
45. ① ② ③ ④ ⑤
46. ① ② ③ ④ ⑤
47. ① ② ③ ④ ⑤
48. ① ② ③ ④ ⑤
49. ① ② ③ ④ ⑤
50. ① ② ③ ④ ⑤

Test 2—Social Studies

1. ① ② ③ ④ ⑤
2. ① ② ③ ④ ⑤
3. ① ② ③ ④ ⑤
4. ① ② ③ ④ ⑤
5. ① ② ③ ④ ⑤
6. ① ② ③ ④ ⑤
7. ① ② ③ ④ ⑤
8. ① ② ③ ④ ⑤
9. ① ② ③ ④ ⑤
10. ① ② ③ ④ ⑤
11. ① ② ③ ④ ⑤
12. ① ② ③ ④ ⑤
13. ① ② ③ ④ ⑤
14. ① ② ③ ④ ⑤
15. ① ② ③ ④ ⑤
16. ① ② ③ ④ ⑤

17. ① ② ③ ④ ⑤
18. ① ② ③ ④ ⑤
19. ① ② ③ ④ ⑤
20. ① ② ③ ④ ⑤
21. ① ② ③ ④ ⑤
22. ① ② ③ ④ ⑤
23. ① ② ③ ④ ⑤
24. ① ② ③ ④ ⑤
25. ① ② ③ ④ ⑤
26. ① ② ③ ④ ⑤
27. ① ② ③ ④ ⑤
28. ① ② ③ ④ ⑤
29. ① ② ③ ④ ⑤
30. ① ② ③ ④ ⑤
31. ① ② ③ ④ ⑤
32. ① ② ③ ④ ⑤
33. ① ② ③ ④ ⑤

34. ① ② ③ ④ ⑤
35. ① ② ③ ④ ⑤
36. ① ② ③ ④ ⑤
37. ① ② ③ ④ ⑤
38. ① ② ③ ④ ⑤
39. ① ② ③ ④ ⑤
40. ① ② ③ ④ ⑤
41. ① ② ③ ④ ⑤
42. ① ② ③ ④ ⑤
43. ① ② ③ ④ ⑤
44. ① ② ③ ④ ⑤
45. ① ② ③ ④ ⑤
46. ① ② ③ ④ ⑤
47. ① ② ③ ④ ⑤
48. ① ② ③ ④ ⑤
49. ① ② ③ ④ ⑤
50. ① ② ③ ④ ⑤

Test 3—Science

1. ① ② ③ ④ ⑤
2. ① ② ③ ④ ⑤
3. ① ② ③ ④ ⑤
4. ① ② ③ ④ ⑤
5. ① ② ③ ④ ⑤
6. ① ② ③ ④ ⑤
7. ① ② ③ ④ ⑤
8. ① ② ③ ④ ⑤
9. ① ② ③ ④ ⑤
10. ① ② ③ ④ ⑤
11. ① ② ③ ④ ⑤
12. ① ② ③ ④ ⑤
13. ① ② ③ ④ ⑤
14. ① ② ③ ④ ⑤
15. ① ② ③ ④ ⑤
16. ① ② ③ ④ ⑤
17. ① ② ③ ④ ⑤
18. ① ② ③ ④ ⑤
19. ① ② ③ ④ ⑤
20. ① ② ③ ④ ⑤
21. ① ② ③ ④ ⑤
22. ① ② ③ ④ ⑤
23. ① ② ③ ④ ⑤
24. ① ② ③ ④ ⑤
25. ① ② ③ ④ ⑤
26. ① ② ③ ④ ⑤
27. ① ② ③ ④ ⑤
28. ① ② ③ ④ ⑤
29. ① ② ③ ④ ⑤
30. ① ② ③ ④ ⑤
31. ① ② ③ ④ ⑤
32. ① ② ③ ④ ⑤
33. ① ② ③ ④ ⑤
34. ① ② ③ ④ ⑤
35. ① ② ③ ④ ⑤
36. ① ② ③ ④ ⑤
37. ① ② ③ ④ ⑤
38. ① ② ③ ④ ⑤
39. ① ② ③ ④ ⑤
40. ① ② ③ ④ ⑤
41. ① ② ③ ④ ⑤
42. ① ② ③ ④ ⑤
43. ① ② ③ ④ ⑤
44. ① ② ③ ④ ⑤
45. ① ② ③ ④ ⑤
46. ① ② ③ ④ ⑤
47. ① ② ③ ④ ⑤
48. ① ② ③ ④ ⑤
49. ① ② ③ ④ ⑤
50. ① ② ③ ④ ⑤

Test 4—Language Arts: Reading

1. ① ② ③ ④ ⑤
2. ① ② ③ ④ ⑤
3. ① ② ③ ④ ⑤
4. ① ② ③ ④ ⑤
5. ① ② ③ ④ ⑤
6. ① ② ③ ④ ⑤
7. ① ② ③ ④ ⑤
8. ① ② ③ ④ ⑤
9. ① ② ③ ④ ⑤
10. ① ② ③ ④ ⑤
11. ① ② ③ ④ ⑤
12. ① ② ③ ④ ⑤
13. ① ② ③ ④ ⑤
14. ① ② ③ ④ ⑤
15. ① ② ③ ④ ⑤
16. ① ② ③ ④ ⑤
17. ① ② ③ ④ ⑤
18. ① ② ③ ④ ⑤
19. ① ② ③ ④ ⑤
20. ① ② ③ ④ ⑤
21. ① ② ③ ④ ⑤
22. ① ② ③ ④ ⑤
23. ① ② ③ ④ ⑤
24. ① ② ③ ④ ⑤
25. ① ② ③ ④ ⑤
26. ① ② ③ ④ ⑤
27. ① ② ③ ④ ⑤
28. ① ② ③ ④ ⑤
29. ① ② ③ ④ ⑤
30. ① ② ③ ④ ⑤
31. ① ② ③ ④ ⑤
32. ① ② ③ ④ ⑤
33. ① ② ③ ④ ⑤
34. ① ② ③ ④ ⑤
35. ① ② ③ ④ ⑤
36. ① ② ③ ④ ⑤
37. ① ② ③ ④ ⑤
38. ① ② ③ ④ ⑤
39. ① ② ③ ④ ⑤
40. ① ② ③ ④ ⑤

Test 5—Math: Part 1

1. ① ② ③ ④ ⑤
2. ① ② ③ ④ ⑤
3. ① ② ③ ④ ⑤
4. ① ② ③ ④ ⑤
5. ① ② ③ ④ ⑤
6. ① ② ③ ④ ⑤
7. ① ② ③ ④ ⑤
8. ① ② ③ ④ ⑤
9. ① ② ③ ④ ⑤
10. ① ② ③ ④ ⑤
11. ① ② ③ ④ ⑤
12. ① ② ③ ④ ⑤
13. ① ② ③ ④ ⑤
14. ① ② ③ ④ ⑤
15. ① ② ③ ④ ⑤
16. ① ② ③ ④ ⑤
17. ① ② ③ ④ ⑤
18. ① ② ③ ④ ⑤

19.

20.

21.

22.

23.

24.

Test 5—Math: Part 1 (cont.)

25.

Test 5—Math: Part 2

26. ① ② ③ ④ ⑤
27. ① ② ③ ④ ⑤
28. ① ② ③ ④ ⑤
29. ① ② ③ ④ ⑤
30. ① ② ③ ④ ⑤
31. ① ② ③ ④ ⑤
32. ① ② ③ ④ ⑤
33. ① ② ③ ④ ⑤
34. ① ② ③ ④ ⑤
35. ① ② ③ ④ ⑤
36. ① ② ③ ④ ⑤
37. ① ② ③ ④ ⑤
38. ① ② ③ ④ ⑤
39. ① ② ③ ④ ⑤
40. ① ② ③ ④ ⑤
41. ① ② ③ ④ ⑤
42. ① ② ③ ④ ⑤
43. ① ② ③ ④ ⑤
44. ① ② ③ ④ ⑤
45. ① ② ③ ④ ⑤
46. ① ② ③ ④ ⑤
47. ① ② ③ ④ ⑤

48.

	/	/	/	
⊙	⊙	⊙	⊙	⊙
⓪	⓪	⓪	⓪	⓪
①	①	①	①	①
②	②	②	②	②
③	③	③	③	③
④	④	④	④	④
⑤	⑤	⑤	⑤	⑤
⑥	⑥	⑥	⑥	⑥
⑦	⑦	⑦	⑦	⑦
⑧	⑧	⑧	⑧	⑧
⑨	⑨	⑨	⑨	⑨

49.

	/	/	/	
⊙	⊙	⊙	⊙	⊙
⓪	⓪	⓪	⓪	⓪
①	①	①	①	①
②	②	②	②	②
③	③	③	③	③
④	④	④	④	④
⑤	⑤	⑤	⑤	⑤
⑥	⑥	⑥	⑥	⑥
⑦	⑦	⑦	⑦	⑦
⑧	⑧	⑧	⑧	⑧
⑨	⑨	⑨	⑨	⑨

Test 5—Math: Part 2 (cont.)

50.

▼ INDEX

REA's Test Prep Books Are The Best!

(a sample of the <u>hundreds of letters</u> REA receives each year)

" I am writing to congratulate you on preparing an exceptional study guide. In five years of teaching this course I have never encountered a more thorough, comprehensive, concise and realistic preparation for this examination. "
Teacher, Davie, FL

" I have found your publications, *The Best Test Preparation...*, to be exactly that. "
Teacher, Aptos, CA

" I used your *CLEP Introductory Sociology* book and rank it 99% — thank you! "
Student, Jerusalem, Israel

" Your *GMAT* book greatly helped me on the test. Thank you. "
Student, Oxford, OH

" I recently got the French *SAT II* Exam book from REA. I congratulate you on first-rate French practice tests. "
Instructor, Los Angeles, CA

" Your *AP English Literature and Composition* book is most impressive. "
Student, Montgomery, AL

" Just a short note to say thanks for the great support your book gave me in helping me pass the test... I'm on my way to a B.S. degree because of you! "
Student, Orlando, FL

(more on front page)